TENTH EDITION

Early Childhood Education Today

George S. Morrison

University of North Texas

PEARSON

Merrill
Prentice Hall

Upper Saddle River, New Jersey
Columbus, Ohio

Library of Congress Cataloging-in-Publication Data

Morrison, George S.
    Early childhood education today / George S. Morrison.—10th ed.
       p. cm.
    Includes bibliographical references and index.
    ISBN 0-13-228621-1 (alk. paper)
  1. Early childhood education—United States. I. Title.
    LB1139.25.M66 2007
    372.21—dc22   2006010958

Vice President and Executive Publisher: Jeffery W. Johnston
Publisher: Kevin M. Davis
Acquisitions Editor: Julie Peters
Editorial Assistant: Michelle Girgis
Development Editor: Karen Balkin
Senior Production Editor: Linda Hillis Bayma
Production Coordination: Norine Strang, Carlisle Publishing Services
Design Coordinator: Diane C. Lorenzo
Text Designer: Candace Rowley
Photo Coordinator: Sandy Schaefer
Cover Designer: Ali Mohrman
Cover image: Corbis
Production Manager: Laura Messerly
Director of Marketing: David Gesell
Marketing Manager: Amy Judd
Marketing Coordinator: Brian Mounts

This book was set in Berkeley by Carlisle Publishing Services. It was printed and bound by R. R. Donnelley & Sons Company. The cover was printed by The Lehigh Press, Inc.

Photo Credits: Photo credits appear on page 566, which constitutes a continuation of this copyright page.

Pearson Education Ltd.   Pearson Education Australia Pty. Limited
Pearson Education Singapore Pte. Ltd.   Pearson Education North Asia Ltd.
Pearson Education Canada, Ltd.   Pearson Educación de Mexico, S.A. de C.V.
Pearson Education—Japan   Pearson Education Malaysia Pte. Ltd.

10 9 8 7 6 5 4 3
ISBN: 0-13-228621-1

For Betty Jane—who has made many sacrifices,
all in the name of deepest love

About the Author

George S. Morrison is professor of early childhood education at the University of North Texas, where he teaches child development and early childhood classes to undergraduate and graduate students. Professor Morrison's accomplishments include a Distinguished Academic Service Award from the Pennsylvania Department of Education, and Outstanding Service and Teaching Awards from Florida International University. His books include *Fundamentals of Early Childhood Education*, 4th Edition; *Teaching in America*, 4th Edition; *Education and Development of Infants, Toddlers, and Preschoolers*; *The World of Child Development*; *The Contemporary Curriculum*; and *Parent Involvement in the Home, School, and Community*.

Dr. Morrison is a popular author, speaker, and presenter. He writes an ongoing column for the *Public School Montessorian* and contributes his opinions and ideas to a wide range of publications. His speaking engagements and presentations focus on the future of early childhood education, the changing roles of early childhood teachers, the influence of contemporary educational reforms, research, and legislation on teaching and learning.

Dr. Morrison's professional and research interests include integrating best practices into faith-based programs; developing programs for young children and their families with an emphasis on early literacy; and the influences of families on children's development. He is also actively involved in providing technical assistance about graduate and undergraduate teacher education programs and early childhood practices to government agencies, university faculty, and private and public agencies in Thailand, Taiwan, and China.

Preface

This is an exciting time to be in the field of early childhood education. In fact, I can think of only one other time during my career when there was so much excitement and challenge: in 1965, with the implementation of Head Start. The excitement and possibility in the air at that time are similar to conditions today because of the interest in universal readiness, universal preschool, early academics, the transformation of kindergarten and the primary grades, and standards and assessment. The field of early childhood education and the roles of early childhood professionals are being transformed! We discuss these changes throughout this book, which focuses on the early care and education of young children from birth to age eight.

These changes bring with them both possibilities and challenges. The possibilities are endless for you as an early childhood education professional to participate in the restructuring of the early childhood profession. The challenges involved will require understanding the unique period of early childhood, collaborating with others, working hard, and committing to the bright promise of high-quality education for all children. Will you take full advantage of these possibilities and challenges and help all young children get the support, care, knowledge, and skills they need to succeed in school and life?

I believe that the way you and I respond to the opportunities we have in front of us today will determine the future of early childhood education. We must be creative in teaching young children and in providing the support that they and their families need.

To that end, this revised edition

- Is comprehensive in its coverage.
- Includes a new DVD, *Early Childhood Education Settings and Approaches*, with every copy of the text so that you can see what it is like to work with young children, as you read about them.
- Is more useful and more applied than ever to help you become an effective teacher. New Competency Builder boxes and more strategies, guidelines, and examples have also been added to this edition.

Comprehensive Coverage

Reviewers consistently state that *Early Childhood Education Today* is comprehensive. Seven core themes are integrated throughout the text and provide a framework for understanding and implementing all that early childhood education encompasses.

- **Professionalism in Practice.** What does it mean to be a practicing early childhood professional today? This text answers this question and helps you become a high-quality professional. Chapter 1, "You and Early Childhood Education: What Does It Mean to Be a Professional?" discusses in detail the many dimensions of professionalism. In addition, two core attributes of professional practice, collaboration and advocacy, are highlighted throughout the text. The Voice from the Field and Program in Action accounts that appear in nearly every chapter illustrate how early childhood teachers dedicate themselves to helping children learn, grow, and develop to their full potential and to helping parents, families, and communities build strong educational programs. As you read about how these teachers put professionalism into practice, you will be inspired to proclaim, "I also teach young children."

- **Theory into Practice.** This text helps you understand how teachers and programs translate theories of learning and educating young children into practice. The Voice from the Field, Program in Action, Diversity Tie-In, and new Competency Builder features provide real-life insights into how teachers in programs across the United States apply early childhood theories, knowledge, and skills to their everyday practices. You will read firsthand about professional colleagues who make theories come alive in concrete ways that truly help children succeed in school and life.

- **Diversity.** The United States is a nation of diverse people, and this diversity is reflected in every early childhood classroom and program. You and your colleagues must have the knowledge and sensitivity to teach all students well, and you must understand how culture, language, socioeconomic status, and gender influence teaching and learning. In addition to two full chapters on diversity (chapter 15, "Multiculturalism: Education for Living in a Diverse Society," and chapter 16, "Children with Special Needs: Appropriate Education for All"), every chapter of this edition emphasizes the theme of diversity through narrative accounts and program descriptions. The theme of diversity is further emphasized by the inclusion in every chapter of a Diversity Tie-In feature, which focuses on issues of diversity, promotes reflection, and shows you how to provide for the diverse needs of all children.

- **Family-Centered, Community-Based Practice.** To effectively meet children's needs, early childhood professionals must collaborate with families and communities. Collaboration is in; solo practice is out! Today, teaching is not an isolated endeavor; successful partnerships at all levels are essential for effective teaching and learning. In addition to an entire chapter on this important topic (chapter 17, "Parent, Family, and Community Involvement: Cooperation and Collaboration"), other chapters provide examples of successful partnerships and their influences on teaching and learning.

- **Timeliness.** This tenth edition is a book for the twenty-first century. The information it contains is timely and reflective of the latest trends and research. Every chapter has been thoroughly revised to reflect changes in the field. I take great pride in ensuring that you and other professionals are well versed in the current state of early childhood education. *Early Childhood Education Today* is a contemporary text, written and designed for contemporary teachers in these contemporary times.

- **Developmentally Appropriate Practice.** The theme of developmentally appropriate practice, which is integrated throughout every chapter of this text, is the solid foundation for all early childhood practice. It is important for you to understand developmentally appropriate practice and become familiar with ways to implement it in your teaching. With all the reforms and changes occurring in the field, your goal is to ensure that all you do is appropriate for all children and their families. Appendix B provides the NAEYC Guidelines for Developmentally Appropriate Practice in Early Childhood Programs, and every chapter includes examples and illustrations of how to apply developmentally appropriate practice.

- **Technology Applied to Teaching and Learning.** Technological and information literacy is essential for living and working in contemporary society. This tenth edition provides you and your colleagues with the knowledge and competencies you need to integrate technology effectively into the curriculum and to use new teaching and learning styles enabled by technology. In addition to chapter 13, "Technology and Young Children: Education for the Information Age," margin notes throughout the text, such as the one shown here, direct you to related information on the Companion Website, located at **www.prenhall.com/morrison**. And included at the end of each chapter is a Linking to Learning section, which provides an annotated list of websites to support your use of the Internet and new technologies as sources of professional growth and development.

Companion Website

To complete a Program in Action activity related to the Reggio Emilia approach, go to the Companion Website at **www.prenhall.com/morrison**, select chapter 6, then choose the Program in Action module.

New DVD: Early Childhood Education Settings and Approaches

In keeping with this book's emphasis on current information, best practices, and professionalism, we have included a new DVD with every copy of the text. *Early Childhood Education Settings and Approaches* contains eight very current, multicultural model programs, running seven to nine minutes each and focusing on:

- Infants and Toddlers
- Child Care
- Kindergarten
- Primary Grades
- Head Start
- Montessori
- Reggio Emilia
- High/Scope

In the Montessori segment of the DVD, observe the sensory materials and experiences that the children engage in.

Each narrated segment depicts children actively playing and learning and teachers discussing their practices. In addition, segment clips with observation and application suggestions appear in the margins of all of the chapters, as shown in the example on the left. These video clips and captions point you to specific scenes in the DVD to help you understand how chapter concepts are practiced in real programs. Seeing in action what you read about in the text and reflecting on what you observe can help you to understand what it is actually like to work with children of different ages and cultures in different types of classrooms.

More Useful, More Applied

This edition was carefully revised to include applied, step-by-step how-to's in Competency Builder features and specific guidelines and strategies in the regular text.

Competency Builders. More than ever before in America's educational history, teachers are being held accountable for children's progress. At the same time, early childhood is a unique developmental period, one that should be respected, with every teacher interacting with every child in developmentally and culturally appropriate ways. Because it is challenging for teachers to balance young children's developmental and learning needs with state and school district standards, which specify what children should know and do, the need for teachers to be competent in all areas of professional practice has perhaps never been greater.

In response to this need, a new feature, **Competency Builder,** is included in most chapters to show you in detail how to be a competent teacher in the areas that early childhood education professionals say are the most important. A list of all of the Competency Builders in the book is on Special Features page xxv. In these features you will learn how to observe young children as a basis for planning and assessing learning experiences; how to preserve and assess learning experiences through documentation; how to effectively communicate with children's family members; how to scaffold children's learning using Vygotsky's theory; and much more. These explicit steps will be useful to you in your practicum or student teaching experience and throughout your teaching career. Studying these features and this text will also help you to pass your certification, state licensure exam, or the PRAXIS.

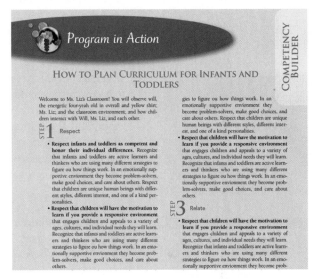

Program in Action

HOW TO PLAN CURRICULUM FOR INFANTS AND TODDLERS

COMPETENCY BUILDER

In-Text Strategies and Applications. You will also find more explicit strategies, guidelines, and detailed how-to's in this edition, as shown in the examples below. Studying these applications will help you to become a competent professional.

1. *Encourage breakfast.* If your school or program does not provide breakfast for children, be an advocate for starting to do that. Providing school breakfasts can be both a nutritional and an educational program.
2. *Provide healthy snacks instead of junk food.* And advocate for healthy foods in school and program vending machines.
3. *When cooking with children, talk about foods and their nutritional value.* Cooking activities are also a good way to eat and talk about new foods.
4. *Integrate literacy and nutritional activities.* For example, reading and discussing labels is a good way to encourage children to be aware of and think about nutritional information.
5. *Make meals and snack times pleasant and sociable experiences.*[25]
6. *Provide parents with information about nutrition.* For example, you can make parents aware of the U.S. Department of Agriculture's new individualized food pyramid (Figure 2.7). You might access the new pyramid online, have children enter their own

FIGURE 7.3 Action Steps to Meet the Cultural Needs of Hispanic Children and Families

- Outreach efforts to parents should include the use of culturally appropriate messages and the involvement of community, religious, social, and economic institutions.
- Early learning guidelines for child care and other educational programs should be respectful of children's home languages, and cultures and give priority to language-rich learning environments that take into account the language(s) spoken by the children.
- Training and professional development of teachers should give priority to research-based strategies to enhance the language, literacy, and school readiness of all children, including children with limited English proficiency.
- Staff recruitment measures should focus on linguistic and cultural minorities to ensure that the professionals working with children are as diverse as the children they serve.
- Child assessment and evaluation outcome measures should be linguistically and culturally appropriate, as well as developmentally appropriate, for all children, including English-language learners.

SPECIAL FEATURES

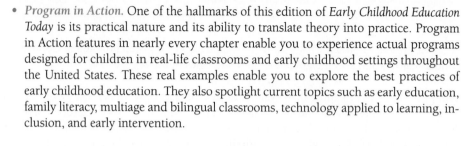

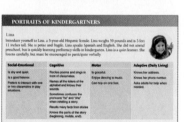

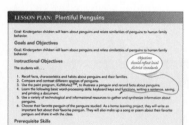

- *Program in Action.* One of the hallmarks of this edition of *Early Childhood Education Today* is its practical nature and its ability to translate theory into practice. Program in Action features in nearly every chapter enable you to experience actual programs designed for children in real-life classrooms and early childhood settings throughout the United States. These real examples enable you to explore the best practices of early childhood education. They also spotlight current topics such as early education, family literacy, multiage and bilingual classrooms, technology applied to learning, inclusion, and early intervention.

- *Voice from the Field.* Teachers' voices play a major role in illustrating practices in *Early Childhood Education Today*. Voice from the Field features allow practicing teachers to explain to you their philosophies, beliefs, and program practices. These teachers mentor you as they relate how they practice early childhood education. Among the contributors are teachers who have received prestigious awards and National Board Certification.

- *Diversity Tie-In.* America's diversity is reflected in today's classrooms. You will need to honor, respect, and provide for the needs of all children, regardless of their culture, language, socioeconomic background, gender, or race. You will also need to be thoughtful about integrating multiculturalism and diversity into your teaching. The Diversity Tie-In in every chapter is designed to introduce you to a topic or issue of diversity you might not have thought about and to encourage you to address it in a way you might not have considered.

- *Portraits of Children.* In a text about children, it is sometimes easy to think about them in the abstract. The Portraits of Children found in chapters 9, 10, 11, 12, and 16 are designed to ensure that we consider children as individuals as we discuss how to teach them. The Portraits of Children are snapshots of children from all cultures and backgrounds, enrolled in real child care, preschool, and primary-grade programs across the United States. Each portrait includes developmental information across four domains: physical, social/emotional, cognitive, and adaptive, or self-help. Accompanying questions challenge you to think and reflect about how you would provide for these children's educational and social needs if you were their teacher.

- *Lesson Plans.* Planning for teaching and learning constitutes an important dimension of your role as a professional. This is especially true today, with the emphasis on ensuring that children learn what is mandated by state standards. The lesson plans in this text let you look over the shoulder of experienced teachers and observe how they plan for instruction. Award-winning teachers share with you how they plan to ensure that their children will learn important knowledge and skills.

  In addition, Competency Builders in chapters 9, 10, 11, and 12 discuss the specific competencies necessary to effectively plan learning activities or lessons for infants and toddlers, preschoolers, kindergartners, and primary-grade students.

- *Margin Notes.* Keeping track of important key terms is a problem often associated with reading and studying. Key terms and concepts are defined in the text as they are presented and are also placed in page margins. In this way, you have immediate access to them for reflection and review, and they maximize your study time by helping you retain essential knowledge.

- *Glossary of Terms.* A glossary of terms at the end of the book incorporates all of the definitions and terms found in the margin notes. The glossary provides a quick and useful reference for study and reflection.

- *Integrated Technology.* Web resources and URLs appear throughout the text, and margin notes cue you to many additional resources, such as projects, self-assessments, and other learning activities found on the Companion Website for this text, located at **www.prenhall.com/morrison**. These links enrich and extend your learning. In addition, at the end of each chapter is a Linking to Learning section, which provides a list of annotated Web addresses for further research, study, and reflection.

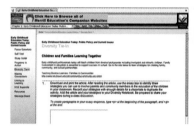

NEW TO THIS EDITION

- **DVD.** A new DVD, *Early Childhood Education Settings and Approaches,* accompanies each copy of the tenth edition so that students can refer to it over and over again. The DVD shows current model programs in multicultural classrooms operated by outstanding teachers and administrators. The DVD takes you inside programs to experience firsthand how teachers interact with young children and to observe the materials, environments, curriculum, and routines of each setting and program. The DVD includes videos of infant-and-toddler, child care, kindergarten, and primary-grade settings and the approaches used by Head Start, Montessori, Reggio Emilia, and High/Scope programs.

- **DVD Margin Notes.** DVD margin notes appear many times in every chapter. These notes show a frame from the DVD and include questions and comments that encourage you to observe the scene and relate what you see to chapter content. In this way you can read the text, view the DVD, reflect on what you observe, and be better prepared to apply theory to practice.

- **Expanded Curriculum Content, Lesson Plans, and Teaching Ideas.** Reviewers of the previous edition suggested expanding coverage of curriculum planning and classroom curriculum ideas and activities for the developmental chapters (9 to 12). In response, lesson plans now include helpful tips supporting students who are learning to write lesson plans, several Competency Builders focus on creating lesson plans, and practical and usable lists of curriculum tips and strategies are included in every chapter. These tips give you a professional tool kit to take into classrooms and other early childhood settings so that you can immediately teach with confidence and help children learn.

- **Ethical Dilemmas.** The Ethical Dilemmas found at the end of every chapter cut to the heart of professional practice. The dilemmas are real scenarios relating to real-life professional practice issues that you will encounter throughout your career. These dilemmas challenge you to think, reflect, and make decisions about children, families, and colleagues. As a result, you will grow in your ability to be a fully practicing professional.

- **Competency Builders.** These features are just what their name implies; they are designed to *build* your *competence* and confidence in performing essential teaching tasks. In early childhood course work, students are increasingly required to demonstrate competency in key areas. Competency Builders have step-by-step guidelines or strategies and provide explicit details that enable you to do key professional tasks expected of early childhood teachers. The Competency Builders are user friendly and can be applied to your professional practice now. In certain cases, they can help you apply state and local standards to practice.

- **New Photos and Artifacts from Contributors' Classrooms.** This edition is enlivened by children's artifacts and photos from a variety of early childhood settings. Many contributors from around the country have provided classroom or center photographs, such as the A. Sophie Rogers laboratory school at The Ohio State University, the Boulder Journey School, California family child care owner Martha Magnia, and many others who did not have time to spare but graciously helped out anyway!

- **Continuing Emphasis on Professional Practice.** Chapter 1 is once again entirely devoted to professional practice and sets the tone and context for the entire text. By beginning with professional practice, you can understand the importance of the early childhood educator's role in shaping the future. You can also recognize that your own professional development is an ongoing responsibility and a necessary part of helping children grow and develop as happily and successfully as possible.

ORGANIZATION AND COVERAGE OF THE TEXT

This edition is extensively revised to reflect current changes in society, research, and the practice of early childhood education. The text is organized in five sections:

- Part 1, "Early Childhood Education and Professional Development," begins with **Chapter 1** on professional development. This chapter is extensively revised and is designed to place professional practice at the heart of being a good teacher and as the compass for all that you do. It helps you engage in professional and ethical practice, provides a Professional Development Checklist, and has expanded coverage of caring. **Chapter 2** provides the context for change and reform that is sweeping across early childhood education today. Strategies to combat childhood obesity and ways to increase physical activity are some of the new additions to this chapter. Through this reorganized chapter, you will gain insight into contemporary educational issues and understand how public policy issues and political agendas shape contemporary practices and programs. **Chapter 3** is extensively revised and is devoted to providing the knowledge and skills necessary to effectively observe and assess children's learning and development, including use of portfolios, photographs, and documentation. Increasingly, assessment is playing a major role in directing instruction and ensuring that all children achieve mandated state and district standards. This chapter provides practical guidelines for observing and authentically assessing young children and explains how to apply the results of observation and assessment to your early childhood practice.

- Part 2, "Foundations: History and Theories," provides a historical overview of the field of early childhood education and descriptions of its theories, ideas, and practices that form its foundation. The two chapters in this section also show how the past influences the present and how the major theories of Montessori, Piaget, and Vygotsky influence programs for young children today. **Chapter 4** traces the history of the field from Martin Luther through Friedrich Froebel up to modern influences on early childhood education practice. **Chapter 5** discusses the importance of learning theories and illustrates how they are used and applied in early childhood settings. It includes expanded information on scaffolding and the zone of proximal development.

- Part 3, "Programs and Services for Children and Families," includes three chapters that illustrate how theories and public policy are transformed into practice in child care, preschools, federal programs, and public schools. **Chapter 6** illustrates how Montessori, High Scope, Reggio Emilia, and Waldorf programs function and operate, as well as expanded content on The Project Approach. **Chapter 7** discusses the important role that child care plays in the American educational system. There is a growing movement to professionalize child care, to ensure that it is of the highest quality and that programs and practices are aligned with current ideas and concepts. **Chapter 8** outlines the powerful role the federal government plays in early childhood today. Head Start has already changed the field of early childhood education, and current changes in Head Start promise to further influence early education and practice. This chapter includes new content on Migrant Head Start, inclusion and collaboration in Head Start, and Head Start's pros and cons.

- Part 4, "The New World of Early Childhood Education," begins with **Chapter 9**, devoted to a discussion of the growth, development, and education of infants and toddlers. Here you will learn how important the early years truly are and how large an impact you can have on young children and their families through your personal interactions with them and by creating enriched environments. **Chapter 10** focuses on the preschool years and outlines some of the tremendous changes that are occurring in how we educate young children. New content includes creating a lesson plan and communicating with families. **Chapter 11** looks at the kindergarten year and forthrightly addresses the educational practices of this formative year, including new content on family literacy and creating lesson plans. **Chapter 12** looks at education in grades one to three and examines how changing practices influence teaching and learning. New content includes strategies for ELLs and lesson planning to meet standards. Taken as a whole, these chapters provide a comprehensive discussion of children's development and ways to implement developmentally appropriate practices, beginning at birth and continuing through age eight.

- Part 5, "Meeting the Special Needs of Young Children," begins with **Chapter 13** and a discussion of technology and young children. It is imperative that young children learn to use technology and that you and other professionals use it to support your teaching and all children's learning. **Chapter 14** suggests ideas for guiding children and helping them to be responsible for their own behavior. These ideas will enable you to confidently manage classrooms and other early childhood settings. **Chapter 15** addresses the ever-important issues of multiculturalism and diversity, including new strategies for supporting ELLs. **Chapter 16** discusses young children's special needs, early intervention, IEPs, and other issues that you need to be aware of for today's inclusive classrooms. These two chapters help you meet children's unique needs in developmentally appropriate and authentic ways. **Chapter 17** stresses the importance of cooperation and collaboration with family and community citizens. This chapter helps you learn how to develop partnerships and confidently interact with parents, families, and communities to provide the best education for all children.

APPENDIXES

Appendix A includes a position statement from NAEYC, Code of Ethical Conduct and Statement of Commitment, which provides practical guidelines for basing your teaching and professional interactions on ethical practices. **Appendix B** presents the NAEYC Guidelines for Developmentally Appropriate Practice in Early Childhood Programs, to ensure that your programs meet the cultural, developmental, gender, and educational needs of all children in ways that are appropriate to them as individuals. **Appendix C** provides a time line of early childhood education history, listing important events from Martin Luther's argument for public support of education for all children in 1524 to Head Start's celebration of its fortieth anniversary in 2005.

SUPPLEMENTS TO THE TEXT

The supplements package for the tenth edition has also been thoroughly revised and up-graded with some exciting new ancillaries. All online ancillaries are available for download by adopting professors via **www.prenhall.com**. Contact your Prentice Hall sales represen-tative for additional information.

FOR INSTRUCTORS

- **NEW** Online Instructor's Manual. This thoroughly restructured and updated *Instructor's Manual* provides professors with a variety of useful resources to support the text, including chapter overviews; teaching strategies (opening motivators, closure) and ideas for classroom activities, discussions, and assessment; transparency masters; and thoughtful ways to integrate the new DVD, the new Ethical Dilemmas, the new Competency Builders, and the robust Companion Website into the course.

- **NEW** Online Test Bank. The revised and updated comprehensive *Test Bank* is a col-lection of multiple choice, matching, and essay (short-answer) questions. The items are designed to assess the student's understanding of concepts and applications.

- **NEW** Online PowerPoint Slides. For each chapter, we provide a new collection of PowerPoint slides, which are available for downloading by instructors. These match the transparency masters provided in the online *Instructor's Manual*.

- Computerized Test Bank Software. Known as TestGen, the computerized test bank software gives instructors electronic access to the Test Bank items, allowing them to create and customize exams. TestGen is available in both Macintosh and PC/Windows versions.

- **NEW** OneKey Course Management. OneKey is Prentice Hall's exclusive new re-source for instructors and students. OneKey is an integrated online course manage-ment resource, featuring everything students and instructors need for work in or outside the classroom, including a Study Guide (Spanish and English), Companion Website material, *Instructor's Manual, Test Bank,* PowerPoint slides, videos from *Early Childhood Education Settings and Approaches,* suggestions for using the NAEYC Code of Ethical Conduct, and more. OneKey is available in WebCT and Blackboard.

FOR STUDENTS

- Companion Website. Located at **www.prenhall.com/morrison**, the Companion Website for this text includes a wealth of resources for both students and professors. Focus Questions help students review chapter content. Students can test their knowl-edge by going to the Multiple Choice and Essay modules and taking interactive quizzes, which provide immediate feedback with a percentage score and correct an-swers. Responses and results can be submitted to instructors via e-mail. The Linking to Learning module contains hot links to all the websites mentioned in the text and assists students in using the Internet to do additional research on chapter topics and key issues. Websites and activities facilitate connections to professional organizations and other groups in the Making Connections module. The Program in Action and Di-versity Tie-In modules provide activities with hot links to articles and websites to en-hance and extend the feature topics in the textbook. The Glossary module and the Professional Development Checklist are also included on this site.

- **NEW** Online Textbook Choice for Student Savings! SafariX Textbooks Online™ is an exciting new choice for students looking to save money. As an alternative to purchasing the print textbook, students can subscribe to the same content online and save up to 50 percent off the suggested list price of the print text. With a SafariX Web-Book, students can search the text, make notes online, print out reading assignments that incorporate lecture notes, and bookmark important passages for later review. For more information, or to subscribe to the SafariX WebBook, visit **www.safariX.com**.

- Student Study Guide. The Student Study Guide provides students with additional opportunities to review chapter content and helps them learn and study more effectively. Each chapter of the guide contains several pages of concept and term identification; open-ended questions requiring short, written answers; and a number of other helpful review resources, including a self-check quiz.

- **NEW** Spanish Student Study Guide. A Spanish language version of the Student Study Guide is available for the first time with the tenth edition. This translation, which has undergone regional geographic reviews, features the same content as the English language version.

ACKNOWLEDGMENTS

In the course of my teaching, service, and consulting, I meet and talk with many professionals who are deeply dedicated to doing their best for young children and their families. I am always touched, heartened, and encouraged by the openness, honesty, and unselfish sharing of ideas that characterize these professional colleagues. I thank all the individuals who contributed to the Voice from the Field, Program in Action, Diversity Tie-In, Competency Builder, and other program features. They are all credited for their contributions, and I am very thankful they have agreed to share with you and me the personal accounts of their professional practice, their children's lives, and their programs.

I am also very grateful to reviewers Tena Carr, San Joaquin Delta College; Pamela Chibucos, Owens Community College; Ann Disque, East Tennessee State University; Stephanie Shine, Texas Tech University; and Kathleen P. Watkins, Community College of Philadelphia, for their very important and helpful feedback. The reviewers challenged me to rethink content and made suggestions for inclusion of new ideas. Many of the changes in this tenth edition are the result of their suggestions.

My editors at Merrill/Prentice Hall continue to be the best in the industry. It was a pleasure to work once again with my editor, Julie Peters, who overflows with creative ideas. I value her remarkable vision and hard work, which help make *Early Childhood Education Today* the leader in the field. Development Editor Karen Balkin is organized, persistent, and adept at managing all of the features that put the tenth edition on the cutting edge. Senior Production Editor Linda Bayma and Production Coordinator Norine Strang (Carlisle Publishing Services) are very attentive to detail and make sure everything is done right. I also appreciated Kathy Termeer's able assistance and can-do attitude in obtaining needed permissions. My copyeditor, Mary Benis, was collaborative, encouraging, and extremely helpful. She constantly challenged me to write better and to view issues from all sides. Together, my colleagues have made this tenth edition one of high and exceptional quality.

TEACHER PREP

MERRILL
PRENTICE HALL

Teacher Preparation Classroom

See a demo at
www.prenhall.com/teacherprep/demo

Your Class. Their Careers. Our Future. Will your students be prepared?

We invite you to explore our new, innovative and engaging website and all that it has to offer you, your course, and tomorrow's educators! Organized around the major courses pre-service teachers take, the Teacher Preparation site provides media, student/teacher artifacts, strategies, research articles, and other resources to equip your students with the quality tools needed to excel in their courses and prepare them for their first classroom.

This ultimate on-line education resource is available at no cost, when packaged with a Merrill text, and will provide you and your students access to:

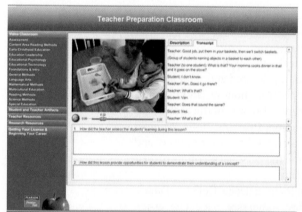

Online Video Library. More than 150 video clips—each tied to a course topic and framed by learning goals and Praxis-type questions—capture real teachers and students working in real classrooms, as well as in-depth interviews with both students and educators.

Student and Teacher Artifacts. More than 200 student and teacher classroom artifacts—each tied to a course topic and framed by learning goals and application questions—provide a wealth of materials and experiences to help make your study to become a professional teacher more concrete and hands-on.

Research Articles. Over 500 articles from ASCD's renowned journal *Educational Leadership*. The site also includes Research Navigator, a searchable database of additional educational journals.

Teaching Strategies. Over 500 strategies and lesson plans for you to use when you become a practicing professional.

Licensure and Career Tools. Resources devoted to helping you pass your licensure exam; learn standards, law, and public policies; plan a teaching portfolio; and succeed in your first year of teaching.

How to ORDER *Teacher Prep* for you and your students:

For students to receive a *Teacher Prep* Access Code with this text, instructors **must** provide a special value pack ISBN number on their textbook order form. To receive this special ISBN, please email **Merrill.marketing@pearsoned.com** and provide the following information:

- Name and Affiliation
- Author/Title/Edition of Merrill text

Upon ordering *Teacher Prep* for their students, instructors will be given a lifetime *Teacher Prep* Access Code.

Brief Contents

Contents

Note: Every effort has been made to provide accurate and current Internet information in this book. However, the Internet and information posted on it are constantly changing, so it is inevitable that some of the Internet addresses listed in this textbook will change.

Special Features

PROGRAMS IN ACTION

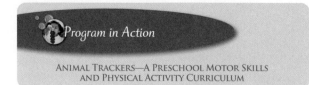

ANIMAL TRACKERS—A PRESCHOOL MOTOR SKILLS
AND PHYSICAL ACTIVITY CURRICULUM

VOICES FROM THE FIELD

ADVOCACY: A VIEW FROM THE FRONT

PART 1

Early Childhood Education and Professional Development

CHAPTER 1

You and Early Childhood Education

WHAT DOES IT MEAN TO BE A PROFESSIONAL?

Whatever you decide to do with your hours in the classroom, use your talents to make it a beautiful and rewarding time for your students.

CHRISTA PEHRSON AND VICKI SHEFFLER, 2002, *USA TODAY* FIRST-TEAM TEACHERS

This is an exciting time to be a member of the early childhood education profession. Early childhood education has changed more in the last ten years than in the previous fifty years, and more changes are in store. Why is early childhood education undergoing dramatic transformation and reform?

First, there has been a tremendous increase in scientific knowledge about young children and the ways they grow, develop, and learn. This new knowledge enables professionals to view young children as extremely capable and naturally eager to learn at a very young age. Second, educators have developed research-based programs and curricula that enable children to learn literally from the beginning of life. Third, research validates the theory that high-quality education in the early years has positive and lasting benefits for children throughout their lives.[1] The way children are reared and educated in the early formative years makes a significant difference in the way they develop and learn. When families, teachers, and other caring adults get it right from the start of children's lives, all of society reaps big dividends. Fourth, the total number of three- and four-year-old children served by forty-four state prekindergarten programs in the 2002–2003 school year rose to 711,000, up from 667,000 the previous year.[2] The demand for teachers and the ongoing public and professional attention will continue to increase as states expand their preschool programs.

Combined, these changes are dramatically altering our understanding of how young children learn and how teachers teach. As a result, the field of early childhood education is entering a new era, which requires professionals who are up-to-date and willing to adapt so that all children will learn and succeed in school and life. You and other early childhood professionals have a wonderful opportunity to develop new and improved programs and to advocate for best practices.

WHAT IS A PROFESSIONAL?

You are preparing to be an early childhood professional, to teach children from birth to age eight. You are going to work with families and the community to bring high-quality education and services to all children. How would you explain the term **early childhood professional** to others? What does *professional* mean?

An early childhood professional has the personal characteristics, knowledge, and skills necessary to teach and conduct programs so that all children learn, as well as the ability to inform the public about children's and families' issues. Professionals are those who promote high standards for themselves, their colleagues, and their students—they are continually improving and expanding their skills and knowledge. A professional is a multidimensional person.

You will discover in your work as an early childhood professional the many opportunities for ongoing professional development which is an extremely important part of your profession. You will realize that as a result of the changing field of early childhood education there are many new job opportunities. Your role as teacher, aide, or administrator, is constantly changing in response to new jobs created by the expanding field of early childhood education. You can expect that you will participate in many professional development activities; will be constantly involved in new programs and practices; and will have opportunities to engage in new and different roles as a professional.

Focus Questions

Who is an early childhood professional?

What can you do to demonstrate the personal, educational, professional practice, and public dimensions of professionalism?

How can you prepare for a career in early childhood education?

What does the future hold for you as an early childhood professional?

Companion Website

To check your understanding of this chapter, go to the Companion Website at **www.prenhall.com/ morrison**, select chapter 1, answer Multiple Choice and Essay Questions, and receive feedback.

Early childhood professional An educator who successfully teaches all children, promotes high personal standards, and continually expands his or her skills and knowledge.

National Association for the Education of Young Children (NAEYC) An organization of early childhood educators and others dedicated to improving the quality of programs for children from birth through the third grade.

Companion Website For more information about NAEYC, go to the Companion Website at **www.prenhall.com/morrison**, select chapter 1, then choose the Linking to Learning module.

THE FOUR DIMENSIONS OF PROFESSIONALISM

Being a professional goes beyond academic degrees and experiences. Professionalism has four integrated dimensions, all of which are important: personal characteristics, educational attainment, professional practice, and public presentation (see Figure 1.1). Each of these dimensions plays a powerful role in determining who and what a professional is and how professionals implement practice in early childhood classrooms. Let's review each of these dimensions and see how you can apply them to your professional practice.

PERSONAL CHARACTERISTICS

I am sure you have heard the saying, "Who you are speaks so loudly I can't hear what you're saying." This is why the personal dimension of professionalism is so important: it includes all the qualities, attitudes, and behaviors you demonstrate as a professional—your character traits, emotional qualities, and physical and mental health.

Character Traits. Ethical behavior—acting on high morals and values—is one very important quality of your personal character. Professional teachers conduct their practices in ways that are legally and ethically proper. Professionals want to do what is right and honest in their relationships with students, colleagues, and parents.

Many professions, such as medicine and law, have unified and universal codes of ethics that govern practice. Although the teaching profession lacks such a code, professional organizations, such as the **National Association for the Education of Young Children (NAEYC)**, have developed codes of ethics that help inform and guide professional practice. You can review the NAEYC Code of Ethical Conduct in appendix A.

Civility is a second important personal characteristic. It includes courtesy, patience, tolerance, respect, and acts of kindness and helpfulness in interaction with children, parents and families, colleagues, and others.

In addition, early childhood professionals should demonstrate dedication, trustworthiness, enthusiasm, understanding, intelligence, and motivation. If we want these qualities in our future professionals, we need to promote them now, in our teaching of young children. Home and early school experiences are critical for developing these character qualities.

FIGURE 1.1 The Four Dimensions of Professionalism

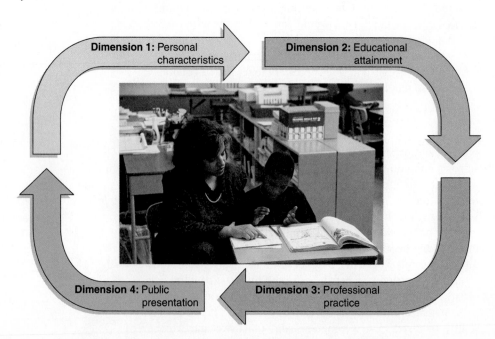

Dimension 1: Personal characteristics

Dimension 2: Educational attainment

Dimension 4: Public presentation

Dimension 3: Professional practice

Emotional Qualities. Some emotional qualities that are crucial for a successful early childhood education professional are love and respect for children and their families, compassion, empathy, friendliness, sensitivity, warmth, and caring.

For the early childhood professional, caring is the most important of these emotional qualities. Professionals care about children; they accept and respect all children and their cultural and socioeconomic backgrounds. As a professional, you will work in classrooms, programs, and other settings where things do not always go smoothly—for example, children will not always learn ably and well, and they will not always be clean and free from illness and hunger. Children's and their parents' backgrounds and ways of life will not always be the same as yours. Caring means you will lose sleep trying to find a way to help a child learn to read and you will spend long hours planning and gathering materials. Caring also means you will not leave your intelligence, enthusiasm, and other talents at home but will bring them into the center, the classroom, administration offices, boards of directors' meetings, and wherever else you can make a difference in the lives of children and their families.

The theme of caring should run deep in your professional preparation and in your teaching. Listen to what Nel Noddings, a prominent teacher educator, has to say about caring:

In the Kindergarten segment of the DVD accompanying this text, the kindergarten teacher emphasizes that teachers must teach children to care for each other. Reflect on your role of caring and teaching children. What does it involve?

> In an age when violence among school-children is at an unprecedented level, when children are bearing children with little knowledge of how to care for them, when the society and even the schools often concentrate on materialistic messages, it may be unnecessary to argue that we should care more genuinely for our children and teach them to care. However, many otherwise reasonable people seem to believe that our educational problems consist largely of low scores on achievement tests. My contention is, first, that we should want more from our educational efforts than adequate academic achievement and, second, that we will not achieve even that meager success unless our children believe that they themselves are cared for and learn to care for others.[3]

The Voice from the Field about caring and kindness illustrates this important point with many examples that you can use in your program or classroom.

Physical Health. Being healthy and fit is an important part of professional practice. When you are healthy, you can do your best and be your best. When you practice good health habits, such as eating a well-balanced diet and staying physically fit, you also set a good example for your students. Wellness and healthy living are vital for the energy, enthusiasm, and stamina that teaching demands.

Mental Health. Good mental health is as important as good physical health. Good mental health includes having a positive outlook on life, the profession, and the future. Having good mental health enables professionals to instill in children good mental health habits. Some of the characteristics of good mental health are optimism, attentiveness, self-confidence, and self-respect.

Early childhood education professionals are often role models for the children they teach. Therefore, if we want children to be caring, kind, tolerant, and sensitive individuals, the adults in their lives should model those behaviors.

EDUCATIONAL ATTAINMENT

The educational dimension of professionalism involves having essential knowledge regarding the profession and professional practice. This includes knowing the history of the profession and the ethics of the profession, understanding the ways children develop and learn, and keeping up-to-date on public issues that influence early childhood and the profession.

CARING AND KINDNESS ARE KEYS TO THE PROFESSION

Kindness is a simple eight-letter word that has the extraordinary power to make the world a better place. As teachers, we have the unique opportunity to promote the practice of kind acts each and every day, in and out of our classrooms.

Someone once said, "We have committed the Golden Rule to memory; let us now commit it to life." In our classroom we teach our students as we would want our own children to be taught. In other words, we practice what we teach by inspiring our students to share kindness with one another and to spread kindness wherever they go. If their first impression is going to be a lasting impression, we want it to be a love of learning *and* a respect for and kindness toward the community and others. To achieve that goal, we teachers must model kindness:

- Show enthusiasm for the subject matter and the students
- Take time to know each student, both personally and academically (e.g., likes, dislikes, strengths, weaknesses, home environment)
- Be friendly and courteous, knowing that our attitudes can change our students' attitudes
- Be supportive and encouraging (e.g., saying "I am very proud of you," "Keep trying," "You're a great example for others")
- Be tactful and discreet, avoid the use of criticism and ridicule
- Do not choose favorites
- Be sensitive to student responses
- Encourage mutual respect and trust by example
- Create nurturing interactions with the students (our classroom motto, "Effort Creates Ability," makes students feel secure in trying new things)

- Provide comfort
- Display a keen sense of respect for all cultures and traditions

CLASSROOM PLEDGES

Each morning we and our students begin the day by reciting three pledges. The first is our Kindness Promise:

Every day, in every way,
I will show kindness to others.

When an unkind act occurs in our classroom, we ask the students involved to repeat the Kindness Promise and to make an apology to the parties involved.

Our second promise is our Helping Hands pledge. It is a quote from Helen Keller:

I am only one, but still I am one.
I cannot do everything, but still I can do something.
And because I cannot do everything, I will not refuse to do the something that I can do.

This is our motto for community service projects in our classroom.

Our last pledge is our learning cheer.

L—Listen to others.
E—Expect to learn each day.
A—Act kindly toward others.
R—Remember the class rules.
N—Never give up on yourself.
1, 2, 3—First grade's cool!

All three pledges remind us that there is more to our classroom than the three Rs. When we think back on our own education, we don't remember the methods of teach-

A major challenge facing all areas of the early childhood education profession is the training and certification of those who care for and teach young children. Training and certification requirements vary from state to state, but more states are tightening standards for child care, preschool, kindergarten, and primary personnel. Many states have mandatory training requirements that individuals must meet before being certified. For example, in North Carolina a lead teacher in a child care program must be at least eighteen years of age and have at least a North Carolina Early Childhood Credential or its equivalent. To receive the North Carolina Early Childhood Credential, teachers must have two early childhood

ing, but we remember our teachers: the ones who inspired us, the ones who took special interest in us, the ones who motivated us to do our best, the ones who encouraged us to dream bigger dreams.

To show acts of kindness in our classroom, we do a number of special activities:

- Pause each morning for a moment of silence. We think kind-and-happy thoughts for our students who are absent, as well as for friends, family, pets, and situations that could benefit from our actions.
- Make a kindness critter, which is like a caterpillar. Each day our class thinks of one new way to show kindness. The teachers write the idea on a new segment of the caterpillar. By the end of the school year, we have a very long critter with almost two hundred ways of showing kindness to others.
- Have regular class meetings to discuss situations in the classroom that relate to kindness (or its absence) and brainstorm solutions for those situations.
- Insist that each student say please and thank you. We also remind our students to say, "I'm sorry."
- Encourage students to compliment each other (e.g., "I like your picture," or "Congratulations, your team won the game."
- Display a rainbow fish in the classroom. Each time the teachers catch someone showing kindness, that person can add a shiny scale to the rainbow fish.
- Form partnerships with organizations in the community. Our local chapter of Parent-Wise has developed a Bee Kind program, which comes to our school, sharing stories and creating hands-on activities that remind the students about the importance of kind acts, no matter how big or small.
- Use Elaine Parke's Caring Habit of the Month series to practice kindness during each month of the year. Posters are displayed throughout the school, and special pencils with the habit for the month printed on them are distributed to students. This program supports the notion that one month is the length of time it takes to turn actions into good habits.

As teachers, we should be the living expression of kindness. Our students should see kindness in our eyes, our faces, and our smiles. Each of us possesses special and unique talents. Whatever you decide to do with your hours in the classroom, use those talents to make it a beautiful, kind, and rewarding time for your students.

KINDNESS OUTSIDE THE CLASSROOM

"Kindness is the golden chain by which society is bound together." There is no better way to promote and foster kindness and compassion in our world than by participating in community service projects.

Teachers have the power to promote random acts of kindness outside the classroom. Here are the ways that we have taken caring and kindness outside our classroom:

- We made a lemonade stand and sold lemonade after each physical education class. We sent the proceeds of the sale to President Bush to be given to the children of Afghanistan.
- We traced the handprint of each of the students in our school onto red, white, or blue pieces of felt. We formed a six-by-eight-foot American flag from those hands and gave it to our state representative. It is now proudly displayed in our state capitol building.
- On Veterans Day we raked the leaves of veterans who live near our school.
- We visited the pediatric floor of our local hospital. We used the bonus points from our Book Club to acquire age-appropriate books and prepared gift bags of hot chocolate, cups, and student-made bookmarks. Our theme was "Warm up with a good book; you'll feel so much better!" The books were given to each sick child as he or she was admitted to the hospital.

Let your light shine! "All the darkness in the world cannot extinguish the light of a single candle."

Contributed by Christa Pehrson and Vicki Sheffler, 2002 *USA Today* First-Team Teachers, Amos K. Hutchinson Elementary School, Greensburg, Pennsylvania.

curriculum courses—six quarter hour credits or four semester hour credits.[4] Courses include the following topics:

- Becoming an early childhood professional
- Understanding the young child—growth and development
- Understanding the young child—individuality, family, and culture
- Developmentally appropriate practices
- Positive guidance
- Health and safety

Many states have career ladders that specify the requirements for progressing from one level of professionalism to the next. Figure 1.2 illustrates the career pathway for early childhood professionals in Oklahoma.

Degree Programs

Associate Degree Programs. Many community colleges provide training in early childhood education that qualifies recipients to be child care aides, primary child care providers, and assistant teachers. For example, Austin Community College in Austin, Texas, offers a two-year associate's degree in early childhood education. Courses in the program include child development, childhood education, wellness of the young child, literacy of the child, and family, school, and community collaboration. Other colleges offer certificate programs, designed to provide the recipient with skills in a specific area and for a specific purpose. For example, at Capital Community College in Hartford, Connecticut, a thirty-credit-hour program yields a certificate in Early Childhood Education and enables students to work with children under five as teacher assistants.

Baccalaureate Programs. Four-year colleges provide programs that result in early childhood teacher certification. The ages and grades to which the certification applies vary from state to state. Some states have separate certification for prekindergarten programs and nursery schools; in other states these certifications are add-ons to elementary (K–6, 1–6, or 1–4) certification.

Master's Degree Programs. Depending on the state, individuals may gain initial early childhood certification at the master's level. Many colleges and universities offer master's-level programs for people who want to qualify as program directors or assistant directors or who may want to pursue a career in teaching.

Certification/Credentialing Programs

CDA National Credentialing Program. At the national level, the Child Development Associate (CDA) National Credentialing Program offers early childhood professionals the opportunity to develop and demonstrate competencies for meeting the needs of young children. A CDA is one who is "able to meet the specific needs of children and who, with parents and other adults, works to nurture children's physical, social, emotional, and intellectual growth in a child development framework."[5]

The CDA program is a major national effort to evaluate and improve the skills of caregivers in center-based preschool settings, center-based infant/toddler settings, family day care homes, home visitor settings, and programs that have specific goals for bilingual children. The program is operated by the Council for Early Childhood Professional Recognition, which offers two options for obtaining the CDA credential, both of which require a candidate to be eighteen years old or older and hold a high school diploma or equivalent.

Direct assessment. The direct assessment option is designed for candidates who have child care work experience in combination with some early childhood education training. The majority of CDA candidates pursue this option.

To obtain the CDA national credential, direct assessment candidates must meet these additional requirements:

- 480 hours of experience working with children within the past five years
- 120 clock hours of training with at least ten hours in each of the following eight CDA training areas and an emphasis in either infant/toddler or preschool concerns:
  - Health and safety
  - Physical and intellectual development
  - Social and emotional development
  - Relationships with families
  - Program operation

Advanced degrees—MS, MA, PhD, EdD, JD, MD, RN

TRADITIONAL
- Occupational Child Care Instructor at technology centers
- Teacher Educator at a two-year college or four-year university
- Teacher/Administrator/Special Educator in a public or private elementary school—certification required
- Instructor/Curriculum Specialist in the armed services
- Child Development Specialist
- Child Guidance Specialist
- Researcher/Writer

RELATED
- Social worker
- Child Advocate/Lobbyist
- Librarian
- Pediatric Therapist— occupational and physical
- Human Resources Personnel in industry
- Child Life Specialist in a hospital
- Speech and Hearing Pathologist— Health Department, public/private school, private practice, university teaching
- Early Childhood Consultant
- Entertainer/Musician/Song Writer for children

- Author and Illustrator of children's books
- Physician/Pediatrician
- Pedodontist (works only with children)
- Dietitian
- Counselor
- Child Psychologist
- Psychiatrist
- Dietetic Assistant
- Recreation Supervisor
- Children's Policy Specialist
- Dental Hygienist
- Scouting Director

- Child Care Center or Playground/Recreation Center Designer
- Probation Officer
- 4-H Agent or County Extension Director
- Adoption Specialist
- Child Care Resource and Referral Director
- "Friend of the Court" Counselor
- Psychometrist
- Attorney with primary focus on children
- Religious Educator
- Certified Child and Parenting Specialist
- Family Mediator

Baccalaureate Level

TRADITIONAL
- Early Childhood Teacher in public school, Head Start, or child care settings
- Special Education Teacher
- Family Child Care Home Provider
- Nanny
- Administrator in Head Start program
- Child Care Center Director/Owner/ Coordinator
- Child Care Center Director in the armed services

- Parents as Teacher's Facilitator
- Director of school-age (out-of-school time) program

RELATED
Some positions will require additional coursework at the baccalaureate level which will be in a field other than early childhood.
- Child Advocate/Lobbyist
- Recreation Director/Worker/Leader
- Web Master

- Journalist/Author/Publisher/ Illustrator of children's books
- Children's Librarian
- Retail Manager of children's toy or bookstores
- Licensing Worker
- Human Resource Personnel in industry
- Music Teacher, Musician/ Entertainer for children
- Recreation Camp Director
- Camp Counselor/ Scout Camp Ranger

- Resource and Referral Trainer/Data Analyst/ Referral Specialist/Child Care Food Program Consultant
- Childbirth Educator
- Gymnastic or Dance Teacher
- Pediatric Nurse Aide
- Child and Parenting Practitioner
- Producer of children's television shows and commercials
- Faith Community Coordinator and Educator

Associate Level

TRADITIONAL
- Head Start Teacher
- Child Care Teacher
- Family Child Care Home Provider
- Nanny
- Child Care Center Director

- School-Age Provider
- Early Intervention/ Special Needs Program
- Para-Teacher/Aide

RELATED
In addition to those listed at the core level:

- Family and Human Services Worker
- LPN—specialized nurse training
- Entertainer for children at theme restaurants and parks
- Social Service Aide

- Playground Helper
- Physical Therapy Assistant
- Nursing Home Aide/ Worker/Technician
- Faith Community Coordinators for families and children

Credential Level

- Head Start Teacher
- Child Care Teacher

- Family Child Care Home Provider
- Nanny

- Child Care Center Director
- Home Visitor

- Nursing Home Aide/Worker

Core Level
These positions require minimum education and training, depending on the position.

TRADITIONAL
- Child Care Teaching Assistant
- Family Child Care Home Provider
- Head Start Teacher Assistant
- Nanny
- Foster Parent
- Church Nursery Attendant

- Related positions which involve working with children in settings other than a child care center, family child care home, Head Start or public school program

RELATED
Positions may require specialized preservice training.

- Children's Storyteller, Art Instructor, or Puppeteer
- Recreation Center Assistant
- Salesperson in toy, clothing, or bookstore
- School Crossing Guard
- Children's Party Caterer
- Restaurant Helper for birthday parties
- Van or Transportation Driver
- Children's Art Museum Guide

- Receptionist in pediatrician's office
- Camp Counselor
- Special Needs Child Care Aide
- Live-in Caregiver
- Respite Caregiver
- Cook's Aide, Assistant Cook, Camp Cook, Head Start or Child Care Center Cook

FIGURE 1.2 Early Childhood Practitioner's Professional Pathway in Oklahoma

Source: Reprinted by permission from the Center for Early Childhood Professional Development, College of Continuing Education, University of Oklahoma, funded by the Oklahoma Department of Human Services/Division of Child Care.

- Professionalism
- Observing and recording children's behavior
- Child growth and development[6]

The candidate must then demonstrate competence in the six CDA areas described in Table 1.1.

Professional Preparation Program (P3). To obtain credentialing through this option, the candidate must identify an advisor to work with during the year of study, which is made up of three phases: fieldwork, course work, and final evaluation.

TABLE 1.1 CDA Competency Goals and Functional Areas

CDA Competency Goals	Functional Areas
I. To establish and maintain a safe, healthy learning environment	1. *Safe:* Candidate provides a safe environment to prevent and reduce injuries. 2. *Healthy:* Candidate promotes good health and nutrition and provides an environment that contributes to the prevention of illness. 3. *Learning environment:* Candidate uses space, relationships, materials, and routines as resources for constructing an interesting, secure, and enjoyable environment that encourages play, exploration, and learning.
II. To advance physical and intellectual competence	4. *Physical:* Candidate provides a variety of equipment, activities, and opportunities to promote intellectual competence. 5. *Cognitive:* Candidate provides activities and opportunities that encourage curiosity, exploration, and problem solving appropriate to the development levels and learning styles of children. 6. *Communication:* Candidate actively communicates with children and provides opportunities and support for children to understand, acquire, and use verbal and nonverbal means of communicating thoughts and feelings. 7. *Creative:* Candidate provides opportunities that stimulate children to play with sound, rhythm, language, materials, space, and ideas in individual ways and to express their creative abilities.
III. To support social and emotional development and to provide positive guidance	8. *Self:* Candidate provides physical and emotional security for each child and helps each child to know, accept, and take pride in himself or herself and to develop a sense of independence. 9. *Social:* Candidate helps each child feel accepted in the group, helps children learn to communicate and get along with others, and encourages feelings of empathy and mutual respect among children and adults. 10. *Guidance:* Candidate provides a supportive environment in which children can begin to learn and practice appropriate and acceptable behaviors as individuals and as a group.
IV. To establish positive and productive relationships with families	11. *Families:* Candidate maintains an open, friendly, and cooperative relationship with each child's family, encourages their involvement in the program, and supports the child's relationship with his or her family.
V. To ensure a well-run, purposeful program responsive to participant needs	12. *Program management:* Candidate is a manager who uses all available resources to ensure an effective operation. The candidate is a competent organizer, planner, record keeper, needs communicator, and a cooperative coworker.
VI. To maintain a commitment to professionalism	13. *Professionalism:* Candidate makes decisions based on knowledge of early childhood theories and practices; promotes quality in child care services; and takes advantage of opportunities to improve competence, both for personal and professional growth and for the benefit of children and families.

Source: Reprinted by permission from the Council for Professional Recognition, *Essentials for Child Development Associates Working with Young Children* (Washington, DC: Author, 1991), 415. Also available online at http://www.cdacouncil.org/rqmts/HV/GoalsandFunctional.htm.

Fieldwork involves study of the council's model curriculum, *Essentials for Child Development Associates Working with Young Children,* which includes the six competency areas listed in Table 1.1. In the second phase, course work, the candidate participates in seminars offered in community colleges and other postsecondary institutions. These seminars are designed to supplement the model curriculum and are administered by a seminar instructor. The third phase is the final evaluation, which takes place in the candidate's work setting or field placement.

The results of all three phases are sent to the council office for review to determine whether the candidate has successfully completed all aspects of the CDA Professional Preparation Program. To date, more than two hundred thousand persons have been awarded the CDA credential. For additional information, you can contact the Council for Early Childhood Professional Recognition.

Teacher Certification. The process of becoming a professional is ongoing and requires that one meet federal, state, and school district requirements for ongoing certification and licensing. All fifty states have requirements that teachers must meet as a condition for continued employment.

In addition, under the No Child Left Behind Act, all teacher aides who work in schools and programs that receive federal poverty funds must become highly qualified by the end of the 2005–2006 school year. To be highly qualified, teacher aides must complete at least two years of college study, earn at least an associate's degree, or pass a test proving their knowledge of reading, writing, and math and their ability to help teach.[7]

National Board for Professional Teaching Standards. National Board Certification is a growing part of the national effort to strengthen standards for the teaching profession. It is a voluntary, advanced teaching credential that goes beyond state licensure by identifying national standards for what accomplished teachers should know and be able to do.

The National Board focuses on education reform in the classroom and certifies teachers who successfully complete its Certification process. The National Board offers a number of certifications, including the Early Childhood/Generalist Certificate. This certificate is designed for teachers of students aged three to eight who engage their students in all subject areas addressed in the Early Childhood/Generalist Standards. The National Board Certification process requires intense self-reflection and is a valuable tool for professional development.[8] Many of the features included in this book were written by National Board certified teachers, including the Voice from the Field by Carole Moyer in this chapter and the lesson plan by Sylvia McCabe in chapter 11.

PROFESSIONAL PRACTICE

Professional practice involves doing what professionals do—teaching and caring for children, working with parents and families, collaborating with community partners, and assuming all the other roles and responsibilities included in the profession. This dimension involves knowing children; developing a philosophy of education; planning; assessing; reporting; reflecting and thinking; teaching; collaborating with parents, families, and community partners; engaging in ethical practice; and seeking continued professional development opportunities.

Knowing Children. **Child development** is the foundation of early childhood professional practice. Child development knowledge enables you to know how children grow and develop across all developmental areas—cognitive, linguistic, social, emotional,

Early childhood educators are professionals who—in addition to teaching and caring for children—plan, assess, report, collaborate with colleagues and families, and behave in ethical ways.

Companion Website For more information about National Board certification, go to the Companion Website at **www.prenhall.com/morrison**, select chapter 1, then choose the Linking to Learning module.

Child development The sum total of the physical, intellectual, social, emotional, and behavioral changes that occur in children from conception through adolescence.

In the Infant and Toddler segment of the DVD, observe how knowledge of child development can help create developmentally appropriate and child-centered environments. How does this knowledge help you be responsive to children's needs?

Philosophy of education
Beliefs about children's development and learning and the best ways to teach them.

and physical—which help make children the unique individuals they are. Competent professionals also really know the children they teach and care for. Knowledge of individual children, combined with knowledge of child growth and development, enables you to provide care and education that is appropriate for every child. Such knowledge is essential for understanding how to conduct developmentally appropriate practice, which is the recommended teaching practice of the profession and is discussed in more detail in chapters 9, 10, 11 and 12.

Developmentally appropriate practice goes far beyond mere knowledge of how children develop.

> Developmentally appropriate practice requires that teachers integrate the many dimensions of their knowledge base. They must know about child development and the implications of this knowledge for how to teach, the content of the curriculum—what to teach and when—how to assess what children have learned, and how to adapt curriculum and instruction to children's individual strengths, needs, and interests. Further they must know the particular children they teach and their families and be knowledgeable as well about the social and cultural context.[9]

Developing a Philosophy of Education. Professional practice includes teaching with and from a **philosophy of education,** which acts as a guidepost to help you base your teaching on what you believe about children.

A philosophy of education is a set of beliefs about how children develop and learn and what and how they should be taught. Your philosophy of education is based on your philosophy of life. What you believe about yourself, about others, and about life infuses and determines your philosophy of education. Knowing what others believe is important and useful, for it can help you clarify what you believe, but when all is said and done, you have to decide what *you* believe. Moment by moment, day by day, what you believe influences what you will teach and how you will teach it.

A philosophy of life and education is more than an opinion. A personal philosophy is based on core values and beliefs. Core values relate to your beliefs about the nature of life, the purpose of life, your role and calling in life, and your relationship and responsibilities to others. Core beliefs and values about education and teaching include what you believe about the nature of children and the purpose of education, the role of teachers, and what is worth knowing.

Your philosophy of education will guide and direct your daily teaching. Your beliefs about how children learn best will determine whether you individualize instruction or try to teach the same thing in the same way to everyone. Your philosophy will also determine whether you help children do things for themselves or whether you do things for them.

As you read through and study this book, make notes and reflect about your developing philosophy of education. The following headings will help get you started:

- I believe the purposes of education are . . .
- I believe that children learn best when they are taught under certain conditions and in certain ways. Some of these are . . .
- The curriculum of any classroom should include certain basics that contribute to children's social, emotional, intellectual, and physical development. These basics include . . .
- Children learn best in an environment that promotes learning. Features of a good learning environment are . . .
- All children have certain needs that must be met if they are to grow and learn to their best ability. Some of these basic needs are . . .
- I would meet these needs by . . .
- A teacher should have certain qualities and behave in certain ways. Qualities I think are important for teaching are . . .

Once you have determined your philosophy of education, write it down and have other people read it. This helps you clarify your ideas and redefine your thoughts, because

10 TIPS FOR BEING A PROFESSIONAL

1. *I am honest and trustworthy.* I present myself to all constituents (students, parents, administration, and the community) in such a way that they know I can be depended on. I am ethical and have integrity so that I never misrepresent the profession, my school, or my district.

2. *I am fair and strive diligently not to discriminate.* I respect and attempt to celebrate the diversity of all cultures represented in our school. My practice is guided by the values of equality, tolerance, and respect for others.

3. *I respect the privacy of others.* I gather personal information for the specific purpose of informing my practice. This personal information is not used for purposes that might harm or compromise the trust of my students or their families.

4. *I honor confidentiality.* I discuss my students' progress, behavior, attitudes, and family circumstances with the support personnel who need the information for the sole purpose of helping me design programs to support my students intellectually, physically, socially, and emotionally. My discussions take place in the proper manner, context, and setting—not in the school halls or in the teachers' lounge.

5. *I acquire and maintain professional competence.* My most important obligation is to achieve quality. I am aware of my students' needs, interests, and abilities. I determine the best ways to impart concepts to my students and, thus, employ multiple paths to learning. I understand the standards for appropriate levels of competence and strive to achieve these standards. I participate in independent study, attend seminars, conferences, and/or courses, and am involved in professional organizations. I collaborate with families, the community, and my colleagues.

6. *I know and respect existing laws pertaining to my profession.* I obey existing local, state, and national laws that are established on an ethical basis. I obey the policies and procedures of my school and district.

7. *I honor contracts, agreements, and assigned responsibilities.* I honor my commitment to provide quality instruction, even when this commitment requires me to use my personal resources, expend extra energy, and work hours that extend past the school day and year. I accept personal accountability for professional work. I am a contributing member of my school community, even when the assigned duties or voluntary tasks do not directly affect my classroom and/or students.

8. *I improve public understanding of teaching and the profession.* I willingly share knowledge with the public by encouraging understanding of the educational process and the methods utilized in my classroom. I wholeheartedly counter any false views related to the profession, my school, and my district. I seek opportunities to speak with policy makers and the community about the importance of supporting education.

9. *I communicate effectively.* My spoken communication is intelligible and suited to the audience. My written communication is free of spelling and grammatical errors. I make provisions for children and parents who have differing levels of understanding and use of the English language.

10. *I am cognizant of my appearance.* I dress appropriately for each situation, but always in a manner that represents the profession in a positive light. As a role model for students, I am purposefully neat in my attire.

Contributed by Carole D. Moyer, National Board certified teacher, early childhood coordinator, Shepard Center, Columbus Public Schools, Columbus, Ohio.

your philosophy should be understandable to others (although they do not necessarily have to agree with you).

Talk with successful teachers and other educators about their philosophies. The accounts of teachers and others in the Voice from the Field features throughout this text are evidence that a philosophy can help you be an above-average teacher. Talking with others and reflecting on their advice exposes you to different points of view and stimulates your thinking. The Voice from the Field by Carole Moyer provides ten powerful tips for molding yourself into a high-quality professional.

Finally, evaluate your philosophy against this checklist:

- Does my philosophy accurately reflect my beliefs about teaching? Have I been honest with myself?
- Is it understandable to me and others?
- Does it provide practical guidance for teaching?
- Are my ideas consistent with one another?
- Does what I believe make good sense?
- Have I been comprehensive, stating my beliefs about (1) how children learn, (2) what children should be taught, (3) how children should be taught, (4) the conditions under which children learn best, and (5) what qualities make up a good teacher?

Planning Thinking about what to teach, how to teach, how to assess what is taught; includes selecting activities, deciding on a time allotment, creating the learning environment, considering the needs of individual children, and preparing assessment.

Planning.   Planning is an essential part of practicing the art and craft of teaching. **Planning** consists of setting goals for children and selecting and developing activities to help achieve those goals. Without planning you can't be a good teacher. Planning will help ensure that all children will learn, which is one of the most important and meaningful challenges you will face as an early childhood education professional. You may have heard it said that all children can learn. What is important is believing that all children *will* learn and then acting on this basic belief. Some essential steps in the planning process are as follows:

1. State what your children will learn and be able to do; these objectives can come from a number of sources. Currently, all fifty states have developed standards regarding what students should know and be able to do in kindergarten through grade three. Standards for preschool education are also commonplace. Program goals represent a second source of objectives. These goals are carefully thought out by staff and families and provide direction for what and how children will learn.
2. Select developmentally appropriate activities and materials that are based on children's interests.
3. Decide how much time to allocate to an activity.
4. Decide how to assess activities and the things that children have learned.

Assessment Making decisions about the needs of students by gathering information on their progress and behavior.

Assessing.   **Assessment** is the process of gathering information about children's behavior and achievement and, on the basis of the data, making decisions about how to meet children's needs. Chapter 3, "Observing and Assessing Young Children," provides practical skills and ideas about how to conduct developmentally appropriate assessment.

Reporting The process of providing to parents information gathered by means of observation, assessment, and children's work products.

Reporting.   **Reporting** to parents and others in an understandable and meaningful way serves several purposes. First, it answers every parent's question, "How is my child doing?" Second, information about children's achievement helps you, as a professional, be accountable to the public for fulfilling your role in helping children learn and be successful. Chapters 9 through 12 and 17 provide specific ideas and examples of reporting children's progress to parents and others.

Reflecting and Thinking.   Professionals are always thinking about and reflecting on what they have done, are doing, and will do. A good guideline for thinking and reflecting is this: think before you teach, think while you are teaching, and think after you teach. This constant cycle of *reflective practice* will help you be a good professional and will help your children learn.

In the Kindergarten segment of the DVD, the teacher talks about teachers, as professionals, being responsible for filling in children's "empty spots." View this segment and reflect on how her comments apply to your professional role.

Teaching.   If you asked most teachers what they do, they would tell you that their job requires them to wear many hats and that their tasks are never done. Teachers' responsibilities and tasks are many and varied. Teaching involves making decisions about what and how to teach, planning for teaching, engaging students in learning activities, managing learning environments, assessing student behavior and achievement, reporting to parents and others, collaborating with colleagues and community partners, and engaging in ongoing professional development. You might feel a little overwhelmed, but you will have a lot of help and support on your journey to becoming a good teacher. Your teacher preparation program, instructors, participating classroom teachers, and this textbook will help you learn how to meet the many responsibilities of becoming a good teacher.

Collaborating with Parents, Families, and Community Partners.   Parents, families, and the community are essential partners in the process of schooling. Knowing how to effectively collaborate with these key partners will serve you well throughout your career. Chapter 17, "Parent, Family, and Community Involvement: Cooperation and Collaboration," will help you learn more about this important topic.

Family education and support is an important responsibility of the early childhood professional. Children's learning begins and continues within the context of the family unit, whatever that unit may be. Learning how to comfortably and confidently work with parents is as essential as teaching children.

Engaging in Ethical Practice.   **Ethical conduct**—the exercise of responsible behavior with children, families, colleagues, and community members—enables you to confidently engage in exemplary professional practice. As previously indicated, the profession of early childhood education has a set of ethical standards to guide your thinking and behavior. NAEYC has developed a Code of Ethical Conduct (see appendix A or review the code online) and a Statement of Commitment, which follows:

Ethical conduct
Responsible behavior toward students and parents that allows you to be considered a professional.

In the Primary Grade segment of the DVD, observe the range of responsibilities teachers have in collaborating with and connecting to parents.

> As an individual who works with young children, I commit myself to furthering the values of early childhood education as they are reflected in the NAEYC Code of Ethical Conduct. To the best of my ability I will
>
>> Ensure that programs for young children are based on current knowledge of child development and early childhood education
>>
>> Respect and support families in their task of nurturing children
>>
>> Respect colleagues in early childhood education and support them in maintaining the NAEYC Code of Ethical Conduct
>>
>> Serve as an advocate for children, their families, and their teachers in community and society
>>
>> Maintain high standards of professional conduct
>>
>> Recognize how personal values, opinions, and biases can affect professional judgment
>>
>> Be open to new ideas and be willing to learn from the suggestions of others
>>
>> Continue to learn, grow, and contribute as a professional
>>
>> Honor the ideals and principles of the NAEYC Code of Ethical Conduct[10]

You can begin now to incorporate professional ethical practices into your interactions with children and colleagues. To stimulate your thinking, the Activities for Further Enrichment at the end of each chapter include an ethical dilemma.

> An ethical dilemma is a situation an individual encounters in the workplace for which there is more than one possible solution, each carrying a strong moral justification. A dilemma requires a person to choose between two alternatives; each has some benefits but also some costs. Typically, one stakeholder's legitimate needs and interest will give way to those of another. . . . "[11]

As you reflect on and respond to each dilemma, use the NAEYC Code of Ethical Conduct as a valuable guide and resource.

> The goal of the NAEYC Code of Ethical Conduct is to inform, not prescribe, answers in tough decisions that teachers and other early childhood professionals must make as they work with children and families. The strategy inherent in the Code is to promote the application of core values, ideals, and principles to guide decision making.[12]

Seeking Ongoing Professional Development Opportunities.   A professional is never a "finished" product; you will always be involved in a process of studying, learning, changing, and becoming more professional. Teachers of the Year and others who share with you their philosophies and beliefs are always in the process of becoming more professional.

Becoming a professional means you will participate in training and education beyond the minimum needed for your current position. You will also want to consider your career objectives and the qualifications you might need for positions of increasing responsibility.

PUBLIC PRESENTATION

The fourth dimension of professionalism is public presentation, which includes advocacy, communicating with others, and representing the profession.

Advocacy The act of engaging in strategies designed to improve the circumstances of children and families. Advocates move beyond their day-to-day professional responsibilities and work collaboratively to help others.

Advocacy. **Advocacy** is the act of pleading the causes of children and families to the profession and the public and engaging in strategies designed to improve the circumstances of those children and families. Advocates move beyond their day-to-day professional responsibilities and work collaboratively to help others. Children and families today need adults who understand their needs and who will work to improve the health, education, and well-being of all young children. You and other early childhood professionals are in a unique position to know and understand children and their needs and to make a difference in their lives.

There is no shortage of issues to advocate for in the lives of children and families. Some of the issues that are in need of strong advocates involve quality programs, abuse and neglect prevention, poverty, good housing, and health. In order to change policies and procedures that negatively affect children, you must become actively engaged. The following are some of the ways in which you can practice advocacy for children and families:

- *Join an early childhood professional organization,* such as NAEYC, the Association for Childhood Education International (ACEI), and the Southern Early Childhood Association (SECA). These organizations have local affiliates at colleges and universities and in many cities and towns and are very active in advocating for young children. You can serve on a committee or be involved in some other way. Contact information on these and other professional organizations can be found at the end of this chapter.
- *Become familiar with organizations that advocate for children and families.*
  - Children's Defense Fund
  - Stand for Children
  - Voices for America's Children
- *Participate in community activities that support children and families.* Help others in your area who work to make a difference for children and families. For example, donate to an organization that supports children and families, volunteer your time at a local event that supports children, or participate in another way in a local organization that supports children and families.
- *Investigate the issues that face children and families today.* Read the news and become informed about relevant issues. For example, subscribe to an e-mail newsletter from a group that supports children and families; news updates are automatically sent on current issues. Then share the news with colleagues, family, and friends.
- *Talk to others about the issues that face children and families.* Identify a specific concern you have for children and families, and talk to others about that issue. For example, if you are concerned about the number of children who do not have adequate health care, learn the facts about the issue in your community, and then talk to people you know about ways to solve that problem in your community. Begin with your own circle of influence: your colleagues, friends, family members, and other social groups in which you are a member.

- *Seek opportunities to share your knowledge of young children.* Inform others about the needs of young children by speaking with groups. For example, volunteer to meet with a group of parents at a local child care program to help them learn how to share storybooks with their young children, or meet with a local civic group that maintains the community park to discuss appropriate equipment for younger children.

- *Identify leaders in a position to make desired changes.* Learn who the leaders are that represent you in local, state, and national government. For example, identify the members of the local school board, and find out who represents you on the board. When issues arise, contact that person to express your concerns and offer solutions.

- *Enlist the support of others.* Contact others to help you disseminate information about an issue. For example, enlist the help of your local PTA in a letter-writing effort to inform town leaders about the need for safety improvements at the local playground.

- *Be persistent.* Identify an issue you are passionate about, and find a way to make a difference. There are many ways to advocate for children and families. Change takes time![13]

Within your own program or classroom, you will face many issues that should inspire you to advocate for your children and their families. The Voice from the Field "Advocacy: A View from the Front" on pages 20–21 identifies many of these issues and suggests specific steps you can take to make a difference.

Communicating with Others. Early childhood professionals must be knowledgeable and informed about their profession and the issues it faces. At the same time, they have to be able to discuss these issues with the public, the media, families, and others in the community. Being articulate about what you do and what the profession does is essential in helping children and families be successful.

Representing the Profession. Representing the profession involves modeling what a professional is and stands for. It is important for professionals to make a good impression; we cannot practice our profession well or receive the respect of parents and the public if we don't always put our best foot forward. How we look and how we behave do make a difference. And like it or not, first impressions count with many people. How we appear to others often sets the tone for interpersonal interactions with them. You should always look your best, do your best, and be your best.

YOUR JOURNEY TOWARD PROFESSIONALISM

These, then, are the four dimensions of professionalism—personal, educational, professional, and public. You should keep all four areas in mind if you want to represent yourself and the profession well. The Professional Development Checklist shown in Figure 1.3 includes some helpful suggestions and reminders.

Your journey toward professionalism is like any other journey. It begins with a well-defined plan and some first steps—one of which can be to complete Figure 1.4 to assess where you are in your journey now. Then you can develop a plan and a time line for achieving your professional goals for the coming year.

A professional is never a "finished" product. Collaborating with other professionals who share your philosophies is an excellent way to continue your professional development. What are some other ways?

FIGURE 1.3 Professional Development Checklist

Dimension 1: Personal

_____ Examine your willingness to dedicate yourself to teaching.

_____ Analyze your attitudes and feelings toward children.

_____ Examine whether your teaching philosophy mirrors your philosophy of life.

_____ Allow your ideas about life to guide your classroom practice.

Dimension 2: Educational

_____ Learn what is involved in teaching.

_____ Ask yourself, "Am I willing to work hard?"

_____ Develop a philosophy of education and teaching.

_____ Visit early childhood programs.

_____ Talk with early childhood professionals.

_____ Enroll in continuing education classes.

_____ Attend professional meetings and conferences.

_____ Read!

_____ Realize that learning is a lifelong process.

_____ Keep up-to-date with changing issues, changing children, and a changing knowledge base.

_____ Good electives in college include keyboarding, first aid, audiovisual aids and media, behavior modification/management, special education, creative writing, and arts and crafts.

Dimension 3: Professional

_____ Ask yourself, "Would I be happier in another field, or do I really want to work with young children?"

_____ Test your attitudes toward children as you interact with them.

_____ Do not fall into the trap of believing that certain children cannot learn because of their cultural or socioeconomic backgrounds.

_____ Realize that all children have the right to be taught by a professional who believes in them.

_____ Use core requirements as a means to explore new and fascinating relationships with education.

_____ Remember that the good professional does not settle for mediocre.

Dimension 4: Public

_____ Branch out from public school settings—explore church schools, child care programs, private and nonprofit agencies, and babysitting as venues to broaden and expand your knowledge of children.

_____ Be willing to adjust to changing circumstances and conditions.

_____ Explore the possibilities for you and your children to get involved in new things.

FIGURE 1.4 Assessing Your Professional Development

Read each of the fifteen desired professional outcomes listed below. Give yourself a 3 if you have fully accomplished the outcome, a 2 if you are making satisfactory progress toward meeting the outcome, and a 1 if you are just getting started on meeting the desired outcome.

Scoring Criteria:

3   Full accomplishment

2   Good progress

1   Need to get started

Desired Professional Outcome	My Rating
1. I have thought about and written my philosophy of teaching and caring for young children.	
2. I have a professional career plan for the next year that includes goals and objectives I will endeavor to meet as a professional.	
3. I engage in study and training programs to improve my knowledge and competence related to teaching and caring for young children.	
4. I am a teachable person.	
5. I have worked or am working on a degree or credential to enhance my personal life and my life as a professional.	
6. I try to improve myself as a person by engaging in a program of self-development.	
7. I practice in my own life and model for others good moral habits and ethical behavior. I encourage others to act ethically.	
8. I act professionally and encourage others to do the same.	
9. I place the best interests of children, parents, and the profession first in decisions about what constitutes quality teaching and care giving.	
10. I know about and am familiar with my profession's history, terminology, issues, contemporary development, and trends.	
11. I consciously and consistently find ways to apply concepts and knowledge about what is best for children to my teaching and care giving.	
12. I belong to a professional organization and participate in professional activities such as celebrations, study groups, committees, and conventions.	
13. I am an advocate for my profession and the needs and rights of children and families.	
14. I involve parents in my program and help and encourage them in their roles as children's primary caregivers and teachers.	
15. I seek the advice of and cooperate with other professionals and professional groups in my work with young children, parents, and families.	
TOTAL POINTS	

Score Results:

40–45   You are already an accomplished professional. You can work on refining your skills. You can be a strong advocate and mentor for others to help them with their careers.

30–39   You have accomplished a lot and are growing in your professional development. You are ready to take the next steps to assume a more active professional role.

0–29   You are ready to build a foundation of professionalism and to develop plans for being a professional. Seek out accomplished professionals for mentorship and coaching.

ADVOCACY: A VIEW FROM THE FRONT

Perhaps the single most important thing I have learned as president of the Association for Supervision and Curriculum Development is the importance of effective advocacy. *

Mary Ellen Freeley

Being in front of the classroom gives you many different views of children. Hector enrolled in your second-grade classroom last week; he is homeless and may be living in a car. Maria's front teeth are full of cavities, and you are very concerned about her future dental health. Isaac wants to sleep most of the day in your classroom; he is an avid video game fan, and you suspect he plays video games into the wee hours of the night. Brandi appears to be thirty pounds overweight and is extremely short of breath when she tries to participate in physical activities. Three-quarters of your children live at or below the poverty level; many of them come to school with torn or worn-out clothing. When you look around your classroom environment, you are not happy with what you see. You believe that you should have more books and materials for your children.

These views from the front dramatically demonstrate that opportunities for advocacy are all around you; you need not look any further than your classroom. When combined with your colleagues' views, your views from the front provide the foundation for you to become involved in local, regional, state, and national advocacy activities.

Here are some things you can do as an advocate in the field of early childhood education, whether as a teacher, administrator, parent, or caregiver:

- Be well informed—know the topic about which you feel passionate and for which you want to advocate. For example, if you want to advocate for homeless children, you need to know as much as possible about the homeless children in your community. You can start by connecting with programs that provide services for homeless children and groups that advocate for homeless people.
- Read and discuss with your colleagues articles, newspapers, and research. What does the latest research say about the achievement gap? about childhood obesity?
- Talk to colleagues about your advocacy goals. Have them help clarify your goals, reasoning, facts and figures, and your arguments.
- Develop your positions on the topics for which you want to advocate. Good advocates know both sides of the issues they're addressing. For example, not everyone supports free access to dental clinics for young children. Why would they hold such a position?

As an effective advocate of quality early childhood programs, you can do quite a few things:

WHY ARE THERE DIVERSITY TIE-INS?

In each chapter of this book, there is a Diversity Tie-In feature designed to do the following:

- Help you become a better person and a teacher who has a wide and deep understanding of the diverse backgrounds of the children you teach
- Enable you to teach all students regardless of their cultural, ethnic, or socioeconomic backgrounds
- Provide you with learning ideas that support all children's intellectual, social, personal, and cultural development, regardless of cultural background, socioeconomic status, and gender
- Help you apply multicultural knowledge and information to your teaching, exploring the opportunities the curriculum provides every day
- Enable you and your children to live happily and productively in a multicultural world

- Seek—and if necessary, demand—adequate funding for early childhood programs. For example, figure out what resources are needed to buy the books you believe are essential for your classroom.
- Support and defend access and equity issues. Do *all* children in your district have access to high-quality programs and teachers?
- Raise awareness about the social and economic issues contributing to the achievement gap between cultures and genders.
- Develop appropriate standards for early childhood programs and practices, standards that address the whole child—academic, social, physical, and emotional. How will your children and families get the nutrition information they need to win the war on obesity?
- Monitor how assessment and testing are used. Does your district use a single test to retain children?
- Support state and federal requirements for highly qualified teachers who are well paid. All children deserve highly qualified teachers; research shows that children in poor schools have the least qualified teachers.[†]
- Offer testimony at public hearings when decisions regarding early childhood education are being deliberated. When you are knowledgeable about your topic and well prepared, you can speak effectively to community groups and the media.
- Join your colleagues and lobby legislators at the local, county, state, and national levels.
- Become the voice for those children who cannot speak out for themselves. Your children may have only your voice to speak publicly about their needs.

As a classroom practitioner, you can advocate for children in many ways:

- Help families understand what it takes in the first five years to get their children ready for school.
- Model teaching strategies that accommodate individual learning styles and meet the multidimensional needs of the whole child.
- Conduct action research in your classroom to add to the body of knowledge on successful practices.
- Help to level the playing field by providing poor children with the varied and rich experiences needed but unavailable in their homes.
- Use what you know about how the brain develops and how children learn as you plan your instruction and activities.
- Collaborate with professionals across disciplines to address health and social welfare issues in classrooms and schools.
- Become a role model for young children, helping them develop a sense of self and well-being as they learn to function in a democratic society.

In a sense, the future of early childhood education is in your hands. It is time for you to remove your white gloves and begin to mold, massage, manipulate, and advocate to ensure that every child has access to quality early childhood educational experiences.

---

*Mary Ellen Freeley (president of ASCD, 2005), keynote speech of the Velma Schmidt Conference on Early Childhood Education, December 2, 2005.

[†]R. M. Ingersoll, *Why Do High-Poverty Schools Have Difficulty Staffing Their Classrooms with Qualified Teachers?* (Washington, DC: Center for American Progress, November 19, 2004). Also available online at http://www.americanprogress.org/atf/cf/{E9245FE4-9A2B-43C7-A521-5D6FF2E06E03}/Ingersoll-FINAL.pdf.

The Diversity Tie-In in this chapter shares some important suggestions to guide you in making sure your professional practice is multicultural.

WHAT IS THE ROLE OF TODAY'S EARLY CHILDHOOD PROFESSIONAL?

The role of the early childhood professional today is radically different from what it was even two or three years ago. Although the dimensions of professionalism and the characteristics of the high-quality professional remain the same, responsibilities, expectations, and roles have changed. Let's examine some of these new roles of the contemporary early childhood professional, which are not so new as much as they are rediscovered and reemphasized.

Companion Website To complete an activity related to multiculturalism and professionalism, go to the Companion Website at **www.prenhall.com/morrison**, select chapter 1, then choose the Diversity Tie-In module.

MULTICULTURALISM AND PROFESSIONALISM: YOU CAN'T HAVE ONE WITHOUT THE OTHER

Think for a moment about all of the classrooms of children across the United States. What do you think their cultural, ethnic, and linguistic makeup is like? More than likely, the demographics of these children are different from those of the children you went to school with in kindergarten or first grade. Consider these data about America's children:

- In 2003, 60 percent of U.S. children were white-alone, non-Hispanic; 19 percent were Hispanic; 16 percent were black-alone; 4 percent were Asian-alone; and 4 percent were all other races.
- The percentage of children who are Hispanic has increased faster than that of any other racial or ethnic group.*

This increase in racial, ethnic, and cultural diversity in America is reflected in early childhood classrooms, which are also receiving increased numbers of children with disabilities and developmental delays (see chapter 16). Consider the student population at Susan B. Anthony Elementary School in Sacramento, California; 63 percent are Asian, 19 percent are Hispanic, 14 percent are African American, and 3 percent are white. Moreover, 88 percent of the children receive free lunches, and 67 percent are English-language learners.†

MEETING THE CHALLENGE

This diverse composition of early childhood classrooms challenges you to make your classroom responsive to the diverse needs of all your children—part of your professional responsibility. Let's look at some of the things you can do to be a responsible professional who is multiculturally aware and who teaches with respect and equity:

1. *Be concerned about your own multicultural development.*
   - Honestly confront your attitudes and views as they relate to people of other cultures. You may be carrying baggage that you have to get rid of to authentically and honestly educate all of your children to their fullest capacity.

In the Kindergarten segment of the DVD, view how the teacher emphasizes literacy. Reflect on the ways this emphasis on emerging literacy impacts the role of today's early childhood professional.

- *Teacher as instructional leader.* Teachers have always been responsible for classroom and program instruction, but this role is now reemphasized and given a much more prominent place in what early childhood teachers do, such as planning for what children will learn, guiding and teaching so that children learn, assessing what children learn, and arranging the classroom environment so that children learn.
- *Intentional teaching of state, district, and program goals and standards.* Intentional teaching occurs when instructors teach for a purpose, are clear about what they teach, and teach so that children learn specific knowledge and skills. In this context, teachers spend more time during the day actually teaching and make a conscious effort to be more involved in each child's learning process. Intentional teaching can and should occur in a child-centered approach for specified times and purposes throughout the school day.
- *Performance-based accountability for learning.* Teachers today are far more accountable for children's learning. Previously, the emphasis was on the process of schooling;

- Read widely about your multicultural role as a professional. At the end of the chapter, some excellent resources are identified for your reading and education.
- Learn about the habits, customs, beliefs, and religious practices of the cultures represented by your children.
- Ask some of your parents to tutor you and help you learn basic phrases for greeting and questioning, the meaning of nonverbal gestures, and the way to appropriately and respectfully address parents and children.

2. *Make every child welcome.*
   - Make your classroom a place where diversity is encouraged and everyone is treated fairly. Create a classroom environment that is vibrant and alive with the cultures of your children. You can do this with pictures, artifacts, and objects loaned by parents.
   - Support and use children's home language and culture. Create a safe environment in which children feel free to talk about and share their culture and language. Encourage children to discuss, draw, paint, and write about what their culture means to them.

3. *Make every parent welcome.*
   - Invite parents and families to share their languages and cultures in your classroom. Music, stories, and customs provide a rich background for learning about and respecting other cultures.
   - Communicate with parents in their home languages.
   - Work with parents to help them (and you) bridge the differences between the way schools operate and the norms of their homes and cultures.

4. *Collaborate with your colleagues.*
   - Ask colleagues to share with you ideas about how to respond to questions, requests, and concerns of children and parents.
   - Volunteer to form a faculty study group to read, discuss, and learn how to meet the cultural and linguistic needs of all children.

5. *Become active in your community.*
   - Learn as much as you can about your community and the cultural resources it can provide. Communities are very multicultural places!
   - Collaborate with community and state organizations that work with culturally and linguistically diverse families and populations. Ask them for volunteers who can help you meet the diverse needs of your children. Children need to interact with and value role models from all cultures.
   - Volunteer to act as a community outreach coordinator to provide families with services, such as family literacy and school readiness information.

You can't be a complete early childhood professional without a multicultural dimension. As you become more multiculturally aware, you will increase your capacity for caring and understanding. And you and your students will learn and grow together.

---

*ChildStats.gov, "America's Children: Key National Indicators of Well-Being 2005," http://childstats.ed.gov/americaschildren/pop3.asp.

†greatschools.net, http://www.greatschools.net/cgi-bin/ca/other4675.

teachers were able to explain their role as "I taught Mario how to. . . . " Today the emphasis is on "What did Mario learn?" and "Did Mario learn what he needs to know and do in order to perform at or above grade level?"

- *Teaching of literacy and reading.* Although the teaching of reading has always been a responsibility of early childhood professionals, this role has been expanded. Today, every early childhood teacher is now a teacher of literacy and reading, subjects neccesary in all content areas, including math and science.
- *Increased emphasis on assessing what children learn.* Today, all teachers use the results of assessment to plan for teaching and learning. Assessment and planning have become a more essential part of the teaching-learning process. Chapter 3, "Observing and Assessing Young Children: Effective Teaching Through Appropriate Evaluation" explores assessment in detail.
- *New meaning of child-centered education.* Early childhood professionals have always advocated child-centered education and approaches. This is certainly true today.

Everything discussed in this book is based on children being the center of the teaching and learning processes. Unfortunately, not all teachers have practiced child-centered approaches, nor have they made children's learning a high priority. This is changing. Included in the child-centered approach are the ideas that children can reach high levels of achievement, that children are eager to learn, and that they are capable of learning more than many people thought they could. A new concept of child-centeredness embraces the whole child in all dimensions: social, emotional, physical, linguistic, and cognitive.

As the field of early childhood continues to change, the details of your role as an early childhood professional will continue to be refined. You will want to devote the time and energy necessary to keep yourself in the forefront of your field.

Honestly analyze your feelings and attitudes toward working with young children. Not everyone has the skills or temperament required for effective teaching of young children.

WHAT DOES THE FUTURE HOLD FOR EARLY CHILDHOOD PROFESSIONALS?

It is always risky to predict what the future holds for you and me as early childhood professionals. However, if the past is any indication of the future, I expect that we will practice our profession under the following conditions:

- *Rapid change.* The field of early childhood education will continue to undergo rapid and dramatic change. Old ways of doing things will be challenged by new ideas and methods. This means that you will have to adapt as the field changes. And you will have to continually transform your thinking as new ways make old habits obsolete.
- *Increased use of technology.* Technology will play an increasingly important and prominent role in how you teach, what you teach, and how children learn. Chapter 13, "Technology and Young Children: Education for the Information Age," discusses in depth the role of technology in early childhood programs and your role in using technology in teaching and learning.
- *Politicization of early childhood education.* Politics have always influenced education in one way or another. However, in the years to come, politics and politicians will play an even greater role in determining what and how children are taught. This means that advocacy will be a major dimension of your professional practice, allowing you to influence decisions on public policy at all levels.
- *Increased emphasis on young children.* The public and politicians are recognizing the critical importance that early years play in children's school and life success. As a result, educators are developing programs for young children and their parents to help the children gain the knowledge and skills that will lead to school and learning readiness. Early childhood will continue to be a time of interest, attention, and action.
- *Acceleration of early childhood teacher education and training.* As the field of early childhood changes, so do the knowledge and skills associated with it. This means that constant and continuous education will play a central role in your professional development. Many teachers will spend as much time educating themselves and being educated as they spend on teaching their children. One way you can continue to educate yourself is by exploring the Linking to Learning section at the end of each chapter in this book. Each Linking to Learning section offers a list of professional or-

ganizations and information sites, many of which have been mentioned in the chapter. Each entry includes a website, where you can access additional information and helpful ideas that will enhance your teaching abilities. Changes that the future holds for the field of early childhood education and for you as a professional are not to be feared but are to be welcomed and embraced. This is a wonderful and exciting time to be in the field of early childhood education. A bright future awaits you and your children.

Companion Website

For additional Internet resources or to complete an online activity for this chapter, go to the Companion Website at **www.prenhall.com/morrison**, select chapter 1, then choose the Linking to Learning or Making Connections module.

LINKING TO LEARNING

RELATED WEBSITES

Children's Defense Fund
http://www.childrensdefense.org/

Provides research and persistent advocacy for children's rights on issues including poverty, discrimination, and gun violence to ensure every child a healthy, fair, and safe start in life and successful passage to adulthood with the help of caring families and communities.

Council for Early Childhood Professional Recognition
http://www.cdacouncil.org

Offers a nationally recognized, competency-based child development associate credential that provides training, assessment, and certification of child care professionals; also offers bilingual specialization.

Early Childhood Education Online
http://www.umaine.edu/eceol

Promotes and facilitates information management and exchange and serves as a resource and benefit for all children, their families, and all people who help them grow and learn.

Early Childhood Education Web Guide
http://www.ecewebguide.com

Provides child care professionals with the most up-to-date Internet resources; checks sites on a weekly basis to ensure their reliability and integrity.

ERIC Education Resources Information Center
http://www.eric.ed.gov/

Provides information to parents and educators on all subjects and grade levels, publishes free biannual newsletters, and sponsors a parent question-answering service (askeric @ ericir.syr.edu) and electronic discussion groups.

Linguistic Diversity and Early Literacy: Serving Culturally Diverse Families in Early Head Start
http://www.ehsnrc.org/publications/cetap.htm

Provides many helpful ideas on how to support the linguistic development of children whose primary language is other than English.

National Association for the Education of Young Children
http://www.naeyc.org

Publishes brochures, posters, videotapes, books, and journals discussing teaching and program ideas, ways to improve parent-teacher relations, and resources for students about safety, language arts, and learning. Offers training opportunities through national, state, and local affiliate groups.

Responding to Linguistic and Cultural Diversity: Recommendations for Effective Early Childhood Education

http://www.naeyc.org/about/positions/PSDIV98.asp

Primarily describes linguistically and culturally diverse children who speak languages other than English. Can also apply to children who speak only English but are linguistically and culturally diverse.

Stand for Children

http://www.stand.org

Advocates for improvements to and funding for programs that give every child a fair chance in life.

Teacher Information Network

http://www.teacher.com

With listings of organizations, resources, sites, and governmental departments, offers a one-stop gateway to all the resources a teacher could want on the Web; chats with other teachers, free e-mail, or news of the latest teaching trends.

Voices for America's Children

http://childadvocacy.org

A national organization committed to working at state and local levels to improve the well-being of children.

ELECTRONIC JOURNALS RELATED TO EARLY CHILDHOOD EDUCATION

Children's Advocate

http://www.4children.org/childadv.htm

A bimonthly newsmagazine published by the Action Alliance for Children; covers California, national, and international policy issues affecting children. Makes highlights from the current issue and selected articles from past issues available on the website.

Clearinghouse on Early Education and Parenting (CEEP)

http://ceep.crc.uiuc.edu/

Part of the Early Childhood and Parenting (ECAP) Collaborative within the College of Education at the University of Illinois at Urbana-Champaign. Works closely with the ECAP Information Technology Group to build print and online resources for the worldwide early childhood and parenting communities.

Early Childhood News

http://www.earlychildhoodnews.com

Focuses on professional development in early childhood education; valuable resource for anyone interested in the field of educating the leaders of tomorrow and the learners of today.

The Future of Children

http://www.futureofchildren.org

An online child advocacy journal published three times a year by the David and Lucile Packard Foundation. Has articles on issues pertaining to the health and well-being of children in our nation.

OTHER PROFESSIONAL ORGANIZATIONS

These agencies are devoted to improving professional practice. Contact them for information about their programs, position statements, and professional and child advocacy initiatives.

Association for Childhood Education International (ACEI)

http://www.acei.org

Southern Early Childhood Association (SECA)

http://www.southernearlychildhood.org

ACTIVITIES FOR FURTHER ENRICHMENT

ETHICAL DILEMMA: "SHOULD I REPORT HER TO . . . ?"

"Kim, you have been teaching here longer than I have, so maybe you can help me. I want to talk to you about the new preschool teacher they hired. I've talked with her a couple of times about how she implements the state preK standards, and she says she isn't too worried about them. I offered to help her with her lesson plans, but she told me she plans as she goes along. She said she knows what to do and developing a written plan gets in the way of her doing what comes naturally for her and the children. She also told me she thinks that the emphasis on early literacy is just a lot of hype—a passing fad. I'm concerned that her children won't be ready for kindergarten.

What should I do? Should I talk to our preschool supervisor and risk damaging my relationship with this new teacher and possibly hurting her career, or should I assume that another teacher's practices are not my business even if they might be harmful to the children?"

APPLICATIONS

1. Recall the teachers who had a great influence on you. Which of their characteristics do you plan to imitate?
2. Put your philosophy of education in writing, and share it with others. Have them critique it for comprehensiveness, clarity, and meaning. How do you feel about the changes they suggested?
3. Metaphors are an effective way of expressing meaning and ideas. They are also a good way to think about yourself, your beliefs, and teaching. For example, some of the metaphors my students have identified for themselves as teachers are leader, coach, and facilitator. Add to this list and then identify one metaphor that best describes your teaching at this time. Use these metaphors to help you develop your philosophy of education.
4. Develop a list of professional goals you wish to accomplish. Earning certification in early childhood education might be one goal. Working toward National Board certification might be a long-term goal. What other professional achievements are important to you?

FIELD EXPERIENCES

1. Attend local meetings of an early childhood professional organization in your area, such as NAEYC or ACEI. What issues is the group addressing? How is the group meeting the needs of its members? of children and families? Would you join the organization you visited?
2. Many local school districts elect and honor a teacher of the year. Contact these teachers and have them share with you the ideas and attitudes that caused their colleagues to elect them teacher of the year. Plan how you will integrate these qualities into your professional development plan.
3. Attend regional and national conferences dedicated to early childhood education. The NAEYC and its local and state affiliates hold well-attended conferences that allow practitioners in every field of early childhood education to gather and learn from one another.
4. Contact the president of the local teachers' union or professional organization and learn about what the group advocates for and what methods it uses to advocate.

RESEARCH

1. Interview five early childhood professionals to determine what they think constitutes professionalism and how professions can be more involved in increasing professionalism.
2. Interview professionals about careers that relate to children and parents. How did they come to their jobs? Is there evidence that they planned for these careers? Do you think you would enjoy an alternative career in education? Why?
3. Interview teachers in various programs and agencies to determine their core beliefs about teaching and the essentials of being a professional. Make a list of these core beliefs, and reflect on them as you continue to consider your philosophy of education.
4. Read current academic articles from scholarly journals such as *Childhood Education* and the *Journal of Research in Childhood Education* to learn about innovative developments in the field of early childhood education.

READINGS FOR FURTHER ENRICHMENT

Catron, C. E., and J. Allen. *Early Childhood Curriculum: A Creative Play Model*, 3rd ed. Upper Saddle River, NJ: Merrill/Prentice Hall, 2003.

Provides information on planning programs with a play-based, developmental curriculum for children from birth to five years of age. Covers basic principles and current research in early childhood curricula.

DeVries, R. *Developing Constructivist Early Childhood Curriculum: Practical Principles and Activities.* New York: Teachers College Press, 2002.

Provides a constructivist interpretation of developmentally appropriate curriculum in early childhood education. Provides the theoretical rationale and practical advice for conducting specific activities in the classroom. Uses descriptive vignettes to show how children's reasoning and teacher interventions are transformed in the course of extended experience with a physical phenomenon or group game.

Isenberg, J. P., and M. Jalongo. *Major Trends and Issues in Early Childhood Education: Challenges, Controversies and Insights,* 2nd ed. New York: Teachers College Press, 2003.

Provides essential social, historical, and philosophical perspectives on the field of early childhood education. Examines a variety of today's most significant and challenging subjects, including child development research, play, program models, assessment, diversity, inclusion, public policy, and advocacy.

Paciorek, K. M., and J. H. Munro, eds. *Early Childhood Education 2005–2006,* 26th ed. New York: McGraw Hill College Division, 2006.

A series of more than seventy-five volumes, each designed to provide convenient, inexpensive access to a wide range of current, carefully selected articles from some of the most respected magazines, newspapers, and journals published today.

Saracho, O., and B. Spodek. *Studying Teachers in Early Childhood Settings.* Greenwich, CT: Information Age, 2003.

Provides a close-up look at teachers in early childhood settings. Covers factors that impact teacher quality, pathways in becoming an early childhood teacher, and beliefs of early childhood teachers.

ENDNOTES

1. L. J. Schweinhart, J. Montie, Z. Xiang, W. S. Barnett, C. R. Belfield, and M. Nores, *Lifetime Effects: The High/Scope Perry Preschool Study Through Age 40* (Ypsilanti, MI: High/Scope Press, 2005).

2. W. Barnett, K. Robin, J. Hudstedt, and K. Schulman, *The State of Preschool: 2003 State Preschool Yearbook* (Rutgers, NJ: National Institute for Early Childhood Education Research, 2004). www.nieer.org/yearbook/pdf/ yearbook.pdf.

3. Nel Noddings, "Teaching Themes of Care," *Phi Delta Kappan* 76, no. 9 (1995): 675.

4. NC Division of Child Development, *North Carolina Early Childhood and Administration Credentials* (2005), http:// ncchildcare.dhhs.state.nc.us/providers/credent.asp.

5. Carol Brunson Phillips, *Field Advisor's Guide for the CDA Professional Preparation Program* (Washington, DC: Council for Early Childhood Professional Recognition, 1991), 2.

6. U.S. Army Child and Youth Services, *CDA (Child Development Associate): What Is It?* http://www.pba.army.mil/cys/more%20training.htm.

7. B. Feller, "Teacher Aides Win Extra Time to Qualify," *New York Times,* June 15, 2005.

8. National Board for Professional Teaching Standards, *Early Childhood/Generalist Standards,* 2nd ed., http://www. nbpts.org/candidates/guide/whichcert/01EarlyChild2004.html.

9. S. Bredekamp and C. Copple, eds., *Developmentally Appropriate Practice in Early Childhood Programs* (Washington, DC: National Association for the Education of Young Children, 1997), 9.

10. S. Feeney and K. Kipnis, *Code of Ethical Conduct and Statement of Commitment* (Washington, DC: NAEYC).

11. S. Feeney and N. K. Freeman, *Ethics and the Early Childhood Educator: Using the NAEYC Code* (Washington, DC: National Association for the Education of Young Children, 1999).

12. Ibid.

13. Used with the permission of Mary Nelle Brunson, assistant chair, Department of Elementary Education, Stephen F. Austin State University, Nacogdoches, Texas.

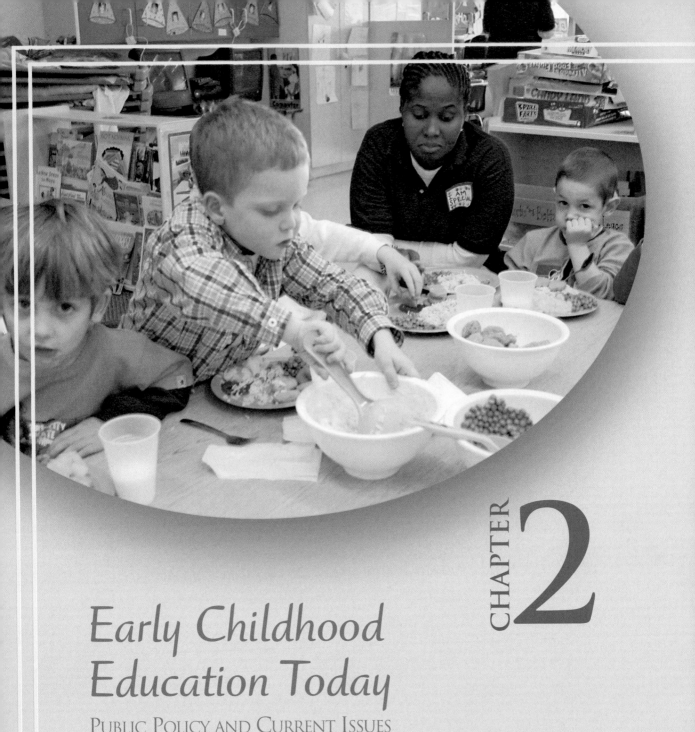

CHAPTER 2

Early Childhood Education Today

PUBLIC POLICY AND CURRENT ISSUES

To prepare children for success in school, policies must provide support for all the contexts that influence child development starting from birth, and must seek to optimize children's functioning across all domains of development.

SCHOOL READINESS: IMPLICATIONS FOR POLICY
CENTER FOR FAMILY POLICY AND RESEARCH, UNIVERSITY OF MISSOURI–COLUMBIA

*I*n this chapter we discuss public policy and current issues as they influence early childhood education. At no time in U.S. history have there been so much interest and involvement by early childhood professionals in the development and implementation of public policy. *Public policy* refers to the responses of government and nongovernmental organizations (NGOs) to public issues. It includes such things as laws; federal, state, and local government guidelines; position statements of professional organizations (e.g., NAEYC's position statements on ethical conduct and on developmentally appropriate practice in appendixes A and B); and court decisions.

At the national level, the federal government's policy of having all children read on grade level by grade three affects state and local education policy and influences the literacy experiences you will provide for young children. The Children's Defense Fund (CDF) is an example of a national NGO that develops and implements public policy on behalf of children and families. (The Companion Website provides additional information about CDF).

Some states have policies designed to ensure that all children enter school ready to learn. These policies give rise to programs to improve children's health and enhance their abilities to achieve at high levels. You might be involved in some of these school readiness programs. At the local level, public schools have developed policies regarding the admittance and education of three- and four-year-old children. More school districts are hiring preschool teachers, and you might be one of them. Public policy drives public and private education from prekindergarten through grade twelve.

PUBLIC POLICY AND CURRENT ISSUES

Agencies develop **public policy** in response to critical societal issues; public policy, in turn, frequently creates public issues. For example, the federal government's policy on standards and testing creates issues about developmentally appropriate testing and teaching of young children. On the other hand, children and families face many issues that dramatically place at risk their education and life outcomes. As a result, governmental agencies and NGOs develop and seek to implement appropriate programs to service the educational, health, and social needs of children and families. For example, the National Association for the Education of Young Children promotes national, state, and local public policies that support a system of well-financed, high quality early childhood education programs in a range of settings, including child care centers, family child care homes, and schools.

Current issues affect how you, as a professional, provide for children's development, education, and care. They influence every dimension of practice from how we teach children to read, to the health care we provide, to the quality of our teaching. We cannot ignore these issues or pretend they do not exist. We must be part of the solution to make it possible for all children to achieve their full potential. Education today is very political, and

Focus Questions

How are public policy and current issues changing early childhood education?

How do social, political, economic, and educational issues influence and change child rearing, early childhood education, and teaching?

What are some implications that contemporary issues have for curriculum, teaching, and the life outcomes of children and families?

How can early childhood programs and teachers help solve contemporary social problems?

Companion Website

To check your understanding of this chapter, go to the Companion Website at **www.prenhall.com/ morrison**, select chapter 2, answer Multiple Choice and Essay Questions, and receive feedback.

FIGURE 2.1   Early Childhood in the News

- It's all work, little play in kindergarten (*DetroitNews.com*)
- If you think it's crowded now ... preschool enrollment likely to rise with Generation Y babies (*Chicago Tribune*)
- Baby talk at root of human understanding (*Seattle Times*)
- NikeGO and the National Head Start Association Launch First-of-Its-Kind Physical Activity Program for Preschool Children (*Nike.Inc*)
- Webcam lets parents peek into day care (*DetroitNews.com*)
- Demands of kindergarten surprise some parents; are they supposed to know that already? (*Cincinnati Enquirer*)
- Cartoon characters caught in adults' food fight (*USAToday.com*)

Public policy   All the plans that local, state, and national governmental and nongovernmental organizations have for implementing their goals.

politicians look to early childhood professionals to help develop educational solutions to social problems.

Daily newspapers provide many examples of critical issues and the nation's interest in young children. Figure 2.1 shows recent newspaper headlines that call attention to young children, parents, families, and child service agencies that illustrate the enormous range of topics relating to young children and families. Other sources of information regarding critical issues affecting early childhood are professional journals such as those identified in chapter 1, agency websites, politicians, education professionals, and community leaders.

FAMILY ISSUES

A primary goal of early childhood education is to meet children's needs in culturally and developmentally appropriate ways. Early childhood professionals agree that a good way to meet the needs of children is through their families, whatever their family unit may be. Review Figure 2.2, which shows the potential benefits of working with children and their families.

Providing for children's needs through and within the family system makes sense for a number of reasons. First, helping families function better means that everyone stands to benefit. When the other people in the family unit—mother, father, grandparents, and others—function better, the children in the family function better, too.

Second, professionals frequently need to address family problems and issues in order to help children effectively. For example, helping parents gain access to adequate, affordable health care means that the whole family, including the children, will be healthier. And when children are healthy, they achieve more.

Third, early childhood professionals can do many things concurrently with children and their families that benefit both. Literacy is a good example. Early childhood professionals are taking a family approach to helping children, their parents, and other family members learn to read, write, speak, and listen. Teaching parents to read helps them understand the importance of supporting their children in the learning process.

Fourth, addressing the needs of children and their families as a whole (i.e., the holistic approach to education and the delivery of services) enables early childhood professionals and others to address a range of social concerns simultaneously. Programs that provide education and support for literacy, health care, nutrition, obesity prevention, healthy living, abuse prevention, and parenting are examples of this family-centered approach. A major trend in early childhood education is that professionals are expanding the family-centered approach to meeting the needs of children and families.

Thus, keeping children healthy becomes an important aspect of early childhood programs. In addition to nutrition and health information children can use at home, childhood

Companion Website   To complete a Program in Action activity related to the importance of physical activity for young children, go to the Companion Website at **www.prenhall.com/morrison**, select chapter 2, then choose the Program in Action module.

Early childhood education professionals provide
- Parenting education to help parents learn basic child-rearing knowledge and skills
- Literacy programs to help children and families learn to read
- Readiness activities and programs designed to get children ready for school
- Family referrals to community agencies that can provide help (e.g., the Special Supplement Nutrition Program for Women, Infants, and Children (WIC), a preventative health and nutrition program that promotes optional growth and development)
- Assistance with problems of daily living

Family and child outcomes as a result of professionals' efforts:
- Less family and child stress
- Healthier families and children
- More involvement of families in their children's education
- Increased school achievement and success
- Reduced child abuse and neglect
- A better quality of life for children and families

FIGURE 2.2   A Model for Meeting the Needs of Children and Families

professionals can include daily activities to support healthy lifestyles. The Program in Action "Animal Trackers" describes a physical activity curriculum designed to do just that.

CHANGING FAMILY UNITS

Families are in a continual state of change as a result of social issues and changing times. Even the definition of what a family is varies as society changes. Consider the following ways families are changing in the twenty-first century:

1. *Structure.* Families now include arrangements other than that of the traditional nuclear family:
   - Single-parent families, headed by mothers or fathers
   - Stepfamilies, including individuals related by either marriage or adoption
   - Heterosexual, gay, or lesbian partners living together with children
   - Extended families, which may include grandparents, uncles, aunts, other relatives, and individuals not related by kinship
2. *Roles.* As families change, so do the roles of parents, family members, and others:
   - More parents work and have less time for their children and family affairs.
   - Working parents combine the roles of parents and employees. The number of hats that parents wear increases as families change.
   - Grandparents and non–family members must learn new parenting roles.

As families continue to change, you and other early childhood professionals must develop creative ways to provide services to children and families of all kinds.

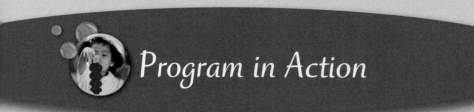

ANIMAL TRACKERS—A PRESCHOOL MOTOR SKILLS AND PHYSICAL ACTIVITY CURRICULUM

Children love to creep and crawl around the room like Lenny the Lizard, throw and catch balls like Maria the Monkey, or even gallop through the playground like Harry the Horse. These are just a few of the animal friends that preschoolers will meet in Animal Trackers as they build motor skills through fun-filled activities, games, and songs.

ENHANCING MOTOR SKILLS

Animal Trackers (AT) was designed as a developmentally appropriate, fun, and skill-building physical activity, movement, and play program for two- to five-year-old children, building on and enhancing the natural acquisition of gross-motor skills during the preschool years. The curriculum was designed to provide teachers with more than just ideas for movement games: AT provides a structured and sequential progression of motor-skills training through carefully designed, age-appropriate, and enjoyable activities. The AT curriculum provides preschoolers with an opportunity to learn and practice the movement motor skills that are basic to physical and sports activities.

THE NEED FOR PHYSICAL ACTIVITY

Studies show that young children do not acquire gross-motor skills at the same age and vary greatly in their proficiency in gross-motor skills. Acquisition of motor skills is a precursor to a variety of physical activities and sports that children may participate in as preschoolers and later as older children.

Daily physical activity is a critical component of child health promotion. The U.S. Surgeon General, the American Academy of Pediatrics, and the Centers for Disease Control encourage children to increase daily physical activity and active play as a general health recommendation, and as a way to help prevent childhood obesity.

The objectives of the AT curriculum are to accomplish the following:

- Increase the frequency and duration of preschool physical activity targeted toward learning and practicing gross-motor skills in a fun and active play format
- Increase the performance of age-appropriate gross-motor skills for preschoolers who participate

Working Parents. More and more families find that both parents must work to make ends meet. An increasing percentage of mothers with children under six are currently employed (nearly 62 percent in 2004; see Figure 2.3), thereby creating a greater need for early childhood programs. This demand focuses increased attention on early childhood programs and encourages early childhood professionals to meet working parents' needs. You can help working parents by effectively communicating with them and providing ways for them to be connected to their children's learning.

Affluent Families. Many parents with middle- and upper-level incomes are willing to invest money in early education for their children. They look for nursery schools and preschool programs that will give their children a good start in life. Montessori schools and franchised operations such as Bright Horizons, Kindercare, and La Petite Academy have benefited in the process. Private preschool education is now a booming business.

Some parents of three- and four-year-olds spend almost as much in tuition to send their children to good preschools as parents of eighteen-year-olds do to send their children to state-supported universities. For example, Crème de la Crème, a series of premium-quality child care and preschool programs, charges $725 a month for their half-day program and $1,344 a month for their full-time program at their Colleyville, Texas, location.

- Train preschool teachers to teach the AT motor-skills activities in an effective and enjoyable way
- Involve parents in the AT program through AT-at-Home child and parent activities

A FOCUS ON STRUCTURED, ACTIVE PLAY

Animal Trackers uses a scope and sequence approach based on goals and objectives that are appropriate for healthy young children, aged three to five. The program includes a balance of skills and concepts designed to enhance the cognitive, motor-affective, and physical development of preschoolers. Movement exploration, guided discovery, and creative problem solving are the predominant teaching strategies employed.

AT activities can easily be integrated into traditional preschool content areas, through innovative cross-curricular content and objectives in math, language, and social skills, designed to build a variety of educational skills through structured active play. Examples include counting, sorting, alphabet recognition and other language skills shapes, following directions, taking turns, and partnering with others. The Creepy-Crawly Things Activity enhances both locomotor and literacy skills.

Creepy-Crawly Things Activity

Have children alternate crawling and creeping by asking them to move like the following and repeating the sound of the letter that begins the name. For example, "Can you creep like a sssss . . . snake? Snake starts with the letter S. Can you crawl like a bbbbbbb . . . baby? Baby starts with the letter B." An alternative is to set up an obstacle course that requires crawling in some places and creeping in others, depending on the obstacle under which the children must move.

Can you creep like a . . .	SNAKE?
Can you crawl like a . . .	BABY?
Can you creep like a . . .	CATERPILLAR?
Can you crawl like a . . .	SPIDER?
Can you creep like a . . .	WORM?
Can you crawl like a . . .	DOG?
Can you creep like a . . .	SNAIL?
Can you crawl like a . . .	CRAB (or lobster)?

EVALUATION IN THE CLASSROOM

Animal Trackers was evaluated in nine Head Start preschool centers (sixteen classrooms, thirty-two teachers, 270 students) in New Mexico, with process measures and pre- and postintervention assessments. The goal was to evaluate program implementation (i.e., frequency, duration, preparatory time, and time spent in structured physical activity). Results showed that AT activities were implemented 4.4 times per week on average with each activity lasting 11.4 minutes, adding almost an hour of structured physical activity to the week. Average teacher prep time for AT activities was seven minutes. Teachers reported that AT was easy to implement in the classroom, that children enjoyed the activities and improved their motor skills with practice. Teachers felt that AT was age and developmentally appropriate and that they would recommend it to others and planned to use it again.

Contributed by Christine L. Williams, MD, MPH, director, Children's Cardiovascular Health Center, Columbia University, Children's Hospital.

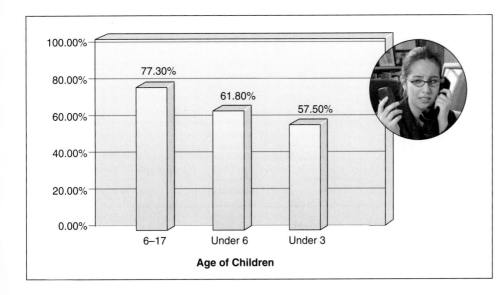

FIGURE 2.3 Mothers in the Workforce with Children of Varying Ages

Unlike previous generations, today the majority of mothers with young children are employed.

Source: U.S. Census Bureau, *Current Population Survey* (2004).

These upper-end preschool programs will continue to grow in number and popularity and may offer employment opportunities that you will want to investigate as you plan your career as an early childhood professional.

Fathers Rediscovered. Fathers are rediscovering the joys of parenting and working with young children, and early childhood education is discovering fathers! Men are now playing a more active role in providing basic care, love, and nurturance to their children. Fathers are more concerned about their role and their participation in family events before, during, and after the birth of their children. Fathers want to be involved in the whole process of child rearing.

Figure 2.4 shows the number of single-parent families headed by fathers of certain races. Also increasing in number are the stay-at-home dads; estimates are as high as two million. And fathers are receiving some of the employment benefits that have traditionally gone only to women, such as paternity leaves, flexible work schedules, and sick leave for family illness.

Because so many men feel unprepared for fatherhood, early childhood programs and agencies such as hospitals and community colleges are providing courses and seminars to introduce fathers to the joys, rewards, and responsibilities of fathering. In addition more agencies are promoting the roles of fathers. For example, Family Support America suggests ten ways to support fathers. These are listed in Figure 2.5.

Single Parents. An important part of your professional preparation is to develop the knowledge and skills necessary for collaborating with single-parent families. The number of one-parent families continues to increase, and certain ethnic groups are disproportionately

When families are involved in their children's education, everyone benefits. What are some culturally appropriate ways you can reach out to the families of the children in your care?

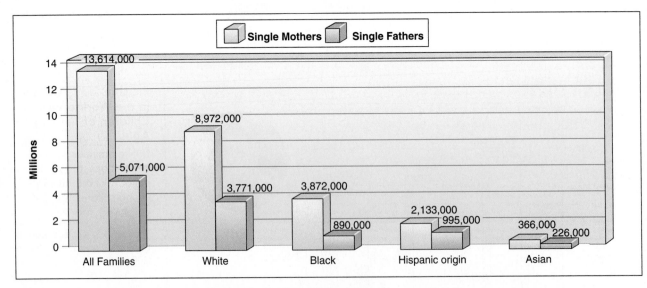

FIGURE 2.4   Families Headed by Single Mothers and Fathers

Families headed by single mothers and fathers are now a way of life for parents and children across the United States.

Source: U.S. Census Bureau, *Current Population Survey* (2004).

FIGURE 2.5 10 Ways to Support Fathers Year-Round

1. Hold a fathers' fair with booths where fathers can bring their kids and brush up on diaper changing, hair braiding, teaching kids how to skate or ride a bike, and so on.

2. Throw a father-child picnic. Post fliers inviting the whole community.

3. Sponsor father-of-the-year awards. Honor fathers who have overcome obstacles in their lives and the lives of their families or fathers who embody the principles of family support.

4. Have an event for noncustodial fathers and their kids. A day of games or an evening of pizza and movies can allow noncustodial dads with visitation rights—who might not be used to spending time with their children—to do so in a supportive environment.

5. Recruit fathers. Go door-to-door with fliers on your program's support and activities for fathers and families.

6. Offer a dads' support group. Many fathers—particularly teen fathers—feel isolated and unsure about their skills as parents and providers.

7. Support noncustodial fathers and their families. Provide counseling, referrals, and tip sheets to help fathers provide nurturing support for their children, covering issues such as paternity establishment, child support, and visitation rights.

8. Make men visible. Recruit men as staff members or volunteers.

9. Involve fathers in program decisions. Make sure fathers are represented on your parent advisory group.

10. Create a mentor program. Train participants in your program to provide one-on-one support to new fathers and fathers seeking to strengthen relationships with their children.

Source: "Family Support America, 10 Ways Your Program Can Support Fathers Year-Round," www.famlit.org/Publications/momentum/August1999/fathers.cfm. Reprinted by permission.

represented, as suggested by Figure 2.4. These increases are attributable to several factors. First, pregnancy rates are higher among lower-socioeconomic groups. Second, teenage pregnancy rates in poor white, Hispanic, and African American populations are sometimes higher because of lower education levels, economic constraints, and fewer life opportunities.

People become single parents for a number of reasons: nearly half of all marriages end in divorce;[1] and some parents, such as many teenagers, are single by default. In addition, liberalized adoption procedures, artificial insemination, surrogate childbearing, and increasing public support for single parents make this lifestyle an attractive option for some individuals. The reality is that more women are having children without marrying.

No matter how people become single parents, they have tremendous implications for early childhood professionals. In response to growing single parenthood, early childhood programs are developing curricula to help children and their single parents. In addition to needing assistance with child care, single parents frequently seek help in child rearing, especially in regard to parenting practices. Early childhood professionals are often asked to conduct seminars to help parents gain these skills. How well early childhood professionals meet the needs of single parents can make a difference in how successful single parents are in providing for the needs of their children and other family members. Thus, your help to single parents can impact how well their children progress in your program.

In the Infant and Toddler segment of the DVD, observe the interactions between teachers and children. How will the great demand for high-quality programs affect your career?

Teenage Parents. Teenage pregnancies continue to be a societal problem, although the teen birthrate has fallen in recent years because of a reduction in sexual activity and the use

In the Head
Start segment of the DVD,
listen to how Head Start
provides education and
services for children in
poverty. What appeals to
you about working in a
Head Start program?

Poverty The condition of
having insufficient income to
support a minimum standard
of living.

of more-effective contraceptive methods.[2] The following facts about teenage pregnancy dramatically demonstrate its continuing extent and effects:

- In 2005, for women aged fifteen through nineteen, there were 41.1 births per 1,000.
- As a group, Latino teenagers have the highest birthrate, with 87.1 births per 1,000.
- Among states, Mississippi has the highest birthrate for teenagers, with 71 births per 1,000. New Hampshire has the lowest birthrate for teenagers with 23 births per 1,000.[3]

Concerned legislators, public policy developers, and national leaders view teenage pregnancy as a loss of human potential. They worry about the demand for public health and welfare services and about an increased number of school dropouts. From an early childhood point of view, teenage pregnancies create greater demand for infant and toddler child care and programs to help teenagers learn how to be good parents. The staff of an early childhood program must often provide nurturance for both children and parents, because the parents themselves may lack emotional maturity, which is necessary to engage in a giving relationship with children. Early childhood professionals must help teenage parents develop parenting skills.

SOCIAL ISSUES

It is almost a given in early childhood education that substandard, unhealthy living conditions are major contributors to poor school achievement and life outcomes. A number of social issues facing children today put their chances for learning and success at risk.

POVERTY

Living in **poverty** means that individuals don't have the income to purchase adequate health care, housing, food, clothing, and educational services. For example, more than one-half of all children who lack insured health care come from poor families.[4] In 2005 poverty for a nonfarm family of four meant an income of less than $19,350. The federal government annually revises its poverty guidelines, which are the basis for distribution of federal aid to schools and student eligibility for academic services, such as Head Start, Title I (a program that provides additional help in math and reading), and free and reduced-price school breakfasts and lunches.

In 2003 children comprised approximately thirty-five percent of the 35.9 million individuals living in poverty. Of those 12.9 million children in poverty, more than four million were under the age of five. Poverty is a greater risk for children living in single-parent homes with female heads of household (see Figure 2.6). Approximately 40 percent of African

**FIGURE 2.6 Families
with Children Living in
Poverty**

Female-headed families
are linked to poverty,
which is also linked to
poor school achievement.

Source: U.S. Census Bureau,
"Annual Demographic Survey,"
Current Population Survey
(2005).

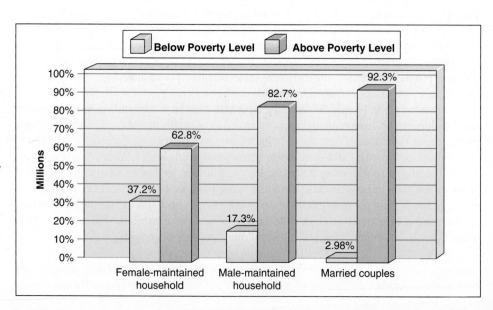

TABLE 2.1 States with Highest Percentage of People in Poverty, 2005

What implications do these data have for public policy and early childhood education?

Rank	State	Percent of Population in Poverty
1.	Arkansas	18.5
2.	New Mexico	18.0
3.	Mississippi	17.9
4.	District of Columbia	17.3
5.	Louisiana	16.9
6.	West Virginia	16.9
7.	Texas	15.8
8.	Alabama	15.1
9.	Tennessee	14.3
10.	N. Carolina	14.2

Source: U.S. Census Bureau, *American Community Survey* (2005). www.uscb.org 2005

American children under the age of five live in poverty, but this figure climbs to 59.7 percent in single-mother households. Poverty rates for Hispanic American children under the age of six are 32.1 percent overall but about 57 percent for those in single-mother homes.[5]

Living in a rural community and in a rural southern state also increases the likelihood that families will live in poverty. As Table 2.1 illustrates, eight of the ten states with the highest poverty rates are in the South. In Mississippi one-third of all children are poor, nearly twice the national average.[6] In addition, living in the inner city increases the chances of being poor. And both rural and urban poverty lead to decreased support for education, meaning that children living in poverty will likely attend schools that have fewer resources and poorer facilities.

The effects of poverty are detrimental to students' achievement and life prospects. For example, children and youth from low-income families are often older than others in their grade level, move more slowly through the educational system, are more likely to drop out, and are less likely to find work. Children in poverty are also more likely to have emotional and behavioral problems and are less likely than others to be "highly engaged" in school.[7] Furthermore, parents in low-income families are less likely to help their children complete homework assignments.

HOUSING

Children's homes and the environments of their homes can have a tremendous impact on their growth, development, and educational achievement. Let's look at some of the ways homes affect young children.

Twenty-three percent of all children under seven living in poverty in the United States live in a home where someone smokes on a regular basis.[8] Estimates are that fifty to sixty-seven percent of all children under five live in a home with at least one adult smoker.[9] Secondhand smoke, also known as environmental smoke (ETS) is a combination of the smoke from a burning cigarette and exhaled smoke. Children exposed to ETS have less lung efficiency and an increased frequency and severity of childhood asthma, chronic respiratory problems, and ear infections.[10] Here are some things you can do to help children in the battle with ETS:

- *Quit.* If you are a smoker, become a nonsmoker.
- *Advocate.* You can be in the forefront of efforts to make sure schools and child care centers are smoke free.
- *Protect.* Ask people not to smoke around children.
- *Educate.* Use newsletters and other forms of family communication to inform parents of the dangers of ETS to themselves and their children.

Beyond the dangers of ETS, six million families in the United States live in substandard housing.[11] Lead poisoning and asthma, which are discussed in the next section, are chronic children's health conditions that are related to the quality and condition of children's homes.[12]

In addition, thirty-seven percent of children live in crowded housing.[13] In certain geographic areas, crowding can be much worse; in Nevada twenty-seven percent of children live in crowded conditions.[14] Crowded housing conditions contribute to communicable diseases, diarrhea and vomiting, and lower respiratory tract infections in infants.[15] Furthermore, crowding produces higher levels of stress and increased parent-child conflicts, which in turn affect academic performance and behavior in school.[16]

Knowing how housing affects children and families will help you be alert to ways that you can work with families and community agencies to improve the quality of housing wherever it is inferior. For example, I once worked with a group of urban teachers who undertook a letter-writing campaign about a slum landlord who ignored the pleas of residents to repair roof leaks and broken plumbing. The campaign attracted public attention and eventually resulted in some relief for the families.

WELLNESS AND HEALTHY LIVING

As you know, when you feel good, life goes much better. The same is true for children and their families. Poor health and unhealthy living conditions are major contributors to poor school achievement and life outcomes. A number of health issues facing children today put their chances for learning and success at risk.

To counteract the national epidemic of childhood obesity in the United States, early childhood professionals are increasingly turning to physical exercise and activities to help children lead healthy lives, now and in the future.

Illnesses. When you think of children's illnesses, you probably think of measles, chicken pox, and strep throat. Actually, asthma, lead poisoning, and obesity are the three leading childhood diseases.

Asthma. Asthma is a chronic inflammatory disorder of the airways, characterized by breathlessness, wheezing, coughing, and chest tightness. It is the most common chronic childhood illness in the United States; according to the Center for Disease Control and Prevention (CDC), an estimated nine million children suffered from asthma in 2005. These soaring rates of asthma have many ill effects, including ten million lost school days every year, two million emergency room visits a year, and loss of learning, physical exercise, and healthy development for the affected children.[17]

Asthma is caused in part by poor air quality, dust, mold, animal fur and dander, allergens from cockroaches and rodents' feces, and strong fumes. Many of these causes are found in poor and low-quality housing. In your role as advocate you can work with the American Lung Association which has two initiatives designed to help children with asthma. One program is the Asthma Friendly School Initiative (AFSI). The other is the Kids With Asthma Bill of Rights designed to help children with asthma talk to their parents and teachers about asthma management.

You will want to reduce asthma-causing conditions in your early childhood program and work with parents to reduce the causes of asthma in their homes. In your school environment, you can prohibit smoking around children, keep the space clean and free of mold, reduce or eliminate carpeting, and have children sleep on mats or cots. You can also work with parents to ensure that their children are getting appropriate asthma medication.

Lead Poisoning.   The CDC estimates that approximately five hundred thousand children under the age of six have elevated blood lead levels.[18] These children are at risk for lower IQs, short attention spans, reading and learning disabilities, hyperactivity, and other behavioral problems.

The major source of lead poisoning is lead-based paint that still exists in many homes and apartments. Approximately eighty percent of homes built before 1978 have lead-based paint in them. Since then, lead has not been used in paint. Other sources of lead are car batteries, cheap children's jewelry, and dust and dirt from lead-polluted soil. Lead enters the body through inhalation and ingestion. Young children are especially vulnerable because they put many things in their mouths, chew on windowsills, and crawl on floors.

Companion Website   For more information about children's health issues, go to the Companion Website at **www.prenhall.com/morrison**, select chapter 2, then choose the Linking to Learning module.

Obesity.   Over the past five years, researchers, nutritionists, and politicians have been calling attention to the growing national crisis of childhood obesity. This generation of children is frequently referred to as the Supersize Generation. Indeed, during the past three decades, the childhood obesity rate has more than doubled for children aged two to five and twelve to nineteen, and it has more than tripled for children aged six to eleven. At present, approximately nine million children over six years of age are considered obese.[19]

Obesity refers to excess fatty tissue in the body.[20] Children are deemed obese if their weight is more than twenty percent greater than the ideal weight for a boy or girl of their age and height.[21] Even though the terms *obesity* and *overweight* are frequently used interchangeably, there are actually three ways of accurately determining obesity:

- Height and weight plotted on a growth chart
- Skin-fold thickness measured on the back of the upper arm with special calipers
- Body/mass index (BMI) determined by a mathematical calculation involving height and weight[22]

Obesity is prevalent in both developed and developing countries, reflecting changes in behavioral patterns, such as decreased physical activity and overconsumption of high-fat, energy-dense foods. Many other individuals become obese because of a biological predisposition to gain weight readily.[23] Current research into childhood obesity reveals numerous causes:

In the Infant and Toddler segment of the DVD, observe how teachers provide for the nutritional needs of young children. Teachers also need to be aware of childhood obesity issues and ways to combat obesity.

- High birth weight
- Obesity in early life—measured at eight and eighteen months
- Rapid weight gain in the first year of life
- Rapid catch-up growth up to two years of age
- Early development of body fat in the preschool years
- More than eight hours of television a week at age three
- Short sleep duration—less than 10.5 hours per night at age three
- Parental obesity[24]

What can you, as an early childhood professional, do to help children and parents win the obesity war? You can start by reading two features in this chapter. The Voice from the Field "Fighting Childhood Obesity in Classrooms" illustrates what can be done with nutrition education, and the Diversity Tie-In "Exercise Is Important for Girls, Too" stresses

Companion Website   To complete a Program in Action activity related to childhood obesity, go to the Companion Website, at **www.prenhall.com/morrison**, select chapter 2, then choose the Program in Action module.

Voice from the Field

FIGHTING CHILDHOOD OBESITY IN CLASSROOMS

Seattle Public Schools fights childhood obesity within the classroom and the cafeteria through strong district-level nutrition policies.

NUTRITION EDUCATION

Fitting nutrition education into a packed, testing-focused curriculum is a real challenge. Add to this the lack of trained nutrition professionals within school buildings, and the challenge becomes even greater. The solution that Seattle Public Schools developed was to invite community partners and volunteers into the schools to provide nutrition education.

One school in Seattle—T.T. Minor Elementary—has benefited from a partnership with a local Washington State University extension office through their Food $ense program, Change: Cultivating Health and Nutrition Through Garden Education. Through this experiential gardening and cooking program, students learn about the food cycle—from seed to the dinner plate. In one of the more popular lessons, students learn about composting from the worms themselves. One-hour lessons are taught over the span of ten weeks by both a Washington State University extension staff member and by the classroom teacher. All lessons are developed using a cross-curricular approach by integrating nutrition into core subject areas (see http://ww.metrokc.gov/dchs/csd/wsu-ce/ FoodSense/CHANGE/).

LINKS TO THE CAFETERIA

Seattle Public Schools has developed programs that link the cafeteria with the classroom. Mission Delicious and You're the Cook! are partnerships with the Seattle Nutrition Action Consortium (SNAC)—a local, USDA-funded nutrition education program aimed at improving the nutritional habits of low-income students and their families. Our students learn how to prepare simple, healthy, and inexpensive recipes (such as yogurt parfaits and pita bites) in the school cafeteria, thus making the connection between didactic and practical learning. To further enhance learning, our teachers are provided supplemental materials for use in the classroom, and students receive take-home materials to share with their families (see http://www.metrokc.gov/health/nutrition/snac.htm).

ETHNIC FOODS

The Ethnic Foods and Education program offers school meals that reflect the ethnic diversity of our student population. The program brings an ethnic food to the lunch menu each month. Classrooms have been an integral part of the program, from submitting student recipes to taste testing foods. Teachers can also take advantage of cross-curricular health and nutrition supplemental lessons that highlight the cultures and health-related components of the foods represented in the program (see http://www.activelivingbydesign.org/index.php?id5409).

DISTRICT POLICIES

The backbone of all of our district's nutrition work is strong district-level policies. Seattle Public Schools nutrition policies (passed in August 2004) ban sales of all foods containing high levels of sugar and fat, improve the quality and appeal of school meal programs, and prohibit contracts with beverage vendors for exclusive pouring rights. The policies also give direction to the school meal program and others to offer fresh, local, organic, non–genetically modified, unirradiated, unprocessed food whenever feasible.

LESSONS LEARNED

Seattle Public Schools has learned some valuable lessons:

- Capitalize on community partners and others who are interested in working with district nutrition services to provide nutrition education and improve food options.
- Integrate nutrition into existing classroom curricula and activities. With the ever-present pressures to raise student test scores, integrating nutrition into existing activities is often the only way to fit it in.
- Understand the importance of district-level support of healthy foods through strong policies. Our policies reflect an institutional agreement that nutrition is important in ensuring student success.

Contributed by Kirsten Frandsen, STEPS nutrition education coordinator, and Carolyn Kramer, MPH, STEPS schools coordinator, Seattle Public Schools, Seattle, Washington.

EXERCISE IS IMPORTANT FOR GIRLS, TOO

Have you ever heard an adult say, "Boys are just more active than girls; they need more time to run and play outdoors" or "The girls are content to play inside; it's the boys who have to get out on the playground"? Knowledgeable preschool teachers know that vigorous physical activity is very important for girls as well as for boys. Both girls and boys need and deserve plenty of time to be physically active indoors and out. Improved aerobic endurance, muscular strength, motor coordination, and growth stimulation of the heart, lungs, and other vital organs are among the benefits of physical activity for children and adolescents. Giving equal opportunity to girls and boys—starting in preschool—is what Title IX of the Educational Amendments of 1972 is all about.

EQUAL OPPORTUNITY FOR ALL CHILDREN

Title IX is the legislation that prohibits sex discrimination in schools, whether in academics or in athletics: "No person in the United States shall, on the basis of sex, be excluded from participation in, denied the benefits of, or subjected to discrimination under any educational program or activity receiving federal aid." Title IX provides for equal treatment and opportunity in athletics while allowing schools the flexibility to choose sports based on student body interest, geographic influence, budget concerns, and gender ratio. The emphasis is on the need for women to have equal opportunities to those for men on the whole, rather than on an individual basis.

The history of female participation in physical activity is a great deal shorter than that of males. It wasn't all that long ago that many physical activities were considered too strenuous or unladylike for young girls and women, who were warned about being tomboys and the possibility of sterility. Although there were some bright spots along the way, it wasn't until the passage of Title IX that girls were given greater opportunities to play high school and college sports. Girls are still less active than boys (they're most inactive between the ages of fourteen and sixteen) but at least are now participating in physical activity and sports in greater numbers than ever before:

- More than 100,000 women now participate in intercollegiate athletics—a fourfold increase since 1971.*

- In 1996, 2.4 million high school girls represented 39 percent of all high school athletes, compared to only 300,000 or 7.5 percent in 1971—an eightfold increase.*

GIRLS' NEED FOR PHYSICAL ACTIVITY

Physical activity, for both genders, helps build and maintain healthy muscles, bones, and joints; increases the body's infection-fighting white blood cells and germ-fighting antibodies; helps control weight; and reduces the risk of developing such illnesses as diabetes, heart disease, and many types of cancer.

Physical activity has additional benefits for girls:

- Because osteoporosis is more prevalent among women, it's especially important for girls to build strong bones when they're young.
- Exercise has been shown to increase strength in girls significantly.
- Estrogen-dependent cancers (breast, ovarian, and endometrial) may occur less often in women who exercise.
- Depression, which is experienced twice as often by adolescent females as by adolescent males, can be impacted positively by exercise. According to a report of the President's Council on Physical Fitness and Sports ("Physical Activity and Sport in the Lives of Girls"), participation in physical activity helps counteract the feelings of hopelessness and worthlessness common to depression and helps instill feelings of success.
- Self-esteem, self-concept, and body image—all of which girls struggle with—are also affected positively by physical activity and exercise.
- Studies show that many high school female athletes received higher grades and standardized test scores than their nonathletic counterparts. They also dropped out at lower rates and were more likely to go on to college.
- Many female executives in Fortune 500 companies were highly involved in athletics.

According to the President's Council, numerous researchers have contended that girls aren't less athletically skilled than boys. Their activities may be different (e.g., jumping rope and performing intricate dance routines), but these activities "still require agility, coordination, strength, and attentional focus. In fact, girls possess the physical capabilities to perform well in all kinds of movement activities. What they may lack is the social support to do so."

The individual who feels competent and confident when moving will most likely continue moving throughout life—that is, will most likely take part in lifelong physical activity and thereby achieve all the health benefits it has to offer. Adolescents and adults who haven't acquired and mastered fundamental movement skills are the ones who shy away from physical activity because the movements required feel unnatural and overly strenuous; learning them at an older age is much more challenging.

Contributed by Rae Pica, children's physical activity specialist and author of *Experiences in Movement* (3rd ed.) and *Your Active Child.*

*"Indicators of Progress Toward Equal Educational Opportunity Since Title IX," *Title IX: 25 Years of Progress* (U.S. Department of Education, June 1997).

Companion Website To complete a Diversity Tie-In activity related to Title IX, go to the Companion Website at **www.prenhall.com/morrison**, select chapter 2, then choose the Diversity Tie-In module.

In the Head
Start segment of the DVD, listen to the teacher discuss program menus for children who are over- and underweight. Observe how good nutrition programs contribute to children's health and overall well-being.

the importance of exercise for good health. Then review the following ten suggestions and commit to supporting them in your early childhood program:

1. *Encourage breakfast.* If your school or program does not provide breakfast for children, be an advocate for starting to do that. Providing school breakfasts can be both a nutritional and an educational program.
2. *Provide healthy snacks instead of junk food.* And advocate for healthy foods in school and program vending machines.
3. *When cooking with children, talk about foods and their nutritional value.* Cooking activities are also a good way to eat and talk about new foods.
4. *Integrate literacy and nutritional activities.* For example, reading and discussing labels is a good way to encourage children to be aware of and think about nutritional information.
5. *Make meals and snack times pleasant and sociable experiences.*[25]
6. *Provide parents with information about nutrition.* For example, you can make parents aware of the U.S. Department of Agriculture's new individualized food pyramid (Figure 2.7). You might access the new pyramid online, have children enter their own data, and then have them share their individualized pyramids with their parents.
7. *Help families understand and practice healthy eating habits.* Encourage parents to set a healthy example for their families so that they can help their young children develop healthy eating habits.[26]
8. *Counsel parents to pull the plug on the television.* TV watching is associated with obesity because children are more likely to snack on fattening foods while they watch and children who watch a lot of television tend to be less physically active. Inactivity promotes weight gain.
9. *Encourage exercise.* You can provide daily opportunities for physical exercise and physical activities in your program, maximizing large-motor muscle activity, such as jumping, dancing, marching, kicking, running, riding a tricycle, or throwing a ball.[27] National obesity experts are now recommending that children engage in at least 60 minutes of physical activity a day.[28]
10. *Be a role model.* You can set a good example for children to follow by modeling appropriate behaviors, such as enjoying a variety of foods, being willing to taste new foods, and enjoying physical activity.[29]

You can do a lot to promote children's health. Do not blame the parents, but work with them to enable them and their children to lead healthy lives.

Stress and Violence. Dramatic changes are occurring in contemporary society. Life is becoming more fast-paced, and more demands are placed on parents, families, and children.

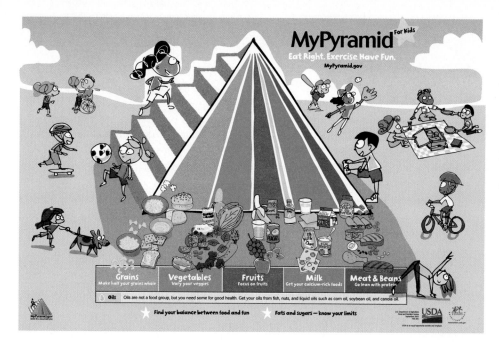

**Figure 2.7
MyPyramid.gov**

Go to www.mypyramid.gov to individualize the pyramid according to each child's age, gender, and physical activity level.

Source: U.S. Department of Agriculture, Food and Nutrition Service, "MyPyramid for Kids" (September 2005), http://www.mypyramid.gov.

As a result, children today are surrounded by stressful situations in homes, child care, and schools. Much of the stress children experience comes from issues we have discussed—poverty, poor housing, poor nutrition, and unhealthy living. Violence and the threat of violence is another stress in children's lives and one that endangers their well-being and life outcomes.

Social issues such as violence have public policy implications for young children, families, and early childhood professionals. Acts of violence within society lead to proposals to provide violence-free homes and educational environments, to teach children to get along nonviolently with others, and to reduce violence on television, in movies, and in video games. Early childhood professionals play important roles in these discussions and decision-making processes. Advocacy is a critical role of the professional. Proposals to reduce violence on television, for example, might include pulling the plug on television; using the V-chip, which enables parents to block out programs with violent content; boycotting companies whose advertisements support programs with violent content; and limiting violence shown during prime-time viewing hours for children. You can play a major role by being an advocate for reducing the media violence that negatively influences children's lives. You might share with parents the guidelines of the American Academy of Pediatrics for children's television viewing (see Figure 2.8).

Programs to prevent and curb bullying are another example of how educators are combating the effects of violence on children. Although in the past the bullying has been dismissed as normal or kids' play, bullying is now related to school and other violence. Bullying includes teasing, slapping, hitting, pushing, unwanted touching, taking personal belongings, name calling, and making sexual comments and insults about looks, behavior, and culture. Schools are starting to fight back against bullies and bullying.

POLICY AND PROGRAMMING TRENDS

BRAIN RESEARCH AND EARLY CHILDHOOD EDUCATION

Early childhood education, like all other forms of education, is becoming much more research based. Over the last decade, the government has turned to research to ensure that federal dollars are being spent on programs and curricula that are effective in helping

FIGURE 2.8 Guidelines for Children's Television Viewing

1. Limit children's total time with entertainment media to no more than one to two hours of quality programming per day.

2. Remove television sets from children's bedrooms.

3. Discourage television viewing for children younger than two years, and encourage more interactive activities that will promote proper brain development, such as talking, playing, singing, and reading together.

4. Monitor the shows children are viewing. Most programs should be informational, educational, and nonviolent.

5. View television programs along with children, and discuss the content.

6. Use controversial programming as a stepping-off point to initiate discussions about family values, violence, sex and sexuality, and drugs.

7. Use the videocassette recorder wisely to show or record high-quality, educational programming for children.

8. Support efforts to establish comprehensive media education programs in schools.

9. Encourage alternative entertainment for children, including reading, athletics, hobbies, and creative play.

Source: Adapted by permission from the American Academy of Pediatrics, Committee on Public Education, "Children, Adolescents, and Television," *Pediatrics* 107, no. 2 (February 2001): 423–426.

children learn to read and that improve overall academic achievement. Today, early childhood education professionals are being encouraged to use research-based instructional strategies, activities, and programs that have been proven to work. One of your professional responsibilities will be to identify and select these kinds of programs.

Research on the brain has enormous implications for early childhood education and for public policy. Brain research provides a strong basis for making decisions about what programs to provide for young children, as well as what environmental conditions promote optimum child development. Brain research underscores the importance of early experiences and the benefits of early intervention services, thus pointing toward a positive economic return on investments in young children.

Public interest in the application of brain research to early childhood education has intensified. In many cases that research affirms what early childhood educators have always intuitively known: good parental care, warm and loving attachments, and positive age-appropriate stimulation from birth onward make a tremendous difference in children's cognitive development for a lifetime.

Brain research also tells us a great deal regarding stimulation and the development of specific areas of the brain. For example, brain research suggests that listening to music and learning to play musical instruments at very early ages stimulate the brain areas associated with mathematics and spatial reasoning. In addition, brain research suggests that gross-motor activities and physical education should be included in a child's daily schedule throughout the elementary years. Regrettably, school systems often cut programs such as physical education and music in times of budget crisis, even though research shows that these programs are essential to a child's complete cognitive development.

Early childhood curricula based on the findings of research strive to apply research findings in a practical way. One example, Zero to Three, focuses on infants, toddlers, and families and is dedicated to promoting the healthy development of America's babies and young children. Based on research, Zero to Three believes that a child's first three years are crucial for developing intellectual, emotional, and social skills and that if these skills are not developed, the child's lifelong potential may be hampered. The organization supports professionals, parents, and policy makers and strives to increase public awareness, inspire leaders, and foster professional excellence through training, always emphasizing the first three years of a child's life.

As research has influenced our ideas about how children learn and what they should learn, basic educational premises have shifted. Early childhood professionals have arrived at the following conclusions about the development of young children:

1. Human development is shaped by a dynamic and continuous interaction between biology and experience.
2. Culture influences every aspect of human development and is reflected in child-rearing beliefs and practices designed to promote healthy adaptations.
3. The growth of self-regulation is a cornerstone of early childhood development that cuts across all domains of behavior.
4. Children are active participants in their own development, reflecting the intrinsic human drive to explore and master one's environment.
5. Child-adult relationships and the effects of these relationships on children are the building blocks of healthy development.
6. The broad range of individual differences among young children often makes it difficult to distinguish normal variations and maturational delays from transient disorders and persistent impairments.
7. The development of children unfolds along individual pathways with trajectories characterized by continuities and discontinuities, as well as by a series of significant transitions.
8. Human development is shaped by the ongoing interplay among sources of vulnerability and sources of resilience.
9. The timing of early experiences can matter, but more often than not, the developing child remains vulnerable to risks and open to protective influences throughout the early years of life and into adulthood.
10. The course of development can be altered in early childhood by effective interventions that change the balance between risk and protection, thereby shifting the odds in favor of more adaptive outcomes.[30]

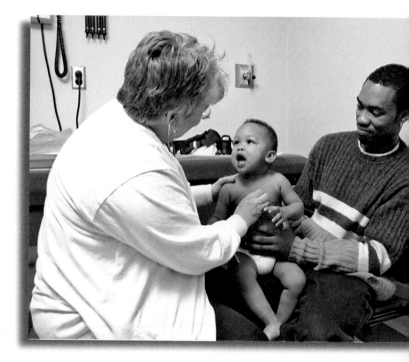

Readiness includes physical growth and general health, such as being well rested and fed and properly immunized. How does children's health status affect their readiness for learning?

GOVERNMENT INVOLVEMENT IN EARLY CHILDHOOD PROGRAMS

Over the past decade there has been increased federal and state funding of early childhood programs, a trend that will continue for a couple of reasons. First, politicians and the public recognize that the early years are the foundation for future learning. Second, spending money on children in the early years is more cost effective than trying to solve problems in the teenage years. As a result, all the states are developing programs for young children. As federal dollars shift to other programs, states are responding by initiating programs of their own, funded from both federal allocations and other sources, including lottery monies and increased taxes on commodities and consumer goods such as cigarettes.

The Florida Department of Education, for example, has an office dedicated to early intervention and school readiness. One of its programs is Florida First Start, a home-school partnership designed to give children at risk of future school failure the best possible start

Companion Website For more information about public policy and early childhood education, go to the Companion Website at **www.prenhall.com/morrison**, select chapter 2, then choose the Linking to Learning module.

in life and to support parents in their role as their children's first teachers. Emphasis is on enabling families to enhance their children's intellectual, physical, language, and social development by involving parents in their children's education during the critical first three years of life. Through early parent education and support services, the program lays the foundation for later learning and future school success, while fostering effective parent-school relationships. Further information is available on the Internet.

In addition, instead of giving monies directly to specific programs, many federal dollars are consolidated into what are known as **block grants**—sums of money given to states to provide services according to broad general guidelines. In essence, the states, not the federal government, then control the way the money is spent and the nature of the programs funded.

Block grants Sums of money given to states to provide services according to broad, general guidelines.

FEDERAL SUPPORT FOR REFORM

At the same time that states are exerting control over education, so is the federal government. One of the dramatic changes occurring in society is the expanded role of the federal government in the reform of public education. We are currently witnessing more federal dollars allocated for specific early education initiatives than ever before. For example, the federal government is providing increased funding to reform Head Start by making it more academic and emphasizing the development of early literacy skills. The critics of federal support for such programs argue that the federal government should not allocate dollars for specific, targeted programs. However, the number and size of federal allocations for reform initiatives will likely continue.

Reforming education so that all children will be able to read on grade level and closing the achievement gap between rich and poor are now two of the top priorities on the national education agenda. The No Child Left Behind Act (Public Law 107-110) and other federal initiatives have focused national attention on developing educational and social programs to serve young children and families. Two areas in particular, reading and school readiness, are now major federal priorities in ensuring that all children succeed in school and life. The Early Reading First programs established in the No Child Left Behind Act provide grants to school districts and preschool programs for the development of model programs to support the school readiness of preschool programs and to promote children's understanding of letters, letter sounds, and the blending of sounds and words. The application of the No Child Left Behind Act to classroom practices is discussed in chapters 8 ("Federal Programs"), 10 ("The Preschool Years"), 11 ("Kindergarten Education"), and 12 ("The Primary Grades"). Both pros and cons are presented.

PUBLIC SUPPORT OF EARLY EDUCATION

Traditionally, the majority of preschool programs were operated by private agencies or agencies supported wholly or in part by federal funds to help the poor, the unemployed, working parents, and disadvantaged children. But times have changed. Parents from all socioeconomic levels exert great pressure on public school officials and state legislatures to sponsor and fund additional preschool and early childhood programs. Increasingly, preschools are providing a full range of services for children and families, with an emphasis on providing for the whole child.

Another trend involves preschool programs conducted in public schools. Currently, California, Florida, New York, North Carolina, Oklahoma, and Texas support preschools; nationwide, about 500,000 preschool children are enrolled in public school programs. As preschool programs admit more three- and four-year-olds, opportunities for teachers of young children will grow.

The spread of preschools reflects changing family patterns, especially the rise in single-parent families and families with two adult wage earners. Demand for preschools also relates to their use in early childhood intervention programs and to the popular belief that three- and four-year-old children are ready, willing, and able to learn.

Parents lobby for public support of early childhood education for a number of reasons. First, because working parents cannot find quality child care for their children, they believe the public schools hold the solution to child care needs. Other parents cannot afford quality child care and believe public preschools are a reasonable, cost-efficient way to meet child care needs. In addition, many people believe that early public schooling is necessary to promote equal opportunity for all. They argue that low-income children begin school already far behind their more fortunate middle-class counterparts and that the best way to keep them from falling hopelessly behind is for them to begin school earlier. It seems sensible to provide services to avoid future school and learning problems. Another reason relates to the growing federal role in early education programs. The federal government provides money for preschool programs based in part on research that supports the importance of early literacy learning as a basis for successful reading. Of course early literacy is not the only thing that young children need to know and do, but it is certainly a major federal emphasis.

The alignment of public schools with early childhood programs is becoming increasingly popular. Some think it makes sense to put the responsibility for educating and caring for the nation's children under the sponsorship of one agency—the public schools. For their part, public school teachers and the unions that represent them are anxious to bring early childhood programs within the structure of the public school system.

It seems inevitable that the presence of public schools in early childhood education will continue to expand. Given that so many public schools offer programs for three- and four-year-olds, can programs for infants and toddlers be far behind?

Early public schooling is a reality for growing numbers of the nation's children. What societal changes are contributing to this trend toward early public schooling?

HOT TOPICS IN EARLY CHILDHOOD EDUCATION

The issues facing early childhood education today are many and varied and have considerable consequences, both positive and negative, for young children. The following hot topics will be discussed throughout this book in order to help you be on the cutting edge of your professional practice.

- *Early literacy and reading.* Professionals regard providing children with the foundation for literacy as one of the key factors necessary for their school success.
- *The politicization of early childhood education.* There has been a dramatic increase in state and federal involvement in the education of young children. For example, the federal government is using Head Start as a means of and model for reforming all of early childhood education. This federalization will likely continue and expand.
- *Use of early childhood programs to promote and support children's readiness for school and learning.* Increasingly, there is a recognition that if children are ready to learn when they enter school, they are more likely to succeed.
- *The increasing use of tests and testing to measure achievement and school performance in the early years.* At the same time, increasing numbers of parents, professionals, and early childhood critics are advocating for less emphasis on high-stakes testing in the early years.
- *Safety and security.* Increasingly in these violent times, parents, the public, and professionals are seeking ways to keep children safe and secure in the learning process.

in the High/ Scope segment of the DVD, observe the classroom routines and choices that children are encouraged to make. Note that High/Scope was originally designed to meet the needs of low-income children and their families.

This is a great time for early childhood education and a wonderful time to be a teacher of young children. Early childhood education has changed more in the last ten years than in the previous fifty. These changes and the issues that accompany them provide many opportunities for you to become even more professional and for all children to learn the knowledge and skills necessary for success in school and life.

Companion Website

For additional Internet resources or to complete an online activity for this chapter, go to the Companion Website at **www.prenhall.com/morrison**, select chapter 2, then choose the Linking to Learning or Making Connections module.

LINKING TO LEARNING

Annie E. Casey Foundation

http://www.aecf.org

Presents the latest information on issues affecting America's disadvantaged children; a friendly, newly updated resource.

Children Now

http://www.childrennow.org

Works to translate the nation's commitment to children and families into action to improve conditions for all children. Recognized nationally for its policy expertise and up-to-date information on the status of children.

Early Childhood Care and Development

http://www.ecdgroup.com

An international, interagency group dedicated to improving the condition of young children at risk by keeping them on the agendas of policy makers, funders, and program developers.

Florida First Start

http://title1.brevard.k12.fl.us/florida_1st_start.htm

A home-school partnership designed to give children at risk of future school failure the best possible start in life and to support parents in their role as their children's first teachers.

National Center for Family Literacy

http://www.famlit.org

Advances and supports family literacy services through programming, training, research, advocacy, and dissemination of information about family literacy.

U.S. Department of Agriculture—Food Pyramid

http://www.foodpyramid.gov

Provides useful information on current nutrition guidelines, including the food pyramid, which promotes a healthy diet.

Zero to Three

http://www.zerotothree.org

Promotes the healthy development of the nation's infants and toddlers by supporting and strengthening families, communities, and those who work on their behalf. A nonprofit organization dedicated to advancing current knowledge; promoting beneficial policies and practices; communicating research and best practices to a wide variety of audiences; and providing training, technical assistance, and leadership development.

ACTIVITIES FOR FURTHER ENRICHMENT

ETHICAL DILEMMA: "MY CHILD'S NOT FAT!"

Your school has set up a pilot program to develop a curriculum for helping overweight children learn good nutrition skills and lose weight. You were asked to select three children from your kindergarten class to participate. One of the children's parents has contacted you and is angry that you selected her child. She believes that her child is not obese and should not be in a program for "fat kids." She believes you are discriminating against her child and is threatening to contact the school board.

What should you do when a parent's needs appear to be in conflict with the best interests of the child? You risk alienating the parent if you insist that her child would benefit from the program. However, if you go along with the parent, the child may suffer.

APPLICATIONS

1. The daily newspapers are an excellent way to keep up-to-date with what is happening in the field of early childhood education. Many articles relate directly to issues of curriculum, practice, and public policy. For example, "Kindergarten Shifts Focus to Academics," an article in the August 15, 2005, *Louisville Courier-Journal,* discusses how the kindergarten curriculum is shifting from playtime to academics. Not all early childhood professionals and parents believe this shift is good for young children, and the topic is creating a lot of discussion (see chapter 11, "Kindergarten Education: Learning All You Need to Know"). For now, list the pros and cons of academics in the kindergarten. Find other examples of education issues covered in the media.

2. Interview single parents and determine what effects they think single parenting has on children. In what ways is single parenting stressful to parents and children? How can early childhood programs support and help single parents? Search for and review research relating to this topic. How does the research agree or disagree with what parents report?

3. Some children in local preschools and child care centers have experienced their parents' divorce, abuse, and other types of stress. What types of problems do early childhood professionals face as they help children whose lives have been affected by these situations?

4. Obesity is an ever-growing concern for the health of children. Visit several preschool and/or child care programs, and see what they are doing to prevent obesity. Based on what you observe, add to the list of obesity prevention ideas discussed in the chapter.

FIELD EXPERIENCES

1. Visit corporations and businesses in your area, and determine what they are doing to support education and family programs.

2. List at least five social, political, and economic conditions of modern society, and explain how these conditions influence how people view, treat, and care for the very young.

3. List at least five significant contributions good early childhood education programs can make to the lives of young children.

4. List at least five cultural factors that can contribute to poor nutrition in young children. For example, some cultures introduce solid foods to infants earlier than is recommended by the American Academy of Pediatrics (see chapter 9). You can also interview various cultural groups and ask them how they think their cultural practices might encourage obesity.

RESEARCH

1. Contact agencies that provide services to single parents, teenage parents, and families in need. How do these programs influence early childhood education programs in your local community?

2. Investigate the types of preschool programs available in your community. Who may attend them? How are they financed? What percentage of the children who attend have mothers working outside the home?

3. Over a period of several weeks or a month, collect articles from newspapers and magazines relating to infants, toddlers, and preschoolers, and categorize them by topic (child abuse, nutrition, etc.). What topics were given the most coverage? Why? What topics or trends are emerging in early education, according to this media coverage? Do you agree with everything you read in the articles? Can you find instances in which information or advice may be inaccurate, inappropriate, or contradictory?

4. Develop a list of environmental concerns in your community that might affect the wellness of children—for example, community centers or schools that still contain lead-based paint. Investigate how other communities have approached such problems and what steps can be taken to improve the conditions in your community.

READINGS FOR FURTHER ENRICHMENT

Endres, J. *Food, Nutrition, and the Young Child*, 5th ed. Upper Saddle River, NJ: Merrill/Prentice Hall, 2004.

Provides early childhood teachers with a basic understanding of food and nutrition as applied to the care of children from birth through age eight; a practical, easy-to-read book.

Klass, C. *The Home Visitor's Guidebook: Promoting Optimal Parent and Child Development.* Baltimore, MD: Paul H. Brookes, 2003.

Contains recent research and presents practical strategies concerning communication, interpersonal skills, trust, respect, boundaries, child development, and diversity.

Moss, P., and P. L. Petrie. *From Children's Services to Children's Spaces: Public Policy, Children and Childhood.* New York: Routledge (UK), 2002.

Explores apparent contradictions and complexities through a critique of the concept of children's services, from the researcher in this field of study.

Robertson, C. *Safety, Nutrition, and Health in Early Education*, 2nd ed. Cliffton Park, NY: Delmar/Thompson Learning, 2003.

Provides information on children's safe environments and good nutrition and health; covers basic information, theory, and health assessment tools. Includes practical applications, caregiving skills, cultural sensitivity, and resources needed for working with children, families, and staff.

Wright, K., D. A. Stegelin, and L. Hartle. *Building Family, School, and Community Partnerships*, 3rd ed. Upper Saddle River, NJ: Merrill/Prentice Hall, 2007.

Profiles today's American families and examines the special relationships among them, their children's schools, and their communities. Through an ecological systems approach, explores the family as a child's first teacher.

ENDNOTES

1. M. L. Munson and P. D. Sutton, *Births, Marriages, Divorces, and Deaths: Provisional Data for November 2004*, National Vital Statistics Reports, vol. 53, no. 19 (Hyattsville, MD: National Center for Health Statistics, 2005).

2. J. Darroch and S. Singh, *Why Is Teenage Pregnancy Declining? The Roles of Abstinence, Sexual Activity and Contraceptive Use* (2004), http://www.alangutt macherinstitute. org/pubs/or_teen_preg_decline.html.

3. Ibid.

4. Carmen DeNavas-Walt, Bernadette D. Proctor, and Robert J. Mills, *Income, Poverty, and Health Insurance Coverage in the United States: 2003* (Washington, DC: U.S. Government Printing Office, 2004). Also available online at http://www.census.gov/prod/2004pubs/p60-226. pdf.

5. U.S. Census Bureau, *Current Population Survey*, 2003.

6. National Center for Education Statistics, *The Condition of Education* 2004 (Washington, DC: U.S. Department of Education, 2004).

7. A. Wigton and A. Weil, *Snapshots of America's Families II: A View of the Nation and 13 States from the National Survey of America's Families*, http://www.urban.org/url.cfm? ID=900841.

8. Child Stats.gov, "Population and Family Characteristics," *America's Children: Key National Indicators of Well-Being 2005*, http://childstats.ed.gov/americas children/pdf/ac.2005/ pop.pdf.

9. American Academy of Otolaryngology–Head and Neck Surgery, *Children and Secondhand Smoke*, http://www.entnet.org/healthinfo/tobacco/secondhand_smoke.cfm.

10. Ibid.

11. National Center for Healthy Housing, *Healthier Homes, Stronger Families: Public Policy Approaches to Healthy Housing*, http://www.centerforhealthyhousing.org/html/healthier_homes_stronger_famil.html.

12. Ibid.

13. Child Stats.gov, "Housing Problems," *America's Children: Key National Indicators of Well-Being 2005*, http://childstats.ed.gov/americaschildren/eco3.asp.

14. Ibid.

15. Children's Hospital of Eastern Ontario, *Medical Officers of Health Join Forces with CHEO to Make Housing a Top Health Priority*, September 2003, http://www.cheo.on.ca/ english/1071_10_sept_03.html.

16. Susan Lang, "CU Study: Home Crowding Has Variety of Harmful Effects for Children," Cornell Chronicle, http://www. news.cornell.edu/Chronicle/99/2.18.99/crowding.html.

17. Tony Proscio, *Healthy Housing, Healthy Families: Toward a National Agenda for Affordable Healthy Housing*, January 2005, http://www.enterprisefoundation.org/majorinitiatives/cdl/hhwhitepaper.asp.

18. Center for Disease Control, *Children's Blood Lead Levels in the United States*, 2005, http://www.cdc.gov/nceh/lead /research/kidsBLL.htm#National%20surveys.

19. Institute of Medicine, *Childhood Obesity in the United States: Facts and Figures*, September 2004, http://www.iom.edu/Object.File/Master/22/606/0.pdf.

20. Bright Futures. "Obesity" in *Bright Futures in Practice: Physical Activity*, http://www.brightfutures.org/physicalactivity/ issues_concerns/48.html.

21. University of Michigan Health System, "Obesity and Overweight," http://www.med.umich.edu/1libr/yourchild/ obesity.htm.

22. The formula for body/mass index is as follows:

$$BMI = \left(\frac{\text{Weight in pounds}}{(\text{Height in inches}) \times (\text{Height in inches})} \right) \times 703$$

However, because children's body fatness changes over

the years and because maturing girls and boys differ in body fatness, the BMI for children and teens is plotted on gender-specific growth charts.

23. M. Deitel, "Overweight and Obesity Worldwide Now Estimated to Involve 1.7 Billion People," editorial, *Obesity Surgery* 13 (2003): 329–330.

24. BBC News, TV Watching Link to Child Obesity," http://news.bbc.co.uk/2/hi/health/4562879.stm.

25. New York State Department of Health, *Preventing Childhood Obesity: Tips for Child Care Professionals,* November 2002, http://www.health.state.ny.us/ prevention/ nutrition/resources/obchcare.htm.

26. Ibid.

27. Ibid.

28. Associated Press, "Children Need an Hour of Exercise per Day," June 22, 2005, http://www.firstcoastnews. com/health/news-article.aspx?storyid=39364.

29. *Preventing Childhood Obesity.*

30. Reprinted by permission from *From Neurons to Neighborhoods: The Science of Early Childhood Development,* © by the National Academy of Sciences (Washington, DC: National Academies Press, 2000), 3–4.

CHAPTER 3

Observing and Assessing Young Children

EFFECTIVE TEACHING THROUGH APPROPRIATE EVALUATION

*. . . assessment should serve one primary purpose:
to improve student learning.*

BOB PETERSON, EDITOR, RETHINKING SCHOOLS

Kindergarten teacher Jesse Jones wants to make sure that Amanda knows the beginning sounds that he has taught the class the last two weeks. First-grade teacher Melynda Seaton wants to see how many words César is familiar with on the class word wall. Third-grade teacher José Gonzalez wants to know if his class can apply to real-life situations what they're learning in class. Decisions, decisions, decisions.

The minutes, hours, and days are filled with assessment decisions. Questions abound: "What is Jeremy ready for now?" "What can I tell Maria's parents about her language development?" "The activity I used in the large-group time yesterday didn't seem to work well. What could I have done differently?" Appropriate assessment can help you find the answers to these and many other questions about how to teach and what is best for children in all areas of development.

WHAT IS ASSESSMENT?

Much of children's lives is subject to and influenced by assessment. Assessment will influence your life as an early childhood professional and will be a vital tool of your professional practice. Assessment well done is one of your most important responsibilities, and it can benefit your children's learning.

Assessment is the process of collecting information about children's development, learning, health, behavior, academic progress, need for special services, and attainment in order to make decisions. Figure 3.1 outlines the purposes of assessment. Notice that all the purposes of assessment involve decisions, which play important roles in children's and teachers' lives.

Assessment occurs primarily through observation, administration of commercial and teacher-made tests, and examination of students' products. You will probably use all three of these assessment procedures in your teaching. Keep in mind that all assessment procedures should inform your instruction so that you can help all children be successful.

APPROPRIATE ASSESSMENT

Early childhood professionals do their best to use assessment in appropriate ways—that is, to support children's learning. However, assessment and the results of assessment are often used inappropriately. One such example is the use of **high-stakes assessment testing** to make life-changing decisions about children. Two examples are noteworthy: In some cases, children are either admitted or not admitted to kindergarten or first grade based on the outcome of a test. In other cases, decisions about whether to promote children are based on the results of a national standardized test.

With so much emphasis on tests, it is understandable that the issue of testing and assessment raises many concerns on the part of parents and professionals. Critics maintain that the standardized testing movement reduces teaching and learning to the lowest common denominator—teaching children what they need to know to get the right answers. Many early childhood professionals believe that standardized tests do not measure children's

Focus Questions

What is assessment, and why is it important?

Why is it important for you to know how to assess?

What are the purposes and uses of assessment and observation?

What are some major ways to assess children's development, learning, and behavior?

What issues are involved in assessment?

Companion Website

To check your understanding of this chapter, go to the Companion Website at **www.prenhall.com/ morrison**, select chapter 3, answer Multiple Choice and Essay Questions, and receive feedback.

Assessment The process of collecting information about children's development, learning, health, behavior, academic process, need for special services, and attainment in order to make decisions.

High-stakes assessment testing An assessment test used to either admit children into programs or promote them from one grade to the next.

In the Kindergarten segment of the DVD, observe the children's different ethnicities. How might assessments used with children from diverse cultures and with varied experiences affect the decision about a child's entrance into kindergarten?

Companion Website To learn more about the uses and abuses of assessment, go to the Companion Website at **www. prenhall.com/morrison**, select chapter 3, then choose the Linking to Learning module.

Authentic assessment Assessment conducted through activities that require children to demonstrate what they know and are able to do; also referred to as *performance-based assessment*.

FIGURE 3.1 Purposes of Assessment

For children
- Identify what children know
- Identify children's special needs
- Determine appropriate placement
- Select appropriate curricula to meet children's individual needs
- Make appropriate instructional decisions
- Select appropriate instructional materials
- Refer children and, as appropriate, their families to programs and agencies for additional services

For families
- Help determine effectiveness of child's program
- Monitor progress and achievement

For early childhood programs
- Make policy decisions regarding what is and what is not appropriate for children
- Determine to what extent programs and services children receive are beneficial and appropriate
- Provide multiple data sources regarding student progress and achievement

For early childhood professionals
- Make lesson and activity plans
- Select materials
- Make instructional decisions about how to implement learning activities
- Report to parents and families about children's developmental status and achievement
- Improve teaching-learning process

For the public
- Provide information regarding children's and a school's achievement performance
- Hold schools and teachers accountable for all children's learning
- Provide a basis to improve school and community programs
- Provide data to compare and evaluate schools and districts
- Make decisions about which schools and programs need increased funding

---

thinking, problem-solving ability, creativity, or responsibility for their own learning. Furthermore, critics believe that group-administered, objectively scored, skills-focused tests—which dominate much of U.S. education—do not support (indeed, may undermine) many of the curricular reforms taking place today. Figure 3.2 identifies the general principles that should guide formal assessment of young children.

AUTHENTIC ASSESSMENT

Authentic assessment is also referred to as *performance-based assessment*. Authentic assessment requires children to demonstrate what they know and are able to do. Meaningless facts and isolated information are considered inauthentic.

FIGURE 3.2 Principles to Guide Formal Assessment of Young Children

- **Make sure assessments benefit children.**
  Gathering accurate information from young children is difficult and potentially stressful. Be sure assessments have a clear benefit—either in direct services to the child or in improved quality of educational programs.
- **Tailor assessments to a specific purpose, and make sure they are reliable, valid, and fair for that purpose.**
  Assessments designed for one purpose are not necessarily valid if used for other purposes. In the past, many of the abuses of testing with young children have occurred because of misuse.
- **Understand that the reliability and validity of assessments increase with children's age.**
  The younger the child, the more difficult it is to obtain reliable and valid assessment data. It is particularly difficult to assess children's cognitive abilities accurately before age six.
- **Make assessments developmentally appropriate.**
  Assessments of young children should address the full range of early learning and development, including physical well-being and motor development; social and emotional development; approaches toward learning; language development; and cognition and general knowledge. Methods of assessment should recognize that children need familiar contexts to be able to demonstrate their abilities.
- **Make assessments linguistically appropriate.**
  Assessment results are easily confounded by language proficiency, especially for children who come from home backgrounds with limited exposure to English and for whom the assessment would essentially be an assessment of their English proficiency. Each child's first- and second-language development should be taken into account when determining appropriate assessment methods and interpreting the meaning of assessment results.
- **Involve parents and early childhood professionals.**
  Assessments should include multiple sources of evidence, especially reports from parents and teachers. Assessment results should be shared with parents as part of an ongoing process that involves them in their child's education.

Source: National Education Goals Panel, "Principles and Recommendations for Early Childhood Assessments" (December 14, 1998): 5–6, http://govinfo.library.cent.edu/Negp/page9-3.htm.

Here are some guidelines for authentic assessment:

- *Assess children based on their actual work.* Use work samples, exhibitions, performances, learning logs, journals, projects, presentations, experiments, and teacher observations.
- *Assess children based on what they are actually doing in and through the curriculum.*
- *Assess what each individual child can do.* Evaluate what each child is learning, rather than comparing one child with another or one group of children with another.
- *Make assessment part of the learning process.* Encourage children to show what they know through presentations and participation.
- *Learn about the whole child.* Make the assessment process an opportunity to learn more than just a child's acquisition of a narrow set of skills.
- *Involve children and parents in a cooperative, collaborative assessment process.* Authentic assessment is child centered.
- *Provide ongoing assessment over the entire year.* Assess children continually throughout the year, not just at the end of a grading period or at the end of the year.

Today many teachers use **portfolios**—a compilation of children's work samples, products, and teacher observations collected over time—as a basis for authentic assessment.

In the High/Scope segment of the DVD, observe that asking children to recall what they did and learned is an authentic method of assessment. How do their responses contribute to teachers' understanding of how to help them learn?

Portfolio A compilation of children's work samples, products, and teacher observations collected over time.

In the Reggio Emilia segment of the DVD, teachers engage in documentation of children's learning. Compare the Reggio method of documentation with the method Linda Sholar used in her Voice from the Field, "How to Document Learning and Build Portfolios for Kindergartners."

Companion Website For more information about authentic assessment, go to the Companion Website at **www.prenhall.com/morrison**, select chapter 3, then choose the Linking to Learning module.

Screening measures Any assessment that gives a broad picture of what children know and are able to do, as well as their physical health and emotional status.

Decisions about what to put in portfolios vary, but examples include written work, artwork, audiotapes, pictures, models, and other materials that attest to what children are able to do. Some teachers let children put their best work in their portfolios; others decide with children what will be included; still others decide for themselves what to include. Portfolios are very useful, especially during parent-teacher conferences, because they include notes about achievement, teacher- and child-made checklists, artwork samples, photographs, journals, and other documentation. The accompanying Voice from the Field on pages 60–61 is a Competency Builder that provides specific suggestions for creating student portfolios based on appropriate and authentic assessment. Competency Builders are features of this text designed to help you increase your teaching competence and performance in specific professional areas. By completing the Competency Builder activities, you will enhance your professional development and contribute to your qualifications as a high-quality teacher.

Some teachers are using technology to develop digital portfolios, which can stand alone or supplement the traditional portfolio. Digital portfolios include books and journals that children keep on computers and then illustrate with digital cameras. Later on in this chapter you will read more about using digital photographs in children's portfolios. However, it is important to remember that portfolios are only one part of children's assessment.

ASSESSMENT FOR SCHOOL READINESS

Because of federal mandates and state laws, many school districts assess children in some manner before or at the time of their entrance into school. Table 3.1 shows formal methods of assessment. Some type of screening occurs at the time of kindergarten entrance to evaluate learning readiness. Unfortunately, children are often classified on the basis of how well they perform on these early screenings. When assessment is appropriate and the results are used to design developmentally appropriate instruction, assessment is valuable and worthwhile. You will want to make sure that all of your assessments of young children are equitable and fair. The Diversity Tie-In on page 62 gives suggestions that will help you achieve that goal.

SCREENING PROCESSES

Screening measures give school personnel a broad picture of what children know and are able to do, as well as their physical and emotional status. As gross indicators of children's abilities, screening procedures provide much useful information for decisions about placement for initial instruction, referral to other agencies, and additional testing that may be necessary to pinpoint a learning or health problem.

Many school districts conduct comprehensive screening programs for children entering preschool and kindergarten. These screening programs are conducted in one day or over several days. Data for each child are usually evaluated by a team of professionals who make instructional placement recommendations and, when appropriate, suggest additional testing and make referrals to other agencies for assistance.

The screening program can involve the following:

- Interviewing parents to gather information about their children's health, learning patterns, learning achievements, personal habits, and special problems
- Conducting health screenings including a physical examination, a health history, and a blood sample for analysis
- Conducting vision, hearing, and speech screenings
- Collecting and analyzing data from former programs and teachers, such as preschools, Head Start, and child care programs
- Administering a cognitive and/or behavioral screening instrument such as those shown in Table 3.1

TABLE 3.1 Formal Measures of Assessment Used in Early Childhood

Assessment Instrument	Age/Grade Level	Purpose
Battelle Developmental Inventory, 2nd edition http://www.assess.nelson.com/test-ind/ bdi.html	Birth to age 8	Assesses key developmental skills in children up to age 8
Boehm Test of Basic Concepts-Revised http://www.cps.nova.edu/~cpphelp/ BTBC-R.html	Kindergarten to grade 2	Assesses children's mastery of basic concepts that are fundamental to understanding verbal instruction and necessary for early school achievement
BRIGANCE® Screens and Inventories http://www.curricassoc.com/brigance/	Prekindergarten to grade 9	Obtains a broad sampling of children's skills and behaviors to determine initial placement, plan appropriate instruction, and comply with mandated testing requirements
Denver Developmental Screening Test-Revised http://www.denverii.com/DenverII.html	Ages 1 month to 6 years	Identifies infants and preschool children with serious developmental delays
Developmental Indicators for the Assessment of Learning, 3rd edition (DIAL-3) http://www.agsnet.com/assessments/ technical/dial.asp	Ages 3 to 6	Identifies children who may have special educational needs
Peabody Individual Achievement Test-Revised (PIAT-R) http://www.cps.nova.edu/~cpphelp/ PIAT-R.html	Kindergarten to grade 12	Provides wide-range assessment of general information, reading recognition, reading comprehension, mathematics, spelling, and written expression
Peabody Picture Vocabulary Test-Revised (PPVT-R) http://www.cps.nova.edu/~cpphelp/ PPVT-R.html	Ages 2.5 to 40	Tests hearing vocabulary; available in two forms
Preschool Child Observation Record, 2nd edition http://www.highscope.org/Assessment/ cor.htm	Ages 2.5 to 6	Measures children's progress in all early childhood programs
Stanford-Binet Intelligence Scales, 5th edition (SB5) http://www.riverpub.com/products/clinical/ sbis/home.html	Ages 2 to 23	Measures fluid reasoning, knowledge, quantitative reasoning, visual-spatial processing, and working memory and can compare verbal and nonverbal performance
Stanford-Binet Intelligence Scales for Early Childhood, 5th edition (Early SB5) http://www.riverpub.com/products/ earlySB5/index.html	Ages 2 to 7.3	Combines a new test observation checklist and software-generated parent report with the subtests from the Stanford-Binet Intelligence Scales, 5th edition
Wechsler Intelligence Scale for Children-Revised (WISC-R) http://www.cps.nova.edu/~cpphelp/ WISC-R.html	Ages 7 to 16	Shows specific patterns of strengths and weaknesses (based on three IQ scores) to indicate how well the child is able to learn and whether there are any specific learning disabilities
Wechsler Preschool and Primary Scale of Intelligence-3rd Edition (WPPSI-III) http://www.cps.nova.edu/~cpphelp/ WPPSI-3.html	Ages 2.6 to 7.3	Measures intelligence of young children and is age appropriate and user friendly

SCREENING INSTRUMENTS AND OBSERVATION RECORDS

Screening instruments provide information for grouping and planning instructional strategies. Most can be administered by people who do not have specialized training. Parent volunteers often help administer screening instruments, many of which can be administered in about thirty minutes.

HOW TO DOCUMENT LEARNING
AND BUILD PORTFOLIOS FOR KINDERGARTNERS

I have used student portfolios to evaluate my kindergarten students for twenty years. A portfolio is a purposeful and systematic collection of children's achievements over time. It is far more than a scrapbook; it is a tool that guides teachers in understanding where children are in their learning and development.

PURPOSE OF PORTFOLIOS

Portfolios serve a number of purposes:

- Providing a record of each student's process of learning
- Supporting learning
- Encouraging children to do their best work
- Guiding instruction

Portfolio entries should meet the following criteria:

- Reflect a student's cognitive, social, emotional, and physical development
- Provide a visual record of a student's process of learning over time
- Encourage input from students, teachers, and parents

CREATING PORTFOLIOS

Throughout the year, you can collect and date samples of students' work to include in their portfolios.

STEP 1 Select quarterly work samples

Look for examples that demonstrate abilities with cutting, writing numbers (let each child decide how far he or she can write), and writing letters of the alphabet and any words or stories (using either invented or conventional spellings).

STEP 2 Allow the children to be involved

Let them select samples of artwork and creative writing (e.g., journal entries, letters or drawings they have done for parents).

STEP 3 Use a table of contents

Consider a checklist format, stapled inside the folder, to keep the volume of materials in the portfolio from becoming overwhelming. A list makes it easy to examine the contents and determine at a glance what data you have to make wise instructional decisions and what information you still need.

STEP 4 Include records for and from parents

Include a parent questionnaire, parent responses to conferences, individual student assessment profiles, and anecdotal records in each portfolio.

APPROPRIATE ASSESSMENT

The success of student portfolios as an evaluation tool depends on the appropriate assessment of individual students and accurate, conscientious documentation of student growth. In my classroom, assessments are ongoing; they occur as children perform daily classroom routines and participate in group time, share time, center time, and recess. Appropriate assessment informs instruction and is aligned to curriculum that reflects local, state, and national standards.

Assessment is the process of observing, recording, and documenting the work children do and how they do it. With each assessment I note the following:

- Which activities the children choose
- How long they work on specific activities
- What their process is for completing activities

I also observe students' learning styles, interest levels, skill levels, coping techniques, strategies for decision making and problem solving, and interactions with other children.

Accurate Documentation

Observations have little value unless they are accurately documented. To manage documentation more accurately and efficiently, I have developed or adapted a variety of forms to make systematic assessments of students' learning. Throughout the year, I use these assessment tools to record information on individual children in each area of their development. I use the symbols that follow and date the occurrence of behaviors, describing and documenting skill proficiency as appropriate.

+ = Progress is noted
✓ = Needs more time and/or experience
* = See comments

The emphasis is on what each child knows or can do at specific times of the year (e.g., at the end of a reporting period). Each child's progress is compared with his or her prior work. When I review these individual assessments, I am able to detect areas of growth and progress over time.

Developing and Using Evaluation Forms

I have also developed several evaluation forms that allow me flexibility in recording observations of students' learning:

1. Daily ongoing assessments of students' learning are useful in planning group and/or individual instruction. They provide additional documentation that supports the individual assessment records.
2. I make anecdotal records (on Post-It notes) of unanticipated events or behaviors, a child's social interactions, and problem-solving strategies.
3. I transfer these notes to a class grid so I can determine at a glance which children I have observed.

The ongoing assessments and the anecdotal records, along with individual assessment profiles, become a part of each student's portfolio, to be used for instructional planning and communicating with parents.

USING ASSESSMENT INFORMATION

I use the information from student portfolios to do the following:

- Plan classroom instruction for individuals and groups
- Identify children who may need additional time or help
- Confer with parents and colleagues

During conferences I share with parents their student's assessment profile for the different areas of development, and together we examine samples of the child's work that support the assessment. Even though progress is visually obvious, I can also point out less obvious progress as we view the samples. I then give conference response forms to parents and ask for comments or suggestions for additional portfolio entries.

With the portfolio I am satisfied that I have gleaned an accurate assessment of and appreciation for each child's total development.

Contributed by Linda Sholar, kindergarten teacher, Sangre Ridge Elementary School, Stillwater, Oklahoma. Photo by Linda Scholar.

Diversity Tie-In

THE UNEVEN PLAYING FIELD OF ASSESSMENT

We readily acknowledge that all children come to school as individuals and with different backgrounds. On the other hand, when we assess children, we can quickly forget issues of individuality and differences in culture, ethnicity, home language, age, home and community environment, maternal and paternal psychological well-being, and socioeconomic background. Children simply do not come to the assessment or testing situation with equal chances for success. Let's consider some of the ways their backgrounds and the testing conditions influence children's approaches to and performance on assessment measures.

Language

- Was the test given to a non-English-speaking child developed for English-speaking children? If so, how will this influence the outcome for the non-English-speaking child? In other words, is the test linguistically appropriate for the children with whom it is being used?
- Is the teacher or other person who administers a test to a non-English-speaking child fluent in the child's language? If the answer is no, what are some ways that this would influence how well a child responds? For example, many teachers learn classical Spanish, the kind spoken in Spain. However, many Spanish-speaking children and their families speak the Spanish of Mexico or Central and South America or a dialect of the languages spoken in these and other Spanish-speaking countries.

Development

- Have the tests administered to a particular age group been developed for that age group? With the trend to test younger children, tests are being used that were developed for older children.
- Can testing procedures be adapted to meet the special needs of different cultures and age groups? For example, are young children allowed to take breaks? Fifty minutes to an hour is much too long for many young children to attend to a testing situation. Can the test be administered in a few sections over a period of time?

Socioeconomic background

- How do children's socioeconomic status influence their achievement and test performance? For example, children who live in families with high incomes score better on achievement tests and have fewer behavior problems than do children from low-socioeconomic households. This link of socioeconomic status to achievement means that we have to provide poor children high-quality preschool programs designed to help them catch up with their more advantaged peers if we expect them to do well on assessments of any kind.*

---

* W. Jean Yeung, Miriam R. Linver, and Jeanne Brooks-Gunn, "How Money Matters for Young Children's Development: Parental Investment and Family Processes," *Child Development* 73, no. 6 (November/December 2002): 1861–1879.

Companion Website

To complete a Diversity Tie-In activity related to assessment, go to the Companion Website at **www.prenhall.com/morrison**, select chapter 3, then choose the Diversity Tie-In module.

BRIGANCE® Preschool Screen II. BRIGANCE® Preschool Screen II is a screening instrument for use in preschool with children ages three to four. The data sheet for a three-year-old child shows the skills, behaviors, and concepts evaluated in that portion of the screening instrument (see Figure 3.3).

DIAL-3. The DIAL-3 (Developmental Indicators for the Assessment of Learning–Revised) in both English and Spanish is designed to screen large numbers of preschool and kindergarten children. Requiring approximately twenty to thirty minutes to administer, the DIAL-3 screens for motor skills, concepts, language skills, self-help, and social development.

A. Child Data

Child's Name: _Calvin Baldwin_

Parents/Guardian: _Carl and Karen Baldwin_

Address: _982 Haines Street_

School/Program: _Ballard School_

Teacher: _Leslie Feingold_

Examiner: _Ben Faust_

	Year	Month	Day
Date of Screening	2006	9	12
Birth date	2003	7	7
Age	3	2	5

B. Basic Screening Assessments

Page	Assessment Number	Skill (Circle the skill for each correct response. Make notes as appropriate.) When deriving standard scores, follow the directions for discontinuing that appear with the assessments where applicable.	Number of Correct Responses	Point Value	Child's Score
3	1A	**Personal Data Response:** Orally gives: ①first name ②last name ③middle name 4. age — Discontinue after 3 in a row incorrect.	3 ×	1 point each	3 /4
4	2A	**Color Recognition:** Points to: ①red ②blue ③green ④yellow ⑤orange — Discontinue after 2 in a row incorrect.	5 ×	2 points each	10 /10
5	3A	**Picture Vocabulary:** Names pictures of: ①boat ②kite ③wagon 4. ladder 5. scissors 6. leaf — Discontinue after 3 in a row incorrect.	3 ×	2 points each	6 /12
6	4A	**Knows Use of Objects:** Knows use of: ①book ②scissors ③refrigerator — Discontinue after 2 in a row incorrect.	3 ×	3 points each	9 /9
7	5A	**Visual Motor Skills:** Copies: ① ② — ③ ○ 4. + — Discontinue after 3 in a row incorrect.	3 ×	3 points each	9 /12
8	6A	**Gross-Motor Skills:** ①Stands on one foot five seconds. ②Stands on other foot five seconds. 3. Walks forward heel-and-toe four steps.			
9	7A	**Number Concepts:** Demonstrates or giving: ①two ②three 3. five — Discontinue after 2 in a row incorrect.	2 ×	3 points each	6 /9
10	8A	**Builds Tower with Blocks:** Builds a tower with: ①6 blocks ②7 blocks ③8 blocks ④9 blocks ⑤10 blocks — Discontinue after 2 attempts without success.	5 ×	2 points each	10 /10
11	9A	**Identifies Body Parts:** Points to or touches: ①chest ②back ③knees ④chin 5. fingernails 6. heels — Discontinue after 3 in a row incorrect.	4 ×	1 point each	4 /6
12	10A	**Repeats Sentences:** Repeats sentences of ①four syllables ②six syllables 3. eight syllables — Give credit for highest level of success and for all lower levels.	2 ×	3 points each	6 /9
13	11A	**Prepositions and Irregular Plural Nouns:** Uses ①prepositions ②irregular plural nouns	2 ×	5 points each	10 /10

Total Score = 79 /100

EXAMPLE OF COMPLETED DATA SHEET

D. Observations

1. Handedness: Right ____ Left ✔ Uncertain ____
2. Grasps pencil with: Fist ____ Fingers ✔
3. Hearing appeared to be normal: (See Functional Hearing and Vision) Yes ✔ No ____ Uncertain ____
4. Vision appeared to be normal: (See Functional Hearing and Vision) Yes ✔ No ____ Uncertain ____
5. Record other observations below or on another sheet. _Cooperated and enjoyed talking_

E. Summary (Complete only if child is screened with a group.) Compared to other children included in this screening:

1. this child scored ____ Lower ____ Average ✔ Higher
2. this child's age is ____ Younger ____ Average ✔ Older
3. the teacher rates this child ____ Lower ✔ Average ____ Higher
4. the examiner rates this child ____ Lower ____ Average ✔ Higher

F. Recommendations _Within normal limits. No further assessment needed at this time._

FIGURE 3.3 Three-Year-Old Child Data Sheet for the BRIGANCE® Preschool Screen II

Source: Reprinted by permission from BRIGANCE® Preschool Screen II, © 2005, CURRICULUM ASSOCIATES®, Inc.

The High/Scope Child Observation Record, Second Edition. The High/Scope Child Observation Record (COR) for ages two and a half to six is used by teachers and other observers to assess young children's development. The High/Scope COR assesses six broad categories: initiative, social relations, creative representation, music and movement, language and literacy, and mathematics and science.

WHAT IS OBSERVATION?

Observation is one of the most widely used methods of assessment. Table 3.2 provides information on and guidelines for observation and other informal methods of authentic assessment.

Observation The intentional, systematic act of looking at the behavior of a child in a particular setting, program, or situation.

Professionals recognize that children are more than what is measured by any particular test. **Observation** is an authentic means of learning about children—what they know and are able to do—especially as it occurs in more naturalistic settings such as classrooms, child care centers, playgrounds, and homes. Observation is the intentional, systematic act of looking at the behavior of a child in a particular setting, program, or situation. Observation is sometimes referred to as kid-watching and is an excellent way to find out about children's behaviors and learning.

PURPOSES OF OBSERVATION

Observation is designed to gather information on which to base decisions, make recommendations, develop curriculum, plan for teaching, select activities and learning strategies, and assess children's growth, development, and learning. When professionals and parents look at children, sometimes they do not really see or concern themselves with what the children are doing or why, as long as they are safe and orderly. Consequently, the significance and importance of critical behaviors may go undetected if observation is done casually and is limited to unsystematic looking.

Systematic observation has specific purposes:

Many school districts conduct a comprehensive screening for children entering kindergarten, which may include assessment of readiness skills, vision, hearing, and speech.

- *To determine the cognitive, linguistic, social, emotional, and physical development of children.* Using a developmental checklist is one way you can systematically observe and chart the development of children. Figure 3.4 shows a checklist you could use to assess children's emergent literacy behaviors.
- *To identify children's interests and learning styles.* Today, teachers are very interested in developing learning activities, materials, and classroom centers based on children's interests, preferences, and learning styles.
- *To plan.* The professional practice of teaching requires planning on a daily, ongoing basis. Observation provides useful, authentic, and solid information that enables you to intentionally plan for activities rather than to make decisions with little or no information.
- *To meet the needs of individual children.* Meeting the needs of individual children is an important part of teaching and learning. For example, a child may be advanced cognitively but overly aggressive and lacking the social skills necessary to play coopera-

TABLE 3.2 Informal Methods of Authentic Assessment

Method	Purpose	Guidelines
OBSERVATION Kid watching—looking at children in a systematic way	Enables teachers to identify children's behaviors, document performance, and make decisions	Plan for observation and be clear about the purposes of the observation.
Anecdotal record Gives a brief written description of student behavior at one time	Provides insight into a particular behavior and a basis for planning a specific teaching strategy	Record only what is observed or heard; should deal with the facts and should include the setting (e.g., where the behavior occurs) and what was said and done.
Running record Focuses on a sequence of events that occurs over time	Helps obtain a more detailed insight into behavior over a period of time	Maintain objectivity and try to include as much detail as possible.
Event sampling Focuses on a particular behavior during a particular event (e.g., behavior at lunchtime, behavior on the playground, behavior in a reading group)	Helps identify behaviors during a particular event over time	Identify a target behavior to be observed during particular times (e.g., fighting during transition activities).
Time sampling Record particular events or behaviors at specific time intervals (e.g., five minutes, ten minutes)	Helps identify when a particular child demonstrates a particular behavior; helps answer the question, "Does the child do something all the time or just at certain times and events?"	Observe only during the time period specified.
Rating scale Contains a list of descriptors for a set of behaviors	Enables teachers to record data when they are observed	Make sure that key descriptors and the rating scale are appropriate for what is being observed.
Checklist A list of behaviors identifying children's skills and knowledge	Enables teachers to observe and easily check off what children know and are able to do	Make sure that the checklist includes behaviors that are important for the program and for learning (e.g., counts from 1 to 10, hops on one foot).
WORK SAMPLE Collection of children's work that demonstrates what they know and are able to do	Provides a concrete example of learning; can show growth and achievement over time	Make sure that the work sample demonstrates what children know and are able to do. Let children help select the items they want to use as examples of their learning.
PORTFOLIO Collection of children's work samples and other products	Provides documentation of a child's achievement in specific areas over time; can include test scores, writing work samples, videotapes, etc.	Make sure the portfolio is not a dumpster but a thoughtful collection of materials that documents learning over time.
INTERVIEW Engaging children in discussion through questions	Allows children to explain behavior, work samples, or particular answers	Ask questions at all levels of Bloom's taxonomy (see chapter 12) in order to gain insight into children's learning.

tively and interact with others. Through observation, you can gather information to develop a plan to help that child learn how to play with others.

- *To determine progress.* Systematic observation, over time, provides a rich and valuable source of information about how individuals and groups of children are progressing in their learning and behavior.

- *To provide information to parents.* Teachers report to and conference with parents on an ongoing basis. Observational information adds to other information, such as test

In the Reggio Emilia segment of the DVD, observe that the emergent curriculum does not occur haphazardly but is based on teachers' observations, which they share with one other.

FIGURE 3.4 Emergent Literacy Behavior Checklist

Child's name _____ Age ____ Date _____

Physical readiness	Observed	Not Observed
Demonstrates visual activity		
Demonstrates hearing activity		
Print concepts		
Recognizes left-to-right sequencing		
Recognizes top, down directionally		
Asks what print says		
Connects meaning between two objects, pictures		
Models reading out loud		
Models adult silent reading (e.g., newspaper, books)		
Recognizes that print has different meanings (e.g., information, entertainment)		
Recognizes local environment print*		
Knows that it is print that is read in stories*		
Comprehension behaviors		
Shows an interest in books and readings*		
Recognizes ten alphabet letters, especially from own name*		
Pays attention to separable and repeating sounds in language (e.g., Peter, Peter, Pumpkin Eater)*		
Questions and comments, demonstrating understanding of literal meaning of story being told*		
Follows oral directions		
Draws correct pictures from oral directions		
Interprets pictures		
Sees links in story ideas		
Links personal experiences with text (e.g., story, title)		
Logically reasons through story plot/conclusions		
Begins to attend to initial or rhyming sounds in salient words*		
Sees patterns in similar stories		

FIGURE 3.4 Continued

Writing behaviors	Observed	Not Observed
Makes meaningful scribbles (i.e., attempts to make letterlike shapes)		
Draws recursive scribbles (i.e., rows of cursivelike writing)		
Makes strings of "letters"		
Uses one or more consonants to represent words		
Uses inventive spellings		
Displays reading and writing attempts, calls attention to self (e.g., look at my story)*		
Writes (i.e., scribbles) message as part of playful activity*		

* From www.readingsuccesslab.com/reading-tips/readingskillschecklist.html.

results and child work samples, and provides a fuller and more complete picture of individual children.

- *To provide professional insight.* Observational information can help professionals learn more about themselves and what to do to help children.

ADVANTAGES OF INTENTIONAL, SYSTEMATIC OBSERVATION

There are a number of advantages to gathering data through observation:

- *Observation enables teachers to collect information that they might not otherwise gather through other sources.* Many of the causes and consequences of children's behavior can be assessed only through observation and not through formal, standardized tests; questioning; or parent and child interviews.
- *Observation is ideally suited to learning more about children in play settings.* Observation affords the opportunity to note a child's social behavior in a play group and discern how cooperatively he or she interacts with peers. Observing a child at play gives professionals a wealth of information about developmental levels, social skills, and what the child is or is not learning in play settings.
- *Observation reveals a lot about children's prosocial behavior and peer interactions.* It can help you plan for appropriate and inclusive activities to promote the social growth of young children. Additionally, your observations can serve as the basis for developing multicultural activities to benefit all children.
- *Observation of children's abilities provides a basis for assessment of what they are developmentally able to do.* Many learning skills are developed sequentially, such as the refinement of large-motor skills before small-motor skills. Through observation, professionals can determine whether children's abilities are within a normal range of growth and development.
- *Observation is useful to assess children's performance over time.* Documentation of daily, weekly, and monthly observations of children's behaviors and learning provides a database for the cumulative evaluation of each child's achievement and development.
- *Observation provides concrete information for use in reporting to and conferencing with parents.* Increasingly, reports to parents involve professionals' observations and children's work samples so that parents and educators can collaborate to determine how to help children develop cognitively, socially, emotionally, and physically.

Intentional observation is a useful, informative, and powerful means of guiding teaching and helping to ensure the learning of all children.

STEPS FOR CONDUCTING OBSERVATIONS

There are four steps involved in the process of systematic, purposeful observation.

Step 1: Plan for Observation. Planning is an important part of the observation process; everything you do should be planned in advance of the observation. A good guide to follow in planning is to ask *who, what, where, when,* and *how* will you observe.

Setting goals for observation is also an important part of the planning process. Goals allow you to reflect on why you want to observe and thus direct your efforts to what you will observe. Your goal might include observing the physical classroom environment for effectiveness, social interactions, or improvements to children's learning activities. Stating a goal focuses your attention on the purpose of your observation. For example, to focus on providing an inclusive classroom or program and fully including an exceptional child, your goals might read like this:

Goal 1: To determine what modifications are necessary in the classroom to provide Dana in her wheelchair with access to all parts of the classroom

Goal 2: To assess the kinds of prosocial behavior other children display to Dana while they interact in the classroom

Observing children at play enables teachers to learn about children's developmental levels, social skills, and peer interactions. How might you use such information to plan play-based activities?

Planning also involves selecting the type of observational tool you will use, one that will meet your goal for observing. To assess the physical modifications necessary to accommodate Dana and to examine students' social interactions with her, you might select an observational tool similar to the checklist in Figure 3.5. Review that figure to see how the teacher used the checklist to achieve Goals 1 and 2.

Step 2: Conduct the Observation. While conducting your observation, it is imperative that you be objective, specific, and as thorough as possible. There are many ways to record your observations, including taking notes, using a checklist or a tally sheet, making a sketch of an indoor or outdoor environment, video taping, or tape-recording. The suggestions in Figure 3.6 on page 70 will help you manage the collection of information. Figure 3.7 on page 71 shows a sample observation form.

Step 3: Interpret the Data. All observations should result in some kind of **interpretation**, which serves several important functions. First, interpretation enables you to use your professional knowledge to make sense of what you have seen. Second, interpretation can help you learn to anticipate behaviors associated with normal growth and development and to recognize what is not representative of appropriate growth, development, and learning for each child. Third, interpretation provides direction for the implementation or modification of programs and curriculum.

Interpreting data includes drawing conclusions about what you have observed and making recommendations for the actions you will take based on what you have observed.

Interpretation Forming a conclusion based on observational and assessment data with the intent of planning and improving teaching and learning.

FIGURE 3.5   Observation Checklist for Inclusive Classrooms

Teacher: _Graciela Gonzalez_   Date: _September 6, 2006_

School: _Mission Hill_   Class: _Kindergarten_

Number of children in class: _18_

Number of children with disabilities in class: _1_

Types of disabilities: _Dana has moderate cerebral palsy (CP) and must use a wheelchair._

Physical Features of the Classroom

1. Are all areas of the classroom accessible to children with disabilities?

   No, Dana cannot access the library/literacy center.

2. Are learning materials and equipment accessible for all children?

   There is not enough room for Dana to manipulate her wheelchair past the easel and the shelf with art materials.

3. Are work and play areas separated to minimize distractions?

   Yes, but pathways are too narrow for Dana's wheelchair.

4. Are special tables or chairs necessary to accommodate children's disabilities?

   Dana has a large work board/table that attaches to her wheelchair.

Academic Features of the Classroom

1. What special accommodations are necessary to help children with disabilities achieve state and local standards?

   I have to check on this.

2. Are principles of developmentally appropriate practice applied to all children, including those with disabilities?

   Yes

3. Is there a wide range of classroom literature on all kinds of disabilities?

   I have a few books — but not enough.

Classroom Interaction

1. Are children with disabilities included in cooperative work projects?

   I will work on this next week.

2. Do nondisabled children interact positively with children with disabilities?

   Dana is a very sociable child. Students interact well with her. Dana could not reach the crayons by herself, so she asked Emma for help. She and Emma seem to get along well.

Play Routines

1. Are children with disabilities able to participate in all classroom and grade-level play activities?

   I need to talk to the P.E. teacher. I also need to observe Dana during lunch and recess to see if she is involved in play and social activities during these times.

FIGURE 3.5 Continued

Conclusions

1. *I need to rearrange my classroom to make sure that Dana has access to all learning centers and materials.*

2. *The children are not as helpful to Dana as I want them to be.*

3. *The classroom library/literacy center needs books relating to children with disabilities.*

4. *There are a lot of questions I don't have the answers to at this time (e.g., meeting state standards).*

5. *I need to include more group work and cooperative activities in my planning.*

Recommendations

1. *I will ask a custodian to help me move a heavy bookshelf. I can move and rearrange the other things. I'll give the new arrangement a trial run and see how it works for all the children.*

2. *In our daily class meetings, I will talk about helpful behaviors and helping others.*

   a. *We can read books about helping.*

   b. *I plan to start a class buddy system; I can pair Dana and Emma.*

3. *In my lesson plans, I need to include activities for learning helpful behaviors.*

4. *I will search for books about children with disabilities.*

   a. *I'll consult with the school librarian.*

   b. *I'll talk to my grade-level leader and ask for money for books.*

5. *I will talk with the director of special education about meeting state standards. Dana is very smart, so I don't anticipate any problems.*

6. *I will develop a lesson involving group work and projects. I will include Dana and observe the children's interactions.*

7. *I will observe Dana at lunch and during recess.*

FIGURE 3.6 Methods of Collecting Observation Data

- *Record* information on self-stick notes, which are easily transferred to student files and folders.

- *Wear* a pocket apron (a carpenter's apron, available at hardware stores, works well) to carry self-stick notes, small tablets, markers, etc.

- *Use* a clipboard to hold a checklist and other forms to record data as you observe.

- *Take* photographs of children's accomplishments or infants' milestones. Take other photos of room arrangements (such as play areas, storage, and circle-time area), children's interactions, teacher-child interactions, and student artifacts. Digital camera images are easily manipulated and transferred to student files.

- *Use* technology whenever possible. For example, a laptop loaded with student files makes it easier to record, store, and manage data after an observation session. In addition, video cameras are a good way to capture certain events and activities.

FIGURE 3.7   Sample Observation Form

Observation Guide

Purpose of observation: _____

Child/class observed: _____   Age/grade:
_____   _____

Observer: _____

Date: _____   Time: _____

Setting: _____

Observation data: What specifically did you observe?

Reflections/conclusions: What is important about your observations? What
implications do your data have?

Recommendations/action plan: How will you use your conclusion to improve your
teaching and help the child/children learn?

Review again the observational checklist in Figure 3.5, and note the teacher's interpretation of data—that is, her conclusions and recommendations.

Step 4: Implement a Plan.   The **implementation** phase is the time that you act on the results or the findings of your observation. For example, although Dana's behavior is appropriate, the other children can benefit from activities designed to help them recognize and respond to the needs of others. In addition, the physical environment of the classroom requires some rearrangement of movable furniture to make the space more accessible for Dana. Implementing—doing something with the results of your observations—is the most important part of the process. Figure 3.8 reviews the four steps of effective observation.

The Program in Action How to Observe Children: "Observing Will" on pages 73–75 is a Competency Builder that will help you learn how to observe in a classroom setting and use your observations as a basis for making decisions about how to teach young children.

Implementation
Committing to a certain action based on interpretations of the observational data.

FIGURE 3.8 Four Steps for Effective Observation

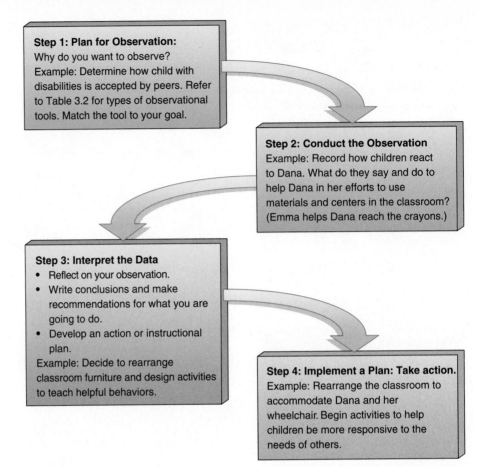

Step 1: Plan for Observation:
Why do you want to observe? Example: Determine how child with disabilities is accepted by peers. Refer to Table 3.2 for types of observational tools. Match the tool to your goal.

Step 2: Conduct the Observation
Example: Record how children react to Dana. What do they say and do to help Dana in her efforts to use materials and centers in the classroom? (Emma helps Dana reach the crayons.)

Step 3: Interpret the Data
• Reflect on your observation.
• Write conclusions and make recommendations for what you are going to do.
• Develop an action or instructional plan.
Example: Decide to rearrange classroom furniture and design activities to teach helpful behaviors.

Step 4: Implement a Plan: Take action.
Example: Rearrange the classroom to accommodate Dana and her wheelchair. Begin activities to help children be more responsive to the needs of others.

Companion Website
To complete a Program in Action activity related to observation skills, go to the Companion Website at **www.prenhall.com/ morrison**, select chapter 3, then choose the Program in Action module.

REPORTING TO AND COMMUNICATING WITH PARENTS

Part of your responsibility as a professional is to report to parents about the growth, development, and achievement of their children. Communicating with parents is one of the most important jobs of the early childhood professional. The following guidelines will help you meet the important responsibility of reporting assessment information to parents:

• *Be honest and realistic with parents.* Too often, we do not want to hurt parents' feelings, so we sugarcoat what we are reporting. However, parents need our honest assessments about their children and what they know, are able to do, and will be able to do.
• *Communicate to parents so they can understand.* What we communicate to parents must make sense to them; they have to understand what we are saying. Reporting to parents often has to be a combination of written (in their language) and oral communication.
• *Share student work samples and portfolios with parents.* Documentation of student progress is a concrete, tangible way to report and share information with family members. The Voice from the Field "Learning to Watch" on pages 76–77 tells how to use photographs both to document and to share children's achievements.
• *Provide parents with ideas and information that will help them help their children learn.* Remember that you and parents are partners in helping children be successful in school and life.

Integrate these ideas for reporting to parents with other related ideas you will find in chapter 17.

Program in Action

HOW TO OBSERVE CHILDREN: OBSERVING WILL

Welcome to Ms. Liz's classroom! You will be observing Will, the energetic four-year-old in overalls and a yellow shirt. He is a bright, only child who is in his first year of school and has a mind of his own. You will also observe Ms. Liz, the classroom environment, and the ways children interact with Will, Ms. Liz, and each other. And by observing, you will try to determine whether Ms. Liz and the classroom environment support active learning. *Active learning* is an important part of early childhood practice. It is a challenge and a goal for all early childhood teachers to promote caring and learning in a child-centered classroom that supports active learning.

Look at the photos of Will, and implement the four steps for effective observation (see Figure 3.8).

STEP 1 — Plan for observation

- Decide *who* you will observe, *how* you will observe (e.g., classroom visit, photos, or video), *what* you will observe, and *where* the observation will take place.
- Write your goal(s) for observation. Our goals for observing Will are to
  - determine if Ms. Liz's classroom supports active learning
  - assess whether Will is happy and learning
  - make recommendations about what features of an active learning environment should be included in a classroom
- Select your observational tool. For observing Will, an anecdotal record will achieve our goals and will provide the data necessary to make conclusions and recommendations. An anecdotal record is a short description of behavior over a period of time; it tells about the child's interaction with the physical and social environment (see Table 3.2 on page 65). It should be as factual as possible. You might use an index card or some other form like the example shown below.

STEP 2 — Conduct the observation

- Observe Will and try to answer the questions accompanying each photograph.

P-1

- Record your observations on index cards or forms you devise.

Ms. Liz is reading one of the children's favorite books. Will asked Ms. Liz if she would please read the book. Before she read it, Ms. Liz asked the children who their favorite characters were and why they wanted to hear the story again. Will said, "I like the way the boy helps the dog."

Anecdotal Record

Child's name: *Will*   Date: *September 8, 2006*

Context: *Ms. Liz's classroom*

Picture 2:   *Will took the book from Ms. Liz. He pushed her arm away as she held on to it. Ms. Liz let Will take the book.*

Picture 3:   *Will held the book in front of him like the teacher. He started to read the book to the class. Ms. Liz looked on and supported him. The other children were not paying attention to Will.*

Ms. Liz then read the story with a lot of expression and enthusiasm. All of the children were attentive. As Ms. Liz read, Will kept moving closer and closer to her.

In P-1 what is Ms. Liz doing to support the children's literacy development? What can you infer from the children's behavior regarding their literacy development?

P-2

Note in P-2 how Ms. Liz supports Will's autonomy and the things he can do for himself. She allows Will to take the picture book from her. Would you have allowed this? Record what she does and how he appears, based on her actions and his ability to show the book to his peers. What can Ms. Liz do to involve the other children in Will's retelling of the story?

P-3

Based on your observation of P-3, what does Will know now about reading? What do you no-tice about the behavior of Will's peers? What does their behavior indicate to you?

P-4

In P-4 you see Will and his friends building a tall tower. What can you tell about Will's willingness to engage in cooperative play with other children? What can you infer about the activity from Will's behavior and facial expression? Observe that the top of the red tower is falling on the child behind Will. Would you allow Will and his peers to build their tower as high as they are building it? Why or why not?

P-5

In P-5 observe how Will responds to the accident of the falling tower. What does Will's behavior tell you? What can you tell about Ms. Liz's behavior? What can you say about the behavior of Ryan, the child in the background behind Ms. Liz?

WHAT ARE CRITICAL ASSESSMENT ISSUES?

With almost everything we talk about in this book, issues surround essential questions about what is appropriate and inappropriate practice and what is best for children and families. Assessment is no different regarding critical issues.

ASSESSMENT AND ACCOUNTABILITY

There is a tremendous emphasis on assessment and the use of tests to measure achievement in order to compare children, programs, school districts, and countries. This emphasis will

P-6

How would you categorize Will's and Megan's play behavior in P-6? Based on your observation, what are some things that Will and Megan are learning? Are the materials appropriate for them to use?

P-7

Observe Will's determination and physical effort in P-7. What are some things you can learn through observation outdoors? What developmental skills is Will enhancing through his outdoor play?

P-8

In the parent-teacher conference depicted in P-8. Observe Will's facial expression and body language. What do they tell you? Does Will's mother seem supportive of him?

STEP 3 Interpret the data

- Review your goals for observing.
- Look at the observation data as a whole. Place your observation in the context of all that you know about young children and all that you know about Will.
- Reflect on your observation and look for patterns.
- Make decisions about what actions you want to pursue, based on your conclusions from the data. Your decision-making process can include consulting with other colleagues and professionals.*

STEP 4 Implement a plan

- Take action based on your interpretation of the data.
- Create a classroom arrangement that would support children's literacy development. Include several areas and use labels to identify materials for use in each area. Incorporate ideas from Ms. Liz's classroom, from your own professional ideas, and from information in this text.
- Share your classroom arrangement plan with teachers and colleagues. Ask them for helpful suggestions and comments.

Thanks to Director Vicki Yun, Ms. Liz, Will Sims, and the children of LaPetite Academy in Dublin, Ohio. Photos by Anthony Magnacca/Merrill.

*Janice Beaty, *Observing the Development of the Young Child*, 6th ed. (Upper Saddle River, NJ: Merrill/Prentice Hall, 2005).

likely continue for a number of reasons. First, the public, including politicians and legislatures, sees assessment as a means of making schools and teachers accountable for teaching all children so they achieve at or above grade level. Second, assessment is seen as playing a critical role in improving education: assessment results can be used to make decisions about how the curriculum and instructional practices can increase achievement. For example, the Good Start, Grow Smart early childhood initiative in the No Child Left Behind Act (see also chapter 8, "Federal Programs and Early Education") calls for an accountability system to ensure that every Head Start center assesses standards of learning in early language and numeracy skills. Therefore, as long as there is a public desire to improve teaching and achievement, we will continue to see an emphasis on the use of assessment for accountability purposes.

LEARNING TO WATCH: USING PHOTOGRAPHS FOR PORTFOLIO-BASED ASSESSMENT

We all watch the young children we teach, noticing their successes and their struggles, talking with them about what we see them doing and learning—but what else can we do with the observations we make?

In early childhood education, the teacher's observations of the young child can be the most important records of the child's growth and development. However, meaningful observation takes practice and an ever-deepening knowledge of individual children, of the principles of early childhood development, and of one's program goals and objectives.

LOOK THROUGH A LENS

We have found that photography is a wonderful strategy for recording children's accomplishments and celebrating the activities of an early childhood program. Frequent photography can also help you improve your own observation skills while you gather material for portfolio-based assessment. Taking pictures throughout the day or the week provides you with a wealth of raw material for individual children's portfolios and for reflection on your own practice.

Jason drew circular shapes on the board after observing peers write letters. His grasp is pronated with a flexed wrist. Note: Continue to watch. Ask specialist to observe and help me with techniques to assist him in using more mature grip.

Traditional 35-millimeter cameras and digital cameras can be very good tools for child observation. Keep a camera handy and snap a few shots at various times of the day. If your camera is digital, take a few minutes at the end of each day to download your photographs to your computer, filing them by date, and then delete them from the camera. You'll be ready to take more pictures in the morning. If you use a 35-mm camera, make dropping off a roll or two of film and picking up double prints from the last batch a routine part of your work week. (If you compare the expenses of 35-mm and digital photos, you may decide that you or your program should invest in a digital camera.)

TAKE A LOOK BACK IN TIME

Once a week, review the photographs you have taken and think about each shot. Does it clearly depict something significant about an individual child, about your program, or about your own development as a teacher? Discard ones that do not provide useful information. Save others, naming each with the date and a child's last name. Write a brief sentence or two about what skill or behavior this photograph illustrates.

Think about how you managed to take the good photographs:

- Did you have a good view of the scene?
- Did you disrupt the children's activity, or did you manage to stay out of their way?
- Is the photo in focus and well lit?

Rubrics Scoring guides that differentiate among levels of performance.

The final Voice from the Field in this chapter, "Kindergarten Assessment—Current Practices," addresses this issue on pages 79–80. The contributing author also emphasizes the value of rubrics in making assessment appropriate and meaningful. **Rubrics** are scoring guides that differentiate among levels of performance. Conventional rubrics use a range of three or more levels—for example, beginning, developing, and proficient. Each of the levels contains specific, measurable performance characteristics, such as "makes few/occasional/frequent spelling errors." Checklists, which provide specific steps for completing tasks to the highest level, are another form of rubric (see Table 3.2).[1]

- Are key elements visible?
  - Facial expressions?
  - Materials or toys that were in use?
  - The learning center or setting?

Next, think about how you can use these photos in your work:

- Print and pass on to parents
- Print and post for children to see and discuss
- Save on disks for individual children
- Print and add to individual children's portfolios
- Include in your program's newsletter or website (being sure to have a signed parental release form for any child whose picture you publish)
- Add to your own professional portfolio

WATCH FOR GROWTH

Accurately linking photographs to assessment and evaluation is a challenge, but one that is worth the effort. To get started, review the expected developmental milestones for the children in your center or class. For many milestones the best form of documentation will be your written notes. For others, the children's work samples are ideal. Which can be documented with photographs? Think about how you might photograph children experiencing each of these milestones:

- Gross-motor breakthroughs, such as pulling up, standing, and walking
- Parallel play
- Letter recognition

This kind of reflection and prior planning will help you make your portfolio photographs more intentional or systematic. Then as you review each week's photographs, you will have a framework for thinking about them and about the children. Perhaps you will notice things that you did not see at first glance: the child who always plays alone, the child who often has trouble sharing, the child who frequently engages others in conversation.

Byron gave one napkin to each peer, demonstrating use of one-to-one correspondence. Note: Next week have him put out napkins prior to peers coming to table to see if he can do this with only spoons at each place.

INVOLVE PARENTS

After you have mastered using a camera frequently and unobtrusively in your early childhood program and have used photographs to document individual children's development and accomplishments, it will be time to think about how photographs can support parent involvement and children's transitions to new programs.

Sending photos home with brief notes attached is an excellent way to report to parents between formal conferences. Including a few particularly significant photographs in a "pass-along portfolio" for a child's next teacher can also be very effective, especially if the new teacher gives the child and the parent time to explain the photographs themselves.

ADD OTHER PORTFOLIO ITEMS

Photographs are just one part of a comprehensive early childhood portfolio. To document individual children's learning and pass on the information to parents and future teachers, you can also use work samples, learning logs, interviews, systematic records, anecdotal records, and narrative reports. Each type of portfolio item has unique value, and each requires practice. We always encourage teachers to implement portfolio techniques one at a time, starting with items that seem the easiest.

When they arrived, Dashon brought a book to his mom and asked her to read to him. This demonstrates enjoyment of reading. Note: This is good progress. A few months ago he would not sit still for a book to be read.

Contributed by Cathy Grace, EdD, professor and director, Early Childhood Institute, Mississippi State University, and Teri Patrick, MEd, education director, Arkansas CARES, University of Arkansas for Medical Sciences, Little Rock, Arkansas. Photos by Cathy Grace and Teri Patrick.

Rubrics have a number of purposes:

- To enable teachers to assess performance based on preestablished criteria
- To make teachers' expectations clear
- To enable children to participate in the evaluation of their own work

To use rubrics effectively in your classroom, you should provide children with models or examples of each level of work and encourage them to revise their work according to the rubric assessment. You should also give children opportunities to contribute to the rubric criteria.

HIGH-STAKES TESTING

We have previously talked about high-stakes testing. This kind of testing occurs when standardized tests are used to make important and often life-influencing decisions about children. Standardized tests have specific and standardized content, administration and scoring procedures, and norms for interpreting scores. High-stakes outcomes include decisions about whether to admit children into programs (e.g., kindergarten), whether children will have to attend summer school, and whether children will be retained or promoted. Generally, the early childhood profession is opposed to high-stakes testing for children through grade three. However, as part of the accountability movement, many politicians and school administrators view high-stakes testing as a means of making sure that children learn and that promotions from one grade to another are based on achievement. Many school critics maintain that in the preK and primary grades there is too much social promotion—that is, passing children from grade to grade merely to enable students to keep pace with their age peers.

As an early childhood professional, part of your responsibility is to be an advocate for the appropriate use of assessment. You will make ongoing, daily decisions about how best to assess your children and how best to use the results of assessment.

Performance-Based Pay. Some states are tying teacher salaries to student achievement, a process called "pay for performance." Denver, Colorado, city schools were the first in the nation to tie student performance to teacher pay.[2] Many school districts allow their teachers to receive extra compensation or bonuses if their schools meet certain student achievement goals. These programs are increasing in other school districts and states across the country. Such plans are based on measuring student achievement with standardized tests, and this means more testing for students of all ages. Performance-based pay programs are not popular with all teachers, but they do seem to be part of many districts' pay plans.

Report assessment findings accurately and honestly to parents. How can such communication build trust? What are other advantages of honest, open communication?

TEST BIAS

Many school district testing programs, as they are currently structured, do not allow all children to demonstrate what they are able to do. There are many gender and ethnic biases in test performance. What is needed are testing programs that include different ways of testing children so that all students are able to demonstrate what they know and are able to do.

HOW YOUNG IS TOO YOUNG?

As mentioned previously, the federal government is currently testing all Head Start children to determine whether they have achieved the knowledge and skills specified in the Head Start Performance Standards (see chapter 8). Testing children at such young ages is a major issue of this testing initiative. Some early childhood professionals believe that four- and five-year-old children are too young to be subjected to such testing.

There are many issues involved in testing young children. For example, *Eager to Learn—Report* cautions early childhood professionals about testing young children and the misuse of test results from young children.

All assessments, and particularly assessments for accountability, must be used carefully and appropriately if they are to resolve, and not create, educational problems. Assessment of

KINDERGARTEN ASSESSMENT—CURRENT PRACTICES

For some time now, federal mandates, state laws, and individual school districts have required assessments for all students. The testing phenomenon now requires assessments for kindergartners, not as a screening tool before entrance to kindergarten, as has been done in many school districts, but as a way for teachers to be accountable to districts and to parents and to align these assessments with the new learning standards. Many school systems have adopted assessments to meet the new standards for kindergarten. For many professionals, assessments are the driving force behind instruction.

Assessment uses are numerous:

- Plan for individual and group instruction
- Identify at-risk students and students with special needs
- Define what each child knows specifically (e.g., how many upper- and lowercase letters can he or she recognize?)
- Discern phonemic awareness skills such as knowledge of rhyming words
- Plan for appropriate group placement in small instructional groupings during literacy and math instruction
- Assist in implementing kindergarten programs and individual lesson plans
- Inform parents of their children's progress

Based on my thirty-plus years of experience, I am convinced that there needs to be a healthy balance between formal assessment through tests and informal assessment through teacher observation and parent feedback. Together, formal and informal assessments comprise a balanced evaluative approach.

PARENT COMMUNICATION

Communication with parents via conferences and report cards is a critical part of the teaching process. Report cards, which align with curriculum standards and assessments, clearly present valuable data to parents. An easy checklist for skill development—such as P (progressing satisfactorily), I (in progress), and N (not yet observed or introduced)—is helpful. A written narrative describing a student's social and emotional growth and development, work habits, and mastery of literacy and math objectives is necessary to tie the checklist to an overview of the whole child to get an accurate picture of the student. The narrative portion of the report card is beneficial because it provides parents an opportunity to know how their child performs in the classroom. I always encourage parents to contact me with questions as follow-up. In some cases I follow up with a parent meeting, or a parent meeting with other colleagues, if I have concerns, such as speech articulation, emotional issues, or personal family problems.

Conferencing with parents is especially important in kindergarten. Developmental and social issues that clarify a student's performance more effectively than a mere checklist or letter grade can be addressed in conversation. Many of these issues may have a very strong impact on a child's ability to learn. Indeed, assessments and conferencing are vital components of sound teaching practice today.

RUBRICS

Standards and assessments are integral parts of the instructional framework and kindergarten curriculum of most school systems. Assessments are used to guide instruction. When used in isolation, such as isolated skills testing, their value is limited. However, when used as part of a classroom lesson, they can be very effective.

For example, looking at a writing sample with a writing rubric for kindergarten is a very explicit and valid form of assessment that is helpful to students. They can gain a beginning understanding of what is expected in a clear and concise manner. A kindergarten writing rubric could look like this:

> *I wrote my name the kindergarten way, using capital and lowercase letters.
> **I made a picture, which matches my words (the text).
> ***I used a capital letter at the beginning of each sentence and a period at the end of each sentence.
> ****I used my best handwriting with spaces between words.

I have used this writing rubric as a kindergartner's self-evaluative measure.

Kindergarten rubrics allow children to know what is generally expected of them and help them complete a specific piece of work. By adapting the rubric for writing, the child's progress is acknowledged. As the circumstances change, the rubrics may become more specific and more challenging and may include higher expectations.

Assessment measures individual differences in students' achievement and needs. Students who are at risk, English language learners, special needs students, gifted students, and average students all must be educated, and assessment is another tool to measure a student's ability and skill. It is clearly a vital component of the kindergarten instructional program today.

As we continue to acquire more research, the assessment process will undergo modifications. Productive assessment strategies will benefit everyone—students, teachers, administrators, and parents—as we all share in this collaborative effort to educate our youngest learners.

Contributed by Sandy Reiss, early childhood educator, Olney, Maryland.

young children poses greater challenges than people generally realize. The first five years of life are a time of incredible growth and learning, but the course of development is uneven and sporadic. The status of a child's development as of any given day can change very rapidly. Consequently, assessment results—in particular, standardized test scores that reflect a given point in time—can easily misrepresent children's learning.[3]

CONCLUSION

Today there is a great deal of emphasis on accountability. Teachers are asked to be accountable to parents, legislators, and the public. Providing for and conducting developmentally appropriate assessment of young children and their programs is one of the best ways you can be accountable for what you do. Conducting appropriate assessment not only make you accountable to parents and the public, but it also enables you to be accountable to young children. You have accepted a sacred trust and have dedicated your life to helping children learn and develop. Effective assessment practices will help you achieve this goal.

Companion Website
For additional Internet resources or to complete an online activity for this chapter, go to the Companion Website at **www.prenhall.com/morrison,** select chapter 3, then choose the Linking to Learning or Making Connections module.

LINKING TO LEARNING

ARCNet
http://arc.missouri.edu/index.html
Created for anyone interested in the world of assessment.

Pathways of School Improvement on the Web
http://www.ncrel.org/sdrs/areas/issues/students/earlycld/ea500.htm
Contains information on current issues, including assessment of the progress and attainments of young children three to eight years of age, and the uses and abuses of assessment.

The Issues: Assessing Young Children
http://www.pbs.org/teachersource/prek2/issues/1201issue.shtm
To read what Dr. Kathy Grace (see Voice from the Field p. 76) has to say about what are issues in assessing young children.

Assessing Young Children's Progress Appropriately
http://www.ncrel.org/sdrs/areas/issues/students/earlycld/ea500.htm

> *Another good source for looking at critical issues relating to the appropriate assessment of children's progress.*

Linking Assessment and Teaching in the Critical Early Years
http://www.nea.org/teachexperience/ask030508.html

> *An excellent source for additional information for assessment through documentation and about linking assessment and teaching.*

A Guide to the Developmentally Appropriate Assessment of Young Children
http://www.beyond-the-book.com/strategies/strategies_090705.html

> *This guide to the developmentally appropriate assessment of young children provides useful information about the appropriate uses of assessment and assessment results.*

ACTIVITIES FOR FURTHER ENRICHMENT

ETHICAL DILEMMA: "TEST OR LEAVE?"

You teach in a preschool program funded with federal dollars. Your administrator has sent out a memo announcing a new testing program. The purpose of this new program is to determine the effectiveness of preschool programs using federal funding. All four-year-olds will be tested on their knowledge, skills, and readiness for kindergarten with a federally developed achievement test. You believe it is developmentally inappropriate to test preschool children using the prescribed federal test.

What should you do? Should you share your concerns with the school administrator and risk her disapproval (or worse), or should you administer a test you believe is inappropriate?

APPLICATIONS

1. Create a developmental checklist similar to that shown in Figure 3.4. Observe an early childhood classroom, and determine how effective you are at spotting dimensions of children's development and learning.
2. Observe a particular child during play or another activity. (Before your observation make sure you follow the steps recommended in this chapter.) Use the information you gather to plan a learning activity for the child. As you plan, determine what information you need that

you didn't gather through observation. When you observe again, what will you do differently?
3. Observe a program that is providing services for children with disabilities. Your purpose is to determine what accommodations need to be made for them.
4. Visit and observe the classrooms of at least two early childhood professionals. A sample observation form you can use is shown in Figure 3.7. You can also check other resources to develop more specific observation guides to track developmental behaviors with individual children. Interview the professionals about the observational practices they use that might be helpful in your own classroom. With their permission, keep copies of checklists and other observation tools, and put them in your professional portfolio and/or idea file.

FIELD EXPERIENCES

1. Interview several kindergarten and primary teachers, and ask them for ideas and guidelines for assessing with portfolios. Which ideas can you use?
2. Review the contents of several children's portfolios. How are they similar and different? What do the contents tell you about the children? About the teachers?
3. Volunteer to serve as an administrator or aide for the DIAL-3 or some other screening device.
4. Interview several early childhood educators to learn about the strategies they use to communicate effectively with parents when reporting assessment results. Make a list of five key guidelines to use when sharing test and assessment data with parents.

RESEARCH

1. Frequently, articles in newspapers and magazines highlight assessment and testing issues. Over a two-week period, read national newspapers online, and determine what assessment and evaluation issues are in the news. Put these materials in your portfolio or teaching file.

2. Visit preK–3 programs in several different school districts. Make a list of the various ways they assess and the instruments and procedures they use. Compare them with the ones identified in this chapter. How and for what purposes are the tests used? What conclusions can you draw from the information you gathered?

3. Research and identify the types of assessments mandated by No Child Left Behind. Interview early childhood teachers, and ask them their opinions about these testing requirements.

4. Investigate what resources are available to parents to help them understand the assessment processes in preschool and/or grades K–1. Make a list of these resources and put them in your professional portfolio or idea file. How do you intend to use these resources?

READINGS FOR FURTHER ENRICHMENT

Anderson, L. W. *Classroom Assessment: Enhancing the Quality of Teacher Decision Making.* Mahwah, NJ: Lawrence Erlbaum, 2002.

Discusses assessing achievement using selection and short-answer tasks, extended response and performance tasks, and classroom behavior and student effort and interpreting assessment results.

Bodrova, E., D. Leong, and O. McAfee. *Basics of Assessment: Primer for Early Childhood Educators.* Washington, DC: NAEYC, 2004.

Provides an overview of basic assessment concepts; creates an understanding of child assessment, including its specialized and often-confusing vocabulary, while focusing on children's development and learning.

Carr, M. *Assessment in Early Childhood Settings: Learning Stories.* Thousand Oaks, CA: Sage, 2001.

Assesses and tracks children's learning in the early years in a way that includes learning dispositions; provides assessment close to children's real experiences, an alternative to mechanistic and fragmented approaches.

Lidz, C. *Early Childhood Assessment.* New York: Wiley and Sons, 2002.

Presents a thorough, step-by-step approach to the comprehensive psychological assessment of young children. Includes specific guidelines and formats for interviewing parents and other caregivers, observing children and caregiver-child interaction, conducting dynamic assessments, writing reports, and evaluating outcomes of recommended interventions.

Wortham, S. *Assessment in Early Childhood Education,* 4th ed. Upper Saddle River, NJ: Merrill/Prentice Hall, 2005.

Explains the assessment challenges posed by the developmental limitations of young children. Offers the most comprehensive coverage available of the types of assessment that are effective with children from birth to age eight and the ways to use them to best advantage.

ENDNOTES

1. Mary Rose, "Make Room for Rubrics," http://teacher.scholastic.com/professional/assessment/roomforubrics.htm.

2. Ann Bradley, "Denver Teachers to Pilot Pay-for-Performance Plan," *Education Week* (September 22, 1999): 5.

3. National Research Council, *Eager to Learn—Report* (Washington, DC: Commission on Behavioral and Social Sciences and Education, 2000).

Foundations: History and Theories

CHAPTER 4

The Past and the Present

PROLOGUE TO THE FUTURE

*The philosophy of the school room in one generation
will be the philosophy of government in the next.*

ABRAHAM LINCOLN

WHY IS THE PAST IMPORTANT?

When we read of the hopes, ideas, and accomplishments of people whom our profession judges famous, we realize that many of today's ideas are built on those of the past. There are at least five reasons to know about the ideas and theories of great educators who have influenced and continue to influence the field of early childhood education.

REBIRTH OF IDEAS

Old ideas and theories are often reborn. Good ideas and practices persist over time and are recycled through educational thought and practices in ten- to twenty-year periods. For example, many practices popular in the 1970s and 1980s such as using phonics to teach reading, family grouping and multifamily grouping, child-centered education, and active learning—are now popular again.

However, old ideas and practices seldom get recycled in exactly their previous form; they are changed and modified as necessary for contemporary society and current beliefs. When you know about former ideas and practices you can more easily recognize them when they are recycled. This knowledge enables you to be an active participant in the recycling process of applying good practices of previous years to contemporary practice. And you can more fully appreciate this recycling if you understand the roots of the early education profession. Take a moment to look at the time line in appendix C. It will help you understand how ideas about early childhood education have been reborn through the years.

BUILDING THE DREAM—AGAIN

Many of today's early childhood practices have their roots in the past. In this sense, building the dream seems like a never-ending process. For example, the idea of universal preschool in the United States has been around since 1830, when the Infant School Society of Boston submitted a petition to incorporate infant schools into the Boston Public Schools.[1] As we discuss in chapter 10, we are *still* trying to implement universal preschool education. Thus, we have inherited the ideas and dreams of a long line of early childhood educators, which we use as a base to build meaningful teaching careers and programs for children and their families. You are both a builder of dreams and an implementer of dreams as you join the ranks of all early childhood professionals.

IMPLEMENTING CURRENT PRACTICE

Understanding the ideas of early educators will help you know how to implement current teaching strategies, whatever they may be. For instance, Rousseau, Froebel, and Montessori all believed children should be taught with dignity and respect. This attitude toward children is essential to an understanding of good educational

Focus Questions

Why is it important for you to have an appreciation for the ideas, professional accomplishments, and contributions of great educators?

What are the basic beliefs of people who have influenced early childhood education: Luther, Comenius, Locke, Rousseau, Pestalozzi, Owen, Froebel, Dewey, Maslow, Erikson, and Gardner?

How have the beliefs and ideas of great educators such as Piaget and Vygotsky influenced early childhood programs?

How is contemporary education influenced by historical people and events?

Companion Website

To check your understanding of this chapter, go to the Companion Website at **www.prenhall.com/ morrison**, select chapter 4, answer Multiple Choice and Essay Questions, and receive feedback.

practice and contributes to good teaching and quality programs. Any program you are involved in should include respect—among many other attributes—as one of its core values.

EMPOWERING PROFESSIONALS

Theories about how young children grow, develop, and learn decisively shape educational and child-rearing practices. Studying the beliefs of the great educators helps parents, you, and other early childhood educators clarify what to do and gives insight into behavior and practice. In this sense, knowing about theories liberates the uninformed from ignorance and empowers professionals and parents. Those who understand historical ideas and theories are able to confidently implement developmentally appropriate practices.

INSPIRING PROFESSIONALS

Exploring, analyzing, and discovering the roots of early childhood education helps inspire professionals. Recurring rediscovery forces people to contrast current practices with what others have advocated. Examining sources of beliefs helps clarify modern practice, and reading and studying others' ideas make us rethink our own beliefs and positions. Thus, knowledge of the great educators and their beliefs helps keep us current. When you pause long enough to listen to what they have to say, you frequently find a new insight or idea that will motivate you to continue your quest to be the best you can be.

HISTORICAL FIGURES AND THEIR INFLUENCE ON EARLY CHILDHOOD EDUCATION

MARTIN LUTHER

Companion Website For links to many of Martin Luther's writings, go to the Companion Website at **www.prenhall.com/morrison**, select chapter 4, then choose the Linking to Learning module.

The primary impact of the Protestant Reformation was religious. However, other far-reaching effects were secular. Two of these effects involved *universal education* and *literacy*, both of which are very much in the forefront of educational practice today.

The question of what to teach is an issue in any educational endeavor. Does society create schools and then decide what to teach, or do the needs of society determine what schools it will establish to meet desired goals? This is a question early childhood professionals wrestle with today. In the case of sixteenth-century European education, Martin Luther (1483–1546) emphasized the necessity of establishing schools to teach children to read. Luther replaced the authority of the hierarchy of the Catholic Church with the authority of the Bible. He believed that individuals were free to work out their own salvation through the scriptures. This meant that people had to learn to read the Bible in their native languages.

This concept marked the real beginning of teaching and learning in people's native languages, or vernacular, as opposed to Latin, the official language of the Catholic Church. After Luther translated the Bible into German, other translations followed, finally making the Bible available to people in their own languages. In this way, the Protestant Reformation encouraged and supported popular universal education and learning to read.

Luther believed the family was the most important institution in the education of children. To this end, he encouraged parents to provide religious instruction and vocational education in the home. Throughout his life Luther remained a champion of education, writing letters and preaching sermons on the subject.

Out of the Reformation evolved other religious denominations, all interested in preserving their faith through education and schooling. Today, many churches, synagogues,

TABLE 4.1   Students Enrolled in Religious Schools

Religion	Number of Students
Roman Catholic	4,440,398
Jewish	198,478
Lutheran Church–Missouri Synod	162,301
Episcopal	100,403
Seventh-Day Adventist	60,681
Islamic	22,951

Source: Private School Universe Survey, National Center for Educational Statistics, U.S. Department of Education (2002).

and mosques operate child care and preK–12 programs. A growing number of parents who want early childhood programs that support their religious values, beliefs, and culture enroll their children in programs operated by religious organizations. For example, over 5.3 million K–12 students are currently enrolled in religious schools.[2] Table 4.1 shows the student enrollment of various religions. What functions do religious shoools serve today?

JOHN AMOS COMENIUS

John Amos Comenius (1592–1670) was born in Moravia, then a province of the Czech Republic, and became a Moravian minister. He spent his life serving as a bishop, teaching school, and writing textbooks. Of his many writings, those that have received the most attention are *The Great Didactic* and *Orbis Pictus* (*The World in Pictures*), considered the first picture book for children.

Orbis Pictus   The first picture book for children; written by John Amos Comenius.

Comenius believed that humans are born in the image of God. Therefore, each individual has an obligation and duty to be educated to the fullest extent of his or her abilities so as to fulfill this godlike image. Since so much depends on education, as far as Comenius was concerned, it should begin in the early years.

> It is the nature of everything that comes into being, that while tender it is easily bent and formed, but that, when it has grown hard, it is not easy to alter. Wax, when soft, can be easily fashioned and shaped; when hard, it cracks readily. A young plant can be planted, transplanted, pruned, and bent this way or that. When it has become a tree, these processes are impossible.[3]

Comenius also believed that education should follow the order of nature, which implies a timetable for growth and learning. Early childhood professionals must observe this pattern to avoid forcing learning before children are ready.

Sensory Education.   Comenius also thought that learning is best achieved when the senses are involved and that **sensory education** forms the basis for all learning. Comenius said that the golden rule of teaching should be to place everything before the senses—for example, that children should not be taught the names of objects apart from the objects themselves or pictures of the objects. *Orbis Pictus* helped children learn the names of things and concepts as they appeared during Comenius's time, through pictures and words. Comenius's emphasis on the concrete and the sensory is a pedagogical principle early childhood professionals still try to fully grasp and implement. Many contemporary programs stress sensory learning, and several early childhood materials promote learning through the senses.

Sensory education Learning experiences involving the five senses: seeing, touching, hearing, tasting, and smelling.

Principles of Teaching. A broad view of Comenius's total concept of education becomes evident in examining some of his principles of teaching:

Following in the footsteps of nature we find that the process of education will be easy

    i. If it begins early, before the mind is corrupted.

    ii. If the mind be duly prepared to receive it.

    iii. If it proceeds from the general to the particular.

    iv. And from what is easy to what is more difficult.

    v. If the pupil be not overburdened by too many subjects.

    vi. And if progress be slow in every case.

    vii. If the intellect be forced to nothing to which its natural bent does not incline it, in accordance with its age and with the right method.

    viii. If everything be taught through the medium of the senses.

    ix. And if the use of everything taught be continually kept in view.

    x. If everything be taught according to one and the same method.

These, I say, are the principles to be adopted if education is to be easy and pleasant.[4]

Comenius's two most significant contributions to today's education are books with illustrations and the emphasis on sensory training found in many early childhood programs. We take the former for granted and accept the latter as a necessary basis for learning.

JOHN LOCKE

The English philosopher John Locke (1632–1704) popularized the *tabula rasa,* or **blank tablet,** view of children. More precisely, Locke developed the theory of and laid the foundation for **environmentalism**—the belief that the environment, not innate characteristics, determines what children will become. The extent of Locke's influence on modern early childhood education and practice is unappreciated by many who daily implement practices based on his theories.

Locke's assumption in regard to human learning and nature was that there are no innate ideas. This belief gave rise to his theory of the mind as a blank tablet, or "white paper." As Locke explains,

Let us suppose the mind to be, as we say, white paper void of all characters, without ideas. How comes it to be furnished? Whence comes it by that vast store which the busy and boundless fancy of man has painted on it with an almost endless variety? Whence has it all the materials of reason and knowledge? To this I answer, in one word, from experience; in that all our knowledge is founded, and from that it ultimately derives itself.[5]

Environmentalism. Locke's belief that the environment forms the mind has implications that are clearly reflected in modern educational practice. The primacy of environmental influences is particularly evident in programs that encourage and promote early education as a means of overcoming or compensating for a poor or disadvantaged environment. Based partly on the idea that all children are born with the same general capacity for mental development and learning, these programs assume that differences in learning, achievement, and behavior are attributable to environmental factors, such as home and family conditions, socioeconomic context, early education, and experiences. Programs of early schooling, especially the current move for public schooling for three- and four-year-olds, work on the premise that some children don't have the readiness experiences necessary for kindergarten and first grade and are at risk for failure in school and life. Today, it is very common to provide public funding for early schooling for those who are considered disadvantaged and to design such programs especially for them.

Because Locke believed that experiences determine the nature of the individual, sensory training became a prominent feature in the application of his theory to education.

**Companion
Website**
For more
information about Comenius's
contributions to educational
thought, go to the
Companion Website at
www.prenhall.com/morrison,
select chapter 4, then choose
the Linking to Learning
module.

Blank tablet The belief that at birth the mind is blank and that experience creates the mind.

Environmentalism The theory that the environment, rather than heredity, exerts the primary influence on intellectual growth and cultural development.

**Companion
Website**
For more
information about John Locke
or Jean-Jacques Rousseau, go
to the Companion Website at
www.prenhall.com/morrison,
select chapter 4, then choose
the Linking to Learning
module.

Locke exerted considerable influence on others, particularly Maria Montessori, who developed her system of early education based on sensory training.

JEAN-JACQUES ROUSSEAU

Jean-Jacques Rousseau (1712–1778) is best remembered by educators for his book *Émile*, in which he raises a hypothetical child from birth to adolescence. Rousseau's theories were radical for his time. The opening lines of *Émile* set the tone not only for Rousseau's educational views but for many of his political ideas as well: "God makes all things good; man meddles with them and they become evil."[6]

Naturalism. Rousseau advocated a return to nature and an approach to educating children called **naturalism.** To Rousseau naturalism meant abandoning society's artificiality and pretentiousness. A naturalistic education permits growth without undue interference or restrictions. Rousseau would probably argue against such modern practices as dress codes, compulsory attendance, frequent and standardized testing, and ability grouping, on the grounds that they are "unnatural."

There is some tendency in American education to emphasize ideas associated with naturalism. For example, family grouping seeks to create a more natural, familylike atmosphere in schools and classrooms; literacy programs emphasize literature from the natural environment (e.g., using menus to show children how reading is important in their everyday lives); and conflict resolution programs teach children how to get along with others. Waldorf schools, which we discuss in chapter 6, are also based on naturalism. Waldorf education recognizes the inherent worth of each child, emphasizes individual freedom, and provides for the developing needs of all children at different ages.

According to Rousseau, natural education promotes and encourages qualities such as happiness, spontaneity, and the inquisitiveness associated with childhood. With his method, parents and teachers allow children to develop according to their natural abilities, do not interfere with development by forcing education, and tend not to overprotect children from the corrupting influences of society. Rousseau felt that Émile's education occurred through three sources: nature, people, and things. He elaborates:

> All that we lack at birth and need when grown up is given us by education. This education comes to us from nature, from men, or from things. The internal development of our faculties and organs is the education of nature. . . . It is not enough merely to keep children alive. They should learn to bear the blows of fortune; to meet either wealth or poverty, to live if need be in the frosts of Iceland or on the sweltering rock of Malta.[7]

Unfolding. Rousseau believed that although parents and others have control over education that comes from social and sensory experiences, they have no control over natural growth. In essence, this is the idea of *unfolding,* in which the nature of children—what they are to be—unfolds as a result of maturation according to their innate timetables. We should observe the child's growth and provide experiences at appropriate times. Some educators interpret this as a laissez-faire, or "let alone," approach to parenting and education.

Educational historians point to Rousseau as dividing the historic and modern periods of education. Rousseau established a way of thinking about the young child that is

Émile Jean-Jacques Rousseau's famous book that outlines his ideas about how children should be reared.

Naturalism Education that follows the natural development of children and does not force the educational process on them.

Rousseau maintained that a natural education encourages spontaneity and inquisitiveness. What should parents and teachers do to provide experiences in which children can develop their natural abilities?

reflected in innovators of educational practice such as Pestalozzi and Froebel. Rousseau's concept of natural unfolding echoes Comenius's concept of naturalness and appears in current programs that stress children's readiness as a factor in learning. Piaget's developmental stages also reinforce Rousseau's thinking about the importance of natural development.

JOHANN HEINRICH PESTALOZZI

Johann Heinrich Pestalozzi (1746–1827) was so impressed by Rousseau's back-to-nature concepts that he purchased a farm and, in 1774, started a school called Neuhof. There Pestalozzi developed his ideas about the integration of home life, vocational education, and education for reading and writing.

Rousseau's influence is most apparent in Pestalozzi's belief that education should follow the child's nature. His dedication to this concept is demonstrated by his rearing of his only son, Jean-Jacques, using *Émile* as a guide. Pestalozzi's methods were based on harmonizing nature and educational practices:

> And what is this method? It is a method which simply follows the path of Nature, or, in other words, which leads the child slowly, and by his own efforts, from sense-impressions to abstract ideas. Another advantage of this method is that it does not unduly exalt the master, inasmuch as he never appears as a superior being, but, like kindly Nature, lives and works with the children, his equals, seeming rather to learn with them than to teach them with authority.[8]

Object Lessons.   Pestalozzi believed that all education is based on sensory impressions and that through the proper sensory experiences, children can achieve their natural potential. This belief led to object lessons. As the name implies, Pestalozzi thought the best way to learn many concepts was through manipulatives—counting, measuring, feeling, touching. Pestalozzi believed the best teachers were those who taught children, not subjects. He also believed in multiage grouping.

Pestalozzi anticipated by about 175 years the many family-centered programs of today that help parents teach their young children in the home. He believed mothers could best teach their children, and he wrote two books—*How Gertrude Teaches Her Children* and *Book for Mothers*—detailing procedures to do this. He felt that "the time is drawing near when methods of teaching will be so simplified that each mother will be able not only to teach her children without help, but continue her own education at the same time."[9]

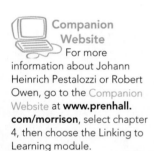

**Companion
Website**
For more information about Johann Heinrich Pestalozzi or Robert Owen, go to the Companion Website at **www.prenhall. com/morrison**, select chapter 4, then choose the Linking to Learning module.

ROBERT OWEN

Quite often, people who affect the course of educational thought and practice are also visionaries in political and social affairs. Robert Owen (1771–1858) was no exception. Owen's influences on education resulted from his entrepreneurial activities associated with New Lanark, Scotland, a model mill town he managed. Owen was an environmentalist; that is, he believed that the environment in which children are reared is the main factor contributing to their beliefs, behavior, and achievement. Consequently, he maintained that society and persons acting in the best interests of society can shape children's individual characters.

He also was a *Utopian,* believing that by controlling the circumstances and consequent outcomes of child rearing, it was possible to build a new and perhaps more perfect society. Such a deterministic view of child rearing and education pushes free will to the background and makes environmental conditions the dominant force in directing and determining human behavior. As Owen explained it,

> Any character, from the best to the worst, from the most ignorant to the most enlightened, may be given to any community, even to the world at large, by the application of proper means; which means are to a great extent at the command and under the control of those who have influence in the affairs of men.[10]

Thus, Owen believed that good traits were instilled at an early age and that children's behavior was influenced primarily by the environment.

Infant Schools. To implement his beliefs, Owen opened an infant school in 1816 at New Lanark, designed to provide care for about a hundred children aged eighteen months to ten years while their parents worked in his cotton mills. This led to the opening of the first infant school in London in 1818. Because part of Owen's motivation for opening the infant schools was to get the children away from their uneducated parents, he also opened a night school for his workers to provide them an education and transform them into "rational beings."

Although we tend to think that early education for children from low-income families began with Head Start in 1965, Owen's infant school came more than a hundred years before. Owen's legacy lived on in the infant schools of England, which eventually developed into kindergartens.

FRIEDRICH WILHELM FROEBEL

Friedrich Wilhelm Froebel (1782–1852) devoted his life to developing a system for educating young children. While Pestalozzi, a contemporary with whom he studied and worked, advocated a system for teaching, Froebel developed a curriculum and educational methodology. In the process, Froebel earned the distinction of being called Father of the Kindergarten. As a result of his close relationship with Pestalozzi and his reading of Rousseau, Froebel decided to open a school and put his ideas into practice.

Froebel's primary contributions to educational thought and practice are in the areas of learning, curriculum, methodology, and teacher training. His concept of children and how they learn is based in part on the idea of unfolding, held by Comenius and Pestalozzi before him. The educator's role, whether parent or teacher, is to observe this natural unfolding and provide activities that will enable children to learn what they are ready to learn when they are ready to learn it. The teacher's role is to help children develop their inherent qualities for learning. In this sense, the teacher is a designer of experiences and activities.

Robert Owen believed that infant schools were an ideal way to provide for the needs of young children while their families worked. What are some issues facing early childhood professionals today as they try to provide quality infant care for working parents?

Kindergarten. Consistent with his idea of unfolding, Froebel compared the child to a seed that is planted, germinates, brings forth a new shoot, and grows from a young, tender plant to a mature, fruit-producing one. He likened the role of educator to that of gardener. In his **kindergarten,** or *garden of children,* he envisioned children being educated in close harmony with their own nature and the nature of the universe. Children unfold their uniqueness in play, and it is in learning through play that Froebel makes one of his greatest contributions to the early childhood curriculum:

> Play is the purest, most spiritual activity of man at this stage and, at the same time, typical of human life as a whole—of the inner hidden natural life in man and all things. It gives, therefore, joy, freedom, contentment, inner and outer rest, peace with the world. It holds the sources of all that is good. A child that plays thoroughly, with self-active determination, persevering until physical fatigue forbids, will surely be a thorough, determined man, capable of self-sacrifice for the promotion of the welfare of himself and others. Is not the most beautiful expression of child-life at this time a playing child?—a child wholly absorbed in his play?—a child that has fallen asleep while so absorbed?
>
> As already indicated, play at this time is not trivial, it is highly serious and of deep significance. Cultivate and foster it, O mother; protect and guard it, O father![11]

Kindergarten The name Friedrich Froebel gave to his system of education for children aged three through six; means "garden of children."

Companion Website For more information about Friedrich Wilhelm Froebel, go to the Companion Website at **www.prenhall.com/morrison,** select chapter 4, then choose the Linking to Learning module.

Gifts Ten sets of learning materials designed to help children learn through play and manipulation.

In the Kindergarten segment of the DVD, the narrator comments that "kindergarten is not what it used to be." As you view this segment of the DVD, compare and contrast the kindergarten as Froebel envisioned it and the way kindergarten is today.

Occupations Materials designed to engage children in learning activities.

Gifts and Occupations. Froebel knew from experience, however, that unstructured play represented a potential danger and that it was quite likely, as Pestalozzi had learned with his son Jean-Jacques, that children left to their own devices may not learn much. Without guidance, direction, and a prepared environment in which to learn, there was a real possibility that little or the wrong kind of learning would occur. According to Froebel, the teacher is responsible for guidance and direction so children can become creative, contributing members of society.

To achieve this end, Froebel developed a systematic, planned curriculum for the education of young children. Its bases were gifts, occupations, songs he composed, and educational games. Froebel's **gifts** were objects for children to handle and explore with a teacher's supervision and guidance. Figure 4.1 identifies all ten gifts. The children formed impressions about the shapes and materials, relating them to mathematics, design (symmetry), and their own life experiences. Froebel himself named only the first six materials as gifts; his followers have since included other materials that Froebel used in his own kindergarten.

Currently, there are ten sets of learning materials, or gifts, designed to help children learn through play and manipulation. The first six gifts are meant to represent solid forms, gift seven represents surfaces, gift eight represents line, gift nine represents the point, and gift ten completes the cycle with the use of point and line to represent the framework of solid forms.

Froebel's most well-known gift, the second, consists of a cube, a cylinder, and a sphere, all able to be suspended in such a way that children can examine their different properties by rotating, spinning, and touching. The sphere, because of its symmetry, has only one loop hole by which it is to be suspended. But the cube and the cylinder have multiple loop holes, so children can suspend the solids in different ways and examine the complexity of these seemingly simple shapes.

A significant idea behind the gifts is the importance for developing minds of examining things around them in a free but structured manner. It is not difficult to imagine a three- or four-year-old playing with the wooden solids and learning from their play.[12]

In addition to his gifts, Froebel also used **occupations,** which provide materials for craft activities, such as drawing, paper weaving, folding paper, modeling with clay, and sewing. These activities were intended to be extensions of the gift play in which children could create and explore different materials. The difference between an occupation and a gift is that a gift can resume its original form whereas an occupation has been permanently altered.

Father of the Kindergarten. Froebel is called the father of the kindergarten because he devoted his life to developing both a program for young children and a system of training kindergarten teachers. Many of his concepts and activities are similar to those that many kindergarten and other early childhood programs provide today. In addition, Froebel's recognition of the importance of learning through play is reinforced by contemporary early childhood professionals who plan and structure their programs around play activities. Other features of Froebel's kindergarten that remain are the play circle (where children sit in a circle for learning) and songs that are sung to reinforce concepts taught with gifts and occupations.

Froebel was the first educator to develop a planned, systematic program for educating young children. He also was the first to encourage young, unmarried women to become teachers, a break with tradition that caused Froebel no small amount of criticism and prompted oposition to his methods. The Voice from the Field on page 94 that follows provides more information about Froebel's kindergarten and efforts to revive his ideas.

THE BEGINNINGS OF KINDERGARTEN IN THE UNITED STATES

Froebel's supporters imported his ideas and kindergarten program, virtually intact, into the United States in the last half of the nineteenth century. Even though Froebel's ideas

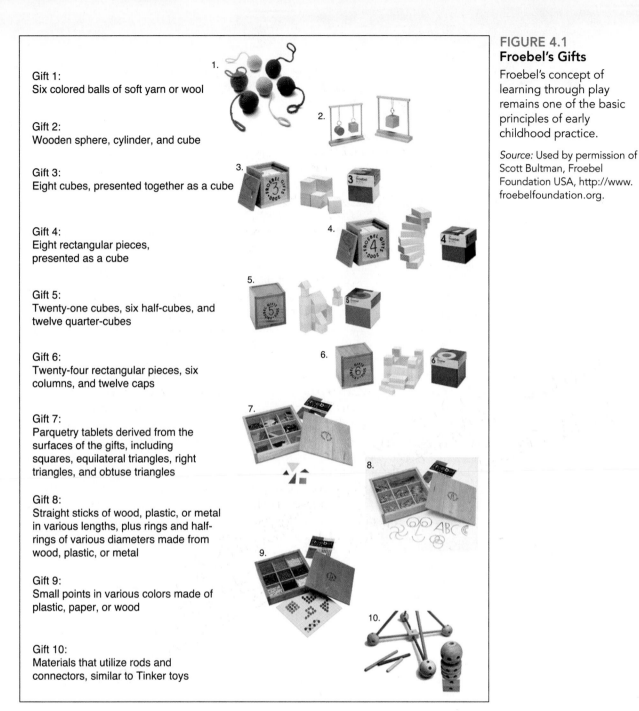

Gift 1:
Six colored balls of soft yarn or wool

Gift 2:
Wooden sphere, cylinder, and cube

Gift 3:
Eight cubes, presented together as a cube

Gift 4:
Eight rectangular pieces, presented as a cube

Gift 5:
Twenty-one cubes, six half-cubes, and twelve quarter-cubes

Gift 6:
Twenty-four rectangular pieces, six columns, and twelve caps

Gift 7:
Parquetry tablets derived from the surfaces of the gifts, including squares, equilateral triangles, right triangles, and obtuse triangles

Gift 8:
Straight sticks of wood, plastic, or metal in various lengths, plus rings and half-rings of various diameters made from wood, plastic, or metal

Gift 9:
Small points in various colors made of plastic, paper, or wood

Gift 10:
Materials that utilize rods and connectors, similar to Tinker toys

FIGURE 4.1
Froebel's Gifts

Froebel's concept of learning through play remains one of the basic principles of early childhood practice.

Source: Used by permission of Scott Bultman, Froebel Foundation USA, http://www.froebelfoundation.org.

seem perfectly acceptable today, they were not acceptable then to those who subscribed to the notion of early education. Especially innovative and hard to accept was the idea that learning could be child centered, based on play and children's interests. Most European and American schools were subject oriented and emphasized basic skills. In addition, Froebel was the first to advocate a communal education for young children outside the home. Until Froebel, most young children were educated in the home by their mothers. The idea of educating children as a group in a special place outside the home was revolutionary.

THE FROEBEL KINDERGARTEN TODAY

The Froebel Kindergarten, more than any other method, was responsible for popularizing early childhood education throughout the world. Froebel created the morning circle, the sand table, the use of paper folding to teach mathematics, the use of block play, the concept of the prepared environment, and the idea of play-based, child-centered education. His method proposes to educate the whole child through activities (and nature study) that support his view that humans are creative beings.

Froebel's work was extremely advanced, anticipating the development of neurology and child psychology, as well as new developments in the fields of mathematics and physics. Today, Froebel's claim that the highest period of brain development is between birth and age three does not seem as far-fetched as it did 170 years ago.

However, in the early 1900s, several factors—including anti-German sentiment and a desire to create a more factorylike approach to education—precipitated a rapid decline of the Froebel Kindergarten method. Froebel's philosophy was labeled romantic. His ideas continued to influence educators, but much of the power and true intention of Froebel's work was lost through misuse of his materials and methods.

Although Froebel wrote mostly in philosophical terms, he put his ideas into practice in his own schools. Froebel kindergarten teachers were highly trained observers of children—the world's first child development specialists. However, many popular books about the Froebel Kindergarten from that era were largely how-to or recipe-like curriculum guides that were sometimes misunderstood.

Because of the lack of modern analysis of Froebel's work and the reliance on outdated and badly translated texts, the Froebel Foundation USA was established in 2001 as a 501(c)(3) nonprofit organization. Its mission is to preserve the history of the Froebel Kindergarten and promote the educational philosophy of Friedrich Froebel to the world at large. The Froebel Foundation USA maintains a large library and archive of books, periodicals, and ephemera dating from the mid-1800s to the present day. The organization reprints some of this historic material and publishes new books, CD-ROMs, videos, and a quarterly newsletter, *The Kindergarten Messenger.*

There is a small but growing Froebel Kindergarten movement worldwide. South Korea, Japan, Canada, Finland, and the UK all have active Froebel centers. The Froebel Foundation USA works closely with other archives and programs around the world.

Contributed by Scott Bultman, ©2003, Froebel Foundation USA, http://www.froebelfoundation.org.

MARGARETHE SCHURZ

Margarethe Schurz (1833–1876) established the first kindergarten in the United States. After attending lectures in Germany on Froebelian principles, she returned to the United States and in 1856 opened her kindergarten in Watertown, Wisconsin. Schurz's program was conducted in German, as were many of the new kindergarten programs of the time, since Froebel's ideas of education appealed especially to bilingual parents. Schurz was instrumental in converting Elizabeth Peabody, the sister-in-law of Horace Mann, to the Froebelian kindergarten system.

ELIZABETH PEABODY

Elizabeth Peabody (1804–1894) opened her kindergarten in Boston in 1860. She and her sister, Mary Mann, also published *Kindergarten Guide.* Peabody realized almost immediately that she lacked the necessary theoretical grounding to adequately implement Froebel's ideas. As a result, she visited kindergartens in Germany and then returned to the United

States to popularize Froebel's methods. Peabody is generally credited as being kindergarten's main promoter in the United States.

MILTON BRADLEY

One element that also helped advance the kindergarten movement was the appearance of appropriate materials. In 1860 toy manufacturer Milton Bradley (1836–1911) attended a lecture by Peabody, became a convert to the kindergarten idea, and began to manufacture Froebel's gifts and occupations. In 1869 Bradley published Froebel's *Paradise of Childhood,* America's first book on kindergarten.

SUSAN BLOW

The first public kindergarten was founded in St. Louis, Missouri, in 1873 by Susan E. Blow (1843–1916) with the cooperation of the St. Louis superintendent of schools, William T. Harris. Elizabeth Peabody had corresponded for several years with Harris, and the combination of her prodding and Blow's enthusiasm and knowledge convinced Harris to open a public kindergarten on an experimental basis. Endorsement of the kindergarten program by a public school system did much to increase its popularity and spread the Froebelian influence within early childhood education. Harris, who later became the U.S. Commissioner of Education, encouraged support for Froebel's ideas and methods.

PATTY SMITH HILL

The kindergarten movement in the United States was not without growing pains. Over a period of time, the kindergarten program, at first ahead of its time, became rigid and teacher centered rather than child centered. By the beginning of the twentieth century, many kindergarten leaders thought that programs and training should be open to experimentation and innovation rather than rigidly tied to Froebel's ideas. Susan Blow was the chief defender of the Froebelian approach. In the more moderate camp was Patty Smith Hill (1868–1946), who thought that kindergarten should remain faithful to Froebel's ideas but should nevertheless be open to innovation. She believed that to survive, the kindergarten movement had to move into the twentieth century, and she was able to convince many of her colleagues. More than anyone else, Hill is responsible for kindergarten as we know it today.

TWENTIETH CENTURY EARLY CHILDHOOD EDUCATORS

MARIA MONTESSORI

Maria Montessori (1870–1952) devoted her life to developing a system for educating young children, and her system has influenced virtually all subsequent early childhood programs. A precocious young woman who considered both mathematics and engineering as a career, she instead chose medicine. Despite the obstacles to entering a field traditionally closed to women, she became the first woman in Italy to earn a medical degree. She was then appointed assistant instructor in the psychiatric clinic of the University of Rome, where her work brought her into contact with mentally retarded children who had been committed to insane asylums.

    Montessori soon became interested in educational solutions for problems such as deafness, paralysis, and "idiocy." As she said, "I differed from my colleagues in that I

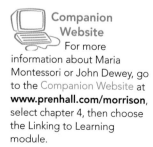

Companion Website For more information about Maria Montessori or John Dewey, go to the Companion Website at **www.prenhall.com/morrison**, select chapter 4, then choose the Linking to Learning module.

In the
Montessori segment of the
DVD, observe how Maria
Montessori's approach to
education helped change the
field of early childhood
education forever.

Children's House
Montessori's first school
especially designed to
implement her ideas.

Progressivism Dewey's
theory of education that
emphasizes the importance of
focusing on the needs and
interests of children rather
than teachers.

Companion
Website
To complete a
Program in Action activity
related to child-centered
programs, go to the
Companion Website at
www.prenhall.com/morrison,
select chapter 4, then choose
the Program in Action
module.

instinctively felt that mental deficiency was more of an educational than medical problem."[13] She wrote of her initial efforts to educate children:

> I succeeded in teaching a number of the idiots from the asylums both to read and to write so
> well that I was able to present them at a public school for an examination together with normal children. And they passed the examination successfully.[14]

This was a remarkable achievement, which aroused interest in both Montessori and her methods. Montessori, however, was already considering something else:

> While everyone else was admiring the progress made by my defective charges, I was trying
> to discover the reasons which could have reduced the healthy, happy pupils of the ordinary
> schools to such a low state that in the intelligence test they were on the level with my own
> unfortunate pupils.[15]

In 1906 Montessori was invited by the director general of the Roman Association for Good Building to organize schools for the young children of the families who occupied the tenement houses constructed by the association. In the first school, named Casa dei Bambini, or **Children's House**, she tested her ideas and gained insights into children and teaching that led to the perfection of her system. Montessori's system is discussed further in chapter 6.

JOHN DEWEY

John Dewey (1859–1952) represents a truly American influence on U.S. education. Through his positions as professor of philosophy at the University of Chicago and Columbia University, his extensive writing, and the educational practices of his many followers, Dewey did more than any other person to redirect the course of education in the United States.

Dewey's theory of schooling, called **progressivism**, emphasizes children and their interests rather than subject matter. From this emphasis come the terms *child-centered curriculum* and *child-centered school*. The progressive education philosophy also maintains that schools should prepare children for the realities of today rather than for some vague future time. As expressed by Dewey in *My Pedagogical Creed,* "Education, therefore, is a process of living and not a preparation for future living."[16] Thus, out of daily life should come the activities in which children learn about life and the skills necessary for living.

What is included in Dewey's concept of children's interests? "Not some one thing," he explained, "it is a name for the fact that a course of action, an occupation, or pursuit absorbs the powers of an individual in a thorough-going way."[17] In a classroom based on Dewey's ideas, children are involved in physical activities, utilization of things, intellectual pursuits, and social interaction. Physical activities include running, jumping, and being actively involved with materials. In this phase the child begins the process of education and develops other interest areas that form the basis for doing and learning. The growing child learns to use tools and materials to construct things. Dewey felt that an ideal expression for this interest was daily living activities, or occupations such as cooking and carpentry.

To promote an interest in the intellectual—solving problems, discovering new things, and figuring out how things work—teachers give children opportunities for inquiry and discovery. Dewey also believed that social interest, referring to interactions with people, is encouraged in a democratically run classroom.

Although Dewey believed the curriculum should be built on the interests of children, he felt that teachers should plan for and capitalize on opportunities to integrate traditional subject matter into the fabric of these interests. Dewey describes a school based on his ideas:

> All of the schools . . . as compared with traditional schools [exhibit] a common emphasis
> upon respect for individuality and for increased freedom; a common disposition to build

upon the nature and experience of the boys and girls that come to them, instead of imposing from without external subject-matter standards. They all display a certain atmosphere of informality, because experience has proved that formalization is hostile to genuine mental activity and to sincere emotional expression and growth. Emphasis upon activity as distinct from passivity is one of the common factors.[18]

Teachers who integrate subjects (such as combining math and literacy experiences), who use thematic units, and who encourage problem-solving activities and critical thinking are philosophically indebted to Dewey. The Project Approach, which is discussed in chapter 6, is also representative of Dewey's child-centered approach. He was not opposed to teaching basic skills or topics; however, he believed, that traditional educational strategies imposed knowledge on children, whereas their interests should be a springboard for involvement with skills and subject matter.

The Program in Action "How to Teach in a Child-Centered Program" on pages 100–101 is a Competency Builder that describes a real-life progressive program and includes guidelines for involving children in active learning. After you read the feature article, look at the observation checklist in Figure 4.2. It can be a valuable tool to help you assess whether programs support child-centered learning.

JEAN PIAGET

Jean Piaget (1896–1980) spent his early career standardizing tests of reasoning for use with children. This experience provided the foundation for his clinical method of interviewing, which he used in studying children's intellectual development. As Piaget recalls, "Thus I engaged my subjects in conversations patterned after psychiatric questioning, with the aim of discovering something about the reasoning process underlying their right, but especially their wrong, answers."[19] This emphasis helps explain why some developers of a Piaget-based early childhood curriculum encourage teachers to use questioning procedures to promote thinking.

Piaget's three children played a major role in his studies, and many of his consequent insights about children's intellectual development are based on his observations and work with them. Using his own children in his studies caused some to criticize his findings. His theory, however, is based on not only his research but also literally hundreds of other studies involving thousands of children. Piaget came to these conclusions about early childhood education:

- Children play an active role in their own cognitive development.
- Mental and physical activity are important for children's cognitive development.
- Experiences constitute the raw materials children use to develop mental structures.
- Children develop cognitively through interaction with and adaptation to the environment.
- Development is a continuous process.
- Development results from maturation and the transactions or interactions between children and their physical and social environments.

Piaget also popularized the age-stage approach to cognitive development and influenced others to apply that theory to other processes, such as moral, language, and social development. He encouraged and inspired many psychologists and educators to develop educational curricula and programs utilizing his ideas and promoted interest in the study of young children's cognitive development that has, in turn, contributed to the interest in infant development and education. Piagetian education is discussed in detail in chapter 5.

Piaget concluded that children's thinking is not wrong but is qualitatively different from adult thought. Can you give two examples of how children's thinking is different from adult thinking?

Companion Website For more information about Jean Piaget, go to the Companion Website at **www.prenhall. com/morrison**, select chapter 4, then choose the Linking to Learning module.

In the High/
Scope segment of the DVD,
observe how the essential
Piagetian concepts listed on
the DVD shape and influence
the High/Scope curriculum for
young children.

FIGURE 4.2 Observation Checklist for Child-Centered Programs

	Yes	No
Physical environment:		
Are learning centers accessible to the children?	___	___
Does the classroom arrangement support children's active leaning?	___	___
Learning environment:		
Are there opportunities for cooperative learning?	___	___
Are children engaged in projects and other extended activites?	___	___
Do the learning materials . . .		
Support a wide range of children's interest?	___	___
Provide for children's different academic and social abilities?	___	___
Teaching environment: Does the teacher . . .		
Support children's efforts to explore, discover, and pursue their interests?	___	___
Make children the center of learning?	___	___
Act as a guide, facilitator, and coach?	___	___
Provide for children's individual differences based on cognitive and physical ability, culture, and gender?	___	___

Companion Website For more information about Lev Vygotsky, go to the Companion Website at **www.prenhall.com/morrison**, select chapter 4, then choose the Linking to Learning module.

LEV VYGOTSKY

Lev Vygotsky (1896–1934), a contemporary of Piaget, increasingly inspires the practices of early childhood professionals. Vygotsky's sociocultural theory of development is particularly useful in describing children's mental, language, and social development. His theory also has many implications for how children's play promotes language and social development. His theory and its application to teaching and learning are discussed in chapter 5.

ABRAHAM MASLOW

Abraham Maslow (1890–1970) developed a theory of motivation based on the satisfaction of needs. Maslow identified self-actualization, or self-fulfillment, as the highest need but maintained that it cannot be achieved until certain basic needs are met. These basic needs include life essentials, such as food, safety, and security; belonging and love; achievement and prestige; and aesthetic needs. Maslow's *hierarchy of needs* is discussed in greater detail in chapter 5; it shows that meeting basic needs in appropriate ways is essential for development.

Companion Website For more information about Abraham Maslow or Howard Gardner, go to the Companion Website at **www.prenhall.com/ morrison**, select chapter 4, then choose the Linking to Learning module.

ERIK ERIKSON

Erik H. Erikson (1902–1994) developed an influential theory of *psychosocial development*. According to Erikson, children's personalities and social skills grow and develop within the context of society and in response to society's demands, expectations, values, and social institutions, such as families, schools, and other child care programs. For Erikson psychosocial development is largely the successful identification with parents, family, and society. Adults, especially parents and teachers, are principal components of these

environments and therefore play a powerful role in helping or hindering children in their personality and cognitive development. For example, school-age children must deal with demands to learn new skills or risk a sense of incompetence—a crisis of "industry versus inferiority." Erikson's theory is also discussed in more detail in chapter 5, which relates his psychosocial theory to children's care and education.

HOWARD GARDNER

Howard Gardner (b. 1943) is well known in educational circles for his theory of *multiple intelligences,* which maintains that instead of a single intelligence, there are actually eight. These are discussed in chapter 5. Gardner and his colleagues at Harvard's Project Zero have been working on the design of performance-based assessments, education for understanding, and the use of multiple intelligences to achieve more personalized curriculum, instruction, and assessment.

According to Gardner's theory of multiple intelligences, children demonstrate many types of intelligences. How would you apply his theory in the early childhood environment?

FROM LUTHER TO THE PRESENT: THE ESSENTIALS OF GOOD EDUCATIONAL PRACTICES

We can identify basic ideas and practices developed over the years that are essential for our work with children and families. Consider how you can apply the following basic concepts to your teaching.

LEARNING ESSENTIALS

- Children need to learn to read and write well.
- Children learn best when they use all of their senses.
- Children's learning is enhanced through the use of concrete materials.
- Children are capable of learning well.
- Education should begin early in life. Today, especially, there is an increased emphasis on beginning education at birth.
- Children should not be forced to learn but should be appropriately taught what they are ready to learn and should be prepared for the next stage of learning. This is a basic of developmentally appropriate practice.
- Learning activities should be interesting and meaningful.
- Social interactions with teachers and peers are a necessary part of development.
- All children have many ways of knowing, learning, and relating to the world.

TEACHING ESSENTIALS

- Teachers must show love and respect for all children.
- Teachers should be dedicated to the teaching profession.
- Teachers should educate all children to the fullest extent of their abilities.

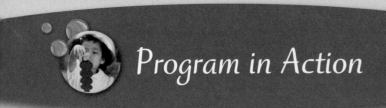

How to Teach in a Child-Centered Program

The City & Country School, founded by Caroline Pratt in 1914, is located in the Greenwich Village district of New York City. It has a current enrollment of 250 students between the ages of two and thirteen and is an example of a progressive school that continues to educate children using the curriculum structure that was set forth over eighty years ago: "giving children experiences and materials that will fit their stage of development and have inherent in them unlimited opportunities for learning." Pratt, a teacher, sought to provide a school environment that suited the way children learn best—by doing.

Basic Values of a Child-Centered Approach

The essence of City & Country's philosophy is faith in children and their desire to learn. When we trust this truly child-centered ideal and set about developing materials, experiences, and environments that foster and guide it, we remain true to Miss Pratt's work. Adults must constantly be open to learn from the children they teach and must be sensitive to their needs and experiences.

- What are the children interested in?
- What is going on in their environment that interests them and is relevant to their lives?

Open-Ended Materials and Methods

It is City & Country School's belief that an early childhood curriculum based on open-ended materials and methods fosters independence, motivation, and interest, all essential components of learning. The younger groups (ages two through seven) use basic, open-ended materials to reconstruct what they are learning about the world and to organize their information and thinking in meaningful ways. Materials such as blocks, clay, water, paint, and wood are chosen because of their simplicity, flexibility, and the challenging possibilities that they offer. Children are encouraged to work out problems among themselves, with help from the teacher only when absolutely necessary.

Children move naturally into the more academic tasks as they need to find out more about what they're already doing. The three Rs are viewed as useful tools to further a child's education, not as ends in themselves;

- Good teaching is based on theories, a personal philosophy of education, goals, and objectives.
- Teaching should move from the concrete to the abstract.
- Observation is a key means of determining children's needs.
- Teaching should be a planned, systematic process.
- Teaching should be child centered rather than adult or subject centered.
- Teaching should be based on children's interests.
- Teachers should collaborate with children as a means of promoting development.
- Teachers should incorporate all types of intelligences in their instruction and activities.

but in no way did Pratt, nor do we, undervalue their importance. In fact, every possible method is used to empower all children with the crucial skill of reading. It can be a natural process for many, but others require extra directed instruction.

THE JOBS PROGRAM

The Lower School curriculum provides a firm foundation for the more formal academic skills that children must master in later years. The Jobs Program was developed to play this central role for students ages eight through thirteen. Each group of students has a specific job to perform that is related to the school's functioning as an integrated community. These jobs provide both a natural impetus for perfecting skills in reading, writing, spelling, and mathematics and a relevant framework for the exploration of social studies and the arts.

Beyond their work with blocks and jobs, children at City & Country are given opportunities to experience art, music, dramatics, foreign languages, science, computers, and woodworking, often integrated with their classroom work.

GUIDELINES FOR A CHILD-CENTERED PROGRAM

Even though children learn naturally, teachers should arrange and manage the classroom environment to stimulate that learning. The following guidelines promote active, independent learning:

GUIDELINE
1
Arrange the classroom to support child-centered learning.

GUIDELINE
2
Provide easily accessible materials and supplies.

GUIDELINE
3
Provide opportunities for children to move around and engage in active learning.

GUIDELINE
4
Provide materials and space for hands-on activities.

GUIDELINE
5
Arrange learning centers and desks so that children can work and play together.

GUIDELINE
6
Support cooperative learning.

GUIDELINE
7
Provide for individual differences and individualized instruction.

GUIDELINE
8
Incorporate project-based activities.

GUIDELINE
9
Provide ample time for children to engage in projects and other cooperative activities.

City & Country School remains committed to its founding principles and will continue to promote and exemplify child-centered education.

Contributed by Kate Turley, principal, City & Country School. Photos courtesy of City & Country School.

COMPETENCY BUILDER

FAMILY ESSENTIALS

- The family is an important institution in children's education and development. The family lays the foundation for all future education and learning.
- Parents are their children's primary educators. However, parents need help, education, and support from early childhood professionals to fulfill this role.
- Parents must guide and direct their children's learning.
- Parents should be involved in all educational programs designed for their children.
- Parents should have knowledge of and training for child rearing.
- Parents and other family members are collaborators in children's learning.
- Parents must encourage and support their children's many interests and their unique ways of learning.

VIEWS OF CHILDREN THROUGH THE AGES

How you and others view children determines how you and they teach and rear them and how society responds to their needs. As you read here about how people view children, try to clarify, and change when appropriate, what you believe. Also, identify social, environmental, and political factors that tend to support each particular view. Sometimes views overlap, so it is possible to integrate ideas from several perspectives into your own particular view of children.

MINIATURE ADULTS

Childhood as we know it has not always been considered a distinct period of life. During medieval times, the notion of childhood did not exist; little distinction was made between children and adults. This concept of children as **miniature adults** was logical for the time and conditions of medieval Europe. Economic conditions did not allow for a long childhood dependency. The only characteristics that separated children from adults were size and age. Children were expected to act as adults in every way, and they did so.[20]

Miniature adults Belief that children are similar to adults and should be treated as such.

In many respects, today is no different. Children are still viewed and treated as adults. Concern is growing that childhood as we knew or remember it is disappearing. Children are viewed as pseudoadults; they even dress like adults, in designer clothes and expensive footwear designed especially for them. Some believe that childhood is not only endangered but already gone. Others fear that, even when allowed a childhood, children are forced to grow up too fast, too soon.[21]

Encouraging children to act like adults and hurrying them toward adulthood causes conflicts between capabilities and expectations, particularly when early childhood professionals demand adultlike behavior from children and set unrealistic expectations. Problems associated with learning, behavior, and social skills can occur when children are constantly presented with tasks and activities that are developmentally inappropriate for them.

SINFUL CHILDREN

Child as sinful View that children are basically sinful, need supervision and control, and should be taught to be obedient.

Based primarily on a religious belief in original sin, the view of the **child as sinful** was widely accepted in the fourteenth through the eighteenth centuries, particularly in colonial North America during the Puritan era of the sixteenth and seventeenth centuries. Misbehavior was a sign of this inherent sin. Those who sought to correct misbehavior forced children to behave and used corporal punishment whenever necessary. Misbehavior was taken as proof of the devil's influence, and "beating the devil out" of the child was an acceptable solution.[22]

This view of inherent sinfulness persists, manifested in the belief that children need to be controlled through strict supervision and insistence on unquestioning obedience to and respect for adults. Many private and parochial or religious schools emphasize respect, obedience, and correct behavior, responding to parents' hopes of rearing children who are less susceptible to the temptations of crime, drugs, and declining moral values. And many Christian religious conservatives advocate a biblical approach to child rearing, encouraging parents to raise their children to obey them. Disobedience is viewed as sinful, and obedience is promoted, in part through strict discipline.

BLANK TABLETS

Earlier we discussed John Locke's belief that children were born into the world as *tabulae rasae,* or blank tablets. Locke concluded, "There is not the least appearance of any settled ideas at all in them; especially of ideas answering the terms which make up those universal propositions that are esteemed innate principles."[23] He believed that children's experiences, through sensory impressions, determined what they learned and, consequently, what they became. The blank tablet view presupposes no innate genetic code or inborn traits; that is, children are born with no predisposition toward any behavior except what is characteristic of human beings. The sum of what a child becomes depends on the nature and quality of experience; in other words, environment is the primary determinant.

The blank tablet view has several implications for teaching and child rearing. If children are seen as empty vessels to be filled, the teacher's job is to fill them—to present knowledge without regard to needs, interests, or readiness for learning. What is important is that children learn what is taught. Children become what adults make of them.

GROWING PLANTS

A perennially popular view of children, which dates back to Rousseau and Froebel, likens them to **growing plants,** with teachers and parents acting as gardeners. This is why Froebel named his program kindergarten–garden of children. Classrooms and homes are gardens in which children grow and mature in harmony with their natural growth patterns. As children grow and mature, they unfold, much as a flower blooms under the proper conditions. In other words, what children become results from natural growth and a nurturing environment. Two key ingredients of this natural unfolding are play and readiness. The content and process of learning are included in play, and materials and activities are designed to promote play.

Children become ready for learning through maturation and play. Lack of readiness to learn indicates that children have not sufficiently matured; the natural process of unfolding has not occurred.

Growing plants View of children popularized by Froebel, which equates children to plants and teachers and parents to gardeners.

PROPERTY

The view that children are **property** has persisted throughout history. Its foundation is that children are the property of their parents or institutions. This view is justified in part by the idea that, as creators of children, parents have a right to them and their labors; parents have broad authority and jurisdiction over their children. Interestingly, few laws interfere with the right of parents to control their children's lives, although this situation is changing somewhat as children are given more rights and the rights they have are protected.

Although difficult to enforce, laws protect children from physical and emotional abuse. In addition, where there are compulsory attendance laws, parents must send their children to school. Generally, however, parents have a free hand in dealing with their children. Legislatures and courts are reluctant to interfere in what is considered a sacrosanct parent-child relationship. A recent and widely publicized Supreme Court decision, *Troxel v. Granville,* reaffirmed this right and declared that parents have a "fundamental right to make decisions concerning the care, custody, and control" of their children.[24] Parents are generally free to exercise full authority over their children; within certain broad limits, most parents feel their children are theirs to do with as they please.

Property Belief that children are literally the property of their parents.

In the Head Start segment of the DVD, observe the way in which Head Start, a social experiment to help poor children and their families, is an example of programs based on the philosophy that children are investments in the future.

INVESTMENTS IN THE FUTURE

Closely associated with the notion of children as property is the view that children represent future wealth or potential for parents and a nation. Since medieval times, people have viewed child rearing as an investment in their future. Many parents assume (not always consciously) that, when they are no longer able to work or must retire, their children will provide for them. This view of **children as investments,** particularly in their parents' future, is being dramatically played out in contemporary society as more middle-aged adults are caring for their own aging and ill parents.

Over the last several decades, some U.S. social policies have been based on the view that children are future investments for society in general. Many programs are built on the underlying assumption that preventing problems in childhood leads to more productive adulthood. And many federal programs have been based on the idea of conserving one of the country's greatest resources—its children.

Children as investments View that investing in the care and education of children reaps future benefits for parents and society.

Companion
Website
To complete a
Diversity Tie-In activity related
to teaching Native American
children, go to the
Companion Website at **www.
prenhall.com/morrison**,
select chapter 4, then choose
the Diversity Tie-In module.

Native American Education.   For many years Native American children were not seen as part of this great resource, and their appropriate education was given little attention. Today, however, attitudes are changing, and programs are focusing on providing high-quality education for Native American children. One such program in California, Project Nee-Sim-Pom, is a collaborative effort that acknowledges the importance of the entire "family"—including home, school, and community—to the academic success of American Indian children.[25] The Diversity Tie-In in this chapter allows you to hear from three Native American teachers who are committed to meeting the academic and cultural needs of their young students.

Return on Investment.   Head Start, Follow Through, and child welfare programs are also products of this view, which has resulted in a human capital, or investment, rationale for child care, preschools, and other services. The High/Scope Perry Preschool program is frequently cited to demonstrate how high-quality preschool programs save taxpayers money. The latest High/Scope preschool research study reports that for each dollar invested, $17.07 is returned to taxpayers. This monetary return results from students who attend high-quality preschools being involved in less crime, staying in school longer, and paying higher taxes as adults.[26] Politicians and public policy makers in particular like research that supports current investments in children reaping large future returns.

PERSONS WITH RIGHTS

Persons with rights   View
that children have certain
basic rights of their own.

A contemporary legal and humanistic view recognizes children as **persons with rights** of their own. Although children are often still treated as economic commodities and individuals who need protection, their rights are beginning to be defined, promoted, and defended. Since children are not organized into political groups, others must act as their advocates. Courts and social service agencies are becoming particular defenders.

The UN Convention on the Rights of the Child, a human rights treaty, went into effect on September 2, 1990, after ratification by more than twenty nations. It has the status of a legally binding treaty for all nations that sign it. The United States has not signed the treaty.

The convention contains fifty-four articles which convey a very strong view of the child as a family member and individual. The convention combines political, civil, economic, and cultural rights. In this sense, the convention acknowledges that health and economic well-being are essential to political freedoms and rights. By extending rights to individual children, the convention challenges the view of children as property. You can access the UN Convention on the Rights of the Child online.

Companion
Website
For more
information about the UN
Convention on the Rights
of the Child, go to the
Companion Website at **www.
prenhall.com/morrison**,
select chapter 4, then choose
the Linking to Learning
module.

Children have rights that would not have been thought possible even ten years ago. Particularly in the area of fetal rights, parents are encountering conflicts between their rights and the lives of their unborn children. For example, many states require places that sell liquor to post a sign reading, "Warning: Drinking alcoholic beverages during pregnancy can cause birth defects." Such questions as What rights of the pregnant woman supersede those of her unborn child? and Does the government or other agency have the right to intervene in a woman's life on behalf of her unborn child? are not easy to answer.

CHILD-CENTERED EDUCATION

As the public increasingly views children as persons with rights, educators are implementing more child-centered approaches. Our discussion of the rights of children fits in nicely with the topic of child-centered education. *Child-centered* is a widely used term that is often misunderstood, leading to heated debates and misinterpretation of instructional practices. It will be helpful to keep these guiding principles about child-centered education in mind as you work with children, parents, and colleagues:

- All children have a right to an education that helps them grow and develop to their fullest; this basic premise is at the heart of our understanding of child-centered

TEACHING NATIVE AMERICAN CHILDREN TODAY

Irene Jones, a Native American Navajo, teaches seventeen Native American kindergarten students at Kenayta Primary School. Kenayta Primary serves 450 Native American children in kindergarten through second grade on the Navajo Nation in Kenayta, Arizona. Irene offers the following insights about what it is like to teach Native American children today.

My children are not as well prepared for school as I would like them to be. They are not prepared because they don't have the social skills to be with other children and to play with others. They don't have the boundaries they need. I have to teach them the social skills necessary to be in a school environment.

Half of my children come to school not knowing any alphabet or their numbers. This is generally true of the children who live in other towns who are bused in from thirty to forty miles away. The other half of my children know their alphabet and numbers. It is really like teaching two classes.

I make a lot of modifications in textbooks and materials so that my children understand what they are to do. My children are very visual learners—I can't just talk—I show them everything. For example, in teaching the letters of the alphabet and in writing, I use visuals and concrete materials. I show my children how to do things—I don't tell them.

Some of my children speak Navajo. At our school we encourage children to retain their language and culture. We have a Navajo culture class, which every child attends once a week.

Darlene Smith teaches in the Navajo Culture and Language Acquisition Program at Kenayta and has dedicated her teaching career to the preservation of Navajo culture and language.

The Navajo tribe wants to have the young children learn their language and culture. I am Navajo, but I had lived off the reservation for a long time and lost a lot of my language skills. I had to get my Navajo language endorsement to teach bilingual, so I went back to school. It was tough for me to learn all of the native language sounds, but I did it. I have taught bilingual now for ten years. The emphasis now is to get more Navajo people to go into teaching. This wasn't always true. This emphasis on Native Americans teaching Native Americans began in the 1980s and 1990s, and I hope it continues. We need to preserve our culture and language, and this is one way to do it.

I teach students to read and write in Navajo, using a Navajo language curriculum that we developed here at Kenayta. The first thing we do is have the children learn their clans. Every child has a clan. There are four basic clans, and then there are clans within clans—they are all related. For example, Harry Yazzie, a kindergartner is a member of the Bitter Water Clan. According to our culture, Harry cannot marry into the Bitter Water Clan or a related clan—this is one reason for him to know his clan. Also, by knowing his clan, he knows his heritage and where he comes from. He also learns respect for the people who he is related to. Children today need to know this cultural information. Unfortunately, I have only thirty minutes for each class, and the children only come once a week, so I don't have a lot of time to teach all I want them to learn.

I think it is important for Navajo children to learn their language and culture. Our language is slowly dying, and if this generation doesn't learn it, I am afraid it will be lost. This is why I am so passionate about teaching our children our culture and language.

At San Felipe Pueblo Elementary School in San Felipe Pueblo, New Mexico, all 490 children are Native American. Anna Beardsley, a native Navajo teacher, teaches twenty-two Native American children.

I teach the children in English. Keres, Tano, and Zuni are the three major language groups of the New Mexico pueblos. At San Felipe the dialect is Keres. The only time we use children's native language is when my aide translates or clarifies directions. If children use more Keres than English when they come to school, my aide uses the native dialect to clarify and help them understand. There is a difference here at San Felipe because some of our teachers are native language speakers, so we are helping our children retain their native language. In the village and school, we encourage the students to retain the language and the culture.

I have taught at several pueblos—there are eighteen pueblos in the state—and teaching varies from pueblo to pueblo. The biggest challenge at the beginning of the school year is to get children to listen and follow directions.

We try our best to have all children achieve to their greatest potential. Our entire curriculum is aligned to the state standards, so we make sure our children are learning what the standards specify. If our children achieve at high levels, then they are more likely to be successful in the real world.

Contributed by Irene Jones, Darlene Smith, and Anna Beardsley through telephone interviews with the author.

education. Therefore, daily interactions with children should be based on the fundamental question, Am I teaching and supporting all children in their growth and development across all domains—social, emotional, physical, linguistic, and intellectual? Such teaching is at the heart of developmentally appropriate practice.

- Every child is a unique and special individual. Consequently, we have to teach individual children and be respectful of and account for their individual uniqueness of age, gender, culture, temperament, and learning style.
- Children are active participants in their own education and development. This means that they should be mentally involved and physically active in learning what they need to know and do.
- Children's ideas, preferences, learning styles, and interests are considered in the planning for and implementation of instructional practices.

Child-centered education has been an important foundation of early childhood education since the time of Froebel. As a professional, you will want to make your teaching and practice child centered. In addition, you will want to advocate for the inherent right of every child to a child-centered education.

A reemphasis on child-centered education is occurring as society in general is becoming more interested in the whole child and efforts to address all of children's needs, not just their academic needs. As a result, there is much more concern for encouraging children to be healthy and lead healthy lifestyles. Providing children with medical immunizations and seeing that all children are fully immunized by age two have received a lot of attention, and programs to help children be free of drugs are common in early childhood and primary programs. Concern for the welfare of children in all areas of their growth and development is evident and attests to the public's growing awareness of their basic rights.

All great educators have believed in the basic goodness of children; the teacher is to provide the environment for this goodness to manifest itself. A central theme of Luther, Comenius, Pestalozzi, Froebel, Montessori, and Dewey is that we must do our work as educators well, and we must really care about those whom we have been called to serve. This indeed is the essence of child-centered education.

Companion Website

For additional Internet resources or to complete an online activity for this chapter, go to the Companion Website at **www.prenhall.com/morrison**, select chapter 4, then choose the Linking to Learning or Making Connections module.

LINKING TO LEARNING

John Amos Comenius
http://www.comeniusfoundation.org/comenius.htm
Biographical information with facts and quotes about Comenius.

John Dewey
http://www.siu.edu/~deweyctr/
The Center for Dewey Studies, housed at Southern Illinois University at Carbondale; offers online documents about Dewey, numerous links, and instructions for joining the John Dewey Internet mailing list.

Erikson Tutorial Home Page
http://facultyweb.cortland.edu/~andersmd/erik/welcome.html

An introduction to and summary of Erik Erikson's eight stages of psychosocial development.

Friedrich Wilhelm Froebel
http://www.infed.org/thinkers/et-froeb.htm

Biography and bibliography of the father of the kindergarten.

Howard Gardner
http://www.pz.harvard.edu/PIs/HG.htm

A biography of Howard Gardner, as well as an account of his work on Harvard's Project Zero.

John Locke
http://www.utm.edu/research/iep/l/locke.htm

The Internet Encyclopedia of Philosophy's entry on John Locke, including his writings and a list of sources.

Martin Luther
http://www.iclnet.org/pub/resources/text/wittenberg/wittenberg-home.html

Provides links to many of Luther's writings online.

Abraham Maslow
http://www.ship.edu/~cgboeree/maslow.html

Tells about Maslow's personality theories and the man himself.

Maria Montessori
http://www.webster.edu/~woolflm/montessori.html

Historical perspective of her life and teaching methods.

Robert Owen
http://www.infed.org/thinkers/et-owen.htm

A bibliography of writings by Robert Owen.

Jean Heinrich Pestalozzi
http://www.infed.org/thinkers/et-pest.htm

A page about Pestalozzi similar to that about Rousseau.

Jean Piaget
http://www.piaget.org/

The Jean Piaget Society's website; an excellent source of information regarding publications and conferences about the work and theories of Piaget.

Jean-Jacques Rousseau
http://www.infed.org/thinkers/et-rous.htm

Contains a brief statement on education by Rousseau, as well as a few links to other Rousseau sites.

Lev Vygotsky
http://www.marxists.org/archive/vygotsky/

The Vygotsky Internet Archive, with biographical and philosophical information.

UNICEF
http://www.unicef.org

Worldwide organization that advocates for measures to give children the best start in life promoting health, education, equality and protection for all children.

ACTIVITIES FOR FURTHER ENRICHMENT

ETHICAL DILEMMA: "WHY DON'T MY KIDS GET THEIR FAIR SHARE"?

You are a novice first-grade teacher in Rocky Springs School District. Your class of twenty-eight students includes fifteen Hispanic students, nine African American students, and four Vietnamese students. Your room is sparsely furnished, many of the tables and chairs need repair, and the classroom library of thirty-seven books is old and worn. Last week at an orientation for preK–3 teachers held across town at the new elementary school, you learned that the students there are 90 percent White and class size averages nineteen. A tour of the classrooms revealed the latest in furniture and equipment with well-stocked classroom libraries. You are concerned about the unequal distribution of resources in the school district; you feel as though your children are not getting their fair share.

What should you do? Should you just keep quiet and hope things get better, or should you advocate for your children by getting a group of your colleagues together and sharing your concerns with them?

APPLICATIONS

1. Reflect on your experiences in elementary school. What experiences were most meaningful? Why? What teachers do you remember best? Why?
2. Interview the parents of children who attend a private or alternative preschool, kindergarten, or elementary school. What are their reasons for sending their children to these schools? Do you agree or disagree with their reasons?
3. To what extent do religious beliefs determine educational practice? Give specific examples from your own experience and from current accounts in newspapers and other media.
4. Reflect on how your philosophy of education has been influenced by the ideas and contributions of great educators. Which of the ideas has influenced you the most? Which ideas of yours have been most challenged by what you have read in this chapter?

FIELD EXPERIENCES

1. Visit early childhood programs in your area. Observe to determine how they apply the basic ideas of historic figures you studied in this chapter.
2. As you visit schools, classrooms, and agencies, keep a journal in which you identify the philosophy or theory you think underlies the particular curriculum, teaching methods, and approach to learning.

Reflect on your observations and consider the implications for your professional practice.

3. Develop an observation guideline based on Gardner's intelligences. Observe children and provide specific examples that demonstrate specific intelligences. Use Figure 5.6 on page 127 as a guide.
4. Visit child care programs in your area, and observe whether the teachers use naturalism in the classroom. Record what you observe in your portfolio or teaching file. What specific naturalistic features did you observe?

RESEARCH

1. Search journals, newspapers, the Internet, and other sources to determine how people, agencies, and legislation are influencing early childhood education. Do you think these influences will be long lasting? Why or why not?
2. A clipping file of newspaper, journal, and magazine articles relating to education is a great way to observe philosophies and theories in action. Many articles will critique how schools are or are not implementing a certain reform or practice. As you read and review these articles, identify the ideas and philosophies that are influencing a particular point of view.
3. You have just been assigned to write a brief historical summary of the major ideas of the key educational pioneers you read about in this chapter. You are limited to fifty words for each person and are to write as though you were the person. For example,

   Locke: "At birth the mind is a blank slate, and experiences are important for making impressions on the mind. I believe learning occurs best through the senses. A proper education begins early in life, and hands-on experiences are an important part of education."

4. Research three of the historical figures discussed in this chapter. Identify in greater detail their influence on early childhood education, and compare their philosophies. What specific theories are similar and different? Which theories are still relevant today? What current practices are based on the people you researched?

READINGS FOR FURTHER ENRICHMENT

Brosterman, N. *Inventing Kindergarten.* New York: Harry N. Adams, 2002.

A comprehensive book about the original kindergarten, a revolutionary educational program invented in the 1830s by German educator Friedrich Froebel. Reconstructs the most successful system ever devised for teaching young children about art, design, math, and natural history. Also includes an exploration of the origins of modern art in the early childhood experiences of some of its greatest creators.

Dewey, John. *Experience and Education,* reprint ed. New York: Collier, 1998.

Dewey's comparison of traditional and progressive education. Provides a good insight into what Dewey believed schools should be like.

Fogarty, R., and J. Bellanca. *Multiple Intelligences: A Collection.* Boston: Allyn and Bacon, 1998.

Contains research and writing about Howard Gardner's multiple intelligences theory. Explores practical applications of the theory and provides supporting evidence that teaching to the multiple intelligences is effective with all learners.

Hymes, J. L., Jr. *Twenty Years in Review: A Look at 1971–1990.* Washington, DC: NAEYC, 1991.

A treasure trove of detail about recent history in early childhood education; chronicles a year's history in each chapter.

Lascarides, V., and B. Hinitz. *History of Early Childhood Education.* New York: Falmer Press, 2000.

Presents a thorough description of the history of early childhood education in the United States; a good collection of historical literature that combines history with theory.

Monroe, W. *Comenius and the Beginnings of Educational Reform.* New York: C. Scribner's Sons, 1900.

Traces the reform movement in education before and up to Comenius, who was responsible for the movement's most significant contributions; also talks about the life of Comenius and his educational writings.

Murphy, Daniel. *Comenius: A Critical Reassessment of His Life and Work.* Dublin: Irish Academic Press, 1995.

Reexamines the principles of Comenius's pedagogic philosophy, giving particular attention to the learner-centered methods of teaching, which constitute his main legacy to world education.

Peltzman, B. *Pioneers of Early Childhood Education.* Westport, CT: Greenwood Press, 1998.

Provides biographies and annotated bibliographies of more than thirty pioneers in early childhood education; gives special attention to multicultural educators.

Wolfe, J. *Learning from the Past: Historical Voices in Early Childhood Education,* 2nd ed. Mayerthorpe, Alberta, Canada: Piney Branch Press, 2002.

Beginning with Plato, examines early childhood education through eleven historical figures, ending with Lucy Sprague Mitchell in the 1900s. Provides a detailed description of a particular era in each chapter. Gives background information about each educator emphasizing their work in early childhood education. Includes illustrations, questions, and available resources.

ENDNOTES

1. Barbara Beatty, "Past, Present and Future," *The American Prospect, Online Edition.* (November 2004), http://www.prospect.org/.

2. Private School Universe Survey, National Center for Educational Statistics, U.S. Department of Education (2002).

3. John Amos Comenius, *The Great Didactic of John Amos Comenius,* ed. and trans. M. W. Keating (New York: Russell & Russell, 1967), 58.

4. Ibid., 127.

5. John Locke, *An Essay Concerning Human Understanding,* ed. Peter H. Nidditch (Oxford: Oxford University Press, 1975), 104.

6. Jean-Jacques Rousseau, *Émile; Or, Education,* trans. Barbara Foxley (New York: Dutton, Everyman's Library, 1933), 5.

7. Jean-Jacques Rousseau, *Émile; Or, Education,* ed. and trans. William Boyd (New York: Teachers College Press, by arrangement with Heinemann, London, 1962), 11–15.

8. Roger DeGuimps, *Pestalozzi: His Life and Work* (New York: Appleton, 1890), 205.

9. Ibid., 196.

10. S. Bamford, *Passages in the Life of a Radical* (London: London Simpkin Marshall, 1844).

11. Friedrich Froebel, *The Education of Man,* trans. M. W. Hailman (New York: Appleton, 1887), 55.

12. Froebel gifts and blocks, http://www.froebelgifts.com.

13. Maria Montessori, *The Discovery of the Child,* trans. M. J. Costelloe (Notre Dame, IN: Fides, 1967), 22.

14. Maria Montessori, *The Montessori Method,* trans. Anne E. George (Cambridge, MA: Bentley, 1967), 38.

15. Montessori, *The Discovery of the Child,* 28.

16. Reginald D. Archambault, ed., *John Dewey on Education—Selected Writings* (New York: Random House, 1964), 430.

17. Henry Suzzallo, ed., *John Dewey's Interest and Effort in Education* (Boston: Houghton Mifflin, 1913), 65.

18. Archambault, *John Dewey on Education,* 170–171.

19. Edwin G. Boring, ed., *A History of Psychology in Autobiography,* vol. 4 (Worcester, MA: Clark University Press, 1952; New York: Russell & Russell, 1968), 244.

20. S. Mintz, *Huck's Raft: A History of American Childhood* (Cambridge, MA: Belknap Press, 2004), 7–13.

21. David Elkind, *The Hurried Child: Growing Up Too Fast Too Soon* (Reading, MA: Addison-Wesley, 1981).

22. Mintz, *Huck's Raft,* 7–13.

23. John Locke, *An Essay Concerning Human Understanding* (New York: Dover, 1999), 92–93.

24. L. S. Vygotsky, *Mind in Society* (Cambridge, MA: Harvard University Press, 1978), 244.

25. California Department of Education, American Indian Early Childhood Education Program, http://www.cde.ca.gov/sp/ai/ec/.

26. L. J. Schweinhart, J. Montie, Z. Xiang, W. S. Barnett, C. R. Belfield, and M. Nores, *Lifetime Effects: The High/Scope Perry Preschool Study Through Age 40* (monographs of the High/Scope Educational Research Foundation, 14) (Ypsilanti, MI: High/Scope Press, 2004), 3.

CHAPTER 5

Theories Applied to Teaching and Learning

FOUNDATIONS FOR PRACTICE

Children's minds, if planted in fertile soil,
will grow quite naturally on their own.

JEAN PIAGET

This chapter discusses the pioneering work of theorists who have contributed to our knowledge and understanding of how children learn, grow, and develop. They have laid the foundation for the practice of *constructivism*, which is based on the theory that children literally construct their knowledge of the world and their level of cognitive functioning. Constructivist theorists include Jean Piaget, Lev Vygotsky, and Howard Gardner. Table 5.1 lists some of these educators' contributions to how children learn. In addition, the chapter discusses the psychosocial theory of Erik Erikson, the basic needs theory of Abraham Maslow, and the cultural context theory of Urie Bronfenbrenner.

THEORIES OF LEARNING AND DEVELOPMENT

LEARNING

How do you learn? How do children learn? We take learning for granted and frequently don't pay much attention to *how* learning occurs. But your belief about how children learn will play a major role in the curriculum you select for them and the way you teach them. Think for a moment about how you would define *learning* and what learning means to you. For some the ability to learn is a sign of intelligence. For others it means the grades children bring home on their reports cards. For many parents, learning is the answer to the "What did you learn in school today?" question.

However, for our purposes, **learning** refers to the cognitive and behavioral changes that result from experiences. The experiences that make up the curriculum are at the core of the learning process and experiences you provide for children should be based on a theory or theories of how children learn.

How will you know whether and what children are learning? You can determine whether learning occurs in a number of ways: by observing what each child is doing, by noting how a child is interacting with other children, by interpreting the results of achievement tests, and by reading stories children have written. These and other methods of observing and assessing learning are discussed in chapter 3.

THEORIES

In general, a theory consists of statements and assumptions about relationships, principles, and data designed to explain and predict a phenomenon. In our case, a **theory** is a set of explanations used to explain how children learn. For example, many professionals use Piaget's theory of cognitive development as a basis for curriculum and practice. His theory is very influential and is applied to many early childhood programs, including those discussed in chapter 6. In fact, Piaget's theory is used more often than any other theory to explain children's thinking and learning and to guide program development.

Focus Questions

What are theories of behavior and learning, and why are they important?

What are the major features of the theories of Piaget, Vygotsky, Maslow, Bronfenbrenner, Erikson, and Gardner?

How can you use theories of learning in your professional practice?

TABLE 5.1 Contributors to Theories of Learning

Contributor	Contributions to Curriculum and Teaching
Jean Piaget (1896–1980)	• Learning involves discovery. • Manipulating objects promotes learning. • Interactions with people, places, and things lead to development of intellect and knowledge.
Lev Vygotsky (1896–1934)	• Learning is social and occurs through personal interactions. • More competent individuals help students scaffold learning. • Group work promotes learning.
Howard Gardner (b. 1943)	• Intelligence is multidimensional. • Human potential is the ability to solve problems. • There are many ways of knowing and expressing knowledge.

Learning Cognitive and behavioral changes that result from experiences.

Learning theories such as Piaget's are important for several reasons.

- They help you think about how children learn. Thinking about and understanding how children learn make it easier for you to plan and teach.
- They enable you to explain to others, especially parents, how learning occurs and what you and they can expect of children. Explaining children's learning on the basis of a theory of learning makes more sense to parents.
- They enable you to evaluate children's learning because you have a basis from which to evaluate; for example, when you observe, you know what you are observing and why.
- They provide you with guidance in developing programs that support and enhance children's learning.

Theory A set of explanations of how children develop and learn.

CONSTRUCTIVISM

Constructivism Theory that emphasizes the active role of children in developing their understanding and learning.

Constructivism is a cognitive theory of development and learning based on the ideas of John Dewey, Jean Piaget, and Lev Vygotsky. The *constructivist approach* supports the belief that children actively seek knowledge; it explains children's cognitive development, provides guidance for how and what to teach, and provides direction for how to arrange learning environments.

> Constructivism is defined in terms of the individual's organizing, structuring and restructuring of experience—an ongoing lifelong process—in accordance with existing schemes of thought. In turn, these very schemes become modified and enriched in the course of interaction with the physical and social world.[1]

Basic Concepts. These are basic constructivist concepts you can use to guide your work with young children:

- Children construct their own knowledge based on what they already know.
- Children are active agents who problem solve and think for themselves.
- Children's experiences with people, places, and things provide a framework for their construction of knowledge.
- Children learn best through experiences and activities that they initiate and find interesting.
- Teaching and learning are child centered.

Companion Website For more information about constructivism, go to the Companion Website at **www. prenhall.com/morrison**, select chapter 5, then choose the Linking to Learning module.

The Constructivist Classroom. The constructivist classroom is child centered and learning centered.

- Children are physically and mentally active.
- Children are encouraged to initiate learning activities.

- Children carry on dialogues and conversations with peers, teachers, and other adults.
- Teachers create and support children's social interactions with peers, teachers, and other adults to provide a context for cognitive development and learning.
- Teachers provide rich social environments characterized by children's collaboration, projects, problem solving, and cooperative learning.
- Teachers arrange classroom desks, tables, and learning centers to support student collaboration and social interaction.
- Teachers create a classroom climate of mutual respect and cooperation.
- Teachers and children are partners in learning.
- Teachers provide guided assistance (see scaffolding discussion later in this chapter).
- Teachers link children's prior knowledge and experiences with current classroom activities and experiences.

Companion Website For more information about Jean Piaget, go to the Companion Website at **www.prenhall. com/morrison**, select chapter 5, then choose the Linking to Learning module.

PIAGET'S THEORY OF LEARNING

Piaget's theory is about cognitive development; it explains how individuals perceive, think, understand, and learn. His theory is basically a logicomathematical theory; that is, cognitive development is perceived as consisting primarily of logical and mathematical abilities.

Generally, the term *intelligence* suggests intelligence quotient, or IQ—that which is measured on an intelligence test. But this is not what Piaget meant by intelligence. Instead, for him intelligence is the cognitive, or mental, process by which children acquire knowledge; hence, intelligence is "to know." It is synonymous with thinking in that it involves the use of mental operations developed as a result of acting mentally and physically in and on the environment.

Active involvement is basic to Piaget's cognitive theory; through direct experiences with the physical world, children develop intelligence. Other basic concepts include adaptation, schemes, assimilation, and accommodation.

One of Piaget's tenets is that children think differently at different stages of cognitive development. How would this affect the way you design learning experiences for children?

ACTIVE LEARNING

Active learning is an essential part of constructivism. Active learning means that children construct knowledge through physical and mental activity and that they are actively involved in problem-setting and problem-solving activities.

Think for a minute about what would happen if you gave six-month-old Emily some blocks. What would she try to do with them? More than likely, she would put them in her mouth; she would want to eat the blocks. On the other hand, if you gave blocks to Emily's three-year-old sister Madeleine, she would try to stack them. Both Emily and Madeleine want to be actively involved with things and people as active learners. Active involvement comes naturally for all children.

Active learning (theory) The view that children develop knowledge and learn by being physically and mentally engaged in learning activities.

Adaptation The process of building schemes through interaction with the environment. Consists of two complementary processes—assimilation and accommodation.

Schemes Organized units of knowledge.

Assimilation The process of fitting new information into existing schemes.

ADAPTATION

The adaptive process operates at the cognitive level much as it does at the physical level. A newborn's intelligence is expressed through reflexive motor actions such as sucking, grasping, head turning, and swallowing. Children develop their intelligence through this process of **adaptation** to the environment via reflexive actions.[2]

Through interactions with their environment, children organize sensations and experiences. The quality of the environment and the nature of children's experiences play a major role in the development of their intelligence.

Schemes. **Schemes** refer to organized units of knowledge that children develop through the adaptation process. Infants use their reflexive actions such as sucking and grasping to build their concepts and understanding of the world.

In the process of developing new schemes, Piaget ascribed primary importance to physical activity. Physical activity leads to mental stimulus, which in turn leads to mental activity. There is not a clear line between physical and mental activity in infancy and early childhood. Consequently, early childhood teachers provide for active learning by arranging classrooms to allow children to explore and interact with people and objects.

Assimilation and Accommodation. **Assimilation** is the taking in of sensory data through experiences and impressions and incorporating this information into existing knowledge of people and objects that has resulted from previous experiences.[3] Through assimilation children use old methods or experiences to understand and make sense of new information and experiences. Emily used assimilation when she put a block in her mouth and ended up sucking on it. The block was fine for sucking but not for eating.

Accommodation is the process by which children change their way of thinking, behaving, or believing to come into accord with reality. Accommodation involves changing old methods to adjust to new situations. Whereas Emily tried to eat the blocks, Madeleine wanted to stack them. Through accommodation she had learned not to try to eat them. Carlos, who is familiar with kittens and cats because he has several cats at home, may, upon seeing a dog for the first time, call it a kitty. He has assimilated dog into his organization of kitty. However, Carlos must change (i.e., accommodate) his model of what constitutes "kittyness" to exclude dogs. He will start to construct, or build, a scheme for dog and thus what "dogness" represents.[4]

The twin processes of assimilation and accommodation, viewed as an integrated and functioning whole, constitute adaptation. Figure 5.1 illustrates both assimilation and accommodation: Julie assimilates the information her father gives her and changes, or accommodates, her existing scheme to reflect her new understanding that she existed in a different form at an earlier time.

Piaget believed that the opportunity to be physically and mentally involved in learning is necessary for mental development in the early years. What are some examples of how children's active involvement contributes to their learning?

Equilibrium. **Equilibrium** is a balance between assimilation and accommodation. Children assimilate, or fit, new data into their already-existing knowledge (i.e., scheme) of reality and the world. If the new data can be immediately assimilated, then equilibrium occurs. However, if children are unable to assimilate the new data, easily, and they try to accommodate their way of thinking, acting, or perceiving to account for the new data and restore equilibrium to their intellectual system.

Children have difficulty with assimilation and accommodation when new experiences are radically different from their past experiences. For this reason Piaget insisted that new experiences must have a connection to previous experiences. It is imperative that you

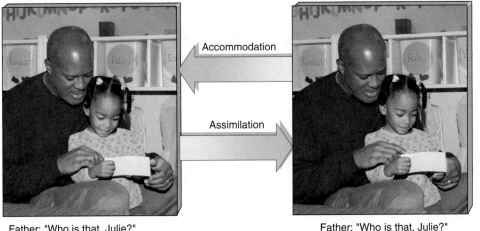

FIGURE 5.1
Assimilation and Accommodation

Source: Text is adapted from K. Bhattacharya and S. Han, "Piaget and Cognitive Development," in M. Orey, ed., *Emerging Perspectives on Learning, Teaching, and Technology* (2001), http://www.coe.uga.edu/epltt/Piaget.htm.

Father: "Who is that, Julie?"
Julie: "That's a baby, Daddy."
Father: "Yes, but that baby is you."

Father: "Who is that, Julie?"
Julie: "That's me, Daddy!"

In order for Julie to understand what her father has told her, she must assimilate the information into her existing internal cognitive structures. Structures are then accommodated as reality is assimilated.

Accommodation
Changing or altering existing schemes or creating new ones in response to new information.

Equilibrium A balance between existing and new schemes, developed through assimilation and accommodation of new information.

learn and understand as much as possible about the children you teach—their culture, family, and community—so that you can tap into and expand on their past experiences.

STAGES OF INTELLECTUAL DEVELOPMENT

Table 5.2 summarizes Piaget's first three developmental stages, provides examples of stage-related characteristics, and gives suggestions of ways that teachers can support each stage. Piaget contended that developmental stages are the same for all children, including the atypical child, and that all children progress through each stage in the same order. Thus, the sequence of growth through the developmental stages does not vary even though the ages at which progression occurs do vary.

Sensorimotor Stage. Piaget's first stage, the **sensorimotor stage,** begins at birth and lasts about two years. During this period children use their senses and motor reflexes—seeing, sucking, grasping—to build their knowledge of the world and to develop intellectually. Reflexive actions help children construct a mental scheme of what is suckable, for example, and what is not (i.e., what can fit into the mouth and what cannot) and what sensations (e.g., warm and cold) occur by sucking. Children use the grasping reflex in much the same way to build schemes of what can and cannot be grasped. Through these innate sensory and reflexive actions, they develop an increasingly complex and individualized hierarchy of schemes. What children become physically and intellectually is related to these sensorimotor functions and interactions.

The sensorimotor period has these major characteristics:

- Dependence on and use of innate reflexive actions
- Initial development of object permanency (i.e., the idea that objects can exist without being seen, heard, or touched)
- Egocentricity, whereby children see themselves as the center of the world and believe events are caused by them
- Dependence on concrete representations (i.e., things) rather than symbols (i.e., words, pictures) for information
- By the end of the second year, less reliance on sensorimotor reflexive actions, and a beginning use of symbols for things that are not present

Sensorimotor stage The stage during which children learn through the senses and motor activities.

In the Infant and Toddler segment of the DVD, the infant and toddler school director mentions that infants and toddlers are sensorimotor beings. Use Piaget's theory to explain this statement.

115

TABLE 5.2 Piaget's Stages of Cognitive Development

Stage	Characteristics	Teacher's Role
Sensorimotor Birth to about 2 years	• Use innate sensorimotor systems of sucking, grasping, and gross-body activities to build schemes • Begin to develop object permanency • "Think" with their senses and their innate reflexive actions • "Solve" problems by playing with toys and using everyday "tools" such as a spoon to learn to feed themselves	• Provide interactive toys, such as rattles, mobiles, and pound-a-peg • Provide many and varied multisensory toys to promote investigation and sensory involvement; include household items such as pots, pans, and spoons • Provide environments in which infants and toddlers can crawl and explore, keeping infants out of their cribs as much as possible • Play hide-and-seek games that involve looking for hidden objects • Provide rich language environments to encourage interaction with people and objects
Preoperational 2 to 7 years	• Depend on concrete representations; "think" with concrete materials • Use the world of here and now as frame of reference • Enjoy accelerated language development; internalize events • Are egocentric in thought and action • Think everything has a reason or purpose • Are perceptually bound • Make judgments based primarily on how things look	• Provide toys and materials for pretend play • Provide building blocks of many kinds (review Froebel's gifts and occupations in chapter 4) • Provide materials for arts and crafts • Provide many and varied kinds of manipulative materials, such as puzzles, counters, and clay • Provide many concrete learning materials and activities • Provide many developmentally appropriate language opportunities involving speaking, listening, reading, and writing
Concrete Operations 7 to 12 years	• Able to reverse thought processes • Able to conserve • Depend on how things look for decision making • Are less egocentric • Structure time and space • Understand numbers • Begin to think logically; can apply logic to concrete situations	• Use props and visual aids, especially when dealing with sophisticated material* • Give students a chance to manipulate and test objects* • Make sure presentations and readings are brief and well organized* • Use familiar examples to explain more complex ideas* • Give opportunities to classify and group objects and ideas on increasingly complex levels* • Present problems that require logical, analytical thinking* • Provide opportunities for role taking, problem solving, and self-reflection.

*Adapted from Anita Woolfolk, *Educational Psychology,* 9th ed. (Boston, MA: Allyn and Bacon, 2004).

Preoperational stage
The stage of cognitive development in which young children are capable of mental representations.

Preoperational Stage. Piaget's second stage, the **preoperational stage**, begins at age two and ends at approximately seven years.

Representation. During the preoperational stage, one of the child's major accomplishments is the ability to use symbols to represent objects and events—symbols such as language, pictures, picture books, maps, drawings, and make-believe play. At about age two, children's ability to use language rapidly accelerates, and at about age three they begin to understand that a picture of a house, for example, stands for a house in the real world. This ability to think symbolically, to visualize things mentally, opens many opportunities for children to develop cognitively and increases their knowledge of their environment.

Children in the preoperational stage make judgments based on how things look. When they look at an object that has multiple characteristics—such as a long, round, yellow pencil—they see whichever of those qualities first catches their eye. Thus, their knowledge is based mainly on what they are able to see, simply because they do not yet have *operational* intelligence, or the ability to think logically.

Conservation. The absence of operations makes it impossible for preoperational children to *conserve,* or determine that the quantity of an object does not change simply because a transformation occurs in its physical appearance. For example, if you show preoperational children two identical rows of coins (see Figure 5.2) and ask whether each row has the same number of coins, the children should answer affirmatively. If you then space out the coins in one row and ask whether the two rows still have the same number of coins, they might insist that more coins are in one row because it's longer. These children are basing their judgment on what they can see—namely, the spatial extension of one row beyond the other row. This example also illustrates that preoperational children are not able to *reverse* thought or action, which requires mentally putting the row back to its original length. Figure 5.2 shows other examples of conservation tasks.

In addition, preoperational children believe and act as though everything happens for a specific reason or purpose. This explains children's constant and recurring questions about why things happen and how things work.

Egocentrism. Preoperational children believe that everyone thinks as they think and act as they do for the same reasons. They have a hard time putting themselves in another's place, and it is difficult for them to be sympathetic and empathetic. The way preoperational children talk reflects their *egocentrism.* For example, in explaining about his dog running away, Matt might say something like this: "And we couldn't find him . . . and my dad he looked . . . and we were glad." Matt assumes you have the same point of view he does and know the whole story. The details are missing for you, not for Matt.

Young children's egocentrism also helps explain why they tend to talk at each other rather than with each other and why they talk to themselves. Perhaps you have observed a four-year-old busily engrossed in putting a puzzle together and saying, "Which piece comes next?" Children use this **self-talk**, which Piaget called *egocentric speech,* to guide themselves. Piaget saw it as further evidence of children's egocentrism, their preoccupation with their own needs and concerns rather than the views of others. Egocentrism, quite simply, is a fact of cognitive development in the early childhood years.

Concrete Operations Stage. Piaget's third stage of cognitive development is **concrete operations.** Children in this stage, from about age seven to about age twelve, begin to use mental images and symbols during the thinking process and can reverse operations.

Concrete operational children begin to understand that change in physical appearance does not necessarily change quality or quantity. They also begin to reverse thought processes, going back and undoing a mental action just accomplished. Other mental operations are also typical of this stage:

- *One-to-one correspondence.* This is the basis for counting and matching objects. Concrete operational children have mastered the ability, for example, to give one cookie to each classmate and a pencil to each member of their work group.
- *Classification of objects, events, and time according to certain characteristics.* For example, a child in the concrete operations stage can classify events as occurring before or after lunch.

> Piaget believed that developmentally, after children are capable of making one-to-one correspondence and classifying and ordering objects, they are ready for higher level thinking activities such as those that involve numeration, time, and spatial relationships.

Self-talk Speech directed to oneself that helps to guide one's behavior.

Concrete operations The stage of cognitive development during which children's thought is logical and can organize concrete experiences.

FIGURE 5.2
**Piagetian
Conservation Tasks**

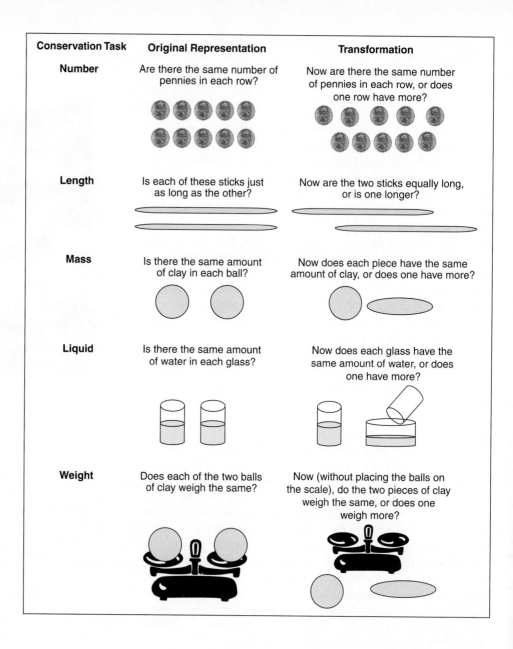

Conservation Task	Original Representation	Transformation
Number	Are there the same number of pennies in each row?	Now are there the same number of pennies in each row, or does one row have more?
Length	Is each of these sticks just as long as the other?	Now are the two sticks equally long, or is one longer?
Mass	Is there the same amount of clay in each ball?	Now does each piece have the same amount of clay, or does one have more?
Liquid	Is there the same amount of water in each glass?	Now does each glass have the same amount of water, or does one have more?
Weight	Does each of the two balls of clay weigh the same?	Now (without placing the balls on the scale), do the two pieces of clay weigh the same, or does one weigh more?

• *Classification involving multiple properties.* Multiple classification occurs when a child can classify objects on the basis of more than one property, such as color and size, shape and size, or shape and color.

• *Class inclusive operations.* Class inclusion also involves classification. For example, if children in this stage are shown five apples, five oranges, and five lemons and asked whether there are more apples or fruit, they are able to respond with "fruit."

The concrete stage does not represent a period into which children suddenly emerge after having been preoperational. The process of development from stage to stage is gradual and continual and occurs over a period of time as a result of maturation and experiences. No simple sets of exercises will cause children to move up the developmental ladder. Rather, ongoing developmentally appropriate activities lead to conceptual understanding.

The "New City School" Program in Action later in this chapter (page 131) is an example of a Piagetian and constructivist theory in action.

LEV VYGOTSKY AND SOCIOCULTURAL THEORY

Lev Vygotsky (1896–1934), a contemporary of Piaget, has had increasing influence on the practices of early childhood professionals. Vygotsky believed that children's mental, language, and social development is supported by and enhanced through social interaction. This view is the opposite of the Piagetian perspective, which sees children as much more solitary developers of their own intelligence and language. For Vygotsky, "Learning awakens a variety of developmental processes that are able to operate only when the child is interacting with people in his environment and in collaboration with his peers. Once these processes are internalized, they become part of the child's independent developmental achievement.[5] Vygotsky further believed that children seek out adults for social interaction, beginning at birth, and that development occurs through these interactions.

ZONE OF PROXIMAL DEVELOPMENT

For early childhood professionals, one of Vygotsky's most important concepts is the **zone of proximal development,** which he defines as follows:

> The area of development into which a child can be led in the course of interaction with a more competent partner, either adult or peer. [It] is not some clear-cut space that exists independently of joint activity itself. Rather, it is the difference between what the child can accomplish independently and what he or she can achieve in conjunction with another, more competent person. The zone is thus created in the course of social interaction.[6]

Zone of proximal development The range of tasks that are too difficult to master alone but that can be learned with guidance and assistance.

Thus, the zone of proximal development (ZPD) represents the range of tasks that children cannot do independently but can do when helped by a more competent person—teacher, adult, or another child. Tasks below the ZPD children can learn independently. Tasks, concepts, ideas, and information above the ZPD children are not yet able to learn, even with help. Figure 5.3 illustrates the ZPD.

In addition, Vygotsky believed that learning and development constitute a dynamic and interactive process:

> Learning is not development; however, properly organized learning results in mental development and sets in motion a variety of developmental processes that would be impossible apart from learning. Thus, learning is a necessary part and universal aspect of the process of developing culturally organized, specifically human, psychological functions.[7]

In other words, learning drives development; the experiences children have influence their development. For this reason it is important for teachers and parents to provide high-quality learning experiences for children.

Observation serves as a basis for assessing children's abilities, achievements, and stage of cognitive development. What do you think this teacher can learn about the children she is observing?

INTERSUBJECTIVITY

Intersubjectivity, another Vygotskian concept, is based on the idea that "individuals come to a task, problem, or conversation with their own subjective ways of making sense of it. If they then discuss their differing viewpoints, shared understanding may be attained. . . . In other words, in the course of communication participants may arrive at some mutually agreed-upon, or intersubjective, understanding."[8] The implication for early childhood education is that social interaction among students and between teachers and students in the classroom promotes learning.[9]

FIGURE 5.3 **The Zone of Proximal Development**

Think about some of the ways you and other more competent persons—such as peers, siblings, and parents—can help children master tasks within this zone.

ZONE OF PROXIMAL DEVELOPMENT

Tasks a child cannot complete, even with help

Tasks or activities that the child can complete independently

SCAFFOLDING

Vygotsky believed that communication or dialogue between teacher and child is very important; it becomes a means of helping children develop new concepts and think their way to higher-level concepts. Assistance in the ZPD is called **scaffolding** and is a major component of teaching; it enables children to complete tasks they could not complete independently. When adults assist toddlers in learning to walk, they are scaffolding them from not being able to walk to being able to walk. Figure 5.4 shows an example of a teacher providing instructional assistance, or scaffolding, for a child during a literacy lesson. The teacher guides and supports the child's language learning by building on what he is already able to do, moving him to a higher level of language use.

Scaffolding is a gradual process of providing different levels of support during the course of an activity. At the beginning of a new task, scaffolding should be concrete and visible; Vygotskian theory maintains that learning begins with the concrete and moves to the abstract. Then, as the task is mastered, scaffolding is slowly withdrawn. Thus, scaffolding builds on children's strengths, enabling the children to grow cognitively and become independent learners. The Voice from the Field "How to Scaffold Children's Learning," on pages 123–124, is a Competency Builder that can help you become a knowledgeable and confident participant with children in their learning. After reading this feature article, look at Figure 5.5, which shows a scaffolding observation form. Try to observe teachers who scaffold their children's learning, and use a form like the one in the figure to identify the specific techniques they use that work.

Scaffolding The process of providing various types of support, guidance, or direction during the course of an activity.

Observe how interaction between the teacher and the child helps to scaffold his learning in the Reggio Emilia segment of the DVD.

ABRAHAM MASLOW AND SELF-ACTUALIZATION THEORY

Abraham Maslow (1890–1970) developed a theory of motivation called *self-actualization*, based on the satisfaction of human needs. Maslow identified self-actualization, or self-

The thought bubble contains the scaffolding script grid (read left to right, starting at lower left), numbered 1-10:

- Would any of you like to ask . . . (10)
- How did you bake the cake? (7)
- I'll bet you mixed the ingredients together. (8)
- I'm not sure I understand. Can you tell me exactly what happened? (9)
- Where were you when this was taken? (4)
- I see you were behind your house. What were you doing? (5)
- What kind of cake was it? (6)
- Can you tell us a story about your photo? (1)
- Can you tell us what is happening here? (2)
- Who is that in the picture? (3)

FIGURE 5.4 A Script for Scaffolding a Child's Language Development

Read the script from left to right, starting at the lower left. Then take a few minutes to write a scaffolding script based on a favorite children's book.

Source: Text reprinted by permission from the University of Texas Center for Reading and Language Arts and the Texas Education Agency, *Implementing the Pre-Kindergarten Guidelines for Language and Early Literacy—Part I: Language Development* (Austin, TX: Texas Education Agency, 2001).

fulfillment, as the highest human need. However, Maslow said that children and adults don't achieve self-actualization until other basic needs such as these are satisfied:

- Life essentials, such as food and water
- Safety and security
- Belonging and love
- Achievement and prestige
- Aesthetic needs

Everyone has these basic needs, regardless of race, gender, sexual orientation, socioeconomic status, or age. Their satisfaction is essential for children to function well and to achieve all they are capable of achieving.

LIFE ESSENTIALS

Just as water is essential for proper brain functions,[10] the same is true of food. We know that when children are hungry, they perform poorly in school. Thus, children who begin school without eating breakfast don't achieve as well as they should and experience difficulty concentrating on their school activities. For this reason many early childhood programs provide children with breakfast, lunch, and snacks throughout the day.[11]

SAFETY AND SECURITY

Safety and security needs also play an important role in children's lives. When children think that their teachers do not like them or children are fearful of what their teachers or others may say and how they may treat them, these children are deprived of a basic need.

In the Head Start segment of the DVD, observe as Romina Pastorelli explains that Head Start programs meet all of children's needs. How is this consistent with Abraham Maslow's hierarchy of needs?

FIGURE 5.5 Scaffolding Observation Form

Teacher: Grade:

Observer: Date:

As you observe, identify specific teacher skills used in the scaffolding of learning. Pay particular attention to how teachers rearrange the classroom environment to support learning, how they interact with particular children, and what they say to children as they support and guide their learning. Record *specific* examples.

Teacher behaviors: What *specific* behaviors are used to scaffold learning?

- Examples
- Clues or suggestions
- Reminders
- Questions
- Encouragement
- Props and materials
- Other

Teacher scripts: What *specific* scripts are used to support children's learning? Scripts can include pictures of the steps in a process, as well as suggestions for what to say or do.

- Example 1
- Example 2

Children's behaviors: What *specific* behaviors indicate that children are learning through scaffolding?

- Private speech
- Asking others for help
- Working cooperatively with others
- Other

Conclusions: What *specific* conclusions can you draw from your obervations?

- What was the most common method used to scaffold?
- How did the teacher individualize scaffolding to meet the needs of particular children?

Recommendations: What *specific* things can you do to develop your skills in scaffolding children's learning?

As a consequence, they do not do well in school, and they become fearful in their relationships with others. The Diversity Tie-In on pages 128–129 promotes antibias education and gives specific ideas to help you establish a fair and equitable classroom environment. In addition, classrooms that have routines and predictability can provide children with a greater sense of security.[12]

LOVE AND BELONGING

Children also need to be loved and feel that they belong within their home and school in order to thrive and develop. All children have a need for affection that teachers can help satisfy through smiles, hugs, eye contact, and nearness. For example, in my work with three- and four-year-old children, many want to sit close to me and want me to put my arms around them. They are seeking love and are looking to their teachers and me to satisfy this basic need.

Companion Website
To complete a Diversity Tie-In activity related to antibias education, go to the Companion Website at **www.prenhall.com/morrison**, select chapter 5, then choose the Diversity Tie-In module.

HOW TO SCAFFOLD CHILDREN'S LEARNING

Vygotsky believed that cognitive development occurs through children's interactions with more competent others—teachers, peers, parents—who act as guides, facilitators, and coaches to provide the support children need to grow intellectually. Much of that support is provided through conversation, examples, and encouragement. When children learn a new skill, they need that competent other to provide a scaffold, or framework, to help them—to show them the overall task, break it into doable parts, and support and reinforce their efforts.

THE SCAFFOLDING PROCESS

Here are the basic steps involved in effective scaffolding. Study them carefully and then look for them in the three examples that follow.

STEP 1 Observe and listen

You can learn a great deal about what kind of assistance is needed.

STEP 2 Approach the child

Ask what he or she wants to do, and ask for permission to help.

STEP 3 Talk about the task

Describe each step in detail—what is being used, what is being done, what is being seen or touched. Ask the child questions about the activity.

STEP 4 Remain engaged in the activity

Adjust your support, allowing the child to take over and do the talking.

STEP 5 Gradually withdraw support

See how the child is able to perform with less help.

STEP 6 Observe the child performing independently

After you have withdrawn all support, check to be sure the child continues to perform the task successfully.

STEP 7 Introduce a new task

Present the child with a slightly more challenging task, and repeat the entire sequence.

EXAMPLE—WORKING A PUZZLE

Celeste has chosen a puzzle to work and dumps the pieces out. She randomly picks up a piece and moves it around inside the frame. She tries another. Look at her face: is she smiling or showing signs of stress? Is she talking to herself?

Perhaps Celeste needs a puzzle with fewer pieces. If so, you can offer her one. But from prior observation, you may know she just needs a little assistance. Try sitting with Celeste and suggesting that you will help. Start by turning all the pieces right side up. As you do this, talk about the pieces you see: this one is red with a little green, this one has a straight edge, this one is curved. Move your finger along the edge.

Ask Celeste whether she can find a straight edge on the side of the puzzle and then whether she can find a piece with a straight edge that matches the color. Ask what hints the pieces give her. Repeat with several other pieces. Then pause to give Celeste the opportunity to try one on her own. As she does, describe what she is doing and the position, shape, and color of the piece. Demonstrate turning a piece in different directions while saying, "I'll try turning it another way." (If you just say, "Turn the piece," she will most likely turn it upside down.)

By listening to you verbalize and by repeating the verbalizing, Celeste is learning to self-talk, that is, to talk herself through a task. By practicing this private speech, children realize they can answer their own questions and regulate their own behavior. When the puzzle is complete, offer Celeste another of similar difficulty and encourage her to try it on her own while you stay nearby to offer assistance as needed, allowing her to take the lead.

EXAMPLE—BAKING

If you are teaching Isaac to bake, you can start by saying, "First we need to get everything out. Let's see what we need." Name the tools you will use as you lay them out.

- Draw pictures on cards to show each ingredient and the spoon(s) or cup(s) you will use to measure.
- Lay the cards out in the proper order, engaging Isaac by asking whether he recognizes each picture, can match it to the ingredient, and can tell you how many cups, teaspoons, etc. are needed.
  - Start with the first card.
  - Ask which cup or spoon should be used and how many times he will fill it.
  - Ask what the ingredient is.
- Encourage Isaac to start the measuring process.
- Observe Isaac. Can he fill the cup with flour? If not, guide his hand. Ask him whether he wants to try mixing, demonstrating if necessary.

The next time Isaac bakes, he will need less scaffolding and will be able to verbalize at least some of the steps for himself.

EXAMPLE—INTERACTING

Three girls are building a house in the block-building area. Joe watches and then asks, "Can I build with you?" In unison the girls respond, "No." When the girls start to move props into the house, Joe picks up a stop sign and places it at the end of the driveway. Arlene sharply reminds him, "We told you no." Joe responds, "But I just wanted to help" and walks away.

This is an opportunity for you to scaffold in a social situation. You must do more than say, "You need to find something else" or "The girls were here first," such as what the teacher in this photo is doing. Implement scaffolding by acknowledging that all the children want to build and helping them figure out how that might work.

Help the girls problem solve strategies for relating to Joe without completely shutting him out. Model appropriate responses: "When the house is finished, you'll be invited to a party" or "Joe, right now there are three of us, and we think it will be too crowded" or "We're building the house. Would you like to plant some trees in the yard?" Have each child draw a picture of the incident that shows an ending in which everyone gains something.

Contributed by Catherine M. Kearn, EdD, early childhood professional and adjunct professor, Carroll College, Waukesha, Wisconsin. Also contributing were Elena Bodrova and Deborah Leong. Photos by Krista Greco/Merrill (p. 123) and Anthony Magnacca/Merrill (above).

ESTEEM

Recognition and approval are self-esteem needs that relate to success and accomplishment. Children who are independent and responsible and who achieve will have high self-esteem. Today, many educators are concerned about how to enhance children's self-esteem; a key way is through increased achievement.

AESTHETICS

Children like and appreciate beauty. They like to be in classrooms and homes that are physically attractive and pleasant. As an early childhood professional, you can help satisfy aesthetic needs by being well dressed and providing a classroom that is pleasant to be in, one that includes plants and flowers, art, and music.[13]

When children have their basic needs met, they can become self-actualized. They can have a sense of satisfaction, be enthusiastic, and be eager to learn. Such children want to engage in activities that will lead to higher levels of learning. Figure 5.6 depicts Maslow's **hierarchy of needs.** As you review and reflect on it, identify ways you can help children meet each of their needs.

Hierarchy of needs
Maslow's theory that basic needs must be satisfied before higher level needs can be satisfied.

ERIK ERIKSON

Erik H. Erikson (1902–1994) developed his *psychosocial development* theory based on the premise that cognitive and social development occur hand in hand and cannot be

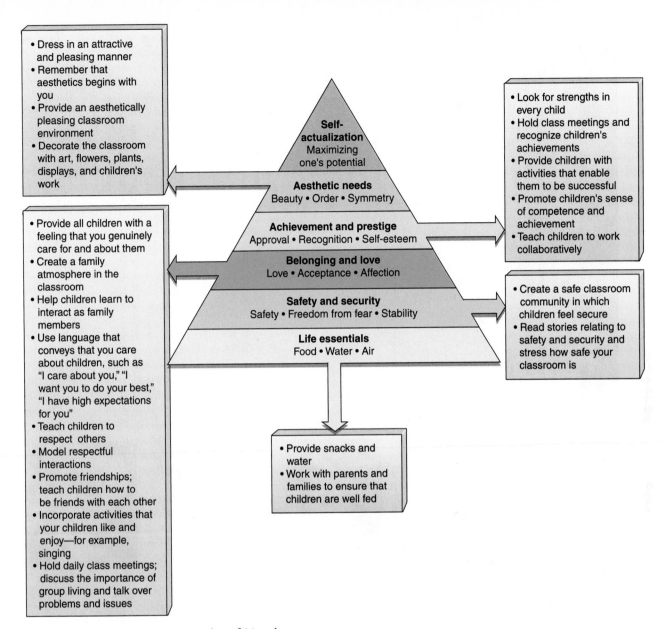

FIGURE 5.6 **Maslow's Hierarchy of Needs**

Source: Maslow's hierarchy of needs data reprinted by permission from Abraham H. Maslow, *Motivation and Personality*, 3rd ed., rev. Robert Frager et al. (New York: Addison Wesley, 1970).

separated. According to Erikson, children's personalities and social skills grow and develop within the context of society and in response to its demands, expectations, values, and social institutions, such as families, schools, and child care programs. Parents and teachers are key parts of these environments and therefore play a powerful role in helping or hindering children in their personality and cognitive development. For example, school-age children must deal with the demands of learning new skills or risk a crisis of *industry*—the ability to do, be involved, be competent, and achieve—versus *inferiority,* marked by failure and feelings of incompetence. Many of the cases of school violence in the news today are connected to children who feel inferior and unappreciated and who lack the social skills to get along with their classmates.[14] Table 5.3 outlines Erikson's stages of psychosocial development and provides suggestions for early childhood educators in each of the four stages.

In the Infant and Toddler segment of the DVD, what are some of the essential ways that high-quality caregivers help promote basic trust in young children? Reflect on the narrator's statement, "You are my child's mother during the day."

125

TABLE 5.3   Erikson's Stages of Psychosocial Development

Stage	Appropriate Age	Characteristics	Role of Early Childhood Educator
I. Basic trust versus mistrust: During this stage, children learn to trust or mistrust their environment and their caregivers. Trust develops when children's needs are met consistently, predictably, and lovingly. Children then view the world as safe and dependable.	Birth to 18 months	Infants learn to trust or mistrust that others will care for their basic needs, including nourishment, warmth, cleanliness, and physical contact.	• Meet children's needs with consistency and continuity. • Identify and take care of basic needs such as diapering and feeding. • Hold babies when feeding them—this promotes attachment and develops trust. • Socialize through smiling, talking and singing. • Be attentive—respond to infants' cues and signals. • Comfort infants when in distress.
II. Autonomy versus shame and doubt: This is the stage when children want to do things for themselves. Given adequate opportunities, they learn independence and competence. Inadequate opportunities and professional overprotection result in self-doubt and poor achievement; children come to feel ashamed of their abilities.	18 months to 3 years	Toddlers learn to be self-sufficient or to doubt their abilities in activities such as toileting, feeding, walking, and talking.	• Encourage children to do what they are capable of doing. • Do not shame children for any behavior. • Provide for safe exploration of classrooms and outdoor areas.
III. Initiative versus guilt: During the preschool years children need opportunities to respond with initiative to activities and tasks, which gives them a sense of purposefulness and accomplishment. Children can feel guilty if they are discouraged or prohibited from initiating activities and are overly restricted in attempts to do things on their own.	3 to 5 years	Children are learning and want to undertake many adultlike activities, sometimes overstepping the limits set by parents and feel guilty.	• Observe children and follow their interests. • Encourage children to engage in many activities. • Provide environments in which children can explore. • Promote language development. • Allow each child the opportunity to succeed.
IV. Industry versus inferiority: In this period, children display an industrious attitude and want to be productive. They want to build things, discover, manipulate objects, and find out how things work. They also want recognition for their productivity, and adult response to their efforts and accomplishments helps develop a sense of self-worth. Feelings of inferiority result when children are criticized or belittled or have few opportunities for productivity.	5 to 8 years	Children actively and busily learn to be competent and productive or feel inferior and unable to do things well.	• Help children win recognition by making things. • Help assure children are successful in literacy skills and learning to read. • Provide support for students who seem confused or discouraged. • Recognize children's achievement and success.

	Visual/spatial—learning visually and organizing ideas spatially. Seeing concepts in action in order to understand them. The ability to "see" things in one's mind in planning to create a product or solve a problem.
	Verbal/linguistic—learning through the spoken and written word. This intelligence was always valued in the traditional classroom and in traditional assessments of intelligence and achievement.
	Mathematical/logical—learning through reasoning and problem solving. Also highly valued in the traditional classroom, where students were asked to adapt to logically sequenced delivery of instruction.
	Bodily/kinesthetic—learning through interaction with one's environment. This intelligence is not the domain of "overly active" learners. It promotes understanding through concrete experience.
	Musical/rhythmic—learning through patterns, rhythms and music. This includes not only auditory learning, but the identification of patterns through all the senses.
	Intrapersonal—learning through feelings, values and attitudes. This is a decidedly affective component of learning through which students place value on what they learn and take ownership for their learning.
	Interpersonal—learning through interaction with others. Not the domain of children who are simply "talkative" or "overly social." This intelligence promotes collaboration and working cooperatively with others.
	Naturalist—learning through classification, categories, and hierarchies. The naturalist intelligence picks up on subtle differences in meaning. It is not simply the study of nature; it can be used in all areas of study.

FIGURE 5.7
Gardner's Eight Intelligences

Note: Gardner (*Intelligence Reframed: Multiple Intelligences for the 21st Century* [New York: Basic Books, 1999]) suggests that there may also be a ninth, existential intelligence. However, he acknowledges that evidence for it is weaker than for the other eight intelligences, hence its exclusion from this figure.

Source: Reprinted by permission from Walter McKenzie, *Multiple Intelligences Overview*, http://surfaquarium.com/MI/overview.htm.

HOWARD GARDNER

Howard Gardner (b. 1943) has played an important role in helping educators rethink the concepts of intelligence. Gardner's philosophy of *multiple intelligences* suggests that people can be smart in many ways. Gardner has identified eight intelligences: visual/spatial, verbal/linguistic, mathematical/logical, bodily/kinesthetic, musical/rhythmic, intrapersonal, interpersonal, and naturalistic. His view of intelligence and its multiple components will undoubtedly continue to influence educational thought and practice. Review Figure 5.7 to learn more about these eight intelligences and their implications for teaching and learning. Then read the Program in Action "New City School" on page 131 to experience how Gardner's theory of multiple intelligences can be put into practice.

Companion Website
To complete a Program in Action activity related to multiple intelligences, go to the Companion Website at **www.prenhall.com/morrison**, select chapter 5, then choose the Program in Action module.

INTEGRATING MULTICULTURAL AND ANTIBIAS EDUCATION INTO EARLY CHILDHOOD PROGRAMS

While on a field trip, four-year-old Ruth observes a man wearing a turban. She points and says, "Why is that man wearing a funny hat?"

While playing with blocks, Joshua says to five-year-old Lior, "Why do you talk so funny?" Lior doesn't respond and says little for the rest of the day.

Children look to adults to model appropriate behavior. If adults do not interrupt acts of unfairness or if such acts are only interrupted occasionally, children have no sense of urgency to counter injustice, nor do they have models of effective methods to begin doing so themselves. Children need the adults in their lives to take responsibility to prevent and counter the damage caused by sexism, heterosexism, racism, ableism, ageism, anti-Semitism and classism by providing fair and accurate messages about people from all cultural groups and by actively challenging the negative messages they witness.

In each of the scenarios cited here, a teacher could have intervened to model appropriate behavior. For example, a teacher could have told Ruth that the funny hat was called a turban and could have explained why the man was wearing it. Similarly, Joshua's teacher could have explained that Lior is from a different country and is just learning English. Further, the teacher could emphasize that calling attention to Lior's difficulties in a negative way is apt to hurt Lior's feelings.

A MODEL PROGRAM

Educators who attend anti-bias workshops provided by the Anti-Defamation League (ADL) come away with the skills and tools to address scenarios such as the ones here, as well as others relating to gender issues, diversity of family composition, physical/mental abilities and economic status. The workshops help participants explore their own biases and the ways they may affect the children in their care. Through interactive, facilitator-led activities, participants come to recognize that they may unintentionally harbor stereotypes about the aptitudes or behavior of children. Although unsettling, that recognition helps them understand that they need to unlearn their own prejudices in order to teach inclusively and fairly.

Intertwining multicultural and antibias lessons into the existing curriculum, instead of teaching isolated multicultural units, makes an antibias approach part of everyday thinking. To assist educators in this integration and to help them ensure that their program environment reflects the diversity of the world and acts as a mirror in which children see themselves reflected, ADL provides all workshop participants with print resources created in collaboration with Sesame Workshop.

Because ADL recognizes that family members play a crucial role in shaping young children's thinking about the world around them, ADL also offers family work-

URIE BRONFENBRENNER AND ECOLOGICAL THEORY

Urie Bronfenbrenner's (b. 1917, d. 2005) ecological theory looks at children's development within the context of the systems of relationships that form their environment. There are five interrelating environmental systems—the microsystem, the mesosystem, the exosystem, the macrosystem, and the chronosystem. Figure 5.8 shows a model of these environmental systems and the ways each influences development. Each system influences and is influenced by the other.

Microsystem The environmental settings in which children spend a lot of their time (e.g., children in child care spend about thirty-three hours a week there).

The **microsystem** encompasses the environments of parents, family, peers, child care, schools, neighborhood, religious groups, parks, and so forth. The child acts on and influences each of these and is influenced by them. For example, four-year-old April might have a physical disability that her child care program accommodates by making the classroom more accessible. Five-year-old Mack's aggressive behavior might prompt his teacher to initiate a program of bibliotherapy.

shops and provides participants with materials that include *Bias-Free Foundations: Early Childhood Activities for Families*. This book contains simple activities to use with children to reinforce the concepts of fairness and acceptance of differences.

FIVE DAILY PRACTICES

The workshops and materials encourage adults to create bias-free environments by incorporating the following practices into their daily lives:

- *Self-exploration.* Make self-assessment a natural activity, examining your own cultural biases and assumptions. For example, a teacher who observes that a student will not make eye contact might realize that the child's cultural background encourages that behavior and thus avoid pressuring the child to make eye contact.
- *Integration.* Integrate culturally diverse information and perspectives throughout the day, instead of relegating equity issues to special or multicultural time. During story time, for example, select books that serve both as a mirror in which children can see themselves reflected and also as a window through which children can explore the world around them.
- *Patience.* Understand that developing antibias behavior is like planting seeds that can one day produce a more just society. Allow time for the process to work.
- *Intervention.* Respond to acts of bias even if they are unintentional, sending the message that discriminatory behavior is hurtful and should not be tolerated or ignored. Silence in the face of injustice conveys the impression that adults condone the behavior or consider it unworthy of attention. Appropriate and timely intervention establishes an environment in which all children feel valued and respected. For instance, a teacher who notices a group of children excluding Susan from their game might say, "I heard you say that Susan couldn't play with you because she is white." The teacher should ask the children for an explanation and should then help them see that their behavior is not acceptable because it hurts Susan's feelings.
- *Creating connections.* Involve parents, other family members and other members of the community in the learning process; they provide the context in which children learn. Connect the home and community with each other and with the larger world. Encourage cultural sharing by offering opportunities for family members to share information about their cultures, such as teaching their child a song or game they enjoyed when they were young.

PROGRAMMATIC SUCCESS

Positive evaluation findings indicate an increase in these behaviors among workshop participants:

- Talking with children about bias and discrimination
- Encouraging children to reflect on their own biases and discriminatory behavior
- Modeling techniques for children to use when they experience bias or discrimination
- Intervening when teasing, name calling, and bias-related incidents occur in the classroom, among family members and among colleagues

For more information, please visit www.adl.org/education/miller.

Contributed by Linda A. Santora, MA, Director, Early Childhood Education Programs, Anti-Defamation League.

The **mesosystem** includes linkages or interactions between microsystems. Interactions and influences there relate to all of the environmental influences in the microsystem. For example, the family's support of or lack of attention to literacy will influence the child's school performance. Likewise, school support for family literacy will influence the extent to which families value literacy.

Mesosystem Links or interactions between microsystems.

The **exosystem** is the environmental system that encompasses those events with which children do not have direct interaction but which nonetheless influence them. For example, when school boards enact a policy that ends social promotion, this action can and will influence children's development. And when a parent's workplace mandates increased work time (e.g., a ten-hour workday), this may decrease parent-child involvement, which influences development.

Exosystems Environments or settings in which children do not play an active role but which nonetheless influence their development.

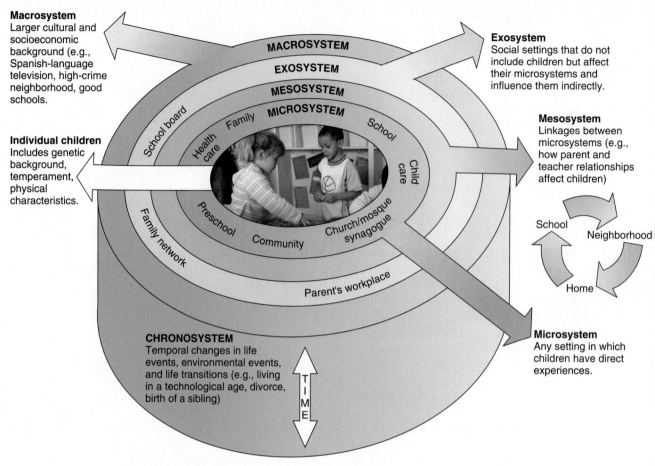

Macrosystem
Larger cultural and socioeconomic background (e.g., Spanish-language television, high-crime neighborhood, good schools.

Individual children
Includes genetic background, temperament, physical characteristics.

MACROSYSTEM
EXOSYSTEM
MESOSYSTEM
MICROSYSTEM

School board · Family
Health care
School
Child care
Family network · Preschool · Community · Church/mosque synagogue
Parent's workplace

Exosystem
Social settings that do not include children but affect their microsystems and influence them indirectly.

Mesosystem
Linkages between microsystems (e.g., how parent and teacher relationships affect children)

School · Neighborhood · Home

Microsystem
Any setting in which children have direct experiences.

CHRONOSYSTEM
Temporal changes in life events, environmental events, and life transitions (e.g., living in a technological age, divorce, birth of a sibling)

TIME

FIGURE 5.8 **Ecological Influences on Development**

Macrosystem The broader culture in which children live (e.g., democracy, individual freedom, and religious freedom).

Chronosystem The environmental contexts and events that influence children over their lifetimes, such as living in a technological age.

The **macrosystem** includes the culture, customs, and values of society in general. For example, contemporary societal violence and media violence influence children's development. Many children are becoming more violent, and many children are fearful of and threatened by violence.

The **chronosystem** includes environmental influences over time and the ways they impact development and behavior. For example, today's children are technologically adept and are comfortable using technology for education and entertainment. In addition, we have already referred to how the large-scale entry of mothers into the workforce has changed family life.

Clearly, there are many influences on children's development. Currently there is a lot of interest in how these influences shape children's lives and what parents and educators can do to enhance positive influences and minimize or eliminate negative environmental influences as well as negative social interactions.

THEORIES RECONSIDERED

Like theories in all other areas of knowledge and understanding, educational theories must stand the tests of time, criticism, and review. They are subject to the scrutiny, testing, and evaluation of professionals and are subsequently accepted, rejected, modified, and refined.

Program in Action

NEW CITY SCHOOL

You don't have to be in early childhood education very long to hear a teacher say, "That boy is just soooo active." Indeed, this statement often has a well-what-can-you-do tone to it. At New City School, an independent school in St. Louis with students three years old through sixth grade, both the tone and the words are different, even though we certainly have lots of active boys. Our statement, "That's a very b-k [bodily-kinesthetic] kid," reflects our focus on Howard Gardner's multiple intelligences. We develop curriculum and look at children (and adults!) from the belief that there are at least eight intelligences: bodily-kinesthetic, spatial, logical-mathematical, musical, linguistic; naturalistic, intrapersonal, and interpersonal. We believe children (and adults!) have strengths in all of these areas, and we work to support children's growth in using and understanding their particular strengths and those of others.

When New City teachers and administrators started working with Howard Gardner's multiple intelligences model about fourteen years ago, we quickly agreed that our preschool program had the fewest changes to make in order to reflect the multiple intelligences. Indeed, preschool programs in general, with their use of centers and choice time, have traditionally given children many opportunities to explore and create. Puzzle areas and art centers offer spatial choices; pretending provides many interpersonal options; games and manipulatives offer logical-mathematical, spatial, and interpersonal choices—the list is long.

A FRAMEWORK

How then has our preschool program changed? Two changes come quickly to mind. First, we, now have a framework with which to plan centers and assessment. Our preschool teachers use the multiple intelligences framework in planning centers and activities, checking themselves to make sure that children have opportunities to use and develop their various intelligences. Remember that b-k kid we talked about in the beginning? Rather than a framework that contains him with rules and time-outs, New City teachers plan centers making sure that there are bodily-kinesthetic activities available during choice time, not just at recess. And teachers now use adjacent halls and even classroom space for activities such as hopscotch, scooter boards, basketball, jump ropes, and the like.

Once children do activities, teachers provide parents and colleagues with assessment information using the multiple intelligence framework. Parents receive information about their children through multiple-page progress reports and portfolio nights. Here again, the multiple intelligences focus is used in showing the children's work and sharing their progress. So the parents of that child with strong bodily-kinesthetic intelligence learn that their child often chooses b-k related activities and that teachers use that bodily-kinesthetic strength in helping him learn other things. He might practice counting while jumping rope or shooting baskets or learn letters by throwing bean bags at alphabet squares.

PERSONAL EMPHASIS

The second change is that we put a strong emphasis on the personal intelligences: intrapersonal, knowing yourself, and interpersonal, knowing how to work and play with others. Believing strongly that these talents can be developed just as a musical or linguistic talent, New City teachers have developed activities and assessment techniques to support growth in the personal intelligences. In our fours/fives classrooms, for example, teachers regularly schedule Buddy Days during choice time. On a Buddy Day, children are paired up by the teachers and must then work together to choose activities for the morning. Teachers model, problem solve, comfort, and support children as they learn to express their interests and accept the interests of their partners.

Over the school year, these children learn to listen, negotiate, delay gratification, and solve problems with a variety of peers. Parents recognize the importance we place on the personals when they read our progress reports; the first page is devoted entirely to the personal intelligences, with assessment topics ranging from teamwork and appreciation of diversity to motivation and problem solving.

The multiple intelligences framework has allowed us to further develop an early childhood program in which all of the intelligences of the children are appreciated.

Contributed by Barbara James Thomson, New City School, 5209 Waterman Ave., St. Louis, Missouri.

Researchers have conducted thousands of studies to test the validity of the theories we have discussed. You will need to put those theories into perspective as you prepare to apply them to your teaching.

PROS AND CONS OF PIAGET'S THEORY

A powerful advantage of Piaget's theory is that it is an elegant explanation of the stages of cognitive development. It enables us to clearly track cognitive development from birth to adolescence; for each stage, Piaget describes what children are and are not able to do. For over half a century, Piaget's theory has provided professionals and researchers with a foundation on which to develop curricula and programs. It is the most widely used theory that explains children's cognitive development.

On the other hand, there are a number of limitations you must consider in applying Piaget's theory. First, Piaget seems to have underestimated the ages at which children can perform certain mental operations. In fact, it appears that he underestimated the intellectual abilities of all children, but particularly younger children. For example, children in the preoperational stage can perform tasks he assigned to the concrete operations stage. And recent advances in infant research suggest that infants have more cognitive tools than Piaget and others thought (more about this in the last section of the chapter).

Second, Piaget's unidimensional view of intelligence, consisting primarily of logico-mathematical knowledge and skills, tends to de-emphasize other views. Professionals now recognize other definitions of intelligence and the ways it develops, such as Howard Gardner's multiple intelligences. You must consider varying definitions of *intelligence* when designing curricula and activities for young children.

Third, Piaget's theory emphasizes that individual children are responsible for developing their own intelligence; he likened children to "little scientists," engaged in a solitary process of intellectual development. Thus, Piaget's approach to cognitive development tends to downplay the role of social interactions and the contributions of others to this process.

VYGOTSKY IN CONTEXT

Vygotsky believed that other people play a major role in children's cognitive development and that children are not alone in their development of mental schemes. For Vygotsky, children develop knowledge, attitudes, and ideas through interactions with more capable others—parents, teachers, and peers. The embracing of Vygotsky's ideas by early childhood professionals helps explain the popularity of many social-based learning processes, such as cooperative learning, multiage grouping, child-teacher collaboration, and peer-assisted teaching.

One characteristic of language and cognitive development that we discussed earlier is that young children talk to themselves. Vygotsky believed that children's *private speech* plays an important role in their cognitive development. He thought that children communicate with themselves to guide their behavior and thinking and that as children develop, their audible private speech becomes silent inner speech that continues to serve the important functions of helping to solve problems and guide behavior. By being attentive to children's private speech, teachers can ask questions that will help children think and solve problems. Additionally, learning environments that permit children to be verbally active while solving problems support their cognitive development.

OTHER PERSPECTIVES

Erikson's theory of psychosocial development is also popular with teachers and schools that work with children. It provides a helpful way to look at children's social development and to consider how children's identity needs change over developmental time. In addition, when teachers and parents endeavor to meet children's psychosocial needs, the children's achievement is encouraged and supported.

Bronfenbrenner's ecological theory is popular because it provides teachers a systematic way to examine how they and others influence children's development and learning. In addition, Bronfenbrenner's theory encourages professionals and others to consider children's lives in more than one setting or environment. What happens in classrooms affects children at home and vice versa. Indeed, it is good to remember that your actions as an early childhood professional will affect children in their many different environments.

NEW DIRECTIONS IN COGNITIVE DEVELOPMENT

As with most theories, new research and discoveries lead to modification and new directions. Since Piaget did his groundbreaking work, several advances have occurred that influence how we view children's cognitive development. First are the ongoing discoveries about genetic influences. For example, the genetic influences on verbal development were not as clearly established in Piaget's time as they are today. This process is discussed in more detail in chapter 9, when infant language development is considered.

Second, research in infant development clearly shows that infants possess a great many more cognitive skills than was previously thought and that they are actively involved in learning. For example, shortly after birth, neonates can discriminate and imitate happy, sad, and surprised facial expressions, indicating an innate ability to compare the sensory information of a visually perceived expression with the movements involved in matching that expression. The developmental significance of such ability may be that it is the starting point of infant psychological development.[15]

Companion Website

For additional Internet resources or to complete an online activity for this chapter, go to the Companion Website at **www.prenhall.com/morrison**, select chapter 5, then choose the Linking to Learning or Making Connections module.

LINKING TO LEARNING

Building an Understanding of Constructivism
http://www.sedl.org/scimath/compass/v01n03/2.html

Describes the basic tenets of constructivism and gives a list of resources.

Constructivism and the Five Es
http://www.miamisci.org/ph/lpintro5e.html

A description of constructivism and the five Es—engage, explore, explain, elaborate, and evaluate.

High/Scope Educational Research Foundation
http://www.highscope.org

An independent, nonprofit research, development, training, and public advocacy organization; attempts to improve the life chances of children and youth by promoting high-quality educational programs.

Jean Piaget and Genetic Epistemology
http://www.gwu.edu/~tip/piaget.html

Detailed description of Piaget's theories concerning genetic epistemology; contains a QuickTime video clip of Piaget discussing this topic.

Multidisciplinary/Cognitive Skills

http://www.ed.gov/pubs/EPTW/eptw10

> *Contains a complete list of projects on cognitive skill development approved by the U.S. Department of Education.*

Resources for the Constructivist Educator

www.odu.edu/educ/act

> *Website for the Association for Constructivist Teaching; provides a rich, problem-solving arena that encourages the learner's investigation, invention, and inference.*

ACTIVITIES FOR FURTHER ENRICHMENT

ETHICAL DILEMMA: "LET'S KEEP SOME FOR US—WHO WILL EVER KNOW?"

You are the director of community relations for the local affiliate of the NAEYC. In the wake of Hurricane Katrina, you have been asked to coordinate the collection of books and other school supplies with the specific purpose of helping flood-ravaged child care centers in Mississippi re-open. Your request for help has been very successful, and your committee has collected more supplies than you anticipated. One of your committee members suggests that you and she divert some of the books to your classroom libraries. Her rationale is that your classroom libraries are outdated and the school board did not include monies for new library books in the latest school budget. "This is our chance to get the books our children desperately need."

What do you do? Do you go along with her plan deceiving those who trusted you to send their donated supplies to flooded centers, so that you can take care of your children's needs, too, or do you send all the books to child care programs in Mississippi?

APPLICATIONS

1. Now is a good time to review the philosophy you developed after reading chapter 1. How do your beliefs fit in with the theories presented in this chapter?
2. Compare Piaget's theory with another theory, such as Montessori's. How are they similar and different?
3. List five concepts of Piaget's theory that you consider most significant for teaching and rearing young children. Explain how Piaget's beliefs and methods may have influenced your philosophy of teaching.
4. Explain how you could apply some portion of each of the theories presented in this chapter to your work with young children.

FIELD EXPERIENCES

1. Constructivists believe that one of the main functions of teachers is to create a climate for learning. Interview early childhood teachers and ask them what elements or features of classrooms are important in supporting learning. From this teacher data, develop a list of characteristics that you will use in your classroom. Place this list in your portfolio or learning file.
2. In a constructivist classroom, children's autonomy and initiative are accepted. Observe classrooms and give examples of how the teachers encourage or discourage initiative and autonomy in their classrooms. Based on your observations, develop plans for how you will support these two important aspects of learning.
3. Visit early childhood classrooms, and observe to determine which theory or theories are being implemented.
4. Observe an early childhood classroom, and identify children demonstrating as many of Gardner's nine intelligences as you can. Was the teacher responding to the children's different intelligences? What strategies did the teacher use to teach children according to their intelligences?

RESEARCH

1. Observe three children—one six months old, one two years old, and one four years old. Note in each child's activities what you consider typical behavior for that age. Can you find examples of behaviors that correspond to Piaget's stages?
2. Observe a child between birth and eighteen months. Can you cite any concrete evidence, such as specific actions or incidents, to indicate how the child is developing schemes of the world through sensorimotor actions?
3. Use the web sites in the Linking to Learning section to find out more information about each of the theories we discussed.
4. Research additional information on the theories of Vygotsky, Erikson, and Bronfenbrenner. Supplement the pros and cons of each theory that were presented in this chapter.

READINGS FOR FURTHER ENRICHMENT

Branscombe, N. Amanda. *Early Childhood Curriculum: A Constructivist Perspective.* Boston: Houghton Mifflin, 2003.

Provides a wealth of practical ideas for integrating constructivist curriculum into preschool and early elementary classrooms.

Hirsh, R. *Early Childhood Curriculum: Incorporating Multiple Intelligences, Developmentally Appropriate Practice, and Play.* Boston: Pearson, 2004.

Outlines the essential aspects of the early childhood curriculum: intelligence and potential, developmentally appropriate practice, healthy relationships, play, values, assessment, and planning.

Martin, D. *Elementary Science Methods: A Constructivist Approach.* Belmont, CA: Wadsworth, 2006.

Guides students in learning by doing. Geared to teachers of preschool through sixth grade students; represents the cutting edge of elementary science teaching with up-to-date investigations into contemporary topics.

Mooney, C. *Theories of Childhood: An Introduction to Dewey, Montessori, Erikson, Piaget & Vygotsky.* St. Paul, MN: Redleaf Press, 2000.

Examines the theoretical foundation of early childhood care. Looks at the ideas of John Dewey, Maria Montessori, Erik Erikson, Jean Piaget, and Lev Vygotsky in relation to early childhood programs and education.

ENDNOTES

1. David M. Brodzinsky, Irving E. Sigel, and Roberta M. Golinkoff, "New Dimensions in Piagetian Theory and Research: An Integrative Perspective," in *New Directions in Piagetian Theory and Practice,* ed. Irving E. Sigel, David M. Brodzinsky, and Roberta M. Golinkoff (Hillsdale, NJ: Erlbaum, 1981), 5.

2. Mary Ann Spencer Pulaski, *Understanding Piaget* (New York: Harper and Row, 1980), 9.

3. P. G. Richmond, *An Introduction to Piaget* (New York: Basic Books, 1970), 68.

4. Ibid.

5. L. S. Vygotsky, *Mind in Society* (Cambridge, MA: Harvard University Press, 1978), 244.

6. Jonathan R. H. Tudge, "Processes and Consequences of Peer Collaboration: A Vygotskian Analysis," *Child Development* 63 (1992): 1365.

7. Ibid.

8. Vygotsky, *Mind in Society,* 90.

9. Tudge, "Processes and Consequences," 1365.

10. K. Carroll, "The Brain and Cooperative Learning—Looking Forward from Spencer Kagan's Workshop," Mid-Atlantic Association for Cooperation in Education, http://www.geocities.com/~maacie/article23.html.

11. M. Hegarty, "Supporting School Success: Fueled to Succeed," http://www.scholastic.com/familymatters/parentguides/backtoschool/fueledtosucceed.html.

12. NAEYC, *Principles of Child Development and Learning That Inform Developmentally Appropriate Practice,* http://www.naeyc.org/about/positions/dap3.asp.

13. Patricia Tarr, "Consider the Walls," *Young Children, Beyond the Journal* (May 2004), http://www.journal.naeyc.org/btj/200405/walls.asp.

14. G. Boeree, "Erik Erikson," http://www.ship.edu/~cgboeree/erikson.html.

15. A. Meltzoff and K. M. Moore, "Resolving the Debate About Early Imitation," *Reader in Developmental Psychology* (1999): 151–155.

PART **3**

Programs and Services for Children and Families

Chapter 6
EARLY CHILDHOOD PROGRAMS
Applying Theories to Practice

Chapter 7
CHILD CARE
*Meeting the Needs of Children,
Parents, and Families*

Chapter 8
THE FEDERAL GOVERNMENT
Supporting Children's Success

Early Childhood Programs

APPLYING THEORIES TO PRACTICE

If education is always to be conceived along the same antiquated lines of a mere transmission of knowledge, there is little to be hoped from it. . . . For what is the use of transmitting knowledge if the individual's total development lags behind?
And so we discovered that education is not something which the teacher does, but that it is a natural process which develops spontaneously in the human being.

MARIA MONTESSORI

CHAPTER 6

*P*arents want their children to attend high-quality programs that will provide them with a good start in life. They want to know that their children are being well cared for and educated. Parents want their children to get along with others, be happy, and learn. How to best meet these legitimate parental expectations is one of the ongoing challenges of early childhood professionals.[1]

THE GROWING DEMAND FOR QUALITY EARLY CHILDHOOD PROGRAMS

The National Association for the Education of Young Children (NAEYC), the nation's largest organization of early childhood educators, accredits 10,845 early childhood programs serving approximately 915,000 children.[2] These programs are only a fraction of the total number of early childhood programs in the United States. Think for a minute about what goes on in these and other programs from day to day. For some children teachers and staff implement well-thought-out and articulated programs that provide for children's growth and development across all the developmental domains—cognitve, linguistic, emotional, social, and physical. In other programs, children are not so fortunate. Their days are filled with aimless activities that fail to meet their academic and developmental needs.

With the national spotlight on the importance of the early years, the public is demanding more from early childhood professionals and their programs. On the one hand, the public is willing to invest more heavily in early childhood programs, but on the other hand, it is demanding that the early childhood profession and individual programs respond by providing meaningful programs.[3] The public demands these things from early childhood professionals:

- *Programs that will help ensure children's early academic and school success.*
  The public believes that too many children are being left out and left behind.[4]
- *The inclusion of early literacy and reading readiness activities in programs and curricula that will enable children to read on grade level in grades one, two, and three.*
  Literacy is the key to much of school and life success, and school success begins in preschool and before.[5]
- *Environments that will help children develop the social and behavioral skills necessary to help them lead civilized and nonviolent lives.*
  In the wake of daily news headlines about shootings and assaults by younger and younger children, the public wants early childhood programs to assume an ever-growing responsibility for helping get children off to a nonviolent start in life.[6]

Focus Questions

Why is there a need for high-quality early childhood education programs?

What are the basic features of high-quality early childhood education programs?

What are the unique characteristics and strengths of early childhood education programs?

How can you apply features of early childhood programs to your professional practice?

Companion Website

To check your understanding of this chapter, go to the Companion Website at **www.prenhall.com/ morrison**, select chapter 6, then answer Multiple Choice and Essay Questions and receive feedback.

Model early childhood program An exemplary approach to early childhood education that serves as a guide to best practices.

As a result of these public demands, there is a growing and critical need for programs that teachers and others can adopt and use. In this chapter we examine and discuss some of the more notable programs for use in early childhood settings. As you read about and reflect on each of these, think about their strengths and weaknesses and the ways each tries to best meet the needs of children and families. Pause for a minute and review Table 6.1, which outlines the **model early childhood programs** discussed in this chapter.

Let's now look at four highly regarded and widely adopted model programs: Montessori, High/Scope, Reggio Emilia, and Waldorf. There is a good probability that you will be associated in some way as a teacher, parent, or advisory board member with one of these programs. In any event, you will want to be informed about their main features and operating principles.

PRINCIPLES OF THE MONTESSORI METHOD

Review again the introductory material on Maria Montessori in chapter 4. The Montessori method has been and is very popular around the world with early childhood professionals and parents. The Montessori approach is designed to support the natural development of children in a well-prepared environment.

Montessori method A system of early childhood education founded on the ideas and practices of Maria Montessori.

Five basic principles fairly and accurately represent how Montessori educators implement the Montessori method in many kinds of programs across the United States. Figure 6.1 illustrates these five basic principles of the **Montessori method**.

FIGURE 6.1 Basic Montessori Principles

These basic principles are the foundation of the Montessori method. Taken as a whole, they constitute a powerful model for helping all children learn to their fullest.

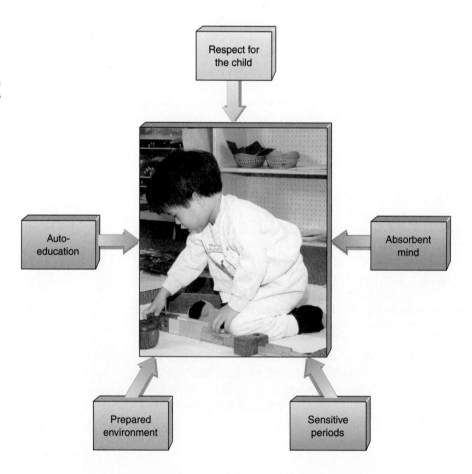

TABLE 6.1 Comparing Models of Early Childhood Education

Program	Main Features	Teacher's Role
Montessori 	• Theoretical basis is the philosophy and beliefs of Maria Montessori. • Prepared environment supports, invites, and enables learning. • Children educate themselves—self-directed learning. • Sensory materials invite and promote learning. • Set curriculum regarding what children should learn—Montessorians try to stay as close to Montessori's ideas as possible. • Children are grouped in multiage environments. • Children learn by manipulating materials and working with others. • Learning takes place through the senses.	• Follows the child's interests and needs • Prepares an environment that is educationally interesting and safe* • Directs unobtrusively as children individually or in small groups engage in self-directed activity* • Observes, analyzes, and provides materials and activities appropriate for the child's sensitive periods of learning* • Maintains regular communications with the parent
High/Scope 	• Theory is based on Piaget, constructivism, Dewey, and Vygotsky. • Plan-do-review is the teaching-learning cycle. • Emergent curriculum is one not planned in advance. • Children help determine curriculum. • Key experiences guide the curriculum in promoting children's active learning.	• Plans activities based on children's interests • Facilitates learning through encouragement* • Engages in positive adult-child interaction strategies*
Reggio Emilia 	• Theory is based on Piaget, constructivism, Vygotsky, and Dewey. • Emergent curriculum is one not planned in advance. • Curriculum is based on children's interests and experiences. • Curriculum is project oriented. • Hundred languages of children—symbolic representation of work and learning. • Learning is active. • Atelierista—a special teacher is trained in the arts. • Atelier—an art/design studio is used by children and teachers.	• Works collaboratively with other teachers • Organizes environments rich in possibilities and provocations* • Acts as recorder for the children, helping them trace and revisit their words and actions*
Waldorf 	• Theoretical basis is the philosophy and beliefs of Rudolf Steiner. • The whole child—head, heart, and hands—is educated. • The arts are integrated into all curriculum areas. • Study of myths, lores, and fairy tales promotes the imagination and multiculturalism. • Main-lesson teacher stays with the same class from childhood to adolescence. • Learning is by doing—making and doing. • Learning is noncompetitive. • The developmental phases of each child are followed.	• Acts as a role model exhibiting the values of the Waldorf school • Provides an intimate classroom atmosphere full of themes about caring for the community and for the natural and living world* • Encourages children's natural sense of wonder, belief in goodness, and love of beauty* • Creates a love of learning in each child

*Information from C. Edwards, "Three Approaches from Europe: Waldorf, Montessori, and Reggio Emilia," *Early Childhood Research & Practice* 4, no.1 (2002). Available online at http://ecrp.uiuc.edu/v4nl/edwards.html.

RESPECT FOR THE CHILD

Respect for the child is the cornerstone on which all other Montessori principles rest. As Montessori said:

> As a rule, however, we do not respect children. We try to force them to follow us without regard to their special needs. We are overbearing with them, and above all, rude; and then we expect them to be submissive and well-behaved, knowing all the time how strong is their instinct of imitation and how touching their faith in and admiration of us. They will imitate us in any case. Let us treat them, therefore, with all the kindness which we would wish to help to develop in them.[7]

Teachers show respect for children when they help them do things and learn for themselves. When children have choices, they are able to develop the skills and abilities necessary for effective learning autonomy, and positive self-esteem. (The theme of respect for children resurfaces in our discussion of guiding behavior in chapter 14.)

THE ABSORBENT MIND

Montessori believed that children educate themselves: "It may be said that we acquire knowledge by using our minds; but the child absorbs knowledge directly into his psychic life. Simply by continuing to live, the child learns to speak his native tongue."[8] This is the concept of the **absorbent mind**.

Absorbent mind The idea that the minds of young children are receptive to and capable of learning. The child learns unconsciously by taking in information from the environment.

Montessori wanted us to understand that children can't help learning. Simply by living, children learn from their environment. Children are born to learn, and they are remarkable learning systems. Children learn because they are thinking beings. But what they learn depends greatly on their teachers, experiences, and environments.

Early childhood teachers are re-emphasizing the idea that children are born learning and with constant readiness and ability to learn. We will discuss these concepts further in chapter 9.

SENSITIVE PERIODS

Sensitive period (Montessori) A relatively brief time during which learning is most likely to occur. Also called a critical period.

Montessori believed there are **sensitive periods** when children are more susceptible to certain behaviors and can learn specific skills more easily:

> A sensitive period refers to a special sensibility which a creature acquires in its infantile state, while it is still in a process of evolution. It is a transient disposition and limited to the acquisition of a particular trait. Once this trait or characteristic has been acquired, the special sensibility disappears. . . .[9]

Although all children experience the same sensitive periods (e.g., a sensitive period for writing), the sequence and timing vary for each child. One role of the teacher is to use observation to detect times of sensitivity and provide the setting for optimum fulfillment. Refer to chapter 3 to review guidelines for observing children.

In the Montessori segment of the DVD, observe the prepared environment, the way it is arranged, and the way it helps children take control of their own learning.

THE PREPARED ENVIRONMENT

Prepared environment A classroom or other space that is arranged and organized to support learning in general and/or special knowledge and skills.

Montessori believed that children learn best in a **prepared environment**, a place in which children can *do things for themselves*. The prepared environment makes learning materials and experiences available to children in an orderly format. Classrooms Montessori described are really what educators advocate when they talk about child-centered education and active learning. Freedom is the essential characteristic of the prepared environment. Since children within the environment are free to explore materials of their own choosing, they absorb what they find there.

AUTOEDUCATION

Montessori named the concept that children are capable of educating themselves **autoeducation** (also known as self-education). Children who are actively involved in a prepared environment and who exercise freedom of choice literally educate themselves. Montessori teachers prepare classrooms so that children educate themselves.

THE TEACHER'S ROLE

Montessori believed that "it is necessary for the teacher to guide the child without letting him feel her presence too much, so that she may be always ready to supply the desired help, but may never be the obstacle between the child and his experience."[10]

The Montessori teacher demonstrates key behaviors to implement this child-centered approach:

- *Make children the center of learning.* As Montessori said, "The teacher's task is not to talk, but to prepare and arrange a series of motives for cultural activity in a special environment made for the child."[11]
- *Encourage children to learn* by providing freedom for them in the prepared environment.
- *Observe children* so as to prepare the best possible environment, recognizing sensitive periods and diverting inappropriate behavior to meaningful tasks.
- *Prepare the learning environment* by ensuring that learning materials are provided in an orderly format and that the materials provide for appropriate experiences for all the children.
- *Respect each child* and model ongoing respect for all children and their work.
- *Introduce learning materials,* demonstrate learning materials, and support children's learning. The teacher introduces learning materials after observing each child.

The Montessori prepared environment makes materials and experiences available for children to explore for themselves. Why is it important to prepare such an organized environment?

Autoeducation The idea that children teach themselves through appropriate materials and activities.

THE MONTESSORI METHOD IN ACTION

In a prepared environment, materials and activities provide for three basic areas of child involvement:

1. Practical life or motor education
2. Sensory materials for training the senses
3. Academic materials for teaching writing, reading, and mathematics

All these activities are taught according to a prescribed procedure.

Companion Website For more information about the Montessori curriculum model, go to the Companion Website at **www.prenhall.com/ morrison,** select chapter 6, then choose the Linking to Learning module.

PRACTICAL LIFE

The prepared environment supports basic, **practical life** activities, such as walking from place to place in an orderly manner, carrying objects such as trays and chairs, greeting a visitor, and learning self-care skills. For example, *dressing frames* are designed to perfect the motor skills involved in buttoning, zipping, lacing, buckling, and tying. The philosophy for activities such as these is to make children independent and develop concentration.

Practical life Montessori activities that teach skills related to everyday living.

Practical life activities are taught through four different types of exercise:

1. *Care of the person*—activities such as using dressing frames, polishing shoes, and washing hands
2. *Care of the environment*—for example, dusting, polishing a table, and raking leaves
3. *Social relations*—lessons in grace and courtesy
4. *Analysis and control of movement*—locomotor activities such as walking and balancing

SENSORY MATERIALS

The **sensory materials** described in Figure. 6.2 are among those found in a typical Montessori classroom. Materials for training and developing the senses have these characteristics:

Sensory materials
Montessori learning materials designed to promote learning through the senses and to train the senses for learning.

In the Montessori segment of the DVD, identify the five senses Montessori believed to be important in learning, and observe how sensory learning materials promote learning through the senses.

- *Control of error.* Materials are designed so that children can see whether they make a mistake; for example, a child who does not build the blocks of the pink tower in their proper order does not achieve a tower effect.
- *Isolation of a single quality.* Materials are designed so that other variables are held constant except for the isolated quality or qualities. Therefore, all blocks of the pink tower are pink because size, not color, is the isolated quality.
- *Active involvement.* Materials encourage active involvement rather than the more passive process of looking.
- *Attractiveness.* Materials are attractive, with colors and proportions that appeal to children.

Sensory materials have several purposes:

Sensory materials such as these help children learn about size, length, and measuring. Children enjoy using hands-on materials to learn about real-life problems.

- To train children's senses to focus on an obvious, particular quality. For example, with the red rods, the quality is length; with the pink tower cubes, size; and with the bells, musical pitch.
- To help sharpen children's powers of observation and visual discrimination as readiness for learning to read.
- To increase children's ability to think, a process that depends on the ability to distinguish, classify, and organize.
- To prepare children for the occurrence of the sensitive periods for writing and reading. In this sense, all activities are preliminary steps in the writing-reading process.

ACADEMIC MATERIALS

The third area of Montessori materials is more academic. Exercises are presented in a sequence that encourages writing before reading. Reading is therefore an outgrowth of writing. Both processes, however, are introduced so gradually that children are never aware they are learning to write and read until one day they realize they are writing and reading. Describing this phenomenon, Montessori said that children "burst spontaneously" into writing and reading. She anticipated contemporary practices by integrating writing and reading and maintaining that writing lays the foundation for learning to read.

Montessori believed that many children were ready for writing at four years of age. Consequently, children who enter a Montessori system at age three have done most of the

Material	Illustration	Descriptions and Learning Purposes
Pink tower		Ten wooden cubes of the same shape and texture, all pink, the largest of which is ten centimeters. Each succeeding block is one centimeter smaller. Children build a tower beginning with the largest block. (Visual discrimination of dimension)
Brown stairs		Ten wooden blocks, all brown, differing in height and width. Children arrange the blocks next to each other from thickest to thinnest so the blocks resemble a staircase. (Visual discrimination of width and height)
Red rods		Ten rod-shaped pieces of wood, all red, of identical thickness but differing in length from ten centimeters to one meter. The child arranges the rods next to each other from largest to smallest. (Visual discrimination of length)
Cylinder blocks		Four individual wooden blocks that have holes of various sizes and matching cylinders; one block deals with height, one with diameter, and two with the relationship of both variables. Children remove the cylinders in random order, then match each cylinder to the correct hole. (Visual discrimination of size)
Smelling jars		Two identical sets of white opaque glass jars with removable tops through which the child cannot see but through which odors can pass. The teacher places various substances, such as herbs, in the jars, and the child matches the jars according to the smells. (Olfactory discrimination)
Baric tablets		Sets of rectangular pieces of wood that vary according to weight. There are three sets—light, medium, and heavy—which children match according to the weight of the tablets. (Discrimination of weight)
Color tablets		Two identical sets of small rectangular pieces of wood used for matching color or shading. (Discrimination of color and education of the chromatic sense)
Cloth swatches		Two identical swatches of cloth. Children identify them according to touch, first without a blindfold but later using a blindfold. (Sense of touch)
Tonal bells		Two sets of eight bells, alike in shape and size but different in color; one set is white, the other brown. The child matches the bells by tone. (Sound and pitch)
Sound boxes		Two identical sets of cylinders filled with various materials, such as salt and rice. Children match the cylinders according to the sound the fillings make. (Auditory discrimination)
Temperature jugs or thermic bottles		Small metal jugs filled with water of varying temperatures. Children match jugs of the same temperature. (Thermic sense and ability to distinguish between temperatures)

FIGURE 6.2 **Montessori Sensory Materials**

sensory exercises by the time they are four. It is not uncommon to see four- and five-year-olds in a Montessori classroom writing and reading. Figure 6.3 shows an example of a child's writing.

Following are examples of Montessori materials that promote writing and reading:

- *Ten geometric forms and colored pencils.* These introduce children to the coordination necessary for writing. After selecting a geometric inset, children trace it on paper and fill in the outline with a colored pencil of their choosing.

FIGURE 6.3 **Writing Sample by Montessori Student Ella Rivas-Chacon**

The Farly
Once upon a time
there was a tiny
Farly who liked her tiny
unicorn soe they
went for a walk.
they were rily happy.
the End

- *Sandpaper letters.* Each letter of the alphabet is outlined in sandpaper on a card, with vowels in blue and consonants in red. Children see the shape, feel the shape, and hear the sound of the letter, which the teacher repeats when introducing it.
- *Movable alphabet with individual letters.* Children learn to put together familiar words.
- *Command cards.* These are a set of red cards with a single action word printed on each card. Children read the word on the card and do what the word tells them to do (e.g., run, jump).

Companion Website To complete a Program in Action activity related to the Montessori method, go to the Companion Website at **www.prenhall.com/morrison,** select chapter 6, then choose the Program in Action module.

MONTESSORI AND CONTEMPORARY PRACTICES

The Montessori approach supports many methods used in contemporary early childhood programs:

- *Integrated curriculum.* Montessori involves children in actively manipulating concrete materials across the curriculum—writing, reading, science, math, geography, and the arts.
- *Active learning.* In Montessori classrooms, children are actively involved in their own learning. Manipulative materials provide for active and concrete learning.

- *Individualized instruction.* Montessori individualizes learning through children's interactions with the materials as they proceed at their own rates of mastery. Montessori materials are age appropriate for a wide age range of children.
- *Independence.* The Montessori environment emphasizes respect for children and promotes success, both of which encourage children to be independent.
- *Appropriate assessment.* In a Montessori classroom, observation is the primary means of assessing children's progress, achievement, and behavior. Well-trained Montessori teachers are skilled observers of children and are adept at translating their observation into appropriate ways of guiding, directing, facilitating, and supporting children's active learning.
- *Developmentally appropriate practice.* The concepts and process of developmentally appropriate curricula and practice (see chapters 9 through 12) are foundational in the Montessori method.

You can gain a good understanding of the ebb and flow of life in a Montessori classroom by reading and reflecting on the Program in Action, which describes a day at Children's House.

This child is learning visual relationships and improving her visual-motor skills while working on a land-water geographic activity. Montessori believed that it is important for children to learn geographic concepts as a basis for learning about their world.

PROVIDING FOR DIVERSITY AND DISABILITY

Montessori education is ideally suited to meet the needs of children from diverse backgrounds, those with disabilities, and those with other special needs such as giftedness. Montessori believed that all children are intrinsically motivated to learn and that they absorb knowledge when they are provided appropriate environments at appropriate times of development. Thus, Montessorians believe in providing for individual differences in enriching environments.

The Circle of Inclusion Project at the University of Kansas identifies ten specific aspects of Montessori education that have direct applicability to the education of children with disabilities:

- *The use of mixed-age groups.* The mixed-age groupings found within a Montessori classroom are conducive to a successful inclusion experience. Mixed-age groups necessitate a wide range of materials within each classroom to meet the individual needs of children, rather than the average need of the group.
- *Individualization within the context of a supportive classroom community.* The individualized curriculum in Montessori classrooms is compatible with the individualization required for children with disabilities. Work in a Montessori classroom is introduced to children according to individual readiness rather than chronological age.
- *An emphasis on functionality within the Montessori environment.* Real objects are used rather than toy replications whenever possible (e.g., children cut bread with a real knife, sweep up crumbs on the floor with a broom, and dry wet tables with cloths). In a Montessori classroom, the primary goal is to prepare children for life; special education also focuses on the development of functional skills.
- *The development of independence and the ability to make choices.* Montessori classrooms help all children make choices and become independent learners in many ways; for example, children may choose any material for which they have had a lesson given by the teacher. This development of independence is especially appropriate for children with disabilities.

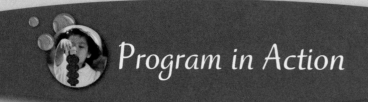
CHILDREN'S HOUSE DAILY SCHEDULE

This sample schedule is typical of a Montessori program. It is structured to allow for activities in all three basic areas of involvement—life, sensory materials, and academic materials—and includes a rest period for the youngest children.

	CLASSROOM ACTIVITIES	BENEFITS FOR CHILDREN
8:00–10:45 **Work Period**	Children spend this uninterrupted time working on individual or small-group activities at a table or on a rug on the floor. Many activities require a lesson from the teacher. Others, such as puzzles, can be used without a lesson. Children who choose an activity that is too difficult for them are offered something that better matches their abilities.	These activities allow children to improve their attention span and concentration skills, small-motor control, eye-hand coordination, attention to detail, perseverance, and the joy of learning. Responsibility for one's own learning is developed as the children make their own choices.
10:45–11:15 **Circle Time**	This group activity includes calling the roll, a peace ceremony, grace and courtesy lessons, stories, songs, games, or lessons on something new in the classroom. Children help set the tables for lunch, feed the animals, water the plants, and perform other chores.	Whole-group lessons are an important time for children to learn how to take turns, participate appropriately in a larger society, share feelings and ideas, enjoy each other's company in songs and games, and learn respect for others.
11:15–11:45 **Outside Play**	Climbing on the play apparatus, sand play, and gardening are a few of the activities available on the playground.	Large-motor control, participation in group games, and learning about the wonders of nature take place as the children play outside.

- *The development of organized work patterns in children.* One objective of the practical life area and the beginning point for every young child is the development of organized work habits. Children with disabilities who need to learn to be organized in their work habits and their use of time benefit from this emphasis.
- *The classic Montessori demonstration.* Demonstrations themselves have value for learners who experience disabilities. A demonstration uses a minimum of language selected specifically for its relevance to the activity and emphasizes an orderly progression from the beginning to the end of the task. Observe several demonstrations by teachers in the enclosed DVD.

Time	Activity	Rationale
11:45–12:25 Lunchtime	The children wash their hands, wait until all are seated before beginning, concentrate on manners and pleasant conversations at the table, take a taste of everything, pack up leftovers, throw away trash, and remain seated until everyone is finished and excused. After lunch, children help clean the tables and sweep the floor.	Respectful behavior at mealtime is learned through modeling and direction from the teacher. Discussions can include manners, healthy nutrition, and family customs. Cooperation and teamwork are fostered as children help each other clean up and transition to the next activity.
12:25–12:50 Outside Play	Climbing on the play apparatus, sand play, and gardening are again available on the playground.	See earlier outside play.
12:50–3:00 Age-Appropriate Activities	Nappers—Children under the age of 4½ sleep or rest in a small-group setting.	Rest rejuvenates these young children for participation in the remainder of the day.
	Pre-kindergarten—Children between 4½ and 5 rest quietly for 30 minutes and then join the kindergarten group.	Working alongside kindergartners encourages pre-kindergarten children to emulate their classmates in academic as well as social skills.
	Kindergarten—Children who are 5 years old by September 30 and are ready for the kindergarten experience continue to work on the lessons that were begun in the morning; they also have more extensive lessons in geography, science, art appreciation, writing, and music.	Kindergarten children benefit from being part of a small group and working to their full potential in any area of their choosing. The joy of learning comes to life as they concentrate on works of intrinsic interest to them.
3:00–3:45 Outside Play	Climbing on the play apparatus, sand play, and gardening are again available on the playground.	See earlier outside play.
3:45–4:00 Group Snack	Children share a snack before starting the afternoon activities.	A snack provides another opportunity to encourage manners and healthy eating.
4:00–5:30 After-School Fun	Activities at this time can include games, art, drama, music, movement, cooking, or an educational video.	Cooperation, teamwork, and creative expression are fostered as children build self-esteem.
5:30 End of Day	All children should be picked up by this time.	Pick-up time offers the children an opportunity to say good-bye to the teacher and each other. It also gives the teacher a chance to speak briefly with parents.

Contributed by Keturah Collins, owner and director, Children's House Montessori School, Reston, Virginia, www.childrenhouse-montessori. com.

- *An emphasis on repetition.* Children with special needs typically require lots of practice and may make progress in small increments.
- *Materials with a built-in control of error.* Materials that have a built-in control of error benefit all children. Because errors are obvious, children notice and correct them without the help of a teacher.
- *Academic materials that provide a concrete representation of the abstract.* Montessori classrooms offer a wide range of concrete materials that children can learn from as a regular part of the curriculum. For children with disabilities, the use of concrete materials is critical to promote real learning.

- *Sensory materials that develop and organize incoming sensory perceptions.* Sensory materials can develop and refine each sense in isolation. A child who cannot see will benefit enormously from materials that train and refine the senses of touch, hearing, and smell, for example.[12]

FURTHER THOUGHTS

In many respects, Maria Montessori was a person for all generations who contributed greatly to early childhood programs and practices. Many of her ideas—such as preparing the environment, providing child-size furniture, promoting active learning and independence, and using multiage grouping—have been fully incorporated into early childhood classrooms. As a result, it is easy to take her contributions, like Froebel's (see chapter 4), for granted. We do many things in a Montessorian way without thinking too much about it.

What is important is that early childhood professionals adopt the best of Montessori for children of the twenty-first century. As with any practice, professionals must adopt approaches to fit the children they are teaching while remaining true to what is best in that approach. Respect for children is never out of date and should be accorded to all children regardless of culture, gender, or socioeconomic background.

HIGH/SCOPE: A CONSTRUCTIVIST APPROACH

High/Scope   An educational program for young children based on Piaget's and Vygotsky's ideas.

The High/Scope Educational Research Foundation is a nonprofit organization that sponsors and supports the **High/Scope** educational approach. The program is based on Piaget's intellectual development theory, discussed in chapter 5. High/Scope provides broad, realistic educational experiences geared to children's current stages of development, to promote the constructive processes of learning necessary to broaden emerging intellectual and social skills.[13] Read the accompanying Program in Action, "High/Scope in Practice," on pages 152–153 to understand how High/Scope works in the classroom.

High/Scope is based on three fundamental principles:

- Active participation of children in choosing, organizing, and evaluating learning activities, which are undertaken with careful teacher observation and guidance in a learning environment replete with a rich variety of materials located in various classroom learning centers
- Regular daily planning by the teaching staff in accord with a developmentally based curriculum model and careful child observations
- Developmentally sequenced goals and materials for children based on the High/Scope "key experiences"[14]

BASIC PRINCIPLES AND GOALS OF THE HIGH/SCOPE APPROACH

The High/Scope program strives to

develop in children a broad range of skills, including the problem solving, interpersonal, and communication skills that are essential for successful living in a rapidly changing society. The curriculum encourages student initiative by providing children with materials, equipment, and time to pursue activities they choose. At the same time, it provides teachers with a framework for guiding children's independent activities toward sequenced learning goals.

The teacher plays a key role in instructional activities by selecting appropriate, developmentally sequenced material and by encouraging children to adopt an active problem-solving approach to learning. . . . This teacher-student interaction—teachers helping

Companion Website   For more information about High/Scope, go to the Companion Website at **www.prenhall.com/morrison,** select chapter 6, then choose the Linking to Learning module.

students achieve developmentally sequenced goals while also encouraging them to set many of their own goals—uniquely distinguishes the High/Scope Curriculum from direct-instruction and child-centered curricula.[15]

The High/Scope approach influences the arrangement of the classroom, the manner in which teachers interact with children, and the methods employed to assess children. The High/Scope curriculum consists of the five interrelated components shown in Figure 6.4. This figure shows how active learning forms the hub of the "wheel of learning" and is supported by the key elements of the curriculum.

THE FIVE ELEMENTS OF THE HIGH/SCOPE APPROACH

Teachers create the context for learning in the High/Scope approach by implementing and supporting five essential elements: active learning, classroom arrangement, the daily schedule, assessment, and the curriculum (content).

Active Learning. The idea that children are the source of their own learning forms the center of the High/Scope curriculum. Teachers support children's **active learning** by providing a variety of materials, making plans and reviewing activities with children, interacting with and carefully observing individual children, and leading small- and large-group active learning activities.

Classroom Arrangement. The classroom arrangement invites children to engage in personal, meaningful, educational experiences. In addition, the classroom contains three or more interest areas that encourage choice.

Active learning (instructional)
Involvement of the child with materials, activities, and projects in order to learn concepts, knowledge, and skills.

FIGURE 6.4
High/Scope Curriculum Wheel

Source: Reprinted by permission of High/Scope Educational Research Foundation, 600 N. River St., Ypsilanti, MI 48198-2898.

In the High/Scope segment of the DVD, listen to and observe the plan-do-review process that is a central feature of the High/Scope approach.

Classroom Arrangement
- 3 or more defined interest areas/centers
- A range of interesting materials
- Organized systems for storage; labels

Daily Schedule
- Plan-Do-Review is incorporated in the schedule
- Consistent from day to day
- Balanced teacher/child-initiated activities
- Children know about changes

Active Learning
These ingredients are incorporated into learning contexts:
- Materials
- Manipulation
- Choice
- Words
- Support

Content
- Teachers are aware of the content to be learned
- Key experiences are used in math, language, the arts, social studies, P.E., etc.
- Time is spent each day focusing on content areas

Assessment
- Attributes of each child are observed and recorded
- Anecdotal records (C.O.R.) are part of the report card
- Portfolios are used
- Teachers evaluate and plan on a daily basis

HIGH/SCOPE IN PRACTICE

The High/Scope educational approach and curriculum for three- to five-year-olds is a developmental model based on the principle of *active learning*. The following beliefs underlie this approach:

- Children construct knowledge through their active involvement with people, materials, events, and ideas, a process that is intrinsically motivated.
- While children develop capacities in a predictable sequence, adult support contributes to their intellectual, social, emotional, and physical development.
- Consistent adult support and respect for children's choices, thoughts, and actions strengthen the children's self-respect, feelings of responsibility, self-control, and knowledge.
- Careful observation of children's interests and intentions is a necessary step in understanding their level of development and planning and carrying out appropriate interactions with them.

In High/Scope programs these principles are implemented throughout the day, both through the structure of the daily routine and in the strategies adults use as they work with the children. The staff of each program plan for the day's experiences, striving to create a balance between adult- and child-initiated activity.

As they plan activities, staff members consider five factors of intrinsic motivation that research indicates are essential for learning: enjoyment, interest, control, probability of success, and feelings of competence. During greeting-circle and small-group time, staff members actively involve the children in decisions about activities and materials as a way of supporting their intrinsic motivation to learn. This emphasis on child choice continues throughout the day, even during activities initiated by adults.

A DAY AT A HIGH/SCOPE PROGRAM

Each program may implement the High/Scope approach in a slightly different way. A typical day's activities at Giving Tree School are described here.

The day begins with greeting circle. After putting their photos on the attendance board, the children gather as the teacher begins a well-known animal finger play, and they join in immediately. Then the teacher suggests that the group make a circus of animals that are moving in many ways. Two children do not want to be animals, and the teacher suggests that these children may want to be the audience. They get chairs and prepare to watch.

The children suggest elephants, bears, and alligators as animals for the group to imitate. Then they parade before the audience, pretending to be those animals and moving to the music. At the close of greeting time, the teacher suggests that the children choose an animal to be as they move to the next activity, small-group time. During small-group time the children make inventions of their choice with recyclable materials the teacher has brought in and pine cones they collected the previous day. Each child uses the materials *in his or her own way*.

As small-group activities are completed, planning time begins. The teacher asks the younger children to indicate their plans for "work" time by going to get something they will use in their play. The older children draw or copy the symbols or letters that stand for the area in which they plan to play. (Each play area is labeled with a sign containing both a simple picture symbol and words for the area.) To indicate his plan, Charlie, age three, gets a small hollow block and brings it to the teacher. "I'm going to make a train. That's all," he says. Aja, age four, brings a dress and a roll of tape. "I'm going to the playhouse to be the mommy, and then I'm going to the art area to make something with tape," she explains. Five-year-old Ashley shows the teacher her drawing of the tub table and the scoops she will use with the rice at the table.

During work time the teachers participate in children's play. Riding on Charlie's train, one teacher shows Tasha how to make the numerals 3 and 5 for train tickets, then joins two children playing a board game, and finally listens to Aja explain how she made a doll bed out of tape and a box. Another teacher helps Nicholas and Charlie negotiate a conflict over a block, encouraging them by listening and asking questions until they agree on a solution.

As the children are given a five-minute warning that it is almost time to clean up, the teachers tell them that today there will be a parade cleanup. When they hear the music, they can parade in any way they want, and when the music stops, they can choose a place nearby to clean up. These playful cleanup strategies are varied every day, and children look forward to the community cleanup process.

At recall time the children gather with their earlier small groups. Standing in a circle, each group rotates a hula hoop through their hands as they sing a short song (one of many such facilitating techniques). When the song ends, the child nearest the tape on the hoop is first to recall his or her work-time experiences. Charlie tells about the train he made out of blocks. Nicholas describes the special speed sticks he played with, Aja shows her doll bed, and Tasha describes her tickets. After their snack the children get their coats on and discuss what they will do outside. "Let's collect more pine cones. We can use them for food for the baby alligators." "Let's go on the swings. I just learned how to pump." "Let's see if we can find more bugs hiding under the rocks. They go there for winter." The teacher responds, "I'd like to help you look for bugs."

KEY EXPERIENCES

As children play, they are actively involved in solving problems, and they are participating in many of the High/Scope key experiences. They are fifty-eight key experiences that fall into ten categories: *social relation and initiative, language, creative representation, music, movement, classification, seriation, numbers, space,* and *time.* Teachers use the fifty-eight key experiences as guides for understanding development, planning activities, and describing the thinking and actions involved in children's play.

The High/Scope approach to learning supports developmentally appropriate, active learning experiences for each child as it encourages decision making, creative expression, problem solving, language and literacy, and other emerging abilities.

Contributed by Betsy Evans, conflict resolution specialist, Kids and Conflict, Gill, Massachusetts, and field consultant, High/Scope Educational Research Foundation.

The classroom organization of materials and equipment supports the daily routine—children know where to find materials and what materials they can use. This encourages development of self-direction and independence. The floor plan in Figure 6.5 shows how room arrangement supports and implements the program's philosophy, goals, and objectives and how a center approach (e.g., books, blocks, computers, dramatic play, art, construction) provides space for large-group activities and individual work. In a classroom where space is at a premium, the teacher makes one area serve many different purposes.

The teacher selects the centers and activities to use in the classroom based on several considerations:

- Interests of the children (e.g., kindergarten children are interested in blocks, housekeeping, and art)
- Opportunities for facilitating active involvement in seriation, number, time relations, classification, spatial relations, and language development
- Opportunities for reinforcing needed skills and concepts and functional use of those skills and concepts

Arranging the environment, then, is essential to implementing a program's philosophy. This is true for Montessori, High/Scope, and every other program.

Daily Schedule. The schedule considers developmental levels of children, incorporates a sixty- to seventy-minute **plan-do-review** process, provides for content areas, is as consistent throughout the day as possible, and contains a minimum number of transitions.

Notice the facial expressions of these children as they engage in active, hands-on learning with manipulative materials. Certainly this picture is worth a thousand words in conveying the power of active learning.

FIGURE 6.5
A High/Scope Kindergarten Classroom Arrangement

Source: Reprinted by permission of High/Scope Educational Research Foundation, 600 N. River St., Ypsilanti, MI 48198-2898.

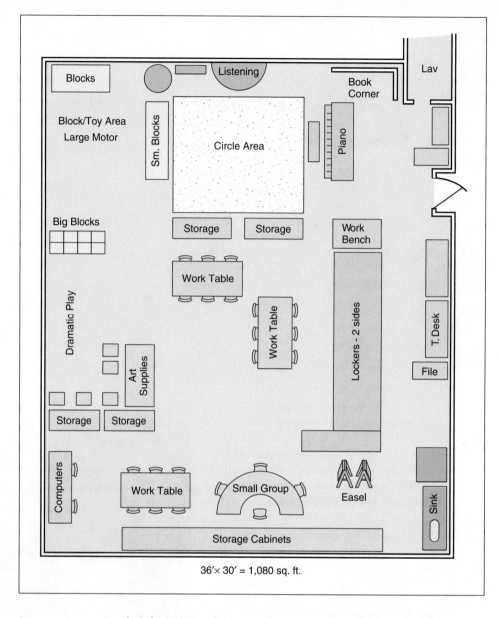

36′ × 30′ = 1,080 sq. ft.

The plan-do-review A sequence in which children, with the help of the teacher, initiate plans for projects or activities; work in learning centers to implement their plans; and then review what they have done with the teacher and their fellow classmates.

Assessment. Teachers keep notes about significant behaviors, changes, statements, and things that help them better understand a child's way of thinking and learning. Teachers use two mechanisms to help them collect data: the key experiences note form and a portfolio. The High/Scope Child Observation Record (see chapter 3) is also used to assess children's development.

Curriculum. The High/Scope curriculum comes from two sources: children's interests and the key experiences, which are lists of observable learning behaviors (see Figure 6.6). Basing a curriculum in part on children's interests is very constructivist and implements the philosophies of Dewey, Piaget, and Vygotsky.

A DAILY ROUTINE THAT SUPPORTS ACTIVE LEARNING

The High/Scope curriculum's daily routine is made up of a plan-do-review sequence and several additional elements. The plan-do-review sequence gives children opportunities to express intentions about their activities while keeping the teacher intimately involved in the whole process. The following five processes support the daily routine and contribute to its successful functioning.

CHAPTER 6
EARLY CHILDHOOD PROGRAMS

Planning Time.   **Planning time** gives children a structured, consistent chance to express their ideas to adults and to see themselves as individuals who can act on decisions. They experience the power of independence and are conscious of their intentions. This supports the development of purpose and confidence.

The teacher talks with children about the plans they have made before the children carry them out. This helps children clarify their ideas and think about how to proceed. Talking with children about their plans provides an opportunity for the teacher to encourage and respond to each child's ideas, to suggest way to strengthen the plans so they will be successful, and to understand and gauge each child's level of development and thinking style. Children and teachers benefit from these conversations and reflections. Children feel reinforced and ready to start their work, while teachers have ideas of what opportunities for extension might arise, what difficulties children might have, and where problem solving may be needed. In such a classroom, children and teachers are playing appropriate and important roles.

Key Experiences.   Teachers continually encourage and support children's interests and involvement in activities that occur within an organized environment and a consistent routine. Teachers plan for **key experiences** that may broaden and strengthen children's emerging abilities. Children generate many of these experiences on their own; others require teacher guidance. Many key experiences are natural extensions of children's projects and interests. Figure 6.6 identifies key experiences for children in pre-K programs.

Work Time.   This part of the plan-do-review sequence is generally the longest time period in the daily routine. The teacher's role during **work time** is to observe children to see how they gather information, interact with peers, and solve problems, and when appropriate, teachers enter into the children's activities to encourage, extend, and set up problem-solving situations.

Cleanup Time.   During cleanup time, children return materials and equipment to their labeled places and store their incomplete projects, restoring order to the classroom. All children's materials in the classroom are within reach and on open shelves. Clear labeling enables children to return all work materials to their appropriate places.

Recall Time.   **Recall time,** the final phase of the plan-do-review sequence, is the time when children represent their work-time experience in a variety of developmentally appropriate ways. They might recall the names of the children they involved in their plan, draw a picture of the building they made, or describe the problems they encountered. Recall strategies include drawing pictures, making models, physically demonstrating how a plan was carried out, or verbally recalling the events of work time. The teacher supports children's linking of the actual work to their original plan.

This review permits children to reflect on what they did and how it was done. It brings closure to children's planning and work-time activities. Putting their ideas and experiences into words also facilitates children's language development. Most important, it enables children to represent to others their mental schemes.

PROVIDING FOR DIVERSITY AND DISABILITY

The High/Scope curriculum is a developmentally appropriate approach that is child centered and promotes active learning. The use of learning centers, active learning, and the plan-do-review cycle, as well as allowing children to progress at their own pace, provides for children's individual and special needs. High/Scope teachers emphasize the broad

Planning time   A time when children plan and articulate their ideas, choices, and decisions about what they will do.

In the High/ Scope segment of the DVD, observe as the teacher leads the children in planning time and helps them begin to make their own decisions and structure their own learning.

Key experiences Activities that foster developmentally important skills and abilities.

Work time   The period of time when children carry out their plans and are engaged in a project or activity.

Recall time   The time in which children form mental pictures of their work-time experiences and discuss them with their teachers.

Companion Website To complete a Program in Action activity related to the High/Scope approach, go to the Companion Website at **www.prenhall.com/ morrison,** select chapter 6, then choose the Program in Action module.

FIGURE 6.6   Key Experiences in a High/Scope Preschool Curriculum

CREATIVE REPRESENTATION
- Recognizing objects by sight, sound, touch, taste, and smell
- Imitating actions and sounds
- Relating models, pictures, and photographs to real places and things
- Pretending and role playing
- Making models out of clay, blocks, and other materials
- Drawing and painting

LANGUAGE AND LITERACY
- Talking with others about personally meaningful experiences
- Describing objects, events, and relations
- Having fun with language: listening to stories and poems, making up stories and rhymes
- Writing in various ways: drawing, scribbling, letterlike forms, invented spelling, and conventional forms
- Reading in various ways: reading storybooks, signs and symbols, one's own writing
- Dictating stories

INITIATIVE AND SOCIAL RELATIONS
- Making and expressing choices, plans, and decisions
- Solving problems encountered in play
- Taking care of one's own needs
- Expressing feelings in words
- Participating in group routines
- Being sensitive to the feelings, interests, and needs of others
- Building relationships with children and adults
- Creating and experiencing collaborative play
- Dealing with social conflict

CLASSIFICATION
- Exploring and describing similarities, differences, and the attributes of things
- Distinguishing and describing shapes
- Sorting and matching
- Using and describing something in several ways
- Holding more than one attribute in mind at a time
- Distinguishing between *some* and *all*
- Describing characteristics that something does *not* possess or what class it does *not* belong to

SERIATION
- Comparing attributes (longer/shorter, bigger/smaller)
- Arranging several things one after another in a series or pattern and describing the relationships (big/bigger/biggest, red/blue/red/blue)
- Fitting one ordered set of objects to another through trial and error (small cup—small saucer/medium cup—medium saucer/big cup—big saucer)

Figure 6.6   Continued

NUMBER

- Comparing the numbers of things in two sets to determine *more, fewer, same number*
- Arranging two sets of objects in one-to-one correspondence
- Counting objects

SPACE

- Filling and emptying
- Fitting things together and taking them apart
- Changing the shape and arrangement of objects (wrapping, twisting, stretching, stacking, enclosing)
- Observing people, places, and things from different spatial viewpoints
- Experiencing and describing positions, directions, and distances in the play space, building, and neighborhood
- Interpreting spatial relations in drawings, pictures, and photographs

TIME

- Starting and stopping an action on signal
- Experiencing and describing rates of movement
- Experiencing and comparing time intervals
- Anticipating, remembering, and describing sequences of events

Source: Reprinted by permission from Nancy Altman Brickman, ed., "Key Experiences in the Preschool Classroom," *Supporting Young Learners* 3 (Ypsilanti, MI: High/Scope Press, 2001): 143–216.

cognitive, social, and physical abilities that are important for all children, instead of focusing on a child's deficits. High/Scope teachers identify where a child is developmentally and then provide a rich range of experiences appropriate for that level. For example, they would encourage a four-year-old who is functioning at a two-year-old level to express his or her plans by pointing, gesturing, and saying single words, and they would immerse the child in a conversational environment that provided many natural opportunities for using and hearing language.[16]

Many early childhood programs for children with special needs incorporate the High/Scope approach. For example, the Regional Early Childhood Center at Rockburn Elementary School in Elkridge, Maryland, operates a full-day multiple-intense-needs class for children with disabilities and typically developing peers and uses the High/Scope approach. The daily routine includes greeting time, small groups (e.g., art, sensory, preacademics), planning time (i.e., picking a center), work time at the centers, cleanup time, recall (i.e., discussing where they "worked"), snacks, circle time with stories, movement and music, and outside time.[17]

FURTHER THOUGHTS

The High/Scope approach represents one approach to educating young children. Whereas Montessori, Emilia Reggio, and Waldorf are European based in philosophy and context, High/Scope puts into practice the learning-by-doing American philosophy. It builds on Dewey's ideas of active learning and teaching in the context of children's interests.

High/Scope is widely used in Head Start and early childhood programs across the United States; High/Scope research has demonstrated that its approach is compatible with Head Start guidelines and performance standards.

There are number of advantages to implementing the High/Scope approach:

- It offers a method for implementing a constructivist-based program that has its roots in Dewey's philosophy and Piagetian cognitive theory.
- It is widely popular and has been extensively researched and tested.
- There is a vast network of teacher training and support provided by the High/Scope Foundation.
- It is research based and it works.

As a result, the High/Scope approach is viewed by early childhood practitioners as one that implements many of the best practices embraced by the profession.

REGGIO EMILIA

Reggio Emilia, a city in northern Italy, is widely known for its approach to educating young children.[18] Founded by Loris Malaguzzi (1920–1994), **Reggio Emilia** sponsors programs for children from three months to six years of age. Certain essential beliefs and practices underlie the Reggio Emilia approach. These basic features define the Reggio approach, make it a constructivist program, and enable it to be adapted and implemented in many U.S. early childhood programs. Read the Program in Action about the Reggio Emilia approach to understand its key elements.

Reggio Emilia An approach to education based on the philosophy and practice that children are active constructors of their own knowledge.

Companion Website For more information about Reggio Emilia, go to the Companion Website at **www.prenhall. com/morrison,** select chapter 6, then choose the Linking to Learning module.

BELIEFS ABOUT CHILDREN AND HOW THEY LEARN

Relationships. The Reggio approach focuses on each child and is conducted in relation to the family, other children, the teachers, the environment of the school, the community, and the wider society. Each school is viewed as a system in which all these interconnected relationships are reciprocal, activated, and supported. In other words, as Vygotsky believed, children learn through social interactions. In addition, as Montessori indicated, the environment supports and is important to learning.

When preparing space, teachers offer the possibility for children to be with the teachers and many of the other children, or with just a few of them. Also, children can be alone when they need a little niche to stay by themselves.

Teachers are always aware, however, that children learn a great deal in exchanges with their peers, especially when they interact in small groups. Such small groups of two, three, four, or five children provide possibilities for paying attention, listening to each other, developing curiosity and interest, asking questions, and responding. Also, groups provide opportunities for negotiation and ongoing dynamic communication.

Hundred Languages. Malaguzzi wrote a poem about the many languages of children. Here is the way it begins:

The child is made of one hundred.
The child has a hundred languages, a hundred hands, a hundred thoughts.
A hundred ways of thinking, of playing, of speaking.[19]

The hundred languages Malaguzzi was referring to include drawing, building, modeling, sculpting, discussing, inventing, discovering, and more. Teachers are encouraged to create environments in which children can use all hundred languages to learn.

In the Reggio Emilia segment of the DVD, observe how interactions of parents, teachers, and children create an active learning community.

Time. Reggio Emilia teachers believe that time is not set by a clock and that continuity is not interrupted by the calendar. Children's own sense of time and their personal rhythms are considered in planning and carrying out activities and projects. The full-day schedule

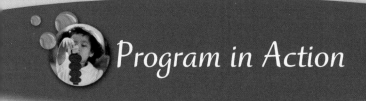

REGGIO EMILIA

Boulder Journey School, a private school for young children in Boulder, Colorado, welcomes 250 children ages six weeks to six years of age and their families. As a school community composed of children, educators, and families, we are inspired and encouraged by our study of the municipal infant-toddler centers and preschools in Reggio Emilia, Italy. Since 1995 we have engaged in an ongoing dialogue with educators in Reggio Emilia, as well as with educators around the world who are also inspired by the Reggio Emilia approach to early childhood education.

We think that the culture of our school emanates from our values, values that define the philosophy and pedagogy of the school. At Boulder Journey School our values are based on a strong image of children as

- **Curious**—From the moment of birth, children are engaged in a search for the meaning of life, seeking to understand the world that surrounds them and the relationships that they form and develop with others in their world.
- **Competent**—Children pose problems and ask questions, form hypotheses and create theories in an effort to answer their questions and find solutions to their problems.
- **Capable**—Using a hundred different languages, children are able to construct, deconstruct, reconstruct, symbolize, represent, and communicate their understandings of the world.
- **Co-constructors of knowledge**—Children interact with other children and adults, sharing their unique identities and experiences, learning as individuals while contributing to the learning of the group.

Recognizing and maintaining an image of children who are filled with ideas that can be extended in depth and breadth is critical as we observe, document, and interpret their explorations and investigations. For example, during the experience captured by the photograph of infants and their teacher examining a glass bulb, the teacher observes the children's use of all their senses: the ways in which they gaze at, touch, and possibly attempt to taste, smell, and listen to the bulb. The teacher documents the experience, combining careful notes with photographs and video. She also notes the ways in which the children interact with one another and with her and how the sharing of ideas contributes to the evolution of the experience. Interpretation

of the documented experience with both colleagues and parents informs the teacher's choices of similar and different materials that can be introduced to the children.

As educators, we are not passive and objective recorders and analyzers of children's learning, but rather active participants in this learning. We are partners, along with families, in the children's research, seeking to make meaning along with them. Our role is to provide a structure that defines the children's research, supports it as it evolves, and makes it visible to others.

Carlina Rinaldi, executive consultant to Reggio Children, stated that as educators we do not produce learning but rather produce the conditions for learning, rich contexts in which children can realize their potential in dialogue with the environment and with others, children and adults. This statement leads us to wonder:

- How can we encourage the emergence of ideas, small moments during which a child or group of children is engaged in the process of thinking and learning?
- How can we nurture these ideas as they develop into long-term investigations?
- In what ways can the traces of these long-term investigations inform and communicate our understanding of how children learn?

At Boulder Journey School we try to answer these questions, considering the environment an essential element in the learning process. We think that the design of the environment of the school should be thoughtful, based on a consideration of the conditions necessary for learning. To encourage the emergence of ideas during small moments that provide possibilities for long-term investigations, the environment and the choice of materials within the environment must be intentional but also fluid, responsive to the children and able to evolve in harmony with the evolution of their ideas.

We also consider the organization of time a vital aspect of our work; time for reflection, dialogue, debate, and

negotiation, which supports and encourages connections among the entire school community. For example, the investigation of the marble blocks, portrayed in the photograph of children attempting to build a block tower, required time for planning, drawing, constructing, and problem solving that led to new plans, drawings, problems, solutions, and subsequent constructions.

Inspired by our study of the schools in Reggio Emilia, Boulder Journey School recognizes the value of building connections. We have built connections among the three protagonists of the learning process—the children, their families, and the educators within each of the classrooms—and we have built those connections throughout the school,

creating a school that thinks of itself as a learning community. For example, our documentation of the children's explorations of light, illustrated in the photograph of two children working with transparent materials on the overhead projector, led to a school-community project in which families contributed materials to be used in conjunction with various sources of light, both natural and artificial. Families anticipated the ways in which the materials would be used; teachers documented the children's explorations of the materials and communicated their observations to families.

Additionally, we have challenged ourselves to think about building connections within our work, recognizing that the learning process in a school is both multifaceted and multidimensional. Although we acknowledge that we must often deconstruct the learning process in order to study individual aspects more closely, we consider it critical to put the pieces back into the entire context. For example, our study of the formation and maintenance of

infant relationships supported our understanding of the role of the environment, which must provide many opportunities for infants to interact with one another, as illustrated in the photograph of two infants in an upholstered tube. Viewing the environment as vital to the development of infant relationships also means giving serious consideration to relationships as a system that is critical to the learning processes of both children and adults.

As a learning community, Boulder Journey School has begun building connections with the community of Boulder, reaching out to learn from this community and most recently building connections focused on what the community can learn from the children. For example, preschool children, parents, and teachers constructed a school grocery store and cafe called the Brown Bag, illustrated in the photograph of two boys at the checkout counter. The children visited several local grocery stores and shared their organization and

pricing system with managers, leading to subsequent classroom investigations of currency and advertising.

We are also striving to build connections both nationally and internationally with other experiences inspired by the Reggio Emilia philosophy of education. We think of Boulder Journey School as a context in which relationships are created and maintained. It is a context of collegiality and collaboration, a context of creativity and expression, and a context in which the culture of the school, composed of its values, is defined and lived.

Contributed by Ellen Hall, owner and director, Boulder Journey School, Boulder, Colorado. Photos courtesy of Boulder Journey School, Boulder, Colorado.

provides sufficient time for being together among peers in an environment that is conducive to getting things done with satisfaction.

Teachers get to know the personal rhythms and learning styles of each child. This is possible in part because children stay with the same teachers and the same peer group for three-year cycles (infancy to three years and three years to six years).

ADULTS' ROLES

Adults play a very powerful role in children's lives; children's well-being is connected to the well-being of parents and teachers.

The Teacher.   Teachers observe and listen closely to children to know how to plan or proceed with their work. They ask questions and discover children's ideas, hypotheses, and theories. They collaboratively discuss what they have observed and recorded, and they make flexible plans and preparations. Teachers then enter into dialogues with the children and offer them occasions for discovering and also revisiting and reflecting on experiences, since they consider learning an ongoing process. Teachers are partners with children in a continual process of research and learning.

The Atelierista.   An **atelierista**, a teacher trained in the visual arts, works closely with teachers and children in every preprimary school and makes visits to the infant/toddler centers.

Atelierista A teacher trained in the visual arts who works with teachers and children.

Parents.   Parents are an essential component of the program and are included in the advisory committee that runs each school. Parents' participation is expected and supported and takes many forms: day-to-day interaction, work in the schools, discussion of educational and psychological issues, special events, excursions, and celebrations.

THE ENVIRONMENT

The infant/toddler centers and school programs are the most visible aspect of the work done by teachers and parents in Reggio Emilia. They convey many messages, of which the most immediate is that this is a place where adults have thought about the quality and the instructive power of space.

The Physical Space.   The layout of physical space, in addition to welcoming whoever enters, fosters encounters, communication, and relationships. The arrangement of structures, objects, and activities encourages choices, problem solving, and discoveries in the process of learning.

The centers and schools of Reggio Emilia are beautiful. Their beauty comes from the message the whole school conveys about children and teachers engaged together in the pleasure of learning. There is attention to detail everywhere: in the color of the walls, the shape of the furniture, the arrangement of simple objects on shelves and tables. Light from the windows and doors shines through transparent collages and weavings made by children. Healthy green plants are everywhere. Behind the shelves displaying shells or other found or made objects are mirrors that reflect the patterns that children and teachers have created.

The environment is also highly personal. For example, a series of small boxes made of white cardboard creates a grid on the wall of a school. On each box the name of a child or a teacher is printed with rubber stamp letters. These boxes are used for leaving little surprises or messages for one another. Communication is valued and favored at all levels.

The space in the centers and schools of Reggio Emilia is personal in still another way: it is full of children's own work. Everywhere there are paintings, drawings, paper sculptures, wire constructions, transparent collages coloring the light, and mobiles moving gently overhead. Such things turn up even in unexpected spaces like stairways and bathrooms. Although the work of the children is pleasing to the eye, it is not intended as decoration, but rather to show and document the competence of children, the beauty of their ideas, and the complexity of their learning processes.

The Atelier.   A special workshop or studio, called an **atelier**, is set aside and used by all the children and teachers in the school. It contains a great variety of tools and resource materials, along with records of past projects and experiences.

Atelier A special area or studio for creating projects.

The activities and projects, however, do not take place only in the atelier. Smaller spaces called miniateliers are set up in each classroom. In fact, each classroom becomes an active workshop with children involved with a variety of materials and experiences that they have discussed and chosen with teachers and peers. In the view of Reggio educators, the children's use of many media is not art or a separate part of the curriculum but an inseparable, integral part of the whole cognitive/symbolic expression involved in the process of learning.

PROGRAM PRACTICES

Cooperation is the powerful mode of working that makes possible the achievement of the goals Reggio educators set for themselves. Teachers work in pairs in each classroom. They see themselves as researchers gathering information about their work with children by means of continual documentation. The strong collegial relationships that are maintained with teachers and staff enable them to engage in collaborative discussion and interpretation of both teachers' and children's work.

Documentation. Transcriptions of children's remarks and discussions, photographs of their activity, and representations of their thinking and learning using many media are carefully arranged by the atelierista, along with the other teachers, to document the work and the process of learning. **Documentation** has many functions:

- Making parents aware of children's experiences and maintaining their involvement
- Allowing teachers to understand children better and to evaluate their own work, thus promoting professional growth
- Facilitating communication and exchange of ideas among educators
- Making children aware that their effort is valued
- Creating an archive that traces the history of the school and the pleasure of learning by many children and their teachers

Curriculum and Practices. The curriculum is not established in advance. Teachers express general goals and make hypotheses about what direction activities and projects

In the Reggio Emilia segment of the DVD, observe how teachers document children's learning and how documentation contributes to both children's and teachers' learning.

Documentation Records of children's work, including recordings, photographs, art, work samples, projects, and drawings.

These documentation panels include children's artifacts, photos, and descriptive captions written by teachers or children. The panels document block work, literacy development, and other activities that the children experience in a day.

might take. On this basis, they make appropriate preparations. Then, after observing children in action, teachers compare, discuss, and interpret together their observations and make choices that they share with the children about what to offer and how to sustain the children in their exploration and learning. In fact, the curriculum emerges in the process of each activity or project and is flexibly adjusted accordingly through this continuous dialogue among teachers and with children.

Projects provide the backbone of the children's and teachers' learning experiences. These projects are based on the strong conviction that learning by doing is of great importance and that to discuss in groups and to revisit ideas and experiences is the premier way of gaining better understanding and learning.

Ideas for projects originate in the experiences of children and teachers as they construct knowledge together. Projects can last from a few days to several months. They may start from a chance event, an idea, or a problem posed by one or more children or from an experience initiated directly by teachers.

The **Project Approach,** which is so popular in early childhood education today, can trace its roots partially to Reggio Emilia practice. With the Project Approach, an investigation is undertaken by a small group of children within a class, sometimes by a whole class, and occasionally by an individual child. The key feature of a project is that it is a search for answers to questions about a topic worth learning more about, something the children are interested in.[20]

The Voice from the Field "How to Use the Project Approach" on pages 164–165 is a Competency Builder that shows how effectively you can use projects to teach young children traditional academic subjects, such as literacy.

Project Approach An in-depth investigation of a topic worth learning more about.

PROVIDING FOR DIVERSITY AND DISABILITY

Like the Montessori approach, Reggio places a high value on respect for each child. In a Reggio program everyone has rights—children, teachers, and parents. Children with disabilities have special rights and are routinely included in programs for all children.

The Grant Early Childhood Center in Cedar Rapids, Iowa, is addressing the challenge of inclusion through Prizing Our National Differences (POND), a program based on the Reggio Emilia approach. The POND program includes all children with disabilities as full participants in general education classrooms with their age-appropriate peers. Four core ingredients of the Reggio approach facilitate successful inclusion at Grant Early Childhood Center:

- Encouraging collaborative relationships
- Constructing effective environments
- Developing project-based curriculums
- Documenting learning in multiple ways[21]

FURTHER THOUGHTS

There are a number of things to keep in mind when considering the Reggio Emilia approach. First, its theoretical base rests within constructivism and shares ideas compatible with those of Piaget, Vygotsky, and Dewey. Second, there is no set curriculum. Rather, the curriculum emerges or springs from children's interests and experiences. This approach is, for many, difficult to implement and does not ensure that children will learn basic academic skills valued by contemporary American society. Third, the Reggio Emilia approach is suited to a particular culture and society. How this approach works and flourishes and meets the educational needs of children in an Italian village may not necessarily be appropriate for meeting the needs of contemporary American children.

Companion Website To complete a Program in Action activity related to the Reggio Emilia approach, go to the Companion Website at **www.prenhall.com/morrison,** select chapter 6, then choose the Program in Action module.

HOW TO USE THE PROJECT APPROACH

Students in the K/1 classroom at University Primary School begin their day reading a daily sign-in question that is intended to provoke a thoughtful response:

Have you ever eaten the flowers of a plant?
Do you think a van is more like a car or a bus?

Such questions are related to the topic under study and are used to engage children in discussing different views during their whole-group meeting later in the morning.

Opportunities for children to express themselves abound at University Primary School. In addition to an hour of systematic literacy instruction, authentic opportunities to read and write occur throughout the day in the course of the children's regular activities.

INTEGRATING LANGUAGE ARTS WITH THE PROJECT APPROACH

The Project Approach involves students in in-depth investigation of worthy real-world topics*; learning becomes meaningful for them as they pursue answers to their own questions. Students can carry out specific literacy-related activities in each phase of project investigation:

PHASE 1 Exploring previous experiences

- Brainstorm what is already known about a project topic
- Write or dictate stories about memories and experiences
- Label and categorize experiences

PHASE 2 Investigating the topic

- Write questions, predictions, and hypotheses
- Write questions to ask experts
- Write questionnaires and surveys
- Write thank-you letters to experts
- Record findings
- Record data
- Make all types of lists (what materials need to be collected, what will be shared with others, who will do which tasks)
- Listen to stories and informational texts read aloud
- Read secondary sources to help answer questions
- Compare what was read with what the experts shared

PHASE 3 Sharing the project with parents and others

- Make charts, displays, and PowerPoint presentations
- Write reports or plays that demonstrate new understanding

WALDORF EDUCATION: HEAD, HANDS, AND HEART

Rudolf Steiner (1861–1925) was very interested in the spiritual dimension of the education process and developed many ideas for educating children and adults that incorporated it. Emil Molt, director of the Waldorf-Astoria cigarette factory in Stuttgart, Germany, was interested in Steiner's ideas and asked him to give a lecture to the workers regarding the education of their children. Molt was so impressed with Steiner's ideas that he asked him to establish a school for employees' children. Steiner accepted the offer, and on September 17, 1919, the Free Waldorf School opened its doors and the Waldorf movement began. Today, Waldorf education has developed into an international movement with close to nine hundred independent schools in fifty-five countries. There are over 157 Waldorf schools in North America.

Waldorf schools emphasize the teaching of the whole child—head, hands, and heart. This is the way Steiner envisioned such education when he planned his school:

- Write invitations to a culminating event
- Share stories orally in readers theater

Throughout all phases of their project investigation, students have authentic contexts to read, spell, write words, and build their vocabulary. In addition, comparing what they knew with what they have learned from the pri-

mary and secondary sources, they develop their analytical thinking and comprehension skills. And they become more fluent readers and writers by using their skills to answer their own questions.

PROVIDING DIRECT INSTRUCTION IN READING AND WRITING

The five reading components articulated in the No Child Left Behind Act—phonemic awareness, phonics, fluency, vocabulary, and comprehension—are taught throughout the students' day within the context of project investigation and during small-group direct literacy instruction. Direct instruction includes a whole-group meeting during which the teacher reads books aloud (i.e., shared reading) for specific purposes. The teacher may choose to highlight the project topic or specific authors or illustrators or to focus on rhyming words or specific patterns of phonemes.

Following the shared reading time, students engage in writing activities related to the books they heard read aloud. These activities may include literature extensions that encourage students to write creatively. They may write a different ending to a story or write a related story from a different point of view. Students may also write their own stories, using the principles of writer's workshop, in which students learn to edit and extend their language skills. The teacher may also introduce extended minilessons on tools of writing, such as alliteration, similes, metaphors, or syllabic rhythms.

After their noon recess, students choose books to read quietly while the teacher provides individual guided reading. Project-related books may be a popular choice. Students conclude their silent reading with approximately ten minutes to engage in buddy reading. During the buddy reading time, students talk about what they have just read with their buddy and read favorite excerpts of their books to their buddy. This collaboration reinforces comprehension skills and instills the love of literature that motivates all children to read. At University Primary School, students are always improving and using their literacy skills to learn.

Contributed by Nancy B. Hertzog, associate professor, Department of Special Education, and director, University Primary School at the University of Illinois at Urbana-Champaign, and by Marjorie M. Klein, former head teacher in the K–1 classroom at University Primary School and now an educational consultant in St. Louis, Missouri. Photo courtesy of Patrick White/Merrill.

*L. G. Katz and S. C. Chard, *Engaging Children's Minds: The Project Approach,* 2nd ed. (Norwood, NJ: Ablex, 2000).

Insightful people are today calling for some form of education and instruction directed not merely to the cultivation of one-sided knowledge, but also to abilities; education directed not merely to the cultivation of intellectual faculties, but also to the strengthening of the will. . . . but it is impossible to develop the will (and that healthiness of feeling on which it rests) unless one develops the insights that awaken the energetic impulses of will and feeling. A mistake often made . . . is not that people instill too many concepts into young minds, but that the kind of concepts they cultivate are devoid of all driving life force.[22]

Although Waldorf schools have many distinguishing characteristics, this dedication to teaching the whole child—head, hands, and heart—appeals to many teachers and parents.

Steiner believed that education should be holistic. In shaping the first Waldorf school, he said that from the start there was to be no classification of children into intellectual "streams," no class lists, no examinations, no holding back in a grade or promoting to a grade, no prizes, no honors boards, no reports, no compulsory homework, and no pun-

Companion Website For more information about Waldorf education, go to the Companion Website at **www.prenhall.com/morrison**, select chapter 6, then choose the Linking to Learning module.

ishments of additional learning material. It was to be a school where teachers and children meet as human beings to share and experience the knowledge of human evolution and development in the world.[23]

BASIC PRINCIPLES

Waldorf education, like the other programs we have discussed, operates on a number of essential principles (see Table 6.1).

Anthroposophy A philosophy developed by Rudolf Steiner that focuses on the spiritual nature of humanity and the universe.

Anthroposophy. **Anthroposophy,** the name Steiner gave to "the study of the wisdom of man," is a basic principle of Waldorf education.

> Anthroposophy, according to Steiner, is derived from the Greek: anthros "man" and sophia "wisdom." Anthroposophy, Steiner claimed, offered a step-by-step guide for spiritual research. Anthroposophical thinking, according to Steiner, could permit one to gain a "new" understanding of the human being—body and spirit.[24]

Anthroposophy is a personal path of inner spiritual work that is embraced by Waldorf teachers; it is not tied to any particular religious tradition. The teacher, through devotion to truth and knowledge, awakens the student's reverence for beauty and truth. Steiner believed that each person is capable of tapping the spiritual dimension, which then provides opportunities for higher and more meaningful learning.

Respect for Development. Waldorf education is based squarely on respect for children's processes of development and their developmental stages. Individual children's development determines how and when Waldorf teachers introduce curriculum topics. Respecting children's development and the ways they learn is an essential foundation of all early childhood programs.

Eurythmy Steiner's art of movement, which makes speech and music visible through action and gesture.

Eurythmy. **Eurythmy** is Steiner's art of movement, which makes speech and music visible through action and gesture and enables children to develop a sense of harmony and balance. Thus, as they learn reading, they are also becoming the letters through physical gestures. According to Steiner, every sound—speech or music—can be interpreted through gesture and body movement; for example, in learning the letter *o,* children form the letter with their arms while saying the sound for *o.* In the main-lesson books that are the children's textbooks, crayoned pictures of mountains and trees metamorphose into letters *M* and *T,* and form drawings of circles and polygons that become the precursor to cursive writing. Mental imagery for geometrical designs supports the fine-motor skills of young children.[25]

Rhythm is an important component of all these activities. Rhythm (i.e., order or pattern in time) permeates the entire school day as well as the school year, which unfolds around celebrating festivals drawn from different religions and cultures.[26]

Nurturing Imagination. Folk and fairy tales, fables, and legends are integrated throughout the Waldorf curriculum. These enable children to explore the traditions of many cultures, thus supporting a multicultural approach to education. They also enrich the imaginative life of the young child and promote free thinking and creativity.

CURRICULUM FEATURES

Common features of the Waldorf curriculum include these:

- Teaching according to developmental stages, the right subject at the right time
- The timing and method of introducing several basic skills, consistent with these developmental stages

- The use of eurythmy in learning
- The inclusion of other arts, as well as handwork
- The sequential linkage between subjects, corresponding to the student's maturity from year to year[27]

The Waldorf curriculum unfolds in main-lesson blocks of three or four weeks. The students create their own texts, or main-lesson books, for each subject. This enables them to delve deeply into the subject.[28]

The accompanying Program in Action introduces the Austin Waldorf School and enables you to experience Waldorf education in action.

PROVIDING FOR DIVERSITY AND DISABILITY

Providing for and being sensitive to diversity is an important aspect of Waldorf education. From first grade the curriculum for all students includes the study of two foreign languages. In addition, the curriculum integrates the study of religions and cultures. As a result, children learn respect for people of all races and cultures.

Waldorf schools can also experience a certain level of success with children who have been diagnosed with disabilities such as dyslexia. Because Waldorf teaches to all of the senses, there is usually a modality that a child can use to successfully learn curriculum material.

Some Waldorf schools are devoted entirely to the education of children with special needs. For example, Somerset School in Colfax, California, offers a variety of programs designed to meet the special needs of students aged six to seventeen years who are unable to participate in regular classroom activities. Teachers, physicians, and therapists work closely with parents to create and implement individualized lesson plans.[29]

FURTHER THOUGHTS

Certainly Waldorf education has much that is appealing: its emphasis on providing education for the whole child, the integration of the arts into the curriculum, the unhurried approach to education and schooling, and the emphasis on learning by doing.

On the other hand, Waldorf education, like the Montessori approach, seems better suited to private, tuition-based education and has not been widely adopted into the public schools.

Several reasons could account for this limited adoption. First, public schools, especially in the context of contemporary schooling, are much more focused on academic achievement and accountability. Second, Waldorf education may not be philosophically aligned with mainstream public education. Waldorf's emphasis on the spiritual aspect of each child may be a barrier to widespread public school adoption. Identification of a student's spiritual self has provoked criticism of Waldorf education, as well as humanistic education and other approaches to holistic practices.

In addition, there are a number of other features of Waldorf education that some critics object to. These include delaying learning to read, not using computers and other technology in the classroom until high school, and discouraging television viewing and the playing of video games.

Although some see Waldorf as too elitist, the schools remain a popular choice for parents who want this type of education for their children. The intimate learning atmosphere of small classes, the range of academic subjects, and the variety of activities can be very attractive.

Companion Website To complete a Program in Action activity related to Waldorf education, go to the Companion Website at **www.prenhall.com/ morrison**, select chapter 6, then choose the Program in Action module.

THE AUSTIN WALDORF SCHOOL

Fundamental to Waldorf education is the recognition that each human being is a unique individual who passes through distinct life stages, and it is the responsibility of education to address the physical, social, emotional, intellectual, and spiritual needs of each developmental stage.

BASIC VALUES

At Austin Waldorf School in Austin, Texas, our guiding values are these:

- A lifelong love of learning
- Creative thinking and self-confidence
- A sympathetic interest in the world and the lives of others
- An abiding sense of moral purpose

Teachers create a school environment that balances academic, artistic, and practical disciplines, as well as providing daily opportunities for both group and individual learning. We develop these qualities in our students.

THE ARTISTIC

Learning in a Waldorf school is an imaginative, enlivening, and creative process. The artistic element is the com-

mon thread in every subject; teachers integrate art, music, drama, storytelling, poetry, and crafts into the curriculum. Thus, students learn with more than their heads; they learn with their heads, hearts, and hands. For example, in first grade the Waldorf student learns to knit. This activity develops the fine-motor skills of the child, ocular tracking, arithmetic (counting stitches), concentration, and focusing on completion of a task. The result—a beautiful piece of handwork and a child with pride.

KINDERGARTEN (AGES 4–6)

Young children learn about the world through their senses and the use of their physical bodies. Teachers create a natural environment that exemplifies truth and beauty and reflects seasonal rhythms. For example, the toys in a Waldorf classroom are made from natural materials (i.e., pieces of wood, baskets of shells or stones, beautifully dyed silks). A simple silk becomes a cape, a sail for a ship, an apron, or a blanket for the nature table, which is filled with treasures found outdoors. Waldorf education nurtures the physical, emotional, spiritual, and social development of the young child in preparation for the responsibilities and challenges of grade school and later life.

Circle Time

During story time, the children sit quietly, engrossed in the tale being told. Their imaginations enriched by the story, they eagerly experience the joy of listening and discovering what comes next. Story and circle time provide the foundation for academics in kindergarten. Teachers teach language arts through the repetition of verses rich in imaginative pictures and rhythms. Through the telling of fairy tales, we promote the development of memory, listening skills, vocabulary, sequencing, imagination, well-articulated speech, and self-expression. Folk tales allow children to explore themes such as farming, grinding grain, house building, and blacksmithing, which are the beginning of social studies, history, and cultural studies.

Our kindergarten students also study mathematics and science. Mathematics includes counting games, rhymes, finger plays, jumping rope, setting the table, and measuring ingredients for baking bread. Science studies include nature walks, gardening, circle themes, water play, and direct experience and observation of plants, insects, and animals.

Art and Movement

Artistic activities and movement abound in the kindergarten. Children participate on a weekly basis in watercolor painting, coloring, beeswax modeling, finger knitting, sewing, and seasonal crafts. Movement activities include eurythmy, rhythmic circle games, jumping rope, swinging, hopping, running, skipping, balancing, climbing, and participating in household tasks. Tasks such as sweeping, hand-washing the cloth napkins used at snack time and then hanging them on a line to dry, caring for the plants and the play area, all instill in the children a sense of reverence and respect for the space in which they spend their time.

The curriculum, which to the young child is play, develops individuals who can think for themselves, be creative in their endeavors, understand the importance of seeing a task to completion, and authentically experience the joy of discovery and learning.

EARLY GRADES

In a Waldorf school, ideally, the teacher who greets a student on the first day of grade one will be the main-lesson class teacher through grade eight. The bond that is created between students and their teachers is extraordinary. A teacher grows with the children and knows the individual strengths and challenges of each child.

Between the ages of seven and fourteen, teachers meet students' specific developmental needs. These are addressed in a structured, socially cooperative, and noncompetitive environment. The curriculum includes comprehensive language arts, math, science, and social studies, classes in German and Spanish, vocal and instrumental music, speech and drama, eurythmy, painting, drawing, modeling, handwork, and woodwork. The school provides a physical education program, which in the middle school expands into competitive team sports.

The Waldorf curriculum is the same in Texas, California, England, and Israel. The differences lie in the freedom of the teachers to bring the curriculum to life through their individuality, human experiences, and teaching style.

THE SCHOOL DAY

The day begins with the class teacher greeting every child at the door of the classroom with "Good morning" and a

handshake. This allows a human connection to be made between the teacher and the students. The class work begins with the main lesson, a two-hour period devoted to the study of a particular academic discipline. The main lesson is taught in blocks lasting from three to four weeks, allowing the children and the teacher to delve deeply into a subject and then digest the content of the lesson. This approach allows for a concentrated, in-depth study while recognizing students' need for variety and time to integrate and comprehend subject matter.

The main lesson is a lively, interactive time, moving between artistic and intellectual activities that engage each student's faculties of thinking, feeling, and willing. Simply put, willing is doing, translating thought into activity. When a young child knits, the thinking (counting stitches), the feeling (creating something beautiful and useful), and the willing (using the hands to work on the project and complete it) work in harmony.

Students' interest and enthusiasm are reflected in their main-lesson books, an artistic representation of what has been learned. Rather than using a standard textbook, the children artistically re-create the rich images and text from the material presented. A main-lesson book is the handwritten intellectual and artistic interpretation of the lesson recorded by the individual child.

Language Arts

Teachers create a rich language environment that draws students forward to mastery of reading and writing.

Teachers preserve the vitality of language through the recitation of playful verses and masterful poetry. Writing down well-loved stories addresses students' needs to be active in the learning process. Reading follows naturally when the content is already intimately connected to the students. In this way learning is less stressful, and all levels of literacy are addressed. Teachers present literature through the art of oral tradition in lively, engaging, and human presentations.

Movement and Math

Movement and math go hand in hand as students step and clap rhythmically through the times tables. Numbers likewise begin with the children's immediate experiences and are made concrete by counting shells or stones kept in a special handmade pouch. A tactile relationship to numbers and counting gives the lesson a sensible meaning, which provides children with a foundation for following more complex mathematical processes.

Knitting and flute playing develop dexterity in head and hand. Exposure to the contrasting sounds of German and Spanish develops inner flexibility, setting the stage for later interest in and appreciation of other cultures and peoples.

Central to Waldorf education is the recognition of the individual human being. Every student

- participates in every subject and every activity
- fully experiences all of his or her potential
- possesses the ability to move through the world with confidence, direction, and purpose

Contributed by Kim Frankel, enrollment director, Austin Waldorf School, Austin, Texas. Photos courtesy of Kim Frankel.

Diversity Tie-In

HOW TO TEACH RESPECT AND TOLERANCE IN ALL EARLY CHILDHOOD PROGRAMS

When I asked my class if anyone had seen the ball that was on my desk and my students said, "A bilingual took it," I knew we had a problem. My third graders were prejudiced against a group of Spanish-speaking children whom they didn't know and had very little contact with. Here are some tips for teaching respect and tolerance that I used to bring the groups together.

1 Start a conversation

Ask an open-ended question. For instance, I asked my third graders, "What does *bilingual* mean?" Most kids had no idea. Some thought it meant "from Mexico" or "not too smart." The first place to start was using our language arts skills to explore the actual definition of *bilingual*.

2 Focus on what kids value

Would you like someone just because you were told to? Kids must earn their peers' respect. So think about what kids value. Kids who can play sports or instruments well gain instant respect. Therefore, take every opportunity to showcase students' talents. Have schoolwide talent shows, poetry readings, events at recess, or impromptu moments if the kids are willing. For instance, one student said she played "America the Beautiful," a song that we were discussing in social studies. When the music room was free, we listened to her. Another student who dances in salsa style brought in a tape and showed us some moves.

Companion Website To complete a Diversity Tie-In activity related to teaching tolerance, go to the Companion Website at **www.prenhall.com/ morrison**, select chapter 6, then choose the Diversity Tie-In module.

Even though all of the program models we have discussed in this chapter are unique, at the same time they all have certain similarities. All of them, regardless of their particular philosophical orientation, have as a primary goal the best education for all children.

As an early childhood professional, you will want to do several things now. First, begin to identify which features of these program models you can and cannot support. Second, decide which of these models and/or features of models you can embrace and incorporate into your own practice. An ongoing rule of the early childhood professional is to decide what you believe is best for children and families before you make decisions about what to teach.

As we end this chapter, there is one more thing for you to consider. All four of these programs emphasize the importance of teachers and children working closely together in order to learn with and from each other. Tolerance and respect make collaboration possible. The accompanying Diversity Tie-In gives you specific ways to promote tolerance and respect in your classroom.

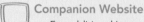**Companion Website**
For additional Internet resources or to complete an online activity for this chapter, go to the Companion Website at **www.prenhall.com/morrison**, select chapter 6, then choose the Linking to Learning or Making Connections module.

3 Use history and current events

Will Smith, Michael Jordan, and Jennifer Lopez make people forget race and color. Find historical and current people who are part of an ethnic group to stand as "cool" models. A well-liked student from the targeted group can help bridge a gap between groups. For instance, my students were pleasantly surprised when a popular kid in our class realized and announced, "I'm bilingual!"

4 Put everyone in the same shoes

If differences are languages, teach a class or hand out papers in another language. If the differences are cultural, give a quiz on a cultural event from the minority group's culture. Discuss with your students how it feels to be confused by language and culture.

5 Focus on the same

Use the curriculum to give kids opportunities to discuss universal kid problems that illustrate how alike we are. For instance, in social studies discuss parental rules or annoying siblings. Use math to talk about allowances and bedtimes.

6 Be a scout

Constantly be on the lookout for special talents and knowledge from your students. Students might not realize that making tamales or tuning pianos is unique. Use the curriculum to ask questions: Has anyone visited Puerto Rico? Does anyone speak two languages or three? Does anyone go to school on Saturdays? You and your students will be amazed at how interesting your class is.

One caution: When students see an individual getting accolades, they might attempt to do or say something to also get attention. To avoid this, discuss with the class that there are two ways to get noticed. One is to do bad things. The class will laugh when you remind them that everyone looks at the toddler who screams at a restaurant. Doing something exceptional or unique is another way. When their funny comments die down, they will agree that the second way is the best.

The best way for any two people to get along is to spend time together and build respect and trust naturally. Therefore, students interacting all day long in little ways will slowly learn to tolerate and appreciate differences. You might even be rewarded by seeing lasting friendships forged.

Contributed by Rebecca Leo, teacher, Enders-Salk Elementary, Schaumburg, Illinois.

LINKING TO LEARNING

American Montessori Society
http://www.amshq.org
Serves as a national center for Montessori information, both for its members and for the general public—answering inquiries and facilitating research wherever possible.

Association Montessori Internationale
http://www.montessori-ami.org/
Founded in 1929 by Dr. Maria Montessori to maintain the integrity of her life's work and to ensure that it would be perpetuated after her death.

ERIC Reggio Emilia Page
http://ceep.crc.uiuc.edu/poptopics/reggio.html
Contains information and resources related to the approach to early childhood education developed in the preschools of Reggio Emilia, Italy.

International Montessori Society
http://imsmontessori.org/
Founded to support the effective application of Montessori principles throughout the world; provides a range of programs and services relating to the fundamental principles of (a) observation, (b) individual liberty, and (c) preparation of the environment.

Merrill-Palmer Institute Reggio Emilia Resources
http://www.mpi.wayne.edu/reggioresources.htm

> *A comprehensive resource listing, including information on Reggio Emilia–related conferences, study tours, and general information on Reggio children, the Reggio Emilia educational philosophy, and contact information for the North American Reggio Network.*

Montessori Online
http://www.montessori.org/

> *Site for the Montessori Foundation, a nonprofit organization dedicated to the advancement of Montessori education. Offers programs and resources to anyone interested in learning about Montessori education.*

Montessori Unlimited
http://www.montessori.com

> *A program that teaches the basis of Montessori—to respect oneself and one's environment—and carries that basis, called practical life, into other areas of learning, including language arts, math, and science.*

North American Montessori Teachers' Association
http://www.montessori-namta.org/

> *A membership organization open to parents, teachers, and anyone else interested in Montessori education.*

ACTIVITIES FOR FURTHER ENRICHMENT

ETHICAL DILEMMA: "SHOULD I BECOME A BOARD MEMBER?"

Lake Country Day School is a private, not-for-profit preschool in your community. Lake Country operates in run-down facilities, serves only low-income children, and has a long waiting list. Lake Country has a reputation of not using its resources wisely, and children entering kindergarten from Lake Country generally do not do well. When board members suggest changes, the director becomes defensive and says, "If you can get someone else to run this place for what you pay me, hire him!"

Over the last several months several board members have resigned. One of your friends has shared with you that she was invited to serve on the board, but she responded, "I'm not going to waste my time on that mess. I have better things to do!" Last evening, the president of the board called and asked whether you would serve. He ended his plea with "I need some help standing up to the director."

What do you do—accept the invitation to be a board member in the hope that you can make a difference and help the children, or do you conclude from what you have heard about Lake Country Day School that it is beyond help?

APPLICATIONS

1. Which of the programs in this chapter do you think best meets the needs of young children? Would you implement one of them in your program? Why?
2. Write three or four paragraphs describing how you think the programs discussed in this chapter have influenced early childhood educational practice.
3. What features of Montessori, High/Scope, Reggio, and Waldorf do you like best? Why? What features do you like least? Why? What features are best for children?
4. Interview a Montessori school director to learn how to go about opening a Montessori school. Determine what basic materials are needed and their cost, then tell how your particular location would determine how you would market the program.

FIELD EXPERIENCES

1. Visit various early childhood programs, including center and home programs, and discuss similarities and differences in class. Which of the programs incorporate practices from programs discussed in this chapter?
2. Compare Montessori materials with those in other kindergartens and preschool programs. Is it possible for teachers to make Montessori materials? What advantages or disadvantages would there be in making and using these materials?

3. Develop a checklist of best practices found in Montessori, High/Scope, Reggio, and Waldorf. Use your checklist to observe other programs. Tell how these programs do or do not demonstrate the best practices.
4. Visit or view on the DVD the four programs discussed in this chapter—Montessori, High/Scope, Reggio, and Waldorf. Observe each program and compare how the teachers implement the different practices. Based on your beliefs, rank the programs from 1 (best liked) to 4 (least liked). Explain why you ranked the programs as you did. Which of the four programs would you like to teach in?

RESEARCH

1. Survey parents in your area to determine what service they desire from an early childhood program. Are most of the parents' needs being met? How is what they want in a program similar to and different from the basic program features discussed in this chapter?
2. Search the AMS, AMI, and NAMTA websites for information about becoming a certified Montessori teacher. Compare the requirements for becoming a certified Montessori teacher with your university training. What are the similarities and differences?
3. Interview public and private school teachers about their understanding of the programs discussed. Do they have a good understanding of the programs? What are the most critical areas of understanding or misunderstanding? Do you think all early childhood professionals should have knowledge of the programs? Why?
4. Research which of the programs discussed in this chapter are available in your area. Which programs are more prevalent? What factors contribute to the prevalence of particular programs in your area?

READINGS FOR FURTHER ENRICHMENT

Cadwell, L. B., and C. Rinaldi. *Bringing Learning to Life: A Reggio Approach to Early Childhood Education* (Early Childhood Education, 86). New York: Teachers College Press, 2003.

Describes real-life classrooms, including details on the flow of the day, parent participation, teacher collaboration, the importance of the environment, documenting students' work, and assessment. Features many illustrations of children's work as well as photos of Reggio-inspired classroom interiors and art materials.

Catron, C. E., and J. Allen. *Early Childhood Curriculum: A Creative Play Model*, 3rd ed. Upper Saddle River, NJ: Merrill/Prentice Hall, 2003.

Provides information on planning programs with a play-based, developmental curriculum for children from birth to five years of age. Covers basic principles and current research in early childhood curricula.

Hendrick, J., ed. *Next Steps Toward Teaching the Reggio Way: Accepting the Challenge to Change.* Upper Saddle River, NJ: Merrill/Prentice Hall, 2004.

More than a presentation of the Reggio Emilia philosophy, also gives a progress report of the steps American and Canadian teachers have taken toward teaching the Reggio Emilia way.

Hohmann, M., et al. *Educating Young Children: Active Learning Practices for Preschool and Child Care Programs.* Ypsilanti, MI: High/Scope Press, 2002.

The official manual for High/Scope curriculum; outlines how to set up a High/Scope classroom, from setting up the learning environment to guiding adult interactions.

Roopnarine, J., and J. Johnson. *Approaches to Early Childhood Education*, 4th ed. Upper Saddle River, NJ: Merrill/Prentice Hall, 2005.

Focuses on models, approaches, and issues that deal with prominent and tested practices in early childhood education. Includes chapters on the family-center model, the Erikson approach, behavioral analysis, Montessori education, and constructivism.

Spietz, H. A. *Montessori Resources: A Complete Guide to Finding Montessori Materials for Parents and Teachers.* Rossmoor, CA: American Montessori Consulting, 2002.

Contains in-depth reviews of products, information on where to buy supplies for integrated lesson planning, recommended computer software, and reviews and recommendations of foreign language products.

Tanner, Laurel. *Dewey's Laboratory school: Lessons for Today.* New York: Teachers College Press, 1997.

A good resource that provides an informative description of how Dewey translated his progressive education ideas into the real world of enabling children to engage themselves in the process of learning.

ENDNOTES

1. National Association for the Education of Young Children, *Summary of NAEYC-Accredited Programs for Young Children*, http://www.naeyc.org/accreditation/center_summary.asp.
2. J. Haberkorn, "Hitting the Books Now Starts at Age 4," *Washington Times*, August 4, 2005.
3. W. Sentell, "Pre-K Classes Popularity Explodes," *Advocate News*, August 2, 2005.

4. Haberkorn, "Hitting the Books."

5. D. Kirp, "All My Children," *New York Times,* July 31, 2005.

6. Ibid.

7. Maria Montessori, *Dr. Montessori's Own Handbook* (New York: Schocken, 1965), 133.

8. Maria Montessori, *The Secret of Childhood,* trans. M. J. Costello (Notre Dame, IN: Fides, 1966), 20.

9. Ibid., 46.

10. Maria Montessori, *The Absorbent Mind,* trans. Claude A. Claremont (New York: Holt, Rinehart & Winston, 1967), 25.

11. Montessori, *Dr. Montessori's Own Handbook,* 131.

12. D. Guess, H. A. Benson, and E. Siegel-Causey, "Concepts and Issues Related to Choice Making and Autonomy Among Persons with Severe Disabilities," *Journal of the Association for Persons with Severe Handicaps* 10, no. 2 (1985): 79–86.

13. High/Scope Educational Research Foundation, *The High/Scope K–3 Curriculum: An Introduction* (Ypsilanti, MI: Author, 1989), 1.

14. Ibid.

15. Ibid., 3.

16. "Educational Programs: Early Childhood," http://www.highscope.org/EducationalPrograms/EarlyChildhood/homepage.htm.

17. Regional Early Childhood Center, http://www.howard.k12.md.us/res/necc.html.

18. This section is adapted from L. Gandini, "Foundations of the Reggio Emilia Approach," in J. Hendrick, ed., *First Steps Toward Teaching the Reggio Way* (Upper Saddle River, NJ: Merrill/Prentice Hall, 1997), 14–25.

19. Reprinted by permission from L. Malaguzzi, "No Way. The Hundred Is There," trans. L. Gandini, in *The Hundred Languages of Children: The Reggio Emilia Approach,* ed. C. Edwards, L. Gandini, and S. Forman (Greenwich CT: Ablex), 3.

20. H. Helm and L. Katz, *Young Investigators: The Project Approach in the Early Years* (New York: Teachers College Press, 2001).

21. R. K. Edmiaston and L. M. Fitzgerald, "How Reggio Emilia Encourages Inclusion," *Educational Leadership* 58, no. 1 (September 2000): 66.

22. R. Steiner, *An Introduction to Waldorf Education,* http://wn.rsarchive.org/Education/IntWal_index.html.

23. G. S. Morrison, *Contemporary Curriculum K–8* (Boston: Allyn and Bacon, 1993), 399.

24. S. F. Foster, "The Waldorf Schools: An Exploration of an Enduring Alternative School Movement" (PhD dissertation, Florida State University, 1981), 18.

25. C. Bamford and E. Utne, "An Emerging Culture: Rudolf Steiner's Continuing Impact in the World," 3, http://www.steinercollege.org/newsletter.html.

26. Ibid.

27. Foster, "The Waldorf Schools," 29.

28. Bamford and Utne, "An Emerging Culture," 4.

29. Somerset School, http://waldorfworld.net/somerset/.

CHAPTER 7

Child Care

MEETING THE NEEDS OF CHILDREN, PARENTS, AND FAMILIES

Early childhood development and education helps prepare children to learn and succeed in preschool, and access to safe, reliable child care allows parents to work and be self-sufficient.

MARIAN WRIGHT EDELMAN

THE WORLD OF CHILD CARE

Child care has many faces and dimensions. Like the children they serve, child care programs have many similarities and differences; no two are the same. Each program is unique in its location, its teachers and administrators, and the children and families it serves. Parents and other primary caregivers make their decisions about using child care based on its affordability, accessibility, and quality. Consider the following real-life scenarios:

- Maria Gloria is a young single parent with two children aged two and four. Maria works in a local convenience store for the minimum wage. "I really can't afford child care, but I have to work. A woman in an apartment three floors up from me keeps my kids and five others while I work. I give her twenty-five dollars a week. It's all I can afford. I'm lucky to have someone to take care of my kids."

- Charlie and Beth Shanker have jobs that pay enough for them to get by on their combined incomes. Charlie drops off their one-year-old daughter, Amanda, and three-year-old son, Jesse, at the Children's Barn child care center on his way to work. "It's not the best, but it's about what we can afford. I have to leave fifteen minutes early because the child care is out of the way. We're looking for something closer, but we haven't found it yet."

- Seven-year-old Chantel Harris walks home and lets herself into the family apartment after school each day. There is no one else at home. Her mother wishes she had more choices. "I know it isn't the best or safest thing to do. I can't afford anyone to take care of her, and the school doesn't offer any kind of programs after school. What am I to do?"

- Amy Charney is a stay-at-home mom. Three mornings a week she takes her four-year-old daughter, Emily, to a Mothers' Day Out (MDO) program at a local church. "It's a great arrangement and very reasonable, in terms of cost. When Emily is in MDO I volunteer in the community, and still she and I get to do a lot of things together. The staff is great and is up-to-date on the latest trends, and I feel Emily is definitely getting ready for school."

- Abby Belanger is an up-and-coming attorney in a prestigious law firm. She is a single mother by choice. Abby's four-year-old daughter, Tiffany, is enrolled in a high-quality, high-end child care program. "I want Tiffany to have the best, and I can afford the best. I want her to have a good start in life so she can go to whatever schools she wants to attend. Education is important to me."

Child care arrangements such as these are duplicated countless times each day all across America. Think a moment about the child care arrangements you know about or are involved with. Child care in America is often referred to as a patchwork of programs and arrangements of varying costs and quality, combining the good, the bad, and the unavailable.

Part of your job and mine as early childhood professionals is to advocate and work for high-quality, affordable, and accessible child care for all children and families. As we will discuss, the kind and quality of care children receive outside their homes make a big

Focus Questions

Why is there a need for child care services?

What are the types of child care offered today?

What constitutes quality in child care programs?

How effective is child care in meeting the needs of children and families?

What are significant issues surrounding child care and its use?

Companion Website

To check your understanding of this chapter, go to the Companion Website at **www.prenhall.com/ morrison**, select chapter 7, answer Multiple Choice and Essay Questions, and receive feedback.

TABLE 7.1   Children in Different Types of Child Care Arrangements

What implications do these data have for you as an early childhood professional?

	Number of Children (in thousands)	Percent in Arrangement
Nonrelative care	6,937	35.4
• Organized care facility	3,933	20.1
• Day care center	2,273	11.6
• Nursery or preschool	1,108	5.7
• Head Start	171	0.9
• School	582	3.0
• Other nonrelative care	3,413	17.4
• In child's home	831	4.2
• In provider's home	2,614	13.3
Family day care	1,426	7.3
Other care arrangements	1,250	6.4
Total children under 5	19,611	100

Source: U.S. Census Bureau, *"Who's Minding the Kids? Child Care Arrangements"* (Spring 2002).

difference in their lives and the lives of their parents and families. As Table 7.1 illustrates, more than 35 percent of the nation's children are in nonrelative child care.

WHAT IS CHILD CARE?

Child care   Comprehensive care and education of young children outside their homes.

Child care is the comprehensive out-of-home care and education of children that supplements the care and education children receive from their families. Child care programs address a variety of needs:

- Providing for children's safety and health needs
- Providing a comprehensive array of services that meet children's physical, social/emotional, and intellectual needs
- Providing educational and readiness programs and activities that support children's abilities to learn and that get them ready for school
- Collaborating with families to help them care for and educate their children

THE POPULARITY OF CHILD CARE

Child care is popular and receiving much public attention for a number of reasons.

Working Parents.   There are more dual-income families and more working single parents today than ever before. For example, 54.1 percent of mothers with children under three are employed, and it is not uncommon for mothers to return to work as early as six weeks after giving birth. The current unprecedented entry of large numbers of mothers into the workforce has greatly impacted the care and education of children in the early years. And the number of working mothers will likely continue to increase and create an even bigger demand for child care of children from six weeks to their entry into a public school program.[1]

Public Policy.   Child care is an important part of many politicians' solutions to the nation's economic and social problems. In this regard, child care is an instrument of public policy; it is used to address political and social issues. For example, child care is an essential part of work-training programs designed to help the needy gain job skills that lead to employment and self-sufficiency. At the same time, many of those programs train the unemployed or underemployed for child care jobs. Thus, many individuals are being gainfully employed as child care workers.

Companion Website   For more information about child care, go to the Companion Website at **www.prenhall.com/morrison**, select chapter 7, then choose the Linking to Learning module.

Politicians also view quality child care as a way of addressing many of the country's social problems through early intervention in children's lives. The reasoning is that if we provide children with quality programs and experiences early in life, we reduce the possibility that they will need costly social services later in life.

As the demand for child care increases, the challenge to you and other early childhood professionals is clear. You and the profession must participate in advocating for and creating quality child care programs that meet the needs of children and families. The Children's Defense Fund (CDF) is an established agency that advocates for children and families on the national level. The Voice from the Field on pages 180–181 in this chapter describes the organization's efforts and the many facets of advocacy. We must all let our voices be heard.

PLACEMENT IN CHILD CARE PROGRAMS

Decisions to place children in child care are personal, individual, and complex. We can say with some assurance that because parents work, they place their children in child care. But it could also be the other way around: because child care is available, some parents choose to work. Decisions relating to child care are not necessarily straightforward but depend on many factors. Consider some of these interesting facts:

In the Child Care segment of the DVD, the child care director explains that working parents create a demand for child care and look for certain qualities in a child care program. What are some desired qualities or features?

- As children grow older, parents are more likely to place them in child care. For example, as children reach three and four years of age, they are more likely to enter center-based programs. Of mothers with children aged 0 to two, 23 percent select center-based programs, whereas 47 percent of mothers with children three to five select center-based programs.[2]
- Latino parents are more likely to enroll their children in center-based programs at age four, whereas whites and African Americans enroll their children in center-based programs at age three.[3]
- Many more affluent parents (70 percent) enroll their children in child care than do low-income parents (45 percent).[4]
- The social support available to families influences their decisions about child care. Families that have a father present in the home and that have supportive family members outside the home use child care less than those families without such social support.[5]
- Young children with more siblings are less likely to be placed in child care.[6]
- Many low-income parents rely on informal arrangements with relatives, neighbors, and babysitters (often referred to as kith and kin) for child care.[7]

TYPES OF CHILD CARE PROGRAMS

Child care is offered in many places and by many persons and agencies that provide a variety of services (see Table 7.2). The options for child care are almost endless. However, regardless of the kind of child care provided, the issues of *quality, affordability,* and *accessibility* are always part of the child care landscape.

CHILD CARE BY RELATIVES AND FRIENDS

Child care is frequently arranged within extended families or with friends. Parents handle these arrangements in various ways. In some cases, children are cared for by grandparents, aunts, uncles, or other relatives. Almost half—47 percent—of grandparents provide child care assistance to their grandchildren.[8] These arrangements satisfy parents' needs to have their children cared for by people with similar lifestyles and values and meet the needs of working parents to have child care beyond normal working hours and on weekends. Such care may also be less costly, and the caregiver-to-child ratio is low.

CHILDREN'S DEFENSE FUND: ADVOCATING FOR CHILDREN AT THE NATIONAL LEVEL

The mission of the Children's Defense Fund (CDF) is to Leave No Child Behind and to ensure every child a *Healthy Start*, a *Head Start*, a *Fair Start*, a *Safe Start*, and a *Moral Start* in life and successful passage to adulthood with the help of caring families and communities. In order to ensure awareness about the legislative process for the unheard needs of millions of children of America, a multifaceted strategy is required. We can ensure that no child is left behind in the richest nation on earth by building a powerful grassroots movement across America.

CDF is organized into five policy areas, including early childhood development, child health, child welfare and mental health, education and youth development, and family income and jobs. The Early Childhood Development Division at CDF focuses predominantly, but not solely, on the following issues: child care, Head Start, preschool, and after-school activities that are a daily concern for millions of working American parents. CDF's Early Childhood Development Division strives to give children a head start in life and ensure that they are safe and secure while their parents are at work.

The Early Childhood Development Division tackles this task by heading up ongoing research projects and data collection, while also sustaining efforts to collaborate with state and local advocates, policy makers, and the media. The Early Childhood Development Division conducts primary and secondary research on the federal, state, and local levels and in collaboration with experts in the field. The information CDF collects is presented through various publications and is readily available in hard copy or online. These reports are distributed widely to members of Congress and their staffs, state policy makers, the media, and advocates. CDF's research offers the most up-to-date and in-depth information available on the state of child care and early education of low-income families; it is widely used as a basis for congressional briefings, hearings, and fact sheets.

In addition to thorough data collection and research, it is essential to work closely with members of Congress and their staffs in order to successfully achieve the aims of child advocacy. At CDF this involves a range of activities:

- Playing a lead role conceiving and drafting federal and state legislation

TABLE 7.2 Variety of Child Care Programs

Child Care Type	Description
Relatives and friends	Children are cared for by grandparents, aunts, uncles, other relatives, or friends, providing both continuity and stability.
Family	An individual caregiver provides care and education for a small group of children in his or her home.
Intergenerational	Child care programs integrate children and the elderly in an early childhood and adult care facility.
Center-based	Center-based child care is conducted in specially designed and constructed centers, churches, YMCAs and YWCAs, and other such facilities.
Employer-sponsored	To meet the needs of working parents, some employers are providing child care at the work site.
Proprietary	Some child care centers are run by corporations, businesses, or individual proprietors for the purpose of making a profit; these programs often emphasize an educational component.
Before- and after-school	Public schools, center-based programs, community and faith-based agencies, and individuals all offer programs that extend the school day with tutoring, special activities, and a safe space.

- Laying the groundwork for child care reauthorization by drafting the Act to Leave No Child Behind, a piece of comprehensive legislation for children and families
- Helping staff draft legislation
- Planning congressional hearings
- Giving staff testimony at congressional hearings using data collected by CDF researchers
- Working with CDF's extensive field network

Members of Congress must also hear directly from their constituents about the need for increased child care investment in their communities. CDF uses a wide variety of targeted strategies to generate constituent activity, including Wednesdays in Washington and at Home, which are special days for constituents to contact their members of Congress. The goal of this program is to convey to elected officials that we want and need them to make children their top priority. Although the specific message changes from week to week, this is the bottom line message of every Wednesday activity.

In addition to Wednesdays in Washington and at Home, CDF uses every means possible to raise public awareness about children's needs and what can be done:

- Visits to expose community leaders and policymakers to children's needs and what they can do
- TV, radio, and print media campaigns
- Town meetings
- Prayer vigils and study circles
- Coalition building
- Sending action alerts to encourage our constituents to contact their members of Congress by phone, fax, or e-mail at key moments throughout the congressional session
- Working closely with advocates in target states that have senators on important committees who have the authority to make decisions about child care funding
- Encouraging state advocates to make a special effort to publicize child care in their states, generate media articles, distribute public service announcements about child care, and encourage their senators and representatives to visit local child care centers
- Providing conference calls for advocates with experts discussing an issue that has risen to the top of the legislative agenda

Clearly, child care and early education advocates must work on many fronts to make change. It is important to collect reasoned and thoughtful data and to publish reports, as well as work directly with elected officials, encourage coalition and constituent activity around child care issues, and also engage the public through the media. However, it is not necessary to be an expert in all or any of these areas. It is vital to simply come forward and make your voice, a voice for children, heard. Advocates must convey their beliefs about what children and families need at every opportunity, with the resources available to them, and in a manner that suits their personal and professional situations. Many people coming together to stand up for children can make a difference.

Get connected. Receive the Early Childhood Development Listserv at http://capwiz.com/cdf/mlm/signup.

Contributed by Yasmine Daniel, director, Early Development Division, Children's Defense Fund.

These types of arrangements allow children to remain in familiar environments with people they know, benefiting from both continuity and stability.

FAMILY CHILD CARE

When home-based care is provided by a nonrelative outside a child's home but in a family setting, it is known as **family child care**, or *family care*. In this arrangement an individual caregiver provides care and education for a small group of children in the caregiver's home. Seven percent of children under five in child care are in family care. It generally involves one of three types of settings: homes that are unlicensed and unregulated by a state or local agency, homes that are licensed by regulatory agencies, or homes that are licensed and associated with an administrative agency.

Both the quantity and the quality of specific services provided in family homes vary from home to home and from agency to agency. However, almost 50 percent of family child care providers spend a substantial amount of their time in direct interaction with the children. Consider the unique features of Bridges Family Child Care in Madison, Wisconsin, and the ways the director, Vic McMurray, and her staff address the issues of quality, accessibility, and affordability such as faith-based organizations and YWCAs:

- Establish sliding-scale fees to encourage affordability
- Offer parents social support

Family child care Home-based care and education provided by a nonrelative outside the child's home; also known as family care.

- Provide information on parenting skills and ideas about what has worked successfully for other families
- Keep parents current on community support services they may be eligible to receive
- Provide a low staff-child ratio of 2:8
- Support children's activities
  - Help-yourself project/art tables
  - Book areas stocked with pillows
  - Regular sessions in music, rhythm, dance, and drama
  - Theme areas, such as a hospital scene, store, and post office
- Encourage children to wash, dress, and toilet independently
- Provide balanced nutrition
  - Serve organic meals and snacks, free from additives, hormones, and pesticides
  - Involve children in cooking, composting, and gardening
- Stress respect for students and staff
- Provide an inclusive environment (including children who are blind, autistic, with cerebral palsy, with Down syndrome, or born to crack-using mothers)
- Offer fair compensation (including health care, continuing education, and paid holidays, vacation, and personal days)

Now read the Program in Action "Magnia Child Care" on pages 184–185 to learn about another family program and the ways it meets the physical and cognitive needs of its children, as well as supporting the parent-caregiver relationship.

In the first DVD note, observe case manager Ronda Lewis as she discusses the nutritional services provided by her child care program. Why are high-quality nutritional services important in a child care program?

INTERGENERATIONAL CHILD CARE

Intergenerational child care programs integrate children and the elderly in an early childhood and adult care facility. The elderly derive pleasure and feelings of competence from interacting with children, and young children receive attention and love from older adults. Intergenerational programs blend the best of two worlds: children and the elderly both receive care and attention in a nurturing environment.

The Friendship Center at Schooley's Mountain in Hackettstown, New Jersey, is an intergenerational child care facility that incorporates senior citizens into its child care programs, which serve children two and a half to six years of age. It recruits elderly residents who can stimulate children through various experiences. For example, seniors at Health Village Retirement Community offer a potpourri of programs and classes to the Friendship Center children on a regular basis—from a French class for prekindergartners to woodworking and a very popular nature trail program. Some of the seniors also visit the children at playtime and push the playground swings, while others teach baking classes, flower arranging, or piano classes. When the children visit the nursing center, they learn to accept the sight of medical equipment, such as wheelchairs and oxygen tanks, and join in programming activities, such as finger painting, with the nursing center residents.

Evidence of the creativity of the children and the involvement of the Village residents is everywhere. The Village Men's Club gave a very special gift to the children—a handcrafted, twenty-four-by-sixteen-foot pirate ship christened *The Friend Ship*. The same group of men worked nine months on the newest playground addition—the Heathosaur, a life-sized, sixteen-by-four-foot wooden dinosaur.

The Child Care segment of the DVD and this textbook discuss different types of child care programs. List and describe as many types of child care programs as you can.

CENTER-BASED CHILD CARE

Center-based child care, as the name implies, is provided to groups of children and families in specially constructed or renovated facilities. For example, KIDCO Child Care Centers in Miami, Florida, operate as a nonprofit corporation out of four renovated warehouses and a former public school. The centers provide care for 450 children, from birth to age five who are primarily Puerto Rican, Dominican, and Haitian. The Program in Action feature about LaCausa on pages 186–187 illustrates another unique center-based

Center-based child care Child care and education provided in a facility other than a home.

program, where staff and administrators strive to provide children and families with quality, affordable, and accessible child care.

Because each state has its own definition of a center-based program, you should research your state's definitions and regulations regarding child care, center care, and other kinds of care. In addition, learn about your state's child care licensing requirements and child staff ratios.

EMPLOYER-SPONSORED CHILD CARE

New responses to child care needs arise as more and more parents enter the workforce. The most rapidly growing segment of the workforce, in fact, is married women with children under one year of age. To meet the needs of working parents, employers are increasingly called on to provide affordable, accessible, quality child care. According to the U.S. Chamber of Commerce, corporate-supported child care is one of the fastest-growing employee benefits. But employer-sponsored child care is not new: the Stride Rite Corporation started the first on-site corporate child care program in Boston in 1971.

On-site child care provides a number of advantages for parents:

- Parents can drop in on breaks for lunch.
- Mothers with infants can stop in to breast-feed.
- Mothers and fathers can stop by to tend to babies.
- Parents can car pool with their children, saving time in the drop-off and pick-up process.
- Parents have the peace of mind knowing their children are close, safe, and well cared for.

Many corporations have child care management programs operate their child care programs for them. And instead of providing on-site care, other employers provide different types of child care assistance, as shown in Figure 7.1.

Companion Website
To complete a Program in Action activity related to LaCausa, go to the Companion Website at **www.prenhall.com/morrison**, select chapter 7, then choose the Program in Action module.

FIGURE 7.1 How Businesses Support Child Care

- *Resource and referral services.* Corporations supply information and counseling to parents on selecting quality care, and they make referrals to local child care providers. These services are offered in-house (i.e., on site) or through community or national resource and referral agencies.

- *Direct aid.* Some companies provide a flat subsidy—a specific amount to help cover the cost of child care. For example, NationsBank, the largest bank in the South, pays its associates with limited incomes up to $35 per week to pay for child care.

- *Voucher systems.* Corporations give employees vouchers with which to purchase services at child care centers.

- *Vendor systems.* Corporations purchase spaces at child care centers and make them available to employees either free or at reduced rates.

- *Contributions to a child care center.* Corporations pay a subsidy to help reduce rates for employees at a particular center.

- *Parent-family leave.* Some corporations provide paid or subsidized leaves of absence for parents in lieu of specific child care services.

- *Other arrangements.* Employers can offer a flexible work schedule so that parents need less or no child care. They may also offer a maternity leave extension and a paternity leave, as well as allowing sick leave to include absence from work to care for a sick child.

MAGNIA CHILD CARE

I have been in the field of early care and education as a licensed family child care provider for sixteen years. My husband and I operate our program in our home. Magnia Child Care is accredited through the National Association for Family Child Care (NAFCC) and serves the needs of families with children from birth through age five. We are licensed for fourteen children and currently have eight enrolled. Because of the quality of our program, we are a training site for child development students from the local community college. As an Early Childhood Mentor Teacher—a program in California that pairs early childhood college students with experienced teachers in the field—I supervise these college students and offer first-hand experiences working with young children.

WHAT IS FAMILY CHILD CARE?

Family child care is the care of children in the provider's home. The provider must meet the necessary state and local licensing requirements, as well as health and safety standards. Family child care offers several benefits to parents that are not necessarily available in other early care settings:

- Smaller ratio of children to adults
- Mixed-age groups of children, allowing siblings to be together
- Consistent primary caregivers
- Flexibility to meet the needs of families
- The nurturing environment of a home

AN APPROPRIATE PROGRAM FOR ALL CHILDREN

At Magnia Child Care, we believe that our primary responsibilities include the following:

▲ Counting freshly picked avocados with center owner Albert Magnia provides an authentic learning experience for young children.

- Meeting the physical and emotional needs of children
- Maintaining a safe and healthy environment
- Supporting the parent-caregiver relationship
- Performing administrative tasks
- Continuing our professional growth and education

Because our program serves infants, toddlers, and preschool children, we offer a developmentally appropriate curriculum based on NAFCC guidelines. Along with planned activities for language and literacy, dramatic play, music and movement, and outdoor experiences, we also respect a child's ability to learn through self-discovery. Children in our program learn about science through their experiences with sand and water. They learn mathematics through the one-to-one ratio as they help pass out spoons or cups for lunchtime. They learn about their community as we take walks in the neighborhood and speak with the postal carrier, a repairman, or a police officer and visit a grocery store.

BACKUP CHILD CARE

Backup child care is a growing form of child care provided to corporate employees. For example, the O'Brien Family Center at PNC Firstside in Pittsburgh provides its employees with up to twenty days of child care a year, which they can use when their regular child care arrangements fall through or when there is a snow day. Employees pay fifteen dollars a day for the child care services. The center has twelve full-time staff and can care for seventy children ages six months to thirteen years. In addition, new parents who wish to return to work during their child's first year receive eight weeks of free infant care.[9] At the backup child

▲
Firm, smooth avocados are new to this child and worthy of the intense investigation that stimulates cognitive development.

Children at Magnia Child Care have opportunities to explore the outdoors on our tricycle path, in our sand box, on the climbing structures and swings, and in the places we've provided for them to discover nature. Indoor activities allow children to play in groups or to investigate on their own. Our schedule also provides a quiet time for rest and napping.

RELATIONSHIPS WITH PARENTS

An important part of our work is the relationships we develop with parents. Together we form a partnership in caring for their children. We learn about the child from the parents, and in turn, the parents learn about their child's growth in our program. Over the years we have

▲
Sharing the Parent File that is filled with articles on topics of interest to parents and information on community resources helps program owner/director Martha Magnia cement the teacher-parent relationship.

collected an assortment of articles on topics of interest to parents that relate to the typical skills of children, guidance suggestions, and dealing with difficult behaviors. Our Parent Files also include information on community resources that are available to children and their families. Coupled with our interactions with parents, this information serves to enhance the confidence of first-time parents as they inquire about their child's development.

AN EFFECTIVE FAMILY CHILD CARE PROVIDER

For an effective family child care provider, a strong background in child development is helpful. Understanding how children learn and how the environment affects their behavior, as well as learning about developmentally appropriate practices, influences the quality of child care. Taking part in professional organizations for early care and education is essential to our continued professional development.

A career in licensed family child care has many benefits. Being the director/owner of your own business is highly rewarding, as is incorporating your own program philosophy and developing your own policies, based on best practices. Your child care program can be flexible and accommodating to meet your needs and those of the families you serve.

Our greatest reward as licensed family child care providers is the pleasure we receive in working with young children and their families. It is gratifying to witness the growth and development of small infants into active, confident, ready-to-learn preschool children.

As with any profession, there are also challenges; unfortunately, some still assume that we are only babysitters. However, we continue to advocate and educate others about the valuable contribution that licensed family child care provides to children, to families, and to our communities.

Contributed by Martha Magnia, owner/director of Magnia Family Child Care and adjunct faculty at Fresno City College, where she teaches child development and family child care courses. Photos also contributed by Martha Magnia.

---

care center operated by J.P. Morgan Chase in Dallas, each employee receives twenty days of free backup childcare.[10]

MILITARY CHILD CARE

The Department of Defense (DoD) military child development system (CDS) provides daily services for the largest number of children of any employer in the United States. Military child care is provided in eight hundred centers in more than three hundred geographic locations, both within and outside the continental United States.

Companion Website
For more information about military child care, go to the Companion Website at **www. prenhall.com/morrison**, select chapter 7, then choose the Linking to Learning module.

Program in Action

La Causa: Innovations in Child Care Practice

It is almost midnight when Lourdes Ortiz wearily steps off the bus that has brought her from her cleaning job at a downtown office building to this street corner in the oldest and poorest neighborhood in Milwaukee. The security guard buzzes her into a large building. Walking down the hall, Lourdes glances at the brightly colored children's art decorating the walls. She enters a dimly lit room. A dozen children are sleeping on cots, covered with beautiful woven Mexican blankets. As the child care teacher helps Lourdes dress her sleeping three-year-old in a snowsuit, they chat softly in Spanish. Carrying Angelina, Lourdes steps out into the frozen darkness for the walk home.

"I just can't take it anymore! Tyrone messes with everything and won't mind when I tell him to quit. The baby cries all the time. Sometimes I'm afraid I'll lose it and hurt somebody," LaKinta Greer tells Carl, while her three children noisily explore the adjacent playroom. The Crisis Nursery worker listens patiently as the exhausted, teary-eyed young mother recounts how she's been struggling to find a job to meet welfare-to-work requirements, how her boyfriend left because he was fed up with all the attention she pays to the kids, how her landlord threatens to evict them because she's two months behind in the rent. It's Sunday afternoon. Carl tells LaKinta that tomorrow he'll work on getting her some long-term help, like rent assistance, and will connect her to the agency's Family Resource Center for parenting education and support. For the short term, he invites her to leave her children here for a few days so she can get some much-needed rest. They will be well cared for in a homelike atmosphere by trained child care providers. Relieved, LaKinta enters the playroom to kiss her kids goodbye.

Marisol Gómez sits at a table in the P.E.A.C.E. Training Academy, laughing with two other assistant child care teachers. The three have just completed a role play in which Marisol as the teacher has tried to help "preschoolers" Karen and Youa resolve their conflict over a riding toy. They are amused because the two teachers sounded exactly like kids fighting. Marisol worries, though, that she did not really support the kids in solving their problem themselves, since she suggested the solution. She motions to the instructor, who has been working with an-

other small group. Sara, a nationally endorsed High/Scope instructor, makes some gentle suggestions, speaking in English and Spanish. On her way back to work at the end of the training session, Marisol waves to her third grader, who is walking to the gym with his classmates, and peeks in on her baby in the infant room.

At La Causa, Inc. quality means so much more than the basics of safety, good nutrition, and a stimulating environment for children. The name of the organization, La Causa, means "The Cause" and has its roots in the rallying cry of the César Chavez movement for civil rights and economic development for Hispanics. In 1972 two Mexican mothers opened La Causa for seventeen children in a small store-front. They wanted quality care for their children that would help them retain their own language and culture while their families were becoming part of the economic and social fabric of their adopted country.

Today, La Causa serves nine thousand children and their parents with accessible, comprehensive services that support the development of the child within the context of family, community, and culture. La Causa's eight buildings are located around Milwaukee's oldest neighborhood. The area is populated largely by immigrant families from Puerto Rico, Mexico, and Central America. In recent years African American and Southeast Asian families have joined the mix. Some of La Causa's programs now reach out beyond the neighborhood to serve the city and the county.

Military families face challenges that are not found in other work environments. Shifting work schedules that are often longer than the typical eight-hour day and the requirement to be ready to deploy anywhere in the world on a moment's notice require a child development system that is flexible in nature yet maintains high standards. Frequent family separations and the need to move, on average, every three years place military families in situations not often experienced in the civilian world. For this population, affordable, high-quality child

La Causa's programmatic centerpiece consists of three child care centers and an elementary school. Even though La Causa's child care facilities all serve the same neighborhood, each has a particular set of services and an atmosphere that offer choices to parents. One small, homey center serves only children under five years of age. The largest center is open practically around the clock—from 5:30 A.M. to 1:30 A.M. This facility cares for infants, toddlers, and preschoolers, as well as children up to twelve years of age before and after their day at the bilingual public school down the block. Soon this center will be open on weekends as well. A new center was recently built to house La Causa's bilingual elementary charter school and a gallery of Mexican art and culture, along with caring for children from four weeks of age through kindergarten.

Working parents need easy access, convenience, support, and familiarity. La Causa's success derives from its extended hours, transportation, nutritious and culturally appropriate meals, sliding fees, and acceptance of government vouchers for care. At La Causa a child can enter at four weeks and move seamlessly through Head Start, kindergarten, and elementary school. Spanish and English speakers mingle easily in the classrooms, as both languages are spoken and valued by their teachers. La Causa's Family Resource Center provides parenting education, a toy lending library, and other opportunities for family support. The Crisis Nursery and Social Services help families at risk to remain intact, keep their children out of the foster care system, and recover from crises.

Families appreciate being served by people who can relate to them culturally and linguistically. La Causa's staff, administration, and board come largely from the communities served; they are 61 percent Latino, 12 percent African American, 1 percent Native American and Asian, and 26 percent Euro-American. The majority of the staff is bilingual in English and Spanish. Most of the teachers and administrators are women from the surrounding neighborhood. The agency has a grow-your-own practice that fosters the development of a multicultural, bilingual staff at all levels by dedicating extraordinary resources to recruitment, training, and advancement.

The child care staff's professional and personal growth is key to La Causa's success at retaining a quality, stable workforce. The P.E.A.C.E. Training Academy provides entry-level and continuing education courses to more than 2,000 child care professionals and paraprofessionals yearly. Course topics include everything from the basics of infant care, to active learning techniques, to working with children with autism. La Causa's educational philosophy includes a commitment to child-centered, developmentally appropriate practices and to fostering the social and emotional skills that prevent violence. Child care personnel are provided with opportunities to develop themselves as nurturers, community peacemakers, and teachers of peace through specially designed courses at the academy. They learn how to take care of their own needs, manage stress and anger, communicate with and understand others better, resolve conflicts, feel pride in their own cultural heritage and interest in others' cultures, and unleash their own creativity and playfulness—all so they can model and teach these skills to children.

La Causa is the first bilingual, multicultural child care center in Wisconsin accredited by the NAEYC. It has been declared a Governor's Center of Excellence and won a *Promesa de un Futuro Brillante* (Promise of a Brilliant Future) Award from the National Latino Children's Institute. The attention La Causa has received is the result of the innovative ways it has found to become a one-stop shop in the cause of child, family, and community development.

Contributed by Fran Kaplan, MSW, EdD, director, P.E.A.C.E. Training Academy, La Causa, Inc., Milwaukee, Wisconsin. Photos also contributed by Fran Kaplan.

care is paramount if they are to be ready to perform their missions and their jobs. It is also important to military personnel that child care services be consistent at installations throughout the military.

Four main components make up the DoD CDS: child development centers, family child care, school-age care, and resource and referral programs. Through these four areas, the DoD serves more than two hundred thousand children (ages six weeks to twelve years) daily. More than 48 percent of the care provided is for infants and toddlers. The system offers full-day, part-day, and hourly (i.e., drop-in) child care; part-day preschool programs; before- and after-school programs for school-age children; and extended-hour care, including nights and weekends.

Child Development Centers.   In child development centers (CDCs), care is usually provided between the hours of 6:00 A.M. and 6:30 P.M. Monday through Friday. Approximately 38 percent of all child care spaces are provided through CDCs. More than 99 percent of all centers are currently accredited by NAEYC.

Family Child Care.   Family child care (FCC) provides in-home care by certified providers. Historically, providers have had to live on the base or in government-leased housing; recently, several of the services expanded this to include military families living in civilian housing. More than nine thousand FCC providers deliver critical services to service members working on shifts, working extended hours or weekends, or preferring a home-based environment for their children. In addition, FCC providers can care for mildly ill children, something CDCs are not set up to do.

School-Age Care.   For children aged six to twelve years, school-age care (SAC) programs are offered before and after school, during holidays, and during summer vacations. The SAC programs complement, rather than duplicate, the school day. Emphasis is placed on SAC programs that meet community needs, reinforce family values, and promote the cognitive, social, emotional, and physical development of children. Not all SAC is provided in CDCs, much of it is provided in youth centers or other suitable facilities.

Resource and Referral Services.   Local resource and referral (R & R) services augment child care systems. R & R services assist parents in finding child care when all spaces on base are full or a parent can't get the preferred child care arrangement through military-provided services. Bridging the gap between those needing child care and those served by military child care services, R & R is a critical component of the system. R & R services at the local level work closely with community agencies to serve as a liaison to nonmilitary child care services.[11]

> Before- and after-school care programs play an increasingly important role in school-based programs and in the lives of children and families. Although opportunities for play and exercise are important in these programs, increasingly parents want them to provide help with homework, time to study, and enrichment activities, such as music and the arts.

BEFORE- AND AFTER-SCHOOL CARE

In many respects, public schools are logical places for before-school and after-school care; they have the administrative organization, facilities, and staff to provide such care. In addition, many taxpayers and professionals have always believed that schools should not sit empty in the afternoons, evenings, holidays, and summers. Thus, using resources already in place for child care makes good sense. The public schools in Dade County, Florida, provide before- and after-school care for more than 3,300 students in 111 before-school centers and more than 25,000 students in 205 after-school centers. Special needs students are mainstreamed at 83 schools, with well over 700 students in after-school care. Parents pay fifteen to thirty dollars per week, depending on the per-child cost at the individual school. Because the programs are school based and managed, the costs of services vary by program.

**TABLE 7.3 Largest Child Care Management Organizations
in the United States**

Organization	Headquarters	Number of Centers
Knowledge Learning Corporation	Portland, OR	2,000
KinderCare Learning Centers	San Rafael, CA	1,250
La Petite Academy	Chicago, IL	670
Bright Horizons Family Solutions	Watertown, MA	550
Childtime Learning Centers	Novi, MI	265

According to the National Study of Before and After School Programs, about 1.7 million children in kindergarten through grade eight are enrolled in 49,500 programs.[12] The three most common sponsors of before- and after-school child care are the public schools, for-profit corporations, and nonprofit organizations.

PROPRIETARY CHILD CARE

Some child care centers are run by corporations, businesses, and individual proprietors for the purpose of making a profit. Some for-profit centers provide before- and after-school elementary and before- and after-school programs as well. Many of these programs emphasize their educational component and appeal to middle-class families who are willing to pay for the promised services. About 35 percent of all child care centers in the United States are operated for profit, and the number is likely to grow. Child care is a thirty-eight billion dollar service industry, with more and more entrepreneurs realizing that there is money to be made in caring for the nation's children. Table 7.3 lists the five largest child care management organizations.

WHAT CONSTITUTES QUALITY CARE AND EDUCATION?

As child care grows and expands across the nation, it forces a number of critical issues. One of these is how to provide and maintain high-quality care for *all* children. Although there is much debate about quality and what it involves, we can nonetheless identify the main characteristics of quality programs that provide care and education for children and families. Figure 7.2 identifies ten components of quality child care as identified by the Center for Prevention and Early Intervention Policy. These ten components pay particular attention to the relationships of child care, the continuity of care, and the responsiveness of caregivers.

APPROPRIATE AND SAFE ENVIRONMENTS

At all age levels, a safe and pleasant physical setting is important. Such an area should include a safe neighborhood free from traffic and environmental hazards, a fenced play area with well-maintained equipment, child-sized equipment and facilities (e.g., toilets and sinks), and areas for displaying children's work, such as finger painting and clay models. The environment should also be attractive and pleasant. The rooms, home, or center should be clean, well lit, well ventilated, and cheerful.

CAREGIVER-CHILD RATIO

The ratio of adults to children should be sufficient to give children the individual care and attention they need. NAEYC guidelines for the ratio of caregivers to children are 1:3 or 1:4 for infants and toddlers and 1:8 to 1:10 for preschoolers, depending on group size.

FIGURE 7.2 10 Components of Quality Child Care

Child care providers and programs can use these ten components to grade the ongoing development of their services to children and families:

- Licensing ensures that a child care setting meets basic health and safety requirements.

- The strongest indicators for long-term education and care are related to the caregivers' education and level of participation in ongoing training in the field of early childhood development and care.

- Learning is an interactive process that involves opportunities for exploration and interaction.

- Group size and ratios determine the amount of time and attention that each caregiver can devote to each child.

- Positive relationships between caregivers and children are crucial to quality child care.

- The active and responsive caregiver takes cues from each child to know when to expand on the child's initiative, when to guide, when to teach, and when to intervene.

- The path to literacy begins with interactions between caregivers and young children.

- Learning involves activities, materials, and opportunities for exploration and interaction.

- High-quality programs incorporate practices reflecting the values and beliefs of the families and the cultures of their communities.

- High-quality child care serves as a protective environment for a child and a source of support for the child's family.

Source: Reproduced by permission of *Zero to Three* from M.A. Graham, A.E. Hogan, B.A. White, and C.A. Chiricos, "Enhancing the Quality of Relationships in Infant-Toddler Child Care: A Developmental Process," *Zero to Three* (July 2003): 15–16.

Child care involves much more than merely providing physical care. All caregivers should provide children with love and affection and should meet each child's full range of social, emotional, and physical needs.

The American Public Health Association and the American Academy of Pediatrics recommend these ratios and standards:

- Child-staff ratios of 3:1 for children under twenty-five months, 4:1 for children twenty-five to thirty months, and 7:1 for children thirty to thirty-five months

- Group sizes of six for children under twenty-five months, eight for children twenty-five to thirty months, and fourteen for children thirty to thirty-five months

- Child care providers who have formal, post–high school training in child development, early childhood education, or a related field

Research shows that when programs meet these recommended child-staff ratios and recommended levels of caregiver training and education, children have better outcomes.[13]

Also, analyses of research data reveal that low-quality care for all children—regardless of whether they were in child care centers or homes or were taken care of by family members—is associated with poorer school readiness and poorer performance on tests of expressive and receptive language skills. In contrast, child care quality was not associated with a child's social behavior.

DEVELOPMENTALLY APPROPRIATE PROGRAMS

Programs should have written, developmentally based curricula for meeting children's needs. A program's curriculum should specify activities for children of all ages, which caregivers can use to stimulate infants, provide for the growing independence of toddlers, and address the readiness and literacy skills of four- and five-year-olds. All programs should include curricula and activities that meet the social, emotional, and cognitive needs of all children. Quality programs use developmentally appropriate practices to implement the curriculum and achieve their program goals.

INDIVIDUAL NEEDS

Good care and education provides for children's needs and interests at each developmental stage. For example, infants need good physical care as well as continual love and affection and sensory stimulation. Toddlers need safe surroundings and opportunities to explore. They need caregivers who support and encourage active involvement. However, within these broad categories of development, individual children have unique styles of interacting and learning that must also be accommodated. Each child must feel valued and respected.

CULTURALLY APPROPRIATE PRACTICE

Developmentally appropriate programs include culturally appropriate practice. Hispanic children remain the largest minority group of underserved children, and the child care issues of access, affordability, and quality are of critical concern to their community. Figure 7.3 provides action steps you can take to meet the needs of young Hispanic children and their families. In addition, the Diversity Tie-In on page 193 in this chapter gives specific strategies you can use to accommodate both Hispanic and Laotian cultures.

FAMILY EDUCATION AND SUPPORT

Parents and other family members should know as much as possible about the program their children attend, their children's growth and development, and the curricular program of activities. It is important to share with parents how services are provided in such critical areas as child development and nutrition. Teachers must place a high priority on daily communication about children's progress.

STAFF TRAINING AND DEVELOPMENT

All teachers should be involved in an ongoing program of training and development. The child development associate (CDA) certification program discussed in chapter 1 is a good beginning for staff members to become competent and maintain necessary skills. Program administrators should also have a background and training in child development and early childhood education. Knowledge of child growth and development is essential for all child care professionals. They need to be developmentally aware and child oriented in all phases of delivering high-quality child care.

Child care providers need to give children opportunities to learn social and academic skills through daily activities such as meal time. What are some ways that you could provide opportunities to ensure that children are learning important nutritional concepts and skills?

In the Child
Care segment of the DVD, the narrator identifies accreditation as one of the hallmarks of program quality. How does accreditation help assure parents of high-quality child care? What six features are essential for accreditation?

Observing children at play enables teachers to learn about their developmental levels, social skills, and peer interactions. How might you use observational information to plan play-based activities?

FIGURE 7.3 Action Steps to Meet the Cultural Needs of Hispanic Children and Families

- Outreach efforts to parents should include the use of culturally appropriate messages and the involvement of community, religious, social, and economic institutions.

- Early learning guidelines for child care and other educational programs should be respectful of children's home languages, and cultures and give priority to language-rich learning environments that take into account the language(s) spoken by the children.

- Training and professional development of teachers should give priority to research-based strategies to enhance the language, literacy, and school readiness of all children, including children with limited English proficiency.

- Staff recruitment measures should focus on linguistic and cultural minorities to ensure that the professionals working with children are as diverse as the children they serve.

- Child assessment and evaluation outcome measures should be linguistically and culturally appropriate, as well as developmentally appropriate, for all children, including English-language learners.

Source: Reprinted by permission from Ray Collins and Rose Ribeiro, "Toward an Early Care and Education Agenda for Hispanic Children," *Early Childhood Research & Practice* (Fall 2004), http://ecrp.uiuc.edu/v6n2/collins.html.

PROGRAM ACCREDITATION

In any discussion of quality, the question invariably arises, Who determines quality? Fortunately, NAEYC has addressed the issue of standards in its Center Accreditation Project (CAP). CAP is a national, voluntary accreditation process for child care centers, preschools, and programs that provide before- and after-school care for school-age children. Accreditation is administered through NAEYC's National Academy of Early Childhood Programs.

The criteria addressed in the accreditation project include interactions among staff and children; curriculum, staff, and parent interactions; administration, staff, and parent interactions; staff qualifications and development; staffing patterns; physical environment; health and safety; nutrition and food service; and program evaluation.[14]

THE EFFECTS OF CARE AND EDUCATION ON CHILDREN

Recent research reveals that high-quality early care and education have influences that last over a lifetime.

A valuable source of research about child care comes from the Study of Early Child Care (SECC) by the National Institute of Child Health and Human Development (NICHD). This is a comprehensive longitudinal study initiated by NICHD in 1989 to answer the many questions about the relationship between child care experiences and characteristics and children's develop-

Diversity Tie-In

HOW TO SUPPORT DIVERSITY IN A MULTICULTURAL CHILD CARE SETTING

Hampton Place Baptist Church is in the low-income region of Oak Cliff, an urban area of Dallas, Texas, that is composed of many minorities. The church provides child care services to primarily Hispanic, Spanish-speaking families. However, we also house a Laotian mission. Our preschool department includes approximately fifteen infants, ten toddlers, and fifteen preschoolers and serves both the Hispanic and the Laotian congregations. Here are some of the considerations and adjustments we make to accommodate these different cultures:

STRATEGY 1

Greet families in a culturally sensitive manner

With Hispanic families, the father is greeted first, then the mother, and the children last.

STRATEGY 2

Provide inclusive artwork

Murals include children with different skin and hair colors.

STRATEGY 3

Use linguistically appropriate materials

Books in English and Spanish should be provided.

STRATEGY 4

Adjust teacher-infant interaction style according to culture

Although most Hispanic infants are calmed with quick, repetitive, choppy phrases and back patting, Laotian infants are calmed through soft, smooth talking, cradling, and gentle rocking.

STRATEGY 5

Meet individual as well as cultural needs

Some infants interact primarily person-to-person; others interact through toys.

STRATEGY 6

Respect different social preferences

Hispanic toddlers tend to interact with peers, but Laotian toddlers tend to keep to themselves and sometimes want to be left alone. A Laotian child may need to be provided with a special place of his or her own.

STRATEGY 7

Apply limits to cultural accommodation when necessary

Discuss compromises with parents. For example, some cultures allow infants to eat items they could choke on. In this case we explain the danger the food presents to the infants and ask parents to bring alternative snacks.

STRATEGY 8

Recognize that all families have individual cultures

Be careful not to stereotype by ethnicity.

Contributed by Amy Turcotte, developmental specialist.

mental outcomes. In 1991 the NICHD researchers enrolled 1,364 children from birth to age three in the study and conducted Phase I from 1991 to 1994. In Phase II, from 1995 to 2000, they followed the 1,226 children who continued to participate through their third year in school. Phase III of the study is currently being conducted to follow more than 1,100 of the children through their sixth year in school.[15] Figure 7.4 gives some of the study's findings on the use of child care and its effects on children and families.

The study results make it clear that professionals must provide high-quality programs and must advocate for that high quality with the public and state legislators.

Companion Website To complete a Diversity Tie-In activity related to multicultural preschools, go to the Companion Website at **www.prenhall.com/morrison**, select chapter 7, then choose the Diversity Tie-In module.

FIGURE 7.4 Selected Results from the NICHD Study of Early Child Care and Youth Development

See what surprises you most as you review these study results. Then try to find other research data that confirm or contradict that finding.

Child care arrangements

- During the first year of life the majority of children in nonparental care experienced more than two different child care arrangements.
- More than one-third experienced three or more arrangements.

Hours in child care

- At their first entry into nonmaternal care, children averaged 29 hours of care per week.
- By twelve months, children in care averaged 33.9 hours a week of care.

Kind of care

- The amount of time the children spent in care rose only slightly after the first year of life; children who were in care for thirty-six months averaged 34.4 hours per week.
- However, the type of care had changed considerably, with 44 percent in center care, 25 percent in child care home, 12 percent cared for by their father or their mother's partner, 10 percent cared for at home by nannies or babysitters, and 9 percent cared for by grandparents

Child care and income

- Families with the lowest nonmaternal income were the most likely to place infants in care before the age of three months, probably because they were the most dependent on the mother's income.
- In contrast, infants from families with the highest maternal and nonmaternal incomes tended to start care between three and five months.
- The higher their mothers' earnings, the more hours infants spent in nonmaternal care; however, the higher the *nonmaternal* earnings in the family, the *fewer* hours they spent in care.

Maternal attitudes and child care

- Mothers who believed their children benefited from their employment tended to place their infants in care earlier and for more hours in nonauthoritarian, nonmaternal care.
- In contrast, mothers who believed maternal employment carried high risks for their children tended to put their infants in care for fewer hours and were especially likely to rely on the infant's father for child care.

Quality of nonmaternal care

- Observations at six months indicated that more-positive caregiving occurred when children were in smaller groups, child-adult ratios were lower, caregivers held less authoritarian beliefs about child rearing, and physical environments were safe, clean, and stimulating.
- Observed quality of care for poor children was generally lower than for nonpoor children when they were cared for by an unrelated caregiver.

Social, emotional, cognitive, and health-related child outcomes

- Observed quality of caregivers' behavior—particularly the amount of language stimulation provided—was positively related to children's performance on measures of cognitive and linguistic abilities at ages fifteen, twenty-four, and thirty-six months.

In the Child Care segment of the DVD, high-quality child care is shown to have a positive impact throughout a child's life. According to Figure 7.4 in the text, what are positive benefits of high-quality child care for young children?

FIGURE 7.4 Continued

- Quality of care was also related to measures of social and emotional development. At twenty-four months, children who had experienced higher-quality care were reported by both their mothers and their caregivers to have fewer behavior problems and were rated higher on social competence by their mothers. At thirty-six months, higher quality care was associated with greater compliance and less negative behavior during mother-child interactions and fewer caregiver-reported behavior problems.

- Over the first three years of life, higher quality child care among the families that used nonmaternal care was also associated with greater maternal sensitivity during mother-child interaction.

- Poor-quality child care was related to an increased incidence of insecure infant-mother attachment at fifteen months, but only when the mother was also relatively low in sensitivity and responsiveness.

Child outcomes

- The extent to which children's child care center classes met professional guidelines was related to developmental outcomes at twenty-four and thirty-six months.

- Children in classes that met the guidelines for child-staff ratio had fewer behavior problems and more positive social behaviors at both ages.

- Three-year-olds in classes that met the standards for caregiver training and higher education showed greater school readiness, better language comprehension, and fewer behavior problems.

- Quality of care continued to be associated with developmental outcomes throughout the preschool years.

Quantity of care

- The quantity of nonmaternal care was a statistically significant predictor of some child outcomes. When children spent more hours in child care, mothers were less sensitive in their interactions with their children (at six, fifteen, twenty-four, and thirty-six months) and children were less positively engaged with their mothers (at fifteen, twenty-four, and thirty-six months).

- Analyses of attachment at fifteen months showed that children who spent more hours in child care *and* had mothers who had relatively insensitive and unresponsive were at heightened risk for insecure infant-mother attachments.

- At twenty-four months, spending more hours in care was associated with mothers' reports of lower social competence and caregivers' reports of more problem behaviors.

- At the kindergarten assessment, quantity of care was associated with both teacher and mother ratings of problem behaviors.

Type of care

- Type of child care was clearly associated with rates of early communicable illnesses.

- Children attending child care centers and child care homes had more ear infections and upper respiratory illnesses than did children cared for at home, especially during the first two years of life.

- The number of other children in the child care setting was also positively related to frequency of upper respiratory illnesses and gastrointestinal illnesses through age three. However, these heightened rates of illness did not seem to have significant adverse developmental consequences over the first three years of life.

FIGURE 7.4 Continued

Family factors and child outcomes

- Analyses of the effects of child care experiences and family factors on child outcomes indicated that family characteristics were more consistent predictors of both social-emotional and cognitive child outcomes through age three than were child care factors.

- In the social-emotional domain, mothers' sensitivity, responsiveness, and overall psychological adjustment predicted infant-mother attachment security at fifteen months; but observed quality and amount of nonmaternal care, age at entry into care, and frequency of changes in care arrangements did not.

- Low-quality nonmaternal care, spending more than ten hours per week in care, and changes in care arrangements did increase the risk of insecure attachments when combined with low maternal sensitivity.

- Secure infant-mother attachment at fifteen months, in turn, predicted more positive infant-mother interaction at twenty-four months and fewer mother-reported behavior problems at thirty-six months.

- Maternal sensitivity during the first two years of life was a better predictor of self-control, compliance, and problem behaviors at twenty-four and thirty-six months than any aspect of children's early nonmaternal care experiences.

- In the cognitive domain, family factors accounted for a much larger share of the variance in cognitive and linguistic outcomes across the first three years of life than child care factors did.

- Maternal vocabulary and the quality of the home environment were significant predictors of cognitive and language development at fifteen, twenty-four, and thirty-six months.

Source: Reprinted by permission from Child Care and Child Development, *Results from the NICHD Study of Early Child Care and Youth Development* (New York: Guilford Press, 2005), 28–35.

Companion Website

For additional Internet resources or to complete an online activity for this chapter, go to the Companion Website at **www.prenhall.com/morrison,** select chapter 7, then choose the Linking to Learning or Making Connections module.

LINKING TO LEARNING

Child Care Bureau

http://www.acf.dhhs.gov/programs/ccb

Includes information on the Child Care and Development Block Grant, links to other Administration on Children and Families sites, and other information within the Department of Health and Human Services, with links to other related child care sites.

Childcare.gov

http://www.childcare.gov

A site for parents, child care programs, and early childhood educators; brings all federal agency resources together in one place.

Connect for Kids
http://www.connectforkids.org

>*A coalition of leaders from diverse organizations advocating for high-quality child care; activities include education, information service, proposing possible solutions, and technical assistance to government offices.*

National Association for the Education of Homeless Children and Youth
http://www.naehcy.org

>*A professional association dedicated to homeless education; has guidelines, goals, and objectives that outline strategies for dealing with government agencies and designing effective programs to help solve problems faced by homeless children, youth, and families.*

National Child Care Information Center
http://nccic.org

>*Sponsored by the Child Care Bureau, Administration for Children and Families, Department of Health and Human Services; provides a central access point for information on child care. Lists the licensure regulations for all fifty states regarding child care, center care, and other kinds of care.*

National Resource Center for Health and Safety in Child Care
http://nrc.uchsc.edu

>*Funded by the Maternal and Child Health Bureau of the Department of Health and Human Service; has the child care licensure regulations for each state. Also has health and safety tips and full-text resources.*

ACTIVITIES FOR FURTHER ENRICHMENT

ETHICAL DILEMMA: "SHOULD I TELL HER?"

Maria, a good friend of yours, has quit her job and opened her own family child care program. She felt that she could make more money by caring for her two children and several other children. Maria's child care is unlicensed and involves eight children, aged two to eight, including her two children, aged four and six. You are concerned that Maria is operating an unlicensed child care program and is caring for too many children; your state licensing laws for family child care allow for a maximum of six children aged two to eight, including the provider's children.

What should you do?

Should you privately discuss your belief that she is out of compliance with state regulations, or should you immediately report Maria to the state child care licensing bureaus. Or should you do nothing and hope that through her CDA training, Maria will realize that it is her professional responsibility to operate a licensed program?

APPLICATIONS

1. Invite people from child care programs, welfare departments, and social service agencies to speak to your class about child care and education. Determine what qualifications and training are necessary to become a child care employee.

2. Which one of the child care programs discussed in this chapter do you think best meets the needs of children and families? What kind of program would you want for your child? Why?

3. Which of the child care programs discussed in the chapter are available in your community? Are some more prevalent than others? What is a possible explanation for the types of child care programs in your community?

4. What before- and after-school programs are available in your area? How do those programs compare to other types of child care programs available? Find out what qualifications are needed to work in one of these settings and what the role of teachers is in it.

FIELD EXPERIENCES

1. Visit various child care programs, including home and center programs, and discuss similarities and differences in class. Which of the programs provides the best services? What changes or special provisions need to be made to improve the success of these kinds of programs?

2. Visit an employer-sponsored child care program, and describe it to your classmates. List the pros and cons of employer-sponsored child care for parents and for employers.

3. Visit several child care programs, and compare and contrast what you see. How are they similar and different? How do you account for this?

4. Visit a before- and after-school child care program at a local school and at a private child care facility. What pros and cons do you observe in each program?

RESEARCH

1. Survey parents in your area to determine what services they desire from child care. Are most of the parents' child care needs being met? How is what they want in a child care program similar to and different from the standards for quality child care discussed in this chapter?
2. Determine the legal requirements for establishing home and center child care programs in your state, city, or locality. What are the similarities and differences in establishing home and center programs? What is your opinion of the guidelines? Why?
3. Link to NAEYC's website (*www.naeyc.org*) and review its Position Statement on Licensing and Public Regulation of Early Childhood Programs. Why does NAEYC believe licensing and regulation of child care are important processes?
4. Conduct a survey to learn the cost of child care services in your area. Arrange your data in a table. What conclusions can you draw?

READINGS FOR FURTHER ENRICHMENT

Catron, C. E., and J. Allen. *Early Childhood Curriculum: A Creative Play Model,* 3rd ed. Upper Saddle River, NJ: Merrill/Prentice Hall, 2003.

Provides information on planning programs with a play-based, developmental curriculum for children from birth to five years of age; covers basic principles and current research in early childhood curricula.

Curtis, A., and M. O'Hagan. *Care and Education in Early Childhood: A Student's Guide to Theory and Practice.* New York: Routledge Falmer, 2003.

Provides a comprehensive and up-to-date review of the key issues in the field of early childhood care and education. Includes discussions on equal opportunities and children's rights, an examination of how children learn, and a look at the learning difficulties they may face. Also compares European perspectives on care and education in the early years.

Halpern, Robert. *Making Play Work: The Promise of After-School Programs for Low-Income Children.* New York: Teachers College Press, 2003.

Describes the historical development, current status, and critical issues facing before- and after-school programs, as they become an important developmental support for low- and moderate-income children.

Lombardi, J. *Time to Care: Redesigning Child Care to Promote Education, Support Families, and Build Communities.* Philadelphia: Temple University Press, 2002.

Lays out seven principles that should shape our image of child care and presents detailed, well-documented discussions of the why, the what, and the how of improving child care systems. Suggests a new view of child care as a potential asset—not as a crisis or a deficit—leading to new opportunities to further the traditional American values of education, family, and quality.

Youcha, Geraldine. *Minding the Children: Child Care in America from Colonial Times to the Present.* Cambridge, MA: Da Capo Press, 2005.

Beyond child care theories and early childhood gurus, a description of how children have actually been reared in America over the last four centuries.

ENDNOTES

1. Bureau of Labor Statistics, U.S. Department of Labor, "Employment Status of Mothers with Own Children Under 3 Years Old by Single Year of Age of Youngest Child and Marital Status, 2003–2004 Annual Averages" (2003–04), http://www.bls.gov/news.release/famee.t06.htm.
2. "Child Care Selection," *Children and Youth Services Review* (January 10, 2005): 4.
3. Ibid.
4. Ibid.
5. Ibid.
6. Ibid.
7. B. Fuller, S. L. Kagan, G. L. Caspary, and C. A. Gauthier, "Welfare Reform and Child Care Options for Low-Income Families," *Children and Welfare Reform* 12, no. 1 (2002), www.futureofchildren.org.
8. Lina Guzman, "Grandma and Grandpa Taking Care of the Kids: Patterns of Involvement," *Child Trends* research brief (July 2004).
9. M. Carpenter, "Study Finds Few Child Care Programs in Pennsylvania Offer High-Quality Early Learning," *Post-Gazette* (December 3, 2002).
10. P. Rivera, "Child Care Service Helps Firms Save," *Dallas Morning News* (December 10, 2002).
11. Military Family Resource Center, http://mfrc.calib.com/myc/mm_cdc.htm.
12. B. Kleiner, M. J. Nolin, and C. Chapman, "Before- and After-School Care, Programs, and Activities of Children in Kindergarten Through Grade Eight: 2001," *Education Statistics Quarterly* 6, no. 1 and 2 (2004). Also available at http://nces.ed.gov/programs/quarterly/vol_6/1_2/4_2.asp.
13. NICHD Early Child Care Research Network, "Child Outcomes When Child Care Center Classes Meet Recommended Standards for Quality," *American Journal of Public Health* 88, no. 7 (1998): 1072–1077.
14. NAEYC, *Accreditation by the National Academy of Early Childhood Programs* (Washington, DC: Author, 1991), 2.
15. The NICHD Study of Early Child Care and Youth Development, http://secc.rti.org/publications.cfm.

The Federal Government

SUPPORTING CHILDREN'S SUCCESS

Head Start provides comprehensive services that children living in poverty need to achieve school readiness.

SARAH GREENE, CEO NATIONAL
HEAD START ASSOCIATION

CHAPTER 8

In chapter 2 we discussed the increasing influence of federal and state governments in early childhood education. One of the remarkable political events of the last decade has been the use of early childhood education to achieve federal and state educational goals and to reform education.

As a result, more federal and state dollars are being poured into early childhood programs, making this a very exciting and challenging time for all early childhood professionals and their programs. However, with increased federal and state funding come mandates, control, and restructuring. Federal and state laws, regulations, and dollars are changing what early childhood programs look like and how they function. Federally funded programs such as Head Start and Early Head Start are leading the way in changing how the early childhood profession cares for and educates young children.

FEDERAL LEGISLATION AND EARLY CHILDHOOD

Federal legislation has had a tremendous influence on the educational process. For early childhood education, the passage of the Economic Opportunity Act of 1964, which funded Head Start, marks the contemporary beginning of federal political and financial support. As you read this chapter, you will learn how and why federal and state governments are changing the field of early childhood education.

NO CHILD LEFT BEHIND ACT OF 2001

The **No Child Left Behind Act of 2001** (NCLB Act) was intended to significantly reform K–twelve education. Since its passage, it has radically and rapidly changed how America conducts its educational business. NCLB emphasizes state and district accountability, mandates state standards for what children should know and be able to do, puts in place a comprehensive program of testing in grades three to twelve, and encourages schools to use teaching methods that have demonstrated their ability to help children learn.

The NCLB Act targets six fundamental areas:

- Accountability
- Literacy
- Programs that work (based on scientific research)
- Professional development
- Educational technology
- Parental involvement

NCLB is a significant educational act that will influence what and how you teach for many years to come. The act has influenced preK education because there is a major emphasis on getting children ready for school. And many federally funded programs now use guidelines and mandates in the No Child Left

Focus Questions

Why are federal agencies so involved in programs that support and educate children and families?

How are federal agencies transforming early childhood education?

What are the essential purposes of federal programs that serve young children and their families?

What are the basic issues involved in the federal funding and control of early childhood programs?

Companion Website

To check your understanding of this chapter, go to the Companion Website at **www.prenhall.com/ morrison**, select chapter 8, answer Multiple Choice and Essay Questions, and receive feedback.

No Child Left Behind Act
Federal law passed in 2001
that has significantly
influenced early childhood
education.

**Companion
Website**
For more
information about the NCLB
Act, go to the Companion
Website at **www.prenhall.
com/morrison**, select chapter
8, then choose the Linking to
Learning Module.

Early Head Start A
federal program serving
pregnant women, infants,
toddlers, and their families.

Head Start A federal early
childhood program serving
poor children aged three to
five and their families.

Entitlement programs
Programs and services
children and families are
entitled to because they meet
the eligibility criteria for the
services.

Behind Act to develop goals and objectives for their own programs. In other words, all facets of programs that serve young children have been and will continue to be influenced by the No Child Left Behind Act.

LITERACY AND READING FIRST

Another far-ranging influence of NCLB is that it puts literacy and reading first by trying to ensure that every child can read on grade level by the end of third grade. This means that efforts to provide young children with the literacy skills they need begins in **Early Head Start** and **Head Start** programs. For example, the Department of Health and Human Services provides Head Start programs with assistance on ways in which they can better prepare children to be ready for school. Particular emphasis is placed on both child and family literacy so that Head Start children can better develop the skills they need to become lifelong readers and parents can better develop the skills they need to improve their own lives and to help their children become reading proficient. Head Start is investing considerable resources in early literacy, including targeting training and technical assistance resources to ensure that every Head Start classroom is promoting reading, vocabulary, and language skills.[1]

FEDERAL PROGRAMS AND EARLY EDUCATION

Every dimension of almost every educational program—public, private, and faith-based—is touched in some way by the federal government. Figure 8.1 shows some of the federal programs that help to provide early care and education.

Head Start (for children aged three to five) and Early Head Start (for children from birth to three) are comprehensive child development programs that serve children, families, and pregnant women. These programs provide comprehensive health, nutritional, educational, and social services in order to help children achieve their full potential and succeed in school and life. Currently, the programs serve poor children and families; thus, they are considered **entitlement programs,** which means that children and families who qualify are entitled to the services. However, only about one-third of eligible children and families receive these services because of the lack of funding to support full implementation.

HEAD START

Head Start was implemented during the summer of 1965. The first programs were designed for children entering first grade who had not attended kindergarten. The purpose of Head Start was literally to give children from low-income families a "head start" on their first-grade experience and, hopefully, on life itself. As public schools have provided more kinder-

---

FIGURE 8.1   Federal Programs That Support Early Care and Education

The federal government's involvement in the field of early childhood care and education
is extensive and far-reaching.

Department of Health and Human Services	**Department of Education**
• Head Start	• Title I PreK and Elementary—helps low income children meet challenging academic standards
• Early Head Start	
• Good Start/Grow Smart	
• Child Care Development Fund	• Early Reading First
• Temporary Assistance for Needy Families—child care(TANF)	• Even Start
	• Special education preschool and infant grants
• Social services block grants to states to support early care and education	• Early childhood educator professional development programs

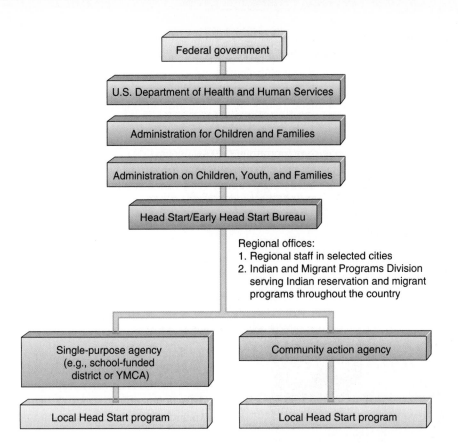

FIGURE 8.2
Organizational Structure of Head Start/Early Head Start

Federal government

U.S. Department of Health and Human Services

Administration for Children and Families

Administration on Children, Youth, and Families

Head Start/Early Head Start Bureau

Regional offices:
1. Regional staff in selected cities
2. Indian and Migrant Programs Division serving Indian reservation and migrant programs throughout the country

Single-purpose agency (e.g., school-funded district or YMCA)

Community action agency

Local Head Start program

Local Head Start program

garten and preschool programs, Head Start now serves younger children. It is administered by the Administration for Children and Families (ACF) in the Department of Health and Human Services. Figure 8.2 shows the organizational structure for Head Start and Early Head Start.

As of 2005 the national Head Start program has an annual budget of more than 6.8 billion dollars and serves some 905,851 low-income children plus their families. There are 1,604 Head Start programs nationwide, with a total of nearly 20,050 centers and more than 48,000 classrooms. The average cost of the Head Start program per child is $7,222 annually. Head Start has a paid staff of 211,950 and 1,353,000 volunteers.[2]

Performance Standards.　Both Head Start and Early Head Start must comply with federal **performance standards,** designed to ensure that all children and families receive high-quality services. These performance standards guide program development and implementation and cover child health and developmental services, education and early childhood development, child safety, child nutrition, child mental health, family and community partnerships, program management, and program governance. In addition, the performance standards stress that local programs should emphasize the professional development of Head Start teachers and should include reading and math readiness skills in the curriculum. Although the Head Start Bureau provides guidance on meeting the performance standards, local agencies are responsible for designing programs to best meet the needs of their children and families.

Objectives.　Five objectives are defined in the Head Start performance standards:

- Enhance children's growth and development
- Strengthen families as the primary nurturers of their children
- Provide children with educational, health, and nutritional services

In the Head Start segment of the DVD, the narrator explains that Head Start is guided by performance standards. How do these standards guide services to children, as well as teachers' professional development?

Companion Website　For more information about Head Start performance standards, go to the Companion Website at **www.prenhall.com/morrison,** select chapter 8, then choose the Linking to Learning module.

Performance standards
Federal guidelines for Head Start and Early Head Start, designed to ensure that all children and families receive high-quality services.

- Link children and their families to needed community services
- Ensure well-managed programs that involve parents in decision making

Standards of Learning. Head Start programs implement *standards of learning* in early literacy, language, and numeracy skills. These nine indicators guide teacher planning and act as standards of learning for Head Start children:

- Develop phonemic, print, and numeracy awareness
- Understand and use language to communicate for various purposes
- Understand and use increasingly complex and varied vocabulary
- Develop and demonstrate an appreciation of books
- In the case of non–English-background children, progress toward acquisition of the English language
- Know that the letters of the alphabet are a special category of visual graphics that can be individually named
- Recognize a word as a unit of print
- Identify at least ten letters of the alphabet
- Associate sounds with written words

In the Head Start segment of the DVD, listen to what teacher Romina Pastorelli identifies as the objectives of Head Start. How do her comments compare with the Head Start objectives identified in this chapter?

The federal government provides Head Start support by training Head Start teachers to use the best methods of early reading and language skills instruction in order to better teach these standards.[3]

Implications. These standards and others embedded in the Head Start performance standards have several implications for Head Start:

- The Head Start curriculum is more academic.
- Literacy and reading are a priority.
- Teachers and programs are more accountable for children's learning.

Child Outcomes Framework. The outcomes framework shown in Figure 8.3 includes the nine indicators of learning as well as many other performance standards that shape the Head Start curriculum. (The nine special indicators appear in boldface and are identified with a ★.) Figure 8.3 is located at the end of this chapter. This outcome framework is important for several reasons:

- It specifies learning outcomes that are essential to children's success in school and life.
- It ensures that all Head Start children in all Head Start programs work toward the same learning outcomes.
- It impacts what children learn in all preschool programs, not just Head Start.

Federally funded programs such as Head Start are designed to provide for the full range of children's social, emotional, physical, and academic needs. Increasingly, however, federal- and state-supported early childhood programs are emphasizing literacy, math, and science skills. How can traditional play-based activities such as this help children learn skills in these three areas?

PROGRAM OPTIONS

Head Start and Early Head Start programs have the freedom to tailor their programs to meet the needs of the children, families, and communities they serve. Every three years local programs conduct a community survey to determine strengths and resources and then design their program option based on these data. There are four program options:

1. The *center-based option* delivers services to children and families using the center as the base, or core. Center-based programs operate either full-day or half-day for thirty-two to thirty-four weeks a year, the minimum required by the Head Start performance standards, or they operate full-year programs. Center staff make periodic visits to family homes.[4]

2. The *home-based option* uses the family home as the base for providing services. Home visitors work with the parents and children to improve parenting skills and to assist parents in using the home as the child's primary learning environment. Twice a month children and families come together for field trips and classroom experiences to emphasize peer group interaction.[5] The home-based option has these strengths:
   • Parent involvement is the keystone of the program.
   • Geographically isolated families have an invaluable opportunity to be part of a comprehensive child and family program.
   • An individualized family plan is based on both a child and a family assessment.
   • The family plan is facilitated by a home visitor, who is an adult educator with knowledge of and training in all Head Start components.
   • The program includes the entire family.

3. The *combination option* combines the center- and home-based options.[6]

4. The *local option* includes programs created specifically to meet unique community and family needs. For example, some Early Head Start programs provide services in family child care homes.[7]

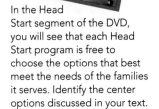

In the Head Start segment of the DVD, you will see that each Head Start program is free to choose the options that best meet the needs of the families it serves. Identify the center options discussed in your text.

The Program in Action "Higher Horizons Head Start" on pages 206–207 provides a good description of a combination program that implements a full-day center-based program for preschool children, as well as home- and center-based services for infants, toddlers, and pregnant women.

Head Start has always prided itself on tailoring its local programs to the children and families in the local community. In fact, this goal of meeting the needs of families and children at the local level is one of the program's strengths, and one that makes it popular with parents.

Companion Website
To complete a Program in Action activity related to Head Start, go to the Companion Website at **www.prenhall.com/morrison**, select chapter 8, then choose the Program in Action module.

ELIGIBILITY FOR HEAD START SERVICES

To be eligible for Head Start services, children must meet age and family-income criteria. Head Start enrolls children aged three to five from low-income families. Income eligibility is determined by whether or not family incomes fall below the official poverty line, which is set annually by the U.S. Department of Health and Human Services. Poverty guidelines for 2005 are shown in Table 8.1.

Ninety percent of Head Start enrollment has to meet the income eligibility criteria. The other 10 percent of enrollment can include children from families that exceed the low-income guidelines. In addition, 10 percent of a program's enrollment must include children with disabilities.

TABLE 8.1 2005 Poverty Guidelines for the Forty-Eight Contiguous States and the District of Columbia

Size of Family Unit	Poverty Guideline
2	$12,830
3	$16,090
4	$19,350
5	$22,610
6	$25,870
7	$29,130
8	$32,390

Source: U.S. Department of State, *2005 Poverty Guidelines* (2005).

HIGHER HORIZONS HEAD START

Higher Horizons Day Care Center, Inc. is a Head Start and Early Head Start program that provides quality early childhood development and family services for low-income families who meet federal poverty guidelines. Higher Horizons offers consistent, comprehensive services that support the core elements of Head Start. The management and staff are committed to delivering the services with pride and excellence.

PROGRAM OPERATION

Higher Horizons operates a full-day, full-year Head Start and Early Head Start program for children from six weeks to five years of age. Early Head Start offers home- and center-based services for infants, toddlers, and pregnant women. Full-day center-based services are provided for preschool children. The twelve-hour operational day accommodates a working parent's schedule in this Washington, DC, suburb.

Families and Children Served

Children, families, and staff at Higher Horizons are representative of the diverse community; over forty-nine of the children speak languages other than English. Some of the many languages represented in the program include Spanish, Creole, Urdu, Somali, Cambodian, Punjabi, and Vietnamese.

Performance Standards

Higher Horizons is guided by Head Start performance standards. Major elements of the standards include early childhood development and health services, family and community partnerships, staffing, and program design and management. Higher Horizons involves parents and community representatives in all aspects of the program, including policy, program design, and curriculum and management decisions. Shared governance is the strength of this Head Start program.

Enrollment

Most new enrollment is completed during the summer months for September programming in Early Head Start and Head Start. Information regarding the family and child is exchanged during the home visit; parents are given the opportunity to discuss the child's growth and development and establish a relationship with the Head Start staff. This is also an opportunity to gain valuable information pertaining to family goals for the child's enrollment in Head Start. Referrals are made to community resources when parents need support with housing, health care, advocacy, credit counseling, parenting skills, and so on.

THE DAY

A routine day for Head Start children at Higher Horizons may include transportation pickup from an apartment complex located off one of the main streets. Children are transported on an agency-owned school bus; others are dropped off daily by parents or caregivers. Transportation is not provided to the infants and toddlers enrolled in the Early Head Start program. All children are checked in and out from home to bus and from bus to the classroom.

Once in the classroom, children are observed for general physical and mental health. Any unusual or observable concerns are reported to the health specialist for follow-up with the teacher and parent. Children are engaged in activities throughout the day, with an afternoon rest period. After the rest period, children begin preparing for departure by bus or receive a snack and participate in organized activities. As the numbers of children de-

Head Start has always been and remains a program for children of poverty. Although it currently reaches a significant number of poor children, increasing federal support for Head Start will likely increase the number of poor children served. However, we must keep in mind that the federal government is using Head Start to reform all of early childhood education. Federal officials believe that the changes they make in the Head Start curriculum—what and how teachers teach and how Head Start operates—will serve as a model for other programs as well.

crease, staff members have the opportunity for individualized instruction.

Mealtime

Meals are served in a family-style setting in each classroom. Children have the opportunity to help with food service, such as table setting. Children help themselves to the food offered at breakfast, lunch, and snack. Adults in the classroom sit at each table, sharing the same food the children eat, and utilize this time to encourage the use of language to discuss both classroom and home activities. The menus are reflective of the diverse population served; meal adjustments are made for children with special dietary needs or food allergies. Special nutrition activities are regularly planned in each classroom.

Children have the opportunity to wash their hands before each meal and brush their teeth after each meal; the classroom staff use these opportunities to discuss the value of good health and hygiene habits.

The Curriculum

Learning in the Head Start classroom is based on the core values of Head Start. Higher Horizons provides a supportive learning environment for children, parents, and staff. The Education Advisory Committee developed the locally designed curriculum "Setting Our Sights." The committee is comprised of Head Start parents, staff, community educators, public school partners, and representatives of the early childhood community. The program promotes respectful, sensitive, and proactive approaches to diversity issues.

The Head Start Child Outcomes Framework (see Figure 8.3 at the end of the chapter) guides. Head Start staff in preschool classes. The staff use multiple sources of information to gain a valid picture of the child in order to individualize programming. They use the information from screenings to determine how they can best respond to each child's individual characteristics, strengths, and needs.

Degreed classroom staff and experienced classroom assistants plan daily activities for the Head Start children, using the curriculum as a guide and a variety of curriculum resources. An array of activities are planned each day, which include computer learning, prereading, prewriting, role play, science and math, physical indoor and outdoor activity, creative arts, and more.

The Higher Horizons "Great Ideas" inclusion model provides services to children with disabilities in a nontraditional manner. Head Start performance standards require that at least 10 percent of the total enrollment is available to children with disabilities. Our unique model is a partnership with the local public school district. Two special education teachers and classroom assistants are housed in the Head Start facility on a full-time basis; they provide direct services to children with disabilities in the Head Start classrooms.

Parent Involvement

Parents play an active role in communicating with classroom staff. Parents are encouraged to visit the classrooms and to participate in two formal conferences and two home visits during a program year. The information gained during these staff-parent conferences enhances the adults' knowledge and understanding of the developmental progress of the children in the program.

STAFF DEVELOPMENT

Staff development is central to providing high-quality, comprehensive, culturally sensitive services to children and families in Early Head Start and Head Start. Head Start requires a systematic approach to staff development. Monthly professional development activities are scheduled for all Head Start staff. Higher Horizons management staff also recognize the value of new teachers having access to help on short notice, responding to new teachers' teaching strategies, and responding to a parent's request for an immediate conference. New teachers are paired with mentors who have time to observe and offer advice, or a small team of teachers convenes for help on short notice.

Higher Horizons Head Start continues to focus on developing and implementing quality programs that reflect current research and best practices and promoting the Head Start goal of social competence in children.

Contributed by Mary Ann Cornish, director, Higher Horizons Head Start, Falls Church, Virginia.

GOOD START, GROW SMART

Good Start, Grow Smart helps state and local communities strengthen early learning for young children to ensure that they enter kindergarten with the skills they will need to succeed at reading and other early learning activities.

The Good Start, Grow Smart initiative addresses three major areas:

1. *Strengthening Head Start.* Through the Department of Health and Human Services, the administration will develop a new accountability system for Head Start to ensure that

Good Start, Grow Smart
The federal government's early childhood initiative designed to help states and local communities strengthen early learning for young children.

every Head Start center assesses standards of learning in early literacy, language, and numeracy skills.

2. *Partnering with states to improve early childhood education.* Good Start, Grow Smart proposes a stronger federal-state partnership in the delivery of quality early childhood programs. This new approach will ask states to develop quality criteria for early childhood education, including voluntary guidelines for prereading and language skills activities that align with state K–twelve standards.

3. *Providing information to teachers, caregivers, and parents.* In order to close the gap between the best research and current practices in early childhood education, the Department of Education will establish a range of partnerships as part of a broad public awareness campaign targeted toward parents, early childhood educators, child care providers, and other interested parties.[8]

In the Head Start segment of the DVD, the teacher identifies different kinds of nutrition programs provided by her Head Start program. How do these compare with the mealtime routines of the Program in Action "Higher Horizons Head Start"?

EARLY HEAD START

Early Head Start (EHS), created in 1994, is designed to

- promote healthy prenatal outcomes for pregnant women
- enhance the development of very young children (birth through age three)
- promote healthy family functioning

In addition to young children, EHS enrolls pregnant women; when the child is born, the mother is provided with family services. EHS is also a program for low-income families who meet federal poverty guidelines. It serves about 63,000 infants and toddlers annually with a budget of $684 million. More than 708 grantees participate in the EHS program.[9] Program services include the following:

- Quality early education both in and out of the home
- Parenting education
- Comprehensive health and mental health services, including services to women before, during, and after pregnancy
- Nutrition education
- Family support services

Head Start's entry into the field of infant and toddler care and education through EHS has achieved two things:

- Head Start now provides services to long-neglected age groups of infants and toddlers.
- EHS has become a leader in the field of infant and toddler education.

Companion Website To complete a Program in Action activity related to migrant education programs, go to the Companion Website at **www. prenhall.com/morrison**, select chapter 8, then choose the Program in Action Module.

OTHER HEAD START PROGRAMS

MIGRANT HEAD START

Migrant Head Start A federal program designed to provide educational and other services to migrant children and their families.

Migrant family A family with school-aged children that moves from one geographic location to another to engage in agricultural work.

Services provided to migrant children and their families are identical to those of other Head Start programs, even as they address the unique needs of migrant children and families. **Migrant Head Start** programs emphasize serving infants and toddlers so that they do not have to accompany their parents to the fields or be left with young siblings.

A **migrant family** is a family with children of compulsory school-attendance age who change their residence by moving from one geographic location to another, for the purpose of engaging in agricultural work. Migrant Head Start provides services tailored to the unique needs of migrant families. Home-based programs are usually located in the southern part of the United States (generally in California, Arizona, New Mexico, Texas, and Florida). They provide services to mobile migrant farm worker families. Upstream programs (generally in Washington, Idaho, Michigan, Illinois, Maine, Indiana, Wisconsin, Nebraska, and Minnesota) provide services to families as they move northward in search of agricultural work during the spring, summer, and fall months.[10] The Program in Action about migrant children on pages 210–211 in New Jersey provides an excellent example of how migrant education programs attempt to meet the unique needs of migrant children and their families.

AMERICAN INDIAN–ALASKA NATIVE HEAD START PROGRAMS

The American Indian–Alaska Native program branch of Head Start provides American Indian and Alaska Native children (birth to age five) and their families with comprehensive health, education, nutritional, social, and developmental services designed to promote school readiness.

Currently, all early childhood programs, including Head Start, emphasize the development of children's early literacy skills by involving parents and grandparents. Literacy skills are seen as a key to success in school and life.

EVEN START FAMILY LITERACY PROGRAM

The Even Start Family Literacy Program, officially authorized in 1989 as the William F. Goodling Even Start Family Literacy Program, was reauthorized as part of the No Child Left Behind Act of 2001.[11]

The purpose of **Even Start** is twofold:

- To provide low-income families with integrated literacy services for parents and their young children (birth through age seven)
- To break the cycle of poverty and illiteracy for low-income families

Even Start implements four program components:

- Adult education
- Early childhood education
- Parenting education
- Interactive literacy activities for parents and their children[12]

Even Start A federal program that provides literacy services for low-income families and children.

OTHER INITIATIVES

TITLE I PROGRAMS

The NCLB Act reauthorized the Elementary Secondary Education Act (ESEA) of 1965. Under this reauthorization, Title I provides financial assistance through state educational agencies (SEAs) to local educational agencies (LEAs) and schools with high numbers or percentages of poor children to help ensure that all children meet challenging state

Companion Website To complete a Program in Action activity related to Title I, go to the Companion Website at **www. prenhall.com/morrison**, select chapter 8, then choose the Program in Action module.

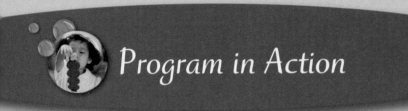

A HELPING HAND FOR MIGRANT CHILDREN IN NEW JERSEY

The children of migrant farm workers are among the most educationally disadvantaged in the nation. Because they must contend with many formidable obstacles to a successful educational experience—such as frequent mobility and a correspondingly high rate of absenteeism, extreme poverty, language differences, low family-literacy levels, poor nutrition, and unmet health needs—they are often in need of supplemental instruction and support services. The U.S. Congress in 1966 created the Migrant Education Program to help meet the unique needs of migrant children and enable them to achieve at the levels of their nonmigratory peers.

In New Jersey, the Garden State, agriculture is still one of the leading industries. Not surprisingly, then, the state is a temporary home to many migrant families and children. To meet the instructional and support needs of these children, the regionally administered Migrant Education Program (MEP) provides supplemental services year-round.

During the regular school year, those services may include after-school tutoring, health and other support services, home/school coordination, advocacy and intervention with local schools where the children are enrolled, parent involvement activities, and records transfer and exchange. In the Elementary and Secondary Education Act, as amended by NCLB, Congress directs the Department of Education to assist the states in developing effective methods for the electronic transfer of student records and in determining the number of migratory children in each state.*

During the summer months, when most crops are cultivated and harvested, the MEP in southern New Jersey experiences a substantial influx of migrant families. To meet their needs, the MEP offers six-week summer school sessions for children in preK through high school. The program design is holistic, providing for the students' academic, health, nutritional, and social/emotional needs in a structured school setting that is warm and nurturing and where learning opportunities abound. School services include transportation, breakfast and lunch, content-rich classroom instruction, physical education, daily computer lab instruction, comprehensive health services, and enrichment activities.

HEALTHY CHILDREN ARE BETTER LEARNERS

A child who cannot see the blackboard properly or who has a distracting ailment is less likely to remain focused on class work and learning. Sadly, many migrant children have unmet health needs and lack access to either preventive or acute care. Consequently, many health services are provided right at the summer school sites, including physical examinations, eye examinations, orthopedic/developmental assessments, and dental triage. Children are then taken in small groups to dental

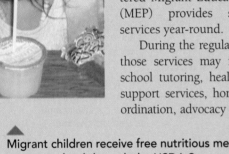

Migrant children receive free nutritious meals during summer school through the USDA Summer Food Service Program.

academic content and student academic achievement standards.[13] In 2004 the federal government spent almost ten billion dollars on Title I services.

Title I focuses on several different objectives, all supporting the goal of giving all children a high-quality education:

- Ensuring that high-quality academic assessments, accountability systems, teacher preparation and training, curriculum, and instructional materials are aligned with

Preschool teacher Patricia Watts guides her students through a creative bead-stringing activity, which incorporates color recognition, counting, and fine-motor skills.

centers for treatment as needed, as well as to other providers for specialty and follow-up care. The children also receive medications, eyeglasses, and lab work as necessary.

EARLY CHILDHOOD SERVICES

The MEP serves children beginning at age three as long as they are out of diapers. Program guides developed especially for migrant education staff correspond directly to the New Jersey Core Curriculum Content Standards. For preschoolers the guides include very specific, age-appropriate activities, each of which is tied to a specific content area and standard. The preschool summer classrooms emphasize healthy social/emotional development, as well as school readiness. Children participate in learning activities that increase vocabulary and English-language proficiency and encourage development of prereading and premath skills. Literacy activities create a foundation for early reading, writing, speaking, and listening skills. Math activities expose the youngsters to very basic numeracy concepts. Mastery of these basic skills, together with exposure to healthy social relationships and development of self-esteem, prepares the children for success in kindergarten and beyond.

Each brightly decorated, inviting classroom is staffed by a certified teacher and an assistant. Various learning centers provide children with a multitude of stimulating activities, and the day is designed to include structured lessons, reading and music, and plenty of time for self-directed play.

A preschool child's day is designed to be highly stimulating and nurturing, full of discovery, laughter, praise, and positive reinforcement. Lessons are presented in creative ways that are fun and are likely to keep children engaged.

Teachers are observant for a variety of learning styles and make accommodations accordingly.

BEYOND THE CLASSROOM—RECREATIONAL CAMP

After lunch the preschool children take a long nap, because when school is dismissed, their day is extended until 6:00 P.M. for an after-school camp care program. The after-school camp is critical, because without it many children would go home to unsupervised settings while their parents labor in the fields. Many of the children reside in farm labor camps or motels; others are even less fortunate, living in cars or vans. The recreational camps are safe and supervised, and they meet the social and emotional needs of the children. Swimming, organized games and sports, arts and crafts, boating, and horseback riding are some of the offerings that children can enjoy. They also receive dinner, their third balanced meal of the day.

TESTAMENT TO SUCCESS

The MEP strives to improve the academic, social/emotional, health, and nutritional status of the migrant children served in the summer program. Summer staff feedback forms are collected each year, asking for observations about any positive impact of the program on participating children. Teachers frequently report progress in English-language proficiency, greater individual self-confidence and pride, improved health, additional mastery of age-appropriate skills, and social enrichment. One teacher described her experience by saying, "I consider it a blessing to have had the opportunity to work with this group of children. They were warm, respectful, and eager to cooperate and learn. My regret is that I didn't get involved in this program earlier, and I am sad to see this session end!" Another wrote a simple but eloquent comment that very succinctly sums up the program: "We are blessed to have these children in our lives—and to have the privilege of opening doors for them."

Contributed by Kathy Freudenberg, director of special projects, Gloucester County Special Services School District, 204 East Holly Avenue, Sewell, NJ 08080. Photos also contributed by Kathy Freudenberg.

*U.S. Department of Education, "Migrant Student Records Exchange Initiative," http://www.ed.gov/admins/lead/account/recordstransfer.html.

challenging state academic standards so that students, teachers, parents, and administrators can measure progress against common expectations for student academic achievement

- Meeting the educational needs of low-achieving children in our nation's highest-poverty schools, limited-English-proficient children, migratory children, children with disabilities, Native American children, neglected or delinquent children, and young children in need of reading assistance

In the Head
Start segment of the DVD,
listen to what project director
Jillian Ramsey says are the
purposes of Even Start.
Compare these to Even Start's
mission as outlined in this
chapter.

Fatherhood initiatives
Various efforts by federal,
state, and local agencies to
increase and sustain fathers'
involvement with their
children and families.

Companion
Website
For more
information about fatherhood
initiatives, go to the
Companion Website at **www.
prenhall.com/morrison**,
select chapter 8, then choose
the Linking to Learning
module.

Companion
Website
For more
information about
partnerships, go to the
Companion Website at **www.
prenhall.com/morrison**,
select chapter 8, then choose
the Linking to Learning
module.

- Closing the achievement gap between high- and low-performing children, especially the achievement gaps between minority and nonminority students and between disadvantaged children and their more advantaged peers
- Providing children with an enriched and accelerated educational program, including the use of schoolwide programs or additional services that increase the amount and quality of instructional time
- Elevating the quality of instruction by providing staff in participating schools with substantial opportunities for professional development
- Affording parents substantial and meaningful opportunities to participate in the education of their children

Programs funded under Title I include Reading First and Even Start.[14] The Program in Action about Title I on pages 214–215 illustrates how this federal program works in an actual elementary school, providing support for low-income children and families.

FATHERHOOD INITIATIVES

The Department of Health and Human Services (DHHS) has developed a special **fatherhood initiative** to support and strengthen the roles of fathers in their families. This initiative is guided by the following principles:

- All fathers can be important contributors to the well-being of their children.
- Parents and partners should be involved in raising their children, even when they do not live in the same household.
- The roles fathers play in families are diverse and are related to cultural and community norms.
- Men should receive the education and support necessary to prepare them for the responsibility of parenthood.
- Government can encourage and promote fathers' involvement through its programs and its own workforce policies.

The DHHS emphasis on the important roles of fathers has, in turn, spawned a Head Start Fatherhood Initiative. It is designed to sustain fathers' involvement in their children's lives and, as a result, enhance the development of their children.

The Early Head Start Research and Evaluation Project has launched research relating to the role of low-income fathers in the lives of their infants and toddlers, in their families, and in the Early Head Start programs in which they participate. The father studies are filling a significant gap in knowledge by increasing the understanding of how fathers and mothers, in the context of the family, influence infant and toddler development.[15]

PARTNERSHIPS AND COLLABORATION

All Head Start programs endeavor to build collaborative relationships with local agencies and programs. These collaborative approaches are designed to better serve children and families and to maximize the use of resources. The Diversity Tie-In in this chapter on page 216 elaborates on how one Head Start program collaborates in providing for children with disabilities, thereby achieving its goals of inclusion. Healthy Beginnings and the QUILT program are two other examples of such collaborative services.

Healthy Beginnings. Healthy Beginnings provides onsite screening at licensed child care sites in seven counties in the Florida Panhandle. Healthy Beginnings collaborates with Head Start's health and nutrition coordinator and the Health Services Advisory Committee, to form a coalition of health and safety providers. Health care professionals visit each licensed child care center in the seven-county area twice a year in a mobile medical van donated by two local hospitals. Only basic screenings (height, weight, health, and dental) are completed because the coalition does not have funding for the liability coverage necessary for blood screenings. (Funding comes from the local Kiwanis Club through its national initiative to provide safe and healthy beginnings for children under five).

The program is producing measurable results—approximately 20 percent of children screened for physical health problems and nearly 50 percent of those screened for dental health needs are referred for further services. The response from parents, particularly working parents who have difficulty scheduling routine health care for their children, is overwhelmingly positive.

QUILT. QUILT (Quality in Linking Together) is the national training and technical assistance project of the federal Administration for Children and Families. It supports local, state, tribal, regional, and national partnerships among Head Start, child care, state-funded preK, and other early education programs aimed at providing quality full-day, year-round services.

QUILT focuses on three major service delivery strategies: onsite technical assistance to states, territories, tribes, and local communities; training at national, regional, and state workshops, forums, and meetings; and development and dissemination of best practice materials and resources.

Here's what people in early education are saying about QUILT's services:

A Head Start state collaboration director: *"What a difference it makes to know that I can rely on QUILT specialists—people who have lived it and done it—from the Head Start side, the child care side, and the public school side. They helped us see the possibilities."*

An executive director of a child care agency: *"So often, families are forced to patch together care that involves two, three, or even four different care providers, each with a different approach, a different set of standards, and a different curriculum. QUILT helped us bring all these players together to create a common community vision—so that we can provide children and families with the quality services they deserve."*

The QUILT project is led by three organizations: the Community Development Institute in Denver, Colorado; the Education Development Center, Inc. in Newton, Massachusetts; and, the National Child Care Information Center in Vienna, Virginia. For further information visit QUILT's website at *www.quilt.org.*[16]

Companion Website To complete a Diversity Tie-In activity related to inclusion and collaboration, go to the Companion Website at **www.prenhall.com/morrison,** select chapter 8, then choose the Diversity Tie-In module.

HEAD START RESEARCH

A question that everyone always asks is, "Do Head Start, Early Head Start, and Even Start programs work?" By *work,* people generally mean, "Do these programs deliver the services they were authorized and funded to deliver, and do these services make a difference in the lives of children and families?"

Over the last five years, the federal government has been much more aggressive in attempting to ensure that the programs it funds provide results. Consequently, we have seen a tremendous increase in federal monies allocated for research of federally funded programs and a corresponding increase in the number of research studies designed to measure the effectiveness of those programs.

A seven-year national evaluation of Early Head Start found these results:

- Three-year-old children completing the program performed better in cognitive and language development than children who did not participate in the program.
- The EHS children developed behavior patterns that prepared them for success in school, such as engaging in tasks, paying attention, and showing less aggression.
- EHS parents showed more positive parenting behavior, reported less physical punishment of their children, and did more to help their children learn at home through activities such as reading to their children.[17]

Program in Action

TITLE I—HELPING CHILDREN BECOME LIFELONG LEARNERS

Title I is a federal aid program for elementary and secondary schools. The money is disbursed to school districts according to the number of low-income families in the district. The school district then allocates the Title I money to those schools that have the largest percentages of low-income students, based on the number of free and reduced-price lunches. A Title I school can use the funds to pay for extra educational services for the children, such as additional teachers, aides, materials, and professional development for the instructional staff. If a school's free and reduced-price lunches total over 40 percent, it is considered a schoolwide Title I school and the funds can be used to benefit the entire school population.

Montevallo Elementary in Montevallo, Alabama, is a schoolwide Title I school with low-income families totaling 57 percent of the school population. More important, it is recognized as a distinguished Title I school. To be so recognized, Montevallo had to demonstrate implementation of a quality program that was in compliance with federal requirements and had to meet certain criteria in numerous areas:

- Opportunity for all children to meet proficient and advanced levels of performance
- Professional development
- Coordination with other programs
- Curriculum and instruction to support achievement of high standards

- Partnerships among schools, parents, and communities.

Achievement data were also considered, and Montevallo had to provide evidence of unusual effectiveness over a three-year period.

VISION AND MISSION

Montevallo Elementary's success story began with a vision "that all students will grow to become lifelong learners who make a positive impact on their communities and the world in which they live" and continued with a mission: "Believing that all students can learn when teachers are provided the knowledge, skills, and support they need to address individual learner needs, Montevallo Elementary School strives to ensure that our learners today are our leaders tomorrow." Our mission is our vision in action.

INCREASED RESOURCES

As a school, Montevallo believes that it is essential to provide instructional opportunities using research-based methods and technologies and ongoing assessment of student performance to guide the instruction. The goal is to improve reading instruction and increase literacy in the school. Title I funds have afforded Montevallo Elementary many instructional opportunities:

The Head Start Impact Study, a congressionally mandated study, arrived at these key findings:

- There are small to moderate statistically significant positive impacts for both three- and four-year-old children on several measures across four of the six cognitive constructs, including prereading, prewriting, vocabulary, and parent reports of children's literacy skills.
- No significant impacts were found for oral comprehension and phonological awareness or for early mathematics skills for either age group.
- For children who entered the study as three-year-olds, there is a small statistically significant impact on problem behaviors, one of the three social-emotional constructs.

- Accelerated Reader—Students reading books on their level and taking a computerized quiz, grades K to five
- STAR Early Literacy—Diagnostic assessment, grades K to two
- STAR Reading—Reading assessment, grades one to five
- Accelerated Math—Math management system (scores and grades assignments and tests), grades one to five
- STAR Math—Math assessment, grades three to five
- Perfect Copy—Writing skills software, grades one to five
- Read 180 Lab—Teacher-computer model used with fourth and fifth grade students reading below grade level
- Literacy Lab—Teacher-directed program for first graders, focusing on phonics and word work
- Modified block schedule in first grade—Dividing a class into thirds, with one-third of students staying with the classroom teacher for a guided reading group, one-third participating in literacy centers in the classroom, and one-third participating in the Literacy Lab

The school has also been able to purchase additional technology to be used in the classrooms. By supplying classrooms with various computers, televisions, and computer software, Montevallo teachers gain access to up-to-date equipment used for instruction and assessment.

STAFF SUPPORT

With Title I funds Montevallo is able to hire substitutes and pay for workshop registrations, giving teachers the opportunity to attend in-services and meet with grade-level teams during the school day to review assessments. Substitute teachers are also used three times a year to free up the assessment team to administer the Dynamic Indicators of Basic Early Literacy Skills assessment in grades K to three and to allow time for all teachers to attend the four Alabama Reading Initiative recertification modules. Ongoing professional development in technology, reading strategies, math, writing, and classroom management has been offered to Montevallo teachers, using Title I funds for registrations, substitutes, and presenters.

PARENT INVOLVEMENT

A Title I school also advocates a parent involvement policy. Principal, teachers, parents, and students all sign a school compact reinforcing each person's role in the educational process. A parent advisory committee is an important part of Title I schools. The committee meets three times a year to review the schoolwide plan, the budget, and parent-school compacts. Funds are also available to provide information on topics such as the No Child Left Behind Act of 2001, stages of child growth and development, state performance standards, and the county school system's curriculum and instruction.

The extra materials, supplies, staff, and professional development opportunities offered to Montevallo Elementary because it qualifies as a Title I schoolwide school are only truly beneficial if they translate into academic growth and progress for the students involved. Our data show yearly growth and indicate that the extra educational services provided for a Title I school make a difference in the lives of Montevallo school children.

Contributed by Christine M. Hoffman, principal, Montevallo Elementary School, Montevallo, Alabama.

- There are no statistically significant impacts on social skills and approaches to learning or on social competencies for three-year-olds.
- No significant impacts were found for children entering the program as four-year-olds.
- For three-year-olds there are small to moderate statistically significant impacts on parent reports of children's access to health care and health status for children enrolled in Head Start.
- For children who entered the program as four-year-olds, there are moderate statistically significant impacts on access to health care, but no significant impacts for health status.
- For children who entered the program as three-year-olds, there are small statistically significant impacts in two of the three parenting constructs, including use of educa-

INCLUSION AND COLLABORATION IN HEAD START

The Head Start program of Upper Des Moines Opportunity, Inc. operates twenty-five fully inclusive preschool classrooms. We have three classrooms specific to toddlers, aged eighteen to thirty-six months. We also have twenty-two classrooms set up for children aged three to five years. Our programs are designated for all children, regardless of race or disability.

Our Head Start programs take pride in the strength of our partnerships with local school districts and other local education agencies. Because of the strength of these relationships, we are able to collaborate in program design and offer natural or least restrictive environments to all children.

In Early Head Start our staff have been trained in case management of children with special needs. They have taken the lead position in coordinating services for our children and their families. These services can be provided in the home, in the classroom, or in a day care setting. Our toddler rooms are facilitated by support service staff trained in specific areas of early childhood development. We use a child study team to continually update staff on individual progress, concerns, and the needs of our children. A child study team consists of professionals such as psychologists,

classroom teachers, special education teachers, and social workers, who assess children and make decisions about their placement and programs of study.

Our Head Start classrooms for children aged three to five offer many opportunities for inclusion. In some centers we dually enroll children, allowing them the opportunity to spend half a day in Head Start and the other half in an early childhood special education (ECSE) classroom. We also have classrooms in which Head Start teachers and ECSE teachers work side by side, allowing for full-day programming for all children in the least restrictive settings. In some of our classrooms the lead teacher has a degree in early childhood special education, and the associate(s) have backgrounds in early childhood; or the lead teacher has a background in early childhood, and the associate(s) are qualified to work with children having special needs. All of our three- to five-year-old classrooms are facilitated by support service staff, and they, too, use the child study team approach to communicate the progress, needs, and concerns of all children.

Contributed by Mary Jo Madvig, early childhood director, Upper Des Moines Opportunity, Inc.

---

tional activities and use of physical discipline. There are no significant impacts on safety practices.

- For children who entered the program as four-year-olds, there are small statistically significant impacts on parents' use of educational activities. No significant impacts were found for discipline or safety practices.[18]

CONCERNS WITH FEDERAL EARLY CHILDHOOD EDUCATION PROGRAMS

As with all programs, Head Start has some associated issues of concern. Some of the issues are inherent in what we have discussed so far, and some are making Head Start a center of national attention.

Accountability.   Part of the federal government's effort to reform Head Start involves making it more accountable for expenditures, children's achievement, and overall program performance. It is likely that Head Start administrators and other personnel will be challenged to enhance performance in all three of these areas. As you might expect, accountability does not come easily for some programs and agencies. However, as we have discussed, part of the changing educational climate is that the public wants to be assured that programs, especially those serving young children, achieve the goals for which they are funded.

Testing Head Start Children.   One of the provisions of NCLB is to annually test children's achievement, beginning in grade three. However, under the provisions of Good Start, Grow Smart, the preschool initiative of NCLB, every four-year-old in Head Start is now tested with the Head Start National Reporting System (NRS) (see chapter 3). That system was first implemented in the fall of 2003 and is being administered twice yearly to all four- and five-year-old children in Head Start whose primary language is English or Spanish. The stated purposes of the test are program self-assessment, training and technical assistance planning, and child outcome monitoring.[19] The implementation of the NRS was the first nationwide skills test of over four hundred thousand four- and five-year-old children.[20]

There is widespread criticism of the NRS, especially from the National Head Start Association (NHSA), a private, nonprofit group that provides support to the Head Start community. NHSA has several problems with the NRS:

- Lack of external validity
- Cultural and linguistic inappropriateness
- Limited scope in relation to Head Start's programming and services
- Lack of clarity about the purpose of the assessment and the use of the data
- Unnecessary testing of every child instead of a sample of children

A report released by the Government Accounting Office (GAO)—a federal agency that investigates matters relating to the receipt, disbursement, and application of public funds—had these recommendations for the Head Start Bureau regarding NRS:

- Determine how NRS data will be used for accountability and targeting technical assistance
- Monitor the effects of the NRS on local Head Start practices
- Use first-year NRS results to conduct further study of the reliability and validity of the NRS
- Compile a detailed, well-organized document on the technical quality of the NRS
- Improve management of the data on NRS participation
- Study the costs and benefits of sampling in administering the NRS[21]

It is likely that controversy will continue to swirl around NRS. However, it is also likely that Head Start children will continue to be tested within the context of the GAO recommendations.

The testing of young children will be a part of Head Start's future and the future of children in other early childhood programs, as well. As an early childhood professional, you will be involved in many discussions related to the testing of young children.

Federal Control and Influence.   One concern about federal legislation, regulations, and funding is that they represent an increasing encroachment of the federal government into state and local educational programs. Historically, the U.S. educational system has been based on the idea that states and local communities should develop and implement educational programs and curricula. Opponents of federal control fear that this highly valued

When children are healthy, they are much more able to benefit from Head Start and other educational programs. Head Start has been a leader in providing for young children's health needs. As a result, other programs such as public school preK programs are also providing for children's health needs.

local control is endangered and may become extinct. Generally, with federal funding comes federal control in the form of regulations and guidelines.

Many other federal and state programs touch the lives of children and influence their physical, cognitive, and social development. For example, the National School Lunch Program is a $3.1 billion annual federal nutrition program that provides breakfast, lunch, and snacks free or at a reduced rate to the nation's children.

The federal legislative and financial influence on early childhood education—indeed, on all of education, from birth through higher education—is vast and significant. You, your colleagues, and the children you teach will be under the direction of federal mandates and guidelines. Consequently, you must be aware of the influence of federal and state governments on you and your profession, and you must be willing to be politically involved in influencing legislation and its implementation in programs and classrooms.

HEAD START'S INFLUENCE

Head Start is big business and serious business. It has a complex operating structure, standards, and regulations. It also has a vast federal bureaucracy of personnel, regional offices, and training centers. Head Start is entrenched in the early childhood field and is now exerting a powerful influence on how the field functions and operates.

In the Head Start segment of the DVD, listen to what Norma Brieler says about the underfunding of Head Start. Compare what she says to the Head Start issues outlined in the Voice from the Field.

National Curriculum. The specter of a national curriculum is closely associated with federal control and Head Start's influence. Head Start began as and is based on local option initiatives; in other words, local Head Start programs have been responsible for developing programs for the people that they represent and serve. Currently, however, there is an ongoing process of erosion that is eating away at the autonomy of local programs to deliver local options within the programs.

Improving Teacher Quality. The School Readiness Act of 2005, which reauthorizes Head Start through 2011, includes an important provision requiring that all Head Start teachers have a BA in child development or a related field by 2011 and that, within three years of the passage of the bill, all teachers have an associate's degree or higher or be enrolled in a program to earn an associate's degree.[22] Achieving this goal with high-quality personnel will certainly challenge administrators of all Head Start programs. Nonetheless, high-quality teachers and other staff are the heart and soul of any educational program and every child deserves the best teacher possible. The debate over teacher qualifications is just one of the numerous Head Start issues about which professionals disagree, as you will see by reading the Voice from the Field "Head Start Issues: The Pros and Cons" on page 219. We can be sure that differing perspectives will continue to be voiced but that Head Start will remain an influential program.

Companion Website

For additional Internet resources or to complete an online activity for this chapter, go to the Companion Website at **www.prenhall.com/morrison,** select chapter 8, then choose the Linking to Learning or Making Connections module.

HEAD START ISSUES: THE PROS AND CONS

ISSUE	PRO	CON
Should Head Start funding be increased?	Three million eligible children are not enrolled in Head Start or Early Head Start. No eligible child who needs the program should be turned away.*†	Head Start already costs a great deal of money ($6.8 billion).
Should Head Start funding come through block grants to the states?	States could provide universal preschool for all children.	States might not offer a full range of comprehensive services for Head Start children.
Should Head Start continue to be administered by the Department of Health and Human Services?	Head Start services are comprehensive, including educational, medical, emotional, and other services.	Head Start should be primarily an educational program and should be administered by the Department of Education.
Should Head Start services remain comprehensive?	Head Start should continue to serve children and their families, which are the most important institution in children's lives.	Head Start should be more educational in order to serve more children with the funds available.
Should Head Start children be tested?	Testing provides accountability, which indicates whether programs are working and money is being well spent.	Neither the tests being used nor the process of testing four-year-olds is developmentally appropriate.
Should Head Start teachers be required to upgrade their professional qualifications? (see the figure below)	Enhancing the qualifications of Head Start teachers through advanced degrees will enhance the quality of Head Start programs.	Enhanced qualifications may be a positive step but should not be required without increased funding to cover the costs.

*H.Blank, "Head Start Under Assault," *The American Prospect* (November2004), http://www.prospect.org/web/page.ww?section=root&name=ViewPrint&articleId=8773.

†National Head Start Association, *Funding Cuts to Head Start and Other Key Programs*, http://www.nhsa.org/advocacy/advocacy_fundingcut.htm.

Degrees and Credentials of Head Start Teachers in 2004

Source: K. Hamm and D. Ewen, *Still Going Strong: Head Start Children, Families, Staff, and Programs in 2004* (CLASP policy brief, 2005), http://www.clasp.org/publications/headstart_brief_6.pdf.

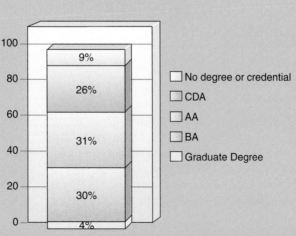

9%
26%
31%
30%
4%

No degree or credential
CDA
AA
BA
Graduate Degree

LINKING TO LEARNING

Fatherhood Initiative
http://fatherhood.hhs.gov/

Presents facts, statistics, and reports in an overview of the Department of Health and Human Services' involvement and activities with the Fatherhood Initiative.

Head Start and Early Head Start Performance Standards
http://www.acf.hhs.gov/programs/hsb/performance/

Details regulations and program performance standards that govern Head Start programs.

Head Start Bureau
http://www2.acf.hhs.gov/programs/hsb

Dedicated to providing comprehensive developmental services to low-income children from birth to age five and social services to their families.

Head Start Information & Publication Center
http://www.headstartinfo.org

A service of the Head Start Bureau that supports the Head Start community and families by providing informational products and services, conference and meeting support, publication distribution, marketing, and outreach efforts.

National Fatherhood Initiative
http://www.fatherhood.org

Offers an online catalog, a listing of online resources, tips and advice for fathers, and relevant links for further information.

National Head Start Association (NHSA)
http://www.nhsa.org

A nonprofit organization dedicated to meeting and addressing the concerns of the Head Start community.

NCLB Act
www.nclb.gov

Presents all of the main features of the No Child Left Behind Act of 2001.

U.S. Department of State Poverty Guidelines
http://travel.state.gov/visa/immigrants/info/info_1327.html

Clearly states the poverty guidelines for the forty-eight contiguous states and the District of Columbia.

ACTIVITIES FOR FURTHER ENRICHMENT

ETHICAL DILEMMA: "WHY CAN'T WE SERVE THEM ALL?"

For the past five years you have worked as a lead teacher at a large Head Start center in a major city. You are a supporter of Head Start and believe in its mission of helping low income children and families. Last week the regional Head Start office released data showing that 1,253 children who are eligible for Head Start in your city are not being served. You believe that all children should have the benefits of Head Start, and you are sick and tired of people saying that children are the nation's greatest resource but not putting their money where their mouths are! In frustration, you meet with Marty, the center director, and tell her that you have talked with a community activist who suggests that you call a meeting of parents with Head Start–eligible children to discuss a plan of action to demand additional funding. However, Marty becomes angry and defensive. "Look, I don't want you to rock the Head Start boat! We have to be satisfied with what we have. Head Start never has been and never will be fully funded."

What do you do? Do you ignore Marty and develop plans to organize the parents, perhaps risking your career and reputation, or do you reluctantly agree with Marty and resign yourself to the fact that there is nothing you can do about a large governmental agency like Head Start, or do you pursue some other course of action to help the children?

APPLICATIONS

1. Not everyone agrees that increases in federal spending on early childhood programs are a good idea. Identify three pros and three cons of increases in federal allocations to early childhood programs.
2. Why have fathers been so neglected in the child-rearing process and early childhood education? What are some specific things you could do to involve fathers in your program?
3. After reviewing current literature and interviewing children, parents, and Head Start personnel, briefly state your opinion concerning the success of Head Start. Give reasons for your comments, and discuss them with your peers.
4. Interview the director of a local Head Start program, and answer these questions:
   a. What are the major challenges facing Head Start today?
   b. If more federal funds were available for Head Start, how would the director spend them?
   c. What changes does the director think should be made in the Head Start program?

FIELD EXPERIENCES

1. Visit a Head Start program and interview teachers about what they believe are the most important services Head Start provides. Likewise, interview parents to determine what Head Start services matter most to them.
2. Visit three Head Start programs and observe their educational programs, using the observation guidelines provided in chapter 3. Evaluate the educational programs, using a scale of high, medium, and low. Then write recommendations for improving each program you observed.
3. Following your visits to local Head Start programs, make a list of their similarities and differences. Explain why a federal program with a common set of guidelines can produce differences in program operations.
4. Visit three elementary schools and/or early childhood learning centers, and make a list of all the programs for which they receive federal support. Could the schools provide the services they do without federal funding? What other programs for young children do you think the federal government should support?

RESEARCH

1. Research the history of Head Start from 1965 to the present, and list what you believe are the major changes Head Start has made during this time. In addition, interview veteran Head Start teachers, and ask them what they identify as the most significant changes in Head Start over the course of their careers. An interesting project would be to initiate an oral history of Head Start that documents significant events in the program by those involved in its development.
2. For each of the Head Start issues we discussed, conduct interviews to gather data about the pros and cons of each. Based on your data, make recommendations regarding each issue.
3. Contact a migrant education office in your area. What are the occupations of migrant parents? What are the major problems faced by these families? What services are being provided for them? Do you think those services are as effective and comprehensive as they should be?
4. Examine the latest poverty-income guidelines published by the federal government. Do you believe these incomes are sufficient for rearing a family? Why or why not? What solutions would you propose to the problem of substandard incomes for a large number of American families?

READINGS FOR FURTHER ENRICHMENT

Shonkoff, J. P., and D. Phillips. *From Neurons to Neighborhoods: The Science of Early Child Development.* Washington, DC: National Academy Press, 2000.
Presents the newest evidence about the importance of early childhood development.

Vihovskis, M. *The Birth of Head Start: Preschool Education Policies in the Kennedy and Johnson Administrations.* Chicago: University of Chicago Press, 2005.
Chronicles the birth of Head Start and its development during its formative years.

Zigler, E., and S. J. Styfco, eds. *The Head Start Debates.* Baltimore: Brookes, 2004.
A compilation of the views of fifty-three top experts about the future of Head Start.

ENDNOTES

1. U.S. Department of Health and Human Services, "Head Start: Promoting Early Childhood Development" (2002), http://www.hhs.gov/news/press/2002pres/ headstart.html.

2. U.S. Department of Health and Human Services, "Head Start Program Fact Sheet" (2004), http://www.acf.hhs.gov/programs/hsb/research/2005.htm.

3. *Good Start, Grow Smart: The Bush Administration's Early Childhood Initiative,* http://www.whitehouse.gov/infocus/earlychildhood/toc.html.

4. U.S. Department of Health and Human Services, *Head Start Program Options,* http://www.acf.hhs.gov/programs/hsb/performance/1306.htm.

5. Ibid.

6. Illinois Head Start Association, "Program Options," *Head Start Program Framework,* http://www.ilheadstart.org/options.html.

7. Ibid.

8. Ibid.

9. Zero to Three Policy Center, "The National Evaluation of Early Head Start: Early Head Start Works" (2005), http://www.zerotothree.org/policy/factsheets/ehs.pdf.

10. U.S. Department of Health and Human Services, "Fact Sheets" (1999), http://www.acf.hhs.gov/news/facts/headst.html.

11. California Department of Education, *Even Start Family Literacy Program,* http://www.cde.ca.gov/sp/cd/op/evenstart.asp.

12. U.S. Department of Education, *William F. Goodling Even Start Family Literacy Program,* http://www.ed.gov/policy/elsec/leg/esea02/pg6.html.

13. U.S. Department of Education, *Title I, Part A Program,* http://www.ed.gov/programs/titleiparta/index.html.

14. U.S. Department of Education, *Title I—Improving the Academic Achievement of the Disadvantaged,* http://www.ed.gov/policy/elsec/leg/esea02/pg1.html.

15. Mathematica Policy Research, "Fatherhood Research in the Early Head Start Research and Evaluation Project," http://www.mathematica-mpr.com/earlycare/fatheroverview.asp.

16. Information contributed by Grace Hardy, QUILT project director, Community Development Institute, 9745 E. Hampden Ave., Suite 310, Denver, CO.

17. U.S. Department of Health and Human Services, *Making a Difference in the Lives of Infants and Toddlers and Their Families: The Impacts of Early Head Start* (Washington, DC: Author, 2002).

18. Administration for Children and Families, *Head Start Impact Study: First Year Findings* (Washington, DC: U.S. Department of Health and Human Services, May 2005).

19. National Head Start Association, Head Start National Reporting System, "Issue Background," http://www.nhsa.org/download/advocacy/fact/HSNRS.pdf.

20. Ibid.

21. Government Accounting Office, "Head Start: Further Development Could Allow Results of New Test to Be Used for Decision Making" (May 2005), http://www.gao.gov/new.items/d05343.pdf.

22. Committee on Education and the Workforce, "Additional Views," (June 16, 2005), http://edworkforce.house.gov/democrats/hr2123views.html.

FIGURE 8.3 Head Start Child Outcomes Framework

DOMAIN	DOMAIN ELEMENT	INDICATORS
Language Development	**Listening and understanding**	◆ Demonstrates increasing ability to attend to and understand conversations, stories, songs, and poems.
		◆ Shows progress in understanding and following simple and multiple-step directions.
		☆ **Understands an increasingly complex and varied vocabulary.**
		☆ **For non-English-speaking children, progresses in listening to and understanding English.**
	Speaking and communicating	☆ **Develops increasing abilities to understand and use language to communicate information, experiences, ideas, feelings, opinions, needs, questions, and other varied purposes.**
		◆ Progresses in abilities to initiate and respond appropriately in conversation and discussions with peers and adults.
		☆ **Uses an increasingly complex and varied spoken vocabulary.**
		◆ Progresses in clarity of pronunciation and towards speaking in sentences of increasing length and grammatical complexity.
		☆ **For non-English-speaking children, progresses in speaking English.**
Literacy	**☆Phonological awareness**	◆ Shows increasing ability to discriminate and identify sounds in spoken language.
		◆ Shows growing awareness of beginning and ending sounds of words.
		◆ Progresses in recognizing matching sounds and rhymes in familiar words, games, songs, stories and poems.
		◆ Shows growing ability to hear and discriminate separate syllables in words.
		☆ **Associates sounds with written words,** such as awareness that different words begin with the same sound.
	☆Book knowledge and appreciation	◆ Shows growing interest and involvement in listening to and discussing a variety of fiction and nonfiction books and poetry.
		◆ Shows growing interest in reading-related activities, such as asking to have a favorite book read; choosing to look at books; drawing pictures based on stories; asking to take books home; going to the library; and engaging in pretend-reading with other children.
		◆ Demonstrates progress in abilities to retell and dictate stories from books and experiences; to act out stories in dramatic play; and to predict what will happen next in a story.
		◆ Progresses in learning how to handle and care for books; knowing to view one page at a time in sequence from front to back; and understanding that a book has a title, author, and illustrator.
	☆Print awareness and concepts	◆ Shows increasing awareness of print in classroom, home, and community settings.
		◆ Develops growing understanding of the different functions of forms of print such as signs, letters, newspapers, lists, messages, and menus.
		◆ Demonstrates increasing awareness of concepts of print, such as that reading in English moves from top to bottom and from left to right, that speech can be written down, and that print conveys a message.
		◆ Shows progress in recognizing the association between spoken and written words by following print as it is read aloud.
		☆ **Recognizes a word as a unit of print,** or awareness that letters are grouped to form words, and that words are separated by spaces.

☆ **Indicates the four specific domain elements and nine indicators that are legislatively mandated.**

FIGURE 8.3 (Continued)

DOMAIN	DOMAIN ELEMENT	INDICATORS
Literacy (cont.)	Early writing	◆ Develops understanding that writing is a way of communicating for a variety of purposes.
		◆ Begins to represent stories and experiences through pictures, dictation, and in play.
		◆ Experiments with a growing variety of writing tools and materials, such as pencils, crayons, and computers.
		◆ Progresses from using scribbles, shapes, or pictures to represent ideas, to using letter-like symbols, to copying or writing familiar words such as one's own name.
	Alphabet knowledge	◆ Shows progress in associating the names of letters with their shapes and sounds.
		◆ Increases in ability to notice the beginning letters in familiar words.
		☆ **Identifies at least ten letters of the alphabet, especially those in one's own name.**
		☆ **Knows that letters of the alphabet are a special category of visual graphics that can be individually named.**
Mathematics	☆Number and operations	◆ Demonstrates increasing interest in and awareness of numbers and counting as a means for solving problems and determining quantity.
		◆ Begins to associate number concepts, vocabulary, quantities, and written numerals in meaningful ways.
		◆ Develops increasing ability to count in sequence to ten and beyond.
		◆ Begins to make use of one-to-one correspondence in counting objects and matching groups of objects.
		◆ Begins to use language to compare numbers of objects with terms such as *more, less, greater than, fewer, equal to.*
		◆ Develops increased abilities to combine, separate, and name "how many" concrete objects.
	Geometry and spatial sense	◆ Begins to recognize, describe, compare, and name common shapes, their parts, and attributes.
		◆ Progresses in ability to put together and take apart shapes.
		◆ Begins to be able to determine whether two shapes are the same size and shape.
		◆ Shows growth in matching, sorting, putting in a series, and regrouping objects according to one or two attributes such as color, shape, or size.
		◆ Builds an increasing understanding of directionality, order and positions of objects, and words such as *up, down, over, under, top, bottom, inside, outside, in front,* and *behind.*
	Patterns and measurement	◆ Enhances abilities to recognize, duplicate, and extend simple patterns using a variety of materials.
		◆ Shows increasing abilities to match, sort, put in a series, and regroup objects according to one or two attributes such as shape or size.
		◆ Begins to make comparisons between several objects based on a single attribute.
		◆ Shows progress in using standard and nonstandard measures for length and area of objects.
Science	Scientific skills and methods	◆ Begins to use senses and a variety of tools and simple measuring devices to gather information, investigate materials, and observe processes and relationships.
		◆ Develops increased ability to observe and discuss common properties, differences, and comparisons among objects and materials.
		◆ Begins to participate in simple investigations to test observations, discuss and draw conclusions, and form generalizations.
		◆ Develops growing abilities to collect, describe, and record information through a variety of means, including discussion, drawings, maps, and charts.
		◆ Begins to describe and discuss predictions, explanations, and generalizations based on past experiences.

FIGURE 8.3 (Continued)

DOMAIN	DOMAIN ELEMENT	INDICATORS
Science (cont.)	Scientific knowledge	◆ Expands knowledge of and abilities to observe, describe, and discuss the natural world, materials, living things, and natural processes. ◆ Expands knowledge of and respect for one's body and the environment. ◆ Develops growing awareness of ideas and language related to attributes of time and temperature. ◆ Shows increased awareness and beginning understanding of changes in materials and cause-effect relationships.
Creative Arts	Music	◆ Participates with increasing interest and enjoyment in a variety of music activities, including listening, singing, finger plays, games, and performances. ◆ Experiments with a variety of musical instruments.
	Art	◆ Gains ability in using different art media and materials in a variety of ways for creative expression and representation. ◆ Progresses in abilities to create drawings, paintings, models, and other art creations that are more detailed, creative, or realistic. ◆ Develops growing abilities to plan, work independently, and demonstrate care and persistence in a variety of art projects. ◆ Begins to understand and share opinions about artistic products and experiences.
	Movement	◆ Expresses through movement and dancing what is felt and heard in various musical tempos and styles. ◆ Shows growth in moving in time to different patterns of beat and rhythm in music.
	Dramatic play	◆ Participates in a variety of dramatic play activities that become more extended and complex. ◆ Shows growing creativity and imagination in using materials and in assuming different roles in dramatic play situations.
Social and Emotional Development	Self-concept	◆ Begins to develop and express awareness of self in terms of specific abilities, characteristics, and preferences. ◆ Develops growing capacity for independence in a range of activities, routines, and tasks. ◆ Demonstrates growing confidence in a range of abilities and expresses pride in accomplishments.
	Self-control	◆ Shows progress in expressing feelings, needs, and opinions in difficult situations and conflicts without harming self, others, or property. ◆ Develops growing understanding of how one's actions affect others and begins to accept the consequences of one's actions. ◆ Demonstrates increasing capacity to follow rules and routines and use materials purposefully, safely, and respectfully.
	Cooperation	◆ Increases abilities to sustain interactions with peers by helping, sharing, and discussion. ◆ Shows increasing abilities to use compromise and discussion in working, playing, and resolving conflicts with peers. ◆ Develops increasing abilities to give and take in interactions; to take turns in games or using materials; and to interact without being overly submissive or directive.

FIGURE 8.3 (Continued)

DOMAIN	DOMAIN ELEMENT	INDICATORS
Social and Emotional Development (cont.)	Social relationships	◆ Demonstrates increasing comfort in talking with and accepting guidance and directions from a range of familiar adults.
		◆ Shows progress in developing friendships with peers.
		◆ Progresses in responding sympathetically to peers who are in need, upset, hurt, or angry and in expressing empathy or caring for others.
	Knowledge of families and communities	◆ Develops ability to identify personal characteristics including gender and family composition.
		◆ Progresses in understanding similarities and respecting differences among people, such as genders, race, special needs, culture, language, and family structures.
		◆ Develops growing awareness of jobs and what is required to perform them.
		◆ Begins to express and understand concepts and language of geography in the contexts of the classroom, home, and community.
Approaches to Learning	Initiative and curiosity	◆ Chooses to participate in an increasing variety of tasks and activities.
		◆ Develops increased ability to make independent choices.
		◆ Approaches tasks and activities with increased flexibility, imagination, and inventiveness.
		◆ Grows in eagerness to learn about and discuss a growing range of topics, ideas, and tasks.
	Engagement and persistence	◆ Grows in abilities to persist in and complete a variety of tasks, activities, projects, and experiences.
		◆ Demonstrates increasing ability to set goals and develop and follow through on plans.
		◆ Shows growing capacity to maintain concentrations over time on a task, question, set of directions, or interactions, despite distractions and interruptions.
	Reasoning and problem solving	◆ Develops increasing ability to find more than one solution to a question, task, or problem.
		◆ Grows in recognizing and solving problems through active exploration, including trial and error, and interactions and discussions with peers and adults.
		◆ Develops increasing abilities to classify, compare, and contrast objects, events, and experiences.
Physical Health and Development	Fine-motor skills	◆ Develops growing strength, dexterity, and control needed to use tools such as scissors, paper punch, stapler, and hammer.
		◆ Grows in hand-eye coordination in building with blocks, putting together puzzles, reproducing shapes and patterns, stringing beads, and using scissors.
		◆ Progresses in abilities to use writing, drawing, and art tools including pencils, markers, chalk, paint brushes, and various types of technology.
	Gross-motor skills	◆ Shows increasing levels of proficiency, control, and balance in walking, climbing, running, jumping, hopping, skipping, marching, and galloping.
		◆ Demonstrates increasing abilities to coordinate movements in throwing, catching, kicking, bouncing balls, and using the slide and swing.
	Health status and practices	◆ Progresses in physical growth, strength, stamina, and flexibility.
		◆ Participates actively in games, outdoor play, and other forms of exercise that enhance physical fitness.
		◆ Shows growing independence in hygiene, nutrition, and personal care when eating, dressing, washing hands, brushing teeth, and toileting.
		◆ Builds awareness and ability to follow basic health and safety rules such as fire safety, traffic and pedestrian safety, and responding appropriately to potentially harmful objects, substances, and activities.

Source: Administration for Children and Families, Head Start Bureau, http://www.hsnrc.org/cdi.

The New World of Early Childhood Education

Infants and Toddlers

FOUNDATION YEARS FOR LEARNING

CHAPTER 9

*Babies are not just cute faces but are the
greatest learning machines in the universe.*

PATRICIA KUHL

Interest in infant and toddler care and education is at an all-time high and will likely continue at this level well into the future. The growing demand for quality infant and toddler programs stems primarily from the conditions discussed in chapter 2. It is also fueled by parents who want their children to have an early start and get off on the right foot so they can be successful in life and work. The popularity of early care and education is also attributable to a changing view of the very young and the discovery that infants are remarkably competent individuals. Let's examine the ways that infants' and toddlers' development and early experiences shape their lives.

WHAT ARE INFANTS AND TODDLERS LIKE?

Think for a minute about your experiences with infants. What characteristics stand out most in your mind? Take a few minutes to review the developmental profiles of Oliver, Conner, Marisa, Hyato, Joseph, Mariafe, Christy, and Daniel in the Portraits of Infants and Toddlers that follow. This chapter will help you understand their development across four domains—social-emotional, cognitive, motor, and adaptive (i.e., daily living). After you read the chapter, reflect on and answer the questions that accompany the portraits.

Have you ever tried to carry on an extended conversation with an infant? They are full of coos, ahas, giggles, smiles, and sparkling eyes! Or have you ever tried to keep up with a toddler? A typical response is, "They are into everything!" The infant and toddler years between birth and age two are full of developmental milestones and significant events. **Infancy**, life's first year, includes the first breath, the first smile, first thoughts, first words, and first steps. During **junior toddlerhood**—from twelve to eighteen months—and **senior toddlerhood**—from eighteen months to two years—two of the most outstanding developmental milestones are walking and rapid language development. Mobility and language are the cornerstones of autonomy that enable toddlers to become independent. How you and other early childhood professionals and parents respond to infants' first accomplishments and toddlers' quests for autonomy helps determine how they grow and master life events.

UNDERSTANDING CHILD DEVELOPMENT

Understanding the major development processes that characterize the formative years of infants and toddlers will help you fully grasp your roles as educator and nurturer. Here are some important considerations:

- Recognize that infants and toddlers are not the miniature adults pictured in many baby product advertisements; children need many years to develop fully and become independent. This period of dependency and professionals' responses to it are critical for children's development.
- Keep in mind that "normal" growth and development milestones are based on averages, and the average is simply the

Focus Questions

How is research influencing the care and education of infants and toddlers?

What are key milestones in infant and toddler development?

How do theories of development explain infant and toddler cognitive, language, and psychosocial development?

How can you and others provide quality programs for infants and toddlers?

Companion Website

To check your understanding of this chapter, go to the Companion Website at **www.prenhall.com/ morrison**, select chapter 9, answer Multiple Choice and Essay Questions, and receive feedback.

PORTRAITS OF INFANTS AND TODDLERS

Oliver

Introduce yourself to Oliver, a four-month-old Caucasian male. He weighs about 18 pounds and is 25 inches long. Oliver is a very alert baby. He loves to put everything he can into his mouth. He gets a little bit cranky when his diaper is changed but loves to get his bath before bedtime.

Social-Emotional	Cognitive	Motor	Adaptive
Is a very friendly boy. Never meets a stranger but is getting more selective with people. Cries only when dirty, scared, or hurting. Laughs all the time along with smiling. Always wants his mom at bedtime rather than his father. Loves to go to child care. Plays with hands and feet and amuses himself.	Follows objects with his eyes. Recognizes mom and dad. Follows sounds with head. Loves to watch and feel the cat. Loves to crinkle paper and eat it. Plays with hands and feet. Constantly has hand in mouth.	Can stand up on his own from a sitting position when holding someone's hands. Can grasp an object hanging down from crib with ease. Can hold an 8-oz. bottle on his own and is able to put it in and out of his mouth without problems. Can sit on his own without support. Can roll from stomach to back and back to stomach.	Does not like changes in his schedule; doesn't cope well with change. Is trying to spoon feed himself. Eats four to five times a day. Chews on everything (teething). Has good sleep habits; sleeps through the night.

Conner

Introduce yourself to Conner, a four-month-old Caucasian male. Conner weighs 17 pounds and is 27 inches long. Conner enjoys other people for a short period of time but becomes very anxious to return to his mother. He is in his most cheerful mode when he wakes up in the morning or from his naps.

Social-Emotional	Cognitive	Motor	Adaptive
Hides face when sleepy. Loves being talked to. Likes to watch little children. Recognizes his mom and dad.	Puts his feet in his mouth. Laughs out loud. Watches every move anyone makes. Chews on everything. Loves to sit in the high chair. Likes to squeeze toys to hear sounds.	Always moves his arms and feet. Reaches for everything. Tries to put everything in his mouth but doesn't always make it. Sits up with support.	Eats about every four hours. Eats rice cereal three times a day. Takes about two naps, about one to two hours long. Just stopped breast feeding; takes formula really well.

Questions about four-month-olds:

- What similarities and differences are there between Oliver and Conner?
- What is a common theme in Oliver's and Conner's cognitive development?
- What roles do toys play in Oliver's and Conner's development?
- Identify three ways play can enhance and influence a child's development.
- What activities can you use to promote development in a four-month-old?
- Compare Oliver's and Conner's development with Tables 9.1 and 9.2.

PORTRAITS OF INFANTS AND TODDLERS (continued)

Marisa

Introduce yourself to Marisa, a ten-month-old Hispanic female. She weighs 25 pounds and is 28 inches long. Marisa is not mobile, she prefers to lie on her back and becomes agitated in other positions. Marisa spends the majority of her awake time observing people and toys.

Social-Emotional	Cognitive	Motor	Adaptive
Does not bother anyone.	Likes to play only with certain toys.	Sits with support.	Eats solid baby food.
Is very quiet.	Likes mirrors.	Rotates in circles on her back.	Drinks formula from a bottle.
Gets frustrated when other babies get too close to her.	Likes music and mobiles	Does not like to be held up in a standing position.	Engages in one activity for several minutes/
Likes her teachers to talk to her.	Follows toys with her eyes and hands.	Does not like to be on her tummy.	Likes to help with dressing herself.
Has her favorite toys.	Understands simple sentences (receptive language).	Does not crawl.	Carries around her favorite stuffed bear.

Hyato

Introduce yourself to Hyato, a ten-month-old Laotian male. He weighs 19 pounds and is 28 inches long. Hyato has recently become very active and does not like being confined in any way. He enjoys personal attention from teachers. Hyato has a good sense of humor and prefers interacting with adults to playing with toys. Look back at the Diversity Tie-In in chapter 7 to review the strategies for accommodating cultural differences in Laotian children.

Social-Emotional	Cognitive	Motor	Adaptive
Likes to play alone in his own space.	Whines for attention.	Crawls around quickly.	Drinks formula and juice from a bottle.
Does not play very much with toys.	Points and babbles at things.	Pulls up on furniture.	Can drink from a cup.
Gets frustrated easily.	Likes push–pull toys.	Walks with support.	Nibbles on crackers.
Likes to play with teachers.	Likes to look for things teacher hides under diaper.	Picks up small pieces of food with fingers.	Holds his own bottle.
Is attached to his own teacher.		Can sit down from a standing position.	Starting to show preference for right hand.
		Can carry things in one hand.	Has trouble sleeping at night.

Questions about ten-month-olds:

- What cultural factors might be affecting Hyato's interaction with toys and people?
- Referring to the weight chart in Table 9.1, how might Marisa's physical characteristics influence her development?
- How might Marisa's and Hyato's different cultures affect their adaptive behavior?
- Based on the descriptions provided, what similarities might exist between Marisa's and Hyato's home lives?
- How might classrooms you are familiar with need to be adjusted for the Hispanic and Laotian cultures?
- Why is it important for you to be sensitive to cultural differences as you care for and teach young children?
- Compare Marisa and Hyato's development with Tables 9.1 and 9.2.

Joseph

Introduce yourself to Joseph, a fifteen-month-old Honduran male. He weighs 26 pounds and is 31 inches tall. Joseph uses his hands to explore and communicate. He knows many words but is not yet speaking. He enjoys expressing himself through actions and noise.

Social-Emotional	Cognitive	Motor	Adaptive
Recognizes his own name.^	Tries to talk.	Paints and scribbles.	Drinks from a baby cup by himself.
Plays with other children.	Likes to explore and discover new things.	Plays with musical instruments.	Likes to snack on crackers.
Smiles and babbies when talked to.	Points to pictures when named.	Picks up food with his fingers.	Uses gestures to ask for things.
	Likes to sit in his teacher's lap and listen to stories.		

Mariafe

Introduce yourself to Mariafe a fifteen-month-old Peruvian female. She weighs 24 pounds and is 30 inches tall. Mariafe speaks only Spanish. She is a bright and cheerful toddler. She is very animated and enjoys pretending and participating in activities that involve music.

Social-Emotional	Cognitive	Motor	Adaptive
Gives things to an adult on request.	Says words like *mama*, *papa*, and *no*.	Dances and bounces up and down to music.	Eats solid foods with spoon.
Laughs when you call her name or make faces at her.	Sings along with music.	Likes to color with crayons.	Is increasingly resistant to naptime.
Makes eye contact and smiles.	Likes to pretend to be different animals.	Enjoys climbing up steps.	Can say when her diaper needs to be changed.
	Knows that her toys don't disappear when she can't see them.		Independent—likes to do things by herself.
	Speaks in two-word utterances using telegraphic speech.		

Questions about fifteen-month-olds:

- Do you think that culture explains some of the differences between Joseph and Mariafe in adaptive development?
- How can you accommodate the different adaptive needs of toddlers in the classroom?
- How strictly should you require Mariafe to adhere to the classroom naptime?
- How would you provide for Mariafe's resistance to naptime?

- What role, if any, has music played in Mariafe's development? What are some ways music can be used to enhance development in all four domains?
- What adjustments can be made to your classroom to encourage exploration and mobility in young toddlers?
- What are some developmental differences between Joseph and Mariafe?
- Compare Joseph and Mariafe's development with Tables 9.1 and 9.2.

Christy

Introduce yourself to Christy, a two-year-old Caucasian female. She weighs 27 pounds and is 32 inches tall. Christy is a shy, yet sociable toddler. She loves attending school and playing with her classmates. Although her words are sometimes difficult to understand, Christy is already sharing stories about what she learns in class.

Social-Emotional	Cognitive	Motor	Adaptive
Does not like big groups of people.	Knows the names of classmates.	Can almost do forward rolls.	Asks for help only when she can't do it by herself.
Laughs a lot.	Speaks in short sentences.	Likes to jump up and down.	Eats with a fork.
Prefers male adults to female.	Shares past events.	Can catch a bouncing ball.	Helps with chores.
Has favorite playmates.	Very egocentric—thinks everything exists for her.		Can dress and undress herself.
			Can open doors by herself.
			Loves to play in and with water.

Daniel

Introduce yourself to Daniel, a two-year-old Hispanic male. He weighs 24 pounds and is 30 inches tall. Daniel is a rambunctious toddler. He is extremely active and tends to involve himself in activities that are dangerous to him and other children. Daniel lacks social skills. However, he is very affectionate to his primary caregiver.

Social-Emotional	Cognitive	Motor	Adaptive
Is beginning to hit others a lot.	Follows simple instructions.	Likes to climb on things.	Feeds himself.
Is very quiet but playful.	Uses gestures to ask for things.	Runa around the room.	Can ask for food and drink.
Loves his big brother and sister.	Says several words.	Throws a ball and retrieves it.	Not quite ready for toilet training.
Does not interact well with others.	Thinks hidden toys have disappeared.	Can peddle a tricycle.	
		Likes to run rather than walk.	

Questions about two-year-olds:

- At six months of age, Daniel was diagnosed with failure to thrive, which means that he was not getting enough nourishment and was not growing at the appropriate rate for his age. Does his overall development reflect this diagnosis? Why or why not?
- What is an *enriched environment?* How can it support the development of toddlers who are developmentally at risk?
- Which of Daniel's behavioral characteristics might be dangerous in the classroom? How can you make your classroom a safe environment for active two-year-olds such as Daniel?
- Do all two-year-olds need the same level of supervision? What kinds of supervision might Daniel and Christy need?
- In what domains are Daniel and Christy most similar? In what domains are they most different? What are some activities that both toddlers can successfully engage in and learn from?
- Compare Christy's and Daniel's development with Tables 9.1 and 9.2.

TABLE 9.1 Average Height and Weight of Infants and Toddlers

Age	Males		Females	
	Height (inches)	Weight (pounds)	Height (inches)	Weight (pounds)
Birth	20.0	8.0	19.5	7.5
3 months	24.0	13.0	23.5	12.5
6 months	26.5	17.5	25.5	16.0
9 months	28.5	20.5	27.5	19.0
1 year	30.0	23.0	29.5	21.0
1½ years	32.5	27.0	33.0	24.5
2 years	34.0	28.0	34.0	26.5
2½ years	36.5	30.0	36.0	28.5
3 years	37.5	31.5	37.5	30.5

Source: National Center for Health Statistics in collaboration with the National Center for Chronic Disease Prevention and Health Promotion (2000), http://www.cdc.gov/growthcharts.

Infancy The first year of life.

Junior toddlerhood Children 12 to 18 months.

Senior toddlerhood Children 18 months to 2 years.

middle ground of development (e.g., Table 9.1 gives the average heights and weights for infants and toddlers). Know the milestones of different stages of development to assess children's progress or lack of it.

- Consider the whole child to assess what is normal for each child.
- Take into account gender, socioeconomic, cultural, and family background, including nutritional and health history, to determine what is normal for individual children. Consider that when children are provided with good nutrition, health care, and a warm, loving environment, development tends toward what is normal for each child.

CULTURE AND CHILD DEVELOPMENT

Culture A group's way of life, including basic values, beliefs, religion, language, clothing, food, and practices.

Many factors influence how children grow and develop; for example, reflect on the influence of parents, siblings, home, and schools. But what about culture? **Culture** is a group's way of life, including basic values, beliefs, religion, language, clothing, food, and various practices. Child rearing, for instance, is influenced by the culture of a particular group. Think for a minute about how the following routines, which are culturally based, affect children's developmental outcomes:[1]

- *Bottle or breast feeding:* Whether children are held during a feeding, whether they are allowed or encouraged to hold the bottle, what feeding position is used, how frequently they are fed, whether a bottle is used to induce sleep
- *Feeding solid foods:* When and which foods are introduced, whether mess and waste are permitted, how much child choice and independence are allowed or encouraged, what utensils are used, where and when feeding occurs
- *Toileting:* At what age toileting begins, whether the goal is independent use of toilet or reduction in number of diapers needed, how much adult involvement or time is required, how toileting accidents are handled, whether diapers, training pants, or disposable pants are used
- *Napping:* How often, how long, and where a child naps; how much adult assistance and participation are required for a child to fall and stay asleep
- *Use of comfort items:* Whether a child is allowed or encouraged to use a pacifier or thumb, blanket, stuffed animal, or other object to provide comfort; if so, when, where, and how often the child is allowed to use it

Teachers and caregivers of infants and toddlers need to consider the cultural practices of their families and form close partnerships with family members. It is very likely that you will experience cultural practices that are different from your own, but it is important that

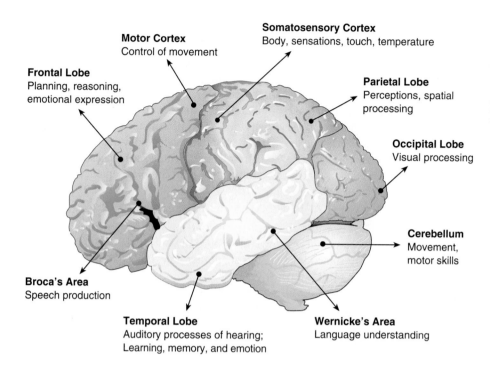

Frontal Lobe
Planning, reasoning, emotional expression

Motor Cortex
Control of movement

Somatosensory Cortex
Body, sensations, touch, temperature

Parietal Lobe
Perceptions, spatial processing

Occipital Lobe
Visual processing

Cerebellum
Movement, motor skills

Broca's Area
Speech production

Temporal Lobe
Auditory processes of hearing; Learning, memory, and emotion

Wernicke's Area
Language understanding

FIGURE 9.1 Brain Regions

Brain research has made educators aware of the importance of providing young children with stimulating activities early in life.

you try to understand them and respect them if they are safe, healthy, and developmentally appropriate for the child.

YOUNG BRAINS: A PRIMER

For the past decade, brain and child development research have received a lot of attention. Brain research has focused especially on the first three years of life, as mentioned in chapter 2. As we discuss these early years now, let's review some interesting facts about infant and toddler brain development and consider the implications they have for you as a professional.

First, review Figure 9.1, which shows the regions of the brain and their functional processes. The brain is a fascinating and complex organ. Anatomically, the young brain is like the adult brain, except smaller. Whereas the average adult brain weighs approximately 3 pounds, at birth the infant's brain weighs ¾ pound; at six months, 1½ pounds; and at two years, 2¾ pounds. So you can see that during the first two years of life the brain undergoes tremendous physical growth. The brain finishes developing at age ten, when it reaches its full adult size.

NEURAL SHEARING

At birth the brain has 100 billion neurons, or nerve cells—all the brain cells it will ever have! As parents and other caregivers play with, respond to, interact with, and talk to young children, brain connections develop and learning takes place. As those connections are repeatedly used, they become permanent. On the other hand, brain connections that are not used or are used only a little may wither away. This withering away, or elimination, is known as **neural shearing**, or **pruning**. Consequently, children whose parents seldom talk or read to them may have difficulty with language skills later in life. This process helps explain why children who are not reared in language-rich environments may be at risk for academic failure.

In the Infant and Toddler segment of the DVD, an expert says that through exploration children make connections and that their brains are like sponges. Why is it beneficial for infants to explore their environment?

Companion Website To learn more about brain development, go to the Companion Website at **www.prenhall.com/morrison**, select chapter 9, then choose the Linking to Learning module.

Neural shearing (pruning)
The selective elimination of synapses.

Synaptogenesis The
rapid development of neural
connections.

SYNAPTOGENESIS

By the time of birth, those billions of neurons will have formed more than 50 trillion connections, or synapses, through a process called **synaptogenesis**, the proliferation of neural connections. This process will continue to occur until the age of ten. During just the first month, the brain will form more than 1,000 trillion more synaptic connections between neurons. These connections and neural pathways are essential for brain development, and it is the experiences that children have that help form these neural connections. Thus, infants whose parents or other caregivers talk to them are more likely to develop larger vocabularies; using different words and speaking to their infants in complex sentences increase the infants' knowledge of words and their later ability to speak in complex sentences.[2]

AGE-APPROPRIATE EXPERIENCES

Sensitive period A period
of developmental time during
which certain things are
learned more easily than at
earlier or later times.

However, children need not just any experiences but the right experiences at the right times. There are developmental windows of opportunity, or **sensitive periods**, during which it is easier to learn something than it is at another time. For example, the critical period for language development is the first year of life. It is during this time that the auditory pathways for language learning are formed. Beginning at birth, an infant can distinguish the sounds of all the languages of the world. But at about six months, through the process of neural shearing, infants lose the ability to distinguish the sounds of languages they have not heard. By twelve months their auditory maps are pretty well in place.[3] It is literally a case of use it or lose it.

There are several conclusions we can draw about the brain:

In the Child
Care segment of the DVD, the
ethnomusicologist asserts that
different kinds of music affect
different parts of the brain.
Review Figure 9.1 and list
ways that music could
influence each region of the
brain.

- Babies are born to learn. They are remarkable learning instruments; their brains make them so.
- Children's brain development and their ability to learn throughout life rely on the interplay between nature (genetic inheritance, controlled by 20,000–25,000 genes)[4] and nurture (the experiences they have and the environments in which they are reared).
- What happens to children early in life has a long-lasting influence on how they develop and learn.
- Critical periods influence learning positively and negatively.
- The human brain is quite "plastic"; it has the ability to change in response to different kinds of experiences and environments.
- The brain undergoes physiological changes in response to experiences.
- An enriched environment influences brain development.

NATURE AND NURTURE

So which of these factors—nature (genetics) or nurture (environment)—plays a larger role? On the one hand, many traits are fully determined by heredity. For example, your eye color is a product of your heredity. Physical height is also largely influenced by heredity—as much as 90 percent. Certainly height can be influenced by nutrition, growth hormones, and other environmental interventions; but by and large, an individual's height is genetically determined. And other traits, such as temperament and shyness, are highly heritable. So we can say that many differences in individuals are due to heredity rather than to environmental factors.

On the other hand, nurture—the environment in which individuals grow and develop—plays an important role in what individuals are and how they behave. For example, the years from birth to age eight are extremely important environmentally, especially for nutrition, stimulation of the brain, affectionate relationships with parents, and opportunities to learn. Think for a moment about other kinds of environmental influence—such as family, school, and friends—that affect development. Review Brofenbrenner's ecological theory in Chapter 5.

A decade or two ago, we believed that nature and nurture were competing entities and that one of these was dominant over the other. Today we understand that they are not

**Companion
Website**
For more
information about the first
three years of life, go to the
Companion Website at
www.prenhall.com/morrison,
select chapter 9, then choose
the Linking to Learning
module.

| Range of | Genetic Expression |

Subaverage Environment

- Indifferent parent(s), lack of affection
- Low level of parent-child interaction
- Few opportunities to go places and do things
- Poor nutrition and habits
- Cramped, cluttered, dirty home
- Not immunized until age of four
- At risk for abuse
- Placed in poor-quality child care
- Mother: high school dropout
- Low socioeconomic status
- Parents: substance abusers

Average Environment

- Receives basic love and affection
- Read and talked to daily
- Good nutrition and physical care
- Average-quality child care
- Mother: high school graduate
- Average socioeconomic status

Above-Average Environment

- Good nutrition and medical care
- Love, affection, and support from extended family, strong family relationships
- Encouraged to "read"
- Engaged in extended conversations
- Many outside opportunities that involve learning
- Enriched opportunities for intellectual stimulation
- High-quality preschool
- Mother: college graduate
- High socioeconomic status

Outcomes

- Slow with language
- Limited vocabulary
- Poor social skills
- Overweight

Outcomes

- Average physical and mental health
- Healthy and happy
- Average language skills
- Average vocabulary

Outcomes

- Talkative
- Independent and assertive
- Socially adept
- Large vocabulary

FIGURE 9.2 **The Interplay of Nature and Nurture**

competing entities; both are necessary for normal development, and it is the interaction between the two that makes us the individuals we are (see Figure 9.2).

HOW DOES MOTOR DEVELOPMENT OCCUR?

What would life be like if you couldn't walk, run, or participate in your favorite activities? Motor skills play an important part in all of life. Even more so for infants and toddlers, motor development is essential because it contributes to their intellectual and skill development. Table 9.2 lists infant and toddler motor milestones.

BASIC PRINCIPLES OF MOTOR DEVELOPMENT

Human motor development is governed by certain basic principles:

- Motor development is sequential.

TABLE 9.2 **Infant and Toddler Motor Milestones**

Children vary in the age at which they achieve major motor milestones. The important thing to observe is that children achieve them.

Age	Milestone
Month 1	• Turns head to one side • Lifts head from a prone position • Holds head with support
Month 2	• Lifts head when held at someone's shoulder • Turns head from side to side when lying on stomach • Lifts and turns head when lying on back • Turns head toward bright colors and lights
Month 3	• Holds chest up and uses the arms for support after being in a prone position • Holds small object in hand • Supports head well when lying on stomach • Sits with support
Month 4	• Rolls over, back to front • Attempts or demonstrates the ability to grasp or maneuver objects • Simultaneously uses both hands to accomplish desired effects
Month 5	• Can support some weight on legs
Month 6	• Sits without support • Lifts head and shoulders while lying on stomach • Plays with toes • Bites and chews • Shakes a rattle • Pulls up to a sitting position if someone grasps baby's hands • Opens mouth to be spoon-fed • Stands with support
Month 7	• Transfers objects from one hand to the other • Enjoys playing games like pat-a-cake and peek-a-boo
Month 8	• Crawls • Stands without support • Pulls up to a standing position • Rolls over from front to back • Sits alone without support
Month 9	• Uses arms and legs to turn • Develops pincer grasp
Month 10	• Able to release an object voluntarily • Gives toy when asked
Month 11	• Walks while holding on to furniture
Month 12	• Tries to climb • Stands while holding on to someone or something • Picks up and manipulates two objects in each hand • Turns pages of a book • Takes first steps
Month 13	• Walks without assistance
Month 14	• Stacks two blocks • Feeds self with assistance
Month 15	• Walks alone
Month 16	• Uses both hands to play

TABLE 9.2   Infant and Toddler Motor Milestones—*Continued*

Age	Milestone
Month 17	• Can build a block tower using 3–4 blocks
Month 18	• Walks backward and up steps • Climbs and utilizes chairs, toys, and tables to reach something
Month 24	• Walks down stairs with support • Can jump in place • Pushes/pulls a light object • Sits directly in a small chair • Runs length of a room without falling • Stands on one foot momentarily

Source: Reprinted by permission from Shane R. May, Mommyguide.com, "Baby's Developmental Milestones from Birth Until Age 2," http://www.mommyguide.com/modules.php?op=modload&name=News&file=article&sid=44.

Cephalocaudal development   The principle that development proceeds from the head to the toes.

Proximodistal development   The principle that development proceeds from the center of the body outward.

• Maturation of the motor system proceeds from gross (large) to fine (small) behaviors. For example, as part of her learning to reach, Maria sweeps toward an object with her whole arm. Over the course of a month, however, as a result of development and experiences, Maria's gross reaching gives way to specific reaching, and she grasps for particular objects.

• Motor development occurs from *cephalo* to *caudal*—from head to foot (tail). This process is known as **cephalocaudal development.** At birth Maria's head is the most developed part of her body; thereafter, she holds her head erect before she sits, and she sits before she walks.

• Motor development proceeds from the *proximal* (i.e., midline, or central part of the body) to the *distal* (i.e., extremities), known as **proximodistal development.** Thus, Maria is able to control her arm movements before she can control her finger movements.

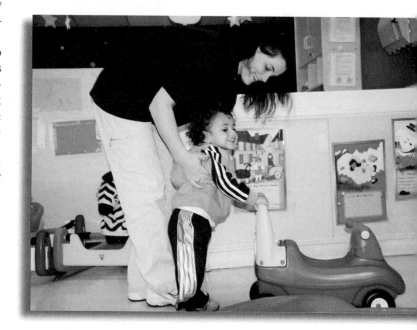

TOILET TRAINING

Motor development plays a major role in social and behavioral expectations. For example, toilet training (also called *toilet learning* or *toilet mastery*) is a milestone of the toddler period that often causes a great deal of anxiety for parents, professionals, and toddlers. Many parents want to accomplish toilet training as quickly and efficiently as possible, but frustrations arise when they start too early and expect too much of their children. Because toilet training is largely a matter of physical readiness, most child-rearing experts recommend waiting until children are two years old before beginning the training process.

The principle behind toilet training is that parents and teachers can help children develop control over an involuntary response. When an infant's bladder or bowel is full, the urethral or sphincter muscles open; the goal of toilet training is to teach

Motor development plays a major role in cognitive and social development. For example, learning to walk enables young children to explore their environment, which in turn contributes to cognitive development. Can you think of other examples?

children to control this involuntary reflex and use the toilet when appropriate. Training involves maturational development, timing, patience, modeling, preparing the environment, establishing a routine, and developing a partnership between the child and parents/teachers. Another necessary partnership is that between parents and the professionals who are assisting in toilet training, especially when parents do not know what to do, are hesitant about approaching toilet training, or want to start the training too soon.

HOW DOES INTELLECTUAL DEVELOPMENT OCCUR?

Reflect on our discussion of cognitive development in chapter 5, and remember that a child's first developed schemata, or schemes, are sensorimotor. According to Piaget, infants do not have "thoughts of the mind." Rather, they come to know their world by acting on it through their senses and motor actions. Piaget said that infants construct (as opposed to absorb) their schemes using reflexive sensorimotor actions.

ASSIMILATION, ACCOMMODATION, AND ADAPTATION AT WORK

Infants begin life with only their billions of neurons and reflexive motor actions to satisfy their biological needs. In response to specific environmental conditions, they modify these reflexive actions through a process of assimilation, accommodation, and adaptation. Recall that *adaptation* consists of two processes, *assimilation* and *accommodation*. Piaget believed that children are active constructors of intelligence through assimilation (taking in new experiences) and accommodation (changing existing schemes to fit new information). During assimilation children adjust their already-existing schemes to interpret what is going on in their environment. Through accommodation children create new schemes or modify existing schemes to fit with the reality of their environments. Patterns of adaptive behavior initiate more activity, which leads to more adaptive behavior, which, in turn, yields more schemes.

Consider sucking, for example, an innate sensorimotor scheme. Kenny turns his head to the source of nourishment, closes his lips around the nipple, sucks, and swallows. As a result of his experiences and maturation, Kenny adapts or changes this basic sensorimotor scheme of sucking to include both anticipatory sucking movements and nonnutritive sucking, such as sucking a pacifier or a blanket.

STAGES OF COGNITIVE DEVELOPMENT: SENSORIMOTOR INTELLIGENCE

Sensorimotor cognitive development consists of six stages (shown in Figure 9.3 and described here). Let's follow Madeleine through these stages of cognitive development:

Stage 1: Birth to One Month. During this stage Madeleine sucks and grasps everything; she is literally ruled by reflexive actions. Because reflexive responses are undifferentiated, Madeleine responds the same way to everything. But sensorimotor schemes help her learn new ways of interacting with the world, and new ways of interacting promote her cognitive development.

Grasping is a primary infant sensorimotor scheme. At birth the grasping reflex consists of closing the fingers around an object placed in the hand. Through experiences and maturation, this basic reflexive grasping action becomes coordinated with looking, opening the hand, retracting the fingers, and grasping, thus developing from a pure, reflexive action to an intentional grasping action. As Madeleine matures in response to experiences, her

In the Infant and Toddler segment of the DVD, the teacher says that babies learn everything through their mouths. Justify this statement based on Piaget's theory of sensorimotor intelligence and the information provided in Figure 9.3.

Stage 1:	Reflexive action	
Age:	Birth to one month	
Behavior:	• Innate reflexive actions—sucking, grasping, crying, rooting, swallowing • Experiences enabling reflexes to become more efficient (e.g., amount of sucking required for nutrition) • Little or no tolerance for frustration or delayed gratification • Beginning to modify reflexes to accommodate the environment	

Stage 2:	Primary circular reactions	
Age:	One to four months	
Behavior:	• Behaviors focused on own body • Acquired adaptions • Reflexive actions gradually being replaced by voluntary actions (e.g., repeatedly putting hand in mouth) • Circular reactions resulting in modification of existing schemes	

Stage 3:	Secondary circular reactions	
Age:	Four to eight months	
Behavior:	• Increased awareness of and response to people and objects in the environment • Ability to initiate activities • Fascination with effects of actions • Beginning of object permanence	

Stage 4:	Coordination of secondary schemes	
Age:	Eight to twelve months	
Behavior:	• Knowledge of cause-effect relationship • Increased deliberation and purposefulness in responding to people and objects • First clear signs of developing intelligence • Continued development of object permanence • Actively searching for hidden objects • Comprehends meanings of simple words • Combines new behavior to achieve goals • Behaves in particular ways to achieve results; likes push-pull toys	

Stage 5:	Experimentation (tertiary circular reactions)	
Age:	Twelve to eighteen months	
Behavior:	• Active experimentation through trial and error, leading to new outcomes • Much time spent experimenting with objects to see what happens; insatiable curiosity • Differentiates self from objects • Realizes that o ut of sight" is not "out of reach" or "out of existence" • Initial understanding of space, time, and causality	

Stage 6:	Representational intelligence	
Age:	Eighteen to twenty-four months	
Behavior:	• Development of cause-effect relationships • Beginning of representational intelligence; child mentally representing objects • Engages in symbolic, imitative behavior • Beginning of sense of time • Egocentric in thought and behavior	

FIGURE 9.3   **Stages of Sensorimotor Cognitive Development**

grasping scheme is combined with the delightful activity of grasping and releasing everything she can get her hands on.

Stage 2: One to Four Months.   The milestone of this stage is the modification of the reflexive actions of stage 1. Sensorimotor behaviors not previously present in Madeleine's repertoire of behaviors begin to appear: habitual thumb sucking (indicating hand-mouth coordination), tracking moving objects with the eyes, and moving the head toward sounds (indicating the beginning of a recognition of causality). Thus, Madeleine starts to direct her own behavior rather than being totally dependent on reflexive actions.

Primary circular reactions
Repetitive actions that are centered on the infant's own body.

Primary circular reactions also begin during stage 2. In the first few months of life, Madeleine's behaviors—that is, her basic reflexive responses—involve her own body. Piaget called this stage primary. And Madeleine repeats the same behaviors over and over again—for example, constantly putting her hand and thumb to her mouth. Consequently, these actions are called circular reactions. By the end of this stage—at four months—Madeleine will have "practiced" her primary circular reactions many times, laying the cognitive and behavioral groundwork for the more coordinated and intentional actions of stage 3.

Stage 3: Four to Eight Months.   Piaget called this stage of cognitive development "making interesting things last." Madeleine manipulates objects, demonstrating coordination between vision and tactile senses. She also reproduces events for the purpose of sustaining and repeating acts. The intellectual milestone of this stage is the beginning of **object permanence**. When infants in stages 1 and 2 cannot see an object, it does not exist for them—out of sight, out of mind. During later stage 3, however, awareness grows that things that are out of sight continue to exist.

Object permanence   The concept that people and objects have an independent existence beyond the child's perception of them.

In addition, **secondary circular reactions** begin during this stage. This process is characterized by repetitive actions intended to get the same response from an object or person; for example, Madeleine repeatedly shakes a rattle to repeat the sound. Repetitiveness is characteristic of all circular reactions. *Secondary* here means that the reaction is elicited from a source other than the infant. Madeleine interacts with people and objects to make interesting sights, sounds, and events happen and last. Given an object, Madeleine uses all available schemes, such as mouthing, hitting, and banging; if one of these schemes produces an interesting result, she continues to use that scheme to elicit the same response. Imitation becomes increasingly intentional as a means of prolonging interest.

Secondary circular reactions   Repetitive actions focused on the qualities of objects, such as their shapes, sizes, colors, and noises.

Stage 4: Eight to Twelve Months.   During this stage, "coordination of secondary schemes," Madeleine uses means to attain ends. For instance, she moves objects out of the way (means) to get another object (end). She also begins to search for hidden objects, although not always in the places they were hidden, indicating a growing understanding of object permanence.

Stage 5: Twelve to Eighteen Months.   This stage, the climax of the sensorimotor period, marks the beginning of truly intelligent behavior. Stage 5 is the *stage of experimentation*. Madeleine's experiments with objects to solve problems are characteristic of intelligence that involves **tertiary circular reactions**; she repeats actions and modifies behaviors over and over to see what will happen (see Figure 9.4). This repetition helps develop understanding of cause-and-effect relationships and leads to the discovery of new relationships through exploration and experimentation.

Tertiary circular reactions
Modifications that infants make in their behavior in order to explore the effects of those modifications.

Physically, stage 5 is also the beginning of the toddler stage, with the commencement of walking. Toddlers' physical mobility, combined with their growing ability and desire to experiment with objects, makes for fascinating and often frustrating child rearing. Madeleine is an avid explorer, determined to touch, taste, and feel all she can. Although the term *terrible twos* was once used to describe this stage, professionals now recognize that there is nothing terrible about toddlers exploring their environment to develop their intelligence. What is important is that teachers, parents, and others prepare environments for exploration. As Madeleine's mom

FIGURE 9.4 **Tertiary Circular Reactions**

Toddlers repeat actions over and over to see what will happen. Here thirteen-month-old Lupe drops her toy to see it bounce! What we can't see is her teacher Amy who constantly picks up the toy and gives it to Lupe, making this wonderful play experience possible.

describes it, "I keep putting things up higher and higher because her arms seem to be getting longer and longer!" Novelty is interesting for its own sake, and Madeleine experiments in many different ways with a given object. For example, she may use any available item—a wood hammer, a block, a rhythm band instrument—to pound the pegs in a pound-a-peg toy.

Stage 6: Eighteen Months to Two Years. This is the stage of transition from sensorimotor to symbolic thought. **Symbolic representation** occurs when Madeleine can visualize events internally and maintain mental images of objects not present. Representational thought enables Madeleine to solve problems in a sensorimotor way through experimentation and trial and error and predict cause-and-effect relationships more accurately. She also develops the ability to remember, which allows her to try out actions she sees others do. During this stage Madeleine can "think" using mental images and memories, which enable her to engage in pretend activities. Madeleine's representational thought does not necessarily match the real world and its representations, which accounts for her ability to have other objects stand for almost anything: a wooden block is a car; a rag doll is a baby. This type of play, known as **symbolic play,** becomes more elaborate and complex in the preoperational period.

In summary, there are several important concepts we need to keep in mind regarding infant and toddler development:

- Chronological ages associated with Piaget's stages of cognitive development are approximate; children can do things earlier than Piaget thought. Focus on children's cognitive behavior, which gives a clearer understanding of their level of development and can guide developmentally appropriate education and caregiving.

Symbolic representation The ability to use mental images to stand for something else.

Symbolic play The ability of a young child to have an object stand for something else.

- Infants and toddlers do not "think" as adults do; they know their world by acting on it and thus need many opportunities for active involvement.
- Infants and toddlers actively construct their own intelligence. Children's activity with people and objects stimulates them cognitively and leads to the development of mental schemata (schemes).
- At birth infants do not have knowledge of the external world. They cannot differentiate between themselves and the external world. For all practical purposes, they are the world.

- The concept of causality, or cause and effect, does not exist at birth. Infants' and toddlers' concepts of causality begin to evolve only through acting on the environment.
- As infants and toddlers move from one stage of intellectual development to another, later stages evolve from, rather than replace, earlier ones. Schemes developed in stage 1 are incorporated and improved on by the schemes constructed in stage 2, and so forth.

Providing an enriched environment is a powerful way to promote infants' and toddlers' overall development. Figure 9.5 identifies some things you can do to create an enriched environment. The Voice from the Field (on pages 246–247) about infant care and development underscores the importance of a holistic approach, paying special attention to relationships.

All children are different, and early childhood educators must provide for the individual needs of each child. Review the Portraits of Infants and Toddlers at the beginning of the chapter, and consider the individual differences in the children portrayed.

LANGUAGE DEVELOPMENT

Language development begins at birth. Indeed, some developmentalists argue that it begins *before* birth. The first cry, the first coo, the first "da-da" and "ma-ma," the first words—all are auditory proof that children are participating in the process of language development. Language helps define us as human and represents one of our most remarkable intellectual accomplishments. But how does the infant go from the first cry to the first word a year later? How does the toddler progress from saying one word to saying several hundred words a year later? Although everyone agrees that children do learn language, not everyone agrees about how. How *does* language development begin? What forces and processes prompt children to participate in one of the uniquely human endeavors?

THEORIES OF LANGUAGE ACQUISITION

Heredity Factors. Heredity plays a role in language development in a number of ways:

- Humans have the respiratory and laryngeal systems that make rapid and efficient vocal communications possible.
- The human brain makes language possible. The left hemisphere is the center for speech and phonetic analysis; it is the brain's main language center. But the right hemisphere also plays a role in our understanding of speech intonations, which enables us to distinguish between declarative, imperative, and interrogative sentences. Without these processing systems, language as we know it would be impossible.

FIGURE 9.5 Creating Enriched Environments for Infants and Toddlers.

Research studies repeatedly show that children who are reared, cared for, and taught in environments that are enriched are healthier, happier, and more achievement oriented.

Include a wide variety of multisensory, visual, auditory, and tactile materials and activities to support all areas of development—physical, social, emotional, and linguistic.

- Hold, play with, and be responsive to infants and toddlers—you are the best toy a child has.
- Provide mirrors for infants and toddlers to look at themselves and others. Talk with the children about how they look. Encourage them to laugh and smile at themselves, you, and others.
- Provide visually interesting things for children to look at—mobiles, pictures, and so on.
- Take infants and toddlers on walks so they can observe nature and people.

Enable children to be actively involved.

- Provide toys and objects that children can manipulate—feel, suck, and grasp.
- Provide objects and containers that children can use to put in or dump out.
- Provide responsive toys that make sounds, pop up, and so on, as children manipulate or act on them.
- Provide safe floor space indoors and grassy areas outdoors so children can explore and move freely.
- Allow infants and toddlers to crawl, pull up, walk, move freely, and explore environments safely.
- Provide activities based on children's interests and abilities—a key to responsive and relational caregiving.
- Provide low, open shelves that allow children to see and select their own materials.

Provide for a full range of language and literacy development.

- Read, read, and read to infants and toddlers. Read aloud with enthusiasm, which shows children how much you love to read.
- Read stories from all kinds of books—stories, poems, and so on.
- Provide books (washable, cloth, etc.) for children to "read," handle, manipulate, and mouth.
- Sing for and with children. Play a wide variety of music. Sing while changing diapers and other teacher-child activities.
- Talk, talk, talk—use the guidelines for supporting literacy in Figure 9.7.

Provide for children's basic emotional needs—safety, security, love, and emotional support.

- Express love and be affectionate to your children. Tell them, "I love you!"
- Give your infants and toddlers your undivided attention—respond to their actions.
- Follow the guidelines for responsive and relational infant and toddler care in the Program in Action: Competency Builder later in this chapter.

Encourage social interactions with other children and adults.

- Play games and engage in activities that include small groups of children.
- Play with toys that involve more than one child—use a wagon and let one child pull another.

Provide for children's health needs.

- Consider massage or touch therapy as a way of getting in touch with your infants and toddlers and as a way of providing for relaxation and muscle stimulation.
- Serve child-sized portions at meal times and let them ask for more.

In the Infant and Toddler segment of the DVD, observe the physical and emotional classroom environment. Comments from school director Becky Raitt and information in Figure 9.5 help explain what infants and toddlers need to thrive in a caring and educational setting.

Voice from the Field

FOCUS ON INFANT CARE AND DEVELOPMENT

The period from birth to age five is a most critical period of life with respect to the rate of development. Children's physical and mental growth reflects experiences with caregivers and surrounding environments. Opportunities for meaningful learning must be brain compatible and developmentally appropriate both in practice and expectation. Our guiding vision of quality extends beyond the realm of good care, education, health, and safety, to the child's total development, including the relationship between child and family within the context of their culture. Our approach deals with the whole child as an integrated entity and is responsive to that individual's needs, desires, and initiatives.

We believe that the four interrelated domains of early development (body, mind, person, and brain) highlight the central accomplishments of early childhood and underscore the obligations of our caregivers. Children are active participants in their own development, together with the adults who care for them. For example, it is crucial for babies to feel good about themselves and think they are learning. We are excited about the things that our babies accomplish. We praise them for pulling up, crawling, waving, smiling, and any number of small accomplishments they make during the day. Babies thrive on the

attention and look to the caregivers for approval. They learn they can make things happen and are delighted that the teacher is excited about it, too.

ENVIRONMENTAL CONSIDERATIONS

These are the environmental considerations we use to support individual development of infants: attachment, trust, mobility, senses, language, and health and safety. Following are specific suggestions to promote each of these areas.

ATTACHMENT

- Attachment is a necessity for learning and development to occur.
- Provide comfortable chairs and floor areas to encourage one-to-one interaction with babies and to support attachment.
- Maintain small group size and low teacher-child ratios; these help to promote attachment as teachers interpret and meet the diverse needs of each child.
- Ensure that each infant has a primary caregiver; the selection is not driven by assignment but by how the personalities are drawn to each other.

Some theorists believe that humans are innately endowed with the ability to produce language. Noam Chomsky hypothesizes that all children possess a structure or mechanism called a *language acquisition device* (LAD), which permits them to acquire language. The young child's LAD uses all the language sounds heard to process many grammatical sentences, even sentences never heard before. The child hears a particular language and processes it to form grammatical rules.

Eric Lenneberg studied innate language acquisition in considerable detail in many different kinds of children, including the deaf. According to Lenneberg,

> All the evidence suggests that the capacities for speech production and related aspects of language acquisition develop according to built-in biological schedules. They appear when the time is ripe and not until then, when a state of what I have called "resonance" exists. The child somehow becomes "excited," in phase with the environment, so that the sounds he hears and has been hearing all along suddenly acquire a peculiar prominence. The change is like the establishment of new sensitivities. He becomes aware in a new way, selecting certain parts of the total auditory input for attention, ignoring others.[5]

The idea of a sensitive period of language development also had a particular fascination for Montessori, who believed there were two such sensitive periods. The first begins at birth and

Trust

- Maintain the familiarity of the environment through association with the same small group.
- Build a trusting relationship between child and caregiver to allow exploration and learning to occur.
- Provide predictable and consistent routines to nurture and create a feeling of security.

Mobility

- Allow babies to play freely on the floor.
- Protect less mobile babies with soft barriers.

Senses

- Stimulate senses with colorful and soft, safe toys.
- Prepare the environment to avoid sensory overload.

Language

- Provide music and rhythm, interesting objects, outside views, pictures, and experiences in which adults talk to infants.
- Recognize that before babies talk, they do a lot of listening.
- Listen to the sounds that infants are hearing and observe their body language.
- Talk to infants about how they are reacting to the sounds and about what they might be thinking.

Health and Safety

- Make health and safety awareness a habit.
- Protect infants from physical danger and biological hazards.

- Embrace children's differences as a natural part of life.

We respect infants' knowledge of what they need and provide a safe environment for their natural development. Because we include children with disabilities throughout the center, it is not unusual to have a baby with a heart monitor or other equipment.

SUPPORT FOR PARENTS

We recognize that a parent is the most important teacher in a child's life. We also understand that relationships with parents of infants are more intense than those with parents of older children; a deeper level of trust is involved, and teachers have a more intimate relationship with infants. As a result, teachers need to communicate in a collaborative manner with parents, rather than taking the role of the expert. For example, a parent or guardian should complete and update a feeding schedule, stating foods to be given, along with preferred times and amounts. The teacher should then keep a daily feeding record for each child, along with times of diaper changes, and share that information with the parent. Teachers should also record notations of a child's activities for the day.

Contributed by Jeanne Roberts, Early Head Start director, and Debbie Moffitt, education coordinator, 0–5 classrooms, New Horizons Center for Children and Families, Macon County, North Carolina.

lasts for about three years. During this time children unconsciously absorb language from the environment. The second period begins at age three and lasts until about age eight. During this time children are active participants in their language development and learn how to use their power of communication. Milestones of language development are illustrated in Figure 9.6.

Environmental Factors. Although the ability to acquire language has a biological basis, the content of the language—syntax, grammar, and vocabulary—is acquired from the environment, which includes parents and others as models for language. Development depends on talk between children and adults and between children and children. Optimal language development ultimately depends on interactions with the best possible language models. Thus, the biological process may be the same for all children, but the content of their language will differ according to environmental factors. Children in language-impoverished homes will not learn language as well as children reared in linguistically rich environments.

				Prespeech								Speech		
0	**1**	**2**	**3**	**4**	**5**	**6**	**7**	**8**	**9**	**10**	**11**	**12 months**	**18 months**	**24 months**
Crying	Social smile	Cooing	"Ah-goo" (the transition between cooing and early babbling)				Babbling (repetition of consonant sounds)			"Dada" "mama" (used appropriately)		Two words	Seven to twenty words	Fifty words
												Three words	Mature jargoning	Two-word sentences
			Razzing (placing the tongue between the lips to produce a "raspberry")					"Dada" "mama" (used inappropriately)			One word	Four to six words Immature jargoning (sounds like gibberish; does not include any true words)	Two-word combinations	Pronouns (*I, me, you*; used inappropriately)

FIGURE 9.6 Language Development in Infants and Toddlers

Source: Adapted by permission from A. J. Capute and P. J. Accardo, "Linguistic and Auditory Milestones During the First Two Years of Life," *Clinical Pediatrics* 17, no. 11 (November 1978): 848.

SEQUENCE OF LANGUAGE DEVELOPMENT

Regardless of the theory of language development you choose to adopt as your own, the fact remains that children develop language in predictable sequences, and they don't wait for us to tell them what theory to follow in their language development! They are very pragmatic and develop language regardless of our beliefs.

Baby signing Teaching babies to use signs or gestures to communicate a need or emotion.

Baby Signing.   Think of the number of ways you use signs, that is, gestures to communicate a need or emotion. You blow a kiss to convey affection or hold your thumb and little finger to the side of your head to signal that you're talking on the telephone. I'm sure you can think of many other examples. Now apply this same principle to young children. Children have needs and wants and emotional feelings long before they learn to talk. As a result, there is a growing movement in support of teaching children to use signs and gestures to communicate desires or signify objects and conditions.

Beginning at about five months, babies can learn signals that stand for something else (e.g., a tap on the mouth for food, squeezing the hand for milk). However, there is no universal agreement about whether to teach babies a common set of signs or to use ones that parents and children themselves make up.

Regardless of the signs used, Linda Acredola and Susan Goodwyn, popularizers of baby signing, identify these benefits:

- Reduces child and parent frustration
- Strengthens the parent-child bond
- Makes learning to talk easier

Baby signs—*left:* monkey (hands up beside armpits with elbows bent and raised); *center:* fish (one arm pointing at a 45° angle with fingers together while other hand is held at that arm's elbow); *right:* Mom (one hand held with all fingers apart and thumb pointing toward mouth).

- Stimulates intellectual development
- Enhances self-esteem
- Provides a window into the child's world[6]

Children are remarkable communicators without words. When they have attentive parents and professionals, they become skilled communicators, using gestures, facial expressions, sound intonations, pointing, and reaching to make their desires known and get what they want. Pointing at an object and saying, "Uh-uh-uh" is the same as saying, "I want the rattle" or "Help me get the rattle." Responsive caregivers can respond by saying, "Do you want the rattle? I'll get it for you. Here it is!" Responsiveness is one attribute of attentive caregivers; it is the ability to read children's signs and signals, anticipating their desires even though no words are spoken.

Holophrasic Speech The ability to communicate progresses from sign language and sounds to the use of single words. Toddlers become skilled at using single words to name objects, to let others know what they want, and to express emotions. One word, in essence, does the work of a whole sentence. These single-word sentences are **holophrases.**

The first words of children are just that, first words. Children talk about people—dada, papa, mama, mummie, and baby (referring to themselves); animals—dog, cat, kitty; vehicles—car, truck, boat, train; toys—ball, block, book, doll; food—juice, milk, cookie, bread, drink; body parts—eye, nose, mouth, ear; clothing and household articles—hat, shoe, spoon, clock; greeting terms—hi, bye, night-night; and a few actions—up, no more, off.

The one-word sentences children use are primarily *referential* (used to label objects, such as "doll") or *expressive* (communicating personal desires or levels of social interaction, such as "bye-bye" and "kiss"). The extent to which children use these two functions of language depends in large measure on caregivers and parents. For example, children's early language use reflects their mothers' verbal style. Thus, how parents speak to their children influences how their children speak.

Motherese or Parentese. Research studies have verified that mothers and other caregivers talk to infants and toddlers differently than adults talk to each other. This distinctive way of adapting everyday speech to young children is called **motherese,**[7] or **parentese.** There are several characteristics of such speech:

- The sentences are short, averaging just over four words per sentence with babies. As children become older, the length of sentences mothers use also becomes longer. Mothers' conversations with their young children are short and sweet.

Holophrase The single words children use to refer to what they see, hear, and feel (e.g., *up, doll*).

Motherese or **parentese** The way parents and others speak to young children in a slow, exaggerated way that includes short sentences and repetition of words and phrases.

In the Infant and Toddler segment of the DVD, listen to what the narrator says about motherese. How does motherese promote infants' and toddlers' language development?

- The sentences are highly intelligible. When talking to their young children, mothers tend not to slur or mumble their words, perhaps because mothers speak more slowly to their children than they do to adults in normal conversation.
- The sentences are unswervingly well formed—that is, they are grammatical sentences.
- The sentences are mainly imperatives and questions, such as "Give Mommie the ball," and "Do you want more juice?" Since mothers can't exchange a great deal of information with their young children, their utterances direct their children's actions.
- Mothers use sentences in which words like *here, that, there* are used to stand for objects or people: "Here's your bottle," "That's your baby doll," "There's your doggie."
- Mothers expand or provide an adult version of their children's communication. When a child points at a baby doll on a chair, the mother may respond by saying, "Yes, the baby doll is on the chair."
- Mother's sentences involve repetitions: "The ball, bring Mommie the ball. Yes, go get the ball—the ball—go get the ball."

Symbolic Representation.   Two significant developmental events occur at about the age of two. First, the development of symbolic representation occurs when something—a mental image, a word—is used to stand for something else not present. Words become signifiers of things—ball, block, blanket. Parents and teachers can help by using the names of things directly ("This is a ball") or indirectly ("Tell me what this is"). They can also use physical labels (*chair*) and use the names of things in conversation with children ("This is a shoe; let's put your shoe on").

The use of words as mental symbols enables children to participate in two processes that are characteristic of the early years: symbolic play and the beginning use of words and sentences to express meanings and make references.

Vocabulary Development.   The second significant achievement that occurs at about two is the development of a fifty-word vocabulary and the use of two-word sentences. This vocabulary development and the ability to combine words mark the beginning of *rapid language development.* Vocabulary development plays a very powerful and significant role in school achievement and life success. Research repeatedly demonstrates that children who come to school with a large vocabulary achieve more than their peers who do not have an expanded vocabulary. And adults are the major source of children's vocabularies.

Telegraphic Speech.   You have undoubtedly heard a toddler say something like "Go out" in response to a suggestion such as "Let's go outside." Perhaps you've said, "Is your juice all gone?" and the toddler responded, "All gone." These two-word sentences are called **telegraphic speech.** They are the same kind of sentences you use when you text message; the sentences are primarily made up of nouns and verbs, generally without prepositions, articles, conjunctions, and auxiliary verbs.

Telegraphic speech   Two word sentences that express actions and relationships (e.g., "Milk gone").

Grammatical Morphemes.   There is more to learning language than learning words; there is also the matter of learning grammar. Grammar is the way we change the meanings of sentences and place events and actions in time: past, present, and future tense. Grammatical morphemes are the principal means of changing the meanings of sentences. A *morpheme* is the smallest unit of meaning in a language. It can be a word, such as *no:* or an element of a word, such as *-ed.* A morpheme that can stand alone, such as *child*, is a *free morpheme.* A morpheme that cannot stand alone is a bound morpheme. *Kicked* consists of the free morpheme *kick* and the bound morpheme *-ed.* Morphological rules govern tenses, plurals, and possessives.

The order in which children learn grammatical morphemes is well documented; the pattern of mastery is orderly and consistent. The first morpheme to be mastered is the present progressive ("I drinking"), followed by prepositions (*in* and *on*), plural (*dolls*), past irregular ("toy fell"), possessive ("Sally's doll"), uncontractible verb ("it is"), articles (*a, the*), past regular (*stopped*), third-person regular ("he runs"), uncontractible auxiliary ("I am going"), contractible verb (*that's*), and contractible auxiliary ("I'm going").[8]

Negatives.   If you took a vote on a toddler's favorite word, *no* would win hands down. When children begin to use negatives, they simply add *no* to the beginning of a word or sentence ("no milk"). As their *no* sentences become longer, they still put *no* first ("*no* put coat on"). Later, they place negatives appropriately between subject and verb ("I no want juice").

When children move beyond the use of the one-word expression *no*, negation progresses through a series of meanings. The first meaning conveys nonexistence, such as "no juice" and "no hat," meaning that the juice is all gone and the hat isn't present. The next level of negation is the rejection of something. "No go out" is the rejection of the offer to go outside. Next, the use of *no* progresses to the denial of something the child believes to be untrue. If offered a carrot stick under the pretense that it is candy, the child will reply, "No candy."[9]

By the end of the preschool years, children have mastered most language patterns. Because the basis for language development is these early years, no amount of later remedial training can make up for development that should have occurred during this sensitive period of language learning.

IMPLICATIONS FOR PROFESSIONALS

A high priority for early childhood professionals is to provide programs that support and facilitate children's language development. Another is to provide a child-staff ratio that supports language development. For example, in a recent study of the effects of a reduced child-staff ratio on children's development, researchers found that in programs with ratios of 1:4 for infants and 1:6 for toddlers, language proficiency improved dramatically when compared to programs with higher ratios.[10] Figure 9.7 provides guidelines that will help you promote children's language development.

The process of language development begins at birth—perhaps even before. What are some specific things parents, teachers, and caregivers can do to promote a child's language development?

PSYCHOSOCIAL AND EMOTIONAL DEVELOPMENT

We discussed Erik Erikson's theory of psychosocial development in chapter 5; review Table 5.3 before reading this section. The first of Erikson's psychosocial stages, basic trust vs. basic mistrust, begins at birth and lasts about one-and-a-half to two years. For Erikson basic trust means that "one has learned to rely on the sameness and continuity of the outer providers, but also that one may trust oneself and the capacity of one's organs to cope with urges,"[11] Whether children develop a pattern of trust or mistrust depends on the "sensitive care of the baby's individual needs and a firm sense of personal trustworthiness within the trusted framework of their culture's life-style."[12]

Basic trust develops when children are reared, cared for, and educated in an environment of love, warmth, and support. An environment of trust reduces the opportunity for conflict between child, parent, and caregiver.

SOCIAL BEHAVIORS

Social relationships begin at birth and are evident in the daily interactions between infants, parents, and teachers. Infants are social beings with a repertoire of behaviors they use to initiate

Providing a language-rich context that supports children's language and literacy is one of the most important things you can do as an early childhood professional.

- *Treat children as partners in the communication process.* Many infant behaviors—such as smiling, cooing, and vocalizing—serve to initiate conversation, and professionals can be responsive to these through conversations.

- *Initiate conversations with infants and toddlers.* Conversations are the building blocks of language development. Attentive and caring adults are infants' and toddlers' best stimulators of cognitive and language development.

- *Talk to infants in a soothing, pleasant voice,* with frequent eye contact, even though they do not talk to you. Most mothers and professionals talk to young children differently from the way they talk to adults. Mothers' language interactions with their toddlers are much the same as with infants. When conversing with toddlers who are just learning language, it is a good idea to simplify verbalization—not by using baby talk, such as "di-di" for diaper or "ba-ba" for bottle, but rather by speaking in an easily understandable way. For example, instead of saying, "We are going to take a walk around the block so you must put your coat on," you would say, "Let's get coats on."

- *Use children's names when interacting with them,* to personalize the conversation and build self-identity.

- *Use a variety of means to stimulate and promote language development,* including reading stories, singing songs, listening to records, and giving children many opportunities to verbally interact with adults and other children.

- *Encourage children to converse and share information* with other children and adults.

- *Help children learn to converse in various settings* by taking them to different places so they can use their language with a variety of people. This approach also gives children ideas and events for using language.

- *Have children use language in different ways.* Children need to know how to use language to ask questions, explain feelings and emotions, tell what they have done, and describe things.

- *Give children experiences in the language of directions and commands.* Many children fail in school settings not because they do not know language but because they have little or no experience in how language is used to give and follow directions. It is also important for children to understand that language can be used as a means to an end—a way of attaining a desired goal.

- *Converse with children about what they are doing and how they are doing it.* Children learn language through feedback—your asking and answering questions and commenting about activities—which shows children that you are paying attention to them and what they are doing.

- *Talk to children in the full range of adult language,* including past and future tenses.

- *Help children learn the names of people and things*—learning names is an important part of vocabulary development.

- *Provide many experiences* so that children have lots of things to talk about.

In the Infant and Toddler segment of the DVD, what important concepts do infants learn by "eating books"?

and facilitate social interactions. Because *social behaviors* are used by everyone to begin and maintain a relationship with others, healthy social development is essential for young children. Regardless of their temperament, all infants are capable of and benefit from social interactions.

Crying is a primary social behavior in infancy. It attracts parents or caregivers and promotes a social interaction of some type and duration, depending on the skill and awareness of the caregiver. Crying has a survival value; it alerts caregivers to the presence and needs of the infant. However, merely meeting the basic needs of infants in a perfunctory manner is not sufficient to form a firm base for social development. Parents and caregivers must react to infants with enthusiasm, attentiveness, and concern for them as unique persons.

Imitation is another social behavior of infants. They have the ability to mimic the facial expressions and gestures of adults. When a mother sticks out her tongue at a baby, after a few repetitions, the baby will also stick out its tongue. This imitative behavior is satisfying to the infant, and the mother is pleased by this interactive game. Since the imitative behavior is pleasant for both persons, they continue to interact for the sake of interaction, which in turn promotes more social interaction. Social relations develop from social interactions, but we must always remember that both occur in a social context, or culture, as the Diversity Tie-In on pages 254–255 so clearly points out.

ATTACHMENT AND RELATIONSHIPS

Bonding and attachment play major roles in the development of social and emotional relationships. **Bonding** is the process by which parents or teachers become emotionally attached, or bonded, to infants. It is the development of a close, personal, affective relationship. It is a one-way process, which some maintain occurs in the first hours or days after birth. **Attachment** is the enduring emotional tie between the infant and the parents and other primary caregivers; it is a two-way relationship.

Attachment behaviors serve the purpose of getting and maintaining proximity; they form the basis for the enduring relationship of attachment. Parent and teacher attachment behaviors include kissing, caressing, holding, touching, embracing, making eye contact, and looking at the face. Infant attachment behaviors include crying, sucking, making eye contact, babbling, and general body movements. Later, when the infant is developmentally able, attachment behaviors include following, clinging, and calling.

Adult speech has a special fascination for infants. Interestingly enough, given the choice of listening to music or listening to the human voice, infants prefer the human voice. This preference plays a role in attachment by making the baby more responsive. Infants attend to language patterns they will later imitate in their process of language development; they move their bodies in rhythmic ways in response to the human voice. Babies' body movements and caregiver speech synchronize to each other: adult speech triggers behavioral responses in the infant, which in turn stimulate responses in the adult, resulting in a "waltz" of attention and attachment. Today, the focus in studying infant social development is on the caregiver-to-infant relationship, not on the individuals as separate entities.[13]

Multiple Attachments.   Increased use of child care programs inevitably raises questions about infant attachment. Parents are concerned that their children will not attach to them. Worse yet, they fear that their baby will develop an attachment bond with the caregiver rather than with them. However, children can and do attach to more than one person, and there can be more than one attachment at a time. Infants attach to parents as the primary teacher as well as to a surrogate, resulting in a hierarchy of attachments in which the latter attachments are not of equal value. Infants show a preference for the primary caregiver, usually the mother.

Parents should not only engage in attachment behaviors with their infants, but they should also select child care programs that employ caregivers who understand the importance of the caregiver's role and function in attachment. High-quality child care programs help mothers maintain their primary attachments to their infants in many ways. The staff keeps parents well informed about infants' accomplishments, but parents are allowed to "discover" and participate in infants' developmental milestones. A teacher, for example, might tell a mother that today her son showed signs of wanting to take his first step by himself. The teacher thereby allows the mother to be the first person to experience the joy of this accomplishment. The mother might then report to the center that her son took his first step at home the night before.

The Quality of Attachment.   The quality of infant-parent attachment varies according to the relationship that exists between them. A primary method of assessing the quality of

Companion Website   To complete a Diversity Tie-In activity related to infant mental health, go to the Companion Website at **www.prenhall.com/morrison** select chapter 9, then choose the Diversity Tie-In module.

Bonding   A parent's initial emotional tie to an infant.

Attachment   An enduring emotional tie between a parent/caregiver and an infant that endures over time.

In the Infant and Toddler segment of the DVD, a teacher talks about the bond that develops between teachers and children. Why is this kind of relationship important for social, emotional, and cognitive development?

INFANT MENTAL HEALTH IN A CULTURAL CONTEXT

Currently, there is a great deal of emphasis on social relations and their influences on infant mental health. We must always remember that social relationships are affected by many processes and contexts, including culture.

Virtually all contemporary researchers agree that children's development is a highly complex process that is influenced by the interplay of nature and nurture. The influence of nurture includes the multiple, nested contexts in which children are reared—home, extended family, child care, community, and society—each of which is embedded in the values, beliefs, and practices of a given culture. The influence of nature is deeply affected by these environments and, in turn, shapes how children respond to their experiences.*

Consequently, it is wise for us to always consider and understand children's culture as we educate and socially interact with them. For example, the Afrocentric model of development encourages us to look at the African worldview and use this as a context to reflect on ways in which African American parents and other family members may think, feel, and act as they relate to and rear their children. Such a perspective would also be helpful to understand how African American parents set goals and guide developmental outcomes for their infants and toddlers. Consider these ten dimensions, which may (or may not) resonate with many African American parents.

1. *Spirituality,* or belief in a supreme being or supreme powers, goes beyond religiosity to focus on the qualities of people rather than on material possessions. For example, when asked what they want for their children in the future, some African American mothers may answer "to be good" (a more spiritual goal) rather than "to graduate from college" (a more material goal).
2. *Communalism,* or an interpersonal orientation, reflects an emphasis on group over individual goals, an emphasis on cooperation rather than

---

FIGURE 9.8 Individual Differences in Attachment

Secure attachment

Secure infants use parents as a secure base from which to explore their environments and play with toys. When separated from a parent, they may or may not cry; but when the parent returns, these infants actively seek the parent and engage in positive interaction. About 65 percent of infants are securely attached.

Avoidant attachment

Avoidant infants are unresponsive/avoidant to parents and are not distressed when parents leave the room. Avoidant infants generally do not establish contact with a returning parent and may even avoid the parent. About 20 percent of infants demonstrate avoidant attachment.

Resistant attachment

Resistant infants seek closeness to parents and may even cling to them, frequently failing to explore. When a parent leaves, these infants are distressed and on the parent's return may demonstrate clinginess, or they may show resistive behavior and anger, including hitting and pushing. These infants are not easily comforted by a parent. About 10 to 15 percent of infants demonstrate resistant attachment.

Disorganized attachment

Disorganized infants demonstrate disorganized and disoriented behavior. They look away from parents and approach them with little or no emotion. About 5 percent of children demonstrate disorganized attachment.

Source: Based on Mary Ainsworth, *Patterns of Attachment: A Psychological Study of the Strange Situation* (Hillsdale, NJ: Lawrence Erlbaum, 1978).

competition, and people-focused versus task-focused activities. Mothers with this orientation may place a high value on young children learning to share their toys or engaging in play activities that involve other children.

3. *Harmony* refers to the importance of integrating one's life into a whole, recognizing one's interdependence with the environment, and seeking unity rather than control.

4. *Expressive communication, or orality,* emphasizes transmitting and receiving information orally, through rhythmic communication and call and response.

5. *Sensitivity* to emotional cues reflects the integration of feelings with cognitions and a synthesis of the verbal and the nonverbal. For example, parents may signal children to alter their behaviors with a simple gesture or look.

6. *Rhythmic movement* is expressed in gross-motor behavior and reflects an interest in flexible yet patterned action.

7. *Multidimensional perception, or verve,* is illustrated in the preference for stimulus variety in learning (e.g., visual, auditory, tactile, motor); both parent and child value experimentation.

8. *Stylistic expressiveness* refers to the valuing of unique style, flair, or spontaneity in expressing oneself (e.g., the way one walks, talks, or wears an article of clothing), but this value is emphasized only when it facilitates group goals.

9. *Time as a social phenomeno* reflects the view that time is spiritual, not material or linear. For example, an event begins when the first person arrives and ends when the last person leaves, rather than at fixed points on a clock. There is also recognition of the linkages of present time to the past and the future.

10. *Positivity* refers to the desire to see good in all situations, no matter how bad they seem on the surface. This positive perspective is thought to stop self-defeating behavior and generate positive problem-solving activity.[†]

As you consider how you can use these ten dimensions in your professional practice, keep in mind that they might not all apply to all African American parents. Groups within African American society might have differences of opinion about any or all of these. It is important for you, therefore, to work closely and individually with all of your parents as you assess their cultural beliefs about parenting and education and the implications that those have for infant and toddler mental health, care, and education.

---

[*]D. A. Phillips and J. P. Shonkoff, *From Neurons to Neighborhoods: The Science of Early Childhood Development* (Washington, DC: National Academy Press, 2000), 23–24.

[†]S. A. Koblinksy and S. M. Randolph, "The Sociocultural Context of Infant Mental Health in African American Families", *Zero to Three* 22, no. 1 (2001): 29–38.

parent-child attachment is the Strange Situation, an observational measure developed by Mary Ainsworth (1913–1999) to assess whether infants are securely attached to their caregivers. The testing episodes consist of observing and recording children's reactions to several events: a novel situation, separation from their mothers, reunion with their mothers, and reactions to a stranger. Based on their reactions and behaviors in these situations, children are described as being securely or insecurely attached, as detailed in Figure 9.8.

The importance of knowing and recognizing different classifications of attachment is that you can inform parents and help them engage in the specific behaviors that will promote the growth of secure attachments.

Fathers and Attachment. Fathers—and their roles in families—are a prominent part of early childhood education today. Many fathers have played important roles in child rearing and have engaged in shared and participatory parenting. Currently, however, there is an increased emphasis on ways to encourage fathers to become even more involved in their families and in child rearing as we discussed in Chapter 8.

Fathers who feed, diaper, bathe, and engage in other caregiving activities demonstrate increased attachment behaviors, such as holding, talking, and looking. Early childhood educators can encourage fathers to participate in all facets of caregiving and can conduct

FIGURE 9.9   Children's Temperaments

Reflect on each of these three temperaments, and provide examples of how each temperament could affect the outcome of children's development.

Easy children
- Few problems in care and training
- Positive mood
- Regular body functions
- Low or moderate intensity of reaction
- Adaptability and positive approach to new situations

Slow-to-warm-up children
- Low activity level
- Slow to adapt
- Withdrawing from new stimuli
- Negative mood
- Low intensity of response

Difficult children
- Irregular body functions
- Tense reactions
- Withdrawing from new stimuli
- Slow to adapt to change
- Negative mood

Source: Based on A. Thomas, S. Chess, and H. Birch, "The Origin of Personality," *Scientific American* 23 (August 1970): 102–109.

training programs that will help fathers gain the skills and confidence needed to assume their rightful places as coparents in rearing responsible children.

TEMPERAMENT AND PERSONALITY DEVELOPMENT

Temperament   A child's general style of behavior.

Children are born with individual behavioral characteristics, which, when considered as a collective whole, constitute **temperament**. This temperament, what children are like, helps determine their personalities, which develop as a result of the interplay of the particular temperament characteristics and the environment.

The classic study to determine the relationship between temperament and personality development was conducted by Alexander Thomas, Stella Chess, and Herbert Birch.[14] They identified nine characteristics of temperament: level and extent of motor activity; rhythm and regularity of functions such as eating, sleeping, regulation, and wakefulness; degree of acceptance or rejection of a new person or experience; adaptability to changes in the environment; sensitivity to stimuli; intensity or energy level of responses; general mood (e.g., pleasant or cranky, friendly or unfriendly); distractibility from an activity; and attention span and persistence in an activity. Thomas and his colleagues developed three classes or general types of children according to how these nine temperament characteristics clustered together: the *easy child,* the *slow-to-warm-up child,* and the *difficult child* (see Figure 9.9).

The importance of developing a match between children's temperament and the caregiver's child-rearing style cannot be overemphasized, particularly in child care programs. As the parenting process extends beyond the natural parents to include all those who care for and provide services to infants, it is reasonable to expect that all who are part of this parenting cluster will accommodate their behavior to take infants' basic temperaments into account.

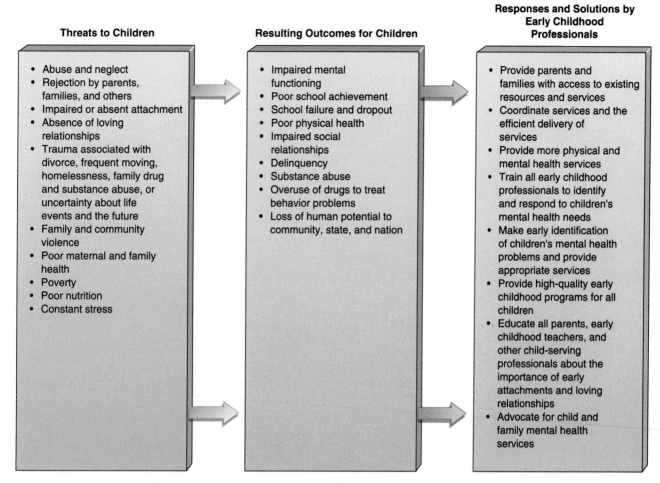

FIGURE 9.10 **Threats to Children's Mental Health, Resulting Outcomes, and Solutions**

INFANT AND TODDLER MENTAL HEALTH

The early childhood profession has always emphasized the importance of providing for children's social and emotional development. One of the benefits of recent research into the importance of early learning is the rediscovery that emotions and mental health play a powerful role in influencing development, especially cognitive development and learning. Think of your own emotions and the ways they influence your daily well-being and approaches to learning. If you are mad or angry right now, your attention is focused elsewhere, and these words cannot carry the importance they would if you were happy, focused, and attentive. Now think about many of the stressful and traumatic events that affect children each day and the negative impacts these have on their lives.

There is growing attention focused on ensuring that all young children are reared and educated in environments that will assure their optimum mental health and well-being, their growth and development to their fullest potential. Figure 9.10 illustrates some causes of poor mental health in children, the associated outcomes, and some remedies available to early childhood professionals, community services providers, mental health experts, and others.

GROWTH OF INFANT MENTAL HEALTH MOVEMENT

The infant mental health movement represents a new direction in early childhood education; efforts are underway to make it a central part of infant/toddler care and education.

Infant/toddler mental health   The overall health and well-being of young children in the context of family, school, and community relationships.

Infant/toddler mental health is a state of emotional and social competence in young children who are developing appropriately within the interrelated contexts of biology, relationships, and culture.[15]

There are a number of reasons for the growth of the infant mental health movement:

- A growing realization that the life and education of children is holistic, not unidimensional
- Brain research findings about how important relationships are in the growth and development of young children; demonstrations that high-quality early environments and nurturing relationships are essential for children's optimal development
- A new and enhanced public awareness about how maternal-child relationships and caregiver-child relationships affect children's mental health; for example, renewed interest in maternal depression and the effects it has on children's development
- Renewed interest in how children are affected by multiple risk factors in their lives, including maternal depression, abusive home environments, absence of fathers from the home, parent and teacher stress, and the lack of continuity of care in homes and child care programs

The field of early childhood is now witnessing burgeoning initiatives designed to strengthen attachments between parents and children and between caregivers/teachers and children and to provide continuity of care for infants and toddlers. Some approaches to promoting continuity of care include the following:

- Screening teachers prior to hiring to determine their beliefs about the importance of relationships and the best ways to provide for them
- Having infants and toddlers and their caregivers choose each other in order to arrive at a best fit
- Providing help and support to grandparents who become the primary caregivers of infants and toddlers
- Having caregivers stay with the same children for several years

SOCIAL ENVIRONMENTS AND INFANT MENTAL HEALTH

Although there are many environments that influence children's development positively and negatively, the infant mental health movement focuses primarily on the social environment as the primary source of mental health influence. Consequently, today there is a great deal of emphasis on the transactions, interactions, and relationships that exist between parents and their child. In a transactional-model approach to infant mental health, emphasis is placed on developing and sustaining positive attachments and relationships between parent(s), child, and caregiver(s).

> Parents and other regular caregivers in children's lives are "active ingredients" of environmental influence during the early childhood period. Children grow and thrive in the context of close and dependable relationships that provide love and nurturance, security, responsive interaction, and encouragement for exploration. Without at least one such relationship, development is disrupted and the consequences can be severe and long-lasting. If provided or restored, however, a sensitive caregiving relationship can foster remarkable recovery.[16]

QUALITY INFANT AND TODDLER PROGRAMS

Before you begin reading about quality infant and toddler programs, visit the real program described in the Program in Action on pages 260–261 to see what a quality program is like.

DEVELOPMENTALLY APPROPRIATE PROGRAMS

All early childhood professionals who provide care for infants and toddlers—indeed, for all children—must understand and recognize the issue of developmental appropriateness, which provides a solid foundation for any program. The NAEYC describes *developmentally appropriate* as having three dimensions:

- What is known about child development and learning—knowledge of age-related human characteristics that permits general predictions within an age range about what activities, materials, interactions, or experiences will be safe, healthy, interesting, achievable, and also challenging for children;
- What is known about the strengths, interests, and needs of each individual child in the group to be able to adapt for and be responsive to inevitable individual variation; and
- Knowledge of the social and cultural contexts in which children live to ensure that learning experiences are meaningful, relevant, and respectful for the participating children and their families.[17]

▲ When making decisions about child care, parents must consider five essential factors: the environment, the professional merit of teachers, staff-child ratios, the quality of care, and the curriculum.

Early childhood professionals must also understand the importance of providing programs for infants and toddlers that are different from programs for older children. NAEYC discusses the necessity of providing unique programming for infants and toddlers:

Developmentally appropriate programs for children from birth to age three are distinctly different from all other types of programs—they are not a scaled-down version of a good program for preschool children. These program differences are determined by the unique characteristics and needs of children during the first three years:

- Changes take place far more rapidly in infancy than during any other period in life.
- During infancy, as at every other age, all areas of development—cognitive, social, emotional, and physical—are intertwined.
- Infants are totally dependent on adults to meet their needs.
- Very young children are especially vulnerable to adversity because they are less able to cope actively with discomfort and stress.

Infants and toddlers learn through their own experience, trial and error, repetition, imitation, and identification. Adults guide and encourage this learning by ensuring that the environment is safe and emotionally supportive. An appropriate program for children younger than three invites play, active exploration, and movement. It provides a broad array of stimulating experiences within a reliable framework of routines and protection from excessive stress. Relationships with people are emphasized as an essential contribution to the quality of children's experiences.[18]

Providing different programs of activities for infants and toddlers first involves helping parents and other professionals recognize that infants, as a group, are different from toddlers and need programs, curricula, and facilities specifically designed for them. It is then necessary to design and implement developmentally appropriate curricula.

It is also important to match professionals with children of different ages. Not everyone is emotionally or professionally suited to provide care for infants and toddlers. Both groups need adults who can respond to their particular needs and developmental characteristics. Infants need especially nurturing professionals; toddlers, on the other hand, need adults who can tolerate and allow for their emerging autonomy and independence.

CURRICULA FOR INFANTS AND TODDLERS

Curricula for infants and toddlers consist of all the activities and experiences they are involved in while under the direction of professionals: feeding, washing, diapering/toileting,

Companion Website
To complete a Program in Action activity related to child care and development, go to the Companion Website at **www.prenhall.com/morrison**, select chapter 9, then choose the Program in Action module.

CHARLIE'S AND EMMA'S VERY, VERY GOOD DAY AT THE BRIGHT HORIZONS FAMILY CENTER

Imagine a warm, sunny, homey room—one part living room, one part playroom/laboratory for messy little scientists—and an adjacent, quiet, comfortable area for cribs and nursing moms. Small cozy spaces, pillows, a couch, places to be together with friends, places to be alone, places to use all your new motor skills, lots of good books, and abundant conversation. And there are always laps, hugs, and smiles.

CHARLIE'S DAY

Twenty-two-month-old Charlie burst through the door, his dad trailing behind with eleven-month-old Emma in his arms. "Bunnies," Charlie said excitedly to his teacher Alicia as he dumped his jacket in his cubby and climbed up next to her on the couch. They talked about his bunny sighting and waved Dad and Emma off. Alicia produced a book on bunnies, which Charlie pored over while she greeted others.

Charlie's friends trickled in, and he and almost-preschooler Jerrod built and crashed walls with the cardboard bricks while waiting for breakfast. After a brief group get-together to welcome each other, sing, and talk about bunnies, new clothes, feeding the fish and the parakeet named Mr. Alejandro (don't ask), and other current events, Charlie's morning was spent experimenting with chemistry and physics (i.e., with colored water and corks at the water table) and a short visit to the infant room to spend time with Emma. He created a picture for Mom and moved around and over things, going in and out of the tent, hiding behind the couch, and spending forty-five minutes in wild abandon tearing about outdoors.

Of course, life has ups and downs—a bump on the knee; an unfortunate, heated dispute with Jeremiah over a wagon, which led to Charlie's temporary banishment from the path and redirection to the slide; having to endure bossy five-year-old Ashley's proudly tying his shoe (Ashley already had the infallible air of the prom queen); and a short pout about not sitting next to Alicia at lunch. Charlie *almost* remembered to go potty but was so busy that he didn't make it in time.

Lunch involved serious eating and silly discussions with Selena, who was teaching them some Spanish by speaking it to them, centering on, "Mi Madre takes me to." Charlie showed Nicholas how he could pour his own milk from the tiny pitcher into his cup. Then it was time for the one story and two poems they always read at nap, a successful trip to the potty, and nap. The nap recharged Charlie's batteries. Snack was ready for each child when he or she woke up, and then the group took a walk to find acorns and leaves for tomorrow's art. The rest of the afternoon was spent with Ashley and Nicholas, playing with real pots, pans, and dishes. Best of all, Jerrod's ten-year-old brother read him a book on the couch after wrestling a bit with him. At 5:30 P.M. it was time to say good-bye and help Dad collect Emma.

EMMA'S DAY

What was the 352nd day of Emma's life like? After a weepy parting from Dad, she spent the day in "conversation"—great responsive language interactions. She explored the world with her mouth, nose, skin, and ears and used her newfound skill of walking (actually, lurching about). She used the couch as a walking rail and a pull-me-up-space and found great delight in using her whole body to explore the concepts of *over, under, around, in,* and *out* as she staggered and crawled around the room, over the footstool, under the table. She played peek-a-boo, hiding in the big box. She splashed her fingers in the soapy tub of water with fourteen-month-old Keesha. She loved seeing her brother Charlie and survived his exuberant hug.

Between her three short naps, she ate lunch, lounged around with a bottle or two, and went for a buggy ride with Keesha, second-favorite caregiver Tony, and two children from next door. She explored the damp grass and trees outside. Of course, Emma spent quite a bit of time being cared for by her primary caregiver Kim, especially during the prime times of diapering and feeding. She was diapered three times, along with the requisite singing and tickle games, and snuggled at least four or five times, reading picture books, rhyming, and having fascinating "conversations" as Kim talked about current events: the birds they saw, the poop in her diaper, the water she drank, Charlie, and the zipper on her coat. Emma also watched closely as fourteen-month-old Nguyen and Tony did a fingerplay together.

Emma was busy. First she helped Kim get the laundry out of the dryer. Then Kim and Emma called Emma's mom to congratulate her on her new promotion. Emma cried after hearing her mom, as did her mom at the wonderful gesture, but it was still worth it. Of course Emma fussed quite a bit and had a fit when Keesha's dad got too close. She also cried a little bit when Kim left, and she burst into tears when Dad arrived, delighted beyond words to have him back. She held him close as he discussed her day with Tony.

This relaxed but full day, left Charlie and Emma ready to go home with enough energy to handle the rush of reuniting with Mom, sharing Charlie's picture and spending some good time together before heading for bed and beginning it all over again the next day.

DECONSTRUCTING THE VERY, VERY GOOD DAY

Taking what we know about the development of children and the development of families, this was an extraordinarily good day for Charlie and Emma.

Family

Emma and Charlie are developing the foundations of their relationship, which will last two lifetimes. They each spend forty-five hours a week at the center; they need time together and they get it. The family is also a strong presence—from Charlie helping Dad with Emma to his picture for Mom and Emma's phone call.

Responsive Interactions with Abundant Language

Charlie and Emma's days are filled with conversations with adults and other children. They aren't just talked to or at, questioned, or responded to. These are real give-and-takes, often initiated by a vocalization by the children. Their days are laced with books, poems, and singing.

Undivided Attention

There are a number of moments during the day when Charlie and Emma each have the undivided attention, the full human presence, of their primary caregiver— sometimes for chatting, sometimes for solace, and sometimes for helping them understand that group life has responsibilities. For that brief moment, the only thing in the world that matters is the interaction between the child and the caregiver.

Exploration

Days are full of exploration inside and out, not only with toys but with materials from real life and nature.

Relationships

Emma and Charlie spend the day in a community, not just a room with children just like themselves. They have relationships with older and younger children and adults throughout the center. When the beloved primary caregiver Alicia or Kim is out, it is still a secure place for them to be.

Teaching and Learning

Both Charlie and Emma learn from other children and teach other children a thing or two.

Expectations

Charlie and Emma are respected as people and expected to behave appropriately. Charlie is learning social graces, and Emma is expected to fuss and cry as she navigates new waters.

Parent Partnership

Charlie and Emma's mother and father are members of the family center community and are respected as the experts on their children. The care Charlie and Emma receive is based on a thorough mutual understanding between the family and the caregivers and on ongoing communication.

Why a Very, Very Good Day?

It wasn't a great day because it wasn't smooth and carefree. There were accidents and tears, teapot tempests, and the sweet sorrow of parting from loved ones. But it was a very, very good day for Charlie and Emma because everything really important that they needed happened. We don't know whether it was a great day for all the other children, but Alicia, Selena, Tony, Kim, and all the other staff members work hard to try to make it great for *each* child and *each* family *every* day. When it all comes together, ain't life grand?

Contributed by Jim Greenman, senior vice president of Bright Horizons Family Solutions, which operates more than 600 high-quality centers and schools in the United States, Canada, and Europe.

FIGURE 9.11 Planning and Implementing Infant/Toddler Curricula

Develop a written plan based on these concepts:
- Knowledge of child development
- Program's philosophy and goals
- Nature of children in program
- Parent's beliefs, culture, and values
- Children's interests, needs, temperaments, and unique individuality

Develop a set of experiences based on these concepts:
- Respect for individual children and their particular interests and needs
- Knowledge of individual children based on observation, screening, assessment, and parent information
- Cultural practices of children and families
- Materials needed to support children's responses

Implement the curriculum:
- Implement and adapt plans as appropriate based on needs of children
- Follow the lead of infants and toddlers in implementing and adjusting the curriculum
- Be available for and responsive to children

Evaluate the curriculum:
- Reflect on and renew the curriculum as appropriate, based on teaching and children's responses
- Have parents provide feedback regarding curriculum effectiveness and learning outcomes

playing, learning and having stimulating interactions, outings, being involved with others, having conversations, participating in stimulating cognitive and language experiences. Professionals must plan the curriculum so that all activities are developmentally appropriate. Figure 9.11 provides a process and a sequence for planning infant and toddler curricula. However, not everyone agrees that planning for infants and toddlers should be such a linear process. Some think that planning should be more circular, that is, based on responses to child and teacher interactions. I believe planning is a combination of linear, circular, and relational processes. The Program in Action on pages 263–265 is a Competency Builder that shows you how to plan a curriculum that promotes relationships and also responds to children's needs and interests.

HEALTHY PROGRAMS FOR YOUNG CHILDREN

The spread of diseases in early childhood programs is a serious concern to all who care for young children; part of their responsibility is to provide healthy care for all children. One of the most important things you can do to promote a healthy environment is to wash your hands frequently and properly. Even though diapering is a prime vehicle for germ transmission, the spread of germs can be greatly reduced through the use of sanitary diapering techniques.

COMMUNITY COLLABORATION

Because families sometimes need assistance in rearing healthy children, communities in which these children live should help. Through collaboration it is possible to make healthy

HOW TO PLAN A CURRICULUM FOR INFANTS AND TODDLERS: DAY TO DAY THE RELATIONSHIP WAY

Talitha (nine-months-old) leans against her teacher while laughing and giving her a quick hug.

Marcus (thirteen-months-old) figures out how to make music with a small drum.

Kareem (eighteen-months-old) climbs into a teacher's lap with a book in his hand.

Tanya (twenty-four-months-old) splashes water with her peers in a small water table.

All of these fortunate infants and toddlers have something in common. They attend programs in which teachers know how to plan a curriculum that is responsive and promotes relationships.

WHAT IS AN INFANT AND TODDLER CURRICULUM?

A curriculum for infants and toddlers includes everything that they experience (from their perspective) from the moment they enter the program until they leave to go home. Every experience makes an impression on how children view themselves, others, and the world. Caring teachers plan a curriculum that is (a) relationship based and (b) responsive to infants' and toddlers' needs, interests, and developmental levels as well their families' goals for their children.

WHY ARE RELATIONSHIPS IMPORTANT IN CURRICULUM?

A relationship is a bond of caring between two people that develops over time. In a relationship-based program, teachers support all the relationships that are key to children's development—parent-child, teacher-child, teacher-family, and child-child relationships. Children need these sustaining, caring relationships to give them a sense of self-worth, trust in the positive intentions of others, and motivation to explore and learn. They need protection, affection, and opportunities to learn to thrive.

HOW CAN YOU PLAN AND IMPLEMENT A RESPONSIVE CURRICULUM?

In a responsive curriculum, teachers interact with children and plan day to day the relationship way. Teachers make daily and weekly changes in the environment and in their interactions in response to each child's needs, interests, goals, and exploration of concepts. How do you do this? First, you *respect,* then you *reflect,* and then you *relate.*

STEP 1 Respect

- **Respect infants and toddlers as competent, and honor their individual differences.** Recognize that infants and toddlers are active learners and thinkers who are using many different strategies to figure out how things work. In an emotionally supportive environment, they become problem solvers, make good choices, and care about others. Respect that children are unique human beings with different styles (e.g., some eat fast and others slow), different interests, and one-of-a-kind personalities. "Each child is valued as a child, not just for what adults want the child to become."*

- **Respect that children will have the motivation to learn if you provide a responsive environment.** It should engage them and appeal to a variety of ages, cultures, and individual needs. Provide opportunities for children to choose from such things as blocks, creative materials, sensory experiences, manipulatives, books, dramatic play, and active play opportunities.

- **Respect that play is the way that infants and toddlers learn.** When infants and toddlers aren't sleeping or eating, they are playing with toys, people, and objects (such as a string or a leaf). As they make choices, infants and toddlers focus on their important goals for learning and nurturing—opening and closing a door on a toy, filling a hole on the playground, playing with a friend, turning a page in a book, putting objects in containers, or climbing on a teacher's lap for a hug. As they play, they explore concepts such as how objects fit into various spaces, cause and effect, object permanence, how to comfort another child, or what they can do with different sizes of paper (e.g., crumple, stack, make into a ball, color on it, cover up toys). Children will pursue their goals in an emotionally supportive and physically interesting environment. For example, a child who feels secure might work on figuring out how to stack blocks for long periods of time. Anything that infants and toddlers decide to do in an interesting and relationship-based program supports their learning in all domains of development at the same time—emotional, social, cognitive, language, and motor. Nurturing and responsive adults stay close by, support children's play, and meet their emotional needs by using all of the strategies described in the next sections.

STEP 2 Reflect

- **Reflect with families to learn about each child's unique interests, explorations, and culture.** If you are open and interested, families will share with you new words that their children are saying, their latest physical accomplishments, blossoming interests in bugs, how they celebrate holidays, or what they want for their children.

- **Reflect through observing children.** Each day observe children to know them well. Each teacher in the room should choose a few children to focus on each week and then take pictures or write notes to capture children's needs, interests, goals, and strategies. You can use an observation and planning guide such as the one shown here to capture your observations. Also, a developmental checklist such as the Ounce[†] allows you to capture the sequence and quality of a child's development over time and then use the information for responsive planning.

- **Reflect on your observations at least weekly with other teachers and often with families.**
  - What is the child trying to do, and how is the child trying to do it?
  - What is the child learning? (Not—what am I teaching?) What concepts (e.g., space, time, social interactions, expressing emotions, ways to open containers) is the child exploring?
  - What is the child telling you he or she needs? (More positive attention, more affection, new strategies to use when another child takes a toy, more room to learn to walk?)

Individual Child Planning Guide

Child s Name: _____

Plans for Week of (Date): _____

Person(s) Completing the Guide: _____

Respect: Child's Emotions, Effort, Goals, Learning, and Relationships

Write an observation or use a photograph or other documentation here—date all notes:

Reflect	Relate
Date all notes: *What am I doing?*	What will you do to support my development and learning?
How am I feeling?	*Responsive Interactions and Building Relationships*
What am I learning? • Emotional:	
• Social with Peers:	*Environment, Toys, Materials, and Experiences*
• Cognitive:	
• Language:	
• Motor:	

Source: Adapted from Wittmer, D. S. & Petersen, S. H. (2006). *Infant and toddler development and respoonsive program planning*, p. 267. Upper Saddle River: NJ: Merrill/Prentice Hall.

- What is new in the child's development? For example, is he or she learning to climb or jump, comfort peers, use two words together, or ask questions?

STEP 3 Relate

- **Relate to children by providing the basics—moment-to-moment responsive adult interactions.** Infants and toddlers need to feel that you really care about them.
  - Comfort distressed children.
  - Respond to children's cues and signals—for example, a frown that indicates discomfort, a cry that indicates distress, a plop in the lap with a book that means "Please read to me," sounds that indicate concentration and enjoyment, and words that communicate.
  - Talk responsively with children, abundantly describe your own and the children's actions, provide reasons and explanations, and engage in cooing, babbling, and word conversations.
  - Sing, read, play with children, and respond in nurturing ways to children's need for sleep, food, and comfort.
  - Guide children to learn how to be prosocial by noticing when they are kind, modeling helpfulness, and demonstrating how to care for others.
  - Be open and receptive to what each child is learning in the moment, and follow each child's lead during play.
  - Encourage the children to experiment and problem solve.
  - When a child becomes frustrated, scaffold the child's learning and motivation by helping just enough to support the child's learning how to do the task.
  - Remember that sometimes you facilitate children's concentration and peer play by sitting near and observing with engaged interest.
- **Relate during routines.** Consider routines such as diapering/toilet learning, feeding/group eating, and nurturing to sleep as central parts of the curriculum for infants and toddlers. Use these times to support children's emotional development and other learning. Talk to children to help them learn language, show affection to help them build a sense of self-worth, and respond to their cues of hunger and tiredness to help them learn to trust themselves and others.
- **Relate by using the observations and reflections to make changes** —day to day and week to week in your interactions, the environment, opportunities, and routines.
  - Plan new ways to support healthy relationships between teachers, children, peers, and families. For example, to help a child who has started to bite peers, plan for a teacher to stay near to help the child learn new behaviors to get needs met.
  - Choose a few new songs to sing, books, toys, changes in the environment, and new opportunities (e.g., art and sensory materials, puzzles, manipulatives, large-motor equipment) based on the children's interests and learning. However, keep most of the environment and materials the same for the children's sense of security and stability. Continue reading favorite books and singing familiar songs while introducing a few new ones each week.

In the following two examples, teachers use the **respect-reflect-relate model** to plan a responsive, relationship-based curriculum. They trust that each child is expressing a need or conveying an interest. They communicate with families, observe the child, reflect on their observations, and then relate by planning changes in the environment, opportunities for the child, and moment-to-moment responsive interactions to build healthy relationships.

> Tommy (twelve months old) was dumping toys out of containers. His teacher observed the dumping and asked, What is he trying to do? How is he trying to do it? What is he learning? What does he need? She asked Tommy's mother how Tommy was playing with his toys at home. Tommy's teacher decided that he was interested in how a container can be full one minute and then empty the next. She provided more containers full of safe objects that Tommy could dump. Soon he also began to fill the containers as he explored different strategies for how objects fit into different spaces.
>
> Another teacher observed Latisha (fifteen months old). She seemed to need to stay near the teacher lately. Her teacher discussed this with Latisha's parents and the other teachers in the room. They decided together that Latisha seemed to need to be near her teacher for protection, affection, and encouragement. Her teacher decided to sit with Latisha more often, give her positive attention, and encourage other children to join them in play.

These teachers were being responsive to Tommy's and Latisha's relationship and learning needs, interests, and developmental changes. When teachers plan the curriculum in a responsive, relationship-based way, infants' and toddlers' motivation to learn and love gets stronger with each caring moment.

Contributed by Donna S. Wittmer and Sandra H. Petersen, authors of *Infant and Toddler Development and Responsive Program Planning: A Relationship-Based Approach* (Upper Saddle River, NJ: Merrill/Prentice Hall, 2006). Donna is a professor of early childhood education at the University of Colorado at Denver and Health Sciences Center. Sandy works for Zero to Three with the National Infant Toddler Child Care Initiative and Early Head Start and is also an instructor for WestEd Laboratories with the Program for Infant and Toddler Caregivers (PITC).

*R. N. Emde and J. K. Hewitt, *Infancy to Early Childhood: Genetic and Environmental Influences on Developmental Change* (Denver, CO: Oxford University Press, 2001), viii.

†TKW Consulting, *Ounce Scale,* http://www.tkwconsulting.com/ounce.htm.

living a reality for all children. Often, the public health community has combined efforts with the early childhood community in order to create the best care for children.

Healthy Child Care America is an excellent example of community collaboration in action. The American Academy of Pediatrics coordinates the Healthy Child Care America campaign in partnership with the U.S. Department of Health and Human Services Child Care Bureau and the Maternal and Child Health Bureau. Healthy Child Care America is based on the principle that, through partnerships, families, child care providers, and health care providers can promote the healthy development of young children in child care and increase access to preventive health services and safe physical environments for children. Linking health care providers, child care providers, and families makes good sense—for maximizing resources, for developing comprehensive and coordinated services, and, most important, for nurturing children.[19]

Companion Website

For additional Internet resources or to complete an online activity for this chapter, go to the Companion Website at **www.prenhall.com/morrison**, select chapter 9, then choose the Linking to Learning or Making Connections module.

LINKING TO LEARNING

Brain Development in Infants and Toddlers: Information for Parents and Caregivers
http://www.nccic.org/poptopics/brain.html

Provides an overview of resources available concerning the brain.

Early Brain Development: What Parents and Caregivers Need to Know
http://www.educarer.org/brain.htm

Presents facts about early brain development that parents and educators need to know.

I Am Your Child Foundation
http://www.iamyourchild.org/

A national public awareness and engagement campaign to make early childhood development a top priority for our nation. Has educated millions of parents and professionals about breakthrough new discoveries in the process of brain development.

KidSource OnLine for Healthcare
http://www.kidsource.com/kidsource/pages/Health.html

Health care articles, online forums, and websites concerning the proper care of young children.

Zero to Three
http://www.zerotothree.org/

Concentrates exclusively on the miraculous first years of life, the critical period when a child undergoes the greatest human growth and development. Seeks to develop a solid intellectual, emotional, and social foundation for young children.

ACTIVITIES FOR FURTHER ENRICHMENT

ETHICAL DILEMMA: "SHOULD I KEEP QUIET?"

You are a teacher of toddlers in the Bent Tree Early Learning Center. Your state guidelines recommend a toddler-adult ratio of 5:1. Generally your room has ten children and two caregivers. However, the administration of Bent Tree overenrolls so that, as your administrator explains, "We can compensate for illnesses and other absences and always be fully enrolled." As a result, more often than not, you have more children than the recommended ratio. Furthermore, when the administration believes the center will be inspected, they shift children around from room to room so they are in compliance with the child-adult ratio. In addition, many times administrators substitute as teachers to comply with ratios.

What should you do—keep quiet and go along with the administration's juggling of child-adult ratios or talk to the administrators about your concern that they are not following state child care regulations?

APPLICATIONS

1. You have been asked to speak to a group of parents about what they can do to promote their children's language development in the first two years of life. Outline your presentation and list five specific suggestions you will make.

2. Observe children between the ages of zero and eighteen months. Identify the six stages of sensorimotor intelligence by describing the behaviors you observed. Cite specific examples of secondary and tertiary reactions. For each of the six stages, develop two activities that would be cognitively appropriate.

3. Why is motor development important in the early years? What are five activities you can include in your program to promote motor development?

4. Identify at least ten games or activities that are beneficial to the developing infant and the growing toddler. Describe the benefits of each of the games or activities you list.

FIELD EXPERIENCES

1. Visit at least two programs that provide care for infants and toddlers. Observe the curriculum to determine whether it is developmentally appropriate. What suggestions would you make for improving the curriculum? Explain what you liked most and least about the program.

2. Visit centers that care for young children of different cultures. List the differences you find. What role does culture play in how we care for and educate children?

3. Review the Competency Builder about planning for infants and toddlers "the relationship way." Then visit infant and toddler programs, and identify the ways the caregiver provides relational care. List the competencies you will need to develop to provide relational child care for infants and toddlers.

4. Review Figure 9.5, which outlines ways to create enriched environments for infant and toddler child care programs. Develop a checklist based on Figure 9.5 (see chapter 3 for help in developing a checklist), and then visit infant and toddler child care programs to assess the ways in which they enrich their environments.

RESEARCH

1. In addition to the qualities cited in this chapter, list and explain five other qualities you think are important for professionals caring for infants and toddlers.

2. Identify customs that are passed down to infants and toddlers as a result of their family's cultural background. How do these customs affect young children's behavior?

3. Interview professionals who care for infants and for toddlers. How are their rules similar and different? Which age group would you prefer to care for? Why?

4. Research baby signing on the Internet, and develop a set of questions you can use to interview parents about baby signing. Then develop a list of pros and cons, and write a statement of your beliefs regarding the teaching of babies to sign.

READINGS FOR FURTHER ENRICHMENT

Hast, Fran, and Ann Hollyfield. *Infant and Toddler Experiences.* St. Paul, MN: Redleaf Press, 1999.

Organized by what the authors call the three Cs—curiosity, connection, and coordination; describes the experiences simply, including materials needed and procedures to keep in mind. Lists specific strategies to help caregivers promote the healthiest development in infants and toddlers.

Herschkowitz, E. C., N. Herschkowitz, and J. Kagan. *A Good Start in Life: Understanding Your Child's Brain and Behavior.* Malden, MA: Joseph Henry Press, 2004.

Seeks to reduce the stress, compiling basic information about child development from conception to age six in one concise book. Written by a neuroscientist and an educator; contains information about the physical stages of early childhood.

Lally, J. Ronald. *Caring for Infants and Toddlers in Groups: Developmentally Appropriate Practice.* Washington, DC: Zero to Three, 2003.

Offers caregivers, directors, trainers, and licensors a great overview of and introduction to child development in the first three years.

Otto, B. *Language Development in Early Childhood,* 2nd ed. Upper Saddle River, NJ: Merrill/Prentice Hall, 2006.

Combines theory, research, and practice to provide a solid foundation for understanding language development from birth to age eight. Provides readers with a basic understanding of the phonetic, semantic, syntactic, morphemic, and pragmatic aspects of language knowledge acquired by young children.

ENDNOTES

1. Klinkner, Joan. *Cultural Sensitivity When Caring for Infants and Toddlers.* Wisconsin Child Care Improvement Project, Inc. http://www.wccip.org/tips/Infant_Toddler/Cultural_Sensitive_Info.html

2. J. Huttenlocher, "Language Input and Language Growth," *Preventive Medicine: An International Journal Devoted to Practice and Theory* 27, no. 2 (March–April, 1998): 195–199.

3. P. Kuhl, *How Babies Acquire Building Blocks of Speech Affects Later Reading, Language Ability,* (July 2001), http://www.sciencedaily.com/print.php?url=/releases/2001/07/010730080042.htm.

4. Professionals and Researchers: Quick Reference and Fact Sheets. March of Dimes Birth Defects Foundation. http://www.marchofdimes.com/professionals/681_1206.asp.

5. Eric H. Lenneberg, "The Biological Foundations of Language," *Readings in Applied Transformational Grammar,* ed. Mark Lester (New York: Holt, Rinehart and Winston, 1970), 8.

6. L. Acredolo and S. Goodwyn, *Baby Signs: How to Talk with Your Baby Before Your Baby Can Talk* (Chicago: Contemporary Books, 1996).

7. E. L. Newport, "Mother, I'd Rather Do It Myself: Some Effects and Non-effects on Maternal Speech Style," in *Talking to Children,* ed. C. E. Snow and C. A. Ferguson (Cambridge: Cambridge University Press, 1977), 112–129.

9. R. Brown, *A First Language* (Cambridge, MA: Harvard University Press, 1973), 281.

0. L. Bloom, *Language Development: Form and Function in Emerging Grammars* (Cambridge, MA: MIT Press, 1970).

10. J. Portner, "Two Studies Link High-Quality Day Care and Child Development," *Education Week* (April 19, 1995): 6.

11. Sue Bredekamp and Carol Copple, eds. *Developmentally Appropriate Practice in Early Childhood Programs,* rev. ed. (Washington, DC: NAEYC, 1997), 9.

12. Erik Erikson, *Childhood and Society,* 2nd ed. (New York: Norton, 1963; first pub., 1950), 249.

13. Ibid.

14. A. Thomas, S. Chess, and H. Birch, "The Origin of Personality," *Scientific American* (1970): 102–109.

15. Charles J. Zeanah, Jr., "Towards a Definition of Infant Mental Health," *Zero to Three,* 22, no. 1 (2001): 13–20.

16. D. A. Phillips and J. P. Shonkoff, *From Neurons to Neighborhoods: The Science of Early Childhood Development* (Washington, DC: National Academy Press, 2000), 7.

17. Ibid.

18. Bredekamp and Copple, *Developmentally Appropriate Practice,* 9.

19. NAEYC, *Developmentally Appropriate Practice in Early Childhood Programs Serving Infants* (Washington, DC: Author, 1989), 547.

The Preschool Years

GETTING READY FOR SCHOOL AND LIFE

Education is for improving the lives of others and for leaving your community and world better than you found it.

MARIAN EDELMAN

arly childhood professionals view the preschool years as a cornerstone of later success in school and life. As a result, the preschool years are playing a more important role in the educational process than they have at any other time in history, and they will continue to be the focus of public attention and financial support.

WHY ARE PRESCHOOLS SO POPULAR?

Preschools are programs for three- to five-year-old children before they enter kindergarten. Today, child care beginning at six weeks is commonplace for children of working parents, and many children are in a school of some kind as early as age two or three. Fifty-five percent of all three- and four-year-olds and 94.5 percent of all five- and six-year-olds are enrolled in some kind of school program.[1]

A number of reasons help explain the current popularity of preschool programs:

- Many parents are frustrated and dissatisfied with efforts to find quality and affordable care for their children. They view public schools as the agency that can and should provide care and education for their children.
- With changing attitudes toward work and careers, more parents are in the workforce, thus placing a greater demand on the early childhood profession to provide more programs and services, including programs for three- and four-year-olds.
- Quality early childhood programs help prevent and reduce behavioral and social problems, such as substance abuse and school dropout. Research supports the effectiveness of this early intervention approach.[2]
- Publicly supported and financed preschools are one means of ensuring that no children, regardless of socioeconomic background, are excluded from the known benefits of quality preschool programs. Given that more than 11.6 million, or 17 percent of American children live in poverty and that more than 8 percent are disabled, affordable quality programs have the potential for positive social change.[3]
- The foundation for learning is laid in the early years, and three- and four-year-old children are ready, willing, and able to learn. Recognizing the strong connection between a child's early development and success later in life, states are funding preschool programs for four- and even three-year-olds.[4] The National Research Council concluded in its study *Eager to Learn: Educating our Preschoolers* that the last thirty years of child development research demonstrate that "two- to five-year-old children are more capable learners than had been imagined, and that their acquisition of linguistic, mathematical, and other skills relevant to school readiness is influenced (and can be improved) by their educational and developmental experiences during those years.[5]

Focus Questions

Why are the preschool years so important?

What are the characteristics of preschoolers' growth and development?

Why are preschools so popular?

What is the role of play in children's learning?

How and why is the preschool curriculum changing?

What are important issues affecting preschool programs?

Companion Website

To check your understanding of this chapter, go to the Companion Website at **www.prenhall.com/ morrison,** select chapter 10, answer Multiple Choice and Essay Questions, and receive feedback.

Companion Website To learn more about preschools, go to the Companion Website at **www. prenhall.com/morrison**, select chapter 10, then choose the Linking to Learning module.

In the Montessori segment of the DVD, the director says that each child is unique. Consider the uniqueness of each child in the Portraits of Preschoolers in this chapter. How do teachers provide for each child in a classroom with many children?

Preschool years The period from three to five years of age, before children enter kindergarten and when many children attend preschool programs.

- From birth to age five, children rapidly develop foundational capabilities on which subsequent development builds. In addition to their remarkable linguistic and cognitive gains, they exhibit dramatic progress in their emotional, social, regulatory, and moral capacities. These critical dimensions of early development are intertwined, and each requires focused attention.[6]

As preschool programs have grown in number and popularity over the last decade, they have also undergone significant changes in purpose. Previously, the predominant purposes of preschools were to help socialize children, enhance their social-emotional development, and get them ready for kindergarten or first grade. Today, although socialization remains a function of the preschool, academics are also playing a major role. Preschools are now promoted as places to accomplish numerous goals:

- *Support and develop children's innate capacity for learning.* The same reasons for providing early education to infants and toddlers also apply to preschool children and their curriculum. Review again the information on the importance of early learning for brain development discussed in chapter 9.
- *Deliver a full range of health, social, economic, and academic services to children and families.* Indeed, family well-being is considered a justification for operating preschools; in fact, increasingly, preschool education is seen as a family affair.
- *Find solutions for pressing social problems.* As was just mentioned, the early years are viewed as a time when interventions are most likely to have long-term positive influence. Thus, preschool programs are seen as a way of lowering the number of dropouts, improving children's health, and preventing serious social problems such as substance abuse and violence.
- *Promote early literacy and math,* as well as readiness for reading and future school achievement.[7]
- *Prepare children to read.* An increasing proportion of children in U.S. schools, particularly in certain school systems, are considered learning disabled, mostly because of reading difficulties. Failure to learn to read adequately for continued school success is especially likely among poor children, members of racial minority groups, and children whose native language is not English. Achieving educational excellence for all children requires an understanding of why these disparities exist, as well as a serious, informed effort to redress them.[8]

It is little wonder that the **preschool years** are playing a larger role in early childhood education and will continue to do so.

WHAT ARE PRESCHOOLERS LIKE?

Today's preschoolers are not like the children of previous decades. Many have already attended one, two, or three years of child care or school. They have watched hundreds of hours of television, and many are technologically sophisticated. Many have also experienced the trauma of family divorce or the psychological effects of abuse. Both collectively and individually, the experiential backgrounds of today's preschoolers are quite different from those of previous generations.

I have stressed the individuality of each child while at the same time understanding the commonalities of development for all children. Within this context of individuality and developmental commonalities, introduce yourself to four preschoolers in the Portraits of Preschoolers. Answer the questions that accompany the portraits, and reflect on how you would meet the needs of these children if they were in your classroom.

PORTRAITS OF PRESCHOOLERS

José

Introduce yourself to José, a three-year-old Puerto Rican male. He weighs 35 pounds and is 3 feet 2 inches tall. José speaks both English and Spanish and is an outgoing child who enjoys participating in a wide variety of activities at school. He eagerly participates in small- and large-group times.

Social-Emotional	Cognitive	Motor	Adaptive
Gets along well and enjoys interacting with other children.	Counts from 1 to 10 in sequence.	Uses brushes, crayons, and markers to draw.	Can put his legs into and pull up pants without help.
At three, he is a leader.	Likes to do puzzles.	Pedals a tricycle.	Opens containers with simple lids without help.
Verbally expresses emotions such as happy and sad.	Repeats simple rhymes.	Likes to build with blocks.	Drinks from a cup.
Prefers to play with favorite friends.	Identifies some colors and shapes.	Loves to climb on everything.	Unafraid—will try anything.
Likes to help other children.			

Gisselle

Introduce yourself to Gisselle, a three-year-old Hispanic female. She weighs 34 pounds and is 3 feet 2 inches tall. Gisselle speaks only Spanish and, unlike José, is reserved and needs encouragement to participate in large-group activities. She enjoys center time, where she interacts with a small group of friends.

Social-Emotional	Cognitive	Motor	Adaptive
Is very shy and sensitive.	Is very curious and asks why a lot.	Enjoys painting pictures.	Drinks milk and water from a cup.
Gets frustrated when other children get too close to her.	Plays matching games with colors and shapes.	Uses fine-motor skills to dress and undress baby dolls.	Dresses herself for school.
Prefers to play with female friends.	Will listen to a short story and reenact it.	Attempts to copy shapes and lines.	Uses the bathroom without assistance.
Enjoys talking with caregiver.			

Questions about three-year-olds:

- What cognitive skills does Gisselle have that will help her be successful in preschool?
- How will José's positive peer relations encourage success in school?
- Could Gisselle's social-emotional development be a risk factor when she enters preschool?
- Identify five developmentally related gender differences between José and Gisselle.
- What types of learning centers are developmentally appropriate for José and Gisselle?
- Teacher-child closeness plays an important role in school success. Which of these two children is more prone to a close teacher relationship? Why?

Emily

Introduce yourself to Emily, a four-year-old Hispanic female. She weighs 36 pounds and is 3 feet 5 inches tall. Emily speaks English and is a very active and assertive preschooler. She likes to be in control of things and is a leader in the classroom. Emily is eager to learn how to read and write.

Social-Emotional	Cognitive	Motor	Adaptive
Pouts when upset.	Puts six- to eight-piece puzzles together.	Would rather run than walk.	Has quiet time in the afternoon but does not nap for long.
Looks forward to and participates in group time.	Identifies all letters of the alphabet.	Loves to dance.	Can snap and upsnap clothing.
Bosses other children around.	Enjoys reading books and magazines.	Likes to ride her bike.	Brushes her teeth without help.
Talks back to adults.		Turns somersaults.	

Benjamin

Introduce yourself to Benjamin, a four-year-old white male. He weighs 33 pounds and is 3 feet 3 inches tall. Benjamin is very sociable and enjoys activities in which he can interact with other children. He is creative and enjoys expressing himself in a variety of ways.

Social-Emotional	Cognitive	Motor	Adaptive
Is interested in learning about new things.	Likes to sing silly songs.	Enjoys playing the piano.	Unzips and zips clothing.
Will take turns when reminded.	Likes to play alliteration games.	Uses scissors to cut on a line.	Washes hands before eating.
Controls anger when upset by clenching his fists.	Tells elaborate fictional stories.	Demonstrates good balance and body control.	Asks for help when needed.
Is talkative; enjoys talking to teachers and peers.	Solves simple problems in his head.	Is very active—likes to be involved in different activities.	Knows how to share things.

Questions about four-year-olds:

- Refer to the portraits and identify developmental changes from three- to four-year-olds.
- How can you use Benjamin's love of songs to develop preliteracy skills?
- Do you think that putting together six- to eight-piece puzzles is developmentally appropriate for Emily, or should she be putting together puzzles with more pieces?

- Why is active learning important for children such as Benjamin?
- What skills do Benjamin and Emily need to develop to be prepared for kindergarten?
- How can you as an early childhood teacher help prepare these preschoolers for transition into kindergarten?

TABLE 10.1   Average Height and Weight of Preschoolers

Age	Males		Females	
	Height (inches)	Weight (pounds)	Height (inches)	Weight (pounds)
3 years	37.5	32.0	37.0	31.0
3 1/2 years	39.0	34.0	38.5	32.5
4 years	40.0	36.0	40.0	35.0
4 1/2 years	41.5	38.0	41.0	38.0
5 years	43.0	40.5	42.5	40.0

Source: National Center for Health Statistics in collaboration with the National Center for Chronic Disease Prevention and Health Promotion (2000), http://www.cdc.gov/growthcharts.

PHYSICAL AND MOTOR DEVELOPMENT

Understanding preschoolers' physical and motor development enables you to understand why active learning is so important. One noticeable difference between preschoolers and infants and toddlers is that preschoolers have lost most of their baby fat and taken on a leaner, lankier look. This slimming down and increasing motor coordination enables them to participate with more confidence in the locomotor activities so necessary during this stage of growth and development. Both girls and boys continue to grow several inches per year throughout the preschool years. Table 10.1 shows the average height and weight for preschoolers.

Preschool children are learning to use and test their bodies. It is a time to learn what they can do individually and how they can do it. Locomotion plays a large role in motor and skill development; it includes activities of moving the body through space—walking, running, hopping, jumping, rolling, dancing, climbing, and leaping. Preschoolers use these activities to investigate and explore the relationships among themselves, space, and objects in space.

Preschoolers also like to participate in fine-motor activities such as drawing, coloring, painting, cutting, and pasting. They need programs that provide action and play, supported by proper nutrition and healthy habits of plentiful rest and good hygiene.

COGNITIVE DEVELOPMENT

Preschoolers are in the preoperational stage of intelligence. As discussed in chapter 5, these children exhibit certain characteristics:

- Grow in their ability to use symbols, including language
- Are not capable of operational thinking (i.e., reversible mental actions), thus *preoperational*
- Center on one thought or idea, often to the exclusion of other thoughts
- Are unable to conserve
- Are egocentric

Preoperational characteristics have particular implications for teachers. You can promote children's learning in numerous ways:

- *Provide concrete materials to help children see and experience concepts and processes.* Children learn from touching and experimenting with actual objects, as well as from pictures, stories, and media. When you read stories about fruit and nutrition, bring in a collection of apples for children to touch, feel, smell, taste, classify, manipulate,

In the Montessori segment of the DVD, observe the concrete learning materials such as the sandpaper letters and the buttoning frame. How do concrete materials support Piaget's theory of preoperational intelligence?

and explore. Collections also offer children an ideal way to learn the names of things, classify, count, and describe.

- *Use hands-on activities that give children opportunities for active involvement in their learning.* Encourage children to manipulate and interact with the world around them so they can construct concepts about relationships, attributes, and processes. Through exploration, preoperational children begin to collect and organize data about the objects they manipulate. For example, when children engage in water play with funnels and cups, they learn about concepts such as measurement, volume, sink/float, bubbles and the prism, evaporation, and saturation.

- *Give children many and varied experiences.* Diverse activities and play environments lend themselves to teaching different skills, concepts, and processes. Children should spend time daily in both indoor and outdoor activities. Give consideration to the types of activities that facilitate large- and fine-motor, social, emotional, and cognitive development. For example, outdoor play activities and games such as climbing, balls, and tricycles enhance large-motor development; fine-motor activities include using scissors, stringing beads, coloring, and writing.

- *Model appropriate tasks and behaviors.* Preoperational children learn to a great extent through modeling. Children should see adults reading and writing daily. Provide opportunities for children to view brief demonstrations by peers or professionals on possible ways to use materials. For example, after children have spent a lot of time in free exploration with math manipulatives, teachers and others can show children patterning techniques and strategies they may want to experiment with in their own play.

- *Provide a literacy-rich environment to stimulate interest and development of language and literacy.* Display class stories and dictations, children's writing, and charts of familiar songs and fingerplays. Have a variety of literature for students to read, including books, magazines, and newspapers. Make sure paper and writing utensils are abundant to motivate children in all kinds of writing. Daily literacy activities should include opportunities for shared, guided, and independent reading and writing; singing songs and fingerplays; and creative dramatics. Read to children every day.

- *Allow children periods of uninterrupted time to engage in self-chosen projects.* Children benefit more from a few extended blocks of time provided for in-depth involvement in meaningful projects than they do from frequent, brief ones. (See, for example, the Project Approach in chapter 6.)

It is essential that programs provide opportunities for children to engage in active play, both in indoor and outdoor settings. What are some things that children can learn through participation in playground activities?

LANGUAGE DEVELOPMENT

Children's language skills grow and develop rapidly during the preschool years. Vocabulary and sentence length increase as children continue to master syntax and grammar. During their third year or earlier, children add helping verbs and negatives to their vocabulary; for example, "No touch," or "I don't want milk." Sentences also become longer and more complex. During the fourth and fifth years, children use noun or subject clauses, conjunctions, and prepositions to complete their sentences.

During the preschool years, children's language development is diverse and comprehensive and constitutes a truly impressive range of learning. Even more impressive is the fact that children learn intuitively, without a great deal of instruction, the rules of language that apply to the words and phrases they use. You can use many of the language practices recommended for infants and toddlers with preschoolers as well.

FIGURE 10.1   Language Development and School Success

- The average child from a higher-income family enters first grade with a 20,000-word vocabulary, compared to the 5,000-word vocabulary of a child from a lower-income home.

- Children who know the alphabet when they start kindergarten are three times more likely to be able to read by the end of first grade.

- Eighty-eight percent of children who have problems reading in first grade will still have problems reading in fourth grade.

Source: Winning Beginning NY, "Key Facts and Statistics on Early Education," http://www. winningbeginningny.org/documents/key_facts.pdf.

I cannot overemphasize the importance of language and vocabulary development. Figure 10.1 shows the dramatic effect of children's early language experiences on their later language development and reading. It also indicates the linkage between family income and vocabulary development, which is strongly correlated with learning how to read and school success. Two of the most important things you can do are to promote vocabulary development with your students and work with parents on ways to promote vocabulary development in the home.

SCHOOL READINESS: WHO GETS READY FOR WHOM?

School readiness is a major topic of discussion about preschool and kindergarten programs. The early childhood profession is reexamining readiness, its many interpretations, and the various ways the concept is applied to educational practices.

For most parents, *readiness* means that their children have the knowledge and abilities necessary for success in kindergarten. But what does readiness for kindergarten really include? Here is what the National Governors Association has to say:

> Years of research on child development and early learning show that several interrelated domains of development define school readiness—physical well-being and motor development, social and emotional development, approaches to learning, language development, and cognition and general knowledge. These domains are important, build on one another, and form the foundation of learning and social interaction. Ready children are those who, for example, play well with others, pay attention and respond positively to teachers' instructions, communicate well verbally, and are eager participants in classroom activities. They can recognize some letters of the alphabet and are familiar with print concepts (e.g., that English print is read from left to right and top to bottom on a page and from front to back in a book.) Ready children can also identify simple shapes (e.g., squares, circles, and triangles), recognize single-digit numerals, and count to 10.[9]

Readiness is no longer seen as consisting solely of a predetermined set of specific capabilities children must attain before entering kindergarten. Furthermore, the responsibility for children's early learning and development is no longer placed solely on the child or the parents but is seen as a shared responsibility among children, parents, families, early childhood professionals, communities, states, and the nation.

Definitions and concepts of readiness vary from state to state and from community to community. North Carolina views readiness as consisting of a two-piece puzzle that is solved when the two pieces fit together. Figure 10.2 shows North Carolina's readiness

FIGURE 10.2   The Readiness Puzzle

Source: Content from North Carolina School Improvement Panel, North Carolina State Board of Education, *School Readiness in North Carolina: Strategies for Defining, Measuring, and Promoting Success for All Children,* pp. 8–9 (2000).

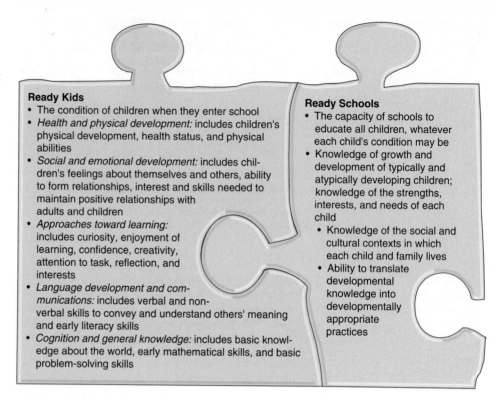

Ready Kids
- The condition of children when they enter school
- *Health and physical development:* includes children's physical development, health status, and physical abilities
- *Social and emotional development:* includes children's feelings about themselves and others, ability to form relationships, interest and skills needed to maintain positive relationships with adults and children
- *Approaches toward learning:* includes curiosity, enjoyment of learning, confidence, creativity, attention to task, reflection, and interests
- *Language development and communications:* includes verbal and non-verbal skills to convey and understand others' meaning and early literacy skills
- *Cognition and general knowledge:* includes basic knowledge about the world, early mathematical skills, and basic problem-solving skills

Ready Schools
- The capacity of schools to educate all children, whatever each child's condition may be
- Knowledge of growth and development of typically and atypically developing children; knowledge of the strengths, interests, and needs of each child
  - Knowledge of the social and cultural contexts in which each child and family lives
  - Ability to translate developmental knowledge into developmentally appropriate practices

puzzle and the components of its two pieces. However, readiness is really no puzzle because the profession knows what children need to know and do in order to be successful in school and life. You and your colleagues must work to ensure that all children are ready for learning, which begins at birth. In addition, you must collaborate with your professional colleagues to make sure that your school is ready for all children.

MATURATION AND READINESS

Some early childhood professionals and many parents believe that time cures all things, including a lack of readiness. They think that as time passes, children grow and develop physically and cognitively and, as a result, become ready to achieve. This belief is manifested in school admissions policies advocating that children remain out of school for a year if they are found not ready for school by a school readiness test.

Assuming that the passage of time will bring about readiness is similar to the concept of unfolding, popularized by Froebel. Unfolding implies that development is inevitable and certain and that a child's optimum degree of development is determined by heredity and a biological clock. Froebel likened children to plants and parents and teachers to gardeners, whose task is to nurture and care for children so they can mature according to their genetic inheritance and maturational timetable. The concept of unfolding continues to be a powerful force in early childhood education; it is based on the belief that maturation is predictable, patterned, and orderly.

Skip ahead to chapter 11, pp. 316–317, to read the Program in Action "A Gift of Time for Nicholas," which describes a developmentally based program that gives young children the time they need to unfold and become ready for kindergarten.

IMPORTANT READINESS SKILLS

Keeping in mind the Readiness Puzzle in Figure 10.2, consider the readiness skills of language, independence, impulse control, interpersonal skills, experiential background, and physical and mental health. All of these are necessary for a successful school experience.

278

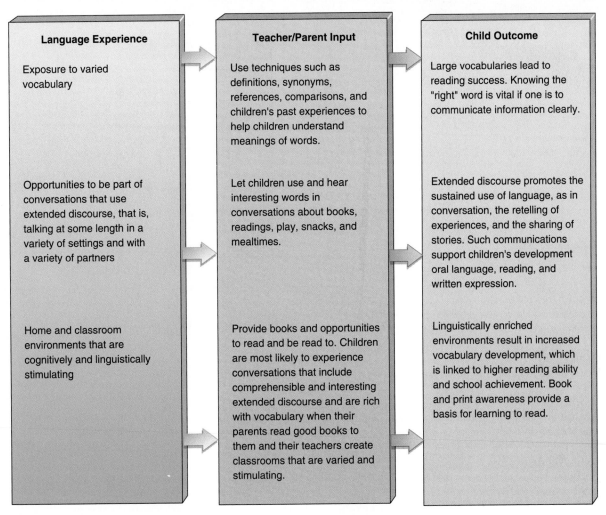

FIGURE 10.3 **Children's Experiences Related to Literacy Success**
The nature and frequency of children's language experiences matter. Be sure to provide experiences and support in all of these areas.

Source: Adapted from D. K. Dickinson and P. O. Tabors, "Fostering Language and Literacy in Classrooms and Homes," *Young Children* (March 2002): 12–13.

Language.   Language is the most important readiness skill. Children need language skills for success in both school and life. Important language skills include *receptive language,* such as listening to the teacher and following directions; *expressive language,* demonstrated in the ability to talk fluently and articulately with teachers and peers, to express oneself in the language of the school, and to communicate needs and ideas; and *symbolic language,* knowing the names of people, places, and things, as well as words for concepts and adjectives and prepositions. Knowledge of the letters of the alphabet is one of the most important factors in being able to learn to read. In addition, vocabulary is essential for school success, as previously illustrated. The language experiences outlined in Figure 10.3 are essential for children's literacy success.

With greater numbers of children of immigrants entering preschools today, you will need to know how to support children with limited English proficiency during the critical preschool years. The Diversity Tie-in "Supporting English Language Learners' Language and Literacy Skills" on pages 280–281 will help you learn techniques to assist these young children in acquiring essential skills.

SUPPORTING ENGLISH LANGUAGE LEARNERS' LANGUAGE AND LITERACY SKILLS

Here are some things you can do to support English language learners (ELLs) in five important literacy domains. As you review and reflect on these activities, consider how you can apply them to your classroom teaching.

WHAT TEACHERS DO	WHAT CHILDREN LEARN
Alphabet Knowledge *Activities that target letter recognition:* Comparing alphabets or writing systems in other languages • Take an alphabet walk around the school, and look for letters in the environment. • Place children in groups of four or five, and have them use their bodies to form letters. • Divide the class in half, and give one half lowercase letter cards and the other half matching uppercase cards. Have the children find their matches. • Teach Spanish-speaking students a song of the English alphabet.	• To identify the letters of the alphabet • To realize that other languages have different alphabets or writing systems
Phonological Awareness *Activities that emphasize the sounds that make up words:* Presenting the sounds of other languages to make words • Word-to-word matching: Do *pen* and *pipe* begin with the same sound? • Sound isolation: What is the first sound in *rose*? • Odd word out: Which word starts with a different sound—*bag, nine, beach, bike*?	• To identify the sounds that make up English words • To realize that other languages have different sounds but all languages use sounds to make words

Independence.   Independence means the ability to work alone on a task, take care of oneself, and initiate projects without always being told what to do. Independence also includes mastery of self-help skills, including but not limited to dressing skills, health skills (toileting, hand washing, using a handkerchief, and brushing teeth), and eating skills (using utensils and napkins, serving oneself, and cleaning up).

Impulse Control.   Controlling impulses includes working cooperatively with others; not hitting other children or interfering with their work; developing an attention span that permits involvement in learning activities for a reasonable length of time; and being able to stay seated for a while. Children who are not able to control their impulses are frequently (and erroneously) labeled hyperactive or learning disabled.

Interpersonal Skills.   Interpersonal skills include getting along and working with peers, teachers, and other adults. Asked why they want their children to attend preschool, parents frequently respond, "To learn how to get along with others." Any preschool pro-

Companion Website   To complete a Diversity Tie-In activity related to English language learners, go to the Companion Website at **www.prenhall.com/morrison**, select chapter 10, then choose the Diversity Tie-In module.

WHAT TEACHERS DO	WHAT CHILDREN LEARN
Book and Print Concepts *Activities that show how books look and how they work:* Showing how books written in other languages look and work • Leave multiple pieces of familiar text posted in the room at children's eye level, available to be read independently. • Use magnetic letters, word tiles, and name cards to emphasize similarities and differences between words and letters.	• That books are written in specific ways, that they have a beginning and ending • That books may look quite different and may even be read in a different way if they are written in other languages
Vocabulary Knowledge *Activities that emphasize words and their meanings:* Emphasizing that there are words in other languages that mean the same thing as words in English • Give each student a card with one word on it, and have them form two circles, one inside the other. When the teacher calls out "inside" or "outside," the students in that circle show their cards to the students in front of or behind them, who must come up with the definitions. The circles then rotate to make new partners.	• That there are lots and lots of words that are used for talking, writing, and reading • That other languages use different words for the same object or concept
Discourse Skills *Activities that encourage telling stories, explaining how the world works, building a fantasy world using English:* Demonstrating that other languages have similar forms although they may seem a bit different • Discuss the storyline of short DVDs, and point out characters, scenes, and time changes; review the story periodically. • Play guessing games like I Spy, and have students give specific clues about a hidden object or picture.	• To use these more sophisticated oral language forms in English • To realize that these or similar forms exist in other languages as well

Sources: Based on The Online Reading Program, *Alphabet Strategy Bank* (2004); W. Ellis, *Phonological Resources* (Phonological Awareness Resources, 1993); Madison Metropolitan School District, *Concepts of Print* (2005); L. Indiana, *Vocabulary Activities* (Teachers Net Gazette, 2003); K. Lowry, *Discourse Planning Skills* (Thames Valley Children's Center, 1994).

gram is an experience in group living, where children have the opportunity to interact with others to become successful in a group setting. Interpersonal skills include working cooperatively with others, learning and using basic manners, and, most important, learning how to learn from and with others.

Experiential Background.   Experiential background is important to readiness because experiences are the building blocks of knowledge, the raw materials of cognitive development. Children must go places—the grocery store, the library, the zoo—and they must be involved in activities—creating things, painting, coloring, experimenting, discovering. Children can build only on the background of information they bring to a new experience. Varied experiences are the context in which children learn words, and the number and kinds of words children know are a major predictor of later school success.

Physical and Mental/Emotional Health.   Children must have good nutritional and physical habits that will enable them to participate fully in and profit from any program.

In the Child
Care segment of the DVD, the narrator talks about programs enriching children's lives. Observe these enrichment activities and reflect on how dance, French, and music enrich children's cognitive, mental, and emotional development.

They must also have positive, nurturing environments and caring professionals to help them develop a self-image for achievement. Today, more attention than ever is paid to children's physical and mental health and nutrition. Likewise, the curriculum at all levels includes activities for promoting wellness and healthy living.

Increasingly, early childhood professionals are taking into account children's emotional development as an important factor in school readiness. A major reason for this new attention is that research clearly shows that young children with aggressive and disruptive behaviors are much less likely to do well in school. Here are several ways you can help develop children's mental/emotional health:

- Observe children, listen to them, and note typical and atypical behavior.
- Use modeling, role play, and group discussion to help children learn appropriate behavior.
- Devote relatively small amounts of class time to instructing children on how to identify and label feelings and how to appropriately communicate with others about emotions and resolve disputes with peers (e.g., using words instead of fists).
- Help parents parent more effectively. This will improve children's emotional and behavioral outcomes and improve families' provision of sensitive, responsive care. In addition, good parenting techniques will help to curtail families' use of inconsistent and harsh practices.

A PROFILE OF PRESCHOOLERS ENTERING KINDERGARTEN

Regardless of what preschoolers *should* know when they enter kindergarten, a longitudinal study of the kindergarten class of 1998–1999 gives us an idea of what they really *do* know:

Cognitive skills and knowledge
- 66 percent recognize letters.
- 29 percent understand the beginning sounds of words.
- 17 percent understand the ending sounds of words.
- 94 percent recognize numbers and shapes and can count to ten.
- 58 percent understand relative size (i.e., sequencing patterns and using nonstandard units of length to compare objects).
- 20 percent understand ordinal sequence, identifying the ordinal position of an object in a sequence (e.g., fifth in line).

Social skills
- Parents report that about 82–89 percent of first time kindergartners often or very often join others in play, make friends, and comfort others.
- Teachers report that about 75 percent are accepting of peer ideas and form friendships.
- Parents report that about 33 percent argue with others often, and less than 20 percent fight with others and get angry easily.
- Teacher ratings are lower, with about 10 percent of first-time kindergartners arguing with others, fighting with others, and easily getting angry.

Physical health and well-being
- The average first-time kindergartner is about 45 inches tall and weighs about 46 pounds.
- About 12 percent of boys and 11 percent of girls have a body mass index that puts them at risk for being overweight.

Approaches to learning
- Parents report that 75 percent persist at tasks.
- 92 percent seem eager to learn.

- 85 percent demonstrate creativity in their work.
- Teachers are slightly more conservative in their ratings, reporting that about two-thirds to three-quarters of beginning kindergartners persist at tasks, seem eager to learn, and pay attention.[10]

These findings suggest that many preschool children come to kindergarten well prepared, physically healthy, and ready to learn; others are not ready for kindergarten, cognitively or socially. You will need to provide for the needs of all children—those who are ready for kindergarten as well as those who are not.

DIMENSIONS OF READINESS

Readiness for life and learning begins at birth and is affected and influenced by many factors. Here are some things to keep in mind about the many dimensions of readiness:

- *Readiness is never ending.* Readiness is a continuum throughout life—the next life event is always just ahead, and the experiences children have today prepare them for the experiences of tomorrow.
- *All children are always ready for some kind of learning.* Children always need experiences that will promote learning and get them ready for the next step.
- *Schools and teachers should promote readiness for children.* Schools should get ready for children and offer a curriculum and climate that allow for a full range of learning.
- *Readiness is individualized.* Three-, four-, and five-year-old children exhibit a range of abilities. Although all children are ready for learning, not all children are ready for learning the same thing at the same time.
- *Readiness is a function of culture.* Teachers have to be sensitive to the fact that different cultures have different values regarding the purpose of school, the process of schooling, children's roles in the schooling process, and the roles of the family and cultures in promoting readiness.
- *Readiness is also a function of family income, maternal education, and parenting practices.* Helping families get their children ready for school is as important as getting the children themselves ready for school.
- *The kinds and quality of experiences children have—or don't have—influence their readiness for learning.*
- *Readiness involves the whole child* —including physical well-being, positive social and emotional development, language development, and enthusiasm for learning.

PLAY AND THE PRESCHOOL CURRICULUM

HISTORY OF PLAY THEORY

The notion that children learn through play began with Froebel, who built his system of schooling on the educational value of play. As discussed in chapter 5, Froebel believed that natural unfolding (i.e., development) occurs through play. Since then, most early childhood programs have incorporated play into their curricula or have made play a major part of the day.

Montessori viewed children's active involvement with materials and the prepared environment as the primary means through which they absorb knowledge and learn. John Dewey also advocated and supported active learning and believed that children learn through play activities based on their interests. Dewey thought that children should have opportunities to engage in play associated with everyday activities (e.g., the house center, post office, grocery store, doctor's office). He felt that play helps prepare children for adult occupations. Today, many curriculum developers and teachers base play activities, such as a dress-up corner, on adult roles.

Piaget believed that play promotes cognitive schemes and is a means by which children construct knowledge of their world. According to Piaget, through active involvement, children learn about things and the physical properties of objects; gain knowledge of the environment and their role(s) in it; and acquire logical-mathematical knowledge—numeration, seriation, classification, time, space, and number. Piaget believed that children learn social knowledge, vocabulary, labels, and proper behavior from others.

Vygotsky viewed the social interaction that occurs through play as essential to children's development. He believed that children learn through social interactions with others the language and social skills (e.g., cooperation and collaboration) that promote and enhance their cognitive development. Viewed from Vygotsky's perspective, adult's play with children is as important as children's play with their peers.

PLAY—CHILDREN'S WORK

Montessori thought of play as children's work and the home and preschool as workplaces where learning occurs through play. This comparison conveys the total absorption, dedication, energy, and focus children demonstrate through their play activities. They engage in play naturally and enjoy it; they do not select play activities because they intentionally set out to learn. They do not choose to put blocks in order from small to large because they want to learn how to seriate, nor do they build an incline because they want to learn the concept of *down* or the principles of gravity. However, the learning outcomes of such play are obvious.

Children's play is full of opportunities for learning, but there is no guarantee that children will learn through play all they need to know when they need to know it. Providing opportunities for children to choose among well-planned, varied learning activities enhances the probability that they will learn what they need to know through play.

Puppets and plays provide many opportunities for children to learn language skills and interact with others.

In the High/Scope segment of the DVD, observe the active play and consider the ways in which play is truly children's work.

PURPOSES OF PLAY

Children learn many things through play. Play activities are essential for their development across all developmental domains—the physical, social, emotional, cognitive, and linguistic. Play enables children to accomplish many things:

- Achieve knowledge, skills, and behaviors
- Learn concepts
- Develop social skills
- Develop physical skills
- Master life situations
- Practice language processes
- Develop literacy skills
- Enhance self-esteem
- Prepare for adult life and roles (e.g., learn how to become independent, make decisions, cooperate/collaborate with others)

The Voice from the Field on pages 286–287 about the value of play illustrates the powerful role of play in enhancing children's literacy and will give you many ideas about how to promote literacy in play settings.

KINDS OF PLAY

Children engage in many kinds of play: social, cognitive, informal, sociodramatic, outdoor, and rough-and-tumble.

Social Play.   Much of children's play occurs with or in the presence of other children. **Social play** occurs when children play with each other in groups. Mildred Parten, children's play researcher now deceased, developed the most comprehensive description and classification of the types of social play, which are shown in Figure 10.4.

Social play   Play of children with others and in groups.

Social play supports many important functions. It provides the means for children to interact with others and learn many social skills. Play provides a context in which children learn how to compromise ("OK, I'll be the baby first, and you can be the mommy"), learn to be flexible, resolve conflicts, and continue the process of learning who they are. Children also learn what skills they have, such as those relating to leadership. In addition, social play provides a vehicle for practicing and developing literacy skills; children have others with whom to practice language and learn. And social play helps children learn impulse control; they realize they cannot always do whatever they want. Finally, social play negates isolation and helps children learn how to have the social interactions so vital to successful living.

In the Child Care segment of the DVD, listen to what the narrator has to say about how the right mix of free play, exploration, and structured enrichment activities support children's growth and development.

Cognitive Play.   Froebel, Montessori, and Piaget all recognized the cognitive value of play. Froebel through his gifts and occupations and Montessori through her sensory materials saw children's active participation with concrete materials as a direct link to knowledge and development. Piaget's theory has influenced contemporary thinking about the cognitive basis for play; from a Piagetian perspective, play is literally cognitive development. Piaget described four stages of play through which children progress as they develop: functional play, symbolic play, playing games with rules, and constructive play.

FIGURE 10.4   Types of Social Play

Reflect on these types of social play and recall examples that you have observed in early childhood classrooms.

- *Unoccupied play:* The child does not play with anything or anyone; the child merely stands or sits without doing anything observable.
- *Solitary play:* Although involved in play, the child plays alone, seemingly unaware of other children.
- *Onlooker play:* The child watches and observes the play of other children; the center of interest is others' play.
- *Parallel play:* The child plays alone but in ways and with toys or other materials similar to the play of other children.
- *Associative play:* Children interact with each other, perhaps by asking questions or sharing materials, but do not play together.
- *Cooperative play:* Children actively play together, often as a result of the organization of the teacher. (This is the least frequently witnessed play in preschools.)

Source: Mildred Parten, "Social Participation Among Pre-School Children," *Journal of Abnormal and Social Psychology* 27 (1933): 243–269.

THE VALUE OF PLAY

Early childhood educators have long recognized the value of play for social, emotional, and physical development. Recently, however, play has achieved greater importance as a medium for literacy development. It is now recognized that literacy develops in meaningful, functional social settings rather than as a set of abstract skills taught in formal pencil-and-paper settings.

ENHANCING LITERACY

Literacy development involves a child's active engagement in cooperation and collaboration with peers; it builds on what the child already knows. Play provides this setting. During observation of children at play, especially in free-choice, cooperative play periods, one can note the functional uses of literacy that children incorporate into their play themes. When the environment is appropriately prepared with literacy materials in play areas, children have been observed to engage in attempted and conceptual reading and writing in collaboration with other youngsters. In similar settings lacking literacy materials, the same literacy activities did not occur.

To demonstrate how play in an appropriate setting can nurture literacy development, consider the following classroom setting in which the teacher has designed a veterinarian's office to go along with a class study on animals, focusing in particular on pets.

The dramatic play area is designed with a waiting room, including chairs; a table filled with magazines, books, and pamphlets about pet care; posters about pets; office hour notices; a No Smoking sign; and a sign advising visitors to check in with the nurse when arriving. On a nurse's desk are patient forms on clipboards, a telephone, an address and telephone book, appointment cards, and a calendar. The office contains patient folders, prescription pads, white coats, masks, gloves, a toy doctor's kit, and stuffed animals for patients.

SCAFFOLDING LITERACY ACTIVITIES

Ms. Meyers, the teacher, guides students in using the various materials in the veterinarian's office during free-play time. For example, she reminds the children to read important information they find in the waiting area, to fill out forms about their pets' needs, to ask the nurse for appointment times, or to have the doctor write out appropriate treatments or prescriptions. In addition to giving directions, Ms. Meyers also models behaviors by partici-

---

Functional play Play involving muscular activities, the only play of the sensorimotor period.

1. **Functional play**, the only play that occurs during the sensorimotor period, is based on and occurs in response to muscular activities and the need to be active. Functional play is characterized by repetitions, manipulations, and self-imitation. Piaget described functional play (which he also called *practice play* and *exercise play*) this way: "The child sooner or later (often even during the learning period) grasps for the pleasure of grasping, swings [a suspended object] for the sake of swinging, etc. In a word, he repeats his behavior not in any further effort to learn or to investigate, but for the mere joy of mastering it and of showing off to himself his own power of subduing reality."[11]

   Functional play allows children to practice and learn physical capabilities while exploring their immediate environments. Very young children are especially fond of repeating movements for the pleasure of it. They engage in sensory impressions for the joy of experiencing the functioning of their bodies. Repetition of language also is common at this level.

Symbolic play The let's-pretend stage of play.

2. **Symbolic play**, the second stage, is also called the let's-pretend stage of play. During this stage, children freely display their creative and physical abilities and social awareness in a number of ways—for example, by pretending to be something else, such as an animal. Symbolic play also occurs when children pretend that one object is another—that a building block is a car, for example—and when they pretend to be another person—a mommy, daddy, or caregiver. As toddlers and preschoolers grow older, their symbolic play becomes more elaborate and involved.

pating in the play center with the children when first introducing materials.

This play setting provides a literacy-rich environment with books and writing materials; allows the teacher to model reading and writing that the children can observe and emulate; provides the opportunity to practice literacy in a real-life situation that has meaning and function; and encourages the children to interact socially by collaborating and performing meaningful reading and writing activities with peers.

The following anecdotes relate the type of behavior Ms. Meyers observed in the play area.

- Jessica was waiting to see the doctor. She told her stuffed animal dog, Sam, not to worry, that the doctor would not hurt him. She asked Jenny, who was waiting with her stuffed animal cat, Muffin, what the kitten's problem was. The girls agonized over the ailments of their pets. After a while they stopped talking, and Jessica picked up the book *Are You My Mother?* and pretended to read to her dog. Jessica showed Sam the pictures as she read.
- Preston examined Christopher's teddy bear and wrote a report in the patient's folder. He read his scribble writing out loud and said, "This teddy bear's blood pressure is twenty-nine points. He should take sixty-two pills an hour until he is better and keep warm and go to bed." At the same time he read, he showed Christopher what he had written so he could understand what to do.

ADDITIONAL IDEAS FOR LITERACY PLAY

When selecting settings to promote literacy in play, choose those that are familiar to children and relate them to themes currently being studied. Suggestions for literacy materials and settings to add to the dramatic play areas include the following:

- A fast-food restaurant, ice cream store, or bakery suggests menus, order pads, a cash register, specials for the day, recipes, and lists of flavors or products.
- A supermarket or local grocery store can include labeled shelves and sections, food containers, pricing labels, cash registers, telephones, shopping receipts, checkbooks, coupons, and promotional flyers.
- A post office to mail children's letters needs paper, envelopes, address books, pens, pencils, stamps, cash registers, and labeled mailboxes. A mail carrier hat and bag are important for children who deliver the mail and need to identify and read names and addresses.
- A gas station and car repair shop, designed in the block area, might have toy cars and trucks, receipts for sales, road maps for help with directions to different destinations, automotive tools and auto repair manuals for fixing cars and trucks, posters that advertise automobile equipment, and empty cans of different products typically found in service stations.

Contributed by Lesley Mandel Morrow, professor and coordinator of early childhood programs, Rutgers University.

3. **Playing games with rules** begins around age seven or eight. During this stage, children learn to play within rules and limits and adjust their behavior accordingly, and they make and follow social agreements. Games with rules are common in middle childhood and adulthood.

Playing games with rules Playing within limits and rules.

4. **Constructive play** develops from symbolic play and represents children's adaptations to problems and their creative acts. Constructive play is characterized by children engaging in play activities to construct their knowledge of the world. They first manipulate play materials and then use these materials to create and build things (e.g., a sand castle, a block building, a grocery store) and experiment with the ways things go together.

Constructive play Play involving the use of modules to build things.

Informal Play. Proponents of learning through **informal**, or **free, play** activities maintain that learning is best when it occurs spontaneously in an environment that contains people and materials with which children can interact. Learning materials may be grouped in centers—a kitchen center, a dress-up center, a block center, a music and art center, a water or sand area, and a free-play center—usually with items such as tricycles, wagons, and wooden slides available nearby for promoting large-muscle development.

Informal, or **free, play** Play in which children play in activities of interest to them.

The atmosphere of this kind of preschool setting tends to approximate a home setting, in which learning is informal, unstructured, and unpressured. Talk and interactions with adults are spontaneous. Play and learning episodes are generally determined by the interests of the children and, to some extent, professionals, based on what they think is best for children. The expected learning outcomes are socialization, emotional development, self-control, and acclimation to a school setting.

In a quality program of free play both indoors and outside, teachers are active participants. Sometimes they observe, sometimes they play with the children, sometimes they help the children, but they never intrude or impose. When well-managed, the free-play format can enable children to learn many things as they interact with interesting activities, materials, and people in their environment.

Sociodramatic Play.

Sociodramatic play Play involving realistic activities and events.

Fantasy play Play involving unrealistic notions and superheroes.

Dramatic, or pretend, play allows children to participate vicariously in a wide range of activities associated with family living, society, and cultural heritage. Dramatic play is generally of two kinds: **sociodramatic play** usually involves everyday realistic activities and events, whereas **fantasy play** typically involves fairytale and superhero play. Dramatic play centers often include areas such as housekeeping, dress-up, occupations, dolls, school, and other situations that follow children's interests. Skillful teachers think of many ways to expand children's interests and then replace old centers with new ones. For example, after a visit to the police station, a housekeeping center might be replaced with an occupations center.

In sociodramatic play, children have an opportunity to express themselves, assume different roles, and interact with their peers. Sociodramatic play centers thus act as a nonsexist and multicultural arena in which all children are equal. We can learn a great deal about children by watching and listening to their dramatic play. For example, one teacher heard a child remark to the doll he was feeding, "You better eat all of this 'cause it's all we got in the house." After investigating, the teacher linked the family with a social service agency that helped them obtain food and assistance.

You must assume a proactive role in organizing and changing dramatic play areas, setting the stage for dramatic play, and participating with children. You must also encourage children who hang back and are reluctant to play, and you must involve those who may not be particularly popular with other children. Because of their background and environment, some children have to be taught how to play.

Outdoor Play.

Children's outside play is just as important as their inside play. Children need to relieve stress and tension through play, and outdoor activities provide this opportunity. However, you should plan for what children will do and what equipment will be available, outdoor play is not a chance for children to run wild.

Outdoor environments and activities promote large- and small-muscle development and body coordination as well as language development, social interaction, and creativity for all children. You should plan to make the playground a learning environment. Figure 10.5 shows some things you can do to make sure children with disabilities can participate in outdoor play.

Dramatic play promotes children's understanding of concepts and processes. Here, play allows children to explore their feelings and ideas about medical practitioners and medical settings.

Many teachers also enjoy bringing the indoor learning environment outdoors, using easels, play dough, or dramatic play props to further enhance learning opportunities. In addition, taking a group of children outdoors for story or music time, sitting in the shade of a tree, brings a fresh perspective to daily group activities. As with indoor activities, provisions for outdoor play involve planning, supervising, and helping children be responsible for their behavior.

FIGURE 10.5   Guidelines for Adapting Outdoor Play for Children with Physical Challenges

- Position a child with physical challenges to achieve maximum range of motion, muscle control, and visual contact with materials and other children. A child might need to lie on his or her side or use a bolster to access materials and interact with other children during activities such as gardening and painting.
- Furnish specifically adapted play and recreation equipment when necessary. This might include modified swings, tricycles, and tables for independent participation in activities.
- Encourage the child to use his or her own means of getting around—whether a wheelchair, walker, or scooter—to participate in the activities and games of other children.
- For a child with limited use of hands and upper body, provide activities for the lower body and feet, such as foot painting, splashing in a wading pool, digging in the garden or sand, and kicking a ball.
- For a child with limited use of feet, legs, and lower body, provide activities such as painting, water table, sandbox, and gardening, which the child can do independently and successfully with the upper body. Always ensure correct positioning of the child's torso.
- Increase the width of balance beams, and modify slippery surfaces to support better balance.
- Use softer balls (e.g., foam balls) or lightweight objects to facilitate throwing and catching when a child lacks strength or endurance.
- Use large balls (e.g., beach balls) and other large objects to make catching easier for a child who is unable to grasp smaller objects.

Source: Reprinted from L. L. Flynn and J. Kieff, "Including *Everyone* in Outdoor Play," *Young Children* 57, no. 3 (2002): 24–25. Reprinted by permission of the National Association for the Education of Young Children.

Rough-and-Tumble Play.   All children, to a greater or lesser degree, engage in rough-and-tumble play. One theory of play says that children play because they are biologically programmed to do so; that is, it is part of children's genetic heritage to engage in play activities. Indeed, there is a parallel between children's rough-and-tumble play and behaviors in the animal kingdom—for example, run-and-chase activities and pretend fighting. Rough-and-tumble play activities enable children to learn how to lead and follow, develop physical skills, interact with other children in different ways, and grow in their abilities to be part of a larger group.

TEACHERS' ROLES IN PROMOTING PLAY

You are the key to promoting meaningful play, which promotes a basis for learning. What you do and what attitudes you have toward play determine the quality of the preschool environment and the events that occur there. Here are some things you can do to support a quality play curriculum:

- Plan to implement the curriculum through play, and integrate specific learning activities with play to achieve specific learning outcomes. Play activities should match children's developmental needs and be free of gender and cultural stereotypes. Be clear about curriculum concepts and ideas you want children to learn through play.
- Provide time for learning through play. Include play in the schedule as a legitimate activity in its own right.
- Create both indoor and outdoor environments that encourage play and support its role in learning.

- Organize the classroom or center environment so that cooperative learning is possible and active learning occurs.
- Provide materials and equipment that are appropriate to children's developmental levels and support a nonsexist and multicultural curriculum.
- Educate assistants and parents about how to promote learning through play.
- Supervise play activities and participate in children's play. Help, show, and model when appropriate, but refrain from interfering.
- Observe children's play to learn how they play and what learning outcomes of play to use in planning your classroom activities.
- Question children about their play, discuss what they did during play, and debrief them about what they have learned through play.
- Provide for safety in indoor and outdoor play.

Providing a safe and healthy environment is an important role that applies to the playground as well as to inside facilities. Outdoor areas should be safe for children to play in. Usually, states and cities have regulations requiring a playground to be fenced and have a source of drinking water, a minimum number of square feet of play area for each child, and equipment that is in good repair. Careful child supervision is a cornerstone of playground safety.

Play is an important part of children's lives and the early childhood curriculum. You and others need to honor, support, and provide many opportunities for children to play.

Companion Website To complete a Program in Action activity related to lesson plans for preschoolers, go to the Companion Website at **www.prenhall.com/morrison**, select chapter 10, then choose the Program in Action module.

Standards Statements of what children should know and be able to do.

THE NEW PRESCHOOL CURRICULUM: STANDARDS AND GOALS

The No Child Left Behind Act of 2001 has dramatically changed all education from preK to grade twelve. In the preschool, NCLB has had its greatest influence on teaching and learning by introducing standards for learning and early reading programs. As a result, the purposes of preschool are changing dramatically; more and more, preschools are seen as places that get children ready for kindergarten. What was traditionally taught in kindergarten is now taught in the preschool through a curriculum that stresses academic skills related to reading, writing, and math as well as social skills.

Increasingly, the responsibility for setting the preschool curriculum is being taken over by state departments of education through **standards,** statements of what preschoolers should know and be able to do. Figures 10.6 and 10.7 list the preschool literacy standards for Oklahoma and New Jersey, respectively. In addition, you can access the full text of the Texas Prekindergarten Curriculum Guidelines online.[12] Keep key concepts like these in mind as you reflect on and plan your preschool curriculum and resulting lessons. The Program in Action "How to Create a Lesson Plan for Preschoolers" on pages 294–295 is a Competency Builder that guides you through the steps involved.

EARLY READING FIRST PROGRAM

The U.S. Department of Education's Early Reading First Program supports preschools and early childhood education providers, especially those serving children from low-income families, so that they can become *preschool centers of educational excellence,* providing children with the foundational skills necessary to become successful readers. Specifically, Early Reading First provides funds to accomplish several goals:

- Support local efforts to enhance early language, cognitive, and reading development skills through strategies and professional development based on scientific research

FIGURE 10.6   Preschool Language Arts Standards for Oklahoma

Oral Language
Standard 1: Listening—The child will listen for information and for pleasure.
Standard 2: Speaking—The child will express ideas or opinions in group or
individual settings.

Literacy
Standard 3: Print awareness—The child will understand the characteristics of
written language.
Standard 4: Phonological awareness—The child will demonstrate the ability to work
with rhymes, words, syllables, and onsets and rimes.
Standard 5: Phonemic awareness—The child will demonstrate the ability to hear,
identify, and manipulate individual sounds in spoken words.
Standard 6: Phonics (letter knowledge and early word recognition)—The child will
demonstrate the ability to apply sound-symbol relationships.
Standard 7: Vocabulary—The child will develop and expand knowledge of words
and word meanings to increase vocabulary.
Standard 8: Comprehension—The child will associate meaning and understanding
with reading.

Writing
Standard 9: Writing process—The child will use the writing process to express
thoughts and feelings.

Source: Oklahoma State Department of Education, "Pre-Kindergarten Curriculum Guidelines,"
http://www.sde.state.ok.us/acrob/Pre-K%20curriculum%20guidelines.pdf.

- Create high-quality language and print-rich environments
- Engage in scientifically proven language and literacy activities that support the age-appropriate development of oral language, phonological awareness, print awareness, and alphabet knowledge
- Use appropriate measures to identify preschool-age children who may be at risk for reading failure
- Integrate scientifically based instructional materials and programs into existing preschool programs.[13]

For example, the purpose of the Minneapolis Early Reading First (MERF) Program is to provide a developmentally appropriate, early education environment in which language and early literacy skills are the focus. The goal of the program is to have children prepared to enter a Minneapolis public school kindergarten classroom. A special curriculum, "Building Language for Literacy," is used to teach important early literacy and language skills needed for school success. The teachers receive frequent training and on-the-job coaching to provide a high-quality experience for children. In addition, language and early literacy skills are measured on a regular basis to help staff improve or change the classroom and instruction. Individual plans are made to help children make the most progress.[14]

APPROPRIATE PRESCHOOL GOALS

All programs should have goals to guide activities and to provide a base for teaching methodologies. Without goals it is easy to end up teaching just about anything. Although the goals of preschools vary by state and individual programs, all should have certain essential goals.

FIGURE 10.7   Preschool Language and Literacy Standards for New Jersey

Expectation 1: Children listen with understanding to environmental sounds, directions, and conversations.

Preschool Learning Outcomes:

1.1 Follows oral directions that involve several actions.

1.2 Identifies sounds in the environment and distinguishes among them (e.g., a phone ringing, a truck passing by or blowing its horn, animal sounds, musical instruments, voices of peers in room, etc.).

1.3 Listens for various purposes (e.g., demonstrating that a response is expected when a question is asked; entering into dialogue after listening to others; repeating parts of stories, poems, or songs).

1.4 Shows interest, pleasure, and enjoyment during listening activities by responding with appropriate eye contact, body language, and facial expressions.

Expectation 2: Children converse effectively in their home language, English, or sign language for a variety of purposes relating to real experiences and different audiences.

Preschool Learning Outcomes:

2.1 Describes previous experiences and relates them to new experiences or ideas.

2.2 Asks questions to obtain information.

2.3 Uses language to express relationships, make connections, describe similarities and differences, express feelings, and initiate play with others.

2.4 Listens and responds appropriately in conversations and group interactions by taking turns and generally staying on topic.

2.5 Joins in singing, finger plays, chanting, retelling, and inventing stories.

2.6 Uses language and imitates sounds appropriate to roles in dramatic play and sets the stage by describing actions and events.

2.7 Uses language to communicate and negotiate ideas and plans for activities.

2.8 Uses new vocabulary and asks questions to extend understanding of words.

2.9 Connects new meanings of words to vocabulary already known (e.g., "It's called *bookend* because the books end").

2.10 Uses complex sentence structure such as compound sentences, if-then statements, and explanations (e.g., "I wanted to make a long snake but Mimi has the scarf," "If I set the table, then you can eat," "Pigs wouldn't like it on the moon because there isn't any mud").

Expectation 3: Children demonstrate emergent reading skills.

Print Awareness:

3.1 Identifies the meaning of common signs and symbols (e.g., pictures, recipes, icons on computers or rebuses).

3.2 Recognizes print in the local environment (e.g., exit sign, area labels, written directions such as the steps for hand-washing).

3.3 Recognizes that a variety of print letter formations and text forms are used for different functions (e.g., grocery list, menu, store sign, telephone book, newspaper, and magazine).

3.4 Identifies some alphabet letters by their shapes, especially those in his or her own name.

3.5 Recognizes own name in a variety of contexts.

3.6 Recognizes that letters form words.

3.7 Recognizes that it is the print that is read in stories.

FIGURE 10.7 Preschool Language and Literacy Standards for New Jersey (continued)

Developing Knowledge and Enjoyment of Books:

3.8 Displays book-handling knowledge (e.g., turning the book right side up, using left to right sweep, turning one page at a time, recognizing familiar books by covers).

3.9 Exhibits readinglike behavior (e.g., pretending to read to self and others and reading own writing).

3.10 Uses a familiar book as a cue to retell a version of the story.

3.11 Shows an understanding of story structure (e.g., commenting on characters, predicting what will happen next, asking appropriate questions, and acting out familiar stories).

3.12 Asks questions and makes comments pertinent to the story being read and connects information in books to his or her personal life experiences.

Phonological Awareness:

3.13 Engages in language play (e.g., manipulating separable and repeating sounds).

3.14 Makes up and chants own rhymes (e.g., when playing in the water table, saying "squishy, wishy, dishy soap," or at lunchtime, when children are conversing, saying "A light is for night").

3.15 Plays with alliterative language (e.g., "Peter, Peter Pumpkin Eater").

Expectation 4: Children demonstrate emergent writing skills.

Preschool Learning Outcomes:

4.1: "Writes" messages as part of play and other activities (e.g., drawing, scribbling, making letterlike forms, using invented spelling and conventional letter forms).

4.2 Attempts to write own name on work.

4.3 Attempts to make own name using different materials, such as magnetic letters, play dough, rubber stamps, alphabet blocks, or a computer.

4.4 Asks adults to write (e.g., asks for labels on block structures, dictation of stories, and a list of materials needed for a project.

Source: New Jersey Department of Education, "Preschool Teaching and Learning Expectations: Standards of Quality" (July 2004), http://www.state.nj.us/njded/ece/expectations.

Social and Interpersonal Skills. Human beings are social, and much of students' learning involves social interactions:

- Getting along with other children and adults and developing good relationships with teachers
- Helping others and developing caring attitudes
- Playing and working cooperatively
- Following classroom rules

Self-Help and Intrapersonal Skills. Children must learn how to manage their behavior and their affairs:

- Taking care of personal needs, such as dressing (e.g., tying, buttoning, zipping) and knowing what clothes to wear
- Eating skills (e.g., using utensils, napkins, and a cup or glass; setting a table)
- Health skills (e.g., how to wash and bathe, how to brush one's teeth)
- Grooming skills (e.g., combing hair, cleaning nails)

Companion Website For more information about the goals of prekindergarten, go to the Companion Website at **www.prenhall.com/morrison,** select chapter 10, then choose the Linking to Learning module.

HOW TO CREATE A LESSON PLAN FOR PRESCHOOLERS

Planning for teaching is a lot like planning for a trip: there are certain essential steps you should follow if you want children to learn new things and have a good time.

- Identifying goals and objectives for teaching and learning is like identifying your destination (e.g., New York City).
- Selecting the methods you will use is like deciding how you are going to get to New York—by car, bus, train, or plane.
- Selecting the materials you will need is similar to selecting what you will need on your trip—clothing, suitcase, tickets, maps.
- Selecting specific activities is like selecting what you will do when you get to New York—walk in Central Park, visit ChinaTown, zip to the top of the Empire State Building.
- Evaluation and assessment come into play after you have taught your lesson, just as you would assess whether you had a good time on your trip.

To prepare yourself to apply these steps to preschool planning, watch any preschool segment in the DVD (such as High/Scope, Montessori, or Reggio Emilia), and observe that preschools today are literacy based and learning oriented. Then suppose that you are asked to create a lesson to develop print and book awareness and follow these steps:

STEP 1 Identify the goals and objectives of your lesson

You may find goals and objectives already selected for you in state or local standards, just as the following preschool goals for print and book awareness come from the Texas preschool guidelines. The goals identify the basic concepts the children are to learn:

- They will understand that illustrations carry meaning but cannot be read.
- They will understand that a book has a title and an author.
- They will begin to understand that print runs from left to right and top to bottom.
- They will begin to understand some basic print conventions (e.g., the concept that letters are grouped to form words and that words are separated by spaces).
- They will begin to recognize the association between spoken and written words by following the print as it is read aloud.
- They will understand that different text forms are used for different functions (e.g., lists for shopping, recipes for cooking, newspapers for learning about current events, letters and messages for interpersonal communication).*

Your lesson will need to address all of these goals in an integrated way. Remember however, that although state standards set goals, you have the creativity to teach your way using your professional knowledge, talents, and abilities.

STEP 2 Select the methods of instruction

How will you teach the children what they are to learn? With your goals or standards in mind, brainstorm developmentally appropriate, culturally relevant, play-based approaches to achieve them:†

- Read "big books" to small groups of five to eight children. (Big books are oversized children's books that teachers use in various reading activities.)
- Call attention to words that occur frequently in the text, such as *a, the, is, you.*

Approaches to Learning.   I am sure you have heard the old saying that you can lead a horse to water but you can't make him drink. In some regards, the same is true for children. Even though on the one hand we talk about children always being ready and eager to learn, on the other hand, professionals understand that all children are not equally ready to learn. Consequently, with today's emphasis on early learning, there is an accompanying emphasis on supporting children's motivation to learn and helping them develop positive disposi-

- Draw attention to letters and punctuation marks in the story.
- Label objects and centers in the classroom.
- Create a word wall in the classroom—an area such as a bulletin board where a collection of words from the books are displayed in alphabetical order.
- Call students' attention to words on the word wall while reading stories.

STEP 3 Select the materials you will need

- Big books with easy-to-read large print and predictable words in the text
- Index cards and markers for making cards for the word wall
- Specially created centers where children can "read" and "write"

STEP 4 Select activities and adapt them for individual needs

As you develop activities, keep in mind children's prior knowledge, their cultural background, and their individual and collective interests, and use them as a basis for the activities:

- Encourage children to play with print. They can pretend to write a shopping list, construct a stop sign, write a letter, make a birthday card. If English-language learners show a preference for writing in their native language, support their efforts.
- Help children understand the relationship between spoken and written language. Encourage them to find letters on a page that are in their names: "Look at this word *big*. It begins with the same letter as the name of someone in this room, *Ben*."
- Play with letters of the alphabet. Read the book *Chicka Chicka Boom Boom*. Place several copies of each letter of the alphabet in a bowl, and ask students to withdraw one letter. When everyone has a letter, ask each student to say the letter's name, and if the letter is in the child's name, have the child keep the letter. Continue until every child has found the letters to spell his or her name.
- Reinforce the forms and functions of print. Point them out in classroom signs, labels, posters, calendars, and so forth.

- Teach and reinforce print conventions. Discuss print directionality (e.g., print in English is written and read from left to right, in Hebrew from right to left, and in Chinese from top to bottom), work boundaries, capital letters, and end punctuation.
- Teach and reinforce book awareness and book handling. Use adaptive technology for children with special needs who are unable to handle books in a conventional manner.
- Promote word awareness by helping children identify word boundaries and compare words.
- Allow children to practice what they are learning. Ask them to listen to and participate in the reading of predictable and patterned stories and books. Ask questions about characters and what might happen next.
- Try using a wordless picture book like *Pancakes*. Page by page, ask the children to tell the story from the pictures. Write their narration on a large piece of paper. Celebrate the story they authored by eating pancakes!
- Provide many opportunities for children to hear good books and participate in read-aloud activities.

STEP 5 Assessment

Give a student a storybook and ask him or her to show you many different elements:

- The front of the book
- The title of the book
- The place to begin reading
- A letter, a word
- The first word of a sentence
- The last word of a sentence
- The first and last word on a page
- Punctuation marks
- A capital letter, a lowercase letter
- The back of the book

---

*Adapted from Texas Education Agency, "Prekindergarten Curriculum Guidelines" (2002), http://www.tea.state.tx.us/curriculum/early/ prekguide. html#2.

†Steps 2–5 adapted from Texas Education Agency, "Print Awareness: Guidelines for Instruction" (2001), http://www.readingrockets.org/ articles/3399.

tions toward learning. This is particularly important for children who are at risk for school failure. **Approaches to learning** (also known as dispositions to learning) include these components:

- Self-regulation of attention and behavior
- Effective social skills to develop a positive relationship with others

Approaches to learning
How children react to and engage in learning and activities associated with school.

- Positive attitude toward learning
- Self-motivation for learning
- Listening skills
- Ability to set goals and develop and follow through on plans
- Understanding, accepting, and following rules and routines
- Finding more than one solution to a question

In the Reggio Emilia segment of the DVD, the narrator says that children are encouraged to see themselves as serious students and engineers of their own learning. How is this view supported by Piaget's and Vygotsky's theories?

Learning to Learn.   Learning how to learn is as important as learning itself—in fact, learning depends on the acquisition of learning skills:

- Self-help skills to promote a good self-image and high self-esteem
- Knowledge of self, family, and culture
- Sense of self-worth
- Persistence, cooperation, self-control, and motivation to learn
- Growing confidence
- Responsibility for age-appropriate tasks
- Turn taking during activities with other children

We want children to be involved in child-initiated and active learning. These children wanted to make pudding after the teacher read the book *Geronimo Stilton's Cookbook*. What are some things children can learn by making and eating pancakes?

Academics.   As academics plays a more central role in preschool curriculum, some key areas of knowledge include these:

- Names, addresses, and phone numbers
- Colors, sizes, shapes, and positions, such as under, over, and around
- Numbers and prewriting skills, shape identification, letter recognition, sounds, and rhyming
- Simple sentence structure
- Simple addition and subtraction
- Ways to handle a book[15]

Language and Literacy.   There is a great emphasis on helping preschool children learn literacy skills. To develop language and literacy skills, preschoolers must work on a variety of capabilities:

- Oral language skills
- Vocabularies
- Conversations with other children and adults
- Proficiency in language
- Literacy skills related to writing and reading
- Letters of the alphabet
- Listening comprehension
- Motivation to read
- Print awareness
- Ways to use and appreciate books[16]

Character Education.   Many schools and school districts identify, with parents' help, the character traits they want all students to demonstrate. Children need multiple opportunities to learn about and demonstrate character traits such as these:

- Positive mental attitude
- Persistence
- Respect for others
- Cooperation

- Honesty
- Trustworthiness
- Sensitivity

Music and the Arts.   Brain research supports the use of music and the arts to encourage learning in all areas. Preschoolers can learn about music and the arts in many ways:

- Varied materials (e.g., crayons, paint, clay, markers) to create original work
- Different colors, surface textures, and shapes to create form and meaning
- Art as a form of self-expression
- Music activities
- Varieties of simple songs
- Movement to music of various tempos
- Dramatic play with others

Wellness and Healthy Living.   When children are not healthy, they cannot achieve their best. Helping children learn healthy habits will help them do well in school. Healthy habits include the following:

- Good nutritional practices
- New foods, a balanced menu, and essential nutrients
- Management of personal belongings
- Ability to dress oneself appropriately
- Personal hygiene, such as washing one's hands and blowing one's nose

Independence.   Skills of independence help children have the confidence they need to achieve in school activities:

- Doing things for themselves
- Taking responsibility for passing out, collecting, and organizing materials
- Learning self-direction

THE DAILY SCHEDULE

What should a preschool day be like? Although a daily schedule depends on many things—your philosophy, the needs of children, parents' beliefs, and state and local standards—the following suggestions illustrate what you can do on a typical preschool day. Because an important preschool trend is toward full-day and full-year programs, this preschool schedule is for a whole-day program.

Opening Activities.   As children enter, greet each individually. Daily personal greetings make children feel important, build a positive attitude toward school, and provide an opportunity for them to practice language skills. Greetings also give you a chance to check each child's health and emotional status.

Children usually do not arrive all at one time, so the first arrivals need something to do while others are arriving:

- Offer free selection of activities or let children self-select from a limited range of quiet activities (such as puzzles, pegboards, or markers to color with).
- Organize arrival time by having children use an assignment board to help them make choices, limit the available choices, and practice concepts such as colors and shapes and recognition of their names. Stand beside the assignment board when children come, and tell each child what the choices are.
- Hand children their name tags and help them put them on the board. Later, children can find their own tags and put them up. Include each child's picture on the name tag.

Group Meeting/Planning. After all children have arrived, plan together and talk about the day ahead, helping children think about what they plan to learn during the day. This is also the time for announcements, sharing, and group songs.

Learning Centers. After the group time, children are free to go to one of various learning centers, organized and designed to teach concepts. Table 10.2 lists types of learning centers you can use and the concepts each is intended to teach.

Bathroom/Hand Washing. Have children wash their hands before any activity in which food is handled, prepared, or eaten.

Snacks. Provide a nutritionally sound and culturally relevant snack that the children can serve (and often prepare) themselves. You will need to find out whether any children have food allergies, such as to peanuts, which can cause serious health risks.

You might try these snack ideas:

- Spread peanut butter on celery sticks and arrange raisins on top.
- Spear banana slices with a stick, dip in juice, and roll in favorite topping.
- In a large bowl, place any type of cereal (Cheerios, Kix, Rice Krispies, etc.). Add pretzel sticks, fish crackers, small snack crackers, oyster crackers, etc. Mix well and place in individual sandwich bags or cups for each child.

Outdoor Activity/Play/Walking. Help children practice climbing, jumping, swinging, throwing, and using body control. Incorporate walking trips and other events into outdoor play.

Bathroom/Toileting. Teach health, self-help, and intrapersonal skills. Allow children to use the bathroom whenever necessary.

Lunch. Make lunch a relaxing time. Serve meals family style, with teachers and children eating together. Let children set their own tables and decorate them with place mats and flowers they have made in the art center or as a special project. Involve children in cleaning up after meals and snacks.

Relaxation. Give children a chance to relax while you read stories and play music. Teach children breathing exercises and relaxation techniques.

Nap Time. Give children who want or need to rest an opportunity to do so. Provide quiet activities for children who do not need to or cannot sleep on a particular day. Don't force children to sleep or lie on a cot or blanket if they cannot sleep or have outgrown their need for an afternoon nap.

Centers or Special Projects. Engage children in center activities or projects. (Projects can also be conducted in the morning, when some may be more appropriate, such as cooking something for a snack or lunch.) Projects can include holiday activities, collecting things, art activities, and field trips.

Group Time. End the day with a group meeting to review the day's activities. Such a meeting develops listening and attention skills, promotes oral communication, stresses that learning is important, and helps children evaluate their performance and behavior.

TABLE 10.2 Learning Centers

Learning centers enable children to engage in active learning in all the developmental domains. Planned well, centers help children meet state and district standards for what they should know and do.

Center	Appropriate Materials	Concepts to Explore and Learn	Center	Appropriate Materials	Concepts to Explore and Learn

Housekeeping	Broom/mop
	Towels
	Sink
		Classification
		Language skills
		Sociodramatic play
		Functions
		Processes
			Science	Science books/
				  magazines
				Plants
				Class pet (fish,
				  hamster, bird)
					Identification of
					  odors
					Functions
					Measure
					Volume
					Texture
					Size
					Relationships

Water/sand	Sand table
	Sand tubs for
	  water
		Texture
		Volume
		Quantity
		Measure
			Manipulatives	Pattern blocks
				Tiles and cubes
				Geoboards
				Tangrams
				Counters
				Spinners
					Classifications
					Spatial
					  relationships
					Shape
					Color
					Size
					Seriation

Blocks	Legos
	Blocks
	Tinkertoys
	Lincoln Logs
		Size
		Shape
		Length
		Seriation
		Spatial relations
			Math	Magnetic numbers
				Estimating jar
				Small cubes
				Balance scale
				Number stamps
					Numerical
					  comparisons
					  (more and less)
					Order and
					  sequence
					Quantity (how
					  much and how
					  many)

Books/
language
	Fiction
	Poetry
	Science
	Math
	Fairy tales
	Materials for
	  writing
		Verbalization
		Listening
		Directions
		How to use books
		Colors
		Size
		Shapes
		Names
					Patterns
					Spatial
					  relationships
					Measurement of
					  volume, length,
					  weight
					Charting

Puzzles/
perceptual
development
	Word search
	Jigsaw puzzles
		Size
		Shape
		Color
		Whole/part
		Figure/ground
		Spatial relations
			Literacy/reading	Bookshelves
				Bean bags
				Chairs
				Tape and CD
				  players and
				  headphones for
				  audio books
				Picture dictionaries
				Stationery
				Postcards
					Reading for
					  pleasure
					Reading with
					  others
					Writing
					Making choices
					  (what to read,
					  materials, etc.)
					Listening
					Vocabulary
					  development

Woodworking	Soft wood of
	  various sizes,
	  shapes, and
	  lengths
	Hammers
	Saws
	Rulers/measuring
	  tapes
	Goggles for eye
	  protection
		Following
		  directions
		Planning
		Whole/part
					Comprehension
					Book familiarity
					Names of authors
					  and books
					Joy and fun of
					  reading and
					  writing

Art	Tablecloths Crayons and markers Coloring books Scissors Glue	Color Size Shape Texture Design Relationships			

Companion
Website
To complete a
Program in Action activity
related to communicating
with families, go to the
Companion Website at **www.
prenhall.com/morrison**,
select chapter 10, then
choose the Program in Action
module.

PRESCHOOL QUALITY INDICATORS

High quality is a major goal for preschool programs. The following quality indicators will help you advocate for high-quality preschool programs for all children:

- Faculty and staff provide for all of the children's needs—physical, social, emotional, cognitive, and language.
- The teachers are well educated and trained.
- Teachers care about all children and believe that all children can learn.
- Classrooms are pleasant, clean, and safe.
- There are sufficient materials and equipment to ensure that children can learn.
- Teacher-child ratios and group sizes are low enough to ensure that all children receive undivided attention and care.
- The curriculum is well organized and aligned with state and local guidelines and standards.
- All staff are sensitive and responsive to the cultural and gender needs of all children.
- Teachers and families collaborate to support children's learning.
- Teachers collaborate with families to help them learn, become better parents, and be their children's first teachers. The Program in Action about communicating with families is a Competency Builder that provides guidelines to help you learn this important skill.

HELPING PRESCHOOLERS MAKE SUCCESSFUL TRANSITIONS

Transition A passage from one learning setting, grade, or program to another.

A **transition** is a passage from one learning setting, grade, program, or experience to another. Young children face many such transitions in their lives. The transition from preschool to kindergarten can influence positively or negatively children's attitudes toward school and learning. You can help ensure that the transition is a happy and rewarding experience. Children with special needs who are making a transition from a special program to a mainstreamed classroom need extra attention and support, as we discuss in chapter 16.

Parents and preschool professionals can help preschool children make transitions easily and confidently in numerous ways. First of all, what happens to children before they come to preschool influences the nature and success of their transitions to kindergarten. Three areas are particularly important: children's home lives, children's skills and prior school-related experiences, and preschool classroom characteristics. Research demonstrates the following in relation to these three areas:

- Children who are socially adjusted have better transitions. For example, preschool children whose parents initiate social opportunities for them are better adjusted socially.
- Rejected children have difficulty with transitions.
- Children whose parents expect them to do well in preschool and kindergarten do better than children whose parents have low expectations for them.
- Children with more preschool experiences have fewer transition adjustments to make.
- Developmentally appropriate classrooms and practices promote easier and smoother transitions for children.

In addition, the preschool and kindergarten staffs can cooperate to work out a transitional plan. Continuity between programs is important for social, emotional, and educational reasons. Children should see their new setting as an exciting place where they will be happy and successful. You might ask the kindergarten teachers to make booklets about their programs, including photographs of the kindergarten children, letters from them, and pictures of kindergarten activities. You can then place these booklets in your reading center, where your preschool children can read about the programs they will attend.

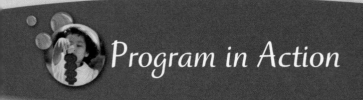

Program in Action

How to Communicate with Families

As children enter preschool, they enter a new world and need lots of support to make a successful transition from home or child care to school. This is also a time of transition for parents, who will have many questions about school, the curriculum, and you. Take a few moments to reflect on and assess your strengths and weaknesses as a communicator. For example, you may be shy or hesitant or may have little experience talking with parents. What is your preferred method of communication—face to face? electronic? written correspondence? How will your communication style affect your interaction with parents? What specific knowledge, skills, and behavior will you have to develop in order to effectively communicate with parents and families?

Communicating with families is essential; authentic, honest, open, and informative communication enables you to teach better, enhances children's learning and achievement, and makes parents partners in their children's education.

Benefits for Teachers

- Helps you know children's interests, abilities, background of knowledge and skills, and their home environments
- Enables you to individualize instruction for each child
- Grounds you in the culture, social and economic status, and educational backgrounds of families
- Optimizes interaction between home and school

Benefits for Families

- Lets them know how their children are progressing academically, socially, and behaviorally
- Informs them of events and activities occurring in the classroom and school
- Enables them to support their children's learning at home and school

Benefits for Children

- Lets them know that their learning is important
- Increases the possibilities that they will learn

- Creates a bond between school and home that supports the children

Strategies for Communicating with Families

There are specific things that you can do to foster effective communication with the families of your students.

STRATEGY 1

At the beginning of the year, send families a welcome letter

Be sure to personalize it. Tell each family how happy you are to have the opportunity to teach their son or daughter. Include other pertinent or interesting information:

- What their child will learn (include the state's and district's standards)
- Where you went to school and whatever personal information you want to share
- How parents can contact you
- What school supplies and class materials are needed

STRATEGY 2

Set a goal of communicating with all families at least every three weeks

To achieve this goal, you will need to communicate with one-third of your parents each week (decide on a certain number each day). Keep communications short and simple.

STRATEGY 3

Use all forms of technology to communicate with families

At the beginning of the school year, find out parents' e-mail addresses if they have them. Contact them via phone, e-mail, or written notes. You might also direct them to a classroom or school website. Learn which method of communication each family prefers and which time of day or evening is best to reach them.

Greet family members as they drop off and pick up their children

Learn and use words and phrases in the parent's home language—for example, "Holá, Señora Martínez—cómo está?"

Learn as much as you can about the families and the children

You might send home a brief questionnaire for parents to complete:

- Share a favorite story about your child
- Tell what your child likes to do with free time
- Tell about your family members and pets
- Share your child's favorite television show, favorite holiday, etc.
- Identify any areas of concern about your child
- Describe your child in fifty words or less

Suggest ways families can help their children succeed in school

Make sure the suggestions are in a language the families can understand. Your tips might include these:

- Read to children, regardless of age
- Help children start and keep collections (e.g., bugs, labels, sports cards, action heroes)
- Help children be organized for school
- Be sure children eat a good breakfast (include suggestions for a nutritious breakfast)
- Limit children's television viewing

Set up a parent/family center in your classroom

Use a bulletin board on which you can post notices and pictures of class activities.

- Post pictures of families and important events in children's family life

Photo by Krista Greco/Merrill.

It is also important to prepare the children and their parents as much as possible for what to expect in the new setting:

- Educate and prepare children ahead of time for any new situation. Children can practice certain routines as they will do them when they enter their new school or grade.
- Alert parents to new and different standards, dress, behavior, and parent-teacher interactions. Preschool professionals, in cooperation with kindergarten teachers, should share curriculum materials with parents so they can be familiar with what their children will learn.
- Let parents know ahead of time what their children will need in the new program (e.g., lunch box, change of clothing).
- Provide parents of special needs children and bilingual parents with additional help and support during the transition.

Perhaps the most effective strategy for a successful transition is to arrange actual visits:

- Offer parents and children an opportunity to visit the new program. Children will better understand its physical, curricular, and affective climates if they visit in advance. And professionals can then incorporate methods into their own program that will help children adjust to the new settings.

- Post a weekly tip sheet (e.g., Five Good Books to Read at Home).
- Furnish diagrams of how to wash hands, brush teeth, etc.

STRATEGY
8

Send children's work home

Attach a note with comments about the work. Occasionally attach another note, asking parents to comment on their children's work. This promotes two-way communication. (See note samples below.)

STRATEGY
9

Organize a parent mentor/buddy system

Parents can help each other learn about the process of schooling and overcome cultural and language barriers, enhancing your communication with parents.

Photo on p. 301 by Krista Greco/Merrill.

Sample Note from Teacher	**Sample Note from Parent**
Dear Family, *This is a picture Pedro drew to describe his favorite part of the story ...*	*Dear Ms. Gloria,* *Pedro likes to draw pictures at home, too. What are some good books I can read to him? When will he ...*

- Exchange class visits between preschool and kindergarten programs. Class visits are an excellent way to have preschool children learn about the classrooms they will attend as kindergartners. Having kindergarten children visit the preschool and tell the preschoolers about kindergarten also provides a sense of security and anticipation.
- Hold a "kindergarten day" for preschoolers in which they attend kindergarten for a day. This program can include such things as riding the bus, having lunch, and participating in kindergarten activities.

The nature, extent, creativity, and effectiveness of transitional experiences for children, parents, and staff will be limited only by the commitment of all involved. If professionals are interested in providing good preschools, kindergartens, and primary schools, we will include transitional experiences in the curricula of all these programs.

PRESCHOOL ISSUES

A number of other issues face preschool children, families, and society today: pushing children, access to quality preschools, universal preschool, funding preschool programs, and the future of preschool education.

PUSHING CHILDREN

Growing numbers of preschool programs are academic in nature; the curriculum consists of many activities, concepts, and skills traditionally associated with kindergarten. Critics think this kind of program puts too much pressure on children because they are not developmentally ready. Pushing children is a persistent and long-standing issue in early childhood education; it revolves around an overemphasis on learning basic skills and expecting young children to behave like older children.

The issue is complex. Some children are able to do more than others at earlier ages; some respond better to certain kinds of learning situations than others do. Some parents and children are able to be involved in more activities than others are. So we must always relate this topic to individual children and their family contexts.

ACCESS TO QUALITY PRESCHOOLS

Access to preschool is another issue facing children, families, and society. Currently, many children do not have access to preschools because there are not enough public preschools available, and many parents cannot afford to pay the tuition at private preschools. Rather than a comprehensive national program of preschools, children and families are confronted with a patchwork of fragmented public and private services that meet the needs of only some children. In addition, available programs of good quality are not equitably distributed. So one of your roles as an early childhood professional is to advocate for access to high-quality preshools for all children.

UNIVERSAL PRESCHOOL

Universal preschool is a program whose time has come, and it is now a permanent part of the American public school system. Preschool is the beginning of public schooling. Of course, it will take many more years before every four-year-old in every state has the opportunity for a public preschool education. The event that tipped the scales toward universal preschool occurred in 2002, when the voters of Florida approved a constitutional amendment requiring public schools to offer prekindergarten to all four-year-old children. Parents are not required to enroll their children, and therein lies one of the issues—whether universal preschool should be compulsory. Some parents do not support compulsory attendance for their young children because of their age and because they would rather have them at home.

FUNDING PRESCHOOL PROGRAMS

One of the ongoing issues of federal, state, and local governments is what they are and are not going to fund. When there is not enough money to fund all priorities, which is always the case, different constituencies compete for funding, and questions of priority abound. Do we fund juvenile justice programs, jails, senior health care, or preschools? Table 10.3 shows the educational and monetary benefits of investing in high-quality preschool programs. You can use these data as you advocate for investing in young children.

THE FUTURE OF PRESCHOOL EDUCATION

The further growth of public preschools for three- and four-year-old children is inevitable. Growth to the point that all children are included will take decades, but it will happen. Most likely, the public schools will focus more on programs for four-year-old children and then, over time, include three-year-olds. A logical outgrowth of this long-term trend will be for the public schools to provide services for even younger children and their families.

One thing is certain: preschool as it was known a decade ago is not the same today, and ten years from now it will again be different. Your challenge is to develop your professional skills so that you can assume a leadership role in the development of quality universal preschool programs.

TABLE 10.3   What Research Says About Investing in Preschool

Program	Results and Benefits
Perry Preschool Project • Children are educated through child-planned activities. • Parents are involved through weekly home visits. • Teachers are trained, supervised, and assessed.	• For every dollar spent, $12.90 was saved in tax dollars. • 66 percent of the program group graduated from high school on time, compared to 45 percent of the control group. • The control group suffered twice as many arrests as the program group.
Chicago Child–Parent Center Program • Parents are required to participate in parent room or classroom activities at least twice a month. • Parent education on nutrition, literacy, development, etc., is provided in the parent room. • Instructional approaches suit children's learning styles.	• For every dollar invested in the program, $7.10 was returned. • Participants had a 51 percent reduction in child maltreatment. • Participants had a 41 percent reduction in special education placement.
Carolina Abecedarian Project • Primary medical care is provided on site. • Each child has individualized educational activities. • Activities promote cognitive, emotional, and social development but focus on language.	• 35 percent attended a four-year college, compared to 13 percent of the control group. • 47 percent had skilled jobs, compared to 27 percent of the control group. • Participants had significantly higher reading and math skills.

Sources: Perry Preschool Project, http://www.highscope.org/Research/PerryProject/perrymain.htm; Child-Parent Center and Expansion Program, http://www.waisman.wisc.edu/cls/Program.htm; and Carolina Abecedarian Project, http://www.fpg.unc.edu/~abc/.

Companion Website

For additional Internet resources or to complete an online activity for this chapter, go to the Companion Website at **www.prenhall.com/morrison,** select chapter 10, then choose the Linking to Learning or Making Connections module.

LINKING TO LEARNING

Administration for Children and Families
www.headstartinfo.org/publications/hsbulletin74/hsb74_04.htm

The organization responsible for federal programs that promote the economic and social well-being of families, children, individuals, and communities.

Concepts of Print
www.madison.k12.wi.us/tnl/langarts/concepts.htm

A website dedicated to the Madison Metropolitan School District.

International Association for the Child's Right to Play
www.ipausa.org

An interdisciplinary organization affiliated with IPA (founded in Denmark in 1961), with membership open to all professionals working for or with children. Includes a position statement on the need for recess in elementary schools and resources on playground games and activities.

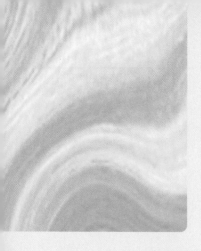

Preschool Teacher

www.preschoolbystormie.com

> *A website dedicated to preK teachers, not necessarily for experts in early childhood education. A place to share ideas used in the classrooms.*

Teachers Net Gazette

Teachers.net/gazette/APR03/vocab.html

> *Features education news, commentary, teaching tips, lessons, pedagogy, classroom crafts, recipes, inspiration, humor, and free printables for the classroom.*

Texas Prekindergarten Curriculum Guidelines

www.tea.state.tx.us/curriculum/early/index.html

> *The preschool curriculum for the state of Texas.*

ACTIVITIES FOR FURTHER ENRICHMENT

ETHICAL DILEMMA: "THERE IS ONLY ONE WAY"

Your school district and your school in particular have a history of low achievement and test scores. The new superintendent has promised the board of education that he will turn the district around in three years. The superintendent has hired a new preschool coordinator because he believes that one of the best ways to close the district's achievement gap is to begin as early as possible. The new preschool coordinator is recommending the adoption of a skills-based curriculum that includes the use of direct instruction and other teacher-centered approaches. According to her, "There is only one way to teach children what they need to know, and that is to directly teach them."

Direct instruction of basic skills and teacher-centered instructional practices are contrary to what you were taught at the university. In addition, these approaches do not fit with your view of child-centered and developmentally appropriate practice.

What do you do? Do you inform the preschool coordinator that you will not use the materials when and if they are adopted, or do you convene a meeting of the other teachers and ask their opinions about the materials, or do you keep your thoughts to yourself and vow to use the new curriculum only when you have to, or do your adopt another plan?

APPLICATIONS

1. Visit preschool programs in your area. Determine their philosophies and find out what goes on in a typical day. Which one would you recommend? Why?
2. Tell how you would promote learning through a specific preschool activity. For example, what learning outcomes would you have for a sand/water area?

What specifically would be your role in helping children learn?
3. Develop a detailed daily schedule that you would use in your preschool.
4. Write a philosophy for a preschool program, and develop goals and objectives for it. Then write a daily schedule that would support your goals.

FIELD EXPERIENCES

1. Collect examples of preschool curricula standards and activities from textbook publishers, teachers, school districts, and state departments of education. Place these in your files for future reference and use.
2. Interview preschool teachers to determine specific ways they believe preschool has changed over the last five years. What implications do these changes have for your teaching?
3. Make arrangements to observe a preschool program. Then read again the Competency Builder on lesson planning, and develop a lesson plan for the preschool children you observed. If possible, make arrangements to teach your lesson to them.
4. Visit a preschool program, and ask to see their program goals. How do they compare to those listed in this chapter? What would you change, add, or delete?

RESEARCH

1. Observe children's play and give examples of how children learn through play and what they learn.
2. Survey preschool parents to learn what they expect from a preschool program. How do parents' expectations compare with the goals of preschool programs you visited?
3. Read and review five articles that relate to today's trend in establishing quality preschool programs. What are the basic issues discussed? Do you agree with these issues? Why?

4. How do parents and others push children? How can pushing harm children? Do you think some children need a push? What is the difference between constructive and destructive pushing?

READINGS FOR FURTHER ENRICHMENT

Catron, C. E., and J. Allen. *Early Childhood Curriculum: A Creative Play Model,* 3rd ed. Upper Saddle River, NJ: Merrill/Prentice Hall, 2003.

Provides information on planning programs with a play-based, developmental curriculum for children from birth to five years of age and covers basic principles and current research in early childhood curricula.

Early Childhood–Head Start Task Force, U.S. Department of Education and U.S. Department of Health and Human Services. *Teaching Our Youngest.* Washington, DC: U.S. Government Printing Office, 2002.

Draws from scientifically based research about what can be done to help children develop their language abilities, increase their knowledge, become familiar with books and other printed materials, learn letters and sounds, recognize numbers, and learn to count.

Eliason, C., and L. Jenkins. *A Practical Guide to Early Childhood Curriculum,* 7th ed. Upper Saddle River, NJ: Merrill/Prentice Hall, 2003.

Focuses on creating a child-centered curriculum that addresses children's needs in all developmental areas. Provides a wealth of meaningful teaching strategies, accompanied by lesson plans and activities.

Hendrick, J., and P. Weissman, *Total Learning: Developmental Curriculum for the Young Child,* 7th ed. Upper Saddle River, NJ: Merrill/Prentice Hall, 2007.

Advocates constructing curriculum based on emerging interests within a practical, flexible, thoughtful, teacher-made plan. Focuses on the developmental needs of children rather than on specific subject areas.

Tompkins, G. *Literacy for the 21st Century: A Balanced Approach,* 4th ed. Upper Saddle River, NJ: Merrill/Prentice Hall, 2006.

Offers a readable, field-tested, and practical approach based on four contemporary theories of literacy learning—constructivist, sociolinguistic, interactive, and reader response. Demonstrates how to implement a literature-based reading program with skills and strategies taught using a whole-part-whole approach.

ENDNOTES

1. "Percent of the Population 3 to 34 Years Old Enrolled in School, by Age Group: Selected Years, 1940 to 2003," *Digest of Education Statistics* (2004).

2. Keith Uhlig, "Wausau-Report: Early Spending Pays Off in Education," *Wausau Daily Herald* (October 19, 2005).

3. R. Rossi and M. Ihejirika, "Preschool Education Seen as Key for Kids," *Chicago Sun Times* (October 17, 2005).

4. J. C. Andrade, "Kindergarten May Be Too Late," *State Legislators* 28, no. 6 (June 2002), 24.

5. B. Bowman, M. S. Donovan, and M. S. Burns, *Eager to Learn: Educating Our Preschoolers* (Washington, DC: National Academy Press, 2001), 25–28.

6. J. P. Shonkoff and D. A. Phillips, eds., *From Neurons to Neighborhoods* (Washington, DC: National Academy Press, 2000), 5.

7. June Kronholz, "Preschoolers' Prep," *Wall Street Journal* (July 12, 2005).

8. M. S. Burns, P. Griffin, and C. E. Snow, eds., *Starting Out Right* (Washington, DC: National Academy Press, 1999), 5.

9. A Governor's Guide to School Readiness, "Building the Foundation for Bright Futures," *National Governors Association* (2005).

10. National Center for Education Statistics, *America's Kindergartners* (1998), 6–10.

11. Jean Piaget, *Play, Dreams, and Imitations in Childhood* (London: Routledge and Kegan Paul, 1967), 162.

12. Texas Education Agency, Prekindergarten Curriculum Guidelines, http://wwwtea.state.tx.us/curriculum/early/prekguide.hml#2.

13. No Child Left Behind, U.S. Department of Education "Early Reading First and Reading First," www.ed.gov/nclb/methods/reading/readingfirst.html.

14. "Minneapolis Early Reading First (MERF) Program," *Minneapolis Public Schools,* schoolchoice.mpls.k12.mn.us./Minneapolis_Early_Reading_First_(MERF)_Program.html.

15. California Department of Education, "Preschool for All," www.cde.ca.gov/eo/in/se/yr05preschoolwp.asp.

16. Texas Education Agency, "Prekindergarten Curriculum Guidelines," www.tea.state.tx.us/curriculum/early/prekguide.html.

CHAPTER 11

Kindergarten Education

LEARNING ALL YOU NEED TO KNOW

*Children are like tiny flowers; they are varied and need care, but each
is beautiful alone and glorious when seen in the community of peers.*

FRIEDRICH FROEBEL

As we begin our discussion of kindergarten children and programs, perhaps you are thinking back to your kindergarten or pre-first-grade school experiences. I am sure you have many pleasant memories that include your teachers and class-mates, as well as what you learned and how you learned it. It is good that you have these fond memories, but we can't use just memories to build our understanding of what today's high-quality kindergartens should be like. If you have not visited a kindergarten program lately, now would be a good time to do so. You will discover that kindergarten educa-tion is undergoing a dramatic change.

- Kindergarten programs are more challenging, and children are being asked to learn at higher levels.
- Kindergarten programs emphasize the basic skills of reading, math, and science while meeting all children's developmental needs.
- More public and private schools and for-profit agencies are provid-ing kindergarten programs.
- Kindergarten is becoming more **universal**, 65 percent of five-year-old children are enrolled in full-day kindergarten, up from just 20 percent three decades ago.[1]
- More states are requiring school districts to provide kinder-garten programs.
- More kindergarten programs—64 percent—are now full day.[2]

As a result of these and other changes we discuss in this chapter, the contemporary kindergarten is a place of high expec-tations and achievement for all children. Figure 11.1 identifies the state requirements for kindergarten. Take some time to re-view Froebel's ideas of kindergarten and its history (see chapter 4) to gain a contrasting context of what kindergartens are like today.

WHO ATTENDS KINDERGARTEN?

Froebel's kindergarten was for children three to seven years of age. In the United States, kindergarten is for five- and six-year-old children before they enter first grade. Since the age at which children enter first grade varies, the age at which they enter kindergarten also differs. Many parents and professionals sup-port an older rather than a younger kindergarten entrance age because they think older children are more ready for kinder-garten and will learn better. Consequently, it is not uncommon to have children in kindergarten who are seven by the end of the year. Whereas in the past, children had to be five years of age prior to December 31 for kindergarten admission, today the trend is toward an older admission age; many school districts re-quire that children be five years old before September 1st of the school year.

CHARACTERISTICS OF KINDERGARTNERS

Kindergarten children are like other children in many ways: They have developmental, physical, and behavioral characteristics that

Focus Questions

What is the history of kindergarten from Froebel to the present?

What are appropriate goals, objectives, and curriculum for kindergarten programs?

How has kindergarten education changed during the last decade?

What issues confront kindergarten education today?

Companion Website

To check your understanding of this chapter, go to the Companion Website at **www.prenhall.com/ morrison**, select chapter 11, answer Multiple Choice and Essay Questions, and receive feedback.

FIGURE 11.1 **State Requirements for Kindergarten**

Source: Adapted by permission from "Full-Day Kindergarten: A Study of State Policies in the United States" (Denver, Co: Education Commission of the States, 2005). Also available online at http://www.ecs.org/ecsmain.asp?page=/html/issuesK12.asp.

Universal kindergarten
The availability of kindergarten to all children.

are the same and characterize them as kindergartners—children five to six years of age. But they also have characteristics that make them unique individuals. Review the portraits of the four kindergarten children included here, and respond to the accompanying questions. You can also develop your own portraits of kindergarten children.

Most kindergarten children, especially those who have attended preschool, are very confident, are eager to be involved, and want to and can accept a great deal of responsibility. They like going places and doing things, such as working on projects, experimenting, and working with others. Socially, kindergarten children are at the same time solitary and independent workers, growing in their ability and desire to work cooperatively with others. Their combination of a can-do attitude and their cooperation and responsibility make them a delight to teach and work with.

Learning centers Places in a classroom where children are free to explore, manipulate, create, and work where their interests take them (e.g., a writing center, a dramatic play center, an art center, a math center).

Kindergarten children have a lot of energy, which they want to use in physical activities such as running, climbing, and jumping. Their desire to be involved in physical activity makes kindergarten an ideal time to involve children in projects of building—for example, making **learning centers** resemble a store, post office, or veterinary office.

Kindergarten children are in a period of rapid intellectual and language growth. They have a tremendous capacity to learn new words and like the challenge. This helps explain their love of big words and their ability to say and use them. This is nowhere more apparent than

PORTRAITS OF KINDERGARTNERS

Lina

Introduce yourself to Lina, a five-year-old Hispanic female. She weighs 39 pounds and is 3 feet 57 inches tall. Lina is petite and fragile; she speaks Spanish and English. She did not attend preschool but is quickly learning preliteracy skills in kindergarten. Lina is a quiet learner: she listens carefully but must be encouraged to participate verbally.

Social-Emotional	Cognitive	Motor	Adaptive
Is shy and quiet.	Recites poems and sings for her parents.	Is graceful.	Knows her address.
Is a good listener.	Names all the letters of the alphabet and knows their sounds.	Enjoys dancing to music.	Knows her phone number.
Prefers to interact with one or two classmates in play situations.		Can hop on one foot.	Asks adults for help when needed.
Tends to talk to her classmates in Spanish, not realizing that they do not understand her.	Sometimes confuses the pronouns *he* and *she* when retelling a story.	Helps her mother make homemade tortillas.	Recognizes her mother's car when being picked up from school in the afternoon.
Seeks approval from the adults in her life (i.e., parents, teacher, grandparents).	Recalls many facts from stories.	Is learning to tie her shoes by herself.	Bathes herself with her mother's supervision.
	Knows the parts of the story—beginning, middle, end).	Loves to write, color, and paint.	

Ganali

Introduce yourself to Ganali, a five-year-old Ghanian male. He weighs 50 pounds and is 4 feet tall. Ganali is physically mature and looks older than his peers. He is a bright, popular boy who enjoys school. Ganali expresses his creativity through drawing and telling stories. Because he is detail oriented, tasks sometimes take him longer to complete.

Social-Emotional	Cognitive	Motor	Adaptive
Enjoys sharing about visits to Africa.	Reads early beginner books.	Is well coordinated.	Knows his phone number and can dial 911.
Knows that his actions have consequences.	Is eager to learn.	Can stand on one foot with his eyes closed.	Knows his home address.
Is a reliable helper in the classroom.	Has an excellent memory and recalls many details from stories.	Likes to draw very detailed and creative pictures.	Knows the city and state that he lives in.
Is a leader.	Is bright and artistic.	Has excellent fine-motor coordination.	Tends to show off in front of strangers.
Is popular and well liked by peers.	Adds simple numbers and understands first and last.	Likes to play throw-and-catch games; says he wants to be a baseball player.	Ties his shoes without assistance.

Questions about five-year-old kindergartners:

- Lina did not attend preschool. Does this appear to have affected her overall development? In what ways can preschool and kindergarten programs contribute to children's development and readiness for first grade?
- Lina is described as shy and quiet. What factors might be influencing these traits? How might temperament influence social-emotional and intellectual development?
- How can you be responsive to Lina's temperament traits?
- How could you integrate Ganali's storytelling about Africa into the classroom curriculum?.

Jamal

Introduce yourself to Jamal, a six-year-old African American male. He weighs 53 pounds and is 4 feet tall. Jamal is quiet and plays with small groups of boys. He is eager to assert his independence but needs help with tasks requiring fine-motor skills. Jamal pays attention during large-group activities but does not like to actively participate.

Social-Emotional	Cognitive	Motor	Adaptive
Is quiet—talks and plays with only a few other boys. Gives yes/no responses during large-group activities. Does not ask questions or share. Is very reserved and easygoing.	Enjoys books about cars, trucks, and machinery. Says he wants to visit a junkyard. Is very interested in how things work. Does not like singing or clapping; will stay in his seat during these activities. Enjoys listening to stories. Likes to write stories. Is reading above his grade level.	Does not color inside lines. Likes to play soccer. Moves slowly in halls and classroom. Has very good writing skills for his age; has very legible printing.	Is very neat—puts things away where they belong. Makes his bed every morning before going to school. Wants to learn how to do things so he does not have to ask for help. Is fascinated by trains; keeps asking his parents to take him on train rides.

Tameka

Introduce yourself to Tameka, a six-year-old African American female. She weighs 45 pounds and is 3 feet, 9 inches tall. Tameka is an assertive kindergartner; she likes to be in control of activities and classmates. Tameka has a strong desire to learn how to read and write and asks many questions during class.

Social-Emotional	Cognitive	Motor	Adaptive
Displays impulsive behavior. Bosses friends. Enjoys talking to any adult. Tattles to the teacher. Is very sensitive to criticism—cries easily. Egocentric. Very possessive of any toys she plays with.	Enjoys "reading" to friends and class, using pictures as cues. Uses puppets to retell stories. Likes writing letters of the alphabet; has neat handwriting. Needs help making the connection between letters and real words. Knows the values of different coins.	Has well-developed gross-motor skills that allow her to jump rope and run gracefully. Likes to dance. Enjoys cutting and pasting, can cut on a line. Is beginning to ride her bicycle without training wheels.	Expresses needs, wants, and dislikes, is very verbal and direct. Opens own milk carton and helps friends open theirs. Enjoys responsibilities, such as taking class roll to the office. Has a strong desire for class to stay on a schedule. Says she wants to be a teacher so she can boss kids around.

Questions about six-year-old kindergartners:

- How might Jamal's motor skills interfere with his desire to learn? Brainstorm some activities that would make writing more enjoyable for children like Jamal, who need to develop fine-motor skills.
- What do you think are some reasons that Jamal cannot tie his shoes?
- How can you encourage all members of your class to participate without discouraging children like Tameka, who tends to dominate activities?
- List some ways, other than copying words, that you can help Tameka make the connection between letters and real words.
- Do you think Jamal and Tameka will be able to meet kindergarten standards?

TABLE 11.1 Average Height and Weight of Kindergarten Children

Age	Males		Females	
	Height (inches)	Weight (pounds)	Height (inches)	Weight (pounds)
5 years	42.5	40.0	42.5	40.0
5 1/2 years	44.0	44.0	44.0	42.0
6 years	45.5	46.0	45.5	44.0
6 1/2 years	46.5	48.0	47.0	47.0
7 years	48.0	50.0	48.0	50.0

Source: National Center for Health Statistics in collaboration with the National Center for Chronic Disease Prevention and Health Promotion (2000), http://www.cdc.gov/growthcharts.

in their fondness for dinosaurs and words such as *brontosaur.* Kindergarten children like and need to be involved in many language activities.

In addition, kindergartners like to talk. Their desire to be verbal should be encouraged and supported, with many opportunities to engage in various language activities, such as singing, telling stories, being involved in drama, and reciting poetry.

From ages five to seven, children's average weight and height approximate each other. For example, at six years boys, on average, weigh forty-six pounds and are about forty-six inches tall, whereas girls, on average, weigh about forty-four pounds and are about forty-six inches tall. At age seven boys and girls weigh, on average, fifty pounds and are forty-eight inches tall (see Table 11.1).

In the Kindergarten segment of the DVD, the narrator says that kindergarten is not like it used to be. Compare and explain the changes cited by the narrator and in your textbook.

READINESS AND PLACEMENT OF KINDERGARTEN CHILDREN

THE ESCALATED CURRICULUM

You may be amazed at how kindergartens are changing. After visiting kindergarten programs, you may be thinking, "Wow, a lot of what they're doing in kindergarten I did in first grade!" Many early childhood professionals would agree. More is expected of kindergarten children today than ever before, and this trend will continue.

A number of reasons account for the escalated curriculum. First, beginning in the 1990s, there has been a decided emphasis on academics in U.S. education, particularly early childhood education. Second, some parents believe an academic approach to learning is the best way for their children to succeed in school and the work world. And third, the standards, testing, and high-quality education reform movement encourages greater emphasis on academics.

These higher expectations for kindergarten children are not necessarily bad. However, achieving them in a developmentally appropriate way is one of the major challenges facing early childhood professionals.

In the Kindergarten segment of the DVD, listen to what the narrator says about the delight of teaching kindergarten. What characteristics of kindergarteners would support this notion?

ALTERNATIVE KINDERGARTEN PROGRAMS

Given the changing kindergarten curriculum, it is not surprising that some children are not ready for many of the demands placed on them. As a result, teachers and schools have developed alternative kinds of kindergarten programs.

Developmental Kindergarten. The **developmental kindergarten (DK)** is a prekindergarten for developmentally or behaviorally delayed kindergarten-age children; it is viewed as one means of helping them succeed in school. School districts have specific criteria for

Developmental kindergarten Designed to provide children with additional time for maturation and physical, social, emotional, and intellectual development.

Today, kindergarten is a universal part of schooling, enrolling children from different cultures and socioeconomic backgrounds and, subsequently, different life experiences. What are some things you can do to ensure that kindergarten experiences meet the unique needs of each child?

Transition kindergarten
Designed to serve children who may be old enough to go to first grade but are not quite ready to handle all of its expectations.

Companion Website
To complete a Program in Action activity related to transition kindergarten, go to the Companion Website at **www. prenhall.com/morrison**, select chapter 11, then choose the Program in Action module.

placing children in developmental kindergartens; some of their placement approaches are identified here:

- Kindergarten-eligible children are given a kindergarten screening test to identify children who have special learning needs. Some states, such as Massachusetts, require that all children take a screening test prior to kindergarten enrollment.
- Prekindergarten children are given a kindergarten readiness test, such as the Kindergarten Readiness Test (KRT),[3] to help determine children's readiness for regular kindergarten. (The placement of children in any program should not be made on the results of one test, an issue we discuss in more detail later in this chapter.)
- Parents and preschool teachers who believe that children are not ready for kindergarten

consult about the placement of individual children. After the DK year teachers, parents, and administrators confer to decide whether the child should be placed in kindergarten or first grade.

Transition Kindergarten.   A **transition kindergarten** is designed to give children the time they need to achieve what is required for entry into first grade. These children are really getting two years to achieve what others would normally achieve in one. A transition class is different from a nongraded program in that the transition class consists of children of the same age, whereas the nongraded classroom has multiage children.

The concept of transition classes implies, and practice should involve, linear progression. Children are placed in a transition kindergarten so that they can continue to progress at their own pace. The curriculum, materials, and teaching practices should be appropriate for each child's developmental age or level.

Proponents of transitional programs believe they offer the following advantages:

- Promote success, whereas retention is a regressive practice that promotes failure
- Provide for children's developmental abilities
- Allow children to be with other children of the same developmental age
- Provide an appropriate learning environment
- Put children's needs ahead of the desire to place them in a particular grade
- Provide time for children to integrate learning—often referred to as the gift of time (read the Program in Action on pages 316–317 with a similar title)

Not all early childhood professionals agree that DK and transitional classes are a good idea. You can read "Still Unacceptable Trends in Kindergarten Entry and Placement" by the National Association of Early Childhood Specialists in State Departments of Education.[4]

Mixed-Age/Multiage Grouping.   **Mixed-age grouping** provides another approach to meeting the individual and collective needs of children. In a multiage group, there is a diversity of abilities, at least a two-year span in children's ages, and the same teacher. The context of multiage groups provides a number of benefits and functions:

- Provides materials and activities for a wider range of children's abilities.
- Creates a feeling of community and belonging. Most mixed-age groups have a feeling of family because children spend at least two years in the group

- Supports children's social development by providing a broader range of children to associate with. Children have more and less socially and academically advanced peers to interact with. Older children act as teachers, tutors, and mentors. Younger children are able to model the academic and social skills of their older class members.
- Provides sustained and close relationships among children and teachers. The teacher encourages and supports cross-age academic and social interactions.
- Supports the scaffolding of learning.
- Provides for a continuous progression of learning.

Looping. **Looping** occurs when a teacher spends two or more years with the same group of same-age children. In other words, a teacher involved in looping would begin teaching a group in kindergarten and would then teach the same group as first graders and perhaps as second graders. Another teacher might do the same with second, third, and fourth graders. The advantages of looping include the following:

- Provides the freedom to expand the curriculum vertically and horizontally over a two-year period
- Gives the teacher the opportunity to monitor a child's progress more closely over a two-year period
- Fosters a family-like atmosphere in the classroom
- Allows teachers to get into the curriculum earlier in the school year because the children know what is expected of them
- Allows for individualized instruction because teachers are more familiar with the strengths and weaknesses of each child
- Provides children with stability
- Grants teachers an opportunity to stay fresh and grow professionally by changing their grade-level assignments every year[5]

Retention. Along with the benefits of early education and universal kindergarten come political issues as well. One of these is the issue of retention. Retained children, instead of participating in kindergarten graduation ceremonies with their classmates, are destined to spend another year in kindergarten. Many of these children are retained, or failed, because teachers judge them to be immature, or they fail to measure up to the district's or teacher's standards for promotion to first grade. Children are usually retained in the elementary years because of low academic achievement or low IQ.

When well-meaning early childhood education professionals retain children, they do so in the belief that they are doing them and their families a favor. These professionals feel that children who have an opportunity to spend an extra year in the same grade will do better the second time around. Teachers' hopes, and consequently parents' hopes, are that these failed children will go on to do as well as their nonretained classmates.

But do children do better the second time around? Despite our intuitive feelings that children who are retained will do better, research evidence is unequivocally contrary to that notion: children do *not* do better the second time around. In addition, parents report that retained children have a more pessimistic attitude toward school, with a resulting negative impact on their social-emotional development.[6]

Mixed-age grouping
Students in two or three grade levels mixed in one classroom with one teacher.

Looping A single-graded class of children staying with the same teacher for two or more years.

In the Montessori segment of the DVD, observe how the Montessori environment supports mixed-age grouping.

Children are born to learn. Learning is not something children get ready for but is a continuous process. What factors do you think are critical for children's readiness to learn?

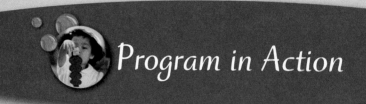

A Gift of Time for Nicholas

The plaque on the classroom door read "Mrs. Parker—Kindergarten." Nicholas reached for the brass doorknob and turned it enough to open it a crack. Mrs. Parker, standing nearby, pushed it open wide and said, "Good morning, Nicholas."

Nicholas could feel his face flush hot and pink as he wrinkled his nose and gave his teacher his best smile. He walked five steps and slid his backpack straps off his shoulders. The backpack fell to the floor with a thud just below the terrarium table next to the cubbies. He unbuttoned his yellow jacket, unzipped his backpack, and tidied his socks. Out came his shiny red lunch box, which he placed on the shelf above the cubbies. As he struggled with the sleeve of his jacket, Mrs. Parker pulled the jacket off one arm as she passed by on her way to the sink. Nicholas glanced her way with a shy smile as the other sleeve slipped off easily. Once his jacket was hung, he let out a big sigh of relief and walked ten steps to his table. He was the first one today. He loved being first. He also loved his teacher and his best friend, Billy, who hadn't arrived yet.

He turned his head toward the long windows, and there it was, still standing—the skyscraper that he and Billy had made the day before at Center Time. Center Time was his favorite. You got to choose what you wanted to do. Mrs. Parker had been so proud of how tall the skyscraper was that she brought the big black marker over, along with a long white strip, and helped the boys sound out the letters, S-K-Y-S-C-R-A-P-E-R. She laid the newly printed word at the base of the building for all the class to see. Everyone gathered around, and Chelsea clapped.

Chelsea is the silly girl who sits beside Nicholas and makes funny faces at him. Nicholas closes his eyes tight to avoid her funny faces, but she makes them anyway. Here comes that funny-face Chelsea right now.

Mrs. Parker gently touched Chelsea's shoulder as she passed by and knelt down next to Nicholas. "Nicholas, did you bring back that important paper I sent home yesterday for Mommy and Daddy to sign?" Nicholas jumped to his feet and ran back to his cubby to find the white paper. His mom had put it in the pocket with the secret zipper. She had told him all about it. It said he needed more time . . . more time to run and jump and play and let nature take its course.

Dad had said, "Yes, Bud! Just think of this year as practice for the big game."

So Nicholas would be going to TK-1 next year. So would his friend Billy and silly funny-face Chelsea. Billy's parents came to school on the same night Nicholas' parents came to watch a movie about TK-1. Everyone already knew the TK-1 teacher, Mrs. Shaw. She was really nice, and she let her class play kick ball.

"Yeah, when you got to go to TK-1, you got to play kick ball and you learned to read, too!" Nicholas had told his parents. He had already read some things like the stop sign and the word *Cheerios* on his cereal box. He loved to listen to stories at the rug, but those stories were just a little too long.

"Time is a gift," his Grandma had said. "You don't get time back." So he was off to TK-1 right after summer vacation. But first, he got to play and swim all summer and celebrate his birthday, too.

Nicholas is not ready for a formal first-grade setting. He needs additional time before he enters the first-grade classroom. Brevard Public Schools recognize that children grow at different rates and this process should not be rushed or altered. Transitional Kindergarten–First Grade (TK-1) is designed for children who are developmentally younger than six.

The Brevard County, Florida, TK-1 program, in effect for over twenty years, upholds a developmental philosophy backed by research concerning the manner in which young children learn:

- Children need a smooth transition from the home environment to the school environment. A working partnership between home and school should be encouraged and fostered for the benefit of the children.
- Children go through predictable stages of development at individual rates of growth that cannot be altered, hurried, or remediated. Activities, materials, and methods of working with children should be differentiated to meet their emotional, social, physical, and intellectual needs.
- Children will develop a positive self-image in a setting where there is total acceptance of individual needs and strengths.
- Children learn to accept and understand their own feelings and those of others through sharing and cooperating in group activities.

- Children learn and grow through active involvement. Opportunities to hop, skip, jump, stretch, balance, climb, catch, and run will enhance physical skills and motor coordination.
- Children learn through concrete experiences and play. Play is the work of children, and manipulative objects are the tools.
- Children learn by using their senses. Experiences must emphasize a multisensory approach to encompass hearing, seeing, touching, tasting, and smelling.
- Children should be taught how to think rather than what to think, thus giving them strong foundations on which to build later experiences.
- Children should be taught to read through a balanced approach involving integrated reading, writing, and language experiences.

QUESTIONS MOST FREQUENTLY ASKED ABOUT OUR TK-1 PROGRAM

Who is the TK-1 program designed for?

The TK-1 program is designed for children who are not ready for the formal first-grade program. These children have already attended kindergarten and are developmentally younger than six.

What is the goal of the program?

The TK-1 year gives children the gift of time to develop physical, social/emotional, language, and cognitive potential. This developmental philosophy, along with research, tells us that children go through predictable stages of development at individual rates of growth that cannot be hurried or altered. The goal of the program is to help children develop a positive self-image in a setting where there is total acceptance of each child's individual needs and strengths.

How are the children chosen for the program?

The Gesell Test (a school readiness screening test) is one instrument used for screening children for placement in the developmental program. The results of this test indicate a child's developmental age, which is differentiated from chronological age. The Gesell Test is an individual test given by a trained, qualified examiner and takes about twenty-five minutes.

The test is given in the spring of the kindergarten year. Recommended placement in TK-1 is also based on chronological age, teacher observation, parent input, and skill mastery as demonstrated on the Literacy Survey and other teacher checklists.

How do parents feel about this placement?

The classroom teacher hosts individual conferences regarding the recommended placement. It is the Gesell Institute's recommendation and district policy that parents have the final decision in the placement of their children in the TK-1 program. More than one parent-teacher conference may be necessary before a decision is finalized. The school also has an informational meeting for all parents considering TK-1, in which they learn more about the program and meet the TK-1 teacher if possible. Parents who accept and go through the program are overwhelmingly glad that they gave their children the gift of time. The school will often have a parent speak at the meeting, someone who has been through the program. Parents feel better when they talk to other parents who have been through the program. This gift of time is invaluable not only now, but also for the student's future as a lifelong learner.

Is this considered a retention on the child's school records?

The student's grade-level assignment for the next school year is written under "Attendance" in the child's records. The term *assigned* rather than *retained* or *promoted* is used to indicate placement for the next year. TK-1 is not considered a retention.

Does the program have its own curriculum and grade-level expectations?

Yes, TK-1 children have their own curriculum and grade-level expectations, which are chosen just for them. They are also given a different report card from the one used in kindergarten and first grade.

How do children adjust to the TK-1 class?

They adjust very well; they have an excellent program and have already had one year in kindergarten. They already know their way around the building, and most faces are familiar to them. Parent volunteers are often used in the program, and the children get used to being comfortable with their new class family.

Would you say your program has been successful?

You would only need to walk through our TK-1 classes to see the answer. Brevard County has been committed to this developmental philosophy for over twenty years and has helped thousands of children make their early years successful.

Contributed by Linda Ridgley, early childhood resource teacher, and Lynn Spadaccini, director of early childhood education and Title I programs, Brevard (Florida) Public Schools.

The ultimate issue of retention is how to prevent failure and promote success. To achieve those goals, many professionals will have to change their views about what practices are best for children and how the factors that create a climate for unsuccessful school experiences can be prevented.

WHAT SHOULD KINDERGARTEN BE LIKE?

All early childhood teachers have to make decisions regarding what curriculum and activities they will provide for their children. When making decisions about what kindergarten should be like, you can consider the ideas and philosophies of the historic figures discussed in chapter 4 and compare them with contemporary practice. Consider Froebel, for example:

> The Kindergarten is an institution which treats the child according to its nature; compares it with a flower in a garden; recognizes its threefold relation to God, man and nature; supplies the means for the development of its faculties, for the training of the senses, and for the strengthening of its physical powers. It is the institution where a child plays with children.[7]

By comparing Froebel's vision of kindergarten with today's practice, we see that many of today's kindergartens are much different from what Froebel envisioned. This difference is entirely appropriate in many ways, for society is vastly different today from what it was in Froebel's time.

DEVELOPMENTALLY APPROPRIATE PRACTICE

This book has emphasized that in all things early childhood professionals do for and with children, their efforts should be **developmentally appropriate**. Developmentally appropriate practice—that is, teaching and caring for young children—facilitates learning that is in accordance with all dimensions of children's physical, cognitive, social, linguistic, cultural, and gender development. Early childhood professionals help children learn and develop in ways that are compatible with how old the children are and who they are as individuals (e.g., their background of experiences and culture).

Talking about developmentally appropriate practice is one thing; actually doing it is another. Here are some things you can do to make your kindergarten program developmentally appropriate and help children learn:

- Make learning meaningful to children by relating it to what they already know. For example, last week Ms. Garcia and her children planted seeds and watched them sprout and grow. They talked about what plants need to grow and why some of their plants died. Yesterday, when the class pet, Fishey, died, Ms. Garcia took the opportunity to extend their discussion about living things and death. And she selected two special books, *Goodbye Mousie* and *Jasper's Day,* to read to the children.
- Individualize your curriculum as much as possible to account for the needs of all children.
- Make learning physically and mentally active. Children should be actively involved in learning activities—building, making, experimenting, investigating, and working collaboratively with their peers.
- Involve children in *hands-on* activities with concrete objects and manipulatives. Emphasize real-life activities as opposed to workbook and worksheet activities.

The Program in Action about creating lesson plans for kindergartners on pages 320–321 is a Competency Builder that incorporates these and other ideas in step-by-step planning for developmentally appropriate learning.

Companion Website To learn more about supporting kindergartners, go to the Companion Website at **www. prenhall.com/morrison**, select chapter 11, then choose the Linking to Learning module.

Developmentally appropriate Based on how children grow, develop, and on individual and cultural differences.

Even though some early childhood educators cannot determine the length of their kindergarten programs, they should be knowledgeable about the options and should be prepared to advocate when appropriate. Both half- and full-day kindergarten programs are available. A school district that operates a half-day program usually offers one session in the morning and one in the afternoon, so that one teacher can teach two classes. Although many kindergartens are half-day programs, there is no general agreement that this system is best. Those who argue for it say that this is all the schooling a five-year-old child is ready to experience and it provides an ideal transition to the all-day first grade. Those in favor of full-day sessions generally feel that not only is the child ready for and capable of a longer program, but also such an approach allows for a more comprehensive program.

The general trend is toward full-day kindergarten programs for all five-year-old children, even though two factors stand in the way of a more rapid transition to full-day programs: tradition and money. Kindergartens have historically and traditionally been half-day programs, although there is ample evidence of full-day programs for four- and five-year-old children. As time passes and society's needs begin to point to full-day programs to prepare children for living in an increasingly complex world, more kindergarten programs will become full-day.

Money is the most important obstacle to the growth of full-day kindergarten programs. Without a doubt, it takes twice as many teachers to operate full-day programs, but as society continues to recognize the benefits of early education and as kindergartens and early childhood programs are seen as one means of solving societal problems, more funding will be forthcoming.

Research supports the attendance of children in full-day kindergarten programs. For example, a study of 17,600 schoolchildren suggests that full-day programs may have both academic and financial benefits:

> The study found that, by the time they reached the third and fourth grades, former full-day kindergartners were more than twice as likely as children without any kindergarten experiences—and 26 percent more likely than graduates of half-day programs—to have made it there without having repeated a grade. . . . . "A lot of research suggests that how students are doing those first few years is very telling of what they'll do later on," said Andrea del Gaudio Weiss, the lead researcher on the study. . . . [8]

In addition, research shows that full-day kindergarten boosts reading achievement.[9]

LITERACY EDUCATION AND KINDERGARTEN CHILDREN

Literacy education is an important and highly visible topic today. Literacy is discussed in virtually all educational circles, and most early childhood educators are talking about how to promote it. It has replaced reading readiness as the main objective of many kindergarten and primary programs. *Literacy* means the ability to read, write, speak, and listen, with an emphasis on reading and writing well, within the context of one's cultural and social setting.

Literacy education is a hot topic for several reasons:

1. Too many children and adults cannot read. The National Adult Literacy Survey estimates that over 50 million Americans are functionally illiterate—at or below a fifth-grade reading level. Furthermore, when we compare the U.S. literacy rate with that of other countries, we do not fare well—many industrialized countries have higher literacy rates.[10] Educators and social policy planners are concerned about this inability

Literacy education
Teaching that focuses on reading, writing, speaking, and listening.

HOW TO CREATE LESSON PLANS
FOR CHILDREN IN KINDERGARTEN

Teaching is more than just my profession—it is my passion! I have an insatiable desire to increase my understanding of the art and science of teaching and am constantly researching and reflecting on ways to improve my practice.

I believe that all students can learn but that success does not look the same for each student. In order to help my children become successful, I let them know I love them and believe in them, and I teach them strategies they can use in school and in life. By focusing on their interests, needs, strengths, learning styles, cultural backgrounds, and previous experiences, I nurture them to work to their full potential and to care and cooperate with one another, laying the foundation for lifelong learning.

It is exciting to be a kindergarten teacher in Montgomery County Public Schools these days. With our new rigorous curriculum and the assessments that go along with it, my ability to assess my children's individual strengths and needs has improved significantly. High-stakes testing has actually improved my creativity; it has forced me to think outside the box and to use as many resources as I possibly can to help my students achieve.

Fifty percent of my students are English language learners, but I strongly recommend the following steps to help *all* children learn:

STEP 1 Know what your students need to know and be able to do

Start by consulting your school's curriculum and the NAEYC Guide for Developmentally Appropriate Practices (see appendix B).

- Know the origin of your school or district standards, whether they are based on national content area standards, NAEYC standards, state learning standards, or other sources
- Develop mastery objectives and criteria for success.
- Know the essential questions, outcomes, and indicators your students will need to master.
- Know the enduring understandings that your students will need for a lifetime.

STEP 2 Preassess your children

You need to know where to begin with each child.

- Use a variety of preassessment tools. A KWHL chart is helpful when assessing the whole class: K—what your students think they *know*, W—what they *want* to find out, H—*how* they can find out, L—what they *learned.*
- Use informal observations and checklists, interview students, have them draw pictures to illustrate background knowledge, and use all-pupil response cards and signs to have students answer questions.

STEP 3 Plan creative and engaging lessons

You must meet the instructional needs of your students, as well as their learning styles and their interests.

- Use a wide variety of activities, songs, dances, finger plays, and games.
- Use concrete models as well as lots of print to support the outcomes.
- Use varied groupings and cooperative learning strategies, such as class buddies and think-pair-share,* so that all children have the opportunity to think and share their answer with someone.
- Use hands-on activities. For example, when teaching children to read high-frequency words, try these ideas:
  - Use magnetic letters to create the words and shaving cream to write the words.
  - Trace over words made of sandpaper.
  - Paint the words in large letters on the playground blacktop, using paintbrushes and water.
  - Sing the song "Popcorn Words."
  - Spell and read the words from a PowerPoint presentation.
  - Use the words on word cards to make sentences.
  - Play high-frequency word bingo.
  - Look for the words in text and highlight them with highlighter tape.
  - Type the words on the computer and have the computer read back what was typed.

- Create authentic books, using students' pictures and predictable patterns, to practice reading the words. For example, on Day 1 we make a book about friends that has three high-frequency words in each sentence and each child's name: "This is my friend _____." Each child gets a copy of the book, made in PowerPoint, and every day for the first month of school and every time a new student joins our class, we read the book together, projected on the TV screen. The children also record themselves reading the book and love to listen to themselves as reader.

STEP 4 Start with an itinerary and close with a summarizer

Before beginning the lesson, share with students the essential components of your plan.

- Use an itinerary, perhaps in the form of a friendly letter, to let students know what they will be doing.
- Share your objectives, sometimes in the form of an essential question, so that students know what they are focusing on and what they are aiming for.
- Activate current student knowledge related to the new learning activities so that students are ready and open for learning.
- Help children make connections from old to new concepts and ideas.
- Have students summarize what they have learned, using pictures or phrases or telling the class or a buddy.

STEP 5 Use a variety of assessments

Using varied assessment techniques allows you to know when each child has mastered an objective and is ready to move on or when you need to reteach something in a different way.

- Use rubrics and checklists as often as possible so that your students know the criteria for success.
- Use ongoing assessments, such as exit cards, on a daily basis to make sure your students are on track. For example, if you are working on rhyming words, ask your children when lining up to go to lunch to tell you a word that rhymes with *man*.
- Have your students set personal goals and graph their progress. For example, students might choose the number of high-frequency words they want to learn over a two-week period, as well as the strategies they are going to use to master their words. When they are ready to read, they can come to you, and you can highlight the new words they have mastered and fill in a graph to show how many total words they have mastered. Children love seeing their graphs

rise and feel empowered by using strategies that work for them.
- Give children choices to show you what they know whenever possible. Children may want to draw a picture, write a story, sing a song, build a structure, or do a puppet show to show what they have learned.

STEP 6 Give timely and specific feedback

Keep the feedback positive, teaching to your students' strengths.

- Include a rubric or checklist right on the activity so that when the children finish it, they can have a quick discussion with you and check off their successes. After you have answered questions or have retaught some material, the children can go back to work on the boxes that are not checked off.
- Include a home-school component so that family members know what is being taught and can provide support or ask questions.

As you prepare to teach, here are some other important ideas to keep in mind:

- Relationships with your students are key. If they know you genuinely care, they will work hard for you.
  - Call each family within the first week of school to share something you really love about their child, and ask whether they have any questions or concerns.
  - Send home daily e-mails letting families know what the children are doing in school and how the families can support them at home.
- Create a caring community in which students respect and support one another.
  - Choose a fun greeting every morning and share news on a daily basis.
  - Use strategies from the Virtues Project (www. virtuesproject.com), as well as class meetings, to create a caring and respectful community.
- Have high and developmentally appropriate expectations for all students, and use encouraging messages:
  - Effective effort leads to achievement!
  - I believe in you!
  - You can do it!
  - I won't give up on you!

Contributed by Dara Feldman, kindergarten teacher at Garrett Park Elementary School, Garrett Park, Maryland, and a National Board certified teacher as well as Disney's 2005 Outstanding Elementary Teacher of the Year.

*"Strategies for Reading Comprehension: Think-Pair-Share," Reading Quest.org, http://curry.edschool.virginia.edu/go/readquest/strat/tps.html.

FIGURE 11.2 Essential Components of Research-Based Programs for Beginning Reading Instruction

1. Children have opportunities to expand their use and appreciation of oral language.

2. Children have opportunities to expand their use and appreciation of printed language.

3. Children have opportunities to hear good stories and informational books read aloud daily.

4. Children have opportunities to understand and manipulate the building blocks of spoken language.

5. Children have opportunities to learn about and manipulate the building blocks of written language.

6. Children have opportunities to learn the relationship between the sounds of spoken language and the letters of written language.

7. Children have opportunities to learn decoding strategies.

8. Children have opportunities to write and relate their writing to spelling and reading.

9. Children have opportunities to practice accurate and fluent reading in decodable stories.

10. Children have opportunities to read and comprehend a wide assortment of books and other texts.

11. Children have opportunities to develop and comprehend new vocabulary through wide reading and direct vocabulary instruction.

12. Children have opportunities to learn and apply comprehension strategies as they reflect on and think critically about what they read.

Source: Texas Reading Initiative, *Beginning Reading Instruction* (Austin, TX: Texas Education Agency Publications Division, 2002).

of the schools to teach all children to read at more than a functional level. Figure 11.2 outlines twelve essential components of research-based programs designed to promote reading.

2. Businesses and industry are concerned about how unprepared the nation's workforce is to meet the demands of the workplace. Critics of the educational establishment maintain that many high school graduates do not have the basic literacy skills required for today's high-tech jobs. Therefore, schools, especially in the early grades, are feeling the pressure to adopt measures that will give future citizens the skills they will need for productive work and meaningful living.

3. State governments are at the forefront of making sure that all children learn to read well and that they read on level by third grade. Not surprisingly, then, the goals for kindergarten learning are higher than they were in the past (see Fig 11.3).

For an example of a lesson plan that promotes literacy and also meets state standards, see "Plentiful Penguins" on pages 324–326. The lesson plan has a number of interesting elements:

- Notice how the lesson integrates many content areas.
- Make a list of the various teaching strategies Sylvia uses to teach her lesson.
- Notice how she connects classroom learning to home learning.
- Consider how Sylvia teaches to state standards.

Explain how you would use the different learning centers identified in the Kindergarten segment of the DVD to implement the state guidelines for kindergarten reading in Figure 11.3.

FIGURE 11.3   State Guidelines for Kindergarten Reading

Indiana
- Identify the front cover, back cover, and title page of a book.
- Follow words from left to right and from top to bottom on the printed page.
- Understand that printed materials provide information.
- Recognize that sentences in print are made up of separate words.
- Distinguish letters from words.
- Recognize and name all uppercase and lowercase letters of the alphabet.

California
- Track and represent the number, sameness/difference, and order of two and three isolated phonemes.
- Track and represent changes in simple syllables and words with two and three sounds as one sound is added, substituted, omitted, shifted, or repeated.
- Blend vowel-consonant sounds orally to make words or syllables.
- Identify and produce rhyming words in response to an oral prompt.
- Distinguish orally stated one-syllable words and separate into beginning or ending sounds.
- Track auditorily each word in a sentence and each syllable in a word.
- Count the number of sounds in syllables and syllables in words.

Kansas
- Identify sounds of both upper- and lowercase letters of the alphabet.
- Identify names of both upper- and lowercase letters of the alphabet.
- Distinguish letters from words by recognizing that words are separated by spaces.
- Demonstrate *phonemic awareness* skills by hearing and orally manipulating.
- Identify and make oral *rhymes* and begin to hear *onsets* and *rimes*.
- Demonstrate an understanding of *graphemes* and *phonemes* in written and spoken language.

Arizona
- Recognize that print represents spoken language and conveys meaning (e.g., his or her own name, Exit and Danger signs).
- Hold a book right side up and turn pages in the correct direction.
- Start at the top left of the printed page, track words from left to right, using return sweep, and move from the top to the bottom of the page.
- Identify different parts of a book (e.g., front cover, back cover, title page) and the information they provide.
- Distinguish between printed letters and words.
- Recognize that spoken words are represented in written language by specific sequences of letters.
- Recognize the concept of words by segmenting spoken sentences into individual words.
- Demonstrate the one-to-one correlation between a spoken word and a printed word.

Sources: Indiana State Department of Education, "Indiana's Academic Standards for Kindergarten" (April 26, 2005), http://www.doe. state.in.us/standards/Docs-2004/English/Word/Grade0K/K-EnglishLA.doc; *California State Board of Education*, "Kindergarten English—Language Arts Content Standards," (August 30, 2005), http://www.cde.ca.gov/be/st/ss/engkindergarten.asp;*Kansas State Department of Education*, "Kansas Curricular Standards for Reading Education" (July 8, 2003), http://www.ksde.org/outcomes/ rwstds 782003.html; *Arizona Department of Education*, "Reading Standards Articulated by Grade Level" (August 12, 2003), http://www.ade. state.az.us/standards/language-arts/articulated.asp.

LESSON PLAN: Plentiful Penguins

Goals and Objectives

Goal: Kindergarten children will learn about penguins and relate similarities of penguins to human family behavior.

Instructional Objectives

The students will . . .

1. Recall facts, characteristics, and habits about penguins and their families.
2. Compare and contrast different species of penguins.
3. Use the paint program KidWorks2™ to illustrate a penguin and record facts about penguins.
4. Learn the following basic word-processing skills: keyboard keys and functions, writing a sentence, saving, and printing a document.
5. Use a variety of technological and informational resources to gather and synthesize information about penguins.
6. Choose their favorite penguin of the penguins studied. As a home learning project, they will write an important fact about their favorite penguin. They will also make up a song or poem about their favorite penguin and share it with the class.

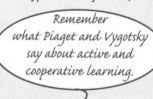

Goals and objectives should incorporate state and local standards.

Prerequisite Skills

1. Students should be familiar with the computer—how to use the mouse, how to type on a keyboard, and how to print.
2. Students will write sentences, using inventive spelling if necessary.
3. Students will use appropriate skills to produce art projects.

Remember what Piaget and Vygotsky say about active and cooperative learning.

Time Frame

Approximately two weeks

Lesson Activities

Activity One: I introduced my students to facts about penguins through nonfiction books.

Activity Two: My students viewed three to four Internet sites about penguins. After viewing these Internet sites and learning about the different types of penguins, they compared and contrasted penguin characteristics.

Activity Three: My students learned the song "All the Penguins" and learned poems about penguins. They made penguins using paper plates and construction paper.

Activity Four: My students gathered in groups and looked at pictures of five different penguins that they had been studying and choose their favorite penguin. As a home learning project, they wrote an important fact about their penguin and drew a picture of their penguin. They also made up a song or poem to bring to class to share with their classmates.

Activity Five: My students used the KidWorks2 paint program to replicate their hand drawing of the penguin and used their keyboarding skills to write a fact about the penguin.

Activity Six: Students' pictures and writings were printed to make a class book to share with others.

Introducing Penguins

I introduced the students to penguins through an integrated curriculum approach. Reading aloud from nonfiction books emphasizes language arts. We talked about the different kinds of penguins and their habitats. I checked for recalled information by asking the students to share facts they remembered about the different penguins. I wrote these facts on chart paper to post in the classroom for reference throughout the unit.

The arts were incorporated as the students learned several poems and a song about penguins, "All the Penguins." They drew pictures, wrote at least one fact about penguins, and made a penguin out of paper plates and construction paper. I provided a variety of learning experiences in order to capitalize on my students' learning styles and interests. I also used a wide range of instructional resources and strategies to integrate developmentally appropriate learning experiences across the content disciplines.

Be sure to start with what students already know.

This lesson can also be introduced using KWL strategies. This technique activates students' prior knowledge by asking them to talk about what they already *know,* what they *want* to learn, and discussing what they have *learned* after the activity.* I use KWL strategies when I begin units as a discussion starter with my students and as a way to pique their curiosity, grab their attention, and activate prior knowledge. My students' questions about what they want to know helped me choose the information to present in the lessons. Writing the information on a chart helped my students remember what they knew and what their questions were. We returned to the chart frequently and reviewed it together as we progressed through the unit. This method helped my students organize their thoughts. It also helped them remember more information accurately.

Internet Research

The students viewed three or four Internet sites about penguins. We used a computer image projected onto a larger screen so that all students could see and understand the navigation and the resources present on the site. I bookmarked these and other penguin sites on the classroom computers so that the students could return to them during independent computer time, in a center, or in the lab.

During independent center time, I sat with a small group of students and demonstrated how to navigate within the penguin sites. After modeling the use of the cursor and the mouse to enhance their searches, I gave each child a turn with the mouse and let each practice these skills individually.

I helped the students in my class use technological resources to access information and to support and extend traditional resources.

Comparing and Contrasting Penguins

The students used the facts and knowledge they gained from their research and the class discussion to compare and contrast penguins.

I use these kinds of group activities to build on prior knowledge and foster appropriate group behavior. These group conversations in my class extend and clarify concepts. They teach the importance of listening to other classmates and increase oral language skills.

Extending classroom activities to the home is a great way to involve parents.

Choosing a Penguin for the Home Learning Project

The students gathered in small groups to look at pictures of the five different penguins we had been studying. Each student chose a favorite penguin. As a home learning project, each student drew a picture of the chosen penguin and wrote an important fact learned through our discussions and research. Each child made up a song or poem to share with the class. They practiced these songs and poems at home with their parents and siblings.

I provide many opportunities for choice in my class. The students have the opportunity to make independent choices as well as making choices together in a group. For example, we made class rules together, planned field trips, and developed rules for safety on those trips. I like to try different decision-making experiences to give them confidence and develop critical-thinking skills. In developing a safe environment, choices allow students to take risks and try new things. Small-group activities also foster social skills.

I am fortunate to have a parent community that supports children's learning. We work together to complete and present home learning projects that are engaging and interesting for both parents and children.

*Donna Ogle, "K-W-L: A Teaching Model That Develops Active Reading of Expository Text," *The Reading Teacher* 39 (February 1986): 564–570.

Learning to Use KidWorks2

I introduced the software program KidWorks2 to the children by showing them how to draw a penguin. The computer screen was projected onto a large TV screen so that all of the children could see what I was doing. We experimented with the different tools in this program to outline and fill in the picture. I expanded the students' growing knowledge of shapes by asking them to describe the pictures I drew.

Incorporate technology to create student interest.

I have found that this projection technique and shared learning experience works well when introducing technology concepts to the whole class. I deliberately make mistakes or choose to erase my work so that the students can feel comfortable experimenting with the software. The students then have a chance to practice what they have learned from my modeling during center time or independent computer time.

I use these technology tools to facilitate the writing process and to develop creativity. Using multiple paths to learning—such as drawing, writing, computer-aided drawing, and other tools—I help my students develop the literacy skills that are critical to success in later years.

Each student used this software program to make an electronic drawing of his or her penguin and type in the important fact. Each of these items was printed separately, instead of typing words directly onto the electronic picture. I have found that this works better for developing writers. These drawings and facts were shared with classmates and parents through the class website, a slide show, and a book. We also e-mailed drawings as attachments to the other kindergarten class.

Contributed by Sylvia McCabe, a kindergarten teacher in the Miami-Dade (Florida) Public Schools and a National Board certified teacher.

Here are some questions to consider about Sylvia's lesson:
- How would you describe an "integrated" approach to teaching?
- What would you say to critics of technology who maintain that kindergarten children are too young to learn with technology?
- How could you apply the KWL approach to your own learning? to your classroom teaching?
- How does Sylvia ensure that her children learn kindergarten state standards?

Review the earlier Competency Builder on creating a lesson plan for kindergartners; then compare those suggestions with the actual lesson described here.

Emergent literacy
Children's literacy development before receiving formal reading and writing instruction in school.

Compare Dr. Dixon-Krauss' definition of *emergent literacy* in the kindergarten segment of the DVD to our definitions here.

EMERGENT LITERACY

Throughout our discussion about literacy and reading, the terms in Figure 11.4 will prove useful.

Emergent literacy involves a range of activities and behaviors related to written language, including those undertaken by very young children who depend on the cooperation of others and/or on creative play to deal with the material. It involves reading- and writing-related activities and behaviors that change over time, culminating in conventional literacy during middle school.[11]

Many literacy approaches emphasize using environmental and social contexts to support and extend children's reading and writing. Children want to make sense of what they read and write. The meaningful part of reading and writing occurs when children talk to each other, write letters, and read good literature or have it read to them. All of this occurs within a print-rich environment, one in which children see others read, make lists, and use language and the written word to achieve goals. Proponents of early literacy maintain that this environment is highly preferable to previous approaches to literacy development.

FIGURE 11.4 Reading/Literacy Terminology

Alphabet knowledge: The understanding that letters have names and shapes and that letters can represent sounds in language

Alphabetic principle: Awareness that each speech sound or phoneme in language has its own distinctive graphic representation, and an understanding that letters go together in patterns to represent sounds

Comprehension: In reading, a basic understanding of the words and the meaning contained within printed material

Grapheme: The letters and letter combinations that represent a phoneme

Onset-rime: Onset—the part of the syllable that precedes the vowel; rime—the remaining part of the syllable

Orthographic awareness: Familiarity with written symbols and an understanding of the relationships between these symbols and the sounds they represent

Phoneme: The smallest unit of speech that makes a difference to meaning

Phonemic awareness: The ability to deal explicitly and segmentally with sound units smaller than a syllable

Phonological awareness: The ability to manipulate language at the levels of syllables, rhymes, and individual speech sounds

Print awareness: The recognition of conventions and characteristics of a written language

The process of becoming literate is viewed as a natural process; reading and writing are processes that children participate in naturally, long before they come to school. No doubt you have participated with or know of toddlers and preschoolers who are literate in many ways. They "read" all kinds of signs (McDonald's) and labels (Campbell's soup) and "write" with and on anything and everything.

The concept of emergent literacy, then, is based on the following beliefs about literacy and the ways children learn:

- Reading and writing involve cognitive and social abilities that children use in the process of becoming literate and gaining meaning from reading, writing, speaking, and listening.
- Most children are involved in activities related to reading and writing long before they come to school; they do not wait until someone teaches them.
- Literacy develops within a social context in which children have the opportunity to interact with and respond to printed language and to other children and adults who are using printed language. In this context, children bring meaning to and derive meaning from reading and writing. Teachers encourage sharing knowledge and ideas through reading and writing.
- Children's cultural identity influences how literacy develops and what form it takes. All children should have opportunities to read the literature of many cultural groups in addition to their own.

The emergent literacy and reading models view reading and written language acquisition as a continuum of development. Think of children as being on a continuous journey toward full literacy development.

APPROACHES TO LITERACY AND READING IN YOUNG CHILDREN

Literacy and reading are certainly worthy national and educational goals, not only for young children but for everyone. However, how best to promote literacy has always been a controversial topic.

Whole Word. One of the most popular methods used for literacy and reading development is the *sight word* approach (also called *whole word* or *look-say*), in which children are presented with whole words (e.g., *cat, bat, sat*) and develop a sight vocabulary that enables them to begin reading and writing. Many early childhood professionals label objects in their classrooms (e.g., door, bookcase, desk) as a means of teaching a sight vocabulary. **Word walls** are very popular in kindergarten and primary classrooms.

Phonics. A second popular approach to literacy and reading is based on *phonics* instruction, which stresses letter-sound correspondence. By learning these connections, children are able to combine sounds into words (*C-A-T*). The proponents of phonics instruction argue that letter-sound correspondence enables children to make automatic connections between words and sounds and, as a result, to sound out words and read them on their own.[12]

From the 1950s until the present time, there has been much debate about which of these two approaches to literacy development—phonics or whole word—is better. Today, there is a decided reemphasis on the use of phonics instruction. One reason is that research evidence suggests that phonics instruction enables children to become proficient readers.[13]

Language Experience. Another method of literacy and reading development, the *language experience approach,* follows the philosophy and suggestions inherent in progressive education philosophy. This approach is child centered and maintains that literacy education should be meaningful to children, growing out of experiences that are interesting to them. Thus, children's own experiences are a key element in such child-centered approaches. Many teachers transcribe children's dictated experience stories and use them as a basis for writing and for reading instruction.

Whole Language. Beginning in about 1980, early childhood practitioners in the United States were influenced by literacy education approaches used in Australia and New Zealand, as well as by approaches from Great Britain, which were popular during the open education movement of the 1960s. These influences gradually developed into what is known as the **whole language approach** to literacy development. Because whole language is a philosophy rather than a method, its definition often depends on who is using the term. This approach, nonetheless, advocates using all aspects of language—reading, writing, listening, and speaking—as the basis for developing literacy. Children learn about reading and writing by speaking and listening; they learn to read by writing, and they learn to write by reading. Other characteristics of the whole language approach include the following:

- It is child centered—that is, children, rather than teachers, are at the center of instruction and learning. Thus, children's experiences and interests serve as the context for topics and as the basis for their intrinsic motivation to read, write, and converse. In this way literacy learning becomes meaningful and functional for children.
- Social interaction is important and a part of the process of becoming literate. Lev Vygotsky (see chapter 5) stressed the social dimensions of learning. He proposed that through interaction with others, especially with more confident peers and with teachers, children are able to develop higher cognitive learning. This process of learning through social interaction is referred to as *socially constructed knowledge.*

Word wall A collection of words from stories displayed on a wall or other display place in the classroom designed to promote literacy learning.

Whole language approach Philosophy of literacy development that advocates the use of all dimensions of language—reading, writing, listening, and speaking—to help children become motivated to read and write.

- Spending time on the processes of reading and writing is more important than spending time on skills to get ready to read. Consequently, from the moment they enter the learning setting, children are involved in literacy activities—that is, being read to; "reading" books, pamphlets, and magazines; scribbling; "writing" notes; and so forth.
- Reading, writing, speaking, and listening are taught as an integrated whole, rather than in isolation.
- Writing begins early; children are writing from the time they enter the program.
- Children's written documents are used as reading materials.
- Themes or units of study are used as a means of promoting interests and content. Generally, themes are selected cooperatively by children and teachers and are used as a means of promoting ongoing involvement in literary processes.

The whole language approach dominated early childhood practice from about 1990 through 1995. However, growing numbers of critics, including parents and the public, maintain that because it is a philosophy rather than a specific approach, it does not teach children skills necessary for good reading. In addition, some teachers have difficulty explaining the whole language approach to parents, and some find it difficult to implement as well. Further, some research has indicated that whole language approaches do not result in the high levels of reading achievement claimed by its supporters. As a result, proponents of phonics instruction are aggressively advocating a return to this approach to best meet the needs of children, parents, and society.

Balance and Support. As with most things, a balanced approach is probably the best, and many early childhood advocates are encouraging literacy approaches that provide a balance between whole language methods and phonics instruction and that meet the specific needs of individual children. One thing is clear: systematic instruction that enables children to acquire skills they need to learn to read is very much in evidence in today's early childhood classrooms. Although the debate over the best approach will likely continue, there will also be increased efforts to integrate the best of all approaches into a unified whole to make literacy education a reality for all children.

A primary goal of kindergarten education is for children to learn how to read. Thus, teachers must instruct, support, and guide them in learning what is necessary to be successful in school and life. Figure 11.5 lists some of the things you can do to motivate children's learning. The Voice from the Field on pages 332–333 tells how one teacher used the results of her action research to motivate her students' growth in literacy. Remember, too, what was said in chapter 5 about Vygotsky's theory of scaffolding children's learning. Figure 5.4 can help you learn how to scaffold children's literacy development.

Companion Website To complete a Diversity Tie-In activity related to Latino family literacy, go to the Companion Website at **www.prenhall.com/morrison**, select chapter 11, then choose the Diversity Tie-In module.

SHARED READING

Because children love books and reading, shared reading is a good way for you to capitalize on their interest and help them learn to read. **Shared reading** is a means of introducing young beginners to reading, using favorite books, rhymes, and poems. Teachers model reading for the students by reading aloud a book or other text and ultimately inviting students to join in.

Shared reading builds on children's natural desire to read and reread favorite books. The repeated reading of texts over several days, weeks, or months deepens children's understanding of them because each time the reading should be for a different purpose: to extend, refine, or deepen a child's abilities to read and construct meaning.

Shared reading is especially good for English language learners because it helps make the written language comprehensible and improves English proficiency. The Diversity Tie-In "Latino Family Literacy" on pages 334–335 includes strategies that promote literacy skills for English-language learners.

Shared reading A teaching method in which the teacher and children read together from text that is visible to all.

FIGURE 11.5   Suggestions for Motivating Children to Read

- Include a variety of different types of books, such as picture books without words, fairy tales, nursery rhymes, picture storybooks, realistic literature, decodable and predictable books, information books, chapter books, biographies, big books, poetry, and joke and riddle books.
- Provide other types of print, such as newspapers, magazines, and brochures.
- Introduce and discuss several books each week (e.g., theme-related, same authors, illustrators, types of books).
- Have multiple copies of popular books.
- Include books in children's home languages.
- Have an easy-to-use system for checking out books.
- Provide a record-keeping system for keeping track of books read (may include a picture-coding system to rate or evaluate a book).
- Showcase many books by placing them so the covers are visible, especially those that are new, shared in read-aloud sessions, or theme-related.
- Organize books on shelves by category or type—perhaps color code.
- Provide comfortable, inviting places to read (e.g., pillows, rugs, a sofa, large cardboard boxes).
- Encourage children to read to friends (include stuffed animals and dolls for pretend reading).
- Have an Author's Table with a variety of writing supplies to encourage children to write about books.
- Have a Listening Table for recorded stories and tapes.

Source: Adapted by permission from Lesley Mandel Morrow, *Literacy Development in the Early Years,* 5th ed. (Boston, MA: Allyn and Bacon, 2004). Copyright © 2004 by Pearson Education.

The shared reading routine requires that you have on hand a big-book form of the book to be read, as well as multiple little-book copies for individual rereading later. You then follow these three steps:

1. *Introduce the book.* Gather the children where they can all see the big book.
   - Show and discuss the book cover: read the title, author, illustrator, and other appropriate book features.
   - Discuss some of the pages in the book, but don't give away the entire story.
   - Invite children to predict what they think will happen in the book. If they have difficulty, model thinking aloud to show them how you would predict. Record their predictions on a chart for later reference.
2. *Read and respond to the book.* Read the book aloud to the children, holding it so they can see each page. As you read, run your hand or a pointer under each line of print to help children develop a sense of left-to-right orientation, speech-to-print match, and other concepts of print. If some children wish to join in, encourage them to do so.

   As you read, you may stop briefly to discuss the story or to respond to reactions, but you should progress through the entire book rather quickly to give children a complete sense of the story. At the conclusion of the reading, encourage children to respond, using questions such as these:
   - Were your predictions right?
   - What did you like in this story?
   - What was your favorite part?
   - What made you happy (or sad)?
   - Who was your favorite character? Why?

Then return to the book, rereading the story and inviting children to read along. Many will feel comfortable doing this right away, but others may not join in until another day. After the second reading, many children will say, "Let's read it again"—especially for books, songs, or rhymes that are lots of fun. Under most circumstances, when children are excited and want to reread, you *should* reread.

After you have read the book again, have children respond, using activities such as these:

- Talk with a friend about a favorite part
- Retell the story to a partner
- Draw a picture about the story and write a word or a sentence about it
- Draw and write about a favorite character
- Write a list of favorite characters

Help children become comfortable with making decisions by giving them only a couple of choices initially.

3. *Extend the book.* You may want to wait until children have read a book several times before extending it, or you may wait unit they have read several books within a thematic unit and combine them for extension activities. Although each repeated reading may seem to be just for fun, each should have a particular focus. You might first invite children to recall what the title was and what the book was about, prompting and supporting them if necessary.

Then tell the children why they are rereading the book, using statements such as the following:

- "As we reread this book, let's think about who the important characters are" (comprehension)
- "In our story today, notice how the author repeats lines over and over" (exploring language)
- "Today, as we reread one of our favorite stories, look for places to use phonic skills we have been learning" (decoding)[14]

KINDERGARTEN CHILDREN AND TRANSITIONS

Young children face many transitions in their lives.[15] They are left with babysitters and enter child care programs, preschools, kindergarten, and first grade. Depending on how adults help children make these transitions, they can be either unsettling and traumatic or happy and rewarding experiences. Under no circumstances should the transition from kindergarten to first grade be viewed as the beginning of real learning.

Leaving kindergarten to enter first grade is a major transition, it may not be too difficult for children whose kindergarten classroom is housed in the same building as the primary grades, but for others whose kindergarten is separate from the primary program or who have not attended kindergarten, the experience can be unsettling. As mentioned in chapter 10, children with special needs who are making a transition from a special program to a mainstreamed classroom need extra attention and support.

Parents and kindergarten professionals can help children make transitions successfully. Many of these suggestions were included for preschool children but are equally effective with kindergartners:

- Educate and prepare children ahead of time for any new situation. For example, children and teachers can visit the new program the children will attend. Also, toward the end of the kindergarten year, children can practice certain routines as they will do them when they enter their new school or grade.
- Alert parents to new and different standards, dress, behavior, and parent-teacher interactions. Kindergarten professionals, in cooperation with first-grade teachers, should share curriculum materials with parents so they can be familiar with what their children will learn.
- Let parents know ahead of time what their children will need in the new program (e.g., lunch box, change of clothing).

ACTION RESEARCH: IMPROVING CLASSROOM PRACTICE

RATIONALE FOR ACTION RESEARCH

Teaching is indeed a social career. We spend our days in continual interaction and communication with others. We debate, discuss, explain, analyze, reiterate, and illuminate for hours on end with children—and for some of us, very young children. The reality of teaching is that there are few opportunities for professional reflection and fewer opportunities still for professional feedback from others. Yet reflection is a necessary component of shaping or reshaping the way we think, act, and evolve into better teachers. Engaging in the process of teacher research provides opportunities to reflect, react, re-create, and evolve into more effective and more energized professionals.

I became a teacher researcher because I knew that there were aspects of my teaching that needed improvement and fresh ideas. Although I routinely attend inservices and various seminars to stay current on philosophical and practical aspects of teaching, the results are often the same. I leave the sessions hoping that I will find the time to institute something from the day's experience that will enhance children's learning. Sometimes I do. Many times, however, the folder full of ideas is filed for another day for consideration and further planning, and I am drawn again into the constant rush of an early childhood world.

Teacher research groups, by their design, set apart time for reflection, create a forum for collaboration, and initiate expansion of ideas and concepts that are practical to the teacher's daily lessons. One benefit of teacher research is that the teacher researcher chooses the target area. The topic is drawn from something that the *teacher* identifies as a puzzlement—not the district, the curriculum committee, or the principal. In my school, our teacher research group is comprised of teachers from different grade levels, speciality areas, and research interests, providing a diverse and resourceful group of professionals with whom to interact.

A COLLABORATIVE PROCESS

Usually six to twelve individuals form a teacher research team at my school. We are provided with one half-day per month during which the school district provides funds for substitute teachers while we meet to share and discuss our research. In teacher research the teacher takes on many roles as an observer of children and learning patterns, a seeker of meaningful impacts on learning, a problem solver, a discoverer, and ultimately a sharer of knowledge. Key elements of the research process include reflective journaling, observation of students' behaviors, professional reading, data collection, and collaborative discussions with fellow teacher-researchers, whom we call critical friends. And all of this often results in systematic, practical, and timely changes in classroom planning and teaching.

- Provide parents of special needs children and bilingual parents with additional help and support during the transition.
- Offer parents and children an opportunity to visit new programs. Children will better understand the physical, curricular, and affective climates of the new program if they visit in advance. Professionals can also incorporate methods into their own program that will help children adjust to new settings.
- Cooperate with the staff of any new program the children will attend, to work out a transitional plan. Continuity between programs is important for social, emotional, and educational reasons. Children should see their new setting as an exciting place where they will be happy and successful.

Three areas are particularly important in influencing the success of transitional experiences: children's skills and prior school-related experiences, children's home lives, and kindergarten classroom characteristics. Read the Diversity Tie-In "Is Poverty Linked to

As the research reveals patterns of learning, immediate changes can be made in a teacher's method or materials to bring about immediate results. These new understandings impact the researcher's students but are also shared with other members of the teacher research team and other teachers in the school and throughout the school system's teacher research network.

In addition, teacher research often leads teachers to resources such as various grants that are available through school districts, governments, or private/commercial businesses. In turn, the research findings are published for a wider audience through the grant submissions and publications, thus impacting many other educators as well.

MY RESEARCH

Each year our principal devotes the last faculty meeting of the year to the teacher research roundtables. At this meeting the teacher researchers informally present their research projects, including their reflections and findings, to the whole staff. After attending one such presentation, I began to consider how I could effectively and expediently modify my teaching practices to impact my children's literacy growth.

I attended a colleague's discussion on how she enhanced her K-1 classroom's writing performance by using shared writing during the free-choice/center time. This prompted me to realize that the children in my classroom did not choose literacy activities during Choice Time. Many children were active in the hands-on math, science, and art centers, but not the reading center. It was then that my research began, because it was then that I identified an area that needed reflective research.

The following September I joined the Teacher Research Committee. My participation took my theoretical training and made it come alive; I was utilizing philosophies I had not acted on since my master's training. Soon I was making significant yet manageable changes in my literacy program. By providing my students with hands-on retelling props to prompt literacy growth, I rediscovered many theoretical tenets from my training: the use of props enhances children's retelling success; stories with predictable text, strong structure, and background knowledge support success; motivation is linked to success . . . and the list goes on.

BENEFITS OF ACTION RESEARCH

The most significant finding in my research is that, ultimately, it is the children who benefit from it:

- Children who speak no English can work through the motions of our favorite fairy tales, demonstrating understanding without the use of one word of English.
- Many children now cheerfully break away from the building blocks, puzzles, or drama centers to retell a story with a friend.
- Story language and comprehension are enhanced as students engage in storytelling with props.
- There is joy in bringing a great story to life.

So significant were my findings that my next research topic shared this knowledge with parents through an at-home story retelling program.

Teacher research also benefits the researchers. It provides meaningful, designated time and resources for them to seek knowledge for specific professional development. And it provides teacher researchers with the opportunity to put their findings into practice through collaboration, reevaluation, and reflection, as well as the privilege of sharing their results through published research papers and presentations at schools and conferences. Action research creates an ongoing reflection that changes teaching forever.

Contributed by Deborah Q. Seidel, EdM, kindergarten teacher, Fairfax County Public Schools, Fairfax, Virginia.

Kindergarten Achievement?" on page 336 for a better understanding of the relationship between childhood poverty and success in school. Research has demonstrated other realities related to transitions:[16]

- Children who are socially adjusted have better transitions. For example, kindergarten children whose parents initiate social opportunities for them are better adjusted socially.
- Rejected children have difficulty with transitions.
- Developmentally appropriate classrooms and practices promote easier and smoother transitions for children.

Companion Website To complete an activity related to poverty and kindergarten achievement, go to the Companion Website at **www.prenhall.com/morrison**, select chapter 11, then choose the Diversity Tie-In module.

KINDERGARTEN ISSUES

Not only is kindergarten education a fascinating topic, but its occurrence almost at the beginning of formal education raises a number of related issues, such as redshirting, high-stakes kindergarten testing, and entrance age.

Diversity Tie-In

LATINO FAMILY LITERACY PROGRAM

The Latino Family Literacy Program is a two-part comprehensive bilingual family literacy project designed to increase parents' involvement in their children's literacy learning. It addresses the growing awareness that the literacy proficiencies of children are closely tied to the adults in their family. This program recognizes that the motivation common to many adult learners is a desire to help their children; the program supports parents' involvement in their children's development and provides a forum in which parents can discuss parenting concerns, family traditions, and education. Each session is designed to establish a family reading routine and provide books materials, and art projects that are culturally and linguistically relevant to the lives of Latino families.

BILINGUAL CHILDREN'S BOOKS

The ten-week program is designed to be presented by a trained teacher, parent center leader, or volunteer parent. Once a week, parents attend a two-hour session and are introduced to bilingual-children's books that they take home and read with their children. The books are returned the following session, and parents are able to discuss what they experience reading with their children and how the books related to their lives.

All books are bilingual so they draw on the linguistic and literacy skills of the entire family. The books are also culturally reflective of Latin families, values, and traditions. This grounding in the Latin culture helps to maintain parents interest in reading with their children. In addition, the books are beautifully illustrated, which assists parents and children in following the story, especially if they have lower-level literacy skills.

FAMILY ALBUM

Each book is accompanied with a writing and art activity that reflects the lives and issues of the participants and contributes to a family album. Parents are given a disposable camera to use at home, taking pictures of their children and their daily experiences. During the weekly class sessions, parents create descriptive text for the photos to use in the family album.

PROGRAM GOALS

The following are the goals of the Latino Family Literacy Program:

- Strengthen parent and child interaction
- Establish and support a family reading routine
- Increase parents' confidence in their ability to assist their children's learning
- Challenge and empower parents to improve their own literacy skills

REDSHIRTING

Academic redshirting The practice of postponing entrance into kindergarten of age-eligible children in order to allow extra time for socioemotional, intellectual, or physical growth.

You may have heard of the practice of **redshirting** college football players—that is, holding a player out a year for him to grow and mature. The theory is that the extra year will produce a better football player. The same practice applies to kindergarten children. The U.S. Department of Education estimates that about 10 percent of entering kindergarten children are redshirted—held out of school for a year.[17] Parents and administrators who practice redshirting think that the extra year gives children an opportunity to mature intellectually, socially, and physically. On the one hand, redshirting might have some benefit for children who are immature and whose birth dates fall close to the cut-off for school entrance. On the other hand, some affluent parents redshirt their children, their sons in particular, because they want them to be the oldest members of the kindergarten class. They reason that their children will be class leaders, will get more attention from the teachers, and will have another year under their belts, all the better to handle the increasing demands of the kindergarten curriculum.

- Support English language skills to parents and children
- Promote enjoyment of reading.

IMPLEMENTING A LATINO FAMILY LITERACY PROGRAM

If you want to implement your own Latino Family Literacy Program, here are some things you can include in each session, along with a possible ten-week schedule:

- A discussion with parents about how the reading with their children went at home.
- An introduction to a new book to take home, including reading the book aloud.
- A discussion of the new books, using questions such as What did you think about the book? What did you like about the book? What do you think the message of the book is? Did you like the illustrations? Why? You might also facilitate a discussion about what takes place in the story and how the characters might feel about what is taking place.
- Work on the day's activity.

Session 1   *We Are a Rainbow/Somos un Arco Iris* by Nancy Maria Grande Tabor
Introduction of participants
Informal assessment of home reading activities (presurvey)

Session 2   *With My Brother/Con Mi Hermano* by Eileen Roe
Distribute disposable cameras
Activity: Have participants identify positive words to describe their child(ren)

Session 3   *Family Pictures/Cuadros de Familia* by Carmen Lomas Garza

Activity: Create a visual depiction of the family tree

Session 4   *A Gift from Papa Diego/Un Regalo de Papá Diego* by Benjamin Alire Saenz
Collect cameras
Activity: Write a letter to a family member.

Session 5   *The Spirit of Tío Fernando/El Espíritu de tío Fernando* by Janice Levy
Activity: Write a letter to their child(ren)

Session 6   *Carlos and the Squash Plant/Carlos y la Planta de Calabaza* by Jan Romero Stevens
Activity: Begin making family album using photos and writing about the photos

Session 7   *Angel's Kite/La Estrella de Angel* by Alberto Blanco
Activity: Continue making family album, being sure to include letters and family tree created in earlier sessions

Session 8   *The Woman Who Outshone the Sun/La Mujer Que Brillaba Aún Más Que el Sol* by Alejandro Cruz Martinez
Activity: Continue making family album

Session 9   *Half Chicken/Medio Pollito* by Alma Flor Ada
Activity: Complete the family album
Informal assessment of reading activity taking place at home (postsurvey)

Session 10   Review and celebration (If funding permits, let participants choose a favorite book to keep in their home libraries.)

Contributed by Charlotte Castignola, director of Parents as Learning Partners, District B, Los Angeles Unified School District.

HIGH-STAKES KINDERGARTEN TESTING

Children at all grade levels are being subjected to more testing. For kindergarten children, this testing includes not only achievement testing but also developmental and readiness screening. Developmental screening is, as the term implies, designed to assess current developmental status and identify children's language, cognitive, and social-emotional delays. Traditionally, this information is used to modify the existing curriculum and/or provide specific learning activities and programs to help children learn. This is what developmental practice is all about.

However, increasing numbers of kindergarten children are confronting readiness screening, designed to determine whether children have the cognitive and behavioral skills necessary for kindergarten success. Unfortunately, many children may be screened out of kindergarten, rather than have a school experience that will help them succeed. And many of the children who are screened out are the children who need a high-quality school program. In addition, there are a number of other concerns with readiness tests:

The Kindergarten segment of the DVD indicates that no conclusive research shows that redshirting works. How would you describe kindergarten readiness to a parent considering redshirting?

IS POVERTY LINKED TO KINDERGARTEN ACHIEVEMENT?

The answer to our question is a resounding yes! The graph illustrates how poverty is linked to the math and reading achievement of kindergarten children. As you will observe, that link is not good in terms of children's school and life outcomes.

Data that show a link of poverty to achievement in kindergarten children are not intended to convey a sense of determinism and lead to the conclusion that all poor, minority children are destined to fail. We know that this is not true. Rather, such data should create a sense of urgency and encourage us to advocate for policies that will help poor children and their families be successful in school and life. Some things you can advocate for and support are these:

- Development of and access to high-quality preschool and kindergarten programs for all children to assure minority and poor children of an equal opportunity to achieve
- Family literacy programs and other programs that will enable families to help their children learn
- Public awareness of how important early learning is and how early learning or the lack of it shapes children's futures
- Entrance of all poor and minority children into early education programs
- Early education programs that ensure that all children will gain the knowledge and skills necessary to achieve in school

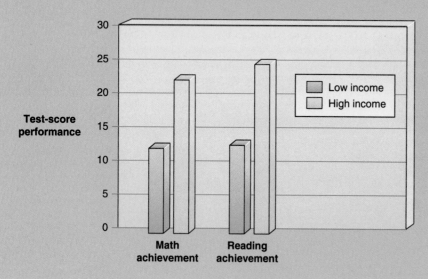

Source: Data from V. E. Lee and D. T. Burkham, *Inequality at the Starting Gate: Social Background Differences in Achievement as Children Begin School* (2002), http://www.epinet.org/books/starting_gate.html.

- Many lack validity; that is, they don't measure what they say they are measuring.
- Many readiness tests measure things that require teaching, such as colors, letters, and shapes. Consequently, children who would benefit most from a kindergarten program are judged not ready.
- There is a mismatch between what readiness tests measure and what kindergarten teachers say is important for school success.[18]

KINDERGARTEN ENTRANCE AGE

Undoubtedly, there will be ongoing debate and discussion about the appropriate age for kindergarten entrance. Current legislative practices indicate that states and school districts will continue to push back the kindergarten entrance age. For example, Maryland recently raised the age at which children can be admitted to kindergarten; children must now be five by September 1 rather than the previous date of December 31. The state's superintendent of schools said the change was necessary because of the increased academic focus in today's kindergartens.[19]

Rather than the constant juggling of entrance ages, what are needed are early childhood programs designed to serve the needs of all children, regardless of the ages at which they enter school. At the heart of this issue is disagreement about whether maturation or school is the more potent factor in children's achievement. Research studies comparing age and school effects suggest that educational intervention contributes more to children's cognitive competence than does maturation.[20]

These and other issues will continue to fuel the educational debates and will make teaching in kindergarten even more fascinating as the years go by.

THE FUTURE OF KINDERGARTEN

From our discussions in this chapter, you may have several ideas about how kindergarten programs will evolve in the next decade. Add these ideas to yours:

- The trend in kindergarten education is toward full-day, cognitive-based programs. Kindergartens give public schools an opportunity to provide all children with the help they need for later success in school and life. Children with different abilities and a society with different needs require that kindergarten programs change accordingly. After all, education is about preparing the children of today for the world of tomorrow.

- Kindergarten curricula will include more writing and reading. This literacy emphasis flows naturally from the realization that reading success plays a major role in school success. The challenge for all professionals is to keep literacy development from becoming a rigid, basic-skills approach.

- Technology (see chapter 13) will be included more in both preschool and kindergarten programs, in keeping with the current growth of technology at all grade levels and as one way of making children in the United States computer literate. Even now, technology as an instructional model exists in growing numbers of early childhood programs. It is no longer something that can be feared or ignored by early childhood professionals.

Companion Website

For additional internet resources or to complete an online activity for this chapter, go to the Companion Website at **www.prenhall.com/morrison**, select chapter 11, then choose the Linking to Learning or Making Connections module

LINKING TO LEARNING

Family Education Network
http://familyeducation.com/topic/front/0,1156,27-2247,00.html
   Tips, activities, and expert advice to keep your kindergartner on the path to academic success.

Inside Kindergarten
http://www.geocities.com/Athens/Aegean/2221
   The personal home page of kindergarten teacher Addie Gaines of the nationally renowned Seneca Elementary, Seneca, MO.

Kindergarten Connection
http://www.kconnect.com

Dedicated to providing valuable resources to primary teachers; offers new hints, tips, and information each week.

National Association for the Education of Young Children (NAEYC)
http://www.naeyc.org/about/positions/PsUnacc.asp

A position statement adopted by the NAEYC ("Still Unacceptable Trends in Kindergarten Entry and Placement"); discusses developmental kindergarten and transitional classes.

National Kindergarten Alliance
http://www.kconnect.com/nka.html

The result of a summit of leaders from various kindergarten associations, organizations, and interest groups that met in January 2000. A national organization that serves kindergarten teachers throughout the United States.

Susan Elizabeth Blow and History of the Kindergarten
http://www.froebelweb.org/images/blow.html

Outlines Blow's contributions to the development of the kindergarten and provides many links to Froebel and interesting kindergarten topics.

ACTIVITIES FOR FURTHER ENRICHMENT

ETHICAL DILEMMA: "NO MORE SOCIAL PROMOTION"

Your school district has implemented a new policy that all kindergarten students must pass a first-grade readiness test before they can be promoted to first grade. Several of your children do not have a passing score on the test. You believe the school district's policy is unfair because it bases promotion on the results of one test score. In addition, you think two of the children who did not pass the readiness test will do well in first grade.

What do you do? Do you keep quiet and say nothing, or do you talk with the school principal and present your case, or do you organize the parents and ask them to help you change the school district's policy, or do you choose another ethically appropriate solution?

APPLICATIONS

1. For each of the changes in kindergarten education discussed in this chapter, identify how it will influence both how and what you will teach. What professional development and/or other help might you need to prepare yourself to meet these new changes in kindergarten?

2. As a teacher, would you support an earlier or later entrance age to kindergarten? If your local legislator asked for specific reasons, what would you say? Ask other teachers and compare their viewpoints.

3. Compare the curricula of a for-profit kindergarten, a parochial school kindergarten, and a public school kindergarten. What are the similarities and differences? To which would you send your child? Why?

4. You have been asked to speak to a parent group about the pros and cons of contemporary approaches to literacy development in kindergarten. What major topics will you include?

FIELD EXPERIENCES

1. Give examples from your observations of kindergarten programs to support one of these opinions: (a) society is pushing kindergarten children, or (b) many kindergartens are not teaching children enough.

2. Develop a list of suggestions about how parents can promote literacy in the home.

3. Use the format of the portraits of Lina and Ganali to develop portraits of two other kindergarten children. Then compare your portraits to those of Lina and Ganali, using the portrait questions as a basis.

4. Review the lesson plan of National Board certified teacher Sylvia McCabe on pages 324–326. Using her lesson plan as a guide, develop a lesson plan for teaching your state standards in literacy, math, and science.

RESEARCH

1. Interview parents to determine what they think children should learn in kindergarten. How do their ideas compare with the ideas in this chapter? with your ideas?

2. State the pros and cons of kindergarten being mandatory for all five-year-old children. At what age should it be mandatory?

3. What are the issues facing kindergarten education in your hometown district? How are they similar to and different from those discussed in this chapter?

4. How might culture, socioeconomic background, and home life affect what should be taught to children in kindergarten? Give specific examples of how you would adjust your teaching from one socioeconomic status or cultural group to another, in order to help the children achieve the kindergarten standards for your state.

READINGS FOR FURTHER ENRICHMENT

Leuenberger, C. *The New Kindergarten: Teaching Reading, Writing & More.* New York: Scholastic Professional Books, 2003.

Offers easy-to-read ideas for setting up learning centers, organizing the day, and meeting state standards. Also gives ideas for getting parents involved and managing behavior.

Morrow, L. M. *Literacy Development in the Early Years,* 5th ed. Boston: Allyn and Bacon, 2004.

Provides a research-based rationale, as well as practical applications based on theory. Embraces integrated language arts and an interdisciplinary approach to literacy development as it addresses the development of writing, reading, and oral language in the home and the school curriculum.

Peck, Betty. *Kindergarten Education: Freeing Children's Creative Potential.* Stroud, Gloucestershire, UK: Hawthorn Press, 2003.

Uses case studies from personal experience and from the research of Froebel and other early pioneers; demonstrates how a holistic, loving approach to preschool education enables creativity, awareness, wonder, and discovery.

Walmsley, B., and Debra Wing. *Welcome to Kindergarten: A Month-by-Month Guide to Teaching and Learning.* Portsmouth, NH: Heinemann, 2004.

A comprehensive resource for kindergarten teachers. Demonstrates how best practices and a student-centered focus can make the first year of school rewarding for kindergartners, parents, and teachers.

ENDNOTES

1. U.S. Census Bureau, "Facts for Features" (August 15, 2005), http://www.census.gov/Press-Release/www/releases/archives/facts_for_features_special_editions/005225.html.

2. National Center for Education Statistics, "Full-Day and Half-Day Kindergarten in the United States" (1999), http://nces.ed.gov/pubs2004/web/2004078.asp.

3. Scholastic Testing Service, "Kindergarten Readiness Test (KRT)" (2005), http://www.ststesting.com/krt.html.

4. NAEYC, "Still Unacceptable Trends in Kindergarten Entry and Placement" (2000), http://www.naeyc.org/about/positions/PsUnacc.asp.

5. Marilyn, Bellis, "Look Before You Loop," *Young Children* (May 1999): 72.

6. P. Mantzicopoulos and D. Morrison, "Kindergarten Retention: Academics and Behavioral Outcomes Through the End of Second Grade," *American Educational Research Journal* 29, no. 1 (1992): 182–198.

7. Friedrich Froebel, *Mother's Songs, Games and Stories* (New York: Arno, 1976), 136.

8. D. Viadero, "Study: Full Day Kindergarten Boosts Academic Performance," *Education Week* (April 17, 2002): 14.

9. Kathleen Kennedy Manzo and Erik W. Robelen, "Study: Full Day Kindergarten Boosts Academic Performance," *Education Week* (June 11, 2003): 9.

10. Literacy Volunteers of America, *Facts on Literacy* (Syracuse, NY: Author, 1994).

11. National Research Council, *Starting Out Right: A Guide to Promoting Children's Reading Success* (Washington, DC: National Academy Press, 1999), 148.

12. Wesley A. Hoover, "The Importance of Phonemic Awareness in Learning to Read," *SEDL Letter* 14, no. 3, http://www.sedl.org/pubs/sedlletter/v14n03/3.html.

13. Ibid., 8.

14. Entire section on shared reading adapted by permission from J. David Cooper, *Literacy: Helping Children Construct Meaning,* 5th ed. (Boston: Houghton Mifflin, 2003), 155–157.

15. "Transitions Smoother Now for Kindergartners," *Pittsburgh Post-Gazette* (August 28, 2005): A-11.

16. K. L. Maxwell and S. K. Elder, "Children's Transition to Kindergarten," *Young Children* 49, no. 6 (1994): 56–63.

17. *Education Statistics Quarterly* (2001), http://nces.ed.gov/programs/quarterly/vol_6/6_3/.

18. D. Stipek, "At What Age Should Children Enter Kindergarten? A Question for Policy Makers and Parents," *Social Policy Report* 16, no. 2 (2002): 10–11.

19. L. Starr, "Kindergarten Is for Kids," *Education World* (June 4, 2002), http://www.education-world.com/a_issues/issues325.shtml.

20. Stipek, "At What Age," 11.

The Primary Grades

PREPARATION FOR LIFELONG SUCCESS

I tell my students that our class is like a wagon train heading out across this great expanse of learning to reach our goal . . . an education. No one will be thrown overboard. . . . Together we are all going to get there.

CHAUNCEY VEATCH, NATIONAL TEACHER OF THE YEAR, 2002

CHAPTER 12

TEACHING IN GRADES ONE TO THREE

As discussed previously, reform is sweeping across the educational landscape, and nowhere is this more evident than in grades one to three. Changes include how schools operate and are organized, how teachers teach, how children are evaluated, and how schools involve and relate to parents and the community. State governments are specifying curriculum and testing agendas. Accountability and collaboration are in; schooling as usual is out.

THE PRIMARY GRADES AND CONTEMPORARY SCHOOLING

As we begin our discussion of living and learning in grades one to three, it will be helpful to look at the nature of primary grades today.

Diversity.   Schools and classrooms are more diverse than ever before. This means that you will be teaching children from different cultures and backgrounds, and you will have to take those differences into account in your planning and teaching. "Strategies for Supporting Children Learning English," a Program in Action on page 342 provides useful strategies, and positive insights to guide you as you help children striving to learn English. In addition to cultural and linguistic differences, diversity is also reflected in socioeconomic status.

Achievement.   The achievement of all students is a high priority. Schools and teachers place a premium on closing the achievement gap that exists between races and socioeconomic levels. High-quality teachers are dedicated to ensuring that all children learn.

Testing.   Testing is a part of contemporary school culture. You will be involved in helping students learn appropriate grade-level content so that they can pass local, state, and national tests. In addition, test data will be used as a basis for planning.

Standards.   The curriculum of schools is commonly aligned with local, state, and national standards. As a result, you will be teaching content designed to help students learn what state standards specify. You won't always get to teach exactly what you want to teach, when you want to teach it, and how you want to teach it. However, good teachers always find ways to include in the curriculum what they believe is important and developmentally appropriate. Teaching to the standards does not have to be dull and boring; you can make learning interesting and relevant to your students' lives.

Academics.   The contemporary curriculum in grades one to three is heavy on reading, math, and science. There is also an emphasis on the arts, social studies, character education, and health

Focus Questions

What are the physical, cognitive, language, psychosocial, and moral developmental characteristics of children in grades one to three?

What are the political and social forces contributing to changes in grades one to three?

How are grades one to three being restructured?

How is the curriculum of the primary grades changing?

Companion Website

To check your understanding of this chapter, go to the Companion Website at **www.prenhall. com/morrison**, select chapter 12, answer Multiple Choice and Essay Questions, and receive feedback.

STRATEGIES FOR SUPPORTING
CHILDREN LEARNING ENGLISH

I currently teach English for Speakers of Other Languages (ESOL) in Miami, Florida. My school's ESOL population comes from various Spanish-speaking countries. I have been teaching two groups of ESOL students, non-English-speaking (ESL-I) and limited-English-speaking (ESL-II), for the past two years. Although earlier in my career I taught first-, third-, and fifth-grade mainstream classes, I have always had limited-English-proficient (LEP) students in my classroom.

TEACHING STRATEGIES

Our daily program is a two-hour block for ESL-I, which includes reading, language arts, and English language instruction; ESL-II students receive English language instruction from me and reading and language arts instruction from their classroom teachers. We begin our day with the class news (shared language-experience approach) and the calendar, when the children share events that have happened out of school and we discuss culturally and historically significant days and months. We then read stories from their grade-level reading textbooks and also from children's magazines so that they have experiences with both literary and informational texts. Using words that we explore from the stories, they complete vocabulary maps so that the words become a meaningful part of their vocabularies. These experiences also give the children the opportunity to use their dictionary skills and expose them to parts of speech and language structure. In addition, I provide my students with composition notebooks so they can record the daily strategies they have learned, such as a main idea table that helps them identify the main idea of a story and its supporting details.

THE CHALLENGE OF STANDARDIZED TESTS

These past two years have given me a clear picture of the effects of standardized testing on students who are learning a new language. Although my children do receive instruction on the information they will encounter on the standardized state assessment test, they receive this instruction for only two hours a day. Direct teaching is the key to success for my ESOL students, and unfortunately these two hours are usually the only exposure they get. Once these children go home, they watch television in Spanish and go to stores and other neighborhood places where they speak Spanish. I want my children to preserve their native tongue, but they need equal exposure to English if they are going to successfully acquire it for communication and academic purposes.

Students are required to take the state test, no matter how long they have been in the United States. Third-grade students are required to take the reading and math portions of the exam, which are all multiple choice. Fourth graders are required to take the reading, writing, and math portions of the exam, which include multiple-choice and long- and short-response items. Math is usually not that difficult for my students; it is universal, and they can use the skills they have learned in their native language. But as far as reading, writing, and content go, the test is very frustrating and unfair for these children, especially the ESL-I students. They have not been given adequate time to learn conversational English, let alone the academic English context skills they need to succeed on the state test.

Even though LEP students are provided with accommodations that help them, such as extra time and the use of a dictionary, they struggle to figure out terms, idiomatic expressions, and the complex structure of the English language, which is so different from their native tongue. And while they are translating, they lose comprehension because fluency and comprehension go hand in hand. Standardized testing doesn't take these issues into consideration.

Contributed by Veneshia Gonzalez, National Board certified teacher–early childhood generalist and ESOL resource teacher, Seminole Elementary School, Miami, Florida.

and wellness through physical education. Many of these other areas, however, are integrated with the basic curriculum.

Obesity Prevention.   Physical education at all levels, preK to twelve, is undergoing a renaissance. One reason for its rejuvenation, especially in the primary and elementary grades, is the concern about the national epidemic of childhood obesity and increases in childhood diabetes. Physical education classes and programs are viewed as a way of providing children with the knowledge and activities they need to get in shape and stay that way for the rest of their lifetimes. The Institute of Medicine recommends that schools do all they can to "ensure that all children and youth participate in a minimum of thirty minutes of moderate to vigorous physical activity during the school day, including expanded opportunities for physical activity through classes, sports programs, clubs, lessons, after-school and community use of school facilities, and walking and biking to school programs."[1]

Planning.   Today's teaching requires extensive planning. You will be involved in a great deal of planning at the individual student, class, grade, school, and district levels. You will also use test data provided by the school and the district to help you plan, in order to ensure that students learn.

Professional Development.   Teachers are involved in frequent and ongoing staff development designed to enhance skills, teach new methods, and ensure that teaching is aligned with standards. A large portion of your professional growth will occur through staff development designed to help you implement district and state standards.

Parent Involvement.   Parent and community involvement is highly valued and encouraged. As a result, you will spend more time and effort promoting and supporting family/parent/community collaboration. We will discuss the specifics of parent/community involvement in chapter 17.

Collaboration.   Teamwork and collaboration are a hallmark of the culture of many schools. Administrators and faculty understand that it takes teamwork to accomplish educational goals. Children with special learning needs rely on a team of professionals to help them succeed—for example, a psychologist, physical therapist, speech therapist, and an occupational therapist.

The primary grades of today are not the same as they were when you were there. Changing times and children demand different approaches. You and other early childhood professionals must look at the education of children in grades one to three with new eyes and a fresh approach.

WHAT ARE CHILDREN IN GRADES ONE TO THREE LIKE?

This text stresses the uniqueness and individuality of children, who also share common characteristics. Those common characteristics guide our practice of teaching, but we must always account for individual needs. All children are unique.

How are children of today different from the children of yesterday?

- Children of today are smarter than children of previous generations: average intelligence test scores have increased about three points over each decade.[2] There are a number of reasons for this: better health and nutrition, better educated parents, better schooling, and access to and involvement with technology, such as computers, electronic games, learning systems, and television.

Companion Website   To complete a Program in Action activity related to strategies for helping English language learners, go to the Companion Website at **www. prenhall.com/morrison**, select chapter 12, then choose the Program in Action module.

In the Primary Grade segment of the DVD, the narrator says that high-stakes testing has changed the way primary-grade teachers teach. Find examples of this change as you read this chapter.

- Many children bring to school a vast background of experiences that contribute to their knowledge and ability to learn.
- However, many children do *not* have a rich background separate from school experiences, and an increasing number are living in poverty. Today, 4.7 million children, or 20 percent of children under age six, live in poverty and come to school unprepared.[3]
- More children are members of minorities, although in many communities and schools, minority children make up the majority. Many children of minority populations come to school with health, home, and learning challenges.

Now let's take a look at six typical children in classrooms today so you can see what they are really like. After you review and reflect on the Portraits of First, Second, and Third Graders, answer the questions that accompany them.

PHYSICAL DEVELOPMENT

Two words describe the physical growth of primary-age children: *slow* and *steady*. Children at this age do not make the rapid and obvious height and weight gains of infants, toddlers, and preschoolers. Instead, they experience continual growth, develop increasing control over their bodies, and explore the things they are able to do. Primary children are building on the development of their earlier years.

From ages seven to eight, children's average weight and height approximate each other, as shown in Table 12.1. The weight of boys and girls tends to be the same until after age nine, when girls begin to pull ahead of boys in both height and weight. However, wide variations appear in both individual rates of growth and development and in the sizes of children. These differences in physical appearance result from genetic and cultural factors, nutritional intake and habits, health care, and experiential background.

MOTOR DEVELOPMENT

Six-year-old children are in the initiative stage of psychosocial development; seven- and eight-year-old children are in the industry stage. Thus, not only are children intuitively driven to initiate activities, but they are also learning to be competent and productive individuals. The primary years are a time to use and test developing motor skills. Children at this age should be actively involved in activities that enable them to use their bodies to learn and develop feelings of accomplishment and competence. Children's growing confidence and physical skills are reflected in games involving running, chasing, and their enthusiasm in organized sports of all kinds. A nearly universal characteristic of children in this period is their almost constant physical activity.

Differences between boys' and girls' motor skills during the primary years are minimal—their abilities are about equal. Teachers therefore should not use gender as a

TABLE 12.1 Average Height and Weight for First- to Third-Grade Children

| Age | Males | | Females | |
	Height (inches)	Weight (pounds)	Height (inches)	Weight (pounds)
7 years	48.0	50.0	48.5	50.0
7 ½ years	49.5	52.5	49.0	53.0
8 years	50.5	56.0	50.5	57.0
8 ½ years	52.0	60.0	51.5	60.0
9 years	53.0	63.0	52.5	64.0

Source: National Center for Health Statistics in collaboration with the National Center for Chronic Disease Prevention and Health Promotion (2004), *http://www.cdc.gov/growthcharts.*

PORTRAITS OF FIRST, SECOND, AND THIRD GRADERS

Kevin

Introduce yourself to Kevin, a seven-year-old Caucasian male with Down syndrome. He weighs 60 pounds and is 3 feet 8 inches tall. Kevin is a very friendly and sociable first grader and enjoys being with his classmates.

Social-Emotional	Cognitive	Motor	Adaptive
Tries hard to fit in with other children. Seeks approval from adults and does not like to disappoint. Is very likable and friendly. Has several classroom buddies he enjoys being with.	Has poor auditory memory. Needs constant prompting and reinforcement with concrete materials. Goes to the school speech therapist three times a week.	Has poor muscle tone. Likes to color and paint using large pencils, crayons, and brushes. Enjoys watching all kinds of sports on television. Is able to participate in soccer with help. Has an occupational therapist who helps with printing, cutting, etc.	Has mild asthma. Is learning how to help himself and be independent, with an emphasis on feeding, dressing, and grooming.

Mei Lei

Introduce yourself to Mei Lei, a seven-year-old Asian female. She weighs 49 pounds and is 4 feet tall. Mei Lei is very sensitive and emotional. She does well in first grade and loves to socialize, even during lessons! Mei Lei learns new concepts easily and enjoys doing school projects that involve creativity. She is very talented in science and math.

Social-Emotional	Cognitive	Motor	Adaptive
Gets her feelings hurt and cries easily. Likes to tell riddles and jokes. Has several best friends. Prefers to spend out-of-school time with her brother, sister, and parents.	Understands basic sentence structure. Likes to read books to herself. Writes short, fictional stories. Can count by 10s to 100.	Enjoys drawing detailed pictures. Likes to climb on the jungle gym. Loves to ride her bicycle. Creates dance routines with her friends.	Does household chores such as sweeping and dusting. Helps cook family meals and fix snacks. Does not like to go places at school (bathroom, office) unaccompanied by a friend.

- Do you think both Kevin and Mei Lei are going to achieve well and be successful in school? What is the basis for your opinion?
- Do you think that Kevin and Mei Lei are at risk in any way? If yes, in what ways? If no, why not?

- What are some major differences between Kevin and Mei Lei? How will these differences influence their learning in years to come?
- What can you do to ensure that Kevin's needs are met in your classroom?

Cameron

Introduce yourself to second grader Cameron, an eight-year-old Caucasian female. She weighs 55 pounds and is 4 feet 2 inches tall. Cameron needs time to adjust to new situations. She enjoys encouraging and supporting her peers. Her attention to detail helps her to be successful in writing and math.

Social-Emotional	Cognitive	Motor	Adaptive
Is very emotionally attached to her parents. Is shy in new situations. Is hesitant to ask questions. Is chatty once comfortable.	Uses periods and question marks appropriately when writing. Writes two-paragraph stories on one subject. Has well-developed math concepts and has mastered all the math standards for her grade. Is interested in details.	Has more developed fine-motor skills than others, especially boys. Can shoot a basketball while jumping. Likes to cheer on teammates when playing games. Wants to be on the school cheerleading squad.	Has limited attention span (around thirty minutes). Knows how to cross a street safely. Needs downtime to rest between activities. Needs help from her parents in new social situations and in meeting new people.

Peter

Introduce yourself to Peter, an eight-year-old Caucasian male who is in the second grade. He weighs 56 pounds and is 4 feet 1 inch tall. Peter is competitive; he wants to be the best and gets frustrated when he makes mistakes. He has a difficult time attending to classroom lessons that do not include active participation.

Social-Emotional	Cognitive	Motor	Adaptive
Shows off in new situations. Needs to stand at least every ten minutes. Is more aggressive than his peers. Gets frustrated easily. Prefers to play only with boys.	Has writing skills. Is confident with individual sounds. Is inquisitive but impatient. Likes to learn about and track weather; wants to be a weather forecaster. Enjoys science. Has difficulty with general math skills.	Has limited fine-motor skills. Does not like to write or paint. Does not like to take turns when playing games at recess. Is action oriented rather than verbal. Likes to pretend he is a superhero, especially Batman.	Is somewhat independent. Earns and manages his allowance at home. Knows how to stop, drop, and roll. Sometimes engages in risky activities at recess and at home.

- What could be some reasons that Peter needs a break every ten minutes?
- How can you structure your class schedule to meet the needs of children like Cameron, who needs a break between activities?
- How is Peter's temperament affecting his behavioral characteristics?
- What might be some reasons for Peter's aggressiveness? Do you think that Peter's aggressiveness and Cameron's shyness are wholly attributable to gender stereotypes?
- What can you do to help a shy child, such as Cameron, be more socially interactive?
- Why might Cameron's fine-motor skills be more developed than Peter's? What could you do to help bridge this gap?
- How can you encourage your students' independence while maintaining control of your classroom?

Chase

Introduce yourself to Chase, a nine-year-old Caucasian male who is in the third grade. He weighs 65 pounds and is 4 feet 7 inches tall. Chase is impulsive and social; he prefers to spend his time playing sports. Chase learns best by active participation and becomes more engaged in learning activities when they directly apply to his life.

Social-Emotional	Cognitive	Motor	Adaptive
Is extremely social.	Has difficulty reading at a third-grade level.	Is aggressive in physical play.	Knows adults who can help in an emergency.
Is trying to establish himself in a group.	Is a hands-on learner.	Can dribble and shoot a basketball very well.	Can take care of all of his personal needs without assistance.
Does not consider how his actions affect others.	Has trouble with word problems and general math.	Understands the rules of sports and games.	Likes to hang out with his older brother's friends, models their behavior.
Is extremely confident, or insecure, depending on the situation.	Likes physical education best.	Wants to be a professional athlete.	
	Has a limited attention span.		

Claudia

Introduce yourself to third grader Claudia, a nine-year-old Hispanic female. She weighs 69 pounds and is 4 feet 5 inches tall. Claudia participates in her school's gifted and talented program. She spends her free time reading or talking with older friends. Recently she has become concerned that her classmates, especially the boys, might think she is too smart.

Social-Emotional	Cognitive	Motor	Adaptive
Talks a lot and has an extensive vocabulary.	Is a voracious reader.	Can walk on a balance beam without falling.	Is very independent and likes to help others.
Prefers a few friends over a group of peers; has a number of friends in fourth and fifth grades.	Can read at a sixth-grade level.	Can hit a baseball, but without direction.	
	Is very curious.		Enjoys being with her aunt, who is a gourmet cook.
	Has an excellent memory.	Likes to play jump rope games.	
Is easily influenced by others.	Has excellent math skills.	Has excellent cursive writing skills.	Likes to wear the latest "tween" fashions.
Is very sensitive to others' feelings.			

- What specific abilities characterize Claudia as gifted?
- Claudia participates in a gifted pull-out program in which she spends two hours a day with other gifted students. How would you provide for Claudia's giftedness in your program?

- Chase and Claudia have different academic and social needs. Is it possible to accommodate their different needs and interests in the same classroom?
- How can you help Claudia accept the fact that she is gifted?
- What can you do to help assure that Claudia remains interested in math?

basis for determining involvement in activities. On the contrary, we should promote all children's involvement in age-appropriate activities.

During the primary years we see evidence of continuing refinement of fine-motor skills in children's mastery of many tasks they previously could not do or could do only with difficulty. They are now able to dress themselves relatively easily and attend to most of their personal needs. They are also more proficient at school tasks that require fine-motor skills such as writing, making artwork, and using computers and other technology. In addition, primary children want to and are able to engage in real-life activities; they want the real thing. This makes teaching them easier and more fun, because many activities have real-life applications.

COGNITIVE DEVELOPMENT

Children's cognitive development during the primary school years enables them to do things that they could not do as preschoolers. A major difference between these two age groups is that older children's thinking has become less egocentric and more logical (see chapter 10). Concrete operational thought is the cognitive milestone that enables children from about age seven to about age twelve to begin to use mental images and symbols during the thinking process; they begin to understand that a change in physical appearance does not necessarily change the quality or quantity of a substance. Thus, they are now capable of performing **operations**, mental actions such as reversibility, one-to-one correspondence, and various types of classification (see chapter 5).

Operations include many logico-mathe- matical activities involving addition and subtraction, greater than and less than, multiplication, division, and equalities. Children at this stage are able to reverse operations when they understand that adding two to three to get five can be reversed by subtracting two from five to get three. They are reversing their thought process by going back and undoing a mental action just accomplished. Because these children are not yet capable of abstract reasoning, their logical operations still require concrete objects and referents in the here and now. Consequently, it is a good idea to use physical materials (e.g., rods, beads, buttons, and blocks) to help them see these operations and support the mental representation.

MORAL DEVELOPMENT

Today, more than at any other time in the last decade, there is much concern about and interest in children's moral development. Especially since September 11, 2001, the nation has focused on issues of good character and moral behavior. In addition, teachers now realize that they cannot separate children's cognitive learning from their moral attitudes about life and learning. Let's review several theories of moral development that can inform your efforts to promote children's moral development and character education.

Piaget's Theory.   Piaget identified two stages of moral thinking typical of children in the elementary grades: **heteronomy**, being governed by others regarding right and wrong, and **autonomy**, being governed by oneself regarding right and wrong.

Although children in the primary grades do not grow physically as rapidly as when they were younger, the years between six and nine are important for cognitive growth. What role should professionals play in these formative years for children?

In the Primary Grade segment of the DVD, the narrator says that children are engaging in higher mental functions. Identify the functions that are characteristic of children in Piaget's concrete operations stage.

Operations   Mental actions that enable children to reason logically.

Heteronomy is characterized by **relations of constraint.** Through first and second grade, children's concepts of good and bad and right and wrong are determined by the judgments of adults. An act is wrong because a parent or teacher says it is wrong. Thus, children's understanding of morality is based on the authority of adults and those values that constrain them.

Gradually, as children mature and have opportunities for experiences with peers and adults (i.e., third grade and beyond), moral thinking may change to **relations of cooperation.** This stage of personal morality is characterized by an exchange of viewpoints among children and between children and adults about what is right, wrong, good, or bad. Autonomy is achieved by social experiences within which children may try out different ideas and discuss moral situations. Autonomous behavior does not mean that children agree or disagree with other children or adults but that they exchange opinions and try to negotiate solutions.

Vygotsky and Moral Autonomy. In chapter 5 we discussed Lev Vygotsky's zone of proximal development and the importance of having children collaborate with more competent peers and adults for cognitive and social development. According to Vygotsky, social interactions provide children with opportunities for scaffolding to higher levels of thinking and behavior. Furthermore, Vygotsky said that part of the professional's pedagogical role was to challenge and help children move to higher levels of thinking and, in this case, moral development. In chapter 14 you will read about specific ways to use scaffolding techniques to help children govern and guide their own behavior.

Kohlberg's Theory. Lawrence Kohlberg (1927–1987), a follower of Piaget, believed children's moral thinking occurs at three developmental levels: preconventional, conventional, and postconventional.[4] Children in the early childhood years are at the **preconventional level,** when morality is basically a matter of good or bad, based on a system of punishments and rewards administered by adults in authority positions.

In Stage 1, the **punishment and obedience orientation,** children respond to the physical consequences of behavior; they base their judgments on whether an action will bring pleasure. In Stage 2, the **instrumental-relativist orientation,** children's actions are motivated by satisfaction of needs. Consequently, interpersonal relations have their basis in mutual convenience based on need satisfaction ("You scratch my back; I'll scratch yours").

Just as Piaget's cognitive stages are fixed and invariant for all children, so too are Kohlberg's moral levels. All individuals move through the process of moral development beginning at level 1 and progressing through each level. No level can be skipped, but each individual does not necessarily achieve every level. Just as intellectual development may become fixed at a particular level of development, so may an individual become fixed at any one of the moral levels.

Implications for Teachers. All of these theories have implications for primary-grade classroom practice:

- All teachers must like and respect children.
- The classroom climate must support individual values. Teachers and schools must be willing to deal with the issues, morals, and value systems children bring to school.
- A sense of justice must prevail in schools, instead of the injustice that can arise from arbitrary institutional values.
- Children must have opportunities to interact with peers, children of different age groups and cultures, and adults in order to move to the higher levels of moral functioning.
- Students must have opportunities to make moral decisions and judgments and discuss the results of their decision making. Responsibility comes from being given opportunities to be responsible.

Heteronomy The stage of moral thinking in which children are governed by others regarding matters of right and wrong.

Autonomy The stage of moral thinking in which children govern their own actions and thoughts about what is right and wrong.

Relations of constraint Children's reliance on others to determine right and wrong.

Relations of cooperation Children's engagement with others in making decisions about good, bad, right, or wrong.

Preconventional level The first level in Kohlberg's theory of moral development, when morality is based on punishment and rewards.

Punishment and obedience orientation The first stage of preconventional moral development, when children make moral decisions based on physical consequences.

Instrumental-relativist orientation The second stage of preconventional moral development, when children's actions are motivated by satisfaction of their needs.

Companion Website To complete a Program in Action activity related to character education, go to the Companion Website at **www. prenhall.com/morrison**, select chapter 12, then choose the Program in Action module.

THE GIRAFFE HEROES PROGRAM

The Giraffe Heroes Program for six- to eight-year-olds provides kindergarten, first-, and second-grade teachers with teaching assistants—Stan and Bea Tall, twin giraffes who go through the program with the class, learning character, service, active citizenship, social skills, and emotional intelligence along with the children. Stan and Bea are young friends, trying, just as the children are, to figure out how the world works and what their roles in it are.

Stan and Bea don't come into the classroom with lists of character traits or lectures on the importance of honesty or perseverance. They just go wherever the children are and help them move from there to experiences that bring forth the children's own innate compassion and desire to contribute to their world. Stan, Bea, and the children learn together to be brave, caring, and responsible.

As classroom puppets with voices on audiotapes, Stan and Bea tell the children stories that give them models for meaningful lives. The heroes of these stories are giraffes because they stick their necks out to make the world a better place. The teacher's guide includes print, audio, and video stories of over thirty human giraffes. These stories of real heroes are from the files of the nonprofit Giraffe Project, which has been finding and commending real heroes since 1982.

HEAR, TELL, BECOME THE STORY

Hearing these stories, kids understand what real heroism is about, despite the cultural messages that tell them that heroes are bulletproof cartoon figures, athletes, or entertainers. That's Stage I of the program, Hear the Story. In Stage II, Tell the Story, the children look in their studies, in the media, and in their communities for real heroes and tell these stories to the class. Then comes putting all they've learned into action—Become the Story, Stage III.

Stan and Bea guide the children through a process called Seven Neckbones (because giraffe and human necks have just seven bones). Doing the Neckbones takes students from looking at problems that concern them through successfully creating and carrying out a service project that addresses one of those problems. Key to the program is the respect given to children's concerns and ideas; they drive the program. The effect on the children is powerful as they realize that their unvoiced concerns can be voiced, that their participation in their community is wanted and valued. In contrast to the lukewarm response sometimes evoked by being directed into a service program, the enthusiasm of students is high when they invent their own programs.

As in all good programs that include service learning, students experience the practical value of academic skills as they carry out their projects. An independent study of the program's contents to determine its essential learnings yielded this list:

Communications

- Listen and observe to gain and interpret information
- Check for understanding by asking questions and paraphrasing

Teachers of primary students should look for opportunities every day to present moral values and decisions. Examples can come from stories or from discussions about heroes in the community. The Giraffe Heroes Program, described in the Program in Action uses exactly this foundation to involve students in meaningful service projects. Children's out-of-classroom experiences can also prompt discussions of moral values. What is most important with any approach is that students have many chances to actually *practice* their moral decision making. Knowing children's stages of moral development will help you guide them in this important area.

- Communicate clearly to a range of audiences
- Develop content and ideas
- Use effective delivery
- Use language to interact effectively
- Work cooperatively as a member of a group
- Seek agreement and solutions through discussion
- Analyze mass communications

Civics

- Examine representative government and citizen participation
- Understand individual rights and accompanying responsibilities
- Identify and demonstrate rights of U.S. citizenship
- Explain how citizen participation influences public policy

Social Studies

- Identify and examine people's interactions with the environment
- Examine cultural differences

Math

- Relate mathematical concepts and procedures to real-life situations

Science

- Examine environmental and resource issues

REVIEWS OF THE PROGRAM

Kids who have done the Giraffe Heroes Program know that they are more than consumers of cereal, cartoons, CDs, and sneakers—they are brave, caring young people who can make good things happen in their world.

In reviewing the Giraffe Heroes Program, Dee Dickinson, founder of New Horizons for Learning, said, "It is never too early to help children develop the character traits the world needs so urgently—altruism, compassion, generosity, and responsible citizenship. The Giraffe Heroes

Program for K–2 offers an engaging, age-appropriate series of lessons that are creative, interesting, humorous, and highly motivating. This program can fit easily into any curriculum and can facilitate the learning of reading, writing, and communication skills. What a great start for lifelong learning!"

Former teacher Paula Mirk, now of the Institute for Global Ethics, said in her review, "Every time I imagine the children who get to experience this approach I think how lucky they are and how much I'd  have used something like this if I'd had it in my own classroom. I predict it will become a significant cornerstone in character education for very young children. What I like best about it is the consistent attention to respecting 'where young children are at' throughout. Text directed at the teacher constantly reminds us that young children deserve very special handling, and then the structure of the curriculum makes such care very easy and a matter of course. The layout and organization of the curriculum is very simple and easy to follow."

THE MATERIALS

Teachers are given lesson plans, scheduling suggestions, ideas on using the program for standard curriculum goals, handout masters, overhead transparencies, and templates for visuals. The guide includes a video about the Giraffe Project from public television that can be used for teacher and parent orientation, and it also includes two audiotapes for the classroom. There are thirty giraffe heroes stories, each with a photograph.

Visit the Giraffe Heroes Project on the Web at http://www.giraffe.org.

Contributed by Jennifer Sand, education director, Giraffe Heroes Program. Photos contributed by Kathy Frazier and Charlie Lawhead.

CHARACTER EDUCATION

Moral development is closely aligned with character education, which is rapidly becoming a part of many early childhood classrooms across the United States. Whereas everyone believes that children have to learn how to count, growing numbers of individuals also believe that schools have to teach children *what* counts. As character education is becoming a higher priority, curricula designed to teach specific character traits are now commonplace. In fact, the early childhood curriculum now consists of the six Rs: *r*eading, *w*riting, a*r*ithmetic, *r*easoning, *r*espect, and *r*esponsibility.

Companion Website
To learn more about character education, go to the Companion Website at **www.prenhall.com/ morrison,** select chapter 12, then choose the Linking to Learning module.

Voice from the Field

TEACHING CHARACTER IN EVERYTHING YOU DO

When I began my teaching career, many students received moral instruction from their home or church. However, times change, and over the years I realized that there was a strong need for the teaching of values in schools. When character education was introduced into our school system, I was asked to be on the task force to develop plans for a curriculum. It was exciting to know that our system valued strong ethics and that we would be encouraged to integrate values into our curriculum.

SCHOOLWIDE INITIATIVES

Teaching with puppets was just one of the techniques I adopted to model concepts to my students and to share character education with the entire school. By working with the school administrators, the guidance counselor, and the elementary-grade teachers, I was able to organize a puppet team. We set up first- and second-semester teams to provide opportunities for more students to participate.

I write the skits using ideas from Thomas Lickona's book *Educating for Character,* William Bennett's *Book of Virtues,* and other literature that stresses morals, along with suggestions made by students and faculty. Using school puppets and ethnically appropriate materials of my own, the skits are performed five to six times a year at our Terrific Kids assemblies, which are sponsored by the local Kiwanis Club. Each assembly emphasizes a monthly character word.

This project has led to the start of two other programs that reinforce positive values: the Kids for Character Club, which meets monthly, and the Hillcrest Hornet TV News, a video shown to our entire school each Friday. Two Kids for Character Club representatives are chosen each semester by their teachers: one student who already models good behavior and one who may need more assistance in consistently demonstrating good character skills. Club activities include decorating character education bulletin boards, making cards for the skilled nursing home of Burlington, and planting flower bulbs on the school grounds. Club members have also encouraged their classmates to fill shoe boxes for distribution to needy children. These opportunities have provided Hillcrest students with opportunities to develop their character skills. As a result, parents and educators who visit our school have noticed the positive environment. The students are polite to each other and respectful of adults, and everyone takes care of our facility.

CHARACTER EDUCATION IN MY CLASSROOM

Although I enjoy these opportunities to promote character education throughout the school, my top priority is

All character education programs seek to teach a set of traditional core values that will result in civic virtue and moral character, including honesty, kindness, respect, responsibility, tolerance for diversity, racial harmony, and good citizenship. Efforts to promote character qualities and values are evident in school and statewide efforts. For example, all school districts in the state of Georgia are required to implement a comprehensive character education program for all children. Some of the traits included are honesty, fairness, responsibility for others, kindness, cooperation, self-control, and self-respect.

In the Voice from the Field "Teaching Character in Everything You Do," Carol Cates, the 1999 North Carolina Educator of the Year, shares some creative ideas for character development.

PRIMARY EDUCATION TODAY

In the last five years, the educational spotlight has cast its beam on the primary grades, where the academic rubber really hits the road. Grades one to three are more academically challenging and rigorous now than they have ever been. Politicians and educational reformers use the third grade as the demarcation for standards of achievement and grade

teaching twenty-two lively first graders. Character education is woven into all of our basic curriculum activities. Children become aware of the positive impact they have on others by demonstrating good character skills.

So that children can broaden their perceptions, I help them understand that their world is larger than their immediate neighborhood. We do many activities:

- Read books that teach character traits, often referring to the list of traits adopted by our school system
- Read the daily newspaper, locating cities and countries on our world and state maps
- Use the special kids sections of the *Times News* (Character Counts and the Kids Scoop pages) to understand the importance of good character skills
- Use visitors and artifacts from other states and countries to help students compare where they live with other areas so that they can appreciate the similarities and differences, eliminate prejudice, and accept cultural differences
- Study the traditions of other cultures and have international tasting parties with food, games, folktales, or stories about the cultures
- Write letters to soldiers for several holidays, including Veterans Day
- Make encouragement cards and small gifts for the cafeteria and maintenance workers and staff
- Send thank-you notes and remembrance cards to parents and grandparents for sharing items or time with our class
- Write to other classes and school groups to express gratitude and encouragement when they have performed for our school

In order to inform parents and let them know how their children are doing, we do a number of other things:

- I give parents an update on their child's character development in report cards.
- I write notes to parents to keep them abreast of their children's progress.
- Students write to their parents when they have disturbed the class with inappropriate behavior. The note indicates the character skill that was not demonstrated (e.g., "I did not show respect"), and the child finishes the note by explaining how he or she will improve the next time that situation occurs.
- Students take home "good" notes that I have made and others we write together.

THE "MORAL" OF THE STORY

Character development is an ongoing process: It needs to be a part of each day's expectations, and children need to learn how to practice virtues and ethics at an early age. When teachers expect and stress values in their classrooms, children understand and use methods of problem solving. When students know they are to practice character skills during transition times each day, these skills continue at home and in the community.

What is the value of teaching character skills all day every day in every way? Consistently teaching children character values that are interwoven with all of the curriculum areas helps children realize that character is a part of everything they do in life and that demonstrating good character is a gift they can share with others.

Contributed by Carol Cates, first grade teacher, Hillcrest Elementary School, North Carolina, and 1999 North Carolina Educator of the Year.

promotion or retention. The federal government talks about all children being able to read on grade level by grade three. Thus, even though all teachers preK through three are responsible for ensuring that all children achieve this goal, it is in the third grade that this goal is measured and decisions are made about whether children will be promoted or retained. In 2002 in Chicago's public schools, 13,308 students in grades three, six, and eight did not qualify for promotion to the next grade.[5] One of your major challenges of teaching in grades one to three will be to ensure that all of your children learn and achieve so that they can be promoted with their peers.

STATE STANDARDS

Review again our discussion of state and national standards in chapter 2 and the ways they are changing teaching and learning in all grades. All fifty states have statewide academic standards, and all have some kind of test to measure how well students are learning and, in many cases, how well students and schools are meeting the set standards. Figure 12.1 shows selected state standards from Florida (first-grade language arts/reading) and California (second-grade science and third-grade mathematics). Standards are not only changing what students learn but are also changing how teachers teach. Let's look at some of the changes standards are making.

In the Primary Grade segment of the DVD, the narrator says that education today is all about passing state standards. Give examples of how you will address standards but also teach in a developmentally appropriate manner.

FIGURE 12.1
Selected State Standards

Sources: Reprinted by permission from the Florida Department of Education, "Sunshine State Standards" (2006), www.flrn.edu/doe/curric/prek12/frame2.htm. Also from the California State Board of Education, "Content Standards," www.cde.ca.gov/be/st/ss/.

Florida—First-Grade Language Arts/Reading

a. Uses prior knowledge, illustrations, and text to make predictions

b. Uses basic elements of phonetic analysis

c. Uses sound/symbol relationships as visual cues for decoding

d. Uses beginning letters and patterns as visual cues for decoding

e. Uses structural cues to decode words

f. Uses context clues to construct meaning

g. Cross-checks visual, structural, and meaning cues to figure out unknown words

h. Knows common words from within basic categories

i. Uses knowledge of individual words in unknown compound words to predict their meaning

j. Uses resources and references to build on word meanings

k. Uses knowledge of suffixes to determine meanings of words

l. Develops vocabulary by listening to and discussing both familiar and conceptually challenging selections read aloud

m. Uses a variety of strategies to comprehend text

n. Knows the main idea or theme and supporting details of a story or informational piece

o. Uses specific details and information from a text to answer literal questions

p. Makes inferences based on text and prior knowledge

q. Identifies similarities and differences between two texts

r. Selects material to read for pleasure

s. Reads aloud familiar stories, poems, and passages

t. Reads for information used in performing tasks

u. Uses background knowledge and supporting reasons from the text to determine whether a story or text is fact or fiction

v. Uses simple reference material to obtain information

w. Alphabetizes words according to the initial letter

x. Uses alphabetical order to locate information

California—Second-Grade Science

Physical Sciences

a. Knows that the position of an object can be described by locating it in relation to another object or to the background

b. Knows that an object's motion can be described by recording the change in position of the object over time

c. Knows the way to change how something is moving by giving it a push or a pull (the size of the change is related to the strength, or the amount of force, of the push or pull)

d. Knows that tools and machines are used to apply pushes and pulls (forces) to make things move

e. Knows that objects fall to the ground unless something holds them up

f. Knows that magnets can be used to make some objects move without being touched

g. Knows that sound is made by vibrating objects and can be described by its pitch and volume

Life Sciences

a. Knows that organisms reproduce offspring of their own kind and that the offspring resemble their parents and one another

b. Knows that the sequential stages of life cycles are different for different animals, such as butterflies, frogs, and mice

c. Knows that many characteristics of an organism are inherited from the parents

d. Knows that characteristics are caused or influenced by the environment

e. Knows that there is variation among individuals of one kind within a population

f. Knows that light, gravity, touch, or environmental stress can affect the germination, growth, and development of plants

g. Knows that flowers and fruits are associated with reproduction in plants

Earth Sciences

a. Knows how to compare the physical properties of different kinds of rocks and knows that rock is composed of different combinations of minerals

b. Knows that smaller rocks come from the breakage and weathering of larger rocks

c. Knows that soil is made partly from weathered rock and partly from organic materials and that soils differ in their color, texture, capacity to retain water, and ability to support the growth of many kinds of plants

d. Knows that fossils provide evidence about the plants and animals that lived long ago and that scientists learn about the past history of Earth by studying fossils

e. Knows that rock, water, plants, and soil provide many resources, including food, fuel, and building materials that humans use

Investigation and Experimentation

a. Makes predictions based on observed patterns and not random guessing

b. Measures length, weight, temperature, and liquid volume with appropriate tools and expresses those measurements in standard metric system units

c. Compares and sorts common objects according to two or more physical attributes (e.g., color, shape, texture, size, weight)

d. Writes or draws descriptions of a sequence of steps, events, and observations

e. Constructs bar graphs to record data, using appropriately labeled axes

f. Uses magnifiers or microscopes to observe and draw descriptions of small objects or small features of objects

g. Follows oral instructions for a scientific investigation

California—Third-Grade Mathematics

a. Understands the place value of whole numbers

b. Calculates and solves problems involving addition, subtraction, multiplication, and division

c. Understands the relationship between whole numbers, simple fractions, and decimals

d. Selects appropiate symbols, operations, and properties to represent, describe, simplify, and solve simple number relationships

e. Represents simple functional relationships

f. Chooses and uses appropriate units and measurement tools to quantify the properties of objects

g. Describes and compares the attributes of plane and solid geometric figures and uses their understanding to show relationships and solve problems

h. Conducts simple probability experiments by determining the number of possible outcomes and makes simple predictions

i. Makes decisions about how to approach problems

j. Uses strategies, skills, and concepts in finding solutions

k. Moves beyond a particular problem by generalizing to other situations

Teacher Roles.   Standards have transformed (some would say reformed) teaching from an input model to an output model. As a result, teachers are no longer able to say, "I taught Mario the use of structural cues to decode words." Now the questions are, "Is Mario able to use and apply decoding skills?" and "Will Mario do well on decoding skills on the state test?" Good teachers have good ideas about what and how to teach, and they always will. However, the time and opportunity to act on those good ideas are reduced by increasing requirements to teach to the standards and teach so that students will master the standards.

Curriculum Alignment.   Teaching issues are as old as teaching itself and involve frequently asked questions, such as What should I teach? and How should I teach it? As usual, the answer is, It depends. It depends on what you and other teachers think is important and what national, state, and local standards say is important. Therein lies the heart of the issue: how to develop meaningful curriculum that is aligned with standards. Learning how to develop a strong lesson plan that also meets state standards is important for all teachers. The Program in Action "How to Plan Lessons That Meet Standards" on pages 360–361 is a Competency Builder that will help you master this critical capability.

Increasing student achievement is at the center of the standards movement. Policymakers and educators view standards, tests, and teaching alignment as a viable and practical way to help ensure student achievement. **Alignment** is the arrangement of standards, curriculum, and tests so that they complement one another. In other words, the curriculum should be based on what the standards say students should know and be able to do; tests should measure what the standards indicate.

Florida has aligned its standards (Florida Sunshine Standards), its assessment system (Florida Comprehensive Assessment Test [FCAT]), and the Governors A+ Program, which grades schools based on how well they score on the FCAT. Such alignment of state standards with curriculum, tests, and school ranking represents a comprehensive approach to educational reform, which is influencing teaching in the elementary grades.

Curriculum alignment is the process of making sure that what is taught—the content of the curriculum—matches what the standards say students should know and be able to do. One way educators achieve alignment is through the use of a **curriculum framework,** a blueprint for implementing content standards. According to the Alaska Department of Education, a curriculum framework serves numerous functions:

Alignment The arrangement of standards, curriculum, and tests so they are in agreement.

Curriculum alignment The process of making sure that what is taught matches the standards.

Curriculum framework A blueprint for implementing content standards.

- A summary of the educational issues facing curriculum development committees
- A discussion of how state goals and standards relate to those issues
- A structure to help district curriculum development committees address the state's student standards
- A guide for planning professional development
- A guide to recommended instructional and assessment strategies
- A description of effective instruction and assessment strategies with an analysis of how they address the standards
- A collection of reference materials to assist curriculum development committees and other educators
- A tool to communicate the goals of the standards to the community[6]

Some school districts also specify or suggest instructional activities and strategies for teachers to use so that the curriculum is implemented in ways that meet the standards.

TEACHING PRACTICES

A lot of change has occurred in the primary grades, with more on the way. Single-subject teaching and learning are out; integration of subject areas is in. Curriculum leaders want to help students relate what they learn in math to what they learn in science, and they want them to know that literacy is applied across the curriculum. Helping students make sense of and apply what they learn to all areas of the curriculum and to life is one goal of contemporary curriculum reform.

In the Primary Grade segment of the DVD, listen to what the narrator says about journal writing and reading. How does journal writing also support math, science, and social studies?

Having students sit in single seats in straight rows, solitarily doing their own work, is out; having them learn together in small groups is in. Textbooks are used in conjunction with hands-on and active learning. Facilitation, collaboration, cooperative discipline, and coaching are in. **Intentional teaching** is becoming more popular as teachers teach children the skills they need for success. Letter grades and report cards are still very popular, although narrative reports (in which professionals describe and report on student achievement), checklists (which describe the competencies students have demonstrated), parent conferences, portfolios containing samples of children's work, and other tools for reporting achievement are being used to supplement letter grades.

Although Dewey's progressive education ideas are still cultivated in the fertile hearts and minds of early childhood professionals, in many respects there is a decided back-to-basics movement in the United States today, and it is influencing the primary curriculum. The primary grades are experiencing the swinging pendulum of educational change, which is moving from less rigorous learning to strong academics.

THINKING ACROSS THE CURRICULUM

We generally think of basic skills as reading, writing, and arithmetic, and many elementary schools give these subjects the major share of time and emphasis. However, some critics believe that the *real* basic skill of education is **thinking**. Their rationale is that if students can think, they can meaningfully engage in subject matter, as well as the rigors and demands of the workplace and life. Increasingly, thinking and problem-solving skills are coming to be regarded as no less basic than math facts, spelling, knowledge of geography, and so on.

As a result, teachers are including the teaching of thinking in their daily lesson plans, using both direct and indirect methods of instruction. A trend in curriculum and instruction today is to infuse the teaching of thinking across the curriculum and make it a part of the culture of a classroom, much as teachers are doing with literacy.

In classrooms that emphasize thinking, students are encouraged to use their power of analysis, and teachers ask higher-level questions. Table 12.2 gives examples of questions teachers can use following Benjamin Bloom's hierarchy of thinking levels. One teaching objective is to ask students questions across the hierarchy, from top to bottom. Teachers are being encouraged to challenge their children to think about classroom information and learning material, rather than merely memorizing acceptable responses.

COOPERATIVE LEARNING

You can probably remember competing with other kids when you were in grade school. You may have tried to see whether you could be the first to raise your hand, leaning out over the front of your seat and frantically waving for your teacher's attention. However, in many of today's primary classrooms, the emphasis is on cooperation, not competition.

Cooperative learning is a teaching and learning strategy in which students are encouraged to work together in small, mixed-ability learning groups of usually four members, with each member responsible for learning and for helping all other members learn. Remember Vygotsky's theory that children learn through interactions with adults and more capable peers. In cooperative learning projects, children experience their peers' thinking and behavioral processes, thereby learning how others solve problems and

Intentional teaching
Developing plans, selecting instructional strategies, and teaching to promote learning.

Thinking   Reasoning about or reflecting on something.

Cooperative learning   A teaching strategy in which small groups of children work together on a variety of learning activities to improve their understanding of a topic, with each member responsible for learning what is taught and helping teammates learn.

Small group communities encourage children to work together, to learn from each other, and to succeed through their combined efforts. What are some things you can do to support small group learning?

TABLE 12.2   Applying Bloom's Taxonomy to Early Childhood Classrooms

Competence	Skills Demonstrated	Sample Questions
Knowledge	• Observation and recall of information • Knowledge of dates, events, places • Knowledge of major ideas • Mastery of subject matter • *Question cues:* list, define, tell, describe, identify, show, label, collect, examine, tabulate, quote, name, who, when, where	• How would you describe the size of an elephant? • Tell me three things that you can do with a soccer ball.
Comprehension	• Understands information • Grasps meaning • Translates knowledge into new context • Interprets facts, compares, contrasts • Orders, groups, infers causes • Predicts consequences • *Question cues:* summarize, describe, interpret, contrast, predict, associate, distinguish, estimate, differentiate, discuss, extend	• How are sounds different (contrasting)? • What is the main idea or point of the book we just read together? Explain.
Application	• Uses information • Uses methods, concepts, theories in new situations • Solves problems using required skills or knowledge • *Question cues:* apply, demonstrate, calculate, complete, illustrate, show, solve, examine, modify, relate, change, classify, experiment, discover	• Construct two buildings in the math area, one tall building and one short building. • How would you organize your paintings to show your mother which one you painted first and which one you painted last?
Analysis	• Seeing patterns • Organization of parts • Recognition of hidden meanings • Identification of components • *Question cues:* analyze, separate, order, explain, connect, classify, arrange, divide, compare, select, explain, infer	• What are the parts of the clarinet? Why do you think the bottom of the clarinet is bell-shaped? • If you see your friend lying down on the playground, crying, what do you suppose happened that caused your friend to do that?
Synthesis	• Uses old ideas to create new ones • Generalizes from given facts • Relates knowledge from several areas • Predicts, draws conclusions • *Question cues:* combine, integrate, modify, rearrange, substitute, plan, create, design, invent, what if?, compose, formulate, prepare, generalize, rewrite	• Can you create a new color by mixing paints? Predict what color the new color will be most like. • Imagine yourself as a Pilgrim boy or girl. How would your life be the same as it is now? How would your life be different than it is now?
Evaluation	• Compares and discriminates between ideas • Assesses value of theories, presentations • Makes choices based on reasoned argument • Verifies value of evidence • Recognizes subjectivity • *Question cues:* assess, decide, rank, grade, test, measure, recommend, convince, select, judge, explain, discriminate, support, conclude, compare, summarize	• Let's decide what the three most important rules of our classroom should be. • Which one of your paintings is your favorite? Why?

Source: Reprinted by permission from Counseling Services—University of Victoria, "Learning Skills Program" (2002), http://www.coun. uvic.ca/learn/program/hndouts/bloom.html.

thus becoming more competent problem solvers themselves. In addition, more capable peers may be able to scaffold less capable students' learning.

Children in a cooperative learning group are assigned certain responsibilities; for example, there is a group leader, who announces the problems or task; a praiser, who praises group members for their answers and work; and a checker. Responsibilities rotate as the group engages in different tasks. Children are encouraged to develop and use interpersonal skills, such as addressing classmates by their first names, saying thank you, and explaining why they are proposing an answer.

Cooperative learning is seen as a way to boost student achievement and positively enhance the climate of the classroom. Supporters maintain that it enables children to learn from each other and to learn cooperative skills. It makes sense that teachers would want to use a child-centered approach that increases student achievement. In addition, if classrooms are frequently too competitive and students who are neither competitive nor high achievers are left behind, cooperative learning would seem to be one of the better ways to reduce classroom competition and foster helping attitudes.

LITERACY AND READING

Just like preschool and kindergarten programs, today's primary grades emphasize literacy development and reading. In fact, this emphasis is apparent in all the elementary grades, from preK to six. Parents and society want children who can speak, write, and read well. As discussed in chapter 11 and as a result of No Child Left Behind, more teachers are adopting a balanced approach. They integrate many different activities into a complete system of literacy development:

- Using the fundamentals of letter-sound correspondence, word study, and decoding, as well as holistic experiences, in reading, writing, speaking, and listening
- Incorporating many reading approaches, such as shared reading (see chapter 11), guided reading (discussed next), independent reading, and modeled reading (reading out loud)
- Using many forms of writing, such as shared writing, guided writing, and independent writing
- Integrating literacy across the curriculum; for example, having students write in journals or composition books about their experiences and investigations in math and science
- Integrating literacy across cultures, that is, using literacy to communicate with and about people in other cultures, part of the mission of World Wise Schools, as described in the accompanying Diversity Tie-In on pages 362–363.
- Using children's written documents as reading material, as well as literature books, vocabulary-controlled and sentence-controlled stories, and those containing predictable language patterns; choosing the best children's literature available to read to and with children
- Organizing literacy instruction around themes or units of study relevant to students
- Having children create stories, write letters, keep personal journals, and share their written documents with others

Connections with others, especially families, are important in making literacy meaningful for children; recall Bronfenbrenner's theory about ecological systems (see chapter 5) and the significance of the home-school connection. The final Voice from the Field on page 364 presents innovative approaches to strengthening these connections in order to support literacy.

GUIDED READING

Guided reading is designed to help children develop and use strategies of independent reading. During guided reading, children read texts that are at their developmentally

In the Primary Grade segment of the DVD, the narrator states that Vygotsky's theory supports the use of cooperative learning. Find specific examples in the DVD of children's learning moving from the social to the internal.

Companion Website To complete a Diversity Tie-In activity related to World Wise Schools, go to the Companion Website at **www.prenhall.com/morrison**, select chapter 12, then choose the Diversity Tie-In module.

Today, teachers provide multiple opportunities for their students to use literacy and reading skills in all subject areas. Here students have to read and follow directions for making a telescope.

HOW TO PLAN LESSONS THAT MEET STANDARDS

When sitting down to create lesson plans, I always keep the following quotation in mind: "You cannot control the wind [i.e., state or district standards] but you can adjust your sails [i.e., personal lesson plans]." As you review the following steps, also review the state standards in Figure 12.1. And remember that lesson plans are to *guide* instruction; they are not a blueprint that must control your every word. You should always follow a wonderful teachable moment, even if it is not written into your lesson plan. You will never regret where it leads you and your students.

STEP 1 Become familiar with both state and district standards

The objectives in my district's teacher's guide are clearly stated and are usually cross-referenced with the broader Florida Sunshine State Standards. Realize that standards encompass broad categories and often do not change significantly from one grade level to another. For example, "Reads for meaning" and "Uses context clues" apply to many grade levels; what changes is the level of presentation.

STEP 2 Incorporate in your plans what will be assessed on high-stakes tests

I work into my lesson plans for all subjects the Florida Comprehensive Assessment Test task cards (e.g., compare/contrast, vocabulary, author's purpose, main idea, details, multiple representations of information, cause and effect) and the big five literacy components—phonological awareness, phonics, vocabulary, comprehension, and fluency.

STEP 3 Plan a week ahead

Planning ahead has several advantages:

- As you plan ahead, you think ahead. Just thinking about what you're going to teach enables you to see how standards and your instructional practices fit together.

- Planning ahead allows you to share ideas with your colleagues, get their advice, and make changes as appropriate.
- Planning ahead gives you time to gather all necessary materials and resources.

STEP 4 Meet with other teachers to coordinate plans

As the chairperson for grade three, I hold a weekly planning meeting with the other third-grade teachers. We explore the information required to be presented the following week and plan together. Because my district uses the same authored curriculum across the county, we all teach from a particular reading series. This is extremely helpful with our somewhat-transient population in Miami and allows for continuity as students move.

STEP 5 Create and save a framework for your lesson plans

Because parts of lessons are repeated week after week, using a consistent framework saves valuable time. On a computer I can cut and paste from week to week, adding or removing entries quickly. The table included on the next page shows a sample format, using Sunshine State Standards for literacy for third grade.

STEP 6 Differentiate instruction

Once the framework for lesson planning is understood, you are ready to "adjust your sails"—that is, differentiate your instruction. As an inclusion teacher (see chapter 16), one-third of my students have exceptional needs, so I differentiate my instruction. I must adjust my presentation rather than expecting my learners to modify themselves to my presentation. Because there are varied abilities and disabilities within any given classroom, instructional practices and approaches should always be adapted to the students served within the classroom. In other words, instruction should meet the learners wherever they are and appeal to them on a multisensory level.

For instance, I plan vocabulary practice daily within every lesson plan (e.g., math vocabulary, science vocabulary, story vocabulary). Because not all students are at the same level in vocabulary development, I do the following:

- Present vocabulary on an overhead
- Use colored markers on the overhead to separate and isolate vocabulary words
- Use hearing and seeing sticks (i.e., rulers with an ear or an eye and a vocabulary word stapled on them). Students raise the stick when they hear or see the vocabulary word.
- Use a highlighter stick (i.e., a yardstick with an index card stapled to the end of it). When the vocabulary words are projected on the wall, I can hold the index card over a word and actually lift the word off the wall by lifting the card.

OTHER PLANNING AND INSTRUCTIONAL GUIDELINES

I recommend overplanning. Activities that you think will take a certain amount of time will often take much less or much more. This is fine—you are working with children! Simply cut and paste a missed lesson into the next week's framework, or discontinue a lesson that is not working for you and move on to your next planned activity.

I also recommend moving your students often. Begin with a whole-group activity, and then transition to a partner activity. I place my students in groups of six rather than having them sit in rows. Within each grouping I place at least two children with special needs and have the group come up with a name and work as a small community. I also set up centers that allow for higher-order processing. Centers give me an opportunity to work with some students who may require more intensive instruction.

Lesson planning is a learned skill, and learned skills take time to master. Ask to see other teachers' lesson plans, ask them what works, and use any ideas that interest you.

Contributed by Lynn Carrier, third-grade teacher, Gulfstream Elementary, Miami, Florida, and 2007 Miami-Dade County Teacher of the Year.

Reading/Language Arts (8:30–10:35 AM): Story Selection—*Across the Wide Dark Sea*

MONDAY	TUESDAY	WEDNESDAY	THURSDAY	FRIDAY
Standard 1: Reads text and determines the main idea	*Standard 2:* Identifies the author's purpose	*Standard 3:* Recognizes when a text is primarily intended to persuade	*Standard 4:* Identifies specific personal preferences relative to fiction and nonfiction reading	*Standard 5:* Reads and organizes information for a variety of purposes
Objective:	Objective:	Objective:	Objective:	Objective:
Activities:	Activities:	Activities:	Activities:	Activities:
ESOL strategies:	ESOL strategies:	ESOL strategies:	ESOL strategies:	ESOL strategies:
Vocabulary:	Vocabulary:	Vocabulary:	Vocabulary:	Vocabulary:
Home learning:	Home learning:	Home learning:	Home learning:	Home learning:
Assessment:	Assessment:	Assessment:	Assessment:	Assessment:

WORLD WISE SCHOOLS

MISSION

The World Wise Schools program puts Peace Corps volunteers in touch with U.S. classrooms so they can correspond. It also produces innovative educational resources that promote cross-cultural understanding and encourage public service among America's youth.

HISTORY

Since its inception in 1989 by Paul D. Coverdell, World Wise Schools has helped more than two million U.S. students communicate directly with Peace Corps volunteers all over the world. Over the past ten years it has expanded its scope by providing a broad range of resources for educators—including award-winning videos, teacher guides, classroom speakers, an e-newsletter, and online resources.

World Wise Schools participants often find that with increased awareness of cultural diversity around the world, students come to value the rich heritage and broad representation of peoples within their own communities.

RESOURCES FOR ELEMENTARY EDUCATORS

Most programs and classroom resources are available free of charge for teachers in the United States. The resources highlighted here are those most appropriate for use with students in kindergarten through grade three and focus on providing connections with children around the world.

Correspondence Match Program

The foundation of the World Wise Schools program, the Correspondence Match Program has helped more than two million U.S. students communicate directly with Peace Corps volunteers in more than eighty countries. Through the exchange of letters, artwork, artifacts, and other educational materials, Peace Corps volunteers lead U.S. students in an exploration of other countries and cultures of the world.

When possible, the Peace Corps volunteer selected for the correspondence match comes from the same city or state as the participating classroom. Teachers may ask to be matched with a volunteer living in a certain region of the world or one who is working in a certain type of program (e.g., agriculture, business, education, forestry, health). Teachers may indicate their preferences on the enrollment form.

To assist teachers with the correspondence, World Wise Schools provides a handbook of ideas on how to fos-

appropriate reading level and have a minimum of new things to learn. The children read in small groups (usually five to eight) with their teacher. The following guidelines should help you learn to use guided reading:

1. *Introduce the book.*
   - Give each student a copy of the book.
   - Show the book cover. Read the title and discuss information on the cover. Ask students to *predict* what is going to happen in the text. Record their predictions.
   - Conduct a picture walk. Turn through the pages, and note the pictures, illustrations, and graphics. Do not give away the ending.
2. *Read and respond to the book.*
   - Direct students to read the book silently to see whether their predictions are accurate. At the very beginning stages of reading, students may read aloud softly to themselves.
   - As the children read, observe their behaviors. Are some having difficulty with certain words or types of words? Are some tracking with their fingers while others are not?
   - Are children applying the decoding skills they have been taught? You can check this when you provide opportunities for them to read sections orally.
   - Look for one or two things you might help the children with. For example, if several children seem to have trouble with the word *day,* print it on the board and

ter an exchange that is rewarding for both students and the volunteer. However, it is up to the individual participants to develop the scope of the correspondence relationship.

The world is out there for you to discover. Teachers interested in corresponding with a Peace Corps volunteer will find information on how to enroll on the World Wise Schools website, www.peacecorps.gov/wws/, or by calling 1-800-424-8580, ×1450.

CyberVolunteer

CyberVolunteer connects teachers and students in the United States with Peace Corps volunteers around the world via e-mail. Members receive an e-mail message once a month from the featured volunteers.

A schedule detailing the name and location of each featured cybervolunteer is provided so that educators can more easily integrate the program into existing lessons. Letters from previous cybervolunteers are available online for review; letters from the current school year are available only to participants. This is not a one-on-one correspondence match; the volunteers' letters are shared with a large group of classrooms through a listserv.

Looking at Ourselves and Others

During Peace Corps service, volunteers look closely at the assumptions and values that shape their perspectives as Americans. They learn about themselves as individuals and as respresentatives of a multifaceted American culture. The activities contained in this pro-gram challenge World Wise students similarly to become more conscious of the values they share with their families, friends, and communities. The materials also provide students with analytical tools that help combat stereotypical thinking and enhance cross-cultural communication.

As your students learn about other countries and cultures, they—like Peace Corps volunteers—will begin to recognize that individuals and groups hold diverse views of the world. They will realize that this diversity often stems from the unique systems of values, beliefs, experiences, and knowledge that link people within cultural groups. In "Neighbors," returned volunteer Orin Hargraves illustrates the profound effect of looking at others from a new perspective. The activities in this guide are designed to help students develop the habit of viewing people and places from multiple points of view.

Presented in a supportive context with opportunities for reflection and application, *Looking at Ourselves and Others* and other World Wise Schools materials can help students join the Peace Corps' exciting and essential mission—right in their own classrooms. The materials are available in print or online.

Contributed by Donna Molinari, marketing specialist, Coverdell World Wise Schools, Washington, DC, www.peacecorps.gov/wws.

help them sequentially decode or read through the word by identifying each sound in order if they have the skills.

- After they have read the book, discuss what students predicted and what actually happened in the text.
- Teach any decoding or comprehension skill or strategy needed.

3. *Extend the book.*
   - Have children reread the book alone or with a partner.
   - Children may also choose to act out or role-play the story with partners.[7]

LOOKING TO THE FUTURE

Although the educational system in general is slow to meet the demands and dictates of society, it is likely that dramatic changes will continue to be seen in grades one to three in the next decade. Their direction will be determined by continual reassessment of the purpose of education and attempts to match the needs of society with the goals of schools. Substance abuse, child and family abuse, violence, and illiteracy are some of the societal problems the schools are being asked to address in significant ways.

Increasingly, schools are asked to prepare children for their place in the world of tomorrow. All early childhood programs must help children and youth develop the skills

In the Primary Grade segment of the DVD, listen to what the narrator says about teaching at this level. What would make it worthwhile? Challenging?

MAKING CONNECTIONS WITH FAMILIES TO STRENGTHEN LITERACY

First-grade teachers Marilyn McNeal and Lara Ernsting of Kirbyville (Missouri) Elementary School work hard at making reading meaningful and fun for their students. They utilize many techniques to strengthen the home/school and community/school connection. They find the following examples key to making reading important and fun for their students.

FAMILY READING NIGHT

Each quarter they host a family reading night. Each child and family is invited to come to the classroom to read favorite titles from the classroom libraries. McNeal and Ernsting provide a snack to go along with the theme and entertainment for the evening. They have discovered that entertainment is the key to family attendance. The students perform choral readings, short skits, poetry, and/or original works. For example, during the first quarter the students were involved in a unit on the study of fairy tales. The family reading night entertainment was a rousing rendition of "Three Bear Rap," followed by teddy-bear-shaped snacks.

READING AT HOME

McNeal and Ernsting continue to involve the parents in reading at home by setting goals for the number of books read outside the classroom. Students chart their progress on individual charts and are rewarded for achieving various levels. McNeal and Ernsting utilize stickers, pencils, erasers, bookmarks, gift certificates, treasure boxes, and the Pizza Hut Book-It program. They find that having the students chart their own progress enables them to see the progress they are making toward the ultimate goal of reading one hundred books outside the classroom environment.

STORY-BITS

McNeal and Ernsting use something their principal introduced at staff meetings, story-bits. The idea originated in an article by Cheryl M. Sigmon in the 4 Blocks column on the teachers net website. Story-bits give students a concrete memento to help recall particular stories. For example, the students received an acorn as a memento for *Chicken Little*. McNeal and Ernsting had each student create a story-bit gift box to store the mementos and sent them home with a letter at the beginning of the year to explain their purpose. When students bring home a memento, they are to retell the story to their parents and save the memento in their story-bit box. The teachers have found that this concrete reminder has helped their students' comprehension levels.

VOLUNTEER READERS

Volunteer readers from the community further emphasize the importance of reading. Volunteers include parents, school personnel (secretaries, janitors, bus drivers, principals, and superintendents), community leaders, DARE officers, local celebrities, and others in the community. The volunteers are encouraged to come and read often. McNeal and Ernsting find that this involvement strengthens the students' awareness of the importance of reading outside the school community.

McNeal and Ernsting believe that no matter how you do it, students need varied exposure and many opportunities to practice their developing skills as readers. Reading should NEVER be a chore. Utilizing the resources around you, you can help students on their quest to becoming avid, excited, and lifelong readers.

Contributed by first-grade teachers Marilyn McNeal and Lara Ernsting and Principal Addie Gaines, Kirbyville (Missouri) Elementary School.

necessary for life success. We know that learning does not end with school and that children do not learn all they will need to know in an academic setting. It makes sense, therefore, to empower students with skills they can use throughout life in all kinds of interpersonal and organizational settings:

- An ability to read and to communicate with others, orally and in writing
- An ability to work well with people of all races, cultures, and personalities
- An ability to direct personal behavior
- The desire and ability to succeed in life—measured not by earning a lot of money but by becoming a productive member of society
- The desire and ability to continue learning throughout life

The future of the primary grades will certainly include an emphasis on academics, higher achievement, and helping all students be successful.

Companion Website

For additional Internet resources or to complete an online activity for this chapter, go to the Companion Website at **www.prenhall.com/morrison,** select chapter 12, then choose the Linking to Learning or Making Connections module.

Research shows that higher achievement occurs when children are engaged in learning tasks that encourage them to think. How can you include practices and activities in your classroom that help students learn to think?

LINKING TO LEARNING

A to Z Teacher Stuff
http://www.atozteacherstuff.com/

Created for teachers by a teacher; designed to help teachers find online lesson plans and resources quickly and easily. Offers ideas on thematic units and lesson plans and contains a large collection of printable worksheets and pages.

Baltimore County Public Schools
http://www.bcps.org

Integrates the teaching of values throughout all curricular areas. Leaves local school values committees responsible for identifying a common core of values to be stressed for their school population. Includes How to Establish a Values Education Program in Your School: A Handbook for School Administrators.

CHARACTER COUNTS! National Homepage
http://www.charactercounts.org/

A nonprofit, nonpartisan, nonsectarian coalition of schools, communities, and nonprofit organizations working to advance character education by teaching the six pillars of character: trustworthiness, respect, responsibility, fairness, caring, and citizenship.

Character Education Partnership

http://www.character.org/

> *A nonpartisan coalition of organizations and individuals dedicated to developing moral character and civic virtue in our nation's youth as one means of creating a more compassionate and responsible society.*

Learning Page

http://www.learningpage.com/

> *A huge collection of professionally produced instructional material for you to download and print. Has lesson plans, books, worksheets, and much more.*

Scholastic Teachers

http://teacher.scholastic.com/

> *Contains great resources for building student success, including lesson plans, activities, reproducibles, and thematic units. Also provides time-saving teacher tools, such as Standards Match, which lets you easily locate classroom resources aligned to your state standards.*

ACTIVITIES FOR FURTHER ENRICHMENT

ETHICAL DILEMMA: "THE SALESPERSON"

One of your colleagues who teaches first grade with you has joined the part-time sales force of a national company that sells a beginning reading program. The program is heavily advertised in the media as being designed to specifically help struggling readers. She has asked you for the names, addresses, and phone numbers of the children in your class who are having trouble with beginning reading.

Do you give your colleague the list, hoping that the program will help your children learn to read, or do you refuse her request and risk alienating her as a coworker or is there some other ethical solution to your dilemma?

APPLICATIONS

1. Identify five contemporary issues or concerns facing society, and tell how teachers in grades one to three could address each of them.
2. Explain how first-grade children's cognitive and physical differences make a difference in how they are taught. Give specific examples.
3. Of the three grades—first, second, or third—decide which you would most like to teach, and explain your reasons.
4. What do you think are the most important subjects of grades one, two, and three? Why? What would

you say to a parent who thought any subjects besides reading, writing, and arithmetic were a waste of time?

FIELD EXPERIENCES

1. Gather information from the websites provided in this chapter. Organize it by topics (e.g., character education), and put it in your teaching portfolio for future use.
2. Inquire whether there are schools in your area that have character education programs, use cooperative learning, or incorporate other curricula that seek to help children be better learners, persons, and citizens. Put information from these programs in your activity file or portfolio.
3. Language and culture play powerful roles in how children learn. Visit classroom and school libraries, and assess whether they have sufficient numbers and kinds of books to support the learning of children from diverse cultures.
4. Teaching reading is an important part of a teacher's role in the primary grades. Observe the teaching of reading in each grade, one to three. Make a list of the things that you will have to do or learn to be an effective teacher of reading.

RESEARCH

1. Interview parents and teachers to determine their views on nonpromotion and the end of social promotion. Summarize your findings. What are your opinions on retention?

2. Compile a list of character traits that you believe are most important to teach young children. Then ask parents and community members what they believe are the most important traits. Compile a complete list.

3. Review your state's standards for grades one, two, and three. Compare these standards to those of two other states in which you might like to teach. What are the similarities and differences? How might the differences influence your teaching?

4. High-quality primary teachers have high efficacy—that is, they believe they are responsible for student learning and can increase it. Efficacious teachers are well organized, use their time well, and communicate clearly. Research the topic of efficacy and add to these three traits. Make an observation form (see chapter 3), and observe classrooms (grades one to three) for efficacious teaching behavior. How do you plan to become an efficacious teacher?

READINGS FOR FURTHER ENRICHMENT

Cunningham, P. *Phonics They Use: Words for Reading and Writing,* 4th ed. Reading, MA: Addison Wesley Longman, 2004.

Offers a coherent collection of practical, hands-on activities to help students develop reading and spelling skills. Stresses a balanced reading program—incorporating a variety of strategic approaches—tied to the individual needs of children.

Cunningham, P., and R. Allington. *Classrooms That Work: They Can All Read and Write,* 3rd ed. Boston: Allyn and Bacon, 2003.

Designed for courses that focus on instructional reading methods for at-risk and culturally diverse student populations; an inexpensive text that assists preservice and in-service teachers in enriching the learning and reading skills of all children.

Glazer, J., and Giorgis, C. *Literature for Young Children,* 5th ed. Upper Saddle River, NJ: Merrill/Prentice Hall, 2004.

A broad introduction to early childhood literature, focusing on literary analysis and specific techniques and methods of effective literature-based education. Includes a number of valuable methods and suggestions designed to enhance both understanding and enjoyment of literature.

ENDNOTES

1. Institute of Medicine, "Schools Can Play a Role in Preventing Childhood Obesity," (September 2004), http://www.iom.edu/Object.File/Master/22/615/0/.pdf.

2. Ulric Neisser, ed., *The Rising Curve: Long-Term Gains in IQ and Related Measures* (American Psychological Association, 1998). Also available online at http://en.wikipedia.org/wiki/Flynn-effect.

3. U.S. Census Bureau, "Historical Poverty Tables" (2005), http://www.census.gov/hhes/www/poverty/histpov/hstpov20.html.

4. Lawrence Kohlberg, "The Claim to Moral Adequacy of a Highest Stage of Moral Judgment," *Journal of Philosophy* 70, no. 18 (1973): 630–646.

5. C. Gewertz, "More Chicago Pupils Flunk Grade," *Education Week* (2002): 13.

6. *Alaska Department of Education and Early Development,* "How to Use the Framework," http://www.eed.state.ak.us/TLS/FRAMEWORKS/langarts/1intro.htm.

7. Guidelines adapted by permission from David Cooper, *Helping Children Construct Meaning,* 5th ed. (Boston: Houghton Mifflin, 2003), 157–158.

Meeting the Special Needs of Young Children

Technology and Young Children

EDUCATION FOR THE INFORMATION AGE

Technology is a tool that can provide another way for children to learn and make sense of their world.

JUDY VAN SCOTER, DEBBIE ELLIS, AND JENNIFER RAILSBACK
NORTHWEST REGIONAL EDUCATIONAL LABORATORY

CHAPTER 13

You need go no further than the daily newspaper (online, of course!) to see how technology is changing the face of education as we know it. A front-page headline declared: "Software for Kids a Growing Proposition." The writer of the article was acknowledging what many people think as they wander the aisles of computer software stores—the fastest-growing software category is for young children under five. For programs with names like *Jumpstart Baby* and *Reader Rabbit Playtime for Baby,* parents spend more than $41 million on young children's software annually.[1]

And curriculum-based software programs such as Leapfrog teach basic skills of reading, math, and science, as well as general technology use. These programs are a growing presence in many early childhood classrooms.

THE COMPUTER GENERATION

Perhaps you are wondering about your role as a teacher in integrating technology into your classroom and programs. You may also wonder how you can use technology to become a better teacher. One thing is certain: children today are technologically oriented. They are the dot-com generation, and their growth, development, and learning are intimately tied to large doses of television, videos, electronic games, and computers in the home and shopping center. Today, more and more students have laptop and hand-held computers that they easily carry back and forth between home and school.

TECHNOLOGY: A DEFINITION

Technology is the application of tools and information to make products and solve problems. With this definition, technology goes far beyond computers and video games, but the most common use of the term refers to electronic and digital applications—in other words, devices you can plug in. Such tools commonly found in early childhood programs include computers, computer programs, television, video recorders, videotapes, tape recorders, cassettes, digital cameras, and various types of assistive technology. As an early childhood professional, you must consider the full range of technology that is applicable to your classroom, learning centers, and activities. The statistics in Figure 13.1 indicate the extent of technology use in education today.

TECHNOLOGICAL LITERACY

Technology is changing and, in the process, changes what the goals of education are, what it means to be educated, and what literacy means. Literacy now has added dimensions: students not only have to read, write, listen, and speak—skills fundamental to participation in a democratic society—but also have to use technology to be truly literate. In society **technological literacy,** the ability to understand and apply technology to meet personal goals, is becoming as important as the traditional components of literacy—reading, writing, speaking, and listening.

Focus Questions

What does technological literacy mean for you, young children, and families?

What challenges do young children face with access to technology and technological equity?

How can technology help special populations of children, such as those with disabilities or with limited English proficiency?

How can you integrate technology into the early childhood learning environment?

How has technology changed parents' roles in their children's education?

Companion Website

To check your understanding of this chapter, go to the Companion Website at **www.prenhall.com/ morrison**, select chapter 13, answer Multiple Choice and Essay Questions, and receive feedback.

FIGURE 13.1 Technology Use in Education Today

- 4.4 to 1 is the ratio of students to computers in all public schools.
- 8 percent of public schools lend laptop computers to students (5 is the median number of laptop computers available for loan in those schools).
- 12 percent of schools in rural areas, 7 percent of urban fringe schools, and 5 percent of city schools lend laptops.
- 10 percent of public schools provide a handheld computer to students or teachers.
- 22 states have established virtual schools.*
- 16 states have at least one cyber charter school.
- 48 states have technology standards for students.
- 8th grade is the target time of No Child Left Behind when every student should be technology literate.
- nearly 62 percent of all households have Internet access.†

*U.S. Department of Education, "Educational Technology Fact Sheet," http://www.ed.gov/about/offices/list/os/technology/facts.html.
†"Census: More Than Half of U.S. Homes Have Net Access," *Tech News World* (October 28, 2005).

Technology The application of tools and information to make products and solve problems.

Technological literacy The ability to understand and apply technological devices to personal goals.

Figure 13.2 shows New Jersey's content standards for technology for preK through grade four. These new dimensions of literacy affect not only how you and your students learn but also how you and they conduct daily life.

TECHNOLOGY USE WITH YOUNG CHILDREN

Children's lives are full of technology. As Figure 13.3 on page 374 illustrates, 70 percent of children aged four to six have used a computer, and 40 percent can load a CD-Rom by themselves. And parents support and value the potential of computers to help their children learn: 72 percent of parents say that using a computer "mostly helps" children's learning. However, we must remember that not all children have the same or equal technology experiences.

Young children's involvement with technology has a number of implications for you as an early childhood teacher:

- You should build on the out-of-school technology experiences that children bring to your classroom. For example, children who are more technologically adept can partner with students who can benefit from one-on-one help.
- You can provide enriched technology experiences for all students, while ensuring that those students who lack technology competence receive appropriate assistance.
- You can involve parents in class programs of technology and enrichment. Parents can help you teach technology skills and can extend in-school technology learning at home.

Above all, you can be an enthusiastic supporter and user of technology and ensure that all children have high-quality technology experiences. The Program in Action "How to Use Technology as a Scaffolding Tool in the Preschool Classroom" on pages 378–380 is also a Competency Builder that will help you introduce technology to young children as an aid in acquiring literacy skills.

Companion Website To learn more about the technology gap between the haves and have-nots, go to the Companion Website at **www.prenhall.com/morrison**, select chapter 13, then choose the Linking to Learning module.

In the High/Scope segment of the DVD, observe the young girl who chose to listen to a story on a tape player with headphones.

FIGURE 13.2   New Jersey Content Standards for Technology (preK–4)

A. Basic computer skills and tools

  1. Use basic technology vocabulary

  2. Use basic features of an operating system (e.g., accessing programs, identifying and selecting a printer, finding help)

  3. Input and access text and data, using appropriate keyboarding techniques or other input devices

  4. Produce a simple finished document using word processing software

  5. Produce and interpret a simple graph or chart by entering and editing data on a prepared spreadsheet template

  6. Create and present a multimedia presentation using appropriate software

  7. Create and maintain files and folders

  8. Use a graphic organizer

  9. Use basic computer icons

B. Application of productivity tools

  1. Social aspects

    a. Discuss the common uses of computer applications, and identify their advantages and disadvantages

    b. Recognize and practice responsible social and ethical behaviors when using technology, and understand the consequences of inappropriate use

      • Internet access

      • Copyrighted materials

      • Online library resources

      • Personal security and safety issues

    c. Practice appropriate Internet etiquette

    d. Recognize the ethical and legal implications of plagiarism of copyrighted materials

  2. Information access and research

    a. Recognize the need for accessing and using information

    b. Identify and use web browsers, search engines, and directories to obtain information to solve real-world problems

    c. Locate specific information by searching a database

    d. Recognize accuracy and/or bias of information

  3. Problem solving and decision making

    a. Solve problems individually and/or collaboratively using computer applications

    b. Identify basic hardware problems and solve simple problems

Source: Printed by permission from New Jersey Department of Education, "New Jersey Core Curriculum Content Standards for Technological Literacy," http://www.state.nj.us/njded/cccs/s8_tech.htm.

In the Kinder-garten segment of the DVD, observe the literacy strategy used. Is it developmentally appropriate? Does it provide equal access for all children?

Companion Website
To complete a Diversity Tie-In activity related to the Internet digital divide, go to the Companion Website at **www.prenhall.com/ morrison**, select chapter 13, then choose the Diversity Tie-In module.

EQUITY IN TECHNOLOGY

Many educators fear that the United States may be creating a new class of illiterates—children who do not have access to and do not know how to use computers and other technology. Table 13.1 shows Internet usage by age and household income, and the Diversity Tie-In on page 381 adds a racial component. These demographics of technological use have serious implications for children, families, and you. Wherever inequities exist, technological

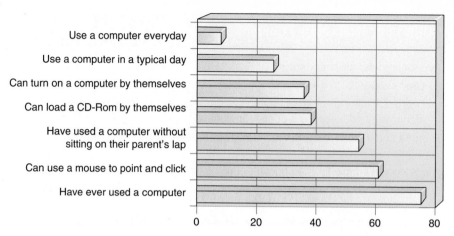

FIGURE 13.3   Computer Use Among Four- to Six-year-Olds

Source: Reprinted by permission from the Henry J. Kaiser Family Foundation, "Zero to Six: Electronic Media in the Lives of Infants, Toddlers and Preschoolers" (#3378; Fall 2003), http:// www.kff.org. The Kaiser Family Foundation, based in Menlo Park, California, is a nonprofit, independent national health care philanthropy and is not associated with Kaiser Permanente or Kaiser Industries.

TABLE 13.1   **Percentage of Internet Users Based on Age and Income**

Percentage of Internet Users within Age Groups		Percentage of Internet Users Within Household Income Groups	
Ages 3–4	19.9	Less than $15,000	31.2
Ages 5–9	42.0	$15,000–$24,999	38.0
Ages 10–13	67.3	$25,000–$34,999	48.9
Ages 14–17	78.8	$35,000–$49,999	62.1
		$50,000–$74,999	71.8
		$75,000 and above	82.9

Source: U.S. Department of Commerce, National Telecommunications and Information Administration, *A Nation Online: Entering the Broadband Age* (2004), http://www.ntia.doc.gov/reports/anol/NationOnlineBroadband04.pdf.

illiteracy can result. We must avoid creating a generation of technology have-nots and must advocate for increased access to technology for *all* students.

Equity means having an opportunity to become technologically literate. In other words, all students must have equitable access to technology that is appropriate for them. Although some may think it a worthy goal for all students to spend the same amount of time on a computer, that may not be equitable—all students may not need the same exposure. Some students may need more or less time to master the objectives of their particular grade and subject. You can partner students with unequal computer skills to create classroom learning communities devoted to increasing technology skills and learning applications.

Parents, teachers, and policymakers must be leaders in ensuring that there are no technological demographic gaps and that all software is free of bias. As discussed in chapter 14 and elsewhere throughout this text, all professionals must consider the diversity present in contemporary society when selecting materials, including computer software, DVDs, films, and other technological applications. These materials must depict children and adults of differing abilities, ages, and ethnic backgrounds and must not stereotype by gender, culture, or socioeconomic class. The software industry has made progress in this regard but still has a long way to go to meet antibias criteria in their products. You must evaluate all software you purchase and continually advocate for unbiased software. Figure 13.4, a soft-

Companion Website
To learn more about selecting appropriate software, go to the Companion Website at **www.prenhall.com/morrison,** select chapter 13, then choose the Linking to Learning module.

FIGURE 13.4 Software Evaluation Checklist

Title of software evaluated: _____

- ❏ The software offers a divergent path and choice-making opportunities.
- ❏ The software is open-ended and invites exploration in a nonthreatening environment.
- ❏ The software provides problem-solving opportunities.
- ❏ The software allows a child to be successful.
- ❏ The software stimulates a child's interest.
- ❏ The software encourages active involvement.
- ❏ The software contains quality animation, graphics, sound, and color.

- ❏ The content reflects a diverse society.
- ❏ The content is developmentally appropriate.
- ❏ The feedback is effective and nonthreatening.
- ❏ The responses to incorrect input are not demeaning.
- ❏ The program is easy to navigate.
- ❏ The program operates at an acceptable speed.
- ❏ The program is easy to exit.
- ❏ The instructions, if any, are clear and easy to follow.
- ❏ The software is compatible with classroom hardware.

Comments:

_____

_____

_____

_____

_____

Source: Reprinted by permission from the Center for Best Practices in Early Childhood, Western Illinois University, Macomb, Illinois.

ware evaluation checklist, will help you in selecting software for young children. In addition, NAEYC's position statement on technology and young children (see Figure 13.5) can guide your software and technology-use decisions.

TECHNOLOGY AND SPECIAL CHILDHOOD POPULATIONS

Technology can have a profound effect on children with special needs, including very young children and students with disabilities.

TECHNOLOGY AND INFANTS, TODDLERS, AND PRESCHOOLERS

Technology is a growing part of the world of very young children. Computers and other devices have a great deal to offer, and there is much that young children can learn via technology in all domains—cognitive, social, emotional, and linguistic. Software is being designed for children as young as nine months; it is often referred to as lapware because children are held in their parents' laps to use it, and it is intended to be used by parents and children together.

You will find many software programs for the very young. For instance, *Jumpstart Baby* and *Reader Rabbit: Playtime for Baby* are aimed specifically at children aged one to three years. *Jumpstart Baby* leads them through eight activities, including wood-block puzzles and

FIGURE 13.5 NAEYC Position Statement on Technology and Young Children

Although there is considerable research that points to the positive effects of technology on children's learning and development, the research indicates that, in practice, computers supplement and do not replace highly valued early childhood activities and materials, such as art, blocks, sand, water, books, exploration with writing materials, and dramatic play. Research indicates that computers can be used in developmentally appropriate ways beneficial to children and also can be misused, just as any tool can. Developmentally appropriate software offers opportunities for collaborative play, learning, and creation. Educators must use professional judgment in evaluating and using this learning tool appropriately, applying the same criteria they would to any other learning tool or experience. They must also weigh the costs of technology with the costs of other learning materials and program resources to arrive at an appropriate balance for their classrooms.

- In evaluating the appropriate use of technology, NAEYC applies principles of developmentally appropriate practice and appropriate curriculum and assessment. In short, NAEYC believes that in any given situation, a professional judgment by the teacher is required to determine if a specific use of technology is age appropriate, individually appropriate, and culturally appropriate.

- Used appropriately, technology can enhance children's cognitive and social abilities.

- Appropriate technology is integrated into the regular learning environment and used as one of many options to support children's learning.

- Early childhood educators should promote equitable access to technology for all children and their families. Children with special needs should have access when this is helpful.

- The power of technology to influence children's learning and development requires that attention be paid to eliminating stereotyping of any group and eliminating exposure to violence, especially as a problem-solving strategy.

- Teachers, in collaboration with parents, should advocate for more appropriate technology applications for children.

- The appropriate use of technology has many implications for early childhood professional development.

Source: Reprinted by permission from NAEYC, "NAEYC Position Statement: Technology and Young Children, Ages 3 Through 8," *Young Children* (September 1996): 11–16.

nursery rhyme sing-alongs. *Reader Rabbit: Playtime for Baby* allows young children to explore colors, shapes, songs, animals, letters, and numbers. There are also software programs for toddlers, such as *Reader Rabbit Toddler,* and *Reader Rabbit: Playtime for Baby and Toddler.*

The market for infant, toddler, and preschool software is growing, with an estimated $50 million spent each year. Programs designed for children under five represent the fastest-growing educational software market. The Voice from the Field "Selecting Software for Young Children" on pages 386–388 offers an evaluation of software interactivity, which can guide you as you choose software for your classroom.

ASSISTIVE TECHNOLOGY AND CHILDREN WITH DISABILITIES

The field of early childhood education is undergoing dramatic changes through its integration with the field of special education. As a result, early childhood professionals are adopting assistive technology to help children and their families. According to Public Law 100–407, the Technology-Related Assistance for Individuals with Disabilities Act of 1988 (Tech Act), **assistive technology** is "any item, device or piece of equipment, or product sys-

Assistive technology
Any device used to promote the learning of children with disabilities.

FIGURE 13.6 Assistive Technology in Real Life

Four-Year-Old Sara

Sara is a four-year-old child who has been diagnosed with cortical blindness. Despite her visual impairment, She is a typical preschooler who enjoys playing in the various classroom centers. To ensure her participation, Sara's teacher has adapted the environment, adding tactile and auditory components and making all materials accessible for her. Because Sara's favorite activity is listening to a story, she enjoys the reading center, which has books on tape. However, her favorite area of the classroom is the computer center. Through adaptive devices and customized software, Sara can not only listen to stories, but also interact with them and with other children at the computer.

Sara's favorite software program is *Just Me and My Dad*. When she wants to listen to certain parts of the program, she presses her jellybean switch to turn the pages. Her teacher has customized the activity by making the software switch-accessible through a software utility program called *Click It!* (IntelliTools). The teacher has also used the *IntelliPics* software to make picture overlays for the IntelliKeys, an adaptive touch sensitive tablet that serves as an alternate input to the computer. Tactile material is added so that Sara can touch and identify parts of the overlay, pressing on areas to hear sounds made by objects on her favorite pages. Sara takes turns with other children, pressing areas on the overlay during small-group activities.

The children can also create their own version of the story through *IntelliPics* or *IntelliPics Studio,* deciding on characters, objects, actions, and words to put into their story. Sara especially enjoys this activity, because she can now tell the other children about her favorite person, her dad, through her recorded voice, sounds she has selected, and pictures from home. Technology is a tool that helps Sara develop not only emergent literacy skills, but also cognitive, social, fine-motor, and communication skills.

Seven-Year-Old James

Assistive technology offers young children with physical disabilities access to the same or similar developmentally appropriate, child-centered, integrated activities engaged in by children without disabilities. With appropriate adaptations and software, young children with disabilities can participate in their own learning. James, a seven-year-old child with multiple disabilities, made images on the computer using *Kid Pix* and adaptive peripherals. By trying different adaptations—such as a switch, a touch screen, an expanded keyboard, and a draw tablet—the teacher discovered that a draw tablet (with an overlay simulating the *Kid Pix* draw screen) was the tool that James could use most successfully. Drawing with a draw tablet is much like drawing on a Magna Doodle or Magic Slate. A stylus is attached to the right or left side of the draw tablet, and the drawing surface is so touch sensitive that even a very light touch creates a line that appears on the monitor. James was able to make the connection between his movements with the stylus and the marks that appeared on the computer screen. As he worked, he told the teacher, "Draw." James also knew when he was successful and exclaimed, "Did it!" to let others know he was pleased with his work. When teachers integrate creative and interactive software with adaptive peripherals, all children have opportunities to gain knowledge and skills and extend their expressiveness.

Source: Reprinted by permission from the Center for Best Practices in Early Childhood, Western Illinois University, Macomb, Illinois.

tem, whether acquired commercially off the shelf, modified, or customized, that is used to increase, maintain, or improve functional abilities of individuals with disabilities."[2]

Assistive technology covers a wide range of products and applications, from simple devices such as adaptive spoons and switch-adapted battery-operated toys to complex devices such as computerized environmental control systems. You will have opportunities to use many forms of assistive technology and modified educational software with all ages of students with special needs. Two real-life examples are described in Figure 13.6.

Uses of Assistive Technology.   Assistive technology is particularly important for students with disabilities who depend on technology to help them communicate, learn, and be mobile. For example, for students with vision impairments, closed-circuit television can

Companion Website To learn more about assistive technology, go to the Companion Website at **www.prenhall.com/morrison**, select chapter 13, then choose the Linking to Learning module.

HOW TO USE TECHNOLOGY AS A SCAFFOLDING TOOL IN THE PRESCHOOL CLASSROOM

Technology can be an exciting tool to help children acquire early literacy skills. Educators and families with young children have access to cameras, printers, scanners, and software that were once the tools only of media production specialists. With this technology, the possibilities for personalizing activities for literacy scaffolds are endless.* However, knowing how to apply the technology to the preschool curriculum remains a barrier for many professionals. Successful use begins with knowing what equipment to buy.

STEP 1 Select the equipment

Technology can be a tool for both educators and children. Several pieces of equipment are needed to create literacy materials and activities.

- **Digital camera** This versatile piece of equipment comes in a variety of models with different features. An inexpensive camera may work just as well as a special model designed for children. There are a number of features to consider:
  - Resolution—the sharpness of the pictures expressed in pixels (the higher the resolution, the better the picture)
  - Optical zoom—magnifies the images using a multifocal-length lens
  - Image capacity—memory capability for images shot at high resolution
  - Expansion slot for memory card
  - LCD display for children to review pictures

- **Digital video camera**
  - This tool documents events in the classroom.
  - Models vary in features.

- A tripod is recommended for children to ease use and avoid accidents.
- **Printer and scanner**
  - A color printer is essential for book making and literacy material creation.
  - Scanners can transfer children's writing samples and artwork into digital format.
  - Printers with scanning capability are suitable for classroom use.
- **Microscope**
  - ProScope (by Bodin) allows children to magnify specimens like butterflies or beetles and view them on the monitor screen.
  - Images can be captured and put into a book or slide show format.
- **PDA (personal digital assistant)**
  - These handheld devices usually include a date book, address book, task list, memo pad, clock, and calculator software. Newer models also have color screens and audio capabilities, enabling them to show multimedia content. Many can also access the Internet.
  - This important documentation tool can record child progress.
  - Children's work can be captured in photo form.
  - Software application is key to use with children's portfolio items.

STEP 2 Learn to use the equipment

Most equipment is fairly user-friendly, requiring very little, if any, instruction to operate.

- Become familiar with all options and test with chosen application.
- Make sure equipment is easy for children to use.
- Adapt the equipment, if necessary.

If training is needed on a certain piece of equipment, the manufacturer may have tutorials that are downloadable from their website. Online training sites, found through an Internet search, may also offer tips and training on using a device.

STEP 3 Choose the software

Before choosing software, decide on the literacy activity:

- For creating simple books or class slide shows, a photo-management type of programs can be used—such as *iPhoto, Kodak EasyShare,* or *Photo Kit Junior.*
- For interactive books, authoring software is best—such as *IntelliPics Studio, HyperStudio,* or even *Microsoft Word.*

Other photo management and authoring software may be available with similar features.

STEP 4 Create literacy activities for the children

By creating their own electronic books, children learn many print concepts, including reading text left to right and top to bottom, separating words with a space, and learning that words have meaning. Books can be created from customized templates or through child-friendly features in software.

- **Electronic book templates**
  - Each child can create a book about him- or herself or can base it on a field trip, class project, or favorite book.
  - Teachers can make templates with authoring software.
  - Children can add their own pictures, voices, and text.
  - Page-turning buttons in the bottom corners of each page allow children to navigate forward and backward through the book.

- **Child-created books** Children in preschool classes can learn to use digital cameras, download pictures to the computer, and use software to create books. When using this technology with children, attach a long strap to the camera so that children can put it around their necks to make sure the camera is not dropped.

  - Explain how to plug the camera into the computer and download the pictures.
  - Show children how to use the photo management application. If needed, prepare photos and import them into the program ahead of time.
  - Teach children how to enter text and sounds into the program.
  - Encourage children to work in small groups to benefit from cooperative play.

STEP 5 Document the learning

- **Daily documentation** Some teachers choose to take digital photos in the classroom on an ongoing basis. Pictures of children's construction, artwork, or play activities can be shared immediately with them. The teacher may also want to share the images with the class as a review of the week's activities and projects.
- **Wall displays** Displaying digital pictures in a hallway or on a classroom wall gives children documentation of events and an opportunity to review and revisit. Children's language skills may be sparked as they review the pictures. They may also dictate a narrative about the pictures and events.
- **Portfolios** Digital photos, scanned photos, writing samples, and artwork can be saved in a child's individual electronic portfolio file. At the end of the year, the teacher can copy the images for families or create an electronic book or movie about each child. Families might also create their own books during a workshop at the end of the year. With simple instructions and a template they could choose the images to place in their children's books. The creation could then be burned on a CD or DVD for families to keep.

STEP 6 Design a universal environment

All children need to have opportunities to participate in literacy-rich technology activities. One way to ensure equal participation is to evaluate the environment and adapt it to meet the needs of all learners. Adaptations can include modifications to book materials, such as page turners, or alternate input for computer users who cannot operate a mouse.[†] The most versatile input devices include these:

- Switches—an input method that uses buttons or pads to press or step on.
- IntelliKeys (IntelliTools)—a touch-sensitive tablet used with customized overlays.
- Touch screen—a touch-sensitive device that is either built into or attached to a monitor.

For more information on using technology or assistive technology with young children, visit the Early Childhood Technology Integrated Instructional System (EC-TIIS) website at www.wiu.edu/ectiis/. Nine online workshops are available for educators and families.

Technology can be a scaffolding tool for literacy when educators and families know how to use equipment and apply it to young children's needs. Children gain print concepts and other early literacy skills, and the technology serves as a valuable documentation tool for educators and families.

Equipment and Software Resources

HyperStudio—Sunburst Technology, www.hyperstudio.com
IntelliKeys, switches, and *IntelliPics Studio*—IntelliTools, www.intellitools.com
iPhoto—Apple, www.apple.com
Kodak EasyShare—Kodak, www.kodak.com
Microsoft Word—Microsoft, www.microsoft.com
Photo Kit Junior—APTE Inc., www.apte.com
ProScope—Bodelin distributor, www.bodelin.com

Contributed by Linda Robinson, assistant director, Center for Best Practices in Early Childhood, Western Illinois University, Macomb, Illinois. Photos also contributed by Linda Robinson, Center for Best Practices in Early Childhood. The center (www.wiu.edu/thecenter/) provides technology and assistive technology training, curricula, and online information to educators and families of young children.

*L. Robinson, "Technology as a Scaffold for Emergent Literacy: Interactive Storybooks for Toddlers," *Young Children* 58, no. 6 (2003): 42–48.
[†]P. Hutinger, M. Beard, C. Bell, J. Bond, L. Robinson, C. Schneider, and C. Terry, *Emerging Literacy and Technology: Working Together.* Macomb: Western Illinois University, Center for Best Practices in Early Childhood Education (2001).

Many children come to school familiar with computers and other technology. Other children have had very limited exposure. What can you do to ensure that all children's technological needs are met?

In the Child Care segment of the DVD, observe how child care programs can be a home away from home. How can you use technology to help children feel at home and connect home and school?

be used to enlarge print, a Braille printer can convert words to Braille, and audiotaped instructional materials can be provided. Closed-captioned television and FM amplification systems can assist students who are deaf or hard of hearing. Touch-screen computers, augmentative communication boards, and voice synthesizers can assist students with limited mobility or with disabilities that make communication difficult.

Technology helps children with vision impairments see and children with physical disabilities read and write. It helps developmentally delayed children learn the skills they need to achieve at appropriate levels and enables other children with disabilities to substi-

THE INTERNET DIGITAL DIVIDE

You and I are so surrounded by technology that we tend to take it for granted; we think that technology is available to and used by everyone. But in the United States there is a great Internet digital divide, a large gap between those who have access to and the skills to use technology and those who—for socioeconomic, cultural, and racial reasons—have limited or no access.

Basic access to a computer is a major issue for many children. Basic access to a computer that is wired to the Internet is yet another issue. Slightly more than half of all black and Latino children have access to a home computer; about 40 percent have Internet access at home. By comparison, 85.5 percent of white children have home computer access, and 77.4 percent can use the Internet at home.*

Look again at Table 13.1, which shows that access to the Internet is also a function of socioeconomic status. Whereas 83 percent of those in families earning more than $75,000 a year use the Internet, only 38 percent of those in families earning between $15,000 and $25,000 do so.

We know that when children have home access to computers, they do use them. In a recent study parents reported that even very young children with home access were using computers: 21 percent of children two and younger, 58 percent of three- to four-year-olds, and 77 percent of five- to six-year-olds. Many of these children first used computers on a parent's lap at around age two and a half and used computers independently by three and a half.†

Why does the digital divide matter?

- Most parents (75 percent) believe that the Internet is a positive learning tool.‡

- Increasingly, students use the Internet as a primary source of information in completing school assignments, leaving lower-income children at a definite disadvantage.
- Access to a home computer increases the likelihood that children will graduate from high school.*

What can you do to help close the digital divide?

- Give children who do not have Internet access or computers at home more time to use both at school.
- Use scaffolding strategies, such as having more technologically literate students team with those who need to develop technological skills.
- Provide time after school for computer use.
- Invite parents without Internet access to a series of family nights devoted to classes on how to use the Internet.
- Work with parents who have computers and Internet access to form technological support groups to help other families.

---

*School News, "Study: 'Digital Divide' Affects School Success," http://www.eschoolnews.com/news/showStoryts.cfm?ArticleID=5999.

†Children's Digital Media Center, Georgetown University, "Research Examines Early Childhood Computer Use," http://cdmc.georgetown.edu/about_press.cfm#research_examines.

‡Tech Soup, "Frequently Asked Questions About the Digital Divide," http://www.techsoup.org/howto/articles/ctc/page3012.cfm.

tute one ability for another and receive the special training they need. In addition, computer-assisted instruction provides software tools for teaching students at all ability levels, including programmed instruction for students with specific learning disabilities. The Center for Best Practices in Early Childhood, featured in the Program in Action on page 389, has been instrumental in promoting assistive technology and facilitating its use.

Opportunities for using many forms of assistive technology are available to even very young children, from birth to age three. Some of these include powered mobility, myoelectric prostheses, and communication devices. Infants as young as three months have interacted with computers, eighteen-month-old children have driven powered mobility devices and used myoelectric hands, and two-year-olds have talked via speech synthesizers. Children with severe physical disabilities can learn how to use switches and scanning techniques.

FIGURE 13.7 Examples of Assistive Technology

Touch Windows 17 (www.riverdeep.net)
- Attaches to computer monitor
- Allows children to touch screen directly, rather than using a mouse
- Can be used on a flat surface, such as a wheelchair tray
- Is scratch resistant and resistant to breakage

BigKeys Keyboard (www.bigkeys.com)
- Has keys four times bigger than standard keyboard keys
- Arranges letters in alphabetical order to assist young children
- Generates only one letter, regardless of how long a key is pressed
- Accommodates children who cannot press down two or more keys simultaneously

Big Red Switch (ablenetinc.com)
- Large, colorful switch to turn devices on and off
- Five-inch diameter surface which is easy to see and activate
- Audible click to help children make cause-effect link

Voice-in-a-Box 6 (www.frame-tech.com)
- Allows children to communicate by pressing on pictures
- Allows for up to thirty-six recorded messages
- Records and rerecords messages
- Has durable and appealing preschool-friendly case

Talk Pad (www.frame-tech.com)
- Is a portable communication device
- Designed to be used by children who need assistance with speech
- Uses an electronic chip that records the voice
- Allows children with language limitations to be active participants in everyday activities

All-Turn-It Spinner (ablenetinc.com)
- Inclusion learning tool that allows all children to participate in lessons on numbers, colors, shapes, matching, sequencing
- A spinner that is controlled by a switch for easy manipulating
- Optional educational overlays, stickers, and books that can be purchased

Tack-Tiles Braille Systems (www.tack-tiles.com)
- Braille literacy teaching toys for all ages
- LEGO-type blocks that form Braille codes, which can be put on a board or magnetized for use on file cabinets or refrigerators
- Tolerant of sudden jarring movements
- Available in several codes, including five languages, mathematics, and music notation

Aurora (www.aurora-systems.com)
- Works with Windows to help people with learning disabilities and dyslexia write and spell better
- Helps people with physical disabilities communicate
- Speeds up typing by predicting words
- Reads back what is typed and reads text from applications for those with reading difficulties
- Allows phrases to be organized into categories for quick conversation

Benefits of Assistive Technology.   Technology permits children with special needs to enjoy knowledge, skills, and behaviors that might otherwise be inaccessible to them. Thus, technology empowers children with special needs; that is, it enables them to exercise control over their lives and conditions of their learning. It enables them to do things previously thought impossible.

In addition, technology changes people's attitudes about children with disabilities. For example, some may have viewed children with disabilities as unable to participate fully in regular classrooms; however, they may now recognize that instead of being segregated in separate programs, these children can be fully included with the assistance of technology. Figure 13.7 will help you expand your vision of how assistive technology can support, extend, and enrich children's learning.

ETHICAL ISSUES AND ASSISTIVE TECHNOLOGY

An extremely important issue in the use of assistive technology is its appropriateness. It should meet the following criteria:

1. A technology should respond to (or anticipate) specific, clearly defined goals that result in enhanced skills for the child.
2. A technology should be compatible with practical constraints, such as available resources or the amount of training required to enable the child, the family, and the early childhood educator to use the technology.
3. A technology should result in desirable and sufficient outcomes: (a) ease of training for the child and the family to use and care for the technology; (b) reasonable maintenance and repair, with regard to time and expense; and (c) monitoring of the technology's effectiveness.[3]

Assistive technology enables children with disabilities to participate in regular classrooms and to learn skills and behaviors not previously thought possible. What are some examples of assistive technologies that would enable this child and others with disabilities to learn?

The mere application of technology is not enough. You and other professionals have to be sensitive to ethical concerns as you work with children, families, and other professionals in applying technology to learning settings and young children's special needs.

IMPLEMENTING TECHNOLOGY IN EARLY CHILDHOOD EDUCATION PROGRAMS

Three challenges confront early childhood teachers in implementing effective programs using technology in their instruction:

1. Their own personal acceptance of technology
2. Confidence that technology has a positive influence on children
3. Decisions about how to use technology in early childhood programs and classrooms

Teachers cannot afford to ignore computers and technology. When they do, they risk having technologically illiterate students; denying children access to skills, knowledge, and learning; and failing to promote an attitude of acceptance of technology. Instead, teachers must promote access to technology and develop creative ways to involve children with it. Figure 13.8 provides some practical advice for infusing technology into your teaching.

SETTING A GOOD EXAMPLE: PERSONAL ACCEPTANCE OF TECHNOLOGY

As an early childhood educator, the first step in using technology in the classroom is accepting technology yourself and learning how to use it effectively and appropriately. Here are guidelines for you to keep in mind:

- Educate yourself on the potential benefits of computers and technology.

Companion Website To complete a Program in Action activity related to the effective use of technology, go to the Companion Website at **www.prenhall.com/morrison**, select chapter 13, then choose the Program in Action module.

FIGURE 13.8   Using Technology in Early Childhood Programs

- Acknowledge that technology infusion is an evolutionary process that has fits and starts in its functionality and practicality.

- Do not be afraid to look to others, whether it's for help infusing the curriculum with technology or for technical assistance. Teachers need to form human networks for planning and troubleshooting. This is somewhat antithetical to teachers' experiences because they typically are alone with their students. However, the social-psychological dimension of sharing, exchanging, and helping one another is critical for success with technology. (This shift in working with others also serves as a model for students as they learn to reach out to other students for assistance.)

- Be prepared for things not to work as expected. The Plan B phenomenon (the need for a backup plan) is very real when working with technology, and teachers need to know how to immediately shift gears when something goes awry technologically.

- Be creative in allowing technology to expand your instructional plans, yet realistic in knowing what students can handle and what the curriculum allows. This is especially important in high-stakes testing.

Source: From S. B. Wepner and Liqing Tao, "From Master Teacher to Master Novice: Shifting Responsibilities in Technology-Infused Classrooms," *The Reading Teacher* 55, no. 7 (2002): 642–651. Reprinted by permission of the International Reading Association and the authors.

- Be willing to try new ways of using technology to help your children learn new knowledge and skills.
- Collaborate with colleagues in your school and school district to explore ways to use technology.
- Collaborate with parents and community members, many of whom have skills that you can use and apply.
- Advocate for and on behalf of gaining access to technology for your classroom and school.

Your confidence and comfort level with technology will set a good example for the children in your care. As you use computers to access information, send e-mails, and keep records of children's accomplishments, they will come to understand that computers are a natural part of schooling and learning. Establishing positive attitudes toward technology is an important part of fostering an appropriate and inviting classroom environment.

DECIDING HOW TO USE TECHNOLOGY IN YOUR PROGRAM

Your next responsibility as an early childhood educator is to determine how to make the most of available technologies to spark your children's learning and imagination. The Voice from the Field "Helping Primary-Grade Children Make the Most of Technology" on pages 390–391 will help you with this challenge. As you make decisions about how to use computers and computer-based technologies in your classroom, here are some considerations to keep in mind.

Meeting Learners' Individual Needs with Technology.   All technology in your classroom should meet children's individual needs. You will want to take children's individual differences into account when deciding how best to involve them in learning activities. Some children will need more help and encouragement; others will naturally want to be more involved. Individual children will have different needs, interests, and abilities and, therefore, will use computers in different ways.

In the High/Scope segment of the DVD, observe how children sit in a group at the computer.

Using Technology to Promote Children's Social Development. Perhaps you have heard critics claim that computers and other technology interfere with children's social development. Let's look at this argument and consider some things you can do to ensure that your use of technology with young children supports and enhances their social development.

Social development involves interacting with and getting along with other children, siblings, parents, and teachers. Social development also includes the development of self-esteem, the feelings children have about themselves. Children's inter-actions and relationships with others enlarge their views of the world and of themselves. Adults expect young children to develop self-regulation, control aggression, and function without constant super-vision. How children meet these expectations has tremendous implications for their self-concept. Children are also learning about adult roles through play and real-life activities. And as they learn about adult activities, they learn to understand others and themselves.

You can use computers and other technology to help children de-velop positive peer relationships, grow in their self-regulation and self-control, explore adult roles, and develop positive self-esteem in the process. Here are some things you can do to accomplish these goals:

- Have children work on projects together in pairs or small groups. Make sure that the computer has several chairs to en-courage children to work together. Learning through technol-ogy is not inherently a solitary activity. You can find many ways to make it a cooperative and social learning experience.
- Provide children with opportunities to talk about their tech-nology projects. Part of social development includes learning to talk confidently, explain, and share information with others.
- Encourage children to explore adult roles related to technol-ogy, such as newscaster, weather forecaster, and photographer. Invite adults from the community to share with children how they use technology in their careers. Invite a television crew to show children how they broadcast from community locations.
- Read stories about technology and encourage children to talk about technology in their lives and the lives of their families.

Assistive technology such as the Alpha Talker II helps this child learn and use a basic core vocabulary. Selecting an appropriate icon enables her to talk and communicate with others. This technology is easily programmed for new words.

As you explore other ways to promote children's social development through tech-nology, remember that all dimensions of children's development are integrated. The cogni-tive, linguistic, social, emotional, and physical dimensions support and depend on each other, and technology can positively support them all.

Promoting Meaningful Learning with Technology. Different educators have vary-ing approaches to and philosophies of learning through computers. For some, the computer and software are a central element of teachers teaching and children learning. Others see computers as a means of providing open-ended discovery learning, problem solving, and computer competence. Different applications promote different kinds of learning experi-ences. You will need to decide which of these applications best suit your learners' needs and interests and your instructional objectives.

Drill Versus Discovery. A major controversy among early childhood professionals in-volves the purpose of computers in the classroom. Some say that the more repetitive drill-and-practice programs have no place in an early childhood program; only software that encourages learning by discovery and exploration is appropriate. Other professionals see drill-and-practice software programs as a valuable means for children to learn concepts and skills they so desperately need to succeed in school—colors, numbers, vocabulary, phonics, and skills such as addition.

In the High/Scope segment of the DVD, listen to what is said about Piaget's theory of active learning. How does classroom technology support active learning?

SELECTING SOFTWARE FOR YOUNG CHILDREN

The software titles listed here are interactive, appeal to the wide range of abilities in a class, nurture children's learning styles, and support activities at home and in the reading center and other areas of the classroom. Interactivity focuses on how many things children can do and how much interaction the software provides. The more interactive the software, the more the child is able to manipulate what happens when the program is used. There are five levels of interactivity, with the first being the least interactive.

LEVEL 1

Level 1 software is intended to be used with beginning computer activities. It offers limited choices and a predetermined path with a fixed response. Software found in this section has fixed graphics that cannot be controlled or manipulated. Many of the software programs at this level are based on stories that have very simple story lines with repeating phrases. Each page contains one sentence or phrase.

One example is "Five Little Ducks," a program on the *Circletime Tales Deluxe* software. This popular story about a mother duck and her five babies can be used with very young children to encourage gesture and verbal imitation. Because there are very few words on the screen at one time, those words can be taught orally, as well as through sign language, for total communication.

Many of the programs suggested at Level 1 are switch programs—that is, they are operated by a switch, rather than a mouse or a keyboard. Children who are beginning switch users can become accustomed to using this device through a simple software program. Often, one press of the switch turns the page in a story; no other interaction is offered at this level. The simple graphics and the limited input of these programs meet the needs of some children. They can attend to one person or object on the screen as they begin to understand their own control of the program. As children progress, they are encouraged to begin to use software with a higher interactivity level.

Software characteristics:
- Minimal choices are offered.
- Path is predetermined.
- Choice of response is fixed.
- Text (if any) is set and cannot be controlled or manipulated.
- Sound control is limited to on/off or up/down.
- Graphics are fixed and cannot be controlled or manipulated.

Software examples:

Animal Tales	*Monkeys Jumping on the Bed*
Camp Frog Hollow	*New Frog and Fly*
Circletime Tales Deluxe	*Press to Play—Animals*
Eensy and Friends	*Rosie's Walk*
Five Green and Speckled Frogs	*Storytime Tales*
Mike Mulligan and His Steam Shovel	*Switch Intro*

LEVEL 2

Level 2 software is slightly more interactive than Level 1. Software such as *JumpStart Toddlers* offers a menu of choices. Although several paths can be chosen, the path is predictable. If children click on a particular picture choice, they will go to the same activity over and over again. The activity has only a few variations of response choices. For example, the peek-a-boo activity contains several different hidden pictures. Sound in this program is limited and cannot be controlled, although the musical tunes do appeal to children. The text found in this program consists of simple labeling words to describe animals and objects found in the pictures. Although the graphics in *JumpStart Toddlers* can be moved for an activity, they cannot be controlled or manipulated into any other form.

Software characteristics:
- Multiple choices are offered.
- Path is divergent but predictable.
- Choice of response is varied.
- Text (if any) is set and cannot be controlled or manipulated.
- Sound control is limited to on/off or up/down.
- Graphics are fixed and cannot be controlled or manipulated.

Software examples:

The Art Lesson	*The Backyard*
Arthur's Birthday	*Bailey's Book House*

Bala Yaga and the Magic
    Geese
The Berenstain Bears Get in
    a Fight
Dr. Seuss's ABC
Fatty Bear's Birthday
    Surprise
Fisher-Price Toddler
Franklin Learns Math
Harry and the Haunted
    House
How Many Bugs in a Box?

Imo and the King
JumpStart Toddlers
Just Me and My Dad
Little Monster at School
More Bugs in a Box
The Playroom
Reader Rabbit Toddler
Sheila Rae the Brave
Stellaluna
The Tortoise and the Hare
The Ugly Duckling

LEVEL 3

Level 3 software, such as *Green Eggs and Ham,* offers a menu of choices. The path is divergent and gives the child moderate control over the path to follow. Response choices are varied. If a child clicks on a particular object, the response may vary from time to time. The text in *Green Eggs and Ham* cannot be controlled or manipulated other than by clicking on a word to hear it spoken or to see it turn into a picture. This program does not allow control of sound other than on and off. The graphics can be clicked on for a response but are fixed and cannot be controlled or manipulated.

Software characteristics:
- Multiple choices are offered.
- Path is divergent, and user is given moderate control.
- Response choice is varied.
- Text (if any) is set and cannot be controlled or manipulated.
- Sound control is limited to on/off or up/down.
- Graphics are fixed and cannot be controlled or manipulated.

Software examples:

3-D Cruiser
A to Zap!
Arthur's Reading Race
Busytown
Darby the Dragon
Dinosaur Adventure 3D
Dr. Seuss: Cat in the Hat
Easy Bake Kitchen Playset
Green Eggs and Ham
How Things Work in
    Busytown
Just Grandma & Me 2.0
Just Me and My Mom
Let's Explore the Farm with
    Buzzy
Let's Explore the Jungle with
    Buzzy

Millie and Bailey Preschool
My First Incredible, Amazing
    Dictionary
My Very First Little People
    Playhouse
Ozzie's World
Playskool Puzzles
Putt Putt Goes to the Moon
Putt Putt Joins the Parade
Ruff's Bone
Sammy's Science House
Thinkin' Things Collection
Time to Play Pet Shop
Tonka Dig'n Rigs Playset
Trudy's Time and Place

LEVEL 4

Software at Level 4 is very interactive. In *Crayola Make A Masterpiece*, a graphic program, children are offered multiple choices with pencils, paintbrushes, a text tool, erasers, and more. With the selection of each of the drawing tools, more choices are offered at the bottom of the computer screen. Different sizes, shapes, and colors can be selected. The child can choose the path of drawing and writing with the many choices. Text in *Crayola Make A Masterpiece* can be controlled and manipulated. Sound control is limited, but recordings can be made to accompany each drawing. The program also offers a slide show choice. Graphics can be controlled and manipulated; children can choose drawing tools, add stamps, mix paint, and create 3-D art with textures.

Software characteristics:
- Multiple choices are offered.
- Path is divergent, and user is given total control.
- Response choice is varied.
- Text (if any) can be controlled or manipulated.
- Sound control is limited.
- Graphics can be somewhat controlled or manipulated.

Software examples:

2 Simple
Amazing Animals
The Amazing Writing
    Machine
Big Job
Blue's Art Time Activities
Chicka Chicka Boom
    Boom
ClarisWorks for Kids
Community Construction
    Kit
Crayola Make A
    Masterpiece

Disney's Magic Artist 3-D
GollyGee Blocks
The Graph Club
Graphers
I Spy
I Spy Junior Puppet
    Playhouse
Kid Works Deluxe
Stanley's Sticker Stories
Storybook Weaver
Write: Outloud

LEVEL 5

Software at Level 5, such as *HyperStudio,* offers the user control over the path, the responses, the text, the sound and sound effects, the graphics, and the content. *HyperStudio* can be compared to a stack of index cards, but the stack does not have to be linear. *HyperStudio* offers added features, including a variety of content ranging from scanned photos to videotape segments. Children using *HyperStudio* can make a variety of choices—from deciding what materials to add to their stack to choosing where to place the materials in the stack and selecting what sound, text, or other content to add to tell a story. Level 5 software is adaptable to the child and curriculum when implemented by the teacher and/or family.

Software characteristics:

The user is given a wide variety of choices and has total control over the following elements:

- Path
- Responses
- Text
- Sound and sound effects
- Graphics
- Content

Software examples:

Blocks in Motion   *Intellipics*
Buildability   *Kid Pix 4*
HyperStudio   *Logo*
i-Movie

Contributed by the Center for Best Practices in Early Childhood, Western Illinois University, Macomb, Illinois.

As with so many things, a middle ground offers an appropriate solution. Many children like drill-and-practice programs and the positive feedback that often comes with them. Other children do not like or do well with skill-drill programs. What is important is that all children have access to a variety of software and instructional and learning activities that are appropriate for them as individuals. This is what a developmentally appropriate curriculum is all about, and it applies to technology and software as well.

Higher-Order Learning.   Technology can support and facilitate critical educational and cognitive processes, such as cooperative learning, group and individual problem solving, critical thinking, reflective practices, analysis, inquiry, process writing, and public speaking. Technology can also promote metacognition—that is, encouraging children to think about their thinking. One such technological application is *LEGO/Logo,* software that links the popular LEGO construction kit with the Logo programming language. Children start by building machines out of LEGO pieces, using not only the traditional building blocks but also new pieces like gears, motors, and sensors. Then they connect their machines to a computer and write computer programs (using a modified version of Logo) to control the machines. For example, a child might build a LEGO house with lights and then program them to turn on and off at particular times. The child might then build a garage and program the door to open whenever a car approaches.

LEGO/Logo engages children in thinking about design and invention. Children have used this software to build and program a wide assortment of creative machines, including a programmable pop-up toaster, a chocolate-carob factory (inspired by the Willy Wonka children's stories), and a machine that sorts LEGO bricks according to their lengths.

The LEGO company now sells a commercial version of *LEGO/Logo* that is used in more than a dozen countries, including more than 15,000 elementary and middle schools in the United States. The Epistemology and Learning Group is currently involved in developing programmable bricks—LEGO bricks with tiny computers embedded inside. With these new electronic bricks, children could build computational capabilities directly into their LEGO constructions.

Technology and Curriculum Integration.   Technology should be integrated as fully as possible into the early childhood curriculum and learning environment so that its use can help promote learning and achieve positive outcomes for all children. Technology integration includes making sure that all technology-based activities remain consistent with the beliefs, principles, and practices of your program. Another aspect of integration is making sure technology use is not seen as a separate or add-on activity. There should not be a computer unit that is separate from work in social studies, science, language arts, and so on. Instead, you could create a computer/technology learning center in your classroom that children have access to, just as they would any other center. Such a center should have software that enables children to work independently, with little or minimal adult supervision.

THE CENTER FOR BEST PRACTICES IN EARLY CHILDHOOD PROMOTES THE EFFECTIVE USE OF TECHNOLOGY

The Center for Best Practices in Early Childhood, a research and development unit at Western Illinois University, develops and promotes practices designed to improve educational opportunities for young children, including those with disabilities. Since 1975 the center, directed by Dr. Patricia Hutinger, has implemented projects in model development, outreach training, personnel preparation, product development, and research, funded through the U.S. Department of Education's Office of Special Education, the Department of Human Services, and the Illinois State Board of Education. In addition to providing training, products, and consultation to Illinois service providers and families of young children with disabilities, the center is nationally recognized for its innovative work in assistive technology, providing services and products through over thirty technology-related projects.

Since the early 1980s, computers, assistive devices, and other technologies have figured prominently in the center's work and products. Center staff provide workshops for teachers, educational support staff, administrators, and families on such topics as selecting and using early childhood software, integrating technology into the preschool curriculum, choosing and using assistive technology, and conducting team-based technology assessments. The center has developed four curricula focusing on the integration of technology into specialized areas, including emergent literacy, expressive arts, and math, science, and social studies to assist young children with disabilities in achieving various skills. Other center products include instructional manuals, CD-ROMs, videotapes, and a website, www.wiu.edu/users/mimacp/wiu/.

Contributed by the Center for Best Practices in Early Childhood, Western Illinois University, Macomb, Illinois.

Finally, educational technology should not be something children get to use only when they have completed other tasks. It should not be used as a reward, nor should it be a supplemental activity.

The Program in Action "Carolina Beach Elementary: A Model School of Technology" on pages 392–393 provides an excellent example of how to integrate technology into the classroom, the curriculum, the school, and the community.

PARENTS AND TECHNOLOGY

Technology has changed the way early childhood professionals teach and the way children learn, so it should come as no surprise that it has also changed parents' roles. With the help of technology, parents now have more resources for participating in, supervising, and directing their children's education. They also have additional responsibilities, like making sure the information their children access on the Internet at home is developmentally appropriate.

TECHNOLOGY TO INCREASE PARENT PARTICIPATION

Even though parenting may seem like a full-time proposition, many parents also have demanding work schedules, and many work two jobs to make ends meet. Juggling the

HELPING PRIMARY-GRADE CHILDREN MAKE THE MOST OF TECHNOLOGY

If schools do not become technologically sophisticated, then the technology sophisticated will not send their children to school.
Phil Schlechty, author and educator

In this new millennium, students have new tools to navigate their worlds. With mouse, keystrokes, and remote controls, they steer through CD-ROMs, videodiscs, channels, and Web pages. Student work displayed in the hallways should show a wide array of technology uses. Colorful graphs, letters, and digital drawings can express the imagination and creativity of students. Software aligned with the curriculum can enable them to become proficient in computer skills as well as content areas. Primary students can write reports and stories, create digital presentations using Kidpix or PowerPoint, and use the Internet for research. Classes can use the digital camera to create bulletin boards, class projects, Web pages, and presentations.

SHARED FILES

Schools with networked systems can set up student access to shared files that will enable students to use templates with instructional activities created by their teachers. An entire class of students can access these on-screen worksheets simultaneously in the computer lab or classroom. This allows for skill practice with immediate feedback and eliminates the need for paper and pencil. Shared files can also be used to save student work, reducing the use of disks, which are easily corrupted. Teachers should make use of the shared files for student assessment, lesson plan templates, sharing ideas, and cross-grade-level sharing. For example, a second-grade teacher might create a digital world map that all second-grade students would access to label the continents.

EQUIPMENT

All primary classrooms should be equipped with two to four computers with Internet access, tape recorders, CD players, and televisions. Overheads, LCD projectors, and VCRs should be available for checkout by the classroom teacher. Classrooms that have a computer conversion device that projects images to televisions for full-class viewing make it easier for the entire class to view the computer screen while the teacher is demonstrating or explaining an activity.

RESEARCH PROJECTS

Children in grades two and three should be encouraged to do research using preselected sites on the Internet. Projects work best if students this age are given one item to research with several specific questions. They will then begin to learn how to take notes and rewrite their answers in paragraph form. One example might be to assign each student an animal and have them find answers to the following questions:

1. What is its habitat like?
2. What does it eat?
3. What does it look like?
4. What is its natural enemy?

demands of parenting and work causes anxiety and concern about parenting and about children's school achievement. Parents' questions and concerns often exceed the capability of teachers and school personnel to respond within the time constraints of the school day. In addition, many parents have difficulty getting to the school for parent conferences, programs, and assistance.

Technology such as e-mail offers new ways to exchange or gain information and to get help and assistance. Other uses of technology to increase parent involvement include school websites, teacher and classroom websites, and phone conferencing. Some teachers use their websites to regularly post pictures of students doing everyday activities in class. In Florida, the Polk County School District uses an online instructional system to help parents as well as students develop critical technology literacy. Parents are encouraged to participate in after-school

After typing a paragraph about the animal, students might copy and paste a picture of the animal on their page. Assignments such as this should reinforce the curriculum and teach skills in research and technology, as well as provide students with the opportunity to discover and explore different modes of learning. Children this age are not afraid to click and love to see the real pictures. It stimulates their interest in science and social studies if they are allowed to research one or two selected sites just before the teacher introduces a topic in class. The main points to remember when surfing the Web with young children are to preview the websites you want them to look at to make sure that they are developmentally appropriate (most are not written for young children) and to have several questions prepared that they are to answer.

ASSESSMENT

Technology assists in the assessment of young students with a variety of different programs. Students like to use technology for assessment because it gives them instant feedback. There are several excellent technology-based, reading-management systems used in elementary schools. Students are tested to find their appropriate reading level, then read books selected from specific catalogs of books that have corresponding reading tests on that level, and then take a computerized test on the book.

EXTENDED LEARNING

Computer programs to extend learning should be utilized regularly in all classrooms. Drawing programs such as Kidpix allow students to apply their knowledge of line, color, and shape in freehand drawings. In order to reinforce certain academic skills, teachers can create templates. For example, a kindergarten teacher might start a pattern in Kidpix and have each student complete the pattern during his or her computer time. As long as the original template is kept, each student can use it. There are also many excellent Internet sites that reinforce math skills on all levels. Young students need to be guided directly to these approved sites to receive maximum curriculum benefits, not left to explore the Internet on their own.

Companies are constantly developing software in all areas of the elementary curriculum. When choosing software, there are several considerations:

1. Is it compatible with your classroom computers (operating system, memory, speed, and color)? Read the label on the back of the CD or in the catalog to make sure. If you still don't know, call the company and tell them what kind of machine you are using.
2. Does it match curriculum standards that you are required to teach?
3. Is it age-level appropriate?
4. Is it fun to play? Kids don't like boring software. Remember, today's students watch a lot of TV and are used to being entertained. Most companies will send you a sample disk to try in your classroom. Let the kids use it for a few days to see whether they like it before you purchase it.

In addition e-mail should be a major source of communication for teachers, staff, and parents. Many teachers compile a group list of all of their students' parents and keep them informed by e-mail of field studies, projects, and upcoming school events.

Technology serves as a tool for learning for all students, from special education to gifted and talented. It levels the playing field by offering a wide variety of programs in different areas of the curriculum that are geared to all levels of learning. It offers students a challenging and fun environment to learn and to practice skills. Technology affords students the opportunity to visit places they will never go and see things they will never see. It brings the world to them at an early age and can be used to spark their quest for knowledge as no other form of media has ever been able to do.

Contributed by Phyllis D. Brown, information technology specialist, Rice Creek Elementary School, Columbia, South Carolina, a 2000–2001 Blue Ribbon School.

programs and in family technology nights. The district's objective is to help parents realize that they don't have to be afraid of technology.[4]

SUPERVISION OF CHILDREN'S INTERNET USE

Parents face a technological challenge in trying to separate the good from the bad on the Internet. One approach is to constantly monitor what their children access. However, for most parents, this is an impractical solution.

Another approach is to use a filter, a computer program that denies access to sites parents specify as inappropriate. One such program, *Cyber Sentinel,* blocks access to chat rooms, stops instant messages, and can be programmed to stop questions such as What is

Companion Website To complete a Program in Action activity related to integrating technology, go to the Companion Website at **www.prenhall.com/morrison**, select chapter 13, then choose the Program in Action module.

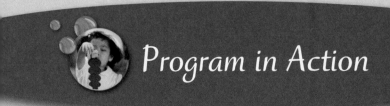
CAROLINA BEACH ELEMENTARY: A MODEL SCHOOL OF TECHNOLOGY

Carolina Beach Elementary School is known in our region and state as a model school of technology. Teachers use technology as a tool for teaching the state-required objectives, as well as a resource for ideas to enrich instruction.

INCORPORATING TECHNOLOGY

Incorporating technology is a priority in our school. We obtained computers and programs through the use of state and county funds, grants, and PTO money. Now we have four desktops and a laptop in every classroom. We also have a computer lab for whole-class instruction and two wireless mobile carts for classroom checkout. Teachers utilize the computer lab to teach technology objectives to their classes. After they master logging on and off the network, students can go to numerous programs to practice independently.

Hands-on training was an essential part of our plan. Teachers received training with the programs and the hardware to learn ways to enhance instruction. Community awareness of how students use technology in our school was also essential. For the past eight years we have held a technology night for students to showcase their technology skills. We invite parents and the community. Several different community services and businesses have participated in sharing how they use technology in the workplace. We also make a presentation at our county technology fair in the spring of each year.

BROADCASTING

Our students start and end the day using technology. On our own school TV channel, students broadcast our morning announcements and our dismissal. Students on the broadcasting teams learn the use of cameras, a mixer board to move from set to set, and a title maker for written messages. Announcers are rotated over a period of time.

TECHNOLOGY TOOLS AND DIVERSE LEARNERS

We have several tools to enhance the curriculum at Carolina Beach Elementary. In science class students study rocks using the ProScope microscope to enhance magnification. In the language arts curriculum, students use Leap Pads and AlphaSmarts to enhance reading skills.

Using technology in the language arts curriculum provides many ways to reach all levels of ability. A teacher can assign different resources for diverse learners. One student who can read might use a program to test his or her comprehension of a story, while a nonreader works on a letter-recognition program.

Technology is also used to help students who are not motivated by traditional teaching methods. Students with poor fine-motor skills for handwriting use a word processing program as a way of expressing themselves and meeting writing objectives. Word processing is also used to help students with other disabilities. Thus, students who would not ordinarily be successful in writing can benefit from word processing. The ultimate goal of the writing curriculum is to be able to communicate effectively.

Students benefit from differentiated instruction because it enables them to be actively involved in the learning process. Students working in small groups use the program *Graph Club* to collect, organize, and display data. They decide as a team what information to gather. For example, "Do you like to go fishing, yes or no?" The small groups ask their classmates this question and place a checkmark in the yes or no column. After the information is collected, the groups use the program *Graph Club*. Each group prints one graph to display their data and then presents it to the whole class. We are convinced by our students' progress that technology has made a significant impact on achievement and motivation at our school.

INTERNET

Teaching students to access information enhances their ability to become lifelong learners. Students use the Internet as a resource to connect with their experiences. For example, when students studied farms, they took a virtual tour of a dairy farm as part of a unit lesson. This gave them a better understanding and provided the background knowledge for all students. Students also know they can go to the Internet to find answers to questions.

MUSIC

At Carolina Beach Elementary School, second and third graders created original accompaniments to a familiar song using the software *GarageBand*. Responsibilities were divided among group members to create different musical parts from the preexisting instrument loops available. Students learned the musical and technological aspects of this software, which provided an appreciation of both music and technology.

FUTURE PLANS

Technology will remain a priority at our school. We will continue to enhance instruction by preparing students for the technology age in which they live.

Contributed by Vickie Holland, technology facilitator; Vicki Hayes, principal; Anita Pope, first-grade teacher; Rachel Taylor, kindergarten teacher; and Sarah Mansbery, music teacher, Carolina Beach (North Carolina) Elementary School. Photos contributed by Carolina Beach Elementary School.

your phone number? *Cyber Sentinel* also has built-in time management that allows parents to control when and for how long their children have access to the Internet. Parents who use America Online can specify three levels of access—Kids Only (under twelve years), Young Teen (thirteen to fifteen), and Mature Teen (sixteen and seventeen). Although many of these solutions are helpful, none can be considered 100 percent effective.

The Children's Online Privacy Act is designed to ensure the privacy rights of children and protect them from unscrupulous individuals and companies. The act requires World Wide Web operators to secure parental permission before they receive children's e-mail or home addresses. To alleviate any privacy concerns, many businesses such as America Online use mail-in parental notification, which allows parents to fill out an information card and mail it back in to the company.[5] Congress also passed the Child Online Protection Act, which calls for commercial website operators who offer harmful material to check the IDs of visitors. It is likely that Congress will continue to legislate ways to protect children aged twelve and under. How do you feel about such legislation? Do you believe it limits freedom of access?

Technology allows children to explore different worlds, access resources, and engage in learning activities on their own. How can you use computers and other technology to appropriately support children's learning?

THE TECHNOLOGICAL FUTURE AND YOU

Undoubtedly you have heard the saying, "You haven't seen anything yet." This remark applies to technology and its application to all school settings—especially the early childhood years from birth to age eight. The vision that each child will acquire the foundational skills and competencies to succeed as an adult in the information age should include children in the very early years.

What will have to happen to bring tomorrow to classrooms today? You must commit to action:

- Use technology and complete the training necessary to be computer literate.
- Dedicate yourself to the developmentally appropriate use of technology and software in your classroom.
- Make sure that technology and all its applications are not just add-ons to the curriculum, activities to do only when there is time, or rewards for good behavior or achievement.

Technology is here to stay and can, just like text-based materials, help all children learn to their fullest potential.

Companion Website

For additional Internet resources or to complete an online activity for this chapter, go to the Companion Website at **www.prenhall.com/morrison,** select chapter 13, then choose the Linking to Learning or Making Connections module.

LINKING TO LEARNING

Early Connections—Technology in Early Childhood Education

http://www.netc.org/earlyconnections/

Helps connect technology with the way children learn. Provides resources and information for educators and care providers in areas such as children's development and technology connections. Also answers many frequently asked questions about children and technology.

KidSites

http://www.kidsites.com/

One of the leading guides to the best in children's websites. Screens all websites listed and includes useful links for parents and teachers.

Reading Rockets: Launching Young Readers

http://www.pbs.org/launchingreaders/

The latest in a long line of complimentary educational websites from the Public Broadcasting Service (PBS). Accompanies the five-part PBS television series Reading Rockets and provides teachers with reading strategies that are proven to work.

SuperKids Educational Software Review

www.superkids.com

Offers teachers and parents objective reviews of educational software. Also has online activities for children.

Technology & Young Children

http://www.techandyoungchildren.org/

Seeks to lead discussions and to share research, information, and best practices regarding technology, so it can be used to benefit children aged birth through eight years.

Web for Teachers

http://www.4teachers.org/

An online space for teachers integrating technology into the curriculum; includes information on many topics, including Internet safety, lessons and WebQuests, project-based learning, activities related to state standards, and much more.

Yahooligans!
http://www.yahooligans.com/

A safe Web guide for children, parents, and teachers. Offers easy information on many topics, in categories such as Around the World, School Bell, Arts and Entertainment, Science and Nature, Computers and Games, and Sports and Recreation.

ACTIVITIES FOR FURTHER ENRICHMENT

ETHICAL DILEMMA: "IT'S UNFAIR!"

You teach third grade in Southwest ISD, a school district that is widely divided by class and socioeconomic status. Your school has over one thousand children who come from low-socioeconomic backgrounds. Ninety percent of the children are eligible for free or reduced lunch, and 85 percent come from a Hispanic background. You are a strong advocate for getting your children the learning materials that they need to learn. A friend of yours teaches across town at Little Oaks Elementary, with five hundred students who are all of white Anglo descent and have a median family income of more than $100,000. Your friend tells you that her school is getting all new computers and software and that the old computers and software are being sent to your school. You think that this is an unfair and inequitable allocation of resources.

What should you do? Call an emergency meeting of your local PTA to mobilize its members to help your school get new computers? Decide that it's not worth the effort to fight about this because many of your past efforts have ended in failure? Or choose some other course of action?

APPLICATIONS

1. Select four software programs for infants and toddlers and four for grades preK–three children. Evaluate the software using Figure 13.4 and these criteria:
   - Is it age appropriate?
   - Are the instructions clear?
   - Is the software easy to use (child friendly)?
   - Does the software accomplish its intended purpose?
   For each program tell whether you would use it, and explain why or why not.
2. Some teachers are not as willing as others to infuse technology into their teaching. Why is this? What are some specific things you will have to do in order to infuse technology into your teaching and work with parents and families?

3. Choose a particular theme in a subject you plan to teach, and write a lesson plan to show how you would integrate technology into that lesson.
4. Develop a plan for using Vygotsky's views (see chapter 5) to promote children's social interaction through computers.

FIELD EXPERIENCES

1. Visit classrooms in your local school districts. What evidence can you find of the integration of technology into the curriculum? What conclusions can you draw?
2. Interview grades preK–three teachers in a local district. What barriers do they say they must contend with in their efforts to include technology in the curriculum? What implications do these barriers have for what you may be able to accomplish as a teacher?
3. Visit classroom programs that provide services to students with disabilities. Cite five ways technology is used to implement curriculum, help teachers teach, and promote learning.
4. Some teachers and parents think children should not be introduced to computers at an early age. List reasons that they might feel this way. Then interview five parents and teachers, and ask them the following questions: At what age should young children use computers? Why do you feel this age is the best?

RESEARCH

1. As Figure 13.1 points out, almost 62 percent of all homes have Internet access. Visit an elementary school and conduct a survey of student access to the Web. Include in your survey the reasons that children don't have access to the Internet. What can schools and teachers do to provide children and their families with access to the Internet?
2. Write a four-paragraph report in which you explain your views about the use of technology in grades preK–grade three programs. Present this to a center director, school principal, or similar person for feedback. Set up a conference for discussion and reaction.

3. Review with several of your classmates the NAEYC Position Statement on Technology and Young Children (Figure 13.5). Tell how and in what ways you agree or disagree with the guidelines.

4. Use the Internet to research whether there is a gender divide between boys and girls in Internet use. Find data on the following: (a) access to the Internet by gender, (b) use of the Internet by gender, and (c) differences in what each group uses the Internet for. What conclusions can you draw from your data?

READINGS FOR FURTHER ENRICHMENT

Hirschbuhl, J. *Annual Editions: Computers in Education,* 11th ed. Guilford, CT: McGraw-Hill/Dushkin, 2003.

A compilation of carefully selected articles from the public press. Addresses the use of computers and the increasingly important roles they play in the lives of children and adults. Also provides the latest information on the application of computer technology in the nation's schools.

Jonassen, D. *Modeling with Technology: Mindtools for Conceptual Change,* 3rd ed. Upper Saddle River, NJ: Prentice Hall, 2005.

Addresses the use of computers to foster critical thinking and problem solving, written to teach current and future teachers how to better engage learners more mindfully and meaningfully in the process of learning. Focuses on how to use technology to support meaningful learning through model building, providing powerful strategies for engaging, supporting, and assessing conceptual change in learners.

Mills, S. C. *Using the Internet for Active Teaching and Learning.* Upper Saddle River, NJ: Merrill/Prentice Hall, 2006.

Helps readers learn to use the Internet to support teaching and learning in today's classrooms. Combines both theory and practice, using Internet technologies and resources to enable project-based active learning in the classroom.

Newby, T. J., D. Stepich, J. Lehman, and J. D. Russell. *Educational Technology for Teaching and Learning,* 3rd ed. Upper Saddle River, NJ: Merrill/Prentice Hall, 2006.

Provides the basics for becoming a knowledgeable educator in the twenty-first century; introduces teachers to the approaches, methods, and procedures for integrating not only computers but also other media into the curriculum.

Thouvenelle, S. *Completing the Computer Puzzle: A Guide for Early Childhood Educators.* Boston: Allyn and Bacon, 2003.

Connects solid knowledge of early education principles with technical computer experiences, emphasizing the role of the teacher and the teacher's responsibility for meaningful integration of computer technology into the early childhood classroom.

ENDNOTES

1. D. Addio, "Software for the Diaper Set," *Pittsburgh Post-Gazette,* July 12, 1998.

2. Technology-Related Assistance for Individuals with Disabilities Act of 1988 as Amended in 1994, http://www.resna.org/taproject/library/laws/techact94.htm.

3. L. Holder-Brown and H.Parette, "Children with Disabilities Who Use Assistive Technology: Ethical Considerations," *Young Children* (September 1992): 74–75.

4. Converge Online, "Helping Parents Become Involved," http://www.convergemag.com/story.php?catid=237&storyid=93739.

5. America Online, Inc., "Privacy Policy" (1998), www.aol.com.

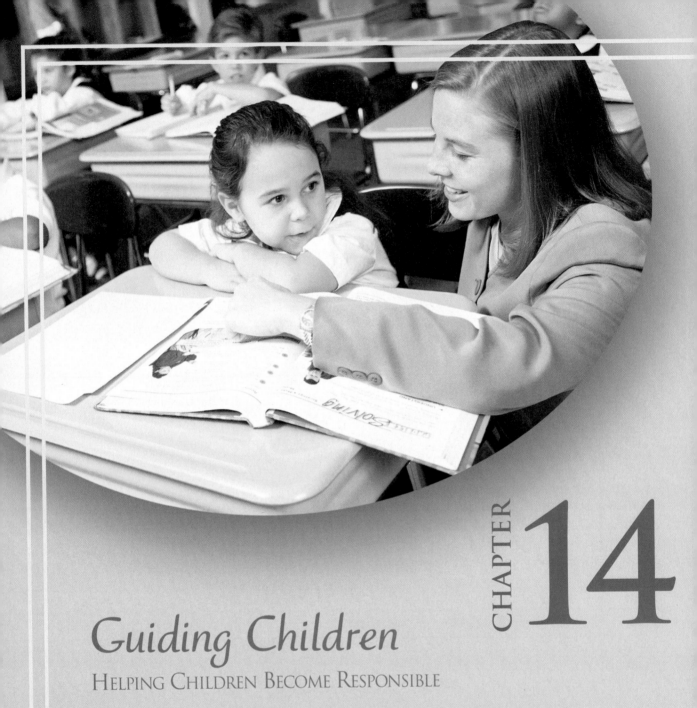

CHAPTER 14

Guiding Children

HELPING CHILDREN BECOME RESPONSIBLE

Consistently teaching children character values interwoven with all of the curriculum areas helps children realize that character is a part of everything they do in life and that demonstrating good character is a gift they can share with others.

CAROL CATES, 1999 NORTH CAROLINA EDUCATOR OF THE YEAR

THE IMPORTANCE OF GUIDING CHILDREN'S BEHAVIOR

Why should you and other early childhood professionals want to know how to best guide children's behavior and help them become responsible? There are a number of reasons.

Academics. Helping children learn to guide and be responsible for their own behavior is as important as helping them learn to read and write. Think for a moment about how many times you have said or have heard others say, "If only the children would behave, I could teach them something!" Appropriate behavior and learning go together; you can't have one without the other. Consequently, one of your primary roles as an early childhood teacher is to help children learn the knowledge, skills, and behaviors that will help them act responsibly.

Lifelong Success. Helping children learn to act responsibly and guide their behavior lays the foundation for lifelong responsible and productive living. As early childhood educators, we believe that the early years are the formative years. Thus, what we teach children about responsible living, how we guide them, and what skills we help them learn will last a lifetime. Society wants educators to prepare responsible children for responsible democratic living.

Preventing Problems. The roots of delinquent and deviant behavior form in the early years. From research we know what behaviors lead to future problems. For example, some characteristics of preschool children are precursors of adolescent behavior problems and delinquency—disruptive behavior, overactive and intense behavior, irritability, noncompliance, intensity in social interactions.[1]

Civility. The public is increasingly concerned about the erosion of civility and what it perceives as a general breakdown of personal responsibility for bad behavior. One reason the public funds an educational system is to help keep society strong and healthy. Parents and the public look to early childhood professionals to help children learn to live cooperatively and civilly in a democratic society. Getting along with others and guiding one's behavior are culturally and socially meaningful accomplishments.

What Is Behavior Guidance? Guiding children's behavior is a process of helping them build positive behaviors. Discipline is not about compliance and control but involves **behavior guidance**, a process by which all children learn to control and direct their behavior and become independent and self-reliant. In this view, behavior guidance is a process of helping children develop skills useful over a lifetime.

As you work with young children, one of your goals will be to help them become independent, able to regulate or govern their own behavior. **Self-regulation** is the "child's capacity to plan, guide, and monitor his or her behavior from within and flexibly

Focus Questions

Why is it important to help children guide their behavior?

What theories of guiding children's behavior can you apply to your teaching?

What are important elements in helping children guide their behavior?

Why is it important to develop a philosophy of guiding children's behavior?

What are important trends and issues in guiding children's behavior?

Companion Website

To check your understanding of this chapter, go to the Companion Website at **www.prenhall.com/ morrison**, select chapter 14, answer Multiple Choice and Essay Questions, and receive feedback.

Behavior guidance The processes by which children are helped to identify appropriate behaviors and use them.

Self-regulation The ability to keep track of and control one's behavior.

Social constructivist approach Approaches to teaching that emphasize the social context of learning and behavior.

Adult–child discourse The talk between an adult and a child, which includes adult suggestions about behavior and problem solving.

Private speech Self-directed speech that children use to plan and guide their behavior.

according to changing circumstances."[2] Three teacher and parent behaviors are essential for promoting self-regulation in children:

1. The use of reasoning and verbal rationales
2. The gradual relinquishing of control
3. A sense of affective nurturance and emotional warmth[3]

This chapter provides you with examples of all three of these essential elements.

A SOCIAL CONSTRUCTIVIST APPROACH TO GUIDING CHILDREN

In chapter 5 we discussed theories of learning and development and ways to use them in your teaching. Review the theories of Piaget, Vygotsky, Maslow, and Erikson so their ideas will be fresh in your mind as we now apply them to guiding children's behavior. Later, I will introduce you to Thomas Gordon's theory of guidance, as practiced in his Teacher Effectiveness Training program.

Piaget's and Vygotsky's theories support a social constructivist approach to learning and behavior. Teachers who embrace a **social constructivist approach** believe that children construct, or build, their behavior as a result of learning from past experiences and from making decisions that lead to responsible behavior. The teacher's primary role in the constructivist approach is to guide children in constructing their behavior and using it in socially appropriate and productive ways. This process begins in homes and classrooms.

In chapter 5 we also discussed Vygotsky's theories of *scaffolding* and the *zone of proximal development (ZPD)*. We can now apply these two concepts to guiding children's behavior and add two other essentials: **adult–child discourse** and **private speech**, or *self-talk*. Foundational to Vygotskian and constructivist theory is the central belief that the development of a child's knowledge and behavior occurs in the context of social relations with adults and peers. This means that learning and development are socially mediated as children interact with more competent peers and adults. Thus, as children gain the ability to master language and appropriate social relations, they are able to intentionally regulate their behavior.

GUIDING BEHAVIOR IN THE ZONE OF PROXIMAL DEVELOPMENT

The ZPD is the cognitive and developmental space that is created when a child is in social interaction with a more competent or knowledgeable person. Teachers take children with the behavioral and social skills they have and guide them to increasingly higher levels of responsible behavior and social interactions. And even though we often think that guiding behavior is a one-on-one activity, your role in guiding behavior also includes large and small groups. Figure 14.1 illustrates again the ZPD and suggests how to guide children's behavior within it. Problem solving is what guiding behavior is all about.

GUIDING BEHAVIOR WITH SCAFFOLDING

Scaffolding is one of the ways teachers guide children in the ZPD. Recall that scaffolding involves informal methods such as conversations, questions, modeling, guiding, and supporting to help children learn concepts, knowledge, and skills that they might not learn by themselves. When more competent others provide help, children are able to accomplish what they would not have been able to do on their own. In other words, children are capable of far more competent behavior and achievement if they receive guidance and support from teachers.

Throughout the Montessori segment of the DVD, observe how the teacher scaffolds children's learning in academic, personal, and social skills.

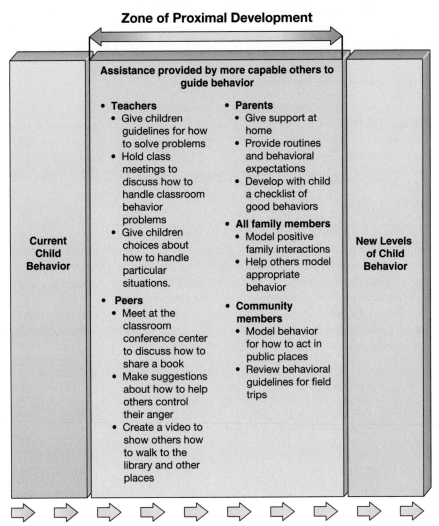

Zone of Proximal Development

Current Child Behavior

Assistance provided by more capable others to guide behavior

- **Teachers**
  - Give children guidelines for how to solve problems
  - Hold class meetings to discuss how to handle classroom behavior problems
  - Give children choices about how to handle particular situations.

- **Peers**
  - Meet at the classroom conference center to discuss how to share a book
  - Make suggestions about how to help others control their anger
  - Create a video to show others how to walk to the library and other places

- **Parents**
  - Give support at home
  - Provide routines and behavioral expectations
  - Develop with child a checklist of good behaviors

- **All family members**
  - Model positive family interactions
  - Help others model appropriate behavior

- **Community members**
  - Model behavior for how to act in public places
  - Review behavioral guidelines for field trips

New Levels of Child Behavior

FIGURE 14.1
Guiding Behavior in the Zone of Proximal Development
The ZPD is constantly moving and changing, depending on children's behavioral accomplishments and the assistance provided by others.

An appropriate target for scaffolding is classroom discussion, often a difficult process for teachers to manage. Teachers can begin by giving students guidance on how to behave during classroom discussions:

- Everyone listens to everyone else's ideas.
- Students who don't understand something ask others to repeat what they said.
- All children get a chance to participate; the teacher may direct the conversation to ensure that all children are involved.
- Children try to state their thoughts clearly.
- At the conclusion of the discussion, participants summarize what was discussed.

ADULT-CHILD DISCOURSE

The scaffolding script that follows is illustrative of adult-child discourse. It is an example of a learning conversation, which invites student participation. This discourse centers on how student authors should act while they are sharing their stories:

Teacher: Maybe we should now think about how to behave as the author during author's chair. What do authors do? Who can remember? Would you like to start?

Tina: The author sits in the author's chair and speaks loud and clear.

Crystal: The author should not fool around, like making faces or having outside conversations.

Shauna: The author should not be shy and should be brave and confident.

The teacher continued to invite students to participate using this type of scaffolding. A list of responsibilities was created and used in subsequent lessons.[4]

You will want to conduct similar discourses with children as you help them develop their skills and behavior. Discourse can also involve talking about how children might solve problems, interact and cooperate with others, understand norms of social conduct, and act on values related to school and family living. Teachers must initiate and guide these discourses and help children learn the new skills that will assist them in developing self-regulation.

PRIVATE SPEECH AND SELF-GUIDED BEHAVIOR

Jennifer, a four-year-old preschooler, is busily engrossed in putting a puzzle together. As she searches for a puzzle piece, she asks herself out loud, "Which piece comes next?" I'm sure you have heard children talk to themselves. More than likely, you have talked to yourself! Such conversations are commonplace among young children.

Private speech plays an important role in problem solving and self-regulation of behavior. Children use it to transfer problem-solving knowledge and responsibility from adults to themselves:

> When adults use questions and strategies to guide children and to help them discover solutions, they elevate language to the status of a primary problem-solving tool. This use of language by adults leads children to use speech to solve problems. Research reveals that the relation of private speech to children's behavior is consistent with the assumption that self-guiding utterances help bring action under the control of thought.[5]

CONSTRUCTIVIST GUIDANCE STRATEGIES

Using our knowledge of Vygotsky's theories, we can develop some strategies to guide children's behavior. Here are some things you can do:

In the Montessori segment of the DVD, observe how the teacher guides the children in resolving their differences.

- Guide problem solving
  "Tanya, what are some things you can do to help you remember to put the books away?"
  "Keyshawn, you and Juana want to use the easel at the same time. What are some ways you can both use it?"
- Ask questions that help children arrive at their own solutions
  "Jesse, you can't use both toys at the same time. Which one do you want to use first?"
  "Mary, here is an idea that might help you get to the block corner. Ask Amy, 'Would you please move over a little so I can get to the blocks?'"
- Model appropriate skills
  Practice social skills and manners (e.g., say please and thank you).
  Listen attentively to children and encourage listening. For example, "Harry has something he wants to tell us; let's listen to what he has to say."

In the short term, telling children what to do may seem like the easiest and most efficient way to manage classroom behavior. However, in the long run, it robs them of growth-producing opportunities to develop skills that will help them guide their behavior throughout their lives. Using strategies such as those listed above is essential and should become a routine part of classroom life.

Thomas Gordon (1918–2002) developed a child guidance program based on teacher-student relationships. He developed Parent Effectiveness Training (PET) for parents and Teacher Effectiveness Training (TET) for teachers. Both programs use communication as the primary means of helping parents and teachers build positive relationships with children, relationships that foster self-direction, self-responsibility, self-determination, self-control, and self-evaluation.[6]

PROBLEM OWNERSHIP

The first cornerstone of the TET approach to guiding behavior is to identify who owns the behavior problem. When a problem arises, as problems inevitably do in teacher-child relationships, you, the teacher, have to determine whether the child or children own the problem or whether you own the problem. For example, preschool teacher Maria Escobar observed that several of her children were noisy and disruptive and were not following the guidelines for using the woodworking center. As Maria thought about the children's lack of self-direction, she concluded that the children owned the problem; they didn't fully understand what the center directions were and how to follow them.

On the other hand, Maria was becoming increasingly irritated with always having to deal with Hector's interrupting behavior during circle time. As Maria thought about Hector's behavior, she realized *she* owned the problem. She was allowing Hector's behavior to irritate her rather than working on specific ways to help Hector learn new ways of behaving and interacting.

> The difference between student-owned and teacher-owned problems is essentially one of tangible and concrete (or *real*) effect. Teachers can separate their own problems from those of their students by asking themselves: "Does this behavior have any *real,* tangible, or concrete effect on me? Am I feeling unaccepting because I am being interfered with, damaged, hurt, or impaired in some way? Or am I feeling unaccepting merely because I'd like the student to act differently, not have a problem, feel the way I think he should?" If the answer is "yes" to the latter, the problem belongs to the student. If it is "yes" to the former, the teacher certainly has a real stake in the problem.[7]

Determining who owns the problem is an essential part of being able to guide children's behavior well.

ACTIVE LISTENING

Active listening is the second cornerstone of TET. It helps you identify who has the problem, and it will help you communicate with children. Active listening involves interactions with a child to provide proof that you understand what the child is talking about. This proof might come in the form of feedback.

Active listening The practice of giving full attention to the person speaking.

Active listening involves seven *attitudes,* or *sets.* Taken as a whole, they will help you practice and perfect active listening, with the goal of helping you help your children guide their behavior:

- Develop a sense of trust in students' ability to solve their own problems.
- Accept the feelings expressed by students.
- Understand that feelings are quite transitory. Many feelings exist only "of the moment."
- Help students with their problems and make time for them.
- Be "with" each student who is experiencing troubles, yet maintain a separate identity. Experience students' feelings as your own, but don't let them become your own.
- Understand that students are seldom able to start out by sharing the real problem.
- Respect the privacy and confidential nature of what students reveal about their lives.[8]

I MESSAGES

I message A method of communication in which speakers reflect on their true feelings about a situation or event.

If, upon reflection, you determine that you own the problem, then you will want to deliver an **I message.** I messages are designed to let others know that you have a problem with their behavior and that you want them to do something to change the behavior. Let's join Maria and Hector again. Maria can send this I message: "Hector, when I am constantly interrupted, I can't teach what I need to, and this makes me feel like I'm not a good teacher." Notice how Maria described the behavior (i.e., interrupting), the consequences of the behavior (i.e., "I can't teach"), and her feelings (i.e., "I'm not a good teacher"). These three components constitute a good I message.

You will want to read more about all of these major concepts associated with Vygotskian, constructivist, and TET ideas and practices and reflect on how you can apply them to your teaching. Using these strategies effectively requires much determination and practice. However, they are worth the effort, and you will be rewarded with beneficial results as you learn to guide children's behavior.

NINE KEYS TO GUIDING BEHAVIOR

The goal of most parents and early childhood professionals is to have children behave in socially acceptable and appropriate ways that contribute to and promote life in a democratic society. Teachers should view children's behavior as a process of learning by doing—with guidance. Children cannot learn to develop appropriate behavior and learn to be responsible by themselves; they must be shown and taught through precept and example. But just as no one learns to ride a bicycle by reading a book on the subject, children do not learn to guide themselves by only being told what to do. They need opportunities to develop, practice, and perfect their abilities to control and guide their own behavior. At the same time they need the guidance, help, support, and encouragement of parents and early childhood professionals. The Voice from the Field "Character, Choice, and Student Behavior" on pages 405–406 shows how one school's proactive approach to guidance brought about amazing changes in behavior.

How can professionals best help children achieve appropriate behavior? Effective guidance of children's behavior consists of these nine essential elements, which we discuss next in this section.

KNOW YOUR PHILOSOPHY OF GUIDING BEHAVIOR

The first rule in guiding children is to know what you believe. Review again your philosophy of education, which you wrote in chapter 1. Unless you know your attitudes toward discipline and behavior, it will be hard to practice a positive and consistent program of guidance, and consistency plays a major role in teaching and guiding. Therefore, develop a philosophy about what you believe concerning discipline and behavior. There are many guidance approaches available.

Knowing what you believe also makes it easier for you to talk to parents, help them guide their children's behavior, and counsel them about discipline. Today, many parents find the challenges of child rearing overwhelming; they do not know what to do and consequently look to professionals for help. Knowing what you believe—based on sound principles of how children grow, develop, and learn—enables you to work confidently with parents.

Parents and early childhood professionals have an obligation to help children learn appropriate behavior by guiding their actions and modeling correct behaviors. What role does setting rules play in guiding behavior?

CHARACTER, CHOICE, AND STUDENT BEHAVIOR

Many educators have responded to rising violence in our schools by supporting ethical or character education in our classrooms. But we have not yet entertained those same principles in guiding our response to student behavior. We profess to want our children to be reasoned, caring humans who will contribute to the good of society, but we tolerate the very opposite in our school discipline procedures. And we have not looked at what we model as a factor in the problem. Our response to behavior problems has been to set the rules and then set the consequences. If the rules do not work, then we set higher consequences. Or conversely, we decide that the problem is a counseling issue and that working with the student on clarifying feelings will make the difference.

RETHINKING OUR APPROACH

More than two years ago, in a district that serves a rural population in upstate New York, we completely revamped the discipline system in the elementary schools we served. This work was undertaken by the school psychologist, the student counselor, and me, the supervisory principal for the district. We gave much thought to what we were doing before we decided what we would change, and we based that though on the principles of moral development and learning theory. We allowed ourselves to question all assumptions about what discipline should look like in a school, and as happens in so many other areas of education, we discovered that much of what was being done was reflex and habit—not thought and vision. In the same way that we find ourselves proclaiming platitudes to our young that came from the mouths of our own parents ("If I've told you once, I've told you a thousand times"), in schools we react as we have always reacted, without asking ourselves whether what we are doing is working—or even if it ever did.

In our deliberations we began with the situation before us, citing the number of children with repetitious behavior problems that were not being changed. We also discussed the fact that, whether or not we choose to label it as such, a good deal of time, is devoted in school to issues of character, if we think of character in terms of the actions that reflect it. Under such a definition, all issues of student discipline are issues of character as well.

PROBLEM SOLVING WITH STUDENTS

We concluded that we could start over and that we could be guided by those same characteristics we so wanted in our students—attributes like respect, caring, honesty, fairness. We also concluded that we wanted real learning to result that would help students use ethical principles in deciding what to say and do and that we would be teachers in this process, not wardens. The result was a structure that took the student our of the trouble situation if it could not be handled within the classroom and took him or her immediately into a problem-solving process. Five adults were on call to provide one-on-one guidance through the process. These were not extra staff but a combination of administrative, teaching, and support staff already with us.

The process itself had five distinct phases: (a) describing the situation or incident; (b) defining what action the student had chosen; (c) identifying what character trait was compromised by the choice of action; (d) generating a number of alternative choices for action, ones that reflected good character; and (e) choosing an action and committing to it.

The process ended when the student had a solution that he or she could commit to and that was workable within the current situation. A solution was not defined as going to detention or staying out of school or doing extra schoolwork. A solution meant reflecting on what went wrong, realizing that we all have choices, and finding a choice that reflected good character. And then, very importantly, making a personal commitment to that choice. Our underlying assumption was that children want to be people of good character, and our experience consistently bore that out.

TAKING TIME

The time necessary to go through the process with a student was anywhere from five minutes to more than one school day, depending on the problem and the student. Our approach was to take whatever time was necessary, our goal being to ensure success for the student. If the student arrived angry or unwilling to work on the problem, the adult mentor would wait until the student was ready, inviting the student to notify the mentor of that readiness.

With that in mind, mentors brought their own work to the problem-solving room and were prepared not to work with the child immediately. The only condition was that the problem would be solved before the student returned to a regular routine. The teacher who sent a student into problem solving also sent a brief description of the problem. Once the student had chosen a solution, the mentor and the student went back to the referring teacher and discussed the viability of the solution. This step was important and was a prerequisite to rejoining the group. If a student failed to use the chosen solution, thus resulting in a continued problem, he or she immediately returned to problem solving.

The students who experienced the greatest difficulty with the process and who thus needed more time were those for whom there was a less-developed understanding of how character looks in action or a lack of connection between ethics and personal choice. Of the students who benefited the most from the process and for whom we could track the greatest growth as we reviewed our cases, many came from homes where there was little or no modeling or support for making good choices. In such cases, we as mentors took the additional step of checking in with the students from time to time to ask how their solutions were working and to give additional encouragement for good decision making.

MAINTAINING THE COMMUNITY

Our results surprised even us. After two years, the decrease in problems—which we tracked through careful record keeping—was 28 percent. An unforeseen result was the effect on school climate. By maintaining the relationship between mentor and student, we remained a support rather than the external controller of imposed behavior. Our sense of community within the school was preserved. And we could hope that we were building the basis in our children for a lifetime of good choices—choices made because they could understand how action reflects character.

Contributed by Margaret Pastor, principal, Stedwick Elementary School, Montgomery Village, Maryland.

KNOW CHILD DEVELOPMENT AND CHILDREN

The foundation for guiding all children is to know what they are like—how they grow and develop. Unfortunately, not all early childhood professionals are as knowledgeable about children as they should be. As a result, they may expect some children to behave in ways that are more appropriate for other children, perhaps younger or older. Here lies part of the problem: children cannot behave well when adults expect too much or too little of them or when adults expect them to behave in ways inappropriate for them as individuals. Thus, a key to guiding children's behavior is to *really know what they are like.*

MEET CHILDREN'S NEEDS

Self-actualization An inherent tendency to reach one's true potential.

Part of knowing children is knowing their needs. Abraham Maslow believed that human growth and development is oriented toward **self-actualization,** the striving to realize one's potential. Maslow felt that humans are internally motivated by five basic needs, which constitute a hierarchy of motivating behaviors, progressing from physical needs to self-fulfillment. Maslow's hierarchy (see chapter 5 for a graphic representation) moves through physical needs, safety and security needs, belonging and affection needs, and self-esteem needs, culminating in self-actualization. Let's look at each of these stages to see how we can apply them to guiding children's behavior.

Physical Needs. Children's abilities to guide their behavior depend in part on how well their physical needs are met. Children do their best in school, for example, when they are well nourished. Thus, parents should provide for their children's nutritional needs by giving them breakfast, and early childhood professionals should stress its benefits.

In the Infant and Toddler segment of the DVD, observe the ways child care requires anticipating children's needs. How does that help children later?

Information on recent brain research, provided in chapter 2, also informs us about nutrition and the brain. For example, the brain needs protein and water to function well. Consequently, many teachers allow children to have water bottles at their desks and allow them to have frequent nutritional snacks.

In addition, the quality of the environment is important. Children cannot be expected to behave appropriately if classrooms are dark and noisy and smell of stale air. And children need adequate rest to do and be their best. The ideal amount of rest is an individual matter, but many young children need eight to ten hours of sleep each night. A tired child cannot meet many of the expectations of schooling.

Safety and Security Needs.   Children can't learn in fear. They should not have to fear parents or professionals and should feel comfortable and secure at home and at school. Asking or forcing children to do school tasks for which they do not have the skills makes them feel insecure, and children who are afraid or insecure become tense. Consider also the dangers many urban children face—such as crime, drugs, or homelessness—or the impact on children who live in an atmosphere of domestic violence. Part of guiding children's behavior includes providing safe and secure communities, neighborhoods, homes, schools, and classrooms.

Need for Belonging and Affection.   Children need the sense of belonging that comes from being given jobs to do, having responsibilities, and helping make classroom and home decisions. Love and affection needs are satisfied when parents hold, hug, and kiss their children and tell them, "I love you." Teachers meet children's affectional needs when they smile, speak pleasantly, are kind and gentle, treat children with courtesy and respect, and genuinely value each child. An excellent way to show respect and affection for children and demonstrate their belonging is to greet them personally when they come into the classroom, center, or home. A personal greeting helps children feel wanted and secure and promotes feelings of self-worth. In fact, all early childhood programs should begin with this daily validation of each child. In the Diversity Tie-In "Do Teacher-Child Relations Really Matter?" on page 408 you can read about the importance of those relationships to as child's healthy intellectual and emotional development.

Need for Self-Esteem.   Children who view themselves as worthy, responsible, and competent act in accordance with these feelings. Children's views of themselves come primarily from parents and early childhood professionals. The foundations for self-esteem are success and achievement. Consequently, it is up to parents and professionals to give all children opportunities for success.

Self-Actualization.   Children want to use their talents and abilities to do things on their own and be independent. Professionals and parents can help young children become independent by helping them learn to dress themselves, go to the restroom by themselves, and take care of their environment. Adults can also help children set achievement and behavior goals ("Tell me what you are going to build with your blocks") and encourage them to evaluate their behavior ("Let's talk about how you cleaned up your room").

These categories highlight the basic needs professionals and parents must consider when guiding children and helping them develop responsibility for their behavior. Read the Program in Action "Positive Guidance" on pages 410–411 for help in developing a program that encourages responsible behavior by first addressing basic needs.

HELP CHILDREN BUILD NEW BEHAVIORS

Internal Control.   Helping children build new behaviors means that you help them learn that they are primarily responsible for their own behavior and that the pleasures and rewards for appropriate behavior are internal, coming from within them, as opposed to always coming from outside (i.e., from the approval and praise of others). We refer to this concept as **locus of control**—the source or place of control. The preferred and recommended locus of control for young and old alike is internal.

Children are not born with inner control; the process begins at birth, continues through the early childhood years, and is a never-ending process throughout life. If the locus of control is external, children are controlled by others and are always told what to do

In the Primary Grade segment of the DVD, observe this boy's behavior in the lunchroom and later in the group listening to a story. What characteristics does he exhibit? How might you empower him?

Locus of control   The source of control over personal behavior, either internal or external.

DO TEACHER–CHILD RELATIONS REALLY MATTER?

Think for a minute about your social relations with others. How others treat you affects you emotionally, physically, and cognitively. The same is true for the children you teach. How you relate to them really matters and affects how well they achieve, as well as how well they do and will behave. What are teacher behaviors that really matter in preventing children's behavior problems? Consider these:

- Responding to children in a timely fashion
- Anticipating student needs and emotions
- Giving frequent feedback
- Providing strong supports for children's academic and social competence in the classroom setting

Researchers have found that the extent to which children can access the instructional and socialization resources of the classroom environment may be, in part, predicated on teacher-child interactions: "[T]he association between the quality of early teacher–child relationships and later school performance can be both strong and persistent. The association is apparent in both academic and social spheres of school performance."*

In addition, teacher–child closeness, such as having an affectionate and warm relationship, can reduce the tendency for aggressive behavior. "Closer teacher–child relationships may provide young children with resources (e.g., emotional security, guidance, and aid) that facilitate an 'approach' orientation—as opposed to an 'avoidant' or 'resistant' stance—toward the interpersonal and scholastic demands of the classroom and school."† The implication for you and other early childhood professionals is that you need to really care for your children and develop strong and affectionate relationships with them.

In one study regarding teacher–child closeness, "females tended to develop higher levels of cooperative participation, school liking, and achievement than did males."‡ This might indicate gender differences in teacher–child relations and suggest that boys are at greater risk of not having a close teacher relationship. Thus, a close teacher–child relationship is particularly important for males; for low-socioeconomic children and minorities; and for all children who might not experience a close relationship with another caring adult.

These findings mean that you need to provide a classroom context that is supportive of and responsive to children's social and affectional needs. This, of course, can be a challenging task, but one that is necessary. How we teachers relate to children helps determine their behavioral outcomes now and in the future.

---

* B. K. Hamre and R. C. Pianta, "Early Teacher-Child Relationships and the Trajectory of Children's School Outcomes Through Eighth Grade," *Child Development* 72 (2001): 625–638.

† G. W. Ladd and K. B. Burgess, "Do Relational Risks and Protective Factors Moderate the Linkages Between Childhood Aggression and Early Psychological and School Adjustment?" *Child Development* 72 (2001): 1579–1601.

‡ Ibid.

---

and how to behave. Parents and professionals must try to avoid developing an external locus of control in children. We want them to control their own behavior. The Program in Action about hard-to-manage children on pages 412–413 is a Competency Builder that will help you help children build new behaviors.

Empowering Children with Responsibility. Helping children build new behaviors creates a sense of responsibility and self-confidence. As children are given responsibility, they develop greater self-direction, which means that you can guide them at the next level in their ZPD. Some professionals and parents hesitate to let children assume responsibilities, but without responsibilities children are bored and frustrated and become discipline problems—the very opposite of what is intended.

To reiterate, guiding behavior is not about compliance and control. And it is not a matter of getting children to please adults with remarks such as, "Show me how perfect you can be," "Don't embarrass me in front of others," "I want to see nice groups," or "I'm wait-

Companion Website To complete a Program in Action activity related to guidance, go to the Companion Website at **www.prenhall.com/morrison**, select chapter 14, then choose the Program in Action module.

ing for quiet." Instead, it is important to instill in children a sense of independence and responsibility for their *own* behavior. For example, you might say, "You have really worked a long time cutting out the flower you drew. You kept working on it until you were finished. Would you like some tape to hang it up?"

Thus, you can do a number of things to empower children:

- *Give children responsibilities.* All children, from an early age, should have responsibilities—that is, tasks that are theirs to do and for which they are accountable. Being responsible for completing tasks—doing such things as putting toys and learning materials away—promotes a positive sense of self-worth and conveys to children that people in a community have responsibilities for making the community work well.
- *Give children choices.* Life is full of choices—some require thought and deliberation; others are automatic, based on previous behavior. But every time you make a decision, you are being responsible and exercising your right to decide. Children like to have choices, and choices help them become independent, confident, and self-disciplined. Making choices is a key to developing responsible behavior and inner control; it lays the foundation for decision making later. Here are several guidelines for giving children choices:
  - Give children choices only when there are valid choices to make. When it comes time to clean up the classroom, do not let children choose whether they want to participate. Instead, let them pick between collecting the scissors or the crayons.
  - Help children make choices. Instead of "What would you like to do today?" say, "Sarah, you have a choice between working in the woodworking center or the computer center. Which would you like to do?"
  - When you do not want children to make a decision, do not offer them a choice.
- *Help children succeed.* Children want to be successful, and you can help them in their efforts. For example, you can arrange the environment and make opportunities available for children to be able to do things. Successful accomplishments are a major ingredient of positive behavior.

Inner control helps children work independently, which is an important social and behavioral skill that is necessary for ongoing school achievement.

ESTABLISH APPROPRIATE EXPECTATIONS

Expectations set the boundaries for desired behavior. They are the guideposts children use in learning to direct their own behavior. When children know what adults expect, they can better achieve those expectations.

Setting appropriate expectations for children means you must first decide what behaviors are appropriate. Up to a point, the more we expect of children, the more and better they achieve. Generally, we expect too little of most children. However, having expectations for children is not enough. You have to help children know and understand what the expectations are and then help them meet these expectations. Some children will need little help; others will need demonstration, explanation, encouragement, and support as they learn.

In the High/Scope segment of the DVD, notice that children are given center choices. How does choice affect behavior?

Set Limits. Setting limits is closely associated with establishing expectations and relates to defining unacceptable behavior. For example, knocking over a block tower built by

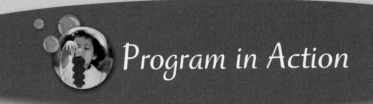

Program in Action

POSITIVE GUIDANCE
Responsible, Motivated, Self-Directed Learners

The Grapevine (Texas) Elementary School staff had a vision. The vision emphasized a desire to encourage all learners to be responsible, intrinsically motivated, and self-directed in an environment of mutual respect. As we looked for a discipline management system that fit this philosophy, we recognized that we needed one that emphasized both personal responsibility for behavior and cooperation instead of competition and one that focused on developing a community of supportive members. We also discovered that we held several beliefs in common that should be the foundation of our discipline management plan:

1. All human beings have three basic needs—to feel connected (the ability to love and be loved), to feel capable (I can accomplish things), and to feel contributive (I count in the communities in which I belong).
2. Problem solving and solutions encourage responsible behavior. Punishment, by contrast, encourages rebellion and resentment.

3. Children can be creative decision makers and responsible citizens when given opportunities to direct the processes that affect the day-to-day environment in which they live.
4. Every inappropriate action does not necessitate a consequence but can be used as a cornerstone of a problem-solving experience, ultimately leading to a true behavior change.

Our desire was, and is, to address the needs of the whole child as we educate our children to be responsible citizens.

ADOPTING THE PLAN

After much research, we decided to implement Positive Discipline as a discipline management system based on the concept of responsibilities rather than rules.* Teachers established the following Grapevine Star Responsibilities:

I will be responsible for myself and my learning.
I will respect others and their property.

someone else and running in the classroom are generally considered unacceptable behaviors. Setting clear limits has several benefits:

1. Helps you clarify in your own mind what you believe is unacceptable, based on your knowledge of child development, children, their families, and their culture.
2. Helps prevent inconsistency.
4. Helps children act with confidence because they know which behaviors are acceptable.
5. Provides children with security; children want and need limits.

As children grow and mature, the limits change and are adjusted to developmental levels, programmatic considerations, and life situations.

Develop Classroom Rules. Although I like to talk about and think in terms of expectations and limits, other early childhood professionals think and talk about rules. Here are some additional guidelines about rules.

You should plan classroom rules from the first day of class. As the year goes on, you can involve children in establishing other classroom rules, but in the beginning, children want and need to know what they can and cannot do. For example, rules might relate to changing small groups and following bathroom routines. Whatever rules you establish, they should be fair, reasonable, and appropriate to the children's age and maturity. And you should keep rules to a minimum—the fewer the better.

Companion Website To learn more about guiding children's behavior, go to the Companion Website at **www.prenhall.com/morrison**, select chapter 14, then choose the Linking to Learning module.

I will listen and follow directions promptly.

I will complete my classwork and homework in a quality manner.

Furthermore, we decided that rewards—whether in the way of stickers, pencils, or award ceremonies—were not on the whole, consistent with encouraging intrinsic motivation and the belief that all children should continuously monitor their own learning and behavior. Rather, the term *reward* should be replaced with *celebration*, and these celebrations should be based on what children find personally significant.

Teachers also discussed the understanding that they would become facilitators of decision-making sessions instead of being generals in command, and they would encourage self-evaluation by students, leading to solutions.

ENGAGING STUDENTS

Throughout the course of the year, students set goals each six-week period (usually one academic goal and one behavioral goal) and conferred with their teachers at the end of the six weeks to determine the extent of their achievement of that goal. At the end of the year, students participated in a celebration of achievement. Each student chose the goal that held the most personal significance and received a certificate that detailed the goal. The principal read each chosen goal in the grade-level celebrations as the students walked across the stage and shook hands with the principal. Teachers, parents, and students all enjoyed this ceremony, which emphasized the worth of each individual and affirmed that learning

was, and is the ultimate goal of education and school (as opposed to a grade or series of marks on a report card).

Irene Boynton, a first-grade teacher, comments that Positive Discipline allows children to experience the rewards of feeling confident and healthy about making respectful, responsible choices because it is the right thing to do, not because they well receive something for their choice.

THE BENEFITS

Teachers at Grapevine Elementary, when asked to comment on Positive Discipline, say such things as, "Is there any other way to teach?" and "We would never go back to playing referee again!" Students no longer ask, "What am I going to get?" in response to a request to go the extra mile for another student or while working on a project. They are developing respect for themselves and for the rights and needs of others. The skills learned through Positive Discipline extend into academic areas, where we find that students are becoming more thoughtful, introspective, self-motivated, and effective problem solvers. We believe that we are fostering a safe, respectful community in which children and adults thrive together in an atmosphere of mutual respect.

Visit Grapevine Elementary on the Web at http://www.gcisd-k12.org/schools/ges/index.html.

Contributed by Alicia King, Belinda Leu, Natalie Finch, and Nancy Robinson (original author), Grapevine (Texas) Elementary School.

* Jane Nelsen, Lynn Lott, and Stephen Glenn, *Positive Discipline in the Classroom* (Rocklin, CA: Prima, 1997).

Remind children of the rules and encourage them to conform to them. Later, review the rules, and have the children evaluate their behavior against the rules. Children are able to become responsible for their own behavior in a positive, accepting atmosphere where they know what the expectations are. You cannot have expectations without having rules.

ARRANGE AND MODIFY THE ENVIRONMENT

Environment plays a key role in children's ability to guide their behavior. For example, if parents want children to be responsible for taking care of their rooms, they should arrange the environment accordingly—providing shelves, hangers, and drawers at child height. Similarly, you should arrange your classroom so that children can get and return their own papers and materials, use learning centers, and have time to work on individual projects.

In child care centers, early childhood classrooms, and family day care homes, early childhood professionals arrange the environment so that it supports the purposes of the program and makes appropriate behavior possible. Room arrangement is crucial to guiding children's behavior; appropriate arrangements signal to children that they are expected to be responsible for their own behavior. An appropriate environment also enables teachers to observe and provide for children's interests through their selection of activities. And it is easier to live and work in an attractive and aesthetically pleasing classroom or center. We all want a nice environment—children should have one, too.

In the Primary Grade segment of the DVD, observe how the environment is set up to engage the children in work.

HOW TO GUIDE HARD-TO-MANAGE CHILDREN TO HELP ENSURE THEIR SUCCESS

Tyrone entered the kindergarten classroom on the first day of the school year, trailing several feet behind his mom, who appeared to be unaware of his presence. She called out a greeting to another mom, and the two of them had an extended discussion about events in the neighborhood. Tyrone glanced around the room and headed purposefully toward the housekeeping center, where he grabbed a baby doll, threw it out of the doll bed, and then ran to the block box and grabbed a large block in each hand. At this point I deflected his trail of destruction and redirected his progress. "Good morning, welcome to my class. My name is Ms. Cheryl. What's your name?" The whirlwind stopped briefly to mumble a response that I could not understand and glared at me in open hostility. "Let's go talk to Mom," I suggested, touching his shoulder and directing him toward his mom.

BACKGROUND

My school is in an area that includes mostly low-socioeconomic households; ours is a Title I school, with 95 percent of our students on free or reduced-fee lunches. In any given year, one-half to two-thirds of our students entering kindergarten have had no preschool experience. Nevertheless, as an early childhood educator, it is my job to help these students develop behaviors that will ensure their success in education. That does not mean that I need only to teach them to write their names, recognize all their letters and numbers, sit quietly in their chairs, and raise their hands before they speak. These tasks are not ends in themselves but are important steps in encouraging children to love learning and to gain the self-regulation that supports it.

UNDERSTANDING BEHAVIOR

In our opening scenario, what important facts should we as educators recognize as signals that Tyrone has some behaviors that require adjustment to ensure his success in school? He seems unaware of the expected protocol for entering a classroom, that is, looking for an adult in charge to give him directions. His mother's apparent lack of interest in her child's behavior could be an indicator that Tyrone does not expect the adults around him to be involved with his activities. He may have been in an atmosphere that requires very little from him when it comes to following rules and, as indicated by his hostility, may see adult intervention as only restrictive rather than supportive and nurturing. Tyrone may even have an undiagnosed speech problem that prohibits adults and other children from understanding his needs. If adults in his world have failed to observe and interact with him, he is also probably lacking in basic language skills and vocabulary, which would limit his understanding. He appears to deal with his world in a very physical manner.

BEHAVIORS NECESSARY FOR SUCCESS IN SCHOOL

The following behaviors are necessary for children to succeed in school:

Behavior #1: *Recognition of authority*—Tyrone was not even aware that an adult was in charge of the classroom.

Behavior #2: *Trust in adults*—The process of building trust is lengthy, but Tyrone needs to learn to see adults as nurturing and supportive.

Behavior #3: *Use of verbal skills rather than physical reactions*—If Tyrone is lacking in language, his teacher

The following guidelines can be helpful as you think about and arrange your classroom or program area to help children guide their own behavior:

- Have an open area in which you and your children can meet as a whole group. This area is essential for story time, general class meetings, and so on. Starting and ending the day with a class meeting allows children to discuss their behavior and say how they can do a better job.

can help provide language experiences: defining words, explaining everything in detail, showing and describing pictures, reading books aloud, helping with activities, and talk, talk, talking.

Behaviors #1 and #2 are especially complex; they stem from children's environments and experiences. However, I am committed to being one of the reasons a child succeeds and will dedicate great amounts of time and energy to changing behaviors that interfere with student learning. I follow certain steps to guide destructive behaviors into more successful ones:

STEP 1 Plan

Before that first day of school, I plan—what activities I will offer my students, what part of the day I will use for centers, how I can show my students the best ways to use materials, where I want them to keep their belongings, how I can explain my expectations about dealing with conflict, how I will deal with behavior that is inappropriate, and what I am going to say about procedures for our classroom.

STEP 2 Be explicit

Many of my students are not accustomed to having an adult schedule their time for six hours, and many behavior problems stem from this new pressure to conform to an unfamiliar structure. Therefore, I want to be sure that all of my students fully understand what I expect. For example, I state exactly how I want them to move about the classroom, the cafeteria, the playground, and the school hallways. If they do not follow my instructions, I require them to practice. Many behaviors that inhibit success in school occur because students are not made aware of appropriate and inappropriate school procedures.

STEP 3 Model behavior

I model or have my students role-play expected behavior in interpersonal actions. Students who take other students' belongings, hit other students, or push and shove other students are taught to handle these issues through conflict-resolution methods. However, it takes numerous rounds of modeling and role-playing to make an impact on behavior that has been ingrained for five years at home and is still the norm when students return home.

STEP 4 Role-play

I spend some time each day having students role-play scenarios with incorrect behavior. We brainstorm about what the correct behavior would be. Hitting, pushing, name calling, destroying property are all common problems among our students. I ask my students how they feel if someone calls them a name (or exhibits any of the other negative behaviors).

STEP 5 Develop classroom rules

I have five classroom rules:

1. We listen to each other.
2. We use our hands for helping, not hurting.
3. We use caring language.
4. We care about each other's feelings.
5. We are responsible for what we say and do.

STEP 6 Reinforce

Helping hard-to-manage children learn to guide their own behavior takes consistent reteaching and reinforcement. I correct every misbehavior I see, either using the "I don't like it when you . . ." statement or stating which rule has been broken. I use a very calm voice when I talk to my students and do not allow them to "tell" on each other. When a student comes to me with a tale of misbehavior, I ask, "Did you tell [specific name] how you feel?" Usually by the end of the first nine-week grading period, my students are using the behaviors and statements we have learned, and the tone of my classroom changes from a volatile one to a caring one. Spending some time at the beginning of the year changing behaviors and stating expectations gives my students the guidance they need to begin and to continue successful student careers.

Contributed by Cheryl Doyle, National Board Certified preschool teacher, Miami, Florida.

- Make center areas well defined and accessible to all children. Make center boundaries low enough so that you and others can see over them for proper supervision and observation.
- Provide for all kinds of activities, both quiet and loud. Try to locate quiet areas together (e.g., reading area and puzzle area) and loud centers together (e.g., woodworking and blocks).

- Have appropriate and abundant materials for children's use. Locate them so that children can easily retrieve them. Having to ask for materials promotes dependency and can lead to behavior problems.
- Make materials easy to store and put away. A general rule of thumb is that there should be a place for everything, and everything should be in its place when not in use.
- Provide children with guidelines on how to use centers and materials.

Supportive classroom
Physical arrangement of the classroom so that it is conducive to the behaviors to be taught.

The Supportive Classroom.   You can arrange the physical setting into a **supportive classroom,** conducive to the behaviors you want to teach. If you want to encourage independent work, you must provide places and time for children to work alone. Disruptive behavior is often encouraged by classroom arrangements that force children to walk over or through other children to get to equipment or materials. The atmosphere of the classroom or the learning environment must be such that new behaviors are possible.

An Encouraging Environment.   The classroom should be a place where children can do their best work and be on their best behavior. It should be a rewarding place. The following are components of an **encouraging environment:**

Encouraging environment   A classroom environment that rewards student accomplishment and independence.

- Opportunities for children to display their work
- Opportunities for freedom of movement (within guidelines)
- Opportunities for independent work
- A variety of work stations and materials based on children's interests

Time and Transitions.   Time, generally more important to adults than to children, plays a major role in every program. The following guidelines relate to time and its use:

- *Do not waste children's time.* Children should be involved in interesting, meaningful activities from the moment they enter the center, classroom, or family day care home.
- *Do not make children wait.* When children have to wait for materials or their turn, you should provide them with something else to do, such as listening to a story or playing in the block center. Problems can occur when children have to wait, because they like to be busy and involved.
- *Allow transition time.* Transitions are times when children move from one activity to another. They should be as smooth as possible and as fun as possible. In one program, teachers sing "It's Cleanup Time!" as a transition from one activity to cleanup and then to another activity.

Routines.   Establish classroom routines from the beginning. Children need the confidence and security of a routine that will help them do their best. A routine also helps prevent discipline problems, because children know what to do and can learn to do it without a lot of disturbance. Parents also need to establish routines in the home; a child who knows the family always eats at 5:30 P.M. can be expected to be there. Consistency plays an important role in managing behavior in both the home and the classroom. If children know what to expect in terms of routine and behavior, they will behave better.

Figure 14.2 identifies strategies you can implement in your classroom to support children in learning self-regulation and guiding their own behavior. As you reflect on these strategies, consider what else you might include.

MODEL APPROPRIATE BEHAVIOR

We have all heard the maxim "Telling is not teaching." Nevertheless, we tend to teach by giving instructions, and, of course, children do need instructions. Professional educators soon realize, however, that actions speak louder than words.

FIGURE 14.2 Strategies for Promoting a Positive Environment

- Emphasize community and a culture of caring
- Set high expectations
- Express clear expectations
- Display consistent behavior
- Develop open communication among all children and adults
- Be an efficacious teacher, one who believes children can and will learn and teaches accordingly
- Obtain sufficient materials to support learning activities
- Establish and maintain routines
- Plan for a daily balance between cooperation and independent learning
- Observe children learning, reflect on how each learns best, and identify trouble areas
- Build positive parent, teacher, and child partnerships

Children see and remember how other people act. After observing another person, a child tries out a new behavior. If this new action brings a reward of some kind, the child repeats it. Proponents of the modeling approach to learning believe that most behavior people exhibit is learned from the behavior of a model(s). They think children tend to model behavior that brings rewards from parents and early childhood professionals.

A model may be someone whom we respect or find interesting and who we believe is being rewarded for the behavior he or she exhibits. Groups can also serve as models. For example, it is common to hear a teacher in an early childhood classroom comment, "I like how Cristina and Carlos are sitting quietly and listening to the story." Immediately following such a remark, you can see the group of children settle down to listen quietly to the story. Models do not necessarily have to be from real life; they can come from books and television. Unfortunately, the modeled behavior does not have to be socially acceptable to be reinforcing.

You can use the following techniques to help children learn through modeling:

- *Show.* For example, show children where the block corner is and how and where the blocks are stored.
- *Demonstrate.* Perform a task while students watch. For example, demonstrate the proper way to put the blocks away and store them. Extensions of this technique might have children practice the demonstration while you supervise or might have a child demonstrate to other children.
- *Model.* Modeling occurs when you practice the behavior you expect of the children. You can also call children's attention to the desired behavior when another child models it.
- *Supervise.* Supervision is a process of reviewing, maintaining standards, and following up. If children are not performing the desired behavior, you will need to review the behavior. You must be consistent in your expectations: children will learn that they do not have to put away their blocks if you allow them not to do it even once. Remember, you are responsible for setting up the environment to enable the children's learning to take place.

As an early childhood professional, you will need to model and demonstrate social and group-living behaviors as well, using simple courtesies ("Please," "Thank you," "You're welcome") and practicing cooperation, sharing, and respect for others.

It is also important not to encourage children's misbehavior; frequently, teachers see too much and ignore too little. Ignoring inappropriate behavior is probably one of the most

Companion Website
To complete an activity related to teacher-child relations, go to the Companion Website at **www.prenhall.com/morrison**, select chapter 14, then choose the Diversity Tie-In module.

overlooked strategies for managing an effective learning setting and guiding children's behavior. Ironically, some early childhood professionals feel guilty when they use this strategy; they believe that ignoring undesirable behaviors is not good teaching. Certainly, it must be combined with positive discipline and teaching, but if you focus on building responsible behavior, there will be less need to solve behavior problems.

For example, if Charlie jumps up during circle time and grabs a book from the book rack in order to get attention, you don't want to reinforce his inappropriate behavior by giving him that attention. Instead, you might ignore his behavior, while at the same time praising other children for sitting quietly and listening to you read the story. After several days of this strategy, Charlie will probably stay in the circle, at which point you can praise him for sitting and listening to the story as the other children are. Ignoring *can* work!

DEVELOP A PARTNERSHIP WITH PARENTS, FAMILIES, AND OTHERS

Involving parents and families is a wonderful way to gain invaluable insights about children's behavior. Parents and early childhood professionals must be partners and work cooperatively in guiding children's behaviors. In addition, involving other persons who are involved with the children is a good idea. Some of these significant others are other teachers, babysitters, before- and after-school care providers, coaches, and club leaders.

In the Reggio Emilia segment of the DVD, how do the teachers involve the parents in discussions about the children? How does this help with guidance?

As we said earlier, an important rule in guiding behavior is to *know your children.* A good way to learn about the children you care for and teach is through home visits. If you do not have an opportunity to visit the home, a parent conference is also valuable. Either way, you should gather information concerning the child's health history and interests; the child's attitude toward schooling; the parents' educational expectations for the child; the school support available in the home (e.g., books, places to study); home conditions that would support or hinder school achievement (such as where the child sleeps); parents' attitudes toward schooling and discipline; parents' support of the child (e.g., encouragement to do well); parents' interests and abilities; and parents' desire to become involved in the school.

A visit or conference also offers an opportunity for you to share ideas with parents. You should, for example, express your desire for children to do well in school; encourage parents to take part in school and classroom programs; suggest ways parents can help children learn; describe some of the school programs; give information about school events, projects, and meetings; and explain your belief about discipline.

In addition, working with and involving parents provides early childhood professionals with opportunities to help parents with parenting skills and child-related problems. The foundation for children's behavior is built in the home, and some parents unwittingly encourage children's misbehavior or antisocial behavior. Parents can promote antisocial behavior in their children by using punitive, negative, or overly restrictive punishment. However, when children are enrolled in child care programs at an early age, professionals have an ideal opportunity to help parents learn about and use positive discipline.

PROMOTE PROSOCIAL BEHAVIOR

One trend in early childhood education is for professionals to focus on helping children learn how to share, care for, and assist others. We call these and similar behaviors *prosocial behaviors.* There is a growing feeling among early childhood professionals that the ill effects of many societal problems, including uncivil behavior and violence, can be reduced or avoided and that efforts to achieve this goal should begin in the preschool and primary years. Consequently, they place emphasis on prosocial behaviors—teaching children the fundamentals of peaceful living, kindness, helpfulness, and cooperation. You can do several things to foster development of prosocial skills in the classroom:

- *Be a good role model for children.* You must demonstrate in your life and relationships with children and other adults the behaviors of cooperation and kindness that you want to encourage in children. Civil behavior begins with courtesy and manners. You can model these and help children to do the same.

- *Provide positive feedback and reinforcement when children perform prosocial behaviors.* When they are "rewarded" for appropriate behavior, children tend to repeat that behavior ("I like how you helped Tim get up when you accidentally ran into him. I bet that made him feel better").

- *Provide opportunities for children to help and show kindness to others.* Cooperative programs between primary classes and nursing and retirement homes are excellent opportunities to practice kind and helping behaviors.

Companion Website For strategies preschoolers can use to get along with others, go to the Companion Website at **www.prenhall.com/morrison**, select chapter 14, then choose the Linking to Learning module.

- *Conduct classroom routines and activities so they are as free of conflict as possible.* Provide opportunities for children to work together and practice skills for cooperative living. Design learning centers and activities for children to share and work cooperatively.

- *When real conflicts occur, provide practice in conflict resolution.* These skills include talking through problems, compromising, and apologizing. But a word of caution regarding apologies: too often an apology is a perfunctory response on the part of teachers and children. Rather than just offering the often-empty words "I'm sorry," it is far more meaningful to help one child understand how another is feeling. To encourage empathic behavior, you can provide examples of conflict resolution: "Erica, please don't knock over Shantrell's building because she worked hard to build it"; "Barry, what's another way that you can tell Pam she's sitting in your chair—instead of hitting her, which hurts?"

- *Conduct classroom activities based on multicultural principles that are free from stereotyping and sexist behaviors* (see chapter 15).

- *Read stories to children that exemplify prosocial behaviors.* Provide such literature for them to read.

- *Counsel and work with parents to encourage them to limit or eliminate children's exposure to violence.* Suggest that they regulate or eliminate watching violence on television, attending R-rated movies, playing video games with violent content, and buying CDs with objectionable lyrics.

It is increasingly important for early childhood professionals to help children learn how to resolve their differences, share, and cooperate. Curricula for helping children peaceably resolve conflict are growing in popularity.

- *Help children feel good about themselves, build strong self-images, and be competent individuals.* Children who are happy, confident, and competent feel good about themselves and are more likely to behave positively toward others.

You can also teach children specific skills for developing prosocial behavior:

- *Do something else.* Teach children to get involved in another activity. Children can learn that they do not always have to play with a toy someone else is playing with. They can get involved in another activity with a different toy; they can do something else now and play with the toy later. Chances are, however, that by getting involved in another activity, they will forget about the toy they were ready to fight for.

- *Take turns.* Taking turns is a good way for children to learn that they cannot always be first, have their own way, or do a prized activity. Taking turns brings equality and fairness to interpersonal relations.

- *Share.* Sharing is good behavior to promote in any setting. Children have to be taught how to share and how to behave when others do not share. Children can be helped to select another toy rather than hitting or grabbing. But keep in mind that during the

FIGURE 14.3   Basic Rights Supporting Positive Behavior

Children's rights

- To be respected and treated courteously
- To be treated fairly in culturally independent and gender-appropriate ways
- To learn behaviors necessary for self-guidance
- To have teachers with high expectations for them
- To learn and exercise independence
- To achieve to their highest levels
- To be praised and affirmed for appropriate behaviors and achievements
- To learn and practice effective social skills
- To learn and apply basic academic skills

Teachers' rights

- To be supported by administrators and parents in appropriate efforts to help children guide their behavior
- To have a partnership with parents so they can be successful
- To be treated courteously and professionally by peers and others

Parents' rights

- To share ideas and values of child rearing and discipline with teachers
- To be involved in and informed about classroom and school discipline policies
- To receive periodic reports and information about their children's behaviors
- To be educated and informed about how to guide their children's behavior

early years, children are egocentric, and acts of sharing are likely to be motivated by expectations of a reward or approval, such as being thought of as a good boy or girl.

In the process of helping children develop self-regulation and positive behavior, everyone involved has certain basic rights. Figure 14.3 lists these basic rights. Perhaps as you read them, you can think of others you want to include.

DEVELOPMENT OF AUTONOMOUS BEHAVIOR

Implicit in guiding children's behavior is the assumption that they can be, should be, and will be responsible for their own behavior. The ultimate goal of all education is to develop *autonomy* in children, which means "being governed by oneself." We want children to regulate their own behavior and make decisions about good and bad, right and wrong, and the way they will behave in relation to themselves and others.

Early childhood educators need to conduct programs that promote autonomy, one aspect of which is exchanging points of view with children.

> When a child tells a lie, for example, the adult can deprive him of dessert or make him write fifty times "I will not lie." The adult can also refrain from punishing the child and, instead, look him straight in the eye with great skepticism and affection and say, "I really can't believe what you are saying because . . . " This is an example of an exchange of points of view that contributes to the development of autonomy in children. The child who can see that the adult cannot believe him can be motivated to think about what he must do to be believed. The child who is raised with many similar opportunities can, over time, construct for himself the conviction that it is best eventually for people to deal honestly with each other.[9]

Autonomous behavior can be achieved only when children consider other people's points of view, which can occur only if they are presented with viewpoints that differ from their own and are encouraged to consider them in deciding how they will behave. However, the ability to take another person's point of view is largely developmental, it is not until around age eight, when children become less egocentric that they are able to decenter and see things from other people's points of view. Long before that, autonomy is reinforced when teachers and parents allow sufficient time and opportunities for children to practice and perform tasks for themselves. Independence is also nurtured when children are allowed to use problem-solving techniques and to learn from their mistakes.

Children can be encouraged to regulate and be responsible for their own behavior through what Piaget referred to as "sanctions by reciprocity," These sanctions "are directly related to the act we want to sanction and to the adult's point of view, and have the effect of motivating the child to construct rules of conduct for himself, through the coordination of viewpoints."[10] Examples of sanctions by reciprocity include exclusion from the group when children have a choice of staying and behaving or leaving; taking away from children the materials or privileges they have abused, while leaving open the opportunity to use them again if the children express a desire to use them appropriately; and helping children fix things they have broken and clean up after themselves.

A fine line separates sanction by reciprocity and punishment. The critical ingredients that balance the scales on the side of reciprocity are your respect for children and your desire to help them develop autonomy rather than obedience. As you read the Program in Action about Hilltop School on pages 420–421, reflect on these questions:

- What other theories, in addition to Maslow's, contribute to practices for helping children guide their behavior?
- How could you implement the three commandments of Hilltop in your classroom or program?
- How would you rate yourself on the rubrics of professional performance applied to the teachers of Hilltop school? Which of the measures would you need the most help in implementing?

PHYSICAL PUNISHMENT

Is it possible to guide children's behavior without physical punishment? More and more, early childhood professionals agree that it is. Whether parents and professionals should spank or paddle as a means of guiding behavior is an age-old controversy. Some parents spank their children, following a "No!" with a slap on the hand or a spank on the bottom; some base their use of physical punishment on their religious beliefs. However, outside the home, spanking is now considered an inappropriate form of guidance. In fact, in some places, such as Florida, physical punishment in child care programs is legislatively prohibited.

There are several problems with spanking and other forms of physical punishment. First, physical punishment is generally ineffective in building behavior in children; it does not show them what to do or provide them with alternative ways of behaving. Second, adults who use physical punishment are modeling physical aggression, saying, in effect, that it is permissible to use aggression in interpersonal relationships. Children who are spanked are thus more likely to use aggression with their peers. Third, spanking and physical punishment increase the risk of physical injury to the child. Because spanking can be an emotionally charged situation, the spanker can become too aggressive, overdo the punishment, and hit the child in vulnerable places. Fourth, parents, caregivers, and teachers are children's sources of security. Physical punishment erodes the sense of security that children must have to function confidently in their daily lives.

The best advice regarding physical punishment is to avoid it; use nonviolent means for guiding children's behavior. More information on physical punishment is available at

Companion Website To complete a Program in Action activity related to collaborative problem solving, go to the Companion Website at **www.prenhall.com/morrison**, select chapter 14, then choose the Program in Action module.

Companion Website To learn more about alternatives to punishment, go to the Companion Website at **www.prenhall.com/morrison**, select chapter 14, then choose the Linking to Learning module.

USING COLLABORATIVE PROBLEM SOLVING TO MODIFY BEHAVIOR AT HILLTOP SCHOOL

Students at Hilltop Elementary School have painted colorful M&M's candies on school windows to remind themselves that the only meltdowns here should be "in your mouth, not in your classroom." Operated by the Rockland Board of Cooperative Educational Services (BOCES) in West Nyack, New York, Hilltop is an alternative school that serves forty-four students with severe behavior and/or academic challenges who are in kindergarten through fifth grade. Hilltop helps students learn how to regulate their behavior so they can have more success in school and in life. In 2002 Hilltop was recognized as a model for other schools when it was awarded the prestigious Magnus Award by the National School Board Association.

A combination of collaborative problem solving and staff-development training helps Hilltop succeed with even the most difficult-to-teach students. Staff are trained about the importance of choice making and self-reflection in students' acquiring two important facets of self-regulation: pattern recognition and impulse control. Students learn how to recognize the important features of an environment or task and attend to these rather than to extraneous features. They learn how to "bystand" their own behaviors, replacing impulsive responses with ones more appropriate to the situation.

THREE SCHOOL COMMANDMENTS

Staff and students use three school commandments to create a shared vision of the expected school climate, as well as a focus for bringing consistent expectations to daily classroom and school routines. Borrowed from Ross Greene's book *The Explosive Child*, the commandments reflect Maslow's hierarchy of needs and establish a guarantee of safety and equity as a contract made between staff and students:

Commandment #1: All students will be safe and learn.
Commandment #2: Fair is not equal.
Commandment #3: Everyone gets what they need.*

Collaborative problem-solving groups are used to teach students how to direct their attention to expectations implicit in the school commandments and adjust their behaviors accordingly. Behaviors corresponding to each

http://www.parentsplace.com, a site where parents can connect, communicate, and celebrate the adventures of parenting; share insights; search through extensive archives of feature articles; and pose questions to a panel of experts.

In the long run, parents and early childhood professionals determine children's behavior. Thus, in guiding the behavior of children entrusted to their care, professionals and others must select procedures that are appropriate to their own philosophies and to children's particular needs. Helping children develop an internal system of control benefits them more than a system that relies on external control and authoritarianism. Developing self-regulation in children should be a primary goal of all professionals.

TRENDS IN GUIDING CHILDREN

As we observe the field of early childhood education, we can clearly see trends in the guidance of young children:

- *Development of democratic learning environments.* In our efforts to help prepare all children to live effectively and productively in a democracy, we are placing increasing emphasis on experiences that will help promote behavior associated with democratic

commandment are taught and demonstrated using cooperative learning techniques.[†]

- Teachers demonstrate what the expected behaviors look and sound like.
- Students are encouraged to role-play prosocial behaviors and use scripts for problem solving and group interactions.
- Charts describing target behaviors are posted in classrooms and are referred to by staff and students.

Daily Meetings

The number of daily collaborative problem-solving meetings varies based on student age. Kindergartners and first graders hold up to nine meetings a day, each meeting lasting approximately five minutes; meetings are held at the beginning and end of each activity block. The older students, second through fifth grades, meet four times a day: at the beginning of the day, before lunch, after lunch, and before dismissal. The format of these meetings is always the same: teachers and students commit to keeping agreed-upon commandments. Follow-up meetings give individuals a chance to reflect on performance as well as receive feedback from the group.

Staff Performance Rubrics

The program's commitment to ongoing professional development is apparent in the measures used to evaluate staff performance in each of six program components:

1. Collaborative problem solving
   - Work with students to identify individual goals related to school commandments
   - Use language intended to refocus students on school commandment to cure and redirect students
2. Supervision of paraprofessional staff
   - Plan specific involvement of paraprofessional in preteaching/reteaching classroom activities
3. Ongoing training
   - Set annual program goals to improve performance in one or more of the program components
4. Building classroom communities
   - Provide students with opportunities to contribute to the lives of other people
5. Best instructional practices
   - Use flexible grouping to ensure that students are not tracked on the basis of a limited number of skills
6. Collaborative partnerships
   - Work collaboratively with parents to promote student success

The actual rubrics describe three levels of performance for each measure, providing a common vision of the level of service the program is committed to. Like the commandments, they ensure consistency in responding to the needs of the children served at Hilltop.

Contributed by Susan E. Craig, Mary Jean Marsico, and Pamela Charles.

* R. Greene, *The Explosive Child* (New York: Harper Collins, 1998).

[†]S. Sharan, *Handbook of Cooperative Learning Methods* (Westport, CT: Greenwood Press, 1994).

---

living. As a result, more professionals are making effects to run their classrooms as democracies. This idea is not new. John Dewey was an advocate of this approach. However, running a democratic classroom is easier said than done. It demands a confident professional who believes that it is worth the effort. Democratic learning environments require that students develop responsibility for their behaviors and learning, that classrooms operate as communities, and that all children are respected by and respectful of others.

- *The use of character education as a means of promoting responsible behavior.* In chapter 12 we discussed reasons for character education and its importance and role in the contemporary curriculum. Character education will continue to grow as a means of promoting fundamental behaviors that early childhood professionals and society believe are essential for living in a democratic society.
- *Teaching civility.* Civil behavior and ways to promote it are of growing interest at all levels of society. The specific teaching of civil behavior—how to treat others well and in turn be treated well—is seen as essential for living well in contemporary society. At a minimum, civil behavior includes manners, respect, and the ability to get along with people of all races, cultures, and socioeconomic backgrounds.

• *Early intervention.* We all know that habits are hard to break and that a behavior once set is difficult to change. Early childhood professionals believe it is essential to help develop appropriate behaviors in the early years, by working with parents and families to help them guide their children's behavior. Waiting to address delinquent behavior is much more costly than promoting right behavior from the beginning of children's lives.

As we have emphasized in this and other chapters, cognitive and social development and behavioral characteristics are interconnected. More early childhood professionals recognize that it does not make sense to teach children reading, writing, and arithmetic but not teach them the skills necessary for responsibly guiding their own behavior.

Companion Website

For additional Internet resources or to complete an online activity for this chapter, go to the Companion Website at **www.prenhall.com/morrison,** select chapter 14, then choose the Linking to Learning or Making Connections module.

LINKING TO LEARNING

Center for Effective Discipline

http://www.stophitting.com

A nonprofit organization that provides educational information to the public on the effects of corporal punishment and on alternatives to its use.

Florida Department of Education

http://www.firn.edu/doe/curric/prek12/index.html

Shows state standards for grades preK through twelve and a wide range of subjects.

National Network for Child Care

http://www.nncc.org

Suggests ways that a preschooler can learn to get along with others and that a caregiver can learn to guide and discipline that preschooler.

Parenting.com

http://www.parenting.com

Offers expert advice on how to deal with topics such as discipline, lying, sharing, shyness, tantrums, and more.

Positive Parenting.com

http://www.positiveparenting.com

Dedicated to providing resources and information to help make parenting more rewarding, effective, and fun.

Virginia Cooperative Extension

http://www.ext.vt.edu

Shows several commonsense strategies for effectively guiding the behavior of young children so they can make positive choices, learn problem-solving skills, and learn respect and responsibility.

ACTIVITIES FOR FURTHER ENRICHMENT

ETHICAL DILEMMA: "JUST GIVE HIM A GOOD WHACK"

Eduardo, age six, has just been assigned to your class. He acts out, hits other children, and screams when he doesn't get his own way. In a team meeting, you ask for ideas on how to help guide Eduardo's behavior. One of your colleagues suggests that when he hits another child, you should "just give him a good whack on the bottom, and he'll soon get the message not to hit others."

How should you handle disagreeing with a colleague over the best course of action to follow when dealing with a child's behavior problems? Should you suggest immediately that giving children a good whack is developmentally and culturally inappropriate, or should you talk after the meeting and share your views that you don't think physical punishment is a way to guide children's behavior, or should you report your colleague to the central administration, or should you pursue another course of action?

APPLICATIONS

1. Develop your own plan for guiding children's behavior in your classroom. Include the following:
   - My core beliefs about guiding children's behavior are . . .
   - I want my children to demonstrate these essential behaviors . . .
   - The five most essential methods I can use to guide children's behavior are . . .
2. What is the difference between normal behavior and acceptable behavior? Give an example of normal behavior that may not be acceptable and another of acceptable behavior that may not be normal.
3. Observe a primary classroom and identify aspects of the physical setting and atmosphere that could influence classroom behavior. Can you suggest improvements?
4. List five methods of guiding children's behavior. Tell why you think each is effective, and give examples.

FIELD EXPERIENCES

1. Observe an early childhood classroom. What guidance system (implicit or explicit) does the teacher use to manage the classroom? Do you think the teacher is aware of the system being used?

2. List ten behaviors that you think are desirable in toddlers, ten in preschoolers, and ten in kindergartners. For each behavior, give two examples of how you would encourage and promote the development of that behavior. Place these ideas in your portfolio or idea file.
3. Challenging behavior is a major classroom issue for many teachers. Observe in preK to grade-one classrooms (follow the guidelines in chapter 3), and document specific challenging behaviors. For each give specific ideas about how you would address it in your classroom.
4. Young children are capable of working together to solve problems and to offer solutions. Observe problem behaviors in a preK classroom (e.g., two girls arguing over who will read a book first or two boys shoving each other over a toy truck). Develop a plan for how to help these children solve their problems. Discuss your plan with preK teachers for their comments and advice.

RESEARCH

1. Many levels of guidance are practiced by parents and early childhood professionals without their being aware of what they are doing or the processes they are using. Observe a mother-child relationship for examples of parental guidance. What specific strategies does the mother use? What is the child's resultant behavior? After further observation, answer these same questions for a teacher–child relationship. In both situations what are the ethical implications of the adult's actions?
2. Observe an early childhood classroom to see which behaviors earn the teacher's attention. Does the teacher pay more attention to positive or negative behaviors? Why do you think the teacher does this?
3. Interview five parents of young children to determine what they mean when they use the word *discipline*. What implications might these definitions have for you if you were their children's teacher?
4. We know that boys are more active than girls and that they receive more attention in the classroom. Use the knowledge and skills you learned in chapter 3 to develop an observation form and then to assess the differences between how teachers guide boys' and girls' behavior. What conclusions can you draw from your data? What implications do your data have for how you will guide children's behavior?

READINGS FOR FURTHER ENRICHMENT

Adams, Suzanne K., and Joan Baronberg. *Promoting Positive Behavior: Guidance Strategies for Early Childhood Settings.* Upper Saddle River, NJ: Merrill/Prentice Hall, 2005.

Equips future teachers to effectively support emotional well-being, reduce problem behavior, and enhance social competence in toddlers, preschoolers, and primary-grade children.

Charles, C. M. *Building Classroom Discipline,* 8th ed. Boston: Allyn and Bacon, 2004.

Presents solutions for reducing types of student misbehavior that impede learning and produce stress; developed by some of the most influential thinkers of the past fifty years. Invites students to pick and choose from the solutions to create systems comfortable to them.

Crone, D. A., and R. H. Horner. *Building Positive Behavior Support Systems in Schools: Functional Behavioral Assessment.* New York: Guilford, 2003.

Presents an up-to-date conceptual model and practical tools for systematically addressing the challenges of problem behavior in schools. Spells out both the whys and the hows of developing and implementing individual behavior support plans. Gives particular attention to the organizational and team-based structures needed to effect change.

Kaiser, Barbara, and Judy Sklar Rasminsky. *Challenging Behavior in Young Children: Understanding, Preventing, and Responding Effectively.* Boston: Allyn and Bacon, 2002.

Presents information and strategies to deal with the challenging behavior that teachers find more and more often in their classrooms. Includes vignettes throughout the book that make strategies come alive.

Keogh, B. *Temperament in the Classroom: Understanding Individual Differences.* Baltimore, MD: Paul H. Brookes, 2003.

Explores the effect of temperament on educational experience and shows readers how individual temperaments of students and teachers influence behavior and achievement.

Marion, M. *Guidance of Young Children,* 7th ed. Upper Saddle River, NJ: Merrill/Prentice Hall, 2007.

Provides a positive, constructivist approach to guidance that respects and protects children and helps them become responsible, competent, independent, and cooperative.

ENDNOTES

1. S. B. Campbell, E. W. Pierce, C. L. March, L. J. Ewing, and E. K. Szumowski, "Hard-to-Manage Preschool Boys: Symptomatic Behavior Across Contexts and Time," *Child Development* 65 (1994): 836–851.

2. R. M. Diaz, C. Neal, and M. Amaya-Williams, *The Social Origins of Self-Regulation: Vygotsky and Education* (Cambridge: Cambridge University Press, 1996), 130.

3. Ibid., 139.

4. L. R. Roehler and D. J. Cantlon, *Scaffolding: A Powerful Tool in Social Constructivist Classrooms* (1996), http://ed-web3.educ.msu.edu/literacy/papers/paperlr2.html.

5. L. E. Berk and A. Winsler, *Scaffolding Children's Learning: Vygotsky and Early Childhood Education* (Washington, DC: NAEYC, 1995), 45–46.

6. T. Gordon, *Teacher Effectiveness Training* (New York: Peter H. Hyden, 1974).

7. Ibid., 40.

8. Ibid., 75–76.

9. K. Constance, *Number in Preschool and Kindergarten* (Washington, DC: NAEYC, 1982), 23.

10. Ibid., 77.

CHAPTER 15

Multiculturalism

EDUCATION FOR LIVING IN A DIVERSE SOCIETY

> It is time for parents to teach young people early on
> that in diversity there is beauty and there is strength.
>
> MAYA ANGELOU

The population of the United States is changing and will continue to change. For example, the population will be less Caucasian, and more students will be black and Hispanic. By 2025, 17 percent of the population will be Hispanic.[1] In addition, America will become even more a nation of blended races. Projections are that by 2050, 22 percent of the population will be of mixed ancestry.

All these demographics have tremendous implications for education. Colleges of education must increase their efforts to recruit and educate minority teachers. In addition, more students will require special education, bilingual education, and other special services. And issues of culture and diversity will shape instruction and curriculum. These demographics will have tremendous implications for your teaching and your children's learning. In part, how you respond to the multicultural makeup and needs of your children will determine how well they fulfill their responsibilities in the years to come. As an early childhood educator, you will want to promote multicultural awareness in your classroom.

MULTICULTURAL AWARENESS

In its simplest form, *multicultural awareness* is the appreciation and understanding of other people's cultures, socioeconomic status, and gender, as well as one's own. As you read this chapter, look for this and other terms in the glossary in Figure 15.1. However, the terms and concepts for describing multicultural education and awareness are not as important as the methods, procedures, and activities of the programs.

Bringing multicultural awareness to the classroom does not mean teaching about certain cultures to the exclusion of others. Rather, multicultural awareness programs and activities focus on minority cultures while making nonminority children aware of the content, nature, and richness of their own. Learning about other cultures while also learning about their own enables children to integrate commonalities and appreciate differences without inferring inferiority or superiority.

THE CULTURES OF OUR CHILDREN

The population of young children in the United States reflects the population at large and thus represents a number of different cultures and ethnicities. Many cities and school districts have populations that express great ethnic diversity, including Asian Americans, Native Americans, African Americans, and Hispanic Americans. For example, the Dade County, Florida, school district has children from 122 countries, each with its own culture. Table 15.1 shows the proportion of minority students in the nation's ten largest school districts.

The great diversity of young children creates interesting challenges for early childhood educators. Many children speak languages other than English, behave differently based on cultural customs and values, and come from varied socioeconomic backgrounds. Yet early childhood professionals must prepare all children to live happily and productively in this society. How to accomplish that task is a major challenge for everyone. The strategies and solutions are not always easy to implement.

Focus Questions

What is multicultural education?

What implications does a multicultural society have for your teaching?

How can you and other early childhood teachers infuse multicultural content into curriculum, programs, and activities?

What contemporary issues influence the teaching of multiculturalism?

How can you educate yourself and young children for living in a diverse society?

Companion Website

To check your understanding of this chapter, go to the Companion Website at **www.prenhall.com/ morrison**, select chapter 15, answer Multiple Choice and Essay Questions, and receive feedback.

FIGURE 15.1 Glossary of Multicultural Terms

Affirmative action: First established by the federal government in 1965, this legal mandate consists of special actions in recruitment, hiring, and other areas designed to eliminate the effects of past discrimination.

Bias-free: Curriculum, programs, materials, language, attitudes, actions, and activities that are free from biased perceptions.

Bilingual education: Education in two languages. Generally, two languages are used for the purpose of academic instruction.

Cultural diversity: Differences in race, ethnicity, language, nationality, or religion among various groups within the community, organization, or nation. A school or classroom is said to be culturally diverse if its students include members of different groups.

Culturally fair education: Education that respects and accounts for the cultural backgrounds of all learners.

Culture: The shared values, norms, traditions, customs, arts, history, folklore, and institutions of a group of people.

Discrimination: Treatment that favors one person or group over another.

Diversity: Difference, variety, and uniqueness. Generally, diversity refers to human qualities that are different from our own and those of groups to which we belong but that are manifested in other individuals and groups. Dimensions of diversity include but are not limited to age, ethnicity, gender, physical abilities or qualities, race, sexual orientation, educational background, income, and religious beliefs.

English as a second language (ESL): Instruction in which students with limited English proficiency attend a special English class.

English for speakers of other languages (ESOL): The term that has begun to replace "ESL" for instruction in which students with limited English proficiency attend a special English class.

English language learners (ELL): Non-English-speaking students who need support to learn the English language.

Homophobia: Aversion to gay or homosexual people or their behavior or an act based on this aversion; irrational fear of, aversion to, or discrimination against homosexuality or homosexuals.

Infusion: The process of making multiculturalism an explicit part of the curriculum throughout all content areas.

Mainstreaming: The educational and social integration of children with special needs into the schoolwide instructional process, usually the regular classroom.

Maintenance bilingual programs: Transitional bilingual programs that also infuse English into content area instruction with the goal of biliteracy.

Multicultural: Pertaining to or representing several different cultures or cultural elements. A *multicultural education* is a compilation of teaching and learning approaches that foster an appreciation and respect for cultural pluralism and promote democratic ideals of justice, equality, and democracy. *Multiculturalism* is an approach to education based on the premise that all peoples in the United States should receive proportional attention in the curriculum.

Multicultural awareness: Ability to perceive and acknowledge cultural differences among people without making value judgments about these differences.

Nonsexist education: Education that promotes attitudes and behaviors consistent with the idea that the sexes are equal.

Prejudice: An opinion formed without enough knowledge or thought that is biased about someone or something.

Race: A group of humans with inherited traits that are distinct enough to characterize its members as a unique people. Such divisions are often used by anthropologists to aid in classification although strict adherence to a classification scheme is limiting and problematic. *Note:* There is no established agreement on any scientific definition of *race*. It has no biological or natural basis but is a socially defined construct that is used to categorize people according to the color of their skin.

Racial profiling: Wrongful and hurtful judgment of an individual or group of individuals based solely on their ethnicity or the color of their skin.

Racism: Unfair behavior whereby one race has and uses power over another.

Stereotype: A generalization or oversimplification about a whole group of people. Gender stereotyping is one example.

Xenophobia: From the Greek word meaning "fear of strangers," the fear or hatred of anything that is foreign or outside one's own group, nation, or culture.

These terms can help you in your professional development and in your work with colleagues and parents.

TABLE 15.1 Proportion of Minority Students in the Ten Largest
Public School Districts in the Continental United States

Name of Reporting District	State	Percentage of Minority Students
Detroit City School District	MI	96.3
City of Chicago School District	IL	90.4
Los Angeles Unified School District	CA	90.1
Houston Independent School District	TX	90.0
Dade County School District	FL	88.7
New York City Public Schools	NY	84.7
Philadelphia City School District	PA	83.3
Broward County School District	FL	58.8
Clark County School District	NV	50.1
Hillsborough County School District	FL	48.2

Source: U.S. Department of Education, National Center for Education Statistics, www.nces.ed.gov/
pubs2002/100_largest/table_08_1.asp.

Promoting **multiculturalism** in an early childhood program has implications far beyond the program itself. Culture influences and affects work habits, interpersonal relations, and a child's general outlook on life. Early childhood professionals must take these multicultural influences into consideration when designing curriculum and instructional processes for young and impressionable children.

> **Companion Website** To learn more about diversity and early childhood education, go to the Companion Website at **www.prenhall.com/ morrison**, select chapter 15, then choose the Linking to Learning module.

> **Multiculturalism** An approach to education based on the premise that all people in the United States should receive proportional attention in the curriculum.

MULTICULTURAL INFUSION

One way to positively change the lives of children and their families is to infuse multiculturalism into early childhood activities and practices. **Multicultural infusion** means that multicultural education permeates the entire curriculum. From a larger perspective, infusion strategies ensure that multiculturalism becomes a part of the entire center, school, and home. Infusion processes used by early childhood programs embody the following precepts:

- Foster cultural awareness
- Promote and use conflict-resolution strategies
- Teach to children's learning styles
- Welcome parent and community involvement

As an early childhood professional, you will want to be constantly developing your multicultural awareness, attitudes, knowledge, and skills.

> **Multicultural infusion** Making multiculturalism an explicit part of curriculum and programs.

FOSTER CULTURAL AWARENESS

Assess Your Attitudes Toward Children. Before working with children to influence their multicultural awareness and education, it is important for you to first assess your own attitudes toward young children and their families to ensure that you are multiculturally sensitive.

- Do you believe that all children can and will learn?
- Are you willing to spend the time and effort necessary to help all children learn?
- Are you willing to teach children individually according to their cultural and individual learning styles?
- Do you have high expectations for all children?

The Infant and Toddler segment of the DVD refers to parents saying, "You are my child's parent during the day." What disposition or attitude will you need in order to teach children whose culture is different from yours?

In the Child
Care segment of the DVD,
observe how language
instruction, dance, music, and
stories from around the world
help to create multicultural
programming.

- Are your expectations for children influenced by their race, socioeconomic status, or gender? What can you do to ensure that you teach all children fairly and equitably?
- Do you feel comfortable with all children?
- Are you familiar with the homes and the communities in which your children live?
- Are you willing to work with the parents and families of your children to learn more about their culture and educational values and preferences?
- Are you willing and able to infuse multiculturalism into your teaching and classroom?

As you reflect on these questions, you may find some areas in which you need work. What is important is that you are willing to learn, change, and become the teacher all children need and deserve.

The lesson plan on "Alaska Animals" provides some interesting elements you might want to include in your own teaching. The lesson plan was contributed by Pam Johnson, a first-grade teacher in Koliganek, Alaska, who was also a 2002 Disney American Teacher Award honoree.

- Ms. Johnson uses a thematic planning sheet, consisting of a web of the topics she will include and possible teaching and learning activities.
- She clearly states the goals and standards for what children will learn.
- The plans include a cooperative learning focus, which indicates how students will learn together and from each other.
- The plan provides for children's multiple intelligences, based on Gardner's theory (discussed in chapter 5).
- Parent involvement and participation are major parts of the plan.

Focus on Fostering Awareness. You must keep in mind that you are the key to a multicultural classroom. The following guidelines can help you in teaching multiculturalism:

- *Recognize that all children are unique.* They all have special talents, abilities, and styles of learning and relating to others. Provide opportunities for children to be different and use their abilities.
- *Get to know, appreciate, and respect the cultural backgrounds of your children.* Visit families and community neighborhoods to learn more about cultures and religions and the ways of life they engender.

Early childhood educators must consider the diverse characteristics of students—including gender, ethnicity, race, and socioeconomic factors—when planning learning opportunities for their classes. What are some ways diversity can enrich the curriculum?

- *Infuse culture (including your children's) into your lesson planning, teaching, and caregiving.* Use all subject areas—math, science, language arts, literacy, music, art, and social studies—to relate culture to all the children and all you do.
- *Use children's interests and experiences to form a basis for planning lessons and developing activities.* This approach makes students feel good about their backgrounds, cultures, families, and experiences. Also, when children can relate what they are doing in the classroom to the rest of their daily lives, their learning is more meaningful.
- *Use authentic situations to provide for cultural learning and understanding.* For example, a field trip to a culturally diverse neighborhood of your city or town provides children an opportunity to understand firsthand many of the details about how people conduct their daily lives. Such an experience provides wonderful opportunities for involving children in writing, cooking, reading, and dramatic play activities. What about setting up a market in the classroom?

LESSON PLAN: Alaska Animals

> *Let state and local standards be your starting point.*

Goals/Standards

Goals are based on standards established by the National Council of Teachers of Mathematics, Benchmarks for Science Literacy, National Science Education Standards, NAEYC/IRA, National Standards for Arts Education, and National Standards for Dance Education.

- Use simple maps with symbols
- Measure lengths
- Estimate weight in pounds
- Classify objects

- Recognize ways in which animals move
- Describe, compare, and classify animals by a variety of means
- Recognize a variety of landforms
- Understand interdependence between living things and their environment
- Use science to understand and describe local environment

- Use technical skills to compose simple nonfiction or fiction stories
- Conduct simple research

- Understand own cultural traditions
- Understand that seasonal changes affect living things
- Know how others lived in the past and what was important to them

- Understand food pyramid
- Describe a balanced meal
- Understand that exercise is important for a healthy lifestyle

- Plan art beforehand
- Reflect on why people dance
- Perform simple songs and dance

Cooperative Learning Focus

> *Vygotsky's theory supports a cooperative learning focus.*

- Cooperative learning groups
- Think pair share
- Team stand and share
- Jigsaw problem solving

> *Incorporate multiple intelligences in your lesson planning.*

Multiple Intelligences

- Linguistic, mathematical, spatial, musical, kinesthetic, naturalist, interpersonal, and intrapersonal

Materials and Resources (items available from district media center)

Adventure of Monty the Moose	*The Eye of the Needle*	*Little Walrus Warning*
The Alaska Animal Alphabet	*More Wild Critters*	*Denali and Friends*
The Alaska Wolf	*Amazing Animals*	*Move Like Animals*
Alaska's Three Bears	*A Caribou Journey*	*Count Alaska's Colors*
Arctic Animal Babies	*Tundra Discoveries*	*Raven and River*
Arctic Animals	*Walrus on Location*	*Wild Critters*
Baby Animals of the North	*Alaska Cookbook*	*Yup'ik Stories*

(continued)

Thematic Planning Sheet

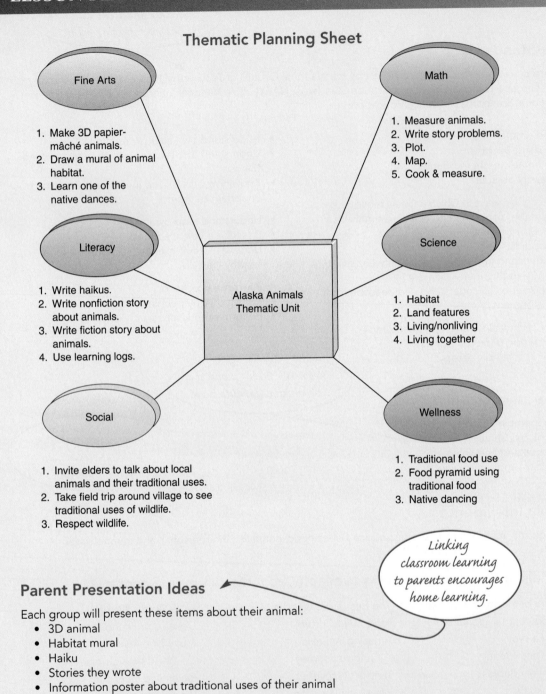

Fine Arts
1. Make 3D papier-mâché animals.
2. Draw a mural of animal habitat.
3. Learn one of the native dances.

Math
1. Measure animals.
2. Write story problems.
3. Plot.
4. Map.
5. Cook & measure.

Literacy
1. Write haikus.
2. Write nonfiction story about animals.
3. Write fiction story about animals.
4. Use learning logs.

Alaska Animals Thematic Unit

Science
1. Habitat
2. Land features
3. Living/nonliving
4. Living together

Social
1. Invite elders to talk about local animals and their traditional uses.
2. Take field trip around village to see traditional uses of wildlife.
3. Respect wildlife.

Wellness
1. Traditional food use
2. Food pyramid using traditional food
3. Native dancing

Linking classroom learning to parents encourages home learning.

Parent Presentation Ideas

Each group will present these items about their animal:
- 3D animal
- Habitat mural
- Haiku
- Stories they wrote
- Information poster about traditional uses of their animal

Whole-Class Activities

- Invite community elders to talk about animals and their traditional uses.
- Ask elders to teach native dances.
- Potluck—We will prepare native foods to share at the presentation.
- Special thanks—Each elder that helped will get a gift made by the students and recognition for the help.

Contributed by Pam Johnson, a first-grade teacher at Koliganek (Alaska) School, and a 2002 Disney American Teacher Award honoree.

- *Use authentic assessment activities to fully assess children's learning and growth.* Portfolios (see chapter 3) are ideal for assessing children in unbiased and culturally sensitive ways. Early childhood professionals should use varied ways of assessing children.
- *Be a role model by accepting, appreciating, and respecting other languages and cultures.* It is important to communicate and demonstrate that uniqueness and diversity are positive.
- *Be knowledgeable about, proud of, and secure in your own culture.* Children will ask about you, and you should share your background with them.

In the Reggio Emilia segment of the DVD, observe the market that has been set up to provide for cultural understanding.

Select Appropriate Instructional Materials.   In addition to assessing your own attitudes and infusing personal sensitivity into a multicultural classroom, you need to carefully consider and select appropriate instructional materials to support that infusion.

Multicultural Literature.   Choose literature that emphasizes people's habits, customs, and general living and working behaviors. This approach stresses similarities and differences regarding how children and families live their *whole* lives and avoids merely noting differences or teaching only about habits and customs. Multicultural literature today is more representative of various cultural groups and provides a more authentic language experience for young children. It is written by authors from particular cultures and contains more true-to-life stories and culturally authentic writing styles. The following books are representative of the rich selection now available:

- *Grannie and the Jumbie: A Caribbean Tale* by Margaret M. Hurst (HarperCollins, 2001). Emanuel's grandmother is always warning him about the evil Jumbie, a boogeyman. He bravely scoffs at her superstitious lectures until the night when he is almost spirited away. Now, when his grannie talks, Emanuel listens.
- *Quilt Alphabet* by Lesa Cline-Ransome (Holiday House, 2001). This homespun alphabet book introduces each letter with a quilt block and clever rhyming riddle. From a basket of apples to a zigzagging country road, this ode to country living is pieced together with poetry. A quilt is defined as "A patch of you, a scrap of me, / Pieces of family history, / Common threads stitched from the heart, / Pieces of us in every part."
- *Under the Quilt of Night* by Deborah Hopkinson (Atheneum, 2002). This historic chronicle traces the escape of a group of slaves and their eventual rescue on the Underground Railroad. Told in prose from the perspective of an adolescent girl, the story explains how quilts were used to mark safehouses. "In most quilts, center squares are red for home and earth," but a quilt with a blue center signals a house that hides runaways.
- *Round Is a Mooncake: A Book of Shapes* by Rosanne Thong (Chronicle, 2000). A little girl's neighborhood becomes a discovery ground of things round, square, and rectangular. Many of the objects are Asian in origin, others are universal: round rice bowls and a found pebble, square dim sum and pizza boxes, rectangular Chinese lace and a very special pencil case. Bright art accompanies this lively introduction to shapes, and a short glossary explains the cultural significance of the objects featured in the book.
- *The Good Luck Cat* by Joy Harjo (Harcourt, 2000). According to Aunt Shelly, Woogie is a good luck cat, and he certainly proves it by surviving one scrape after another. But when he doesn't come home, we wonder if this good luck cat's luck has run out. This is a light, charming celebration of a young girl's friendship with a cat. And it's a children's picture book featuring Native American characters in which culture isn't the main theme.
- *Shades of Black: A Celebration of Our Children* by Sandra L. Pinkney (Scholastic, 2000). Using simple poetic language, illuminated by brilliant photographs, this is a remarkable book of affirmation for African American children. Photographic portraits and striking descriptions of varied skin tones, hair texture, and eye color convey a strong sense of pride in a unique heritage. *Shades of Black* is a joyous celebration of children,

Companion Website   To learn more about additional multicultural education resources for educators, go to the Companion Website at **www.prenhall.com/ morrison**, select chapter 15, then choose the Linking to Learning module.

as well as a gracious invitation to readers of all ages and cultures to explore and embrace the rich diversity among African Americans.

• *The Three Pigs* by David Wiesner (Clarion Books, 2001). Once upon a time, three pigs built three houses out of straw, sticks, and bricks. Along came a wolf, who huffed and puffed. . . . So you think you know the rest? Think again. It's never safe to assume too much. When the wolf approaches the first house, for example, and blows it in, he somehow manages to blow the pig right out of the story frame. One by one, the pigs exit the fairy tale's border and set off on an adventure of their own.

Themes.   Early childhood professionals can use thematic units to strengthen children's understanding of themselves, their culture, and the cultures of others. The lesson plans in this book are theme-based. Thematic choices from a variety of cultures can help children identify cultural similarities and encourage understanding and tolerance. Consider the following suggestions:

• Getting to know myself, getting to know others
• What is special about you and me?
• Growing up in the city
• Growing up in the country
• Tell me about Africa (South America, China, etc.)

Multicultural Accomplishments.   Add to classroom activities, as appropriate, the accomplishments of people from different cultural groups, women of all cultures, and individuals with disabilities. The following criteria are most important when picking materials for use in a multicultural curriculum for early childhood programs:

• Represent people of all cultures fairly and accurately.
• Represent people of color, many cultural groups, and people with exceptionalities.
• Be sure that historic information is accurate and nondiscriminatory.
• Be sure that materials do not include stereotypical roles or language.
• Ensure gender equity—that is, boys and girls must be represented equally and in nonstereotypical roles.

Avoid Sexism and Gender-Role Stereotyping.   Current interest in multiculturalism in general and nondiscrimination in particular has prompted concern about sexism and gender-role stereotyping. **Sexism** is "the collection of attitudes, beliefs, and behaviors which result from the assumption that one sex is superior. *In the context of schools,* the term refers to the collection of structures, policies, practices and activities that overtly or covertly prescribe the development of girls and boys and prepare them for traditional sex roles."[2]

Sexism   Prejudice or discrimination based on sex.

Title IX of the Education Amendments Acts of 1972, as amended by Public Law 93-568, prohibits such discrimination in the schools: "No person in the United States shall, on the basis of sex, be excluded from participation in, be denied the benefits of, or be subjected to discrimination under any education program or activity receiving Federal financial assistance."[3] Since Title IX prohibits sex discrimination in any educational program that receives federal money, early childhood programs as well as elementary schools, high schools, and universities cannot discriminate against males or females in enrollment policies, curriculum offerings, or activities.

Sexual harassment
Unwelcome sexual behavior and talk.

You and other early childhood professionals need to be concerned about the roots of sexism and **sexual harassment** and realize that these practices have their beginnings in children's early years in homes, centers, and preschools. Early childhood professionals must continue to examine personal and programmatic practices, evaluate materials, and work with parents to eliminate sexism and to ensure that girls—indeed, all children—are not shortchanged in any way.

Parents and teachers can provide children with less restrictive options and promote a more open framework in which gender roles can develop freely. The following are some suggestions for avoiding gender stereotypes:

- *Provide opportunities for all children to experience the activities, materials, toys, and emotions traditionally associated with both sexes.* Give boys as well as girls opportunities to experience tenderness, affection, and the warmth of close parent–child and teacher–pupil relationships. Conversely, girls as well as boys should be able to behave aggressively, get dirty, and participate in what are typically considered male activities, such as woodworking and block building.

- *Determine what physical arrangements in the classroom promote or encourage gender-role stereotyping.* Are boys encouraged to use the block area more than girls? Are girls encouraged to use the quiet areas more than boys? Do children hang their wraps separately— a place for boys and a place for girls? All children should have equal access to all learning areas of the classroom; no area should be reserved exclusively for one sex. In addition, examine any activity or practice that promotes segregation of children by gender or culture. Cooperative learning activities and group work offer ways to ensure that children of both sexes work together.

- *Examine the classroom materials you are using and determine whether they contain obvious instances of gender-role stereotyping.* When you find examples, modify the materials or do not use them. Let publishers know your feelings, and tell other faculty members about them.

- *Become conscious of words that promote sexism.* In a lesson on community helpers, taught in most preschool and kindergarten programs at one time or another, many words carry a sexist connotation. *Fireman, policeman,* and *mailman,* for example, are all masculine terms; nonsexist terms are *firefighter, police officer,* and *mail carrier.* You should examine all your curricular materials and teaching practices to determine how you can make them free of sexism.

- *Examine your behavior to see whether you are encouraging gender stereotypes.* Do you tell girls they cannot empty wastebaskets but they can water the plants? Do you tell boys they should not play with dolls? Do you tell girls they cannot lift certain things in the classroom because they are too heavy for them? Do you say that boys aren't supposed to cry? Do you reward only the females who are always passive, well behaved, and well mannered?

- Follow these guidelines in your teaching:
  - Give all children a chance to respond to questions. Research consistently shows that teachers do not wait long enough after they ask a question for most children, especially girls, to respond. Therefore, quick responders—usually boys—answer most of the questions. By waiting longer, you will be able to encourage more girls' answers.
  - Be an active professional. Just as we want children to engage in active learning, so too professionals should engage in active involvement in the classroom to ensure that they interact with all children, not just a few.
  - Help all children become independent and do things for themselves. Discourage behaviors and attitudes that promote helplessness and dependency.
  - Use portfolios, teacher observations, and other authentic means of assessing children's progress (see chapter 3) to provide bias-free assessment. Involving children in the evaluation of their own efforts is also a good way of promoting children's positive images of themselves.

You can combat the development of sexist attitudes by encouraging students in your classroom to engage in activities that challenge traditional gender-role stereotypes.

In the Reggio Emilia segment of the DVD, observe the atelierista and the pedigogista discussing their roles and interacting with the children. How might their roles support antibias and multicultural learning?

- *Have a colleague or parent observe you in your classroom to determine what gender-role behaviors you are encouraging.* Because we are often unaware of our behaviors, self-correction can begin only after someone points out the behaviors to us. Obviously, unless you begin with yourself, eliminating gender-role stereotyping will be next to impossible.
- *Counsel with parents to show them ways to promote nonsexist child rearing.* If society is to achieve a truly nonsexist environment, parents will be the key factor, for it is in the home that many gender-stereotyping behaviors are initiated and practiced.
- *Do not encourage children to dress in ways that lead to gender stereotyping.* Females should not be encouraged to wear frilly dresses, then forbidden to participate in an activity because they might get dirty or spoil their clothes. Children should be encouraged to dress so they will be able to participate in a range of both indoor and outdoor activities. This is an area in which you may be able to help parents by discussing how dressing children differently can contribute to more effective participation.

Implement an Antibias Curriculum and Activities.   The goal of an *antibias curriculum* is to help children learn to be accepting of others, regardless of race, ethnicity, gender, sexual orientation, socioeconomic status, or disability. Children participating in an antibias curriculum become comfortable with diversity and learn to stand up for themselves and others in the face of injustice. Additionally, in this supportive, open-minded environment, children learn to construct a knowledgeable, confident self-identity.

Young children are constantly learning about differences and need a sensitive teacher to help them form positive, unbiased perceptions about variations among people. As children color pictures of themselves, for example, you may hear a comment such as, "Your skin is white and my skin is brown." Many teachers are tempted, in the name of equality, to respond, "It doesn't matter what color we are—we are all people." Although this remark does not sound harmful, it fails to help children develop positive feelings about themselves. A more appropriate response might be, "Amanda, your skin is a beautiful dark brown, which is just right for you; Christina, your skin is a beautiful light tan, which is just right for you." A response such as this positively acknowledges each child's different skin color, which is an important step in developing a positive self-concept.

Through the sensitive guidance of caring teachers, children learn to speak up for themselves and others. By living and learning in an accepting environment, children find that they have the ability to change intolerable situations and can have a positive impact on the future. This is part of what empowerment is all about, and it begins in the home and in early childhood programs. An antibias curriculum should start in early childhood and continue throughout the school years.

The Voice from the Field "Preparing Teachers for Diversity Through Antibias Education" on pages 438–440 provides an important perspective as well as a lesson plan.

Companion Website   To learn more about implementing an antibias curriculum, go to the Companion Website at **www.prenhall.com/morrison**, select chapter 15, then the Linking to Learning module.

PROMOTE AND USE CONFLICT-RESOLUTION STRATEGIES

We all live in a world of conflict. Television and other media bombard us with images of violence, crime, and international and personal conflict. Unfortunately, many children live in homes where conflict and disharmony are a way of life rather than an exception. Increasingly, early childhood professionals are challenged to help children resolve conflicts in peaceful ways. *Conflict-resolution strategies* help children learn how to solve problems, disagree in appropriate ways, negotiate, and live in harmony with others.

Your goal is to have children reach mutually agreeable solutions to problems without the use of power (e.g., fighting, hitting, pushing, or shoving). The following no-lose method of conflict resolution may help you achieve your goal:

1. Identify and define the conflict in a nonaccusatory way ("Vinnie and Rachael, you have a problem—you both want the green paint").
2. Invite the children to participate in fixing the problem ("Let's think of how to solve this problem").

3. Generate possible solutions with the children; accept a variety of solutions, and avoid evaluating them ("Yes, you could both use the same paint cup. . . . You could take turns").

4. Examine each idea for merits and drawbacks, with the children decide which to try, and thank them for thinking of solutions ("Vinnie, that's a good idea—putting paint in the two paper cups so that both you and Rachael can use the green paint at the same time").

5. Put the plan into action ("See whether the two of you can get the green paint into the paper cups without help").

6. Follow up to evaluate how well the solution worked (After a few minutes, "Looks like your idea of how to solve your green paint problem really worked").[4]

TEACH TO CHILDREN'S LEARNING STYLES AND INTELLIGENCES

Although every child has a unique learning style, we can cluster learning styles for instructional purposes. It makes sense to consider these various styles and account for them when organizing the environment and developing activities in early childhood programs.

"Learning style is the way that students of every age are affected by their (a) immediate environment, (b) own emotionality, (c) sociological needs, (d) physical characteristics, and (e) psychological inclinations when concentrating and trying to master and remember new or difficult information or skills."[5]

- Environment—sound, light, temperature, design
- Emotionality—motivation, persistence, responsibility, need for either structure or choice
- Sociological needs—learning alone, with others, in a variety of ways (perhaps including media)
- Physical characteristics—perceptual strengths, intake, day or night energy levels, mobility
- Psychological, inclinations—global/analytic, hemispheric preference, impulsive/reflective

Not all children learn in the same way. As a result, it is important to assess each child's learning style and teach each child appropriately. What style of learning works best for you?

There are many ways you can provide for children's learning styles while responding appropriately to diversity in your program. For example, Dunn et al. suggest the following ways to adapt the learning environment to children's individual learning styles[6]:

Noise Level.   Provide earplugs or music on earphones (to avoid distractions for those who need quiet); create conversation areas or an activity-oriented learning environment separated from children who need quiet. Or establish silent areas, providing individual dens or alcoves with carpeted sections; suggest earphones without sound or earplugs to insulate against activity and noise.

Light.   Place children near windows or under adequate illumination; add table or desk lamps. Or create learning spaces under indirect or subdued light away from windows; use dividers or plants to block or diffuse illumination.

Authority Figures Present.   Place children near appropriate professionals, and schedule periodic meetings with them; supervise and check assignments often. Or permit isolated study if self-oriented, peer groupings if peer oriented, or multiple options if learning in several ways is indicated.

PREPARING TEACHERS FOR DIVERSITY THROUGH ANTIBIAS EDUCATION

Because early childhood classrooms today are increasing in diversity, teachers must become prepared to instruct children who may be racially, ethnically, culturally, and linguistically different. Teachers must also know how to work with children who learn differently and may have special learning needs. It is important to prepare teachers to focus on all aspects of diversity and to address the biases that may occur in teaching children who are different.

USE DEVELOPMENTALLY APPROPRIATE PRACTICE

In instructing young children, developmentally appropriate practice (DAP) is the significant approach. The NAEYC states three areas that early childhood educators need to understand in regard to DAP: knowledge of the child's development, knowledge of the individual needs of the child, and knowledge of the cultural and social context in which the child lives. Instructing teachers to be aware and knowledgeable of social and cultural context is crucial to the care of the young child. Contextual knowledge assists the teacher in being culturally sensitive and modeling appropriate behavior for young children.

EXPLORE CULTURAL VALUES

I have found that preservice teachers must explore their own cultural values, beliefs, and instructional practices while learning about others. At the institution where I teach, undergraduate teacher candidates in early childhood education are required to take a multicultural education course, as well as participate in activities that infuse diversity into the other major-level courses. At the beginning of the multicultural course, preservice teachers are required to write a reflective paper defining themselves and the ways they believe they will influence the lives of the young children they will teach.

USE AN ANTI-BIAS CURRICULUM

Many undergraduate students begin their exploration of diversity with a strong focus on racial and external differences. However, I have found it helpful to share research and recommendations from Louise Derman-Sparks and the Antibias Curriculum Task Force regarding antibias curriculum. Antibias curriculum allows teachers to go beyond the tourist curriculum of celebrating holidays and festivals of different cultural and ethnic groups. Antibias curriculum helps teachers address discrimination and the prevention of prejudices through instruction. This type of knowledge challenges the preservice teacher to really look at the many dimensions diversity contains.

EXPLORE PERSONAL VALUES

During the course, preservice teachers must explore stereotypes, prejudice, and discrimination related to ability, age, appearance, belief, socioeconomic status, family composition, and racial, gender, and language differences. Teacher candidates are required to keep a journal exploring these concepts in relation to their personal beliefs. Reflection is an important piece of growth. An undergraduate student, Cara Tucker, shared some of her reflections:

> I did not realize that gender, age, disabilities, and religion were also considered multicultural and diversity issues. . . . It is very difficult to not put people into stereotypical categories, but it is something that we should all be aware of. . . . We do not live in a world where discrimination is acceptable anymore. It is imperative that we progress in regard to multicultural and diversity issues. If I had not taken this class, I would probably not be as sensitive to other groups of people who come from different backgrounds, cultures, and countries. . . . These ideas will only help me become a better educator.

USE ANTI-BIAS INSTRUCTION

After exploration of self, the preservice teachers and I explore resources and methods of teaching young children through antibias instruction. We share children's books, materials, and activities; and teacher candidates evaluate lesson plans posted on the Internet for diversity in development and attention to the needs of diverse learners. Teacher candidates also develop lesson plans that contain antibias objectives, as well as objectives addressing the educational goals of the lesson. This process helps preservice teachers actively think about how they will address the differences and similarities in young children.

During one semester, two teacher candidates developed antibias lesson plans utilizing the children's book

It's Okay to Be Different by Todd Parr. Included here is a full lesson plan developed by teacher candidate Sharon Boeck, who taught the lesson to four-year-olds to address the concept of appearances and physical differences.

Another teacher candidate, Marni Donovan, developed a lesson using the same children's book to teach four-year-olds an antibias lesson about ability differences. Her lesson included bringing in an assistance dog to the class. The children were able to learn more about persons with ability differences and see how animals assist in making some individuals' lives easier.

PROFESSIONAL GROWTH

Learning about self and others is an ongoing process but a necessary part of professional development. Reflection on self as a practitioner, review of materials for diversity, and stressing the need for antibias instruction can be difficult. Preservice teachers may become uncomfortable with the process, but it is necessary for growth to occur. In the words of another former teacher candidate, "*By opening my eyes to the different children I will encounter while teaching, I have been taught the most important role . . . teaching children not only about multiculturalism, but also about themselves.*"

Title of lesson activity name: We Are All Alike, We Are All Different

Domain(s): Language arts/math/social studies/social and emotional development/creative expression

Content standards: Plan with state standards.

Language arts:
Listens to and follows spoken directions.
Responds to questions.
Listens to story read aloud.

Mathematics:
Matches like objects.
Classifies and sorts.
Explains sorting and classifying.
Participates in creating and using real
  pictorial graph of data representation.
Uses mathematical language involving measurement.

Social studies:
Begins to understand family structures and roles.

Social and emotional development:
Recognizes self as a unique individual and becomes
  aware of the uniqueness of others.
Develops personal preferences.

Creative expression:
Experiments with a variety of materials and activities
  for sensory experience and exploration.
Always begin with what children know.

Prior knowledge:
Teacher candidate came in prior to the lesson and asked each child questions about eye color, hair color, hair texture, favorite food, and favorite activity. Teacher candidate then created a chart/graph from the findings.

Outcome statement/antibias objective:
This will be a lesson on embracing differences and finding uniqueness in everyone. Many examples of same and different will be demonstrated through creative expression, matching objects, sorting and classifying objects, and using a variety of nonstandard and standard means of measurement.

Specific objectives, students will:
Identify and match several objects and shapes that go together and pick out objects that are different.
Demonstrate how objects are different or the same and big or small.
Discover that their fingerprints are different from everyone else's in the world.
Discover that their facial features are unique.
Discover how their classmates are sometimes different from themselves and at other times the same.
Draw their faces with creative expressions and use a variety of mediums.

Materials:
Book: *It's Okay to Be Different* by Todd Parr
Book: *We Are All Alike ... We Are All Different* by
  the Cheltenham Elementary School kindergartners
Drawing paper
Markers
Colored pencils
Yarn/string for hair

Index cards
Stamp pad
Magnifying glass
Chart
Star stickers
Assorted laminated objects on sticks, alike and different
Mirrors (optional)

Motivation/mind capture:
The teacher candidate will show the chart that she created from the information the children gave her prior to the lesson.

Procedures:
The teacher candidate will read *It's Okay to Be Different*. See Chapter 11 for shared reading ideas. The teacher candidate will ask, "How are you the same as your friends?" and "How are you different from your friends?"

Activity #1:

Each student will be handed a laminated object on a stick and asked to locate another classmate with the same object. Several students will be picked out by the teacher candidate. The class is to identify for the teacher what is the same about the chosen students.

Activity #2:

Students will go back to their seats and create a self-portrait. Students will pay close attention to their hair color, hair texture, and eye color.

Activity #3:

Using a stamp pad and index cards, the students will have their thumbprints made. The students will be provided with a magnifying glass and will examine the differences between their thumbprints and their classmates'.

Closure:

Students will review the concepts of different and same. The teacher will tell the students that she is creating a book on differences and uniqueness, using each student's self-portrait.

Adaptation for students with specific learning needs:

Students may have a buddy to assist them.

Assessment:

A copy of the teacher/class-created book will be displayed in the classroom for the students to read, review, and enjoy. At the end of the school year, the teacher will make another chart, and the students can note all the growth, changes, and differences.

Contributed by Raynice Jean-Sigur, PhD, assistant professor of early childhood education, Kennesaw State University, and by Cara Tucker, Sharon Boeck, and Marni Donovan, undergraduate teacher candidates, Kennesaw State University, Kennesaw, Georgia.

Visual Preference. Use pictures, filmstrips, films, graphs, single-concept loops, transparencies, computer monitors, diagrams, drawings, books, and magazines; supply resources that require reading and seeing; use programmed learning (if student needs structure) and written assignments and evaluations. Reinforce knowledge through tactile, kinesthetic, and then auditory resources.

Tactile Preference. Use manipulative and three-dimensional materials; resources should be touchable and movable as well as readable; allow children to plan, demonstrate, report, and evaluate with models and other real objects; encourage them to keep written or graphic records. Use real-life experiences such as visits, interviewing, building, designing, and so on. Introduce information through activities such as baking, building, sewing, visiting, or acting. Reinforce through kinesthetic, visual, and then auditory resources.

Kinesthetic Preference. Provide opportunities for real and active experiences; visits, projects, acting, and floor games are appropriate. Introduce information through real-life activities (e.g., planning a part in a play or a trip). Reinforce through tactile resources—such as electroboards, task cards, and learning circles—then through visual and auditory resources.

Mobility. Provide frequent breaks, assignments that require movement to different locations, and schedules that permit mobility in the learning environment; require results, not immobility. Or provide a stationary desk or learning station where most of the child's responsibilities can be completed without requiring excessive movement.

WELCOME PARENT AND COMMUNITY INVOLVEMENT

As an early childhood professional, you will work with children and families of diverse cultural backgrounds. You will need to learn about their cultural backgrounds so that you can respond appropriately to their needs. Let's take a look at the Hispanic culture and its implications for parent and family involvement.

Throughout Hispanic culture there is a widespread belief in the absolute authority of the school and teachers. In many Latin American countries it is considered rude for a parent to intrude in the life of the school. Parents believe that it is the school's job to educate and the parent's job to nurture and that the two jobs do not mix. A child who is well educated is one who has learned moral and ethical behavior.

Hispanics, as a whole, have strong family ties, believe in family loyalty, and have a collective orientation that supports community life; they have been found to be field dependent (i.e., learning best in group and highly organized environments) and sensitive to nonverbal indicators of feeling.[7] These traits are represented by an emphasis on warm, personalized styles of interaction, a relaxed sense of time, and a need for an informal atmosphere for communication. Given these preferences, a culture clash may result when Hispanic students and parents are confronted with the typical task-oriented style of most American teachers.

Although an understanding of the general cultural characteristics of Hispanics is helpful, it is important not to overgeneralize. Each family and child are unique, and care should be taken not to assume values and beliefs just because a family speaks Spanish and is from Latin America. It is important that teachers spend the time to discover the particular values, beliefs, and practices of the families in the community. You will find the next Voice from the Field on pages 442–444 about Latino child development helpful as you get to know the Hispanic children and families in your program or school.

You can use the following guidelines to involve Hispanic parents:

In the Head
Start segment of the DVD, observe how family involvement encourages communication and cultural understanding.

- *Use a personal touch.* It is crucial to use face-to-face communication in the Hispanic parents' primary language when first making contact. It may even take several personal meetings before the parents gain sufficient trust to actively participate. Home visits are a particularly good way to begin to develop rapport. Written flyers or articles sent home have proven to be ineffective even when written in parents' home languages.
- *Provide bilingual support.* All communication with Hispanic parents, written and oral, must be provided in Spanish and English. Many programs report that having bicultural and bilingual staff helps promote trust.[8]
- *Use nonjudgmental communication.* To gain the trust and confidence of Hispanic parents, teachers must avoid making them feel that they are to blame for something or are doing something wrong. Parents need to be supported for their strengths, not judged for perceived failings.
- *Address real concerns.* To keep Hispanic parents actively engaged, activities planned by the early childhood program must respond to a real need or concern of the parents. Teachers should communicate clearly what parents will get out of each meeting and how the meeting will help them in their role as parents.
- *Provide strong leadership and enlist administrative support.* Flexible policies, a welcoming environment, and a collegial atmosphere all require administrative leadership and support. As with other educational projects and practices that require innovation and adaptation, the efforts of teachers alone cannot bring success to parent involvement projects. Principals must also be committed to project goals.
- *Participate in staff development focused on Hispanic culture.* All staff must understand the key features of Hispanic culture and its impact on their students' behavior and learning styles. It is educators' obligation to learn as much about the children and their culture and background as possible.
- *Facilitate community connections.* Many Hispanic families could benefit from family literacy programs, vocational training, ESL programs, improved medical and dental services, and other community-based social services. A school or early childhood program can serve as a resource and referral agency to support the overall strength and stability of the families.

WHAT EARLY CHILDHOOD PROFESSIONALS SHOULD KNOW ABOUT LATINO CHILD DEVELOPMENT

Early childhood professionals are increasingly asked to understand the needs of children and families from cultures other than their own. One group that is experiencing dramatic growth is the Latino or Hispanic population. From 1980 to 2006, the Latino population in the United States has more than doubled. Latinos or Hispanics are defined as persons whose origins are Mexican, Puerto Rican, Cuban, Central or South American, or some other Spanish origin. Mexican-origin individuals represent 67 percent of the population identified by the U.S. Census Bureau as Hispanic, and many of these individuals are immigrants. Because the field of early childhood education has a professional responsibility to provide appropriate programs and services to all children, understanding the culture and value orientations of Latinos is important.

In understanding diversity, one should distinguish aspects of development that are *culturally specific* and those aspects that are *universal*, or common to all humans regardless of their cultural background. For example, toilet training occurs for all infants, regardless of culture; however, the timing of the appearance of this ability is likely influenced by a culture's expectations. Thus, we need to keep in mind both universal and culturally specific developmental processes in understanding diverse populations.

Latinos are often seen as having a similar family history and maintaining exactly the same set of values. However, this is a simplistic way of thinking about this population; Latinos are, in fact, a very heterogeneous group. Although Latinos may be similar in their language and possibly their religious heritage, other differences exist such as country of origin, urban/rural differences, migratory histories, and, most importantly, acculturation status. All of these factors need to be considered in understanding how culture influences individual children and families.

THE ROLE OF SOCIOECONOMIC STATUS AND ACCULTURATION

Socioeconomic Status

One of the most important factors in understanding cultural differences of Latinos is the role of socioeconomic status. Because cultural background and socioeconomic background are highly interrelated, what we think is culturally specific might be more a function of the group's adaptation to their socioeconomic conditions. Research suggests that when social class is similar, some differences between middle-income Anglos and middle-income Latinos decrease. For example, differences are found between low-income Latinos and middle-income Anglo mothers in their styles of interacting with their preschool children on a teaching task. Yet those differences substantially decrease when comparisons are made between middle-income Latinos and middle-income Anglos. When socioeconomic status is held constant, both groups perform similarly.

Why should social class matter in understanding cultural differences? Social class standing is an important determinant of such resources as housing, employment opportunities, medical services, and most significantly, educational opportunities. Unfortunately, Latinos as a group have higher rates of poverty than many non-Latino groups. Thus, in much of the research on Latinos, low-income status is mixed up with cultural factors, making it difficult to understand the influence of culture. Some experts even argue that it is not possible to separate the effects of culture from socioeconomic class because they highly influence each other.

Acculturation

For Latinos residing in the United States, the level of acculturation also plays an important role. Acculturation refers to the degree to which an individual is able to function effectively in the dominant culture. Acculturation includes the ability to speak the language of the dominant culture and have knowledge of the dominant culture's values and cultural expressions (e.g., foods, arts). These factors play a major role in determining an individual's ability to adapt to and function in the dominant society. However, it is important to note that acculturation is not a linear process whereby, as one becomes more acculturated, the values and attitudes of one's native culture are relinquished. It is possible that as individuals become more acculturated, they can function effectively in both their own culture and the broader dominant culture. This is referred to as biculturalism and is viewed by many as the ideal outcome of the acculturation process.

In order to effectively understand and service Latinos, the early childhood professional needs to recognize where children and families are located within the acculturation spectrum. More important, when working with families, it is often the case that children and their parents will differ on acculturation, creating stronger-than-average generational divisions.

PARENTAL ORIENTATION

Early childhood professionals need to consider how parental orientation may differ from the specific goals and objectives of a particular intervention program. When working with immigrant families, it is sometimes appropriate to indicate how the expectations of the school explicitly differ from the target group's orientation. For many immigrant families, adaptation and innovation are a way of life, and accepting different ways of doing things is part and parcel of the immigrant experience. However, for second-generation or more acculturated groups reared in the United States, such explicit contrast might not suffice. In these instances, practitioners must become familiar with the degree of acculturation that characterizes the group and adjust their services accordingly.

Another important factor in understanding Latino child development is parental orientation to children. Specifically, early childhood professionals should ask themselves, What are the child-rearing practices that the parents use, and what are the parents' overall goals for their children's development? Previous research on parental beliefs suggests that cultural background is an important determinant of parental ideas. For example, in research with low-income immigrant Latino parents, expectations for their children's skill development differs from that of Latinos born in the United States. This research suggests that foreign-born Latinos perceive the behavioral capabilities of young children as developing later than do U.S.-born Latinos. It may be that foreign-born Latinos have a different perspective on children's development that is more maturational in nature. That is, non-U.S.-born Latino parents may see young children's development as occurring naturally and not requiring much direct intervention and stimulation. Thus, the early emphasis on cognitive stimulation promoted in the United States may be somewhat inconsistent with their expectations.

CHILD-REARING PRACTICES

A maturational approach to child rearing may stem from the social and historic backgrounds of Latino groups living in the United States. In cultures in which children are expected to take part in the activities of adults, such as sibling caretaking and the economic maintenance of the family, certain parent–child patterns will emerge. In more rural, traditional cultures, parents may socialize their children by stressing observation and immediate assistance in task development rather than the explicit instruction valued by middle-class U.S. parents.

The often-referenced proposition that parents are the first teachers of their children is generally acceptable within the context of early development. Yet the role of parents as teachers of school-related tasks may vary in families of Latino heritage. The role of parents as teachers of their own children may not be congruent with a family's cultural values, perceptions of parenting, and socioeconomic reality. For example, Latino children are less likely to live in nuclear families in which the mother has the exclusive responsibility for child rearing. In Latino families siblings may play both a caretaking role and a mentoring role to younger children by helping them with their school work. Thus, the focus on the mother as the exclusive socializer of the children may overlook the important role of other family members. Early childhood professionals need to understand a family's value orientation about child development, recognize and be sensitive to parental perceptions about teaching young children, and see other members of the family as important contributors to a child's development.

CHILDHOOD SOCIALIZATION

Latinos hold certain values and beliefs that relate to childhood socialization. The following sections present an overview of important core values and beliefs that will vary in individual families depending on their acculturation level, socioeconomic standing, and ethnic loyalty. It is very important to see these core values as broad generalizations subject to adaptations to local conditions.

Familialism

This value is viewed as one of the most important culture-specific values of Latinos. *Familialism* refers to strong identificaiton and connection to the immediate and extended family. Behaviors associated with familialism include strong feelings of loyalty, reciprocity, and solidarity. Familialism is manifested through (a) feelings of obligation to provide both material and emotional support to the family, (b) dependence on relatives for help and support, and (c) reliance on relatives as behavioral and attitudinal role models.

Respeto

Associated with familialism is the cultural concept of *respeto,* an extremely important underlying tenet of interpersonal interaction. Basically, *respeto* ("respect") refers to the deference ascribed to various members of the family or society because of their position. Respect is accorded to the position and not necessarily the person. For example, respect is expected toward elders, parents, older siblings within the family, and teachers, clergy, nurses, and doctors outside the family. With respect comes deference; that is, the person will not question the individual in an authority position, will exhibit courteous behavior in front of them, and will appear to agree with information presented to them by the authority figure.

Bien Educado

A person exhibiting the characteristics associated with *respeto* is said to be *bien educado*. Important here is that the term *educado* (educated) refers not to formal education but to the acquisition of appropriate social skills and graces within the Latino cultural context. For traditional Latinos, receiving a degree from a prestigious university would not qualify one as well educated. A well-educated individual demonstrates proper social behavior as defined by core cultural values.

By both acknowledging and honoring important cultural values and beliefs, the early childhood professional communicates respect toward children and families. Taken a step further, the modification of professional practice to account for cultural differences, although challenging, is an even more critical component. When working with Latino groups, it is suggested that the early childhood professional demonstrate high degrees of courtesy, understand that indirect communication on the part of the child and parent is a reflection of *respeto* to teachers as authority figures, and view the broader family configuration as an important resource for understanding Latino family dynamics. Within this general framework, the professional must accommodate individual differences and local community conditions.

Contributed by Marlene Zepeda, PhD, professor, Department of Child and Family Studies, California State University, Los Angeles, California.

BILINGUAL EDUCATION PROGRAMS

For most people, *bilingual education* means that children will be taught a second language. Some people interpret this to mean that a child's native language (often referred to as the *home language*)—whether English, Spanish, French, Italian, Chinese, Tagalog, or any of the other 125 languages in which bilingual programs are conducted—will tend to be suppressed. For other people, bilingual education means that children will be taught in both the home language and the primary language of the country. The Bilingual Education Act, Title VII of the Elementary and Secondary Education Act (ESEA), sets forth the federal government's policy toward bilingual education:

> The Congress declares it to be the policy of the United States, in order to establish equal educational opportunity for all children and to promote educational excellence (A) to encourage the establishment and operation, where appropriate, of educational programs using bilingual educational practices, techniques, and methods, (B) to encourage the establishment of special alternative instructional programs for students of limited English proficiency in school districts where the establishment of bilingual education programs is not practicable or for other appropriate reasons, and (C) for those purposes, to provide financial assistance to local educational agencies.[9]

REASONS FOR INTEREST IN BILINGUAL EDUCATION

Diversity is now a positive aspect of U.S. society. Ethnic pride and identity have caused renewed interest in languages and a more conscious effort to preserve children's native languages. In the nineteenth and early twentieth centuries, foreign-born individuals and their children wanted to camouflage their ethnicity and lose their native language because it seemed unpatriotic or un-American. Today, however, we hold the opposite viewpoint.

A second reason for interest in bilingual education is an emphasis on civil rights. Indeed, much of the concept of providing children with an opportunity to know, value, and use their heritage and language stems from people's recognition that they have a right to their culture. Just as we extend rights to children with disabilities today, so do we view children with other languages as people with rights.

A third reason for interest in bilingual education includes efforts to ban the use of languages other than English in state and municipal activities and prohibit the use of bilingual

**TABLE 15.2 The Top Twenty Languages Other Than English
Most Commonly Spoken in U.S. Homes**

Language	Total Speakers over Five Years Old
Spanish	28,101,052
Chinese	2,022,143
French	1,643,838
German	1,383,442
Tagalog	1,224,241
Vietnamese	1,009,627
Italian	1,008,370
Korean	894,063
Russian	706,242
Polish	667,414
Arabic	614,582
Portuguese / Portuguese Creole	564,630
Japanese	477,997
French Creole	453,368
Other Indic languages	439,289
African languages	418,505
Greek	365,436
Hindi	317,057
Persian	312,085
Urdu	262,900

Source: U.S. Census Bureau, Census 2000 Summary File 3, Matrix PCT10, http://factfinder.census.gov.

education to help children learn English. One attempt to curtail the implementation of bilingual programs includes the passage of English-only laws by state governments. What these laws mean and what they prohibit varies from state to state. Some declare English the official language of the state; some limit or prohibit the provision of non-English-language assistance and services; others limit or prohibit bilingual education programs. Currently, sixteen states have English-only laws. In addition, in some states such as California (Proposition 227) and Arizona (Proposition 203), voters have passed state statutes that specifically prohibit native language instruction in the public schools for most children with limited English proficiency.

Yet another reason for bilingual interest is the number of people who speak a language other than English. According to the Census Bureau, forty-seven million, or about one in five, residents of the United States speak a language other than English, with Spanish now the second most common language. Table 15.2 shows the twenty most common languages (other than English) spoken in U.S. homes. Pay particular attention to the fastest-growing languages, such as Tagalog and Vietnamese. The Asian school-age population is expected to double by the year 2020.

These data show an increasing probability that you will work with parents, children, and families in a language other than English. They also give you some idea what languages parents and children you work with will speak. Moreover, these increases will necessitate culturally appropriate material and activities. As individual professionals and as a body, we cannot ignore the need to develop appropriate curriculum materials for children of all cultures. To do so would add to the risk of language-minority children being cut off from mainstream life and the American dream. But there is also a need to develop training programs for early childhood professionals to enable them to work in culturally sensitive ways with parents, families, and children.

PROGRAMS FOR STUDENTS WITH LIMITED ENGLISH PROFICIENCY

Early childhood programs and schools can choose from a number of responses to the need for English language learning among children with limited English proficiency (LEP).

Companion
Website
To complete a
Diversity Tie-In activity related
to helping English language
learners, go to the
Companion Website at
www.prenhall.com/morrison,
select chapter 15, then
choose the Diversity Tie-In
module.

TABLE 15.3 Types of Programs for English Language Learners

Program	Description	Goal
English as a second language (ESL)	Students receive specified periods of instruction aimed at the development of English language skills, with a primary focus on grammar, vocabulary, and communication rather than academic content areas. Academic content is addressed through mainstream instruction, where no special assistance is provided.	English language fluency
Structured immersion (or sheltered immersion)	Students are limited English proficient, usually from different language backgrounds. Instruction is in English, with an adjustment made to the level of English so that subject matter is more easily understood. Typically, there is no native language support.	English language fluency
Transitional bilingual education	Most students are English language learners. They receive some degree of instruction through their native language. However, within the program there is a rapid shift toward using primarily English.	Transition to English as rapidly as possible
Maintenance bilingual education	Most students are English language learners and from the same language background. They receive significant amounts of instruction in their native language.	Academic proficiency in both languages
Two-way bilingual programs	About half of students are native speakers of English; the other half are English language learners from the same language group. Instruction is in both languages.	Proficiency in both languages
English language development or ESL pull-out	Students are usually at beginning-level proficiency and are integrated in mainstream, English-only classrooms in other subjects with no assistance. Students are pulled out for instruction aimed at developing English grammar, vocabulary, and communication skills, rather than academic content.	English language fluency
Immersion with primary-language support	This is used when only a few students in each grade level are English language learners. Bilingual teachers tutor small groups of students by reviewing particular lessons covered in mainstream classes, using students' primary language.	English language fluency

Source: Adapted with permission from R. Linquanti, "Types of Instructional Program Models" (WestEd, 1999). Also available online at http://www.wested.org/policy/pubs/fostering/originals/models.doc.

Programs for the education of English language learners are shown in Table 15.3. Review these now. Which of the programs do you like the best? Which one of the approaches would you select for your program or school?

Regardless of the approach you choose, the Diversity Tie-In on pages 447–448 "How to Help English Language Learners Succeed" is a Competency Builder that gives some excellent ideas you can use to help *all* English language learners in your classroom.

ISSUES IN BILINGUAL EDUCATION

As you might expect, programs to help children learn English are controversial. Critics of immersion programs assert that when the focus is only on teaching English, children are at risk of losing the ability to speak and use their native language. On the other hand, proponents of immersion programs maintain that English is the language of schooling and U.S. society and it is in children's best interest to learn English as quickly and fluently as possible. Further, they maintain that it is the parents' responsibility to help maintain native language and culture. Parents do want their children to be successful in both school and society, but some regret that their children do not maintain their native language because of the role it plays in culture and religion.

Critics of transitional bilingual programs maintain that it takes children too long to learn English and that it is too costly to maintain a child's native language. On the other hand, proponents of transitional programs say that it makes sense to help children learn English while preserving native language and culture.

Diversity Tie-In

How to Help English Language Learners Succeed

My attempts to learn Spanish have given me a lot of empathy for English language learners. Perhaps you have had the same experience of frustration with comprehension, pronunciation, and understandable communication. English language learners face these same problems and others. Many come from low socioeconomic backgrounds. Others come to this country lacking many of the early literacy and learning opportunities we take for granted.

INCREASING NUMBERS

Many school districts across the country have seen their numbers of English language learners skyrocket. For example, in the Winston-Salem/Forsyth County School District in North Carolina, more than 8 percent of the 47,000 student population are English language learners, representing fifty-two different native languages.

The chances are great that you will have English language learners in your classroom wherever you choose to teach. There are a number of approaches you can use to ensure that your children will learn English and that they will be academically successful.

TIPS FOR SUCCESS

Judith Lessow-Hurley, a bilingual expert, says, "It's important to create contexts in which kids exchange meaningful messages. Kids like to talk to other kids, and that's useful."* Lessow-Hurley also supports sheltered immersion (see Table 15.3). She says, "A lot of what we call 'sheltering' is simply good instruction—all kids benefit from experiential learning, demonstrations, visuals, and routines. A lot of sheltering is also common sense—stay away from idioms, speak slowly and clearly, [and] find ways to repeat yourself."†

Here are some other general tips Lessow-Hurley offers for assisting English language learners, along with some explicit classroom strategies:

STRATEGY 1
Develop content around a theme

The repetition of vocabulary and concepts reinforces language and ideas and gives English language learners better access to content.

STRATEGY 2
Use visual aids and hands-on activities to deliver content

Information is better retained when a variety of senses are used.

- Rely on visual cues as frequently as possible.
- Have students create flashcards for key vocabulary words. Be sure to build in time for students to use them.
- Encourage students to use computer programs and books with cassette tapes.

STRATEGY 3
Use routines to reinforce language

This practice increases the comfort level of second-language learners; they then know what to expect and associate the routine with the language.

- One helpful routine is daily reading.
- Use pictures, gestures, and a dramatic voice to help convey meaning.

▲ **Picture yourself in this classroom. Which of the activities suggested here would you select to help your students learn English?**

STRATEGY 4
Engage English language learners with English speakers

Cooperative learning groups of mixed language abilities give students a meaningful content for using English.

- Pair English language learners with native speakers to explain and illustrate a specific word or phrase frequently heard in the classroom.

Classroom activities such as those suggested here can help English language learners gain important skills.

- Ask the students to make a picture dictionary of the words and phrases they are learning, using pictures they have cut out of magazines.
- Have small groups make vocabulary posters of categories of common words, again using pictures cut from magazines.

Permit students to demonstrate their knowledge and comprehension in alternative ways. For example, one teacher has early primary students hold up cardboard "lollipops" (green or red side forward) to indicate a yes or no answer to a question.

It's better to get students talking; they acquire accepted forms through regular use and practice. A teacher can always paraphrase a student's answer to model Standard English.[‡]

Photo on p. 447 by Michael Newman/PhotoEdit, Inc.; photo on this page from B. Daemmrich/The Image Works.

*"Acquiring English: Schools Seek Ways to Strengthen Language Learning," *Curriculum Update,* Association for Supervision and Curriculum Development (Fall 2002): 6.

[†] Ibid.

[‡] Ibid, 7.

TRENDS IN MULTICULTURAL EDUCATION

As with most areas of early childhood education, we can identify trends that will affect multicultural curricula, programs, and practices:

Companion Website To complete a Program in Action activity related to multicultural education, go to the Companion Website at **www.prenhall.com/morrison**, select chapter 15, then choose the Program in Action module.

- Multicultural curricula are becoming more pluralistic, including knowledge and information about many cultures. As a result, more children will examine a full range of cultures rather than looking at only two or three, as is often the current practice. Read "The Chinese American International School of San Francisco," a Program in Action on pages 449–450 to learn more about a full-time multicultural program.
- More early childhood teachers are recognizing that young children are able to learn about multicultural perspectives. Consequently, multicultural activities and content are being included in curricula from the time children enter preschool programs. Thus, kindergarten children might be encouraged to look at Thanksgiving through the eyes of both Native Americans and Pilgrims, instead of being taught only the Pilgrims' point of view.
- Many early childhood professionals are being challenged to preserve children's natural reactions to others' differences before they adopt or are taught adult stereotypical reactions. Young children are, in general, understanding and accepting of differences in others.
- Increasing amounts of material are becoming available to aid in teaching multicultural education. Consequently, teachers will have ever-more decisions to make regarding the kind of materials they want and can use. Because materials are not all of equal value or worth, this abundance will mean that professionals will need to be increasingly diligent when selecting appropriate materials for young children.
- There is a growing recognition that effective multicultural education is good for all. Whereas in the past some teachers and parents have resisted multicultural teaching, more and more the public is accepting and supportive of multicultural education for all children.

THE CHINESE AMERICAN INTERNATIONAL SCHOOL OF SAN FRANCISCO

DESCRIPTION AND PHILOSOPHY

The Chinese American International School (CAIS) of San Francisco was established in 1981 by a multiethnic group of parents, educators, and civic leaders. It remains the nation's only full-time school from prekindergarten through eighth grade that offers instruction in English and Mandarin Chinese as equal languages in all subjects.

The school's mission emphasizes fluency in both English and Mandarin Chinese, internationalism, intellectual flexibility, and the development of character and emotional and social maturity as a foundation for active participation and leadership in the modern world.

No prior Chinese language knowledge is necessary for children to enter the program. Children of every ethnicity are enrolled in the school, with 95 percent of the families speaking no Mandarin Chinese at home.

The program is a fifty-fifty foreign language immersion program, whereby all subjects in the curriculum are taught in and through Mandarin Chinese. Mandarin Chinese is an equal language of instruction and communication with English and not simply the object of study itself, as in traditional foreign language classes.

Parents gravitate to this program for several different reasons: Asian Americans of second, third, or fourth generation seek a link to their cultural and historical heritage; international business professionals want their children to enjoy the advantage of fluency in the language and culture; families who have studied research results send their children to the school for the social and cognitive benefits of bilingual education.

THE PREKINDERGARTEN AND KINDERGARTEN CHILDREN

Entering students in prekindergarten are immediately immersed in both English and Mandarin Chinese so that by the completion of kindergarten they have developed basic proficiency in both languages. Each class is taught by an English teacher and a Chinese teacher with the help of teaching assistants. All teachers are native speakers of the language they use for instruction.

The English kindergarten curriculum utilizes the Montessori method, giving careful attention to each child's developmental level and individual learning style. Through lessons and everyday life-skill experiences, the children develop a fine sense of order and enhanced ability to concentrate, following a complex sequence of steps. Hands-on learning materials make abstract concepts clear and concrete. Along with the opportunity to explore, this curriculum teaches the children to be independent, responsible, caring individuals.

The Chinese prekindergarten and kindergarten curriculum provides similar opportunities for the children to grow and learn. It focuses on social interaction skills and respect for others as the children acquire listening and speaking skills in the foreign language. The Chinese immersion curriculum is concrete, multisensory, hands-on, and project oriented. A science class on flotation, for example, would require children to test and record flotation of real objects, enabling them to learn the objects' names as well as to express concepts related to flotation in the Chinese language.

In a typical school day, children sing dramatized songs, produce art and craft projects, play games, listen to stories, and familiarize themselves with some written characters. The teacher uses Chinese exclusively, making use of movements, facial expressions, voice inflections, pictures, toys, and a myriad of props to ensure comprehension and participation. Children are allowed to demonstrate their understanding in multiple ways.

Together, the Chinese and English teachers in the prekindergarten programs encourage children to organize, hypothesize, explore, invent, discover, and test their experiences. An emphasis is placed on the development of each child's creativity, concentration, initiative, self-confidence, self-discipline, imagination, and love of learning. This lays the foundation for a challenging elementary school curriculum, which emphasizes both oral and written communication in the two languages.

THE ELEMENTARY CURRICULUM

In elementary school, science, social studies, language arts, and mathematics share equal prominence in both the

English and Chinese classes. In a fifty-fifty bilingual immersion program, students spend half a day in an English classroom, learning in much the same way as students in a monolingual school do. Then, in the second part of the day, they enter a different classroom, filled with Chinese writing and media. They then study subjects with the Chinese teacher, just as they did with the English teacher, but express themselves in Chinese. On the following day, the model repeats itself, beginning with Chinese in the morning and English in the afternoon.

Close coordination between the English and the Chinese teachers allows the development of common themes for study materials and cultural celebrations. Teachers reinforce—but do not repeat or translate—each other's activities. For instance, whereas the Chinese teacher assumes the responsibility for the celebration of Chinese festivals such as Chinese New Year, the English teacher leads the celebration of American holidays like Thanksgiving. In the course of the celebrations, children can learn language and content simultaneously. Besides immersion in the culture, they acquire second-language vocabulary through cooking, costume designing, and dramatization of events.

PROFESSIONAL DEVELOPMENT

Current enrollment in the new San Francisco Civic Center campus has grown to four hundred students, with most grade levels incorporating multiple sections. The earliest graduates of CAIS are now enrolled in universities throughout the United States, most continuing their Chinese studies. Alumni in high school regularly serve as counselors and aides during the school's summer session. Summer sessions also serve as training periods for new faculty, who work closely with a master/mentor teacher for several years before assuming full curricular responsibility.

The growing interest in teaching the Chinese language at all age levels and in the elementary curriculum in particular led to the development of a separate unit of the school devoted to teacher training and curricular development. The Institute for Teaching Chinese Language and Culture is supported by two national foundations in its role as the creator of a graduate training program in the CAIS immersion methodology. The elementary school serves as the laboratory practicum for teachers coming for training from throughout the United States and Asia.

You can visit the Chinese American International School on the Web at http://www.cie-cais.org/.

Contributed by Juliana Carnes, teacher, and Shirley, Lee, principal, Chinese American International School, San Francisco, California. Photo on p. 449 courtesy of Emily Ching; photo on this page from EMG Education Management Group.

Even though we have a long way to go to ensure that all classrooms and curricula provide for children's multicultural needs, we are making progress. You can be at the forefront of making even greater advances by educating both yourself and young children to live in a diverse society.

Companion Website

For additional Internet resources or to complete an online activity for this chapter, go to the Companion Website at **www.prenhall.com/morrison,** select chapter 15, then choose the Linking to Learning or Making Connections module.

LINKING TO LEARNING

Multicultural Book Reviews
http://www.isomedia.com/homes/jmele/homepage.html
A useful site for educators to preview existing and new titles in multicultural education.

Multicultural Pavilion
http://www.edchange.org/multicultural/

Strives to provide resources for educators, students, and activists to explore and discuss multicultural education; facilitates opportunities for educators to work toward self-awareness and development; and provides forums for educators to interact and collaborate toward a critical, transformative approach to multicultural education.

Multicultural Perspectives in Mathematics Education
http://jwilson.coe.uga.edu/DEPT/Multicultural/mathED.html

Explores multicultural dimensions of mathematics, a field often regarded as difficult to teach multiculturally.

National Association for Multicultural Education
http://www.nameorg.org/

Brings together individuals and groups with interests in multicultural education from all levels of education, different academic disciplines, and diverse educational institutions and occupations. Has six points of consensus regarding multicultural education that are central to NAME's philosophy and serve as NAME's goals.

National Clearinghouse for English Language Acquisition
http://www.ncela.gwu.edu/

Funded by the U.S. Department of Education's Office of English Language Acquisition, Language Enhancement & Academic Achievement for Limited English Proficient Students to collect, analyze, and disseminate information relating to the effective education of linguistically and culturally diverse learners in the United States.

National Multicultural Institute
http://www.nmci.org

Operated by the Washington-based National Multicultural Institute; explores many facets of diversity.

ACTIVITIES FOR FURTHER ENRICHMENT

ETHICAL DILEMMA: "WE SHOULDN'T CATER TO THEM!"

You have just been hired to teach first grade in River Bend School District, which has had an influx of minority students over the past few years. The minority students are almost the majority. Not everyone thinks that the rapid increase in the minority student population is beneficial to the school district or town. Some of your colleagues think that the school district is bending over (too far) backward to meet minority students' needs. At your first meeting with Harry Fortune, your new mentor teacher, he remarked, "Respecting minorities and catering to them are two different things. I'm going to stress with my parents that this is America and American culture comes first, and that includes speaking English!"

What do you do? Do you agree with your mentor teacher, adopt a policy of English first, or do you seek out the director of multiculturalism for your school district, Linda Strang, and discuss Harry's comments with her, or do you pursue another course of action?

APPLICATIONS

1. The classroom environment and certain educational materials may promote sexism and gender-role stereotyping. Examine the environment of selected classrooms to determine the extent of sexist practices. Make recommendations based on your findings for minimizing or eliminating any such practices.

2. Effective educational programs provide children with opportunities to develop an understanding of other persons and cultures. Consider how you would accomplish the following objectives in your classroom:
   a. Provide children with firsthand, positive experiences with different cultural groups.
   b. Help children reflect on and think about their own cultural identity.
   c. Help children learn how to obtain accurate information about other cultural groups.

3. How does a teacher modify the classroom environment, classroom routines, learning activities, student groupings, teaching strategies, instructional materials, assessments, and homework assignments to meet all students' cultural needs? Visit several classrooms and take notes on what you observe. Compare and discuss your observations with classmates who have visited different settings across all early childhood grade levels.

4. Cite at least five ways in which culture influences child-rearing practices. Identify five implications these practices have for you as a teacher of children from diverse backgrounds.

FIELD EXPERIENCES

1. In addition to the books mentioned in this chapter, select ten children's books that have multicultural content. Decide how you would use these materials to promote awareness and acceptance of diversity. Read these books to children and get their reactions.

2. Survey ten teachers and your classmates, asking them what the term *multicultural* means. Ask them to share with you activities to promote multiculturalism. Put these activities in your teaching file.

3. Use the knowledge and skills learned in chapter 3 to develop an observational checklist. Then visit classrooms with diverse student populations, and observe the children during play activities. Follow a particular child from a diverse background, and note what appropriate materials are available and how other children and the teacher interact with him or her. Try to determine whether the child's cultural needs are being met. If not, hypothesize why not. Discuss your observations with your colleagues.

4. Observe children in both school and nonschool settings to see how students' dress reflects gender stereotyping and how parents' behaviors promote gender stereotyping also.

RESEARCH

1. Examine children's books and textbooks to determine instances of sexism. What recommendations would you make to change such practices?

2. Stories and literature play an important role in transmitting to children information about themselves and what to expect in life.

a. What books and literature played an important role in your growing up? In what way?

b. Identify five children's books that you think would be good to use with children, and indicate why you think so.

3. Get permission to teach in a third-grade classroom for about an hour. Have the children write "Who I Am" poems—four or five lines, each beginning with "I am. . . ." Have the children share their poems with each other. Later, analyze the children's poems, and draw several conclusions about children's identities.

4. Interview five parents from diverse cultural backgrounds, and ask them to identify at least three cultural concepts they think should be taught in their children's classrooms. How can you incorporate their ideas into your classroom?

READINGS FOR FURTHER ENRICHMENT

Bennett, C. I. *Comprehensive Multicultural Education: Theory and Practice,* 5th ed. Boston: Allyn and Bacon, 2003.

Provides teachers with the historical background, basic terminology, and social science concepts of multicultural education. Also provides a curriculum model with six goals and numerous lesson plans illustrating how each goal can be implemented in the classroom.

Flor Ada, A. *A Magical Encounter: Latino Children's Literature in the Classroom,* 2nd ed. Boston: Allyn and Bacon, 2003.

Brings literature to the classroom as a vehicle for language and concept development, for creative expression, and for the development of higher-thinking skills.

Howes, C. *Teaching 4- to 8-Year-Olds: Literacy, Math, Multiculturalism, and Classroom Community.* Baltimore: Paul H. Brookes, 2003.

Explains developmentally appropriate teaching practices in four crucial areas: literacy, mathematics, multiculturalism, and classroom community.

Jones, T. G., and M. L. Fuller. *Teaching Hispanic Children.* Boston: Allyn and Bacon, 2003.

Presents information about the role of national origins and cultural backgrounds in teaching and learning and discusses why it is important for teachers to know about culture in general and about Hispanic cultural groups in particular.

Tiedt, P. L., and I. M. Tiedt. *Multicultural Teaching: A Handbook of Activities, Information, and Resources,* 7th ed. Boston: Allyn and Bacon, 2006.

Provides activities and information to enable the teacher to explore the many kinds of diversity in the classroom. Guides readers to examine their own diversity first in order to better understand how diversity affects everyone. Presents model lesson plans, fully developed thematic units, and a variety of instructional strategies, as well as a wealth of resources that support multicultural teaching.

ENDNOTES

1. U.S. Census Bureau, "U.S. Interim Projections by Age, Sex, Race, and Hispanic Origin" (2004), http://www.census.gov/.

2. *Federal Register* (August 11, 1975), 33803.

3. *Federal Register* (June 4, 1975), 24128.

4. Marian Marion, *Guidance of Young Children,* 6th ed. (Upper Saddle River, NJ: Merrill/Prentice Hall, 2003), 58.

5. Marie Cabo, Rita Dunn, and Kenneth Dunn, *Teaching Students to Read Through Their Individual Learning Styles* (Boston: Allyn and Bacon, 1991), 2.

6. Rita Dunn, Kenneth Dunn, and Gary Price, *Learning Styles Inventory* (Lawrence, KS: Price Systems, 1987), 14–19.

7. N. Williams, *The Mexican American Family* (Dix Hills, NY: General Hill, 1990).

8. L. Espinosa, *Hispanic Parent Involvement in Early Childhood Programs* (Washington, DC: Office of Educational Research and Improvement, 1995).

9. *Bilingual Education Act,* statute 2372, section 703, Title VII of the *Elementary Secondary Education Act,* statute 2268, vol. 92 (November 1978).

CHAPTER 16

Children with Special Needs

APPROPRIATE EDUCATION FOR ALL

*Good schools, like good societies and good families,
celebrate and cherish diversity.*

DEBORAH MEIER, EDUCATOR

Children with special needs are in every program, school, and classroom in the United States. As an early childhood professional, you will teach students who have a variety of special needs. They may come from low-income families or various racial and ethnic groups, and they may have exceptional abilities or disabilities. In fact, some students may have more than one exceptionality; they may be **twice exceptional**. For example, students may be gifted and also have a learning disability.

Students with special needs are often discriminated against because of their disability, socioeconomic background, language, ethnicity, or gender. You will be challenged to provide for all your students an education that is appropriate for their physical, intellectual, social, and emotional abilities and to help them achieve their best. To meet the challenge, you should learn as much as you can about the special needs of children and collaborate with other professionals to identify and develop teaching strategies, programs, and curricula for them. Most of all, you need to be a strong advocate for meeting all children's individual needs.

As we begin our study of children with special needs, let's examine the Portraits of Kenly Marie and Jake and reflect on how appropriate services have helped them grow and develop. Thereafter, review Figure 16.1 and discuss with your peers the questions included there.

CHILDREN WITH DISABILITIES

Children with special needs and their families need education and services that will help them succeed. You will be a part of the process of seeing that they receive such services. Unfortunately, quite often children with disabilities are not provided appropriate services and fail to reach their full potential. This is one reason for laws to help ensure that they have special education and related services and that schools and teachers have high expectations for them. The federal government has passed many laws protecting and promoting the rights and needs of children with disabilities. One of the most important federal laws is PL 101-476, the Individuals with Disabilities Education Act (IDEA), passed in 1990. Congress periodically updates IDEA, with the latest revision in 2004.

As with many special areas, the field of special needs has a unique vocabulary and terminology. The glossary in Figure 16.2 will help you as you read the chapter and as you work with children and families. As the fields of early childhood and special education slowly integrate, early childhood educators must learn more about the field of early childhood special education and the terminology associated with it.

INDIVIDUALS WITH DISABILITIES EDUCATION ACT (IDEA)

The purpose of the **Individuals with Disabilities Education Act (IDEA)** is to ensure that all children with disabilities have available to them

> a free appropriate public education which emphasizes special education and related services designed to meet their unique needs, to assure that the rights of the disabled children and their parents or guardians are protected, to assist states and localities to provide for the education of all disabled children, and to assess and assure the effectiveness of efforts to educate disabled children.[1]

Focus Questions

What are the reasons for the current interest in educating children with special needs?

What are the legal, political, educational, and social bases for mainstreaming and inclusion of children in early childhood programs?

What issues relate to teaching children with special needs?

How do programs for the gifted meet children's needs?

What is your role in identifying and reporting child abuse?

Companion Website

To check your understanding of this chapter, go to the Companion Website at **www.prenhall.com/ morrison**, select chapter 16, answer Multiple Choice and Essay Questions, and receive feedback.

WITH APPROPRIATE INTERVENTIONS, SUCCESS COMES NATURALLY

Kenly Marie of Farmington, Utah, graduated from Knowlton Elementary Preschool in the Davis School District. Kenly, age 5½, has Down syndrome and has completed her three years of preschool in an inclusive setting with a remarkably devoted teacher, Mrs. Chris Mooney.

Shortly after her birth, Kenly began receiving early intervention services through a program at Utah State University, including occupational, physical, and speech therapy. She completed her early intervention years in Davis County. Days after her third birthday, Kenly transitioned to the Davis District preschool program. Her mother was concerned that Kenly would be in over her head with typical peers because of her delays. At age three, Kenly was not walking, had limited speech, and was still in diapers.

Instead, Kenly rose to the challenge. Utilizing her talent to model others' behavior, Kenly realized she, too, should learn to walk, and did so within two months of beginning preschool. Her expressive language began blooming as she interacted with typical peers, and this progress was strengthened with speech therapy sessions within the classroom. She now follows the classroom routine, sings along with all the songs, says the Pledge of Allegiance, is toilet trained, and has begun to grasp which behaviors are socially appropriate through her interaction with the other kids.

The laws under the Individuals with Disabilities Education Act (IDEA) have helped Kenly build a firm foundation on which she will build her life. She is now excited about attending kindergarten in her neighborhood elementary school, Reading Elementary. Her parents are anxious to see quality special education services continued, maximizing the educational benefit to Kenly.

Parents of children with disabilities must remain involved in every single aspect of their children's lives. They must mediate, orchestrate, and advocate in order to ensure positive outcomes for their children. Added to the ordinary routines of life, this devotion can be exhausting. With all the challenges that accompany a child with disabilities—behavior issues, medical expenses, safety issues, staying informed on current disability and legislative issues, finding qualified child care, applying for services, constant evaluations, endless appointments—parents must be able to depend on IDEA to guarantee their children's rights to free and appropriate education in the least restrictive environment, thus helping them reach their fullest potential. Kenly's ultimate goal is to live a full and independent life in her community, which is only possible through a successful and adequately supported educational experience.

Jake attends Kent City Community Schools in Kent City, Michigan. He is eight years old and in second grade but no longer requires special education services. Earlier in his educational career, Jake was labeled as having an emotional impairment. Consequently, he was in a preprimary impaired classroom for one year and in a self-contained kindergarten program for children who were emotionally impaired for another year. In first grade he received limited resource room assistance.

Jake had a difficult time controlling his behavior from an early age. His mother worked with him on his social/emotional health and sought the help of the school system when he was only three. The school set up a behavioral plan for Jake that was in accordance with the provisions of IDEA and was carried out in the classroom and at home. The school staff and Jake's family worked closely together to make his discipline plan as consistent as possible.

Halfway through Jake's kindergarten year a great deal of improvement was noted in his behavior. His temper tantrums disappeared, his social skills grew to age level, and he was much less confrontational. Jake is an extremely intelligent child, and he worked hard at achieving his behavioral goals.

Last spring Jake was exited from all special education services. The behavior plans and special education services had helped him achieve his goals. The real praise for Jake's exit from special education services belongs to Jake himself for working so hard at learning to control his behavior and to his mother for supporting him in his education. A shining example of the importance and influence of early childhood intervention, Jake is a true success story.

Contributed by the Council for Exceptional Children.

FIGURE 16.1 Children with Disabilities: Some Facts, Figures, and Questions

Facts and Figures

- Low birth weight is found in 32 percent of children in early intervention*; African American babies are most likely to have low birth weight.
- Two-thirds of children in early intervention are described as difficult to understand; 70 percent have some trouble communicating.
- 26 percent of children entering early intervention have some trouble with use of their legs or feet.
- 67 percent of children entering early intervention live in a two-adult household.
- 41 percent of families in the early intervention system have an annual income of less than $25,000.
- Children with disabilities comprise 5.5 percent of students enrolled in LEP services.
- Hispanic preschoolers represent 20 percent of the general population but only 13.9 percent of preschoolers with disabilities.
- African American students (ages 6 through 21) represent only 14.8 percent of the general population but comprise 18.9 percent of students with mental retardation.
- Although American Indian/Alaskan Native students represent only 1 percent of the general population, they represent 8.5 percent of students with mental retardation.

Questions

- Might Hispanics with disabilities be underrepresented in these data? Why might this occur?
- Why do you think African American students are overrepresented in the population of students with disabilities? What other statistic helps explain this?
- What is the primary developmental delay with children in early intervention?
- Why is early intervention important for success in school?
- What unique challenges do LEP students with disabilities face? What challenges do you face as the teacher of such students?

*Early intervention is mandated in IDEA, Part C, for infants and toddlers with disabilities who are under the age of three. Disabilities include diagnosed developmental delays, and physical or mental conditions that have a high probability of resulting in developmental delay, as well as other at-risk conditions at the state's discretion.

Source: U.S. Department of Education, Twenty-Fourth Annual Report to Congress on the Implementation of the Individuals with Disabilities Education Act (Washington, DC, 2002).

Twice exceptional
Students with dual exceptionalities who may be gifted and have a disability, for example.

Individuals with Disabilities Education Act (IDEA) A federal act providing a free and appropriate education to youth between ages three and twenty-one with disabilities.

Companion Website To complete a Diversity Tie-In activity related to this topic, go to the Companion Website at **www.prenhall.com/morrison**, select chapter 16, then choose the Diversity Tie-In module.

IDEA defines **students with disabilities** as

those with mental retardation, hearing impairments (including deafness), speech or language impairments (including blindness), serious emotional disturbance, orthopedic impairments, autism, traumatic brain injury, other health impairments, or specific learning disabilities; and who, by reason thereof, need special education and related services.[2]

About 10 to 12 percent of the nation's students have some type of disability. Table 16.1 lists the number of persons from ages three to twenty-one with disabilities in the various categories covered under IDEA. The Diversity Tie-In "Is Special Education a Boys' Club" on page 464 gives data that will help you examine the gender differences among special education students."

Students with disabilities
Children with physical or mental/emotional impairments or specific learning disabilities who need special education and related services.

FIGURE 16.2 Glossary of Terms Related to Children with Special Needs

Adaptive education: Modifying programs, environments, curricula, and activities in order to provide learning experiences that help all students achieve desired educational goals. The purpose of adaptive education is to respond effectively to student differences and to enhance each individual's ability to succeed.

Children with disabilities: The expression that replaces former terms such as *handicapped*. To avoid labeling children, do not use the phrase *disabled children*.

Coteaching: The process by which a regular classroom professional and a special educator or a person trained in exceptional student education team teach a group of regular and mainstreamed children in the same classroom.

Cross-categorical classroom: A classroom or other setting with students having a variety of disabilities or delays.

Disability: A physical or mental impairment that substantially limits one or more major life activities.

Early intervention: Providing services to children and families as early in the child's life as possible in order to prevent or help with a special need(s).

English language learners: Students with a primary language other than English.

Exceptional student education: Replaces the term *special education*; refers to the education of children with special needs.

Full inclusion: The mainstreaming or inclusion of all children with disabilities in natural environments, such as playgrounds, family care centers, child care centers, preschool, kindergarten, and primary grades.

Individualized education program (IEP): A written plan for a child stating what will be done, how it will be done, and when it will be done.

Integration: A generic term that refers to educating children with disabilities along with typically developing children. Such education can occur in mainstream, reverse mainstream, and full-inclusion programs.

Least restrictive environment (LRE): The use of special classes, separate schooling, or other removal of children with disabilities from the regular educational environment only when the nature or severity of the disability is such that education in regular classes with the use of supplementary aids and services cannot be achieved satisfactorily.

Limited English proficiency (LEP): Describes children who have limited English skills.

Mainstreaming: The social and educational integration of children with special needs into the general instructional process, usually a regular classroom program.

Natural environment: Any environment that is natural for any child to be in, such as home, child care center, preschool, kindergarten, primary grade, and playground.

Normalized setting: A place that is normal, or best, for the child.

Reverse mainstreaming: The process by which typically developing children are placed in programs for children with disabilities, who are in the majority.

In the Head Start segment of the DVD, listen to what the Head Start Training Specialist says is included in the training Head Start teachers receive to help them work with children with disabilities.

Free and appropriate education (FAPE) Education suited to children's age, maturity, condition of disability, past achievements, and parental expectations.

IDEA has established seven basic principles to follow as you provide education and other services to children with special needs:

1. *Zero reject:* IDEA calls for educating all children and excluding none from an education. Before IDEA many children were excluded from educational programs or were denied an education.
2. *Nondiscriminatory evaluation:* A fair evaluation is required to determine whether a student has a disability and, if so, what the student's education should consist of.
3. *Multidisciplinary assessment:* In this team approach a group of people use various methods in a child's evaluation to ensure that a child's needs and program will not be determined by one test or one person.
4. *Appropriate education:* IDEA provides for a **free and appropriate education (FAPE)** for all students between the ages of three and twenty-one. *Appropriate* means that children must receive an education suited to their age, maturity, condition of disability, past achievements, and parental expectations.

TABLE 16.1 Individuals Aged Six to Twenty-One Served by IDEA

Type of Disability	Number Served	Percent of Total Served
Specific learning disabilities	2,846,135	49.1
Speech or language impairments	1,083,750	18.7
Mental retardation	592,424	10.2
Emotional disturbance	476,156	8.2
Multiple disabilities	127,000	2.2
Hearing impairments	70,245	1.2
Orthopedic impairments	73,306	1.3
Other health impairments	336,560	5.8
Visual impairments	25,296	0.4
Autism	97,329	1.7
Deafness/blindness	1,573	Trace
Traumatic brain injury	20,693	0.4
Developmental delay	44,867	0.8
Total	5,795,334	100.0

Source: International Center for Disability Information, "U.S. Disability Data Tables" (2002), http://www.icdi.wvu.edu/disability/US%20Tables/US1.htm.

5. *Least restrictive placement/environment:* Students with disabilities must, to the maximum extent appropriate for each, one be educated with students who do not have disabilities. The **least restrictive environment (LRE)** is not necessarily the regular classroom, although 80 percent of children with disabilities are educated in the regular classroom.

6. *Procedural due process:* IDEA provides schools and parents with ways to resolve their differences by mediation or by having hearings before impartial hearing officers or judges.

7. *Parents and student participation:* IDEA specifies a process of shared decision making whereby educators, parents, and students collaborate in deciding the student's educational plan.

Least restrictive environment (LRE) Placement that meets the needs of students who are disabled in as regular a setting as possible.

REFERRAL, ASSESSMENT, AND PLACEMENT

Under IDEA and other guidelines that specify the fair treatment of children with disabilities and their families, educators must follow certain procedures in developing a special plan for each child. Referral of the student for exceptional student services can be made by a teacher, parent, doctor, or other professional. The referral is usually followed by a comprehensive individual assessment to determine whether the child possesses a disability and is eligible for services. In order for testing to occur, parents or guardians must give their consent.

If a child is eligible for exceptional student services, the child study team meets to develop an individualized education program (IEP) for the child (see Figure 16.3). Essentially, the IEP is a contract or agreement that specifies how the child will be educated and what services will be provided in the process. The child study team includes a parent or parent representative, the student when appropriate, a special education teacher, a regular education teacher, a representative of the school district, and a principal, assistant principal, or coordinator of exceptional student services. The IEP must be reviewed annually and revised as appropriate. The child study team is also responsible for dismissing students from exceptional student education services when they are able to function in a regular classroom without the services.

Companion Website To learn more about IDEA, go to the Companion Website at **www.prenhall.com/morrison**, select chapter 16, then choose the Linking to Learning module.

INDIVIDUALIZED EDUCATION PROGRAMS AND FAMILY SERVICE PLANS

Because IDEA requires **individualization of instruction,** schools must provide for all students' specific needs, disabilities, and preferences, as well as those of their parents. Individualization

Individualization of instruction Providing for students' specific needs, disabilities, and preferences.

FIGURE 16.3 IEP Team Members

An IEP team member can fill more than one of the team positions if properly qualified and designated. For example, the school system representative may also be the person who can interpret the child's evaluation results.

Source: Office of Special Education and Rehabilitative Services, *A Guide to the Individualized Education Program* (Washington, DC: U.S. Department of Education, 2000). Also available online at http://www.ed.gov/parents/needs/speced/iepguide/iepguide.pdf.

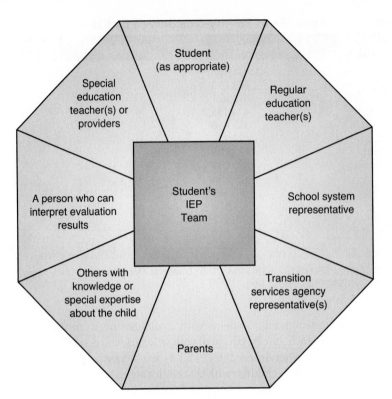

Special education teacher(s) or providers

Student (as appropriate)

Regular education teacher(s)

A person who can interpret evaluation results

Student's IEP Team

School system representative

Others with knowledge or special expertise about the child

Transition services agency representative(s)

Parents

Individualized education program (IEP) A plan for meeting an exceptional learner's educational needs, specifying goals, objectives, services, and procedures for evaluating progress.

Individualized family service plan (IFSP) A plan designed to help families reach their goals for themselves and their children, with varied support services.

Companion Website To learn more about IEPs, go to the Companion Website at **www.prenhall.com/morrison,** select chapter 16, then choose the Linking to Learning module.

of instruction also means developing and implementing an **individualized education program (IEP)** for each student. The IEP must specify what will be done for the child, how and when it will be done, and by whom it will be done, and this information must be in writing. Figure 16.4 outlines the purposes and functions of the IEP, and Figure 16.5 shows a sample IEP. In developing the IEP, a person trained in diagnosing disabling conditions, such as a school psychologist, must be involved, as well as a classroom professional, the parent, and, when appropriate, the child.

In 1986 Congress passed PL 99-457, the Education of the Handicapped Act Amendments, which was landmark legislation relating to infants, toddlers, and preschoolers with disabilities. This law extended to children with disabilities between the ages of three and five the same rights that are extended to children with disabilities under IDEA and establishes a state grant program for infants and toddlers with disabilities. Most states participate in the infant and toddler grant program.

The process of helping young children with disabilities begins with referral and assessment and results in the development of an **individualized family service plan (IFSP)**, which is designed to help families reach the goals they have for themselves and their children. IDEA provides funds for infants and toddlers to receive early intervention services through the IFSP, which includes the following:

- Multidisciplinary assessment developed by a multidisciplinary team and the parents.
- Planned services to meet developmental needs, including, as necessary, special education, speech and language pathology and audiology, occupational therapy, physical therapy, psychological services, parent and family training and counseling services, transition services, medical diagnostic services, and health services.
- Supporting information—a statement of the child's present levels of development; a statement of the family's strengths and needs in regard to enhancing the child's development; a statement of major expected outcomes for the child and family; the criteria, procedures, and timelines for determining progress; the specific early intervention services necessary to meet the unique needs of the child and family; the pro-

FIGURE 16.4 Purposes and Functions of an IEP

- Protects children and parents by ensuring that planning will occur.
- Guarantees that children will have plans tailored to their individual strengths, weaknesses, and learning styles.
- Helps professionals and other instructional and administrative personnel focus their teaching and resources on children's specific needs, promoting the best use of everyone's time, efforts, and talents.
- Helps ensure that children with disabilities will receive a range of services from other agencies. The plan must specify how a child's total needs will be met.
- Helps clarify and refine decisions about what is best for children, where they should be placed, and how they should be taught and helped.
- Ensures that children will not be categorized or labeled without discussion of their unique needs.
- Requires at least annual review, encouraging professionals to consider how and what children have learned, determine whether what was prescribed was effective, and prescribe new or modified strategies.

In the Reggio Emilia segment of the DVD, observe the multiple ways the teachers document children's learning. How would documenting learning in several ways support the inclusion of children with special needs in an early childhood classroom?

jected dates for initiation of services; the name of the case manager; and transition procedures from the early intervention program into a preschool program.

Steps That Lead to Effective IFSPs. A successful IFSP process depends on numerous components:[3]

- *Identify family concerns, priorities, and resources.* The family's concerns, priorities, and resources guide the entire IFSP process. Early intervention should be seen as a system of services and supports available to families to enhance their capacity to care for their children. The notion of partnership between the intervention team and the family must be introduced and nurtured at this beginning point.

- *Identify the family's activity settings.* All children develop as the result of their everyday experiences. It is important to document valued, enjoyable routines (e.g., bath time, eating, play activities) and analyze them to see whether they offer the sustained engagement that leads to learning opportunities. Likewise, it is important to identify the community activity settings (e.g., child care, gymboree, swimming) that provide opportunities for learning.

- *Conduct a functional assessment.* An effective assessment process itself has several components:
  - Addresses the family's questions about enhancing their child's development, focusing on each family member's concerns and priorities
  - Collects information for a specific purpose (e.g., the evaluation conducted by the early interventionist at the beginning of the IFSP process determines whether the child is eligible for services)

All early childhood programs should address the individual needs of children with disabilities. How can you use IEPs to ensure that those needs are being met?

FIGURE 16.5 A
Sample IEP Form

Source: Excerpted and adapted from the Missouri Department of Elementary and Secondary Education, Division of Special Education (2005), http://dese.mo.gov/divspeced/Compliance/IEP/IEP-FORM.doc.

THE INDIVIDUALIZED EDUCATION PROGRAM FOR:

Name: First	Middle	Last

IEP CONTENT (Required):

Date of IEP Meeting: / /	Initiation Date of IEP: / /
Projected Date of Annual IEP Review: / /	Parent(s)/Legal Guardian(s) provided copy of this IEP: / /

PARTICIPANTS IN IEP MEETING AND ROLE(S)

The names and roles of individuals **participating in developing** the IEP meeting must be documented.

Name of Person and Role Signatures are not required. If a signature is used it only indicates attendance, not agreement.	Method of Attendance
Parent/Guardian	
Parent/Guardian	
Student	
LEA Representative	☐ in person (* required participant)
Special Education Teacher	☐ in person ☐ excused ☐ in writing (if applicable)
Regular Classroom Teacher	☐ in person ☐ excused ☐ in writing (if applicable)
Individual Interpreting Instructional Implications of Evaluation Results	☐ in person ☐ excused ☐ in writing (if applicable)
Part C Representative (if applicable)	
Other:	
Other:	

1. Present Level of Academic Achievement and Functional Performance

- How the child's disability affects his/her involvement and progress in the general education curriculum; or for preschool children, participation in age-appropriate activities.

- The strengths of the child

- Concerns of the parent/guardian for enhancing the education of the child

- Changes in current functioning of the child since the initial or prior IEP

- A summary of the most recent evaluation/re-evaluation results

- A summary of the results of the child's performance on:
  - ▶ general state (MAP/MAP-A):
  - ▶ district-wide assessments:

- For students participating in alternative assessments, a description of benchmarks or short-term objectives
  - ☐ N/A Objectives/benchmarks are on goal page(s)
  - ☐ Objectives/benchmarks described below:

2. Special Considerations: Federal and State Requirements

Note: For the first six items below, if the IEP team determines that the child needs a particular device or service (including an intervention, accommodation, or other program modification) information documenting the team's decision regarding the device or service must be included in the appropriate section of the IEP. These must be considered annually.

Is the student blind or visually impaired?
☐ No
☐ Yes. If yes, complete Form A: Blind and Visually Impaired.

Is the student deaf or hearing impaired?
☐ No
☐ Yes. The IEP Team has considered the child's language and communication needs, opportunities for direct communication with peers and professionals in the child's language and communication mode, academic level, and full range of needs including opportunities for direct instruction in the child's language and communication mode in the development of the IEP.
Does the student use an assistive hearing device? ☐ No ☐ Yes If, yes, acknowledge the next two items.
☐ Assistive hearing device monitoring will be done on a daily basis and during evaluation procedures.
☐ Evaluation of hearing aid/amplification system is completed annually. Date last completed: / / . (month/day/year)

Does the student exhibit behaviors that impede his/her learning or that of others?
☐ No
☐ Yes. If yes, strategies including positive behavior interventions and supports must be considered by the IEP team, and if determined necessary, addressed in this IEP. If a behavior intervention plan is developed it must be a part of the IEP.

Does the student have limited English proficiency?
☐ No
☐ Yes. The student's language needs are addressed in this IEP.

Does the student have communication needs?
☐ No
☐ Yes. The student's communication needs are addressed in this IEP.

Does the student require Assistive Technology device(s) and/or services?
☐ No
☐ Yes. The student's assistive technology needs are addressed in this IEP.

Extended School Year:
☐ No. The student is not eligible for ESY services.
☐ Yes. The student is eligible for ESY services. **Complete Form B**
☐ The need for ESY services will be addressed at a later date. Will be addressed by   /   (month/year).
Attach IEP Addendum page and Form B

Post-secondary Transition Services: (must be addressed not later than the first IEP to be in effect when the child turns 16, and updated annually thereafter.)
☐ Transition services not required.
☐ Transition services required. **Complete Form C.**

Transfer of Rights: Notification must be given beginning not later than one year before the student is 18 informing the student of the rights under IDEA that will transfer to the student upon reaching the age of majority.
☐ N/A for this student/IEP
☐ Notification was given: /   /   (month/day/year).

State Assessments
Are there state assessments administered for this student's age/grade level?
☐ No
☐ Yes. If yes, **Complete Form D**.

District-wide Assessments
Are there district-wide assessments administered for this student's age/grade level?
☐ No
☐ Yes. If yes, **Complete Form E.**

3. IEP Goal(s) with Objectives/Benchmarks and Reporting Form
Annual Measurable Goals

Annual Goal #: _____

Progress toward the goal will be measured by: **(check all that apply)**

☐ Work samples	☐ Curriculum based tests	☐ Portfolios		☐ Checklists
☐ Scoring guides	☐ Observation chart	☐ Reading record		☐ Other:

Periodic Progress Report	**Progress Toward the Goal**							
Date of Report	/ /	/ /	/ /	/ /	/ /	/ /	/ /	/ /
Making progress toward annual goal								
Not making progress toward annual goal								
Goal not addressed this reporting period								
Goal met								

Comments:

Measurable Benchmarks/Objectives: (Optional: *only required for children taking alternate assessments if benchmarks/objectives not discussed in the Present Level.*)

Annual Goal #: _____

Progress toward the goal will be measured by: **(check all that apply)**

☐ Work samples	☐ Curriculum based tests	☐ Portfolios		☐ Checklists
☐ Scoring guides	☐ Observation chart	☐ Reading record		☐ Other:

Periodic Progress Report	**Progress Toward the Goal**							
Date of Report	/ /	/ /	/ /	/ /	/ /	/ /	/ /	/ /
Making progress toward annual goal								
Not making progress toward annual goal								
Goal not addressed this reporting period								
Goal met								

Comments:

Diversity Tie-In

IS SPECIAL EDUCATION A BOYS' CLUB?

Much discussion has focused on there being more boys than girls in special education. For example, the graph included here shows that about 60 percent of students identified with mental retardation are male. Some call special education a boys' club.

Why is it that more boys are in special education? Several thoughts come to mind: boys exhibit more behavior problems than girls, boys are more aggressive than girls, and perhaps there is a natural bias toward boys. However, a look behind the figures provides another possible explanation: instead of boys being *over*represented in special education, girls may be *under*represented.

Researchers who studied this issue found that the boys who were admitted to special education were appropriately placed and needed the services. However, they con-

cluded: We believe . . . that while there is a tendency to refer to the issue of disproportionate representation of males in special education as a problem of male overrepresentation, it may well be a viable alternative explanation for the disproportionate number of males is that females who do need some academic support and special education services but who do not exhibit concomitant behavior problems are not being referred or served in special education.

Sources: M. L. Wehmeyer and M. Schwartz, "Disproportionate Representation of Males in Special Education Services: Biology, Behavior, or Bias?" *Education and Treatment of Children* 24 (2001): 28–45; A. Vaishnav and B. Dedman, "Special Ed Gender Gap Stirs Worry," *Boston Globe,* July 8, 2002.

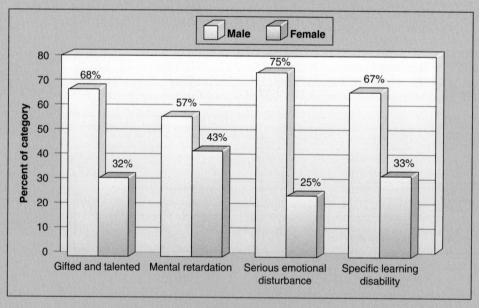

Source: Data from the U.S. Department of Education, Office for Civil Rights, "OCR Elementary and Secondary School Survey" (2002), http://205.207.175.84/ocr2002r/eng/wdsview/dispviewp.asp.

- Reflects a complete and accurate picture of the child's strengths, needs, and preferences for activities, materials, and environments
- Has a person familiar to the child conduct observations and other assessments in settings familiar to the child (e.g., home, outdoor play area, child care program)
- *Collaboratively develop expected outcomes.* After assessment information is collected, the team meets to review the information and the family's concerns, priorities, and re-

sources to develop statements of expected outcomes or goals. Active family involvement is essential. Collaborative goals focus on enhancing the family's capacity and increasing the child's participation in valued activities.

- *Assign intervention responsibilities.* After outcomes are identified, the early intervention team assigns responsibilities for services that support those outcomes. An IFSP requires an integrated, team approach to intervention. A **transdisciplinary team model** is one method of integrating information and skills across professional disciplines. In that model all team members (including the family) teach, learn, and work together to accomplish a mutually agreed upon set of intervention outcomes. Individuals' roles are defined by the needs of the situation rather than by the function of a specific discipline. With a transidisciplinary model, one or a few people are primary implementers of the program; other team members provide ongoing direct or indirect services, such as consultation. For example, an occupational therapist might observe a toddler during meals and then recommend to the parent how to physically assist the child.

- *Identify strategies to implement the plan.* This step involves working closely as a team to increase learning opportunities, using the child's surroundings to facilitate learning, selecting the most effective strategies to bring about the desired outcomes, and identifying reinforcers that best support the child's learning. Implementation may involve a toddler participating in a library story hour one afternoon a week, a physical therapist showing family members how to use adaptive equipment, or a service coordinator completing the paperwork to pay for a child's transportation from home to needed services. Effective strategies should share several characteristics:

  - Help promote generalization of outcomes—that is, the child performs new skills in a variety of environments after intervention has ended. For example, both service providers and family members can encourage a child to request desired objects with gestures in numerous environments, such as home, playgroup, and child care.

  - Target several outcomes during one activity—in one activity a child may use a variety of skills from a number of developmental areas. For example, during mealtimes a toddler may use communication skills to request more juice, fine-motor skills to grasp a spoon, and social skills to interact with a sibling.

  - Help a child become more independent—strategies might offer assistance during mealtimes, prompt a response during a self-care routine, or provide pull-on clothing to enable the child to dress without assistance.

  - Look like a typical activity in a natural environment—for instance, a child developing fine-motor skills should color, draw pictures, play with puzzles, build with blocks, pick up toys, use eating utensils, and play finger games.

  Ideally, interventions should emphasize functional competencies and should include both social and nonsocial activities.

- *Evaluate early intervention to ensure quality.* Both ongoing and periodic evaluations are essential to any early intervention program. Ongoing monitoring of a child's progress requires keeping records in a systematic manner in order to answer critical questions:

  - To what extent and at what rate is the child making progress toward desired outcomes?

  - Are the selected intervention strategies and activities promoting gains in development?

  - Do changes need to be made in the intervention plan?

Periodically reviewing the IFSP provides a means of sharing results about the child's progress and integrating these results into the plan. Part C of IDEA requires that the IFSP be evaluated and revised annually and that periodic reviews be conducted at least every six months (or sooner if requested by the family). This ongoing process provides a continual support to the family and child.

Transdisciplinary team model Professionals from various disciplines working together to integrate instructional strategies and therapy and to evaluate the effectiveness of their individual roles.

FIGURE 16.6

Services Provided Through an IFSP

When we think about intervention and support services for young children, we need to think of the full range of services that can benefit them and their families.

Source: 34 *Code of Federal Register (CFR)* § 303.12(d).

Assistive technology devices and services

Audiology

Family training, counseling, and home visits

Health services

Medical services for diagnosis or evaluation

Nursing services

Nutrition services

Occupational therapy

Physical therapy

Psychological services

Service coordination

Social work services

Special instruction

Speech-language pathology

Transportation and related costs

Vision services

Benefits of Family-Centered Services. Services that can be provided through the IFSP include, but are not limited to, those listed in Figure 16.6. Family-centered services are an important component of early childhood programming now, and they will become even more important. Programs that embrace and utilize family-centered services achieve some important benefits:

- Improving child developmental and social adjustment outcomes
- Decreasing parental stress as a result of accessing needed services for their children and themselves
- Recognizing the family's role as decision maker and partner in the early intervention process
- Helping families make the best choices for their children by providing comprehensive information about the full range of resources in their communities
- Accommodating individual child, family, and community differences through creative, flexible, and collaborative approaches to services
- Valuing children and families for their unique capacities, experiences, and potential
- Seeking meaningful and active family involvement in the planning and implementation of family-centered and community-based services
- Obtaining potential health care savings due to ongoing monitoring of health status and referral for primary health care and nutritional services[4]

Keep in mind the following ideas when striving for effective individual and family service plans:

- Appropriate methods and techniques for teaching children with disabilities are essential as a basis for writing and implementing the IEP and the IFSP.
- Working with parents is an absolute must for every classroom professional. You should learn all you can about parent conferences and communication, parent involvement, and parents as volunteers and aides (see chapter 17).
- Working with all levels of professionals offers a unique opportunity for the classroom professional to individualize instruction.

- As individual education becomes a reality for all children and families, early childhood professionals will need skills in assessing student behavior and family background and settings.
- Professionals must know how to find and use a wide range of instructional materials, including the various media technologies. You cannot hope to individualize without a full range of materials and media to accommodate students' visual, auditory, and tactile/kinesthetic learning styles.

MAINSTREAMING AND INCLUSION

Mainstreaming implies the placement of students with disabilities in general classrooms, called natural environments. *Natural environments* are the ones in which students would be placed if they did not have a disability. Today most educators agree that special needs should be met as much as possible in the general education classroom.

A variety of adaptations can be used to ensure that all students, regardless of abilities, have equal access to a quality education. **Adaptive education** is aimed at providing learning experiences that help each student achieve desired educational goals. Education is adaptive when school learning environments are modified to respond effectively to student differences and to enhance an individual's ability to succeed in such environments.

The Full Inclusion Debate. Inclusion supports the right of all students to participate in natural environments. **Full inclusion** means that students with disabilities receive the services and support appropriate to their individual needs entirely in the general classroom. **Partial inclusion** means that students receive some of their instruction in the general classroom and some in pull-out classrooms, or resources rooms, where they work individually or in small groups with special education teachers. Read the Voice from the Field about teaching in an inclusive classroom on pages 468–469 and the Program in Action "Inclusion . . . Yours, Mine, Ours" on pages 470–471 to gain greater insight into this important classroom challenge.

Full inclusion receives a lot of attention and is the subject of great national debate for several reasons:

- Court decisions and state and federal laws mandate, support, and encourage full inclusion; many of them relate to basic civil rights. For example, in the 1992 case *Oberti v. Board of Education of the Borough of Clementon School District,* the judge ruled that Rafael, an eight-year-old child with Down syndrome, should not have to earn his way into an integrated classroom but had a right to be there from the beginning.
- Some teachers feel they do not have the training or support necessary to provide for the disabilities of children in full-inclusion classrooms. These teachers believe they cannot provide for children with disabilities even with the assistance of aides and special support services.
- Some parents of children with disabilities are dissatisfied with separate programs, which they view as a form of segregation. They want their children to have the academic and social benefits of attending general education classrooms.
- Some people believe the cost of full inclusion outweighs the benefits. Nationally, the average cost of educating a regular classroom student is $4,745, compared with

Inclusive classrooms educate students with disabilities in the least restrictive educational environment. What would you say to a parent of a child without a disability who questions the idea of an inclusive classroom?

Mainstreaming The concept that a student with a disability should be integrated with nondisabled peers to the maximum extent possible and appropriate to the needs of the child.

Adaptive education Modifications in any classroom, program, environment, or curriculum that help students achieve desired educational goals.

Full inclusion An approach whereby students with disabilities receive all instruction and support services in a general classroom.

Partial inclusion An approach whereby students with disabilities receive some instruction in a general classroom and some in a specialized setting.

Voice from the Field

TEACHING IN AN INCLUSIVE CLASSROOM

Inclusive education is a catalyst for important role changes for today's regular and special education teachers. No longer should regular and special educators operate as two distinct entities but should merge into one unified system, designed to meet the unique needs of all students within the classroom. Inclusion has promoted a partnership between regular classroom teachers and special educators. Teachers are now cast in the roles of facilitators, coteachers, consultants, coaches, counselors, and itinerants. Inclusion has also helped eliminate the stigma placed on individuals with disabilities by heightening the awareness of the likenesses and differences we all possess.

TEAMWORK

Teamwork is an important component of an inclusive classroom. Working together assists in identifying areas of breakdown in student learning. The team—composed of parents, special and regular educators, and related service providers—share their expertise to provide an optimal learning experience for each child. Working with parents collaboratively makes the education of their children twice as effective.

SETTING GOALS

Inclusive classroom teachers must define the goals for their program and then assess the effectiveness of those goals, based on student outcome and teacher satisfaction. Identification of goals should be a collaborative effort of both regular and special educators. Goals of an inclusive program may include these:

- Form a partnership between the two disciplines, and define roles to blend the strengths of both professionals
- Provide appropriate instructional programs to maximize all students' learning potential
- Provide specialized, individualized instructional strategies for students experiencing difficulty within the classroom
- Modify the regular classroom curriculum to enable all students to learn in that setting
- Utilize multisensory learning centers to address the unique needs of all students
- Improve communication among the special educator, general educator, and parents

$8,310 for an exceptional education student in a special education program. This latter cost can be higher for some students and in some school districts.[5]

- Some professionals think that the money spent on separate special education facilities and programs would be better used for full-inclusion programs.

As with any worthy goal, there are both pros and cons associated with inclusive classrooms.

The Pros of Teaching in an Inclusive Classroom. These are just some of the positive aspects associated with an inclusive classroom:

- Provides a full range of educational services in the most natural and appropriate setting for children with disabilities.
- May allow children with disabilities to receive more services and a more appropriate education.
- Fosters increased self-esteem in children with disabilities as a result of higher expectation.s
- Allows all children to learn new social skills.
- Provides ongoing opportunities for socialization among regularly developing children and children with disabilities.

Companion Website To complete a Program in Action activity related to inclusion, go to the Companion Website at **www. prenhall.com/morrison**, select chapter 16, then choose the Program in Action module.

PROFESSIONAL BENEFITS

The opportunities of the inclusive classroom outweigh the challenges. An inclusive partnership breaks the pattern of teaching in isolation; it combines the general educator's knowledge of what to teach with the special educator's knowledge of how to utilize varied instructional strategies. The classroom is then equipped to accommodate the learning and behavioral needs of all students.

The special educator is given these opportunities:

1. Utilize the regular educator's content area expertise
2. Gain knowledge of the daily expectations of the regular education classroom
3. Devote more time and energy to assisting students with motivation, effort, and responsibility
4. Acquire moral support from a colleague
5. Share specialized skills to benefit all students
6. Improve student self-esteem
7. Increase ability to communicate with families

The regular education teacher is given these opportunities:

1. Develop an awareness of specialized teaching strategies (i.e., multisensory methods of instruction)
2. Increase teaching time
3. Promote greater understanding of specific disabilities and accommodations/modifications
4. Work collaboratively with a peer

5. Increase student self-esteem via classroom successes
6. Decrease the teacher-student ratio
7. Increase ability to communicate with families

The shared expertise of regular and special educators can create instructional programs that allow all children to learn in the regular classroom. An inclusive classroom allows students and teachers to be risk takers within a school culture that values different outcomes for different individuals. Working together, educators can look at individual students from different angles and concentrate on meeting learning needs in the least restrictive environment.

This collaboration creates a dynamic classroom situation that promotes increased learning and positive experiences, a win-win situation for both students and teachers. A successful inclusive classroom provides interactive tasks based on learning styles and individual needs. Active learning strategies (e.g., cooperative learning, peer tutoring, critical thinking groups) engage students and enhance the higher-order thinking skills necessary for success in the future while fostering lifelong learning. An inclusive classroom can produce enlightened and intellectually curious individuals with cooperative and appropriate social skills.

Contributed by Susan Hentz, educational consultant and Florida Council of Exceptional Children 2002 Teacher of the Year.

- Provides opportunities for all children to form meaningful friendships with a wide range of peers.
- Enables all children to learn about and value diversity and to develop moral and ethical principles.
- Provides opportunities to educate school personnel, parents, and the public about the needs of children with disabilities.

The Cons of Teaching in an Inclusive Classroom.   Here are some of the negative aspects associated with full inclusion:

- The regular classroom may need to be redesigned to accommodate children with special needs.
- The inclusive classroom may be a more distracting learning environment.
- Classroom resources and size may be inadequate to accommodate all children.
- Parents of children with disabilities may have less input into their children's education and classroom.
- Children may have difficulty adapting.
- An inclusive classroom may be stressful for more medically involved children.
- Children may receive less one-on-one attention.
- Inclusion increases responsibilities, planning time, and workload for teachers.

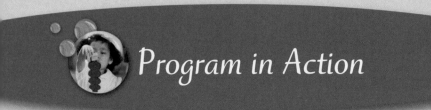
INCLUSION . . . YOURS, MINE, OURS

Alimacani Elementary School is a National Model Blue Ribbon school located in Jacksonville, Florida. The faculty, staff, and community have consistently worked together to live up to their vision: "Alimacani is a place where education is a treasure and children are inspired to reach for their dreams."

THE CASE FOR INCLUSION

The school serves preK to grade five students and originally included self-contained classes for kindergarten children with varying exceptionalities. After several years of using this traditional model and mainstreaming individually as appropriate, frustration ran high. Although the children with disabilities were occasional visitors to the kindergarten classes, they were never a part of the general classroom community. Our team of kindergarten teachers brainstormed ideas of how to better meet the needs of all our students and, after many difficult conversations, decided to include the entire population of children with special needs in regular kindergarten classes, matching children with teacher strengths.

DEVELOPING THE MODEL

We were anxious and unsure in the beginning. We would have to teach with other teachers and give up ownership of children and space. All of our roles would change. We had read about the benefits of collaboration with colleagues, but we knew that the reality of so intimate a bond would require trust, respect, a great deal of faith, and a strong sense of humor!

Despite our reservations and uncertainty, we were full of enthusiasm. Our expectations changed daily, and even our assignments changed as we enrolled and identified a record number of kindergarten children with special needs. Eighteen children with a variety of special needs were included in three different kindergarten classes during that initial year, including children with Down syndrome, autism, mild physical and mental disabilities, attention deficit (hyperactivity) disorder, Asperger's syndrome, fetal alcohol syndrome, learning disabilities, and developmental

- Regular education teachers may be resistant to ideas and practices associated with inclusive education.
- Teachers may need specialized training to teach children with disabilities.

Clearly, teaching in an inclusive classroom presents many challenges. The Voice from the Field "How to Teach in an Inclusive Classroom" on page 474 is a Competency Builder that should help you meet those challenges successfully.

The Need for a Continuum of Services. The policy of the Council for Exceptional Children (CEC), a professional organization of special educators, is as follows:

> CEC believes that a continuum of services must be available for all children, youth, and young adults. CEC also believes that the concept of inclusion is a meaningful goal to be pursued in our schools and communities. In addition, CEC believes children, youth, and young adults with disabilities should be served whenever possible in general education classrooms in inclusive neighborhood schools and community settings. Such settings should be strengthened and supported by an infusion of especially trained personnel and other appropriate supportive practices according to the individual needs of the child.[6]

A *continuum of services* implies a full and graduated range of services available for all individuals, from the most restrictive placements to the least. For students with disabilities,

delays. In partnership with parents of the children with disabilities and parents of typically developing children, we stretched, bent, and broadened our ideas. In most cases, by the end of the year, visitors to our classrooms could not identify the children with disabilities from their typically developing peers. They also could not always identify general education teachers from special educators.

SUCCESSFUL TRANSITION

To say that the first year was a success is an understatement. Without exception, we felt that we had done a better job of educating exceptional children than we had ever done in our self-contained model. We also learned that we did not have to sacrifice the many for the few. Our typically developing population of kindergartners thrived with the new responsibilities of helping their peers. As we developed alternative methods of instruction for children with special needs, we found many of those same methods reaching our typically developing children, At the end of the year, we were extremely proud of *all* of our kindergartners as they marched ahead into first grade.

This is not to say that there were no roadblocks, but we tried to turn each obstacle into an opportunity. We detoured, we had traffic jams, and occasionally we even had head-on collisions, but we used each experience as a learning and building block. For example, out of one of our moments of frustration, we developed our website http://www.rushservices.com/Inclusion as a voice for teachers and parents to exchange information. Since then we have logged on thousands of participants from all over the world who have willingly shared their insights and inspirations, their challenges, and many successes.

CONCLUSIONS

Even with our own success, we have come to believe that inclusion is not for everyone. We believe that there must continue to be an array of services to meet individual needs. And we believe that we must learn to look first at the needs of our students and then design programs and assign personnel to make learning successful.

We have chosen as our symbol the starfish. You may be familiar with the story of the person who comes upon a beach filled with starfish washed ashore. She spots a young man throwing starfish back into the ocean, one at a time, and questions him as to why he is taking the time to throw the starfish back into the sea. After all, there is no way he can save all of the starfish on the beach. The young man answers that his efforts do make a difference to each starfish he is able to save. Well, that is how we feel at Alimacani. We are walking that same beach, making a real difference, one starfish at a time.

Contributed by Dayle Timmons, Marie Rush, Kerry Rogers, and Lori Medlock of Alimacani Elementary School, Jacksonville, Florida. Photos contributed by Kerry Rogers. You can visit the inclusive classrooms of Kerry Rogers and Lori Medlock at http://www.rushservices.com/Inclusion.

---

a continuum of services would identify institutional placement as the most restrictive and a general education classroom as the least restrictive. Figure 16.7 shows this continuum of services.

There is considerable debate over whether such a continuum is an appropriate policy. Advocates of full inclusion say that the approach works against developing truly inclusive programs. Figure 16.8 on page 473 presents the policy on inclusion of the Division for Early Childhood of the Council for Exceptional Children. The Voice from the Field "Inclusion in a Preschool Setting" on pages 475–476 shows the importance of a commitment to inclusion. Given the great amount of interest in inclusion, discussion regarding both its appropriateness and the best ways to implement it will likely continue for some time.

Another type of classroom that includes children with disabilities is a **cross-categorical classroom,** which include children with different categories of disability. Read the Program in Action "Teaching in a Cross-Categorical Classroom" on page 477 for insight into this unique approach.

CONSULTATION AND COLLABORATION

As an early childhood professional, you will participate in **consultation**, seeking advice and information from colleagues. You will also engage in **collaboration**, working cooperatively

Companion Website To complete a Program in Action activity related to cross-categorical classrooms, go to the Companion Website at **www.prenhall.com/morrison**, select chapter 16, then choose the Program in Action module.

Cross-categorical classroom A classroom or other setting of students with a variety of disabilities or delays.

Consultation Seeking advice and information from colleagues.

Collaboration Working jointly and cooperatively with other professionals, parents, and administrators.

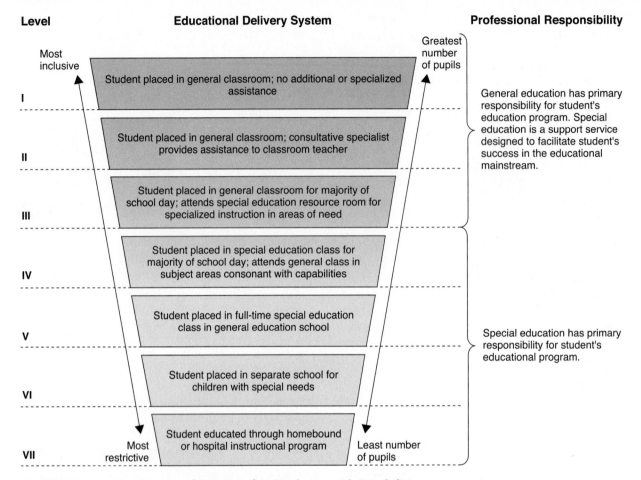

| Level | Educational Delivery System | Professional Responsibility |

FIGURE 16.7 Continuum of Services for Students with Disabilities

Service options range from the most physically integrated, with the regular classroom teacher meeting most of a child's needs, to the least integrated, a residential setting providing a therapeutic environment.

Source: From Michael L. Hardman et al., *Human Exceptionality: School, Community, and Family,* 8th ed (Boston: Allyn and Bacon, 2005). Copyright 2005 by Pearson Education. Reprinted by permission of the publisher.

with a range of special educators, other professionals, parents, and administrators to provide services to students with disabilities and students at risk. Some of those professionals include the following:

- Diagnosticians, who are trained to test and analyze students' strengths and weaknesses
- Special educators, who are trained to instruct students with special needs
- **Itinerant teachers,** who travel from school to school, providing assistance and teaching students
- **Resource teachers,** who provide assistance with materials and planning
- Physical therapists, who treat physical disabilities through nonmedical means
- Occupational therapists, who direct activities that develop muscular control and self-help skills
- Speech and language pathologists

Consultation with experienced teachers, experts in the field of special education, and administrators will enable you to see your options more clearly, gain important knowledge and insight, and consider teaching and learning strategies you might not have thought of on your own. With collaboration you will be able to implement those strategies and new approaches with the help and support of others.

Itinerant teachers
Professionals who travel from school to school, providing assistance and teaching students.

Resource teachers
Professionals who provide assistance with materials and planning for teachers of exceptional students.

FIGURE 16.8 The Division for Early Childhood's Position Statement on Inclusion

Inclusion, as a value, supports the right of all children, regardless of abilities, to participate actively in natural settings within their communities. Natural settings are those in which the child would spend time had he or she not had a disability. These settings include, but are not limited to, home, preschool, nursery schools, Head Start programs, kindergartens, neighborhood school classrooms, child care, places of worship, and recreational (such as community playgrounds and community events) and other settings that all children and families enjoy.

DEC supports and advocates that young children and their families have full and successful access to health, social, educational, and other support services that promote full participation in family and community life. DEC values the cultural, economic, and educational diversity of families and supports a family-guided process for identifying a program of service.

As young children participate in group settings (such as preschool, play groups, child care, kindergarten), their active participation should be guided by developmentally and individually appropriate curriculum. Access to and participation in the age-appropriate general curriculum becomes central to the identification and provision of specialized support services.

To implement inclusive practices DEC supports

(a) The continued development, implementation, evaluation, and dissemination of full inclusion supports, services, and systems that are of high quality for all children

(b) The development of preservice and inservice training programs that prepare families, service providers, and administrators to develop and work within inclusive settings

(c) Collaboration among key stakeholders to implement flexible fiscal and administrative procedures in support of inclusion

(d) Research that contributes to our knowledge of recommended practice

(e) The restructuring and unification of social, educational, health, and intervention supports and services to make them more responsive to the needs of all children and families

Ultimately, the implementation of inclusive practice must lead to optimal developmental benefit for each individual child and family.

Source: Reprinted by permission from the Division for Early Childhood of the Council for Exceptional Children, "Position Statement on Inclusion" (adopted 1993, reaffirmed 1996, revised 2000) http://www.dec-sped.org/pdf/positionpapers/position%.2.Inclusion.pdf.

With Colleagues.   Discussing with colleagues, especially exceptional education educators, students' needs and the best ways to meet those needs is an essential component of successful teaching and learning in an inclusive classroom. As a classroom teacher, you will be expected to provide information and ideas about content knowledge, curriculum objectives, curriculum sequence, and content evaluation. Exceptional education educators can be expected to contribute information about disabilities, learning and motivation strategies that work with students with disabilities, and ideas about how to adapt curriculum to meet students' special needs.

Itinerant Special Educators.   Many school districts use the services of a special education itinerant teacher, who can be a valuable resource to you, your students, and their parents. This traveling teacher provides information, assists you in making helpful modifications to the classroom environment, coaches you in some new instructional techniques, and in some cases works directly with the child(ren) for part of each week.

In the Reggio Emilia segment of the DVD, the narrator says that emergent curriculum does not unfold haphazardly. Observe how the teachers help each other. How can this collaboration benefit children with disabilities as well as typically developing children?

Voice from the Field

HOW TO TEACH IN AN INCLUSIVE CLASSROOM

Effective teaching in inclusive classrooms requires many competencies. Listed here are important guidelines to help you understand what you will need to know and do to become a competent and compassionate teacher in an inclusive classroom:

GUIDELINE 1 Understand students and their needs

- Learn the characteristics of students with special needs
- Learn about legislation affecting students with special needs
- Become comfortable with students with special needs
- Learn about and use assistive and educational technologies

GUIDELINE 2 Develop skill in instructional techniques

- Modify instruction for students with special needs
- Use a variety of instructional styles and media and increase the range of learning behaviors

- Individualize instruction and integrate the curriculum
- Provide instruction for students of all ability levels
- Modify assessment techniques for students with special needs

GUIDELINE 3 Manage the classroom environment

- Physically adapt the learning environment to accommodate students with special needs
- Foster social acceptance of students with special needs
- Provide inclusion in varied student groupings
- Use peer tutoring
- Guide and manage the behavior of all students
- Motivate all students

GUIDELINE 4 Collaborate with other professionals and parents

- Work closely with special educators and other specialists
- Work with and involve parents
- Participate in planning and implementing IEPs

In the Reggio Emilia segment of the DVD, listen to what the narrator says about Jerome Bruner's concept of "negotiated meaning" and how children work in a stress-free, nonregimented environment.

Embedded instruction
Instruction that is included as an integral part of normal classroom routines.

The itinerant teacher can give you and the parents information about a child's disability, explain any jargon or medical terms that may be present in evaluation reports, and refer the parents to helpful resources, such as pertinent websites or parent support groups. In addition, the itinerant teacher may talk with you about how the physical environment is working for a child with a disability. Is the room fully accessible, is the equipment appropriate, and does the child seem to find all areas of the room inviting? The itinerant teacher may also loan equipment to you and help you provide more visual support for the child, such as a picture-schedule or markings on the floor to indicate where children sit and line up.

The itinerant teacher will probably study the social environment in your classroom, too. He or she may ask if there is enough adult attention available to the child and, if not, how scheduling might be modified to help. In many instances, the itinerant teacher can help with classroom routines for at least part of each week. Often, the itinerant teacher can also offer friendship activities or cooperative projects to help the child with a disability interact with the other children in positive ways.

School districts are required to provide specialized instruction to students with disabilities, but the itinerant teacher will look for opportunities for **embedded instruction**

INCLUSION IN A PRESCHOOL SETTING

THE VISION

Inclusion in the mainstream of life is always the desired path. Once the commitment to inclusion is born, any obstacles must be viewed only as opportunities to develop strategies that support the ideal, an inclusive classroom. Anything less deprives children of a potent learning experience, of learning naturally from their peers.

However, in developing best practices for challenged children, typical children must never be utilized only as facilitators for their special needs friends. Typical children must also have best practices in place to support their highest need and achievement. Each child must be served to his or her highest purpose, and the inclusive classroom should never aspire to less.

THE BEGINNING

At the Palma Ceia Presbyterian Preschool, in Tampa, Florida, we are entering our twenty-fifth year of service to the community as a fully inclusive early childhood education program. As the

founder, I can attest to the changes in the community ethos that at first rejected this model but now embraces it by placing so many children on the waiting list that three-quarters of those waiting are never able to be enrolled.

Our small community program began in an opposite way to that of most inclusive programs. It was initiated to accommodate three children with special needs who were not being served. As our first school year unfolded, a four-year-old typically developing sibling expressed a desire to come, too, and out of that most simple and natural request, inclusion was born at Palma Ceia.

THE CHALLENGE

Because the first staff members had expertise in special education, we had to improve our knowledge base in early childhood education in order to teach our new "playmate." Remember—begin with the end in mind, and then figure out the strategies. Our goal was inclusion, so we had to figure out our strategies to meet our newest stu-

dent's needs. We investigated curricular materials at her level and had to learn to individualize so that all four of our students were being challenged and our typical student was not just playing a miniteacher role. After all, our newest student would be starting kindergarten the next year, and her readiness was very important in her life.

The presence of typical children led to staff training, which led to a better understanding of typical early childhood development. In turn, this knowledge influenced us to see how teaching and learning could be accomplished in a more natural way with our special needs children.

We learned that special needs children could be incidental learners, too: they learned from each other, not only from teachers. And they did not always need extrinsic reinforcement to succeed. The presence of typical children, kept our understanding of the developmental norms sharper, improved our assessment skills, and helped us to emphasize the developmental milestones for our special needs population.

THE RIGHT ATTITUDE

In the development and current success of our school, attitude has played a role of great magnitude. As our school grew, we could have decided not to serve particular children, but we always said, "We'll try." Each diagnosis led us to new confidence as we researched and remained open to new learning. We found the answers because we looked for them. Again, to succeed with children, you must begin with the goal and then research and design specific strategies to support that child. Often, you will find a possible path to success, and you will find you can do more than you think.

COLLABORATION

We began to receive more referrals of children with diagnoses of autism (pervasive developmental delay) and problem behaviors. Although we tried standard guidance strategies, which had worked for us in the past, we found these children to be very challenging in our community program. We were reluctant, however, to admit that we could not serve their needs.

We were extremely fortunate to have in our community a nationally known researcher and author in the Department of Child and Family Studies at the University of

South Florida. With Dr. Lise Fox we developed a true collaboration, in which the university helped to build our capacity to serve children with problem behaviors and our preschool provided the university researchers with a community perspective, a site for data collection, and a community home for university students. We called our collaboration First Steps Together.

The collaboration did indeed build our capacity, and now our school is much more able to implement Positive Behavior Support (PBS) plans for children experiencing problem behaviors. Based on person-centered values and effective procedures, PBS reduces problem behaviors by enriching the environment, developing adaptive alternatives, and enhancing a person's competence and lifestyle. The children have responded well, and the staff takes pride in our greater professionalism.

The collaboration has yielded far more than staff training, however. University and preschool staffs have presented together at local, state, and national conferences, coauthored papers for publication, and hosted two students at the school in their work toward master's theses.

THE TEACHER'S PERSPECTIVE

No perspective can be ignored. Through our desire to serve the children, we grew in awareness of the perspective of teachers. Our accreditation by the NAEYC and national research led us to understand that a significant part of nurturing children is nurturing their teachers. Inclusion can be difficult, and we did not find success in browbeating teachers into teaching special needs children without the support necessary to succeed.

Instead, we found success in respecting teachers and their perspectives, helping them understand their strengths, and assigning children based on team perspective. In special education, few teachers have had experience or training in all the challenging conditions that may present themselves. So accommodating teachers' understanding of their own strengths leads to a culture of trust, a culture of choice making for teachers as well as for children, and a strengthening of skills needed to support children over time.

KEYS TO SUCCESSFUL INCLUSION

So what makes inclusion work?

- Use best practices for all children
- Keep low staff-to-child ratios, at or below those recommended by the NAEYC
- Use assessment and observation to identify each child's developmental level
- Hire a mix of special educators and early childhood educators
- Use speech therapists and occupational therapists
- Use phrases that help develop understanding (e.g., "He or she needs. . . . ")
- Handle challenges in a matter-of-fact way
- Find materials, posters, toys, and props to support inclusion goals (e.g., let children play with dolls using wheelchairs, walkers, and other supports)
- Use sign language in the context of music and movement and have access to Braille at the writing center

In our hearts, we know what is right to do: Decide to include all children, and then figure out how. You will be able to do more than you think, and you can find the help you need to succeed. If you say yes, I can promise you a wonderful and eventful journey, one that is richer and deeper than any easy ride. Inclusion is possible, it is desirable, and it should be embraced.

Contributed by Nancy King Little, director and founder, Palma Ceia Presbyterian Church Preschool, Tampa, Florida, and *Parent and Child* Early Childhood Professional Award winner. Photo also contributed by Nancy King Little.

Naturalistic methods
Incorporating instruction into opportunities that occur naturally or routinely in the classroom.

that can use **naturalistic methods.** In these cases, the instruction will blend right into normal classroom routines. For example, if the child has a social objective to greet classmates using their names, a natural opportunity might prompt this behavior with a greeting-song during arrival time or opening-circle time and again when classmates enter an area where the child is working during free-choice time.

The itinerant teacher can be a careful observer to help you discover ways to engage a child more effectively during group instruction. In some cases the itinerant teacher might get directly involved, providing direct instruction in a small-group format with a few typically developing classmates. If this can be done at the same time that the rest of the class is working in small groups, it can blend in as a natural part of the classroom routine.

In a collaborative teaching experience with an itinerant special education teacher, you can learn a lot and share together the joy of watching young children with special needs succeed in their very own neighborhood schools.[7]

TEACHING IN A CROSS-CATEGORICAL CLASSROOM

The Early Childhood Special Education Program, Mascoutah District #19, is housed at Scott Elementary School on the Scott Air Force Base in Illinois. It is a *cross-categorical* program, which means that it serves different types of disabilities, including, but not limited to, cerebral palsy, autism, Down syndrome, and delays in cognitive, language, motor, and social skills. The teachers provide each student with an individualized education program (IEP), which shows individualized goals and objectives and the services provided. In addition to a certified early childhood teacher and an instructional aide, each classroom may benefit from individual care aides, social workers, speech and language pathologists, and occupational, physical, and music therapists.

FOUR ESSENTIALS

In order to meet the individual needs of its students, this special education program has integrated its educational philosophy in four specific areas.

Classroom Environment

Consistency is the most important aspect of classroom environment. Day to day, the classroom must be user friendly, comfortable, and able to meet as many needs as possible; and the schedule should be predictable to accommodate students who are upset by changes in their environment. Many teachers also provide an open classroom that welcomes parents.

Student/Staff Interaction

Interaction stems from the teacher's ability to fill many roles: teacher, social worker, nurse, police officer, and sometimes friend. Teachers do not look at their students as people with disabilities, but as individuals who require different approaches, attitudes, stimuli, and schedules. The teachers can never become complacent—their attitude is one of looking forward, not resting on a recent success. The teachers lead by example,

and by the end of the year, students have learned how the teachers treat them, and often they treat each other in the same way.

Behavior Management

Behavior management is aimed at helping children learn to guide and direct their own behavior. Teachers begin with four or five classroom rules, such as Keep your hands and feet to yourself. All rules are based on safety and respect. In the beginning, teacher direction is easier for the children to understand and gives them an immediate solution to behavioral problems. For instance, "Stop" is more effective than "No."

Student Needs

Students with special needs are treated as typically developing students for whom teachers provide adaptive materials when necessary. Engaging students as often as possible is the primary goal. For example, if a student is autistic and appears unresponsive, teachers persist. Although a child cannot be forced to make eye contact, a teacher can do many things to get into the student's line of vision. What varies with each teacher and each student is the how and when: teachers must gauge how far to go with each child, how to expand an activity, and when to move on or stop. These teaching skills and techniques are highly individualized and take time to master. Some teachers invite older students to assist in addressing social skills; others incorporate music to determine which sensory modes are most useful.

Above all, teachers who work in a cross-categorical classroom are flexible. They are required to work on deficit areas of development but end up addressing whatever needs attention that particular day—toileting, feeding, writing, or just interacting.

Contributed by Scott Simon, preschool teacher, Scott Elementary School, Scott Air Force Base, Illinois, and *Parent and Child* Early Childhood Professional Award winner.

With Parents.   The development of an IEP requires that you work closely with parents in developing learning and evaluation goals for students with disabilities. Also, some parents may want to spend time in your classroom to help you meet the needs of their children. All parents have information about their children's needs, growth, and development that will be helpful to you as you plan and teach.

With Paraprofessionals.   You may have one or more full- or part-time aides in your classroom, depending on the number of students with disabilities and the nature of their disabilities. Classroom assistants can help you in providing multimodal instruction and assessing students' skills.

With Administrators.   Administrators can help you with the legal, political, and procedural matters of teaching students with special needs in your classroom. Administrators can also help by providing more planning time and opportunities for special education and general education teachers to plan together and by employing a "floating" substitute to aid teachers and increase release time for teacher planning. In addition, in supporting coteaching partnerships, administrators can give you access to a network of other services, information, and resources.

ATTENTION DEFICIT HYPERACTIVITY DISORDER

Attention deficit hyperactivity disorder (ADHD) Difficulty with attention and self-control, which leads to problems with learning, social functioning, and behavior that occur in more than one situation and have been present for a significant length of time.

Students with **attention deficit hyperactivity disorder (ADHD)** generally display cognitive delays and have difficulties in three specific areas: attention, impulse control, and hyperactivity. To be classified as having ADHD, a student must display for a minimum of six months at least six of the characteristics listed in Figure 16.9 to a degree that is maladaptive and inconsistent with developmental level.

ADHD is diagnosed more often in boys than in girls and occurs in about 20 percent of all students. About half of the cases are diagnosed before age four. Frequently, the term *attention deficit disorder* (ADD) is used to refer to ADHD, but ADD is a form of learning disorder, whereas ADHD is a behavioral disorder. There are three components of successful programs for children with ADHD: academic instruction, behavioral intervention, and classroom accommodation.

Academic Instruction.   You can apply these principles of effective teaching when you introduce, conduct, and conclude each lesson during the school day.[8]

Introducing Lessons
- *Provide an advance organizer.* Prepare students for the day's lesson by quickly summarizing the order of various activities planned. Explain, for example, that a review of the previous lesson will be followed by new information and that both group and independent work will be expected.
- *Review previous lessons.* Review information from previous lessons on this topic. For example, remind children that yesterday's lesson focused on learning how to regroup in subtraction. Then review several problems before describing the current lesson.
- *Set learning expectations.* State what students are expected to learn during the lesson. For example, explain to students that a language arts lesson will involve reading a story about Paul Bunyan and identifying new vocabulary words in the story.
- *Set behavioral expectations.* Describe how students are expected to behave during the lesson. For example, tell children that they may talk quietly to their neighbors as they do their seatwork or they may raise their hands to get your attention.
- *State needed materials.* Identify all materials that the children will need during the lesson, rather than leaving them to figure that out on their own. For example, specify that children need their journals and pencils for journal writing or their crayons, scissors, and colored paper for an art project.

FIGURE 16.9   Characteristics of ADHD

Inattention

- Often fails to give close attention to details or makes careless mistakes in schoolwork, work, or other activities
- Often has difficulty sustaining attention in tasks or play activities
- Often does not seem to listen when spoken to directly
- Often does not follow through on instructions and fails to finish school work, chores, or duties in the workplace (but not as a result of oppositional behavior or failure to understand instructions)
- Often has difficulty organizing tasks and activities
- Often avoids, dislikes, or is reluctant to engage in tasks that require sustained mental effort (such as schoolwork or homework)
- Often loses things necessary for tasks or activities (e.g., toys, school assignments, pencils, books, or tools)
- Is often easily distracted by extraneous stimuli

Hyperactivity

- Often fidgets with hands or feet or squirms in seat
- Often leaves seat in classroom or in other situations in which remaining seated is expected
- Often runs about or climbs excessively in situations in which it is inappropriate (in adolescents or adults, may be limited to subjective feelings of restlessness)
- Often has difficulty playing or engaging in leisure activities quietly
- Is often on the go or acts as if driven by a motor
- Often talks excessively

Impulsivity

- Often blurts out answers before questions have been completed
- Often has difficulty awaiting turn
- Often interrupts or intrudes on others (e.g., butts into conversations or games)

Source: Reprinted with permission from the *Diagnostic and Statistical Manual of Mental Disorders, Fourth Edition, Text Revision* (Copyright 2000). American Psychiatric Association.

- *Explain additional resources.* Tell students how to obtain help in mastering the lesson. For example, refer children to a particular page in the textbook for guidance on completing a worksheet.

Conducting Lessons

- *Support the student's participation in the classroom.* Provide ADHD students with private, discreet cues to stay on task and an advance warning that they will be called on shortly. Avoid bringing attention to differences between ADHD students and their classmates. At all times avoid the use of sarcasm and criticism.
- *Use audiovisual materials.* Use a variety of audiovisual materials to present academic lessons. For example, use an overhead projector to demonstrate how to solve an addition problem requiring regrouping. The students can work on the problem at their desks while you manipulate counters on the projector screen.
- *Check student performance.* Question individual students to assess their mastery of the lesson. For example, you can ask students doing seatwork (i.e., lessons completed by students at their desks) to demonstrate how they arrived at the answer to a problem, or you can ask individual students to state in their own words how the main character felt at the end of the story.

- *Perform ongoing student evaluation.* Identify students who need additional assistance. Watch for signs of a lack of comprehension, such as daydreaming or visual or verbal indications of frustration. Provide these children with extra explanations, or ask another student to serve as a peer tutor for the lesson.
- *Help students correct their own mistakes.* Describe how students can identify and correct their own mistakes. For example, remind students that they should check their calculations in math problems, and reiterate how they can check their calculations. Also remind them of particularly difficult spelling rules and ways to watch out for easy-to-make errors.
- *Help students focus.* Remind students to keep working and to focus on their assigned task. For example, you can provide follow-up directions or assign learning partners. These practices can be directed at individual children or at the entire class.
- *Use follow-up directions.* Effective teachers of children with ADHD guide them with follow-up directions:
  - *Oral directions* —After giving directions to the class as a whole, provide additional oral directions for a child with ADHD. For example, ask whether the child understood the directions, and then repeat the directions together.
  - *Written directions* —Provide follow-up directions in writing. For example, write the page number for an assignment on the chalkboard, and remind the child to look at the board if he or she forgets the assignment.
- *Use cooperative learning strategies.* Have students work together in small groups to maximize their own and each other's learning. Use strategies such as think-pair-share, in which teachers ask students to think about a topic, pair with a partner to discuss it, and share ideas with the group.
- *Individualize instructional practices:*
  - *Partnered reading activities* —Pair the child with ADHD with another student who is a strong reader. Have the partners take turns reading orally and listening to each other.
  - *Storytelling* —Schedule storytelling sessions in which children can retell a story that they have read recently.
  - *Word bank* —Keep a word bank or dictionary of new or hard-to-read sight-vocabulary words.
  - *Computer games for reading comprehension* —Schedule computer time for children to have drill-and-practice with sight-vocabulary words.
  - *Backup materials for home use* —Make available to students a second set of books and materials that they can use at home.
- *Use organizational and study-skill strategies:*
  - *Assignment notebooks* —Provide the child with ADHD with an assignment notebook to help organize homework and seatwork.
  - *Color-coded folders* —Provide the child with color-coded folders to help organize assignments for different academic subjects (e.g., reading, mathematics, social science, and science).
  - *Homework partner* —Assign the child a partner to help record homework and seatwork in the assignment notebook and to help file work sheets and other papers in the proper folders.
- *Assist students with time management:*
  - *Use a clock or wristwatch* —Teach the child with ADHD how to read and use a clock or wristwatch to manage time when completing assigned work.
  - *Use a calendar*—Teach the child how to read and use a calendar to schedule assignments.
  - *Practice sequencing activities*—Provide the child with supervised opportunities to break down a long assignment into a sequence of short, interrelated activities.
  - *Create a daily activity schedule*—Tape a schedule of planned daily activities to the child's desk.

Behavioral Intervention. The purpose of behavioral intervention in the school setting is to assist ADHD students in displaying the behaviors that are most conducive to their own learning and that of classmates. Well-managed classrooms prevent many disciplinary problems and provide an environment that is most favorable for learning. Consequently, behavioral intervention should be viewed as an opportunity for teaching in the most effective and efficient manner, rather than as an opportunity for punishment.[9]

- *Define the appropriate behavior while giving praise.* Praise should be specific for the positive behavior displayed by the student; that is, the comments should focus on what the student did right and should include exactly what part(s) of the student's behavior were desirable. Rather than praising a student for not disturbing the class, for example, a teacher should praise the student for quietly completing a math lesson on time.
- *Give praise immediately.* The sooner approval is given regarding appropriate behavior, the more likely the student is to repeat it.
- *Vary the statements given as praise.* The comments used by teachers to praise appropriate behavior should vary; when students hear the same praise statement repeated over and over, it may lose its value.
- *Be consistent and sincere with praise.* Appropriate behavior should receive consistent praise. Consistency among teachers is important to avoid confusion on the part of students with ADHD. Similarly, students will notice insincere praise, which will make praise less effective.

Classroom Accommodation. Children with ADHD often have difficulty adjusting to the structured environment of a classroom, determining what is important, and focusing on their assigned work. Because they are easily distracted by other children or by nearby activities in the classroom, many children with ADHD benefit from accommodations that reduce distractions in the classroom environment and help them stay on task.[10]

- *Seat the child near the teacher.* Assign the child with ADHD a seat near your desk or the front of the room. This seating assignment allows you to monitor and reinforce the child's on-task behavior.
- *Seat the child near a student role model.* This arrangement enables children to work cooperatively and to learn from their peers.
- *Provide low-distraction work areas.* As space permits, teachers should make available a quiet, distraction-free room or area for quiet study time and test taking. Students should be directed to this room or area privately and discreetly in order to avoid the appearance of punishment.

The Medication Controversy. The use of drugs to control children's behavior, rather than teaching them to control their own behavior, is a growing concern for many early childhood professionals. Growing numbers of teachers and other education professionals object to medication being prescribed for this purpose. See Table 16.2 for a list of commonly prescribed medications, along with their intended and unintended effects.

STRATEGIES FOR TEACHING CHILDREN WITH DISABILITIES

Sound teaching strategies work well for all students, including those with disabilities, but you must plan how to create inclusive teaching environments. The following ideas will help you teach children with disabilities and create inclusive settings that enhance the education of all students:

- *Accentuate the positive.* One of the most effective strategies is to emphasize what children can do rather than what they cannot do. Children with disabilities have talents and abilities similar to those of other children.

TABLE 16.2 ADHD Medications

All of these medications share the same potential benefits for children: reduced impatience and impulsiveness, better control of emotions, improved relationships with family and friends, less difficulty completing schoolwork, and increased self-esteem.

Drug	Intended Effects	Side Effects
Ritalin • Short-acting form: begins working in about 30 minutes, peaks at 2 hours, is gone at 4 hours • Long-acting form: lasts about 8 hours • Safety and effectiveness not established in children under 6 years of age	• Affects children as related stimulants (like cocaine) affect adults • Sharpens short-term attention span	• Headaches, abdominal pain, nervousness, insomnia, dizziness, cardiac arrhythmia, and weight loss • Produces "valleys" when it wears off • Long-term use linked to abnormalities in brain development (like those found with cocaine)
Adderall • Approved for unrestricted use for ADHD in 1996 • A cocktail drug that combines four drugs from the amphetamine family • Lasts about 6 hours per dose • May take more than a few doses to achieve full effect	• Can be less harsh than Ritalin • May produce fewer peaks and valleys	• Restlessness, dizziness, insomnia, headache, dryness of the mouth, and weight loss • High potential for abuse and addiction, especially among people who do not have ADHD
Concerta • A reformulation of Ritalin • Approved in 2000 • Lasts 12 hours • Cannot adjust dosage	• Provides more even action than Ritalin	• Headache, upper respiratory tract infection, stomachache, vomiting, loss of appetite, sleeplessness, increased cough, sore throat, sinusitis, and dizziness • Reduced stature, tics, moodiness, and psychosis • Not recommended for children under the age of 6

Sources: Attention Deficit Disorder Help Center, "ADHD Medication Information," http://www.add-adha-help-center.com/adhd_medication_information.htm; Robert Brayden, "Ritalin: Pros and Cons," http://www.med.umich.edu/1libr/pa/pa_ritalin_hhg.htm.

In the Primary Grade segment of the DVD, the narrator says that cooperative learning helps children of mixed abilities. How does such a learning environment support and accommodate children's special learning needs?

- *Use appropriate assessment.* Include work samples, cumulative records, and appropriate assessment instruments. Parents and other professionals who have worked with individual children are sources of valuable information and can contribute to accurate and appropriate plans for them.
- *Use concrete examples and materials.*
- *Develop and use multisensory approaches to learning.*
- *Model what children are to do.* Rather than just telling them what to do, have a child who has mastered a certain task or behavior model it for others. Also, ask each child to perform a designated skill or task with supervision. Give corrective feedback.
- *Let children practice or perform a certain behavior.* Then involve them in their own assessment of that behavior.
- *Make the learning environment a pleasant, rewarding place to be.*
- *Create a dependable classroom schedule.* Young children develop a sense of security when daily plans follow a consistent pattern. Allowing for flexibility is also important, however.
- *Encourage parents to volunteer at school and to read to their children at home.*
- *Identify appropriate tasks children can accomplish on their own.* Create opportunities for them to become more independent of you and others.

- *Use cooperative learning.* Cooperative learning enables all students to work together to achieve common goals. Cooperative learning has five components:
  - *Positive interdependence.* Group members establish mutual goals, divide the prerequisite tasks, share materials and resources, assume shared roles, and provide feedback to each other.
  - *Face-to-face interaction.* Group members encourage and facilitate each other's efforts to complete tasks through direct communication.
  - *Individual accountability/personal responsibility.* Individual performance is assessed, and results are reported back to both the individual and the group, which holds members accountable for completing their fair share of responsibility.
  - *Interpersonal and small-group skills.* Students are responsible for getting to know and trust each other, communicating accurately and clearly, accepting and supporting each other, and resolving conflicts in a constructive manner.
  - *Group processing.* Group reflection includes describing which contributions of members are helpful or unhelpful in making decisions and which group actions should be continued or changed.
- *Use circle of friends.* With this technique classmates volunteer to be part of a student's circle, which meets as a team on a regular basis. The teacher coordinates the circle and helps the group solve problems or concerns that arise. Students in the circle provide friendship and support so that no student is isolated or alone in the class.[11]
- *Use Classwide Peer Tutoring* (CWPT) *program.* CWPT involves whole classrooms of students in tutoring activities that improve achievement and student engagement, particularly for at-risk, low-income students. Having opportunities to teach peers seems to reinforce students' own learning and motivation, according to Charles R. Greenwood, the program developer.[12]
- *Develop a peer buddy system.* In a peer buddy system, classmates serve as peer buddies (i.e., friends, guides, or counselors) to students who are experiencing problems. Variations are to pair an older student with a younger one who is experiencing a problem or to pair two students who are experiencing similar problems.[13]
- *Use learning centers.* Multisensory learning centers can assist in meeting the diverse needs in an inclusive classroom; they can address various instructional levels with emphasis on visual, auditory, and kinesthetic pathways to learning. See the suggestions of Susan Hentz in Figure 16.10.

In the High/Scope segment of the DVD, observe how the plan-do-review approach accommodates the learning needs of children with disabilities.

Because they have a great deal of knowledge about their children, parents should be involved in helping plan objectives and curricula for their children who are gifted and talented. What are some issues teachers and parents might plan for children?

GIFTED AND TALENTED CHILDREN

In contrast to children with disabilities, children identified as gifted and talented are not covered under IDEA provisions, and Congress has passed other legislation to provide for these children specifically. The Jacob K. Javits Gifted and Talented Students Education Act of 1988 defines *gifted and talented children* as those who "give evidence of high performance capabilities in areas such as intellectual, creative, artistic, or leadership capacity or in specific academic fields, and who require services or activities not ordinarily provided by the school in order to fully develop such capabilities.[14] The definition distinguishes between *giftedness,* which is characterized by above-average intellectual ability, and *talented,* which refers to

FIGURE 16.10 Learning Centers in Inclusive Classrooms

Learning center rules should be set up before your first rotation and should be consistent.

- Be sure to model appropriate center behaviors, role-play, and practice.
- Post procedures/visual aids at each center to be used as a reference.

Basic centers can be used all year, with activities within the centers continually changing based on the needs of the students.

Author's Nook/Writing Center

This center should have a large, comfortable space for writing. Available materials include colored pencils, crayons, markers, white boards, paper, greeting cards.

Alphabet chart

Examples of good writing

Magnetic letters

Shower curtain—for word wall or a large floor storyboard

Publishing materials

Mailbox: student letters

Alphabet stamps

Wikki Stix

Picture stamps/stickers for rebus stories

Story starters—pictures

Listening/Sound Stage/ Auditory Center

This center can be a desktop or a corner in the classroom. Headphones would be useful. Tapes or CDs can be commercial or teacher/parent-made.

Books on tape

Tape recorder

Spelling review tests

Directions for reading stories, etc.

Songs, poems, riddles

Language master

Tapes of parent readers

Student-made tapes/CDs

Math/Manipulative Center

A good place for this center is near the calendar board. The center can provide opportunities for daily graphing.

Linking cubes

Scales

Stacking items

Pattern blocks

Plastic counters

Math Geo Safari

Fraction models

Play money

Library/Reading Center

This center should have comfortable seating in a secluded atmosphere. Encourage silent reading, buddy reading, and oral reading. Books can be sorted by units of study, student-made books, holidays, featured authors, journals, magazines, etc.

Puppets

Flannel-board stories

Magnetic storyboards

Pocket charts: rebus, words

Books: shelves, tubs, boxes, baskets

Flashcards: letters, words

Poetry box

Technology/Computer Center

Be sure to keep computers away from windows to keep the glare of sunlight off the screens. Computers should have a variety of multilevel software and living books.

Learning games

Telecommunications

Cross-curricular software

Source: Contributed by Susan Hentz, educational consultant and Florida Council of Exceptional Children 2002 Teacher of the Year.

individuals who excel in such areas as drama, art, music, athletics, and leadership. Students can have these abilities separately or in combination; for example, a talented five-year-old may be learning disabled, and a student with orthopedic disabilities may be gifted.

Figure 16.11 outlines the characteristics displayed in each of the areas of giftedness; you can use these to help identify gifted children in your program. Although children may not display all of the identified markers, the presence of several of them can alert parents and professionals to make appropriate instructional, environmental, and social adjust-

Visual/Performing Arts

outstanding in sense of spatial relationships
unusual ability for expressing self feelings, moods, etc. through dance, music, drama
good motor coordination
exhibits creative expression
desire for producing "own product" (not content with mere copying)
observant

Leadership

assumes responsibility
high expectation for self
and others
fluent, concise self-
expression
foresees consequences
and implications of
decisions
good judgment in
decision making
likes structure
well liked by peers
self-confident
organized

Creative Thinking

independent thinker
exhibits original thinking in oral and written expression
comes up with several solutions to a given problem
possesses a sense of humor
creates and invents
challenged by creative tasks
improvises often
does not mind being different from the crowd

**General Intellectual
Abilities**

formulates abstractions
processes information in
complex ways
observant
excited about new ideas
enjoys hypothesizing
learns rapidly
uses a large vocabulary
inquisitive
self-starter

Specific Academic Ability

good memorization ability
advanced comprehension
acquires basic-skills knowledge quickly
widely read in special-interest area
high academic success in special-interest area
pursues special interests with enthusiasm and vigor

FIGURE 16.11   Characteristics of Various Areas of Giftedness

Source: Reprinted by permission from the National Association for Gifted Children (NAGC), Washington, DC. This chart may not be further reproduced without the permission of NAGC.

ments. Professionals tend to suggest special programs and sometimes special schools for the gifted and talented, which would seem to be a move away from providing for these children in regular classrooms. Regular classroom professionals can provide for gifted children through enrichment and acceleration. *Enrichment* allows children to pursue topics in greater depth and in different ways than the curriculum specifies. *Acceleration* permits children to progress academically at a quicker pace.

In regular classrooms early childhood professionals can also use parents and resource people to tutor and work in special ways with these children and can provide opportunities for the children to assume leadership responsibilities. For example, gifted and talented children may be interested in tutoring other students who need extra practice or help. Tutoring can cut across grade and age levels. Students can also help explain directions and procedures to the class. In addition, professionals can encourage them to use their talents and abilities outside the classroom by becoming involved with other people and agencies.

Professionals can foster creativity through classroom activities that require divergent thinking (e.g., "Let's think of all the different uses for a paper clip"). They must challenge these children to think, using higher-order questions that encourage the children to explain, apply, analyze, rearrange, and judge. Many schools have resource rooms for gifted and talented students, where children can spend a half day or more every week working with a professional who is interested and trained in working with them. Resource room pullout is the most popular of these methods.

ABUSED AND NEGLECTED CHILDREN

Many of our views of childhood are highly romanticized. We tend to believe that parents always love their children and enjoy caring for them. We also envision family settings full of joy, happiness, and harmony. Unfortunately for children, their parents, and society, these

assumptions are not always true. In fact, the extent of child abuse is far greater than we might imagine. In 2003 an estimated one million children were victims of child abuse and neglect; 2.9 million were reported to protective service agencies throughout the U.S.[15]

Child abuse is not new; abuse—in the form of abandonment, infanticide, and neglect—has been documented throughout history. The attitude that children are property partly accounts for this record. Parents have believed, and some still do, that they own their children and can do with them as they please.

The extent to which children are abused is difficult to ascertain but is probably much greater than most people realize. Valid statistics are difficult to come by because definitions of child abuse and neglect differ from state to sate and reports are categorized differently. Because of the increasing concern over child abuse, social agencies, hospitals, child care centers, and schools are becoming more involved in identification, treatment, and prevention of this national problem.

Public Law 93-247, the Child Abuse Prevention and Treatment Act, defines *child abuse and neglect* as the

> physical or mental injury, sexual abuse, negligent treatment or maltreatment of a child under the age of eighteen by a person who is responsible for the child's welfare under circumstances which indicate that the child's health or welfare is harmed or threatened thereby as determined in accordance with regulations prescribed by the secretary.[16]

In addition, all states have some kind of legal or statutory definition of child abuse and mistreatment, and many define penalties for child abuse.

Just as debilitating as physical abuse and neglect is *emotional abuse,* which occurs when parents, teachers, and others strip children of their self-esteem. Adults take away children's self-esteem by continually criticizing, belittling, screaming and nagging, creating fear, and intentionally and severely limiting opportunities. Because emotional abuse is difficult to define legally and difficult to document, the unfortunate consequence for emotionally abused children is that they are often left in a debilitating environment.

Table 16.3 will help you identify abuse and neglect, both of which adversely affect children's growth and development. Remember that the presence of a single characteristic does not necessarily indicate abuse. You should observe a child's behavior and appearance over a period of time and should generally be willing to give parents the benefit of the doubt about a child's condition.

REPORTING CHILD ABUSE

As a teacher you are a mandatory reporter of child abuse. Other mandatory reporters include physicians, nurses, social workers, counselors, and psychologists. Each state has its own procedures and set of policies for reporting child abuse. You need to be very familiar with your state and district policies about how to identify child abuse and how to report it.

Children today are subjected to many stressful situations in their community environment and home life and on television. As early childhood professionals, what can we do to reduce or eliminate stresses that imperil children's lives and learning?

Companion Website

To learn more about how to prevent child abuse, go to the Companion Website at **www.prenhall. com/morrison**, select chapter 16, then choose the Linking to Learning module.

TABLE 16.3 Indicators of Child Abuse

Abuse Type	Physical Indicators	Behavioral Indicators
Physical abuse	Unexplained bruises and welts • On torso, back, buttocks, thighs or face • Identifiable shape of object used to inflict injury (belt, electrical cord, etc.) • Appear with regularity after absence, weekend, or vacation Unexplained burns • On soles of feet, palms, back, buttocks, or head • Hot water, immersion burns (glove-like, sock-like, or doughnut-shaped burn on buttocks or genitals) Unexplained fractures or dislocations Bald patches on scalp	Child states he/she "deserves" punishment Fearful when others cry Behavioral extremes • Aggressive • Withdrawn Frightened of parents or caretakers Afraid to go home Child reports injury by parents or caretakers Inappropriate/immature acting out Needy for affection Manipulative behaviors to get attention Tendency toward superficial relationships Unable to focus—daydreaming Self-abusive behavior or lack of concern for personal safety Wary of adult contact
Physical neglect	Not meeting basic needs • Food, shelter, clothing Failure to thrive • Underweight, small for age Persistent hunger Poor hygiene Inappropriate dress for season or weather Consistent lack of supervision Unattended physical problems or medical needs Abandonment	Begging or stealing food Early arrival at or late departure from school Frequent visits to the school nurse Difficulty with vision or hearing Poor coordination Often tired or falling asleep in class Takes on adult roles and responsibilities Substance abuse Acting out behavior Child verbalizes a lack of care-taking
Sexual abuse	Difficulty walking or sitting Torn, stained, or bloody undergarments Pain, swelling, or itching in genital area Pain when urinating Bruises, bleeding, or tears around the genital area Vaginal or penile discharge Sexually transmitted diseases • Herpes, crabs, vaginal warts • Gonorrhea, syphilis • HIV, AIDS Excessive masturbation	Unwilling to change for gym or participate in physical education activities Sexual behavior or knowledge inappropriate to the child's age Sexual acting out on younger children Poor peer relations Delinquent or runaway behavior Report of sexual assault Drastic change in school performance Sleep disorders/nightmares Eating disorders Aggression Withdrawal, fantasy, infantile behavior Self-abusive behavior or lack of concern for personal safety Substance abuse Repetitive behaviors • Hand-washing, pacing, rocking
Emotional abuse and neglect	Speech disorders • Stuttering • Baby talk • Unresponsiveness Failure to thrive • Underweight, small for age Hyperactivity	Learning disabilities Habits • Sucking, biting, rocking Sleep disorders Poor social skills Extreme reactions to common events Unusually fearful Overly compliant behaviors • Unable to set limits Suicidal thoughts or actions; self-abusive Difficulty following rules or directions Child expects to fail so does not try

Source: Reprinted by permission from "Child Abuse: What Is It? What Can You Do?" Childhelp USA® (2003).

The following guidelines should govern your response to a child with suspected abuse or neglect:

- *Remain calm.* A child may retract information or stop talking if he or she senses a strong reaction.
- *Believe the child.* Children rarely make up stories about abuse.
- *Listen without passing judgment.* Most children know their abusers and often have conflicted feelings.
- *Tell the child you are glad that he or she told someone.*
- *Assure the child that abuse is not his or her fault.*
- *Do what you can to make certain that the child is safe from further abuse.*
- *Do not investigate the case yourself.* Call the police or the child and family services agency.

How child abuse is reported varies from state to state. In Washington, DC, for example, if child abuse or neglect is suspected, you are to immediately call the reporting hotline at (202) 671-SAFE. To make a report, you would need to provide the following information:

- Name, age, sex, and address of the child who is the subject of the report, names of any siblings and the parent, guardian, or caregiver
- Nature and extent of the abuse or neglect, as you know it (and any previous abuse or neglect)
- Any additional information that may help establish the cause and identity of persons responsible
- Your name, occupation, contact information, and a statement of any actions taken concerning the child

SEEKING HELP

What can be done about child abuse? There must be a conscious effort to educate, treat, and help abusers and potential abusers. The school is a good place to begin. Federal agencies are another source of help. For information, contact any of the following organizations:

- National Clearinghouse on Child Abuse and Neglect Information, which helps coordinate and develop programs and policies concerning child abuse and neglect; *http://nccanch. acf.hhs.gov/*
- Childhelp USA, which handles crisis calls and provides information and referrals to every country in the United States; hotline 1-800-422-4453 or 4-A-CHILD.
- National Committee to Prevent Child Abuse (NCPCA), a volunteer organization of concerned citizens that works with community, state, and national groups to expand and disseminate knowledge about child abuse prevention; *http://www.nal.usda.gov/ pavnet/pm/pmnatcom.htm*

Companion Website To complete a Program in Action activity related to homeless children, go to the Companion Website at **www.prenhall.com/ morrison**, select chapter 16, then choose the Program in Action module.

HOMELESS CHILDREN

While walking down a city street, you may have encountered homeless men and women, but have you seen a homeless child? Homeless children are the neglected, forgotten, often abandoned segment of the growing homeless population in the United States. The National Coalition for the Homeless estimates that there are as many as 1.35 million homeless children, living either with homeless families or on their own and states children are the fastest-growing population among the homeless.[17]

Homelessness has significant mental, physical, and educational consequences for children. It results in developmental delays and can produce high levels of distress. Homeless children observed in day care centers exhibit such problem behaviors as short attention spans, weak impulse control, withdrawal, aggression, speech delays, and regressive behavior. They are at greater risk for health problems, and if they do enter school, they face many problems related to previous school experience (e.g., grade failure) and attendance (e.g., long trips to attend school). In addition, childhood homelessness is a strong risk factor for adult homelessness. Fortunately, more agencies are now responding to the unique needs of homeless children and their families. The final Program in Action in this chapter describes the efforts of one faith-based agency to meet the educational needs of homeless children.

Public Law 107-110, the McKinney-Vento Homeless Education Act of 2001, provides that "each State educational agency shall assure that each child of a homeless individual and each homeless youth has access to the same free, appropriate public education, including a public preschool education, as provided to other children and youth."[18]

Companion Website

For additional Internet resources or to complete an online activity for this chapter, go to the Companion Website at **www.prenhall.com/morrison,** select chapter 16, then choose the Linking to Learning or Making Connections module.

Program in Action

CHILDREN WHO ARE POOR AND HOMELESS AND THEIR EDUCATIONAL NEEDS

The creation of a safe, healthy, loving atmosphere for families is the mission of Holy Family Home and Shelter, which opened on February 3, 1989. The shelter enables homeless children to attend school, the one constant in their young and troubled lives. Children living at Holy Family attend the local schools in Willimantic, Connecticut. However, if they wish to stay in their own school, transportation must be provided, according to the provisions of The Education of Students in Homeless Situations in the 2001 No Child Left Behind Act, along with the McKinney-Vento Act, which was reauthorized in 2001. Keep in mind that the shelter is merely temporary housing, not a change of address.

THE KEY

In August of 1993, Holy Family Home and Shelter began an education program called The Key. This program does not replace the public school curriculum but is an enhancement, helping the children with their educational needs. Our plan includes a preschool, toddler time, and an after-school tutoring program. One problem that is prevalent among the school-age children is homework—when to do it, how to do it, and who can help. Tutors, students, and professors from the University of Connecticut and Eastern Connecticut State University have been a vital force in the after-school program. Once the children in the shelter regain their educational footing with the additional help from the shelter, their grades improve, social attitudes change for the better, and the children become less stressed.

In order for people to free themselves from the world of poverty and homelessness, they need a key to open the door to prosperity and homeownership. This key is education—thus, the name for the education program. In the evolution of the program, the name has changed from The Key to the Holy Family Home and Shelter Education Program, but education is still the key that unlocks the door to personal freedom.

YEAR-ROUND ACTIVITIES

Although teachers at Holy Family may change from time to time, the essence of the program does not. Our newest teacher, Marja Prewitt, has a wealth of international classroom experience and was able to expand on the education program over the summer months. Holy Family's education program does not run on the local academic calendar but provides for year-round learning. When there is no school, the children engage in educational hands-on projects, such as making shadow puppets or creating holiday pastries. Field trips to local historical museums and state parks help to broaden the children's educational vistas.

VARIED SUPPORT

The children who come into homeless shelters carry a huge burden of abuse, neglect, and nightmarish experiences. Often we encounter children with behavioral problems. Sometimes these problems can be addressed by the school system and the educational coordinator. At other times it is necessary to hospitalize a child for his or her general well-being and protection. There is an outpatient hospital program for children called the Joshua Program, which has counseling as well as an educational component.

We try to bring out the best in our children, highlight their skills and talents, and build their self-esteem as opportunities arise. Validating a child's existence is accomplished partly with birthday parties and special holiday events. Occasionally an outside group will come and celebrate the day with the children. However, if that is not possible, the shelter staff makes sure the day is recognized. Gifts are given, and cake and ice cream are part of the celebration. Such celebrations help make the stay in the shelter less traumatic for the children.

OUTREACH

Another component of the education program is an outreach program to neighborhoods where former families now live. This program called Books to the Streets and developed by Miriam Epstein, a Holy Family volunteer, brings new and gently used books, bookmarks, and book buddies (small stuffed animals) to our former resident children and other children in the neighborhoods. Volunteers inscribe each book with a positive message and then go out to the various neighborhoods to distribute the books to the children. This program continues to grow.

Another program, Books to Dreams, which was also started by Epstein, brings books, bookmarks, and book buddies into the soup kitchens and shelters in all of eastern Connecticut. At this time Books to Dreams spans the state from the Rhode Island border to Hartford. Children who would not otherwise have their own books to read and keep now have the start of their own libraries. Each shelter and soup kitchen is provided with a book box to allow parents to choose books for their young children and older children to choose what interests them.

Contributed by Sister M. Peter Bernard. SCMC, director of public relations and volunteers, Holy Family Home and Shelter, Willimantic, Connecticut.

LINKING TO LEARNING

Council for Exceptional Children
http://www.cec.sped.org/
> Publishes extremely up-to-date news regarding education-related legislation; contains numerous links to other sites.

Council for Learning Disabilities
http://www.cldinternational.org

An international organization of and for professionals who represent diverse disciplines and who are committed to enhancing the education and life span development of individuals with learning disabilities. Establishes standards of excellence and promotes innovative strategies for research and practice through interdisciplinary collegiality, collaboration, and advocacy.

IDEA Practices
http://www.ideapractices.org

Answers your questions about the IDEA, keeps you informed about ideas that work, and supports your efforts to help all children learn, progress, and realize their dreams.

Illinois State Board of Education
http://www.isbe.net/

Features all types of educational information, including current issues, news, and reports on early childhood education.

National Association for the Education of Homeless Children and Youth (NAEHCY)
http://www.naehcy.org/

A professional organization specifically dedicated to homeless education. Established to ensure research-based strategies for effective approaches to the problems faced by homeless children, youth, and families. Has created guidelines, goals, and objectives that outline strategies for dealing with government agencies and designing effective programs.

National Dissemination Center for Children with Disabilities
http://www.nichcy.org/

National information and referral center that provides information on disabilities and disability-related issues for families, educators, and other professionals.

Office of Special Education and Rehabilitation Services
http://www.ed.gov/about/offices/list/osers/index.html?src-mr

Supports programs that assist in educating children with special needs, provides for the rehabilitation of youth and adults with disabilities, and supports research to improve the lives of individuals with disabilities.

Teaching Children with Attention Deficit Hyperactivity Disorder
http://www.ed.gov/teachers/needs/speced/adhd/adhd-resource-pt2.doc

Provides many excellent ideas and specific strategies for teaching students with ADHD.

ACTIVITIES FOR FURTHER ENRICHMENT

ETHICAL DILEMMA: "THEY DON'T NEED TO KNOW EVERYTHING"

You are a first-year teacher and are participating in your first team meeting relating to the referral, assessment, and placement process for one of your students. You want to make sure that seven-year-old Krystal gets all of the services she deserves. During the meeting you ask the district supervisor of special education services whether Krystal's parents have been notified about today's meeting and given an opportunity to participate in the meeting. The supervisor's comment is, "Oh, let's not worry about that now. Parents don't need to know everything! We can get a lot of this done and just tell them what we are going to do." Under IDEA, parents are en-titled to be members of any group that makes decisions about the educational placement of their child.

What do you do? How can you be the best advocate for Krystal? Do you tell the district supervisor what rights parents have, or do you keep quiet and say nothing until you have time to think about what you should do, or do you select some other course of action?

APPLICATIONS

1. Visit a center where children with special needs are included, and observe the children during play activities. Follow a particular child and note the materials available, the physical arrangement of the environment, and the number of other children involved with the child. Try to determine whether the child is really engaged in the play activity. Hypothesize

about why the child is or is not engaged. Discuss your observations with your colleagues.

2. Develop a file or notebook in which you can keep suggestions for adapting curricula for children with special needs.

3. Visit an early childhood special education classroom and a regular preschool classroom, and compare the types of behavior management problems and techniques found in each setting.

4. Spend some time in mainstreamed inclusive classrooms. What specific skills would you need in order to become a high-quality professional in such settings?

FIELD EXPERIENCES

1. Visit several public schools to see how they are providing individualized and appropriate programs for children with disabilities. What efforts are being made to involve parents?

2. Visit agencies and programs that provide services for people with disabilities. Before you visit, list specific features, services, and facilities you will look for.

3. How is curriculum and instruction in a class for gifted and talented students different from that in other classes? Get permission to visit and observe such a class. Then compare that class with others you have observed or experienced. On the basis of your observations, describe how you might teach a student who is gifted and talented within your inclusive classroom.

4. Contact local schools in your area, and ask them what activities and services they provide for students before and after school. How are these designed to meet students' special needs?

RESEARCH

1. Interview parents of children with disabilities. What do they feel are their greatest problems? What do they consider the greatest needs of their children? List specific ways the parents have been involved with educational agencies. How have those agencies resisted providing for their children's needs?

2. What programs does the federal government support for children with special needs in your area? Give specific information.

3. Discuss with people of another culture their culture's attitudes toward children with disabilities. How are they similar or different from your attitudes?

4. How does a teacher modify the classroom environment, classroom routines, learning activities, stu-

dent groupings, teaching strategies, instructional materials, assessments, and homework assignments to meet all students' needs? What human and material resources for successful inclusion are available to teachers and to students with special needs? How do students show social acceptance of their classmates with special needs? Visit an inclusive classroom and take notes on what you observe. Compare and discuss your observations with classmates who have visited different settings across all grade levels.

READINGS FOR FURTHER ENRICHMENT

Cimera, R. E. *The Truth About Special Education: A Guide for Parents and Teachers.* Lanham, MD: Scarecrow Press, 2003.

Contains a step-by-step discussion of the special education process and has hundreds of additional resources for parents, including professional organizations, support groups, and useful websites to help parents and students minimize the anxiety often associated with enrolling in a special education program.

Cook, R. E., M. D. Klein, A. Tessier, and S. Daley. *Adapting Early Childhood Curricula for Children in Inclusive Settings,* 6th ed. Upper Saddle River, NJ: Merrill/Prentice Hall, 2004.

Reflects the most recent developments in the field, presenting the skills necessary for teachers to assist infants, young children, and their families to meet their special challenges and to develop to their fullest potential.

Haager, D., and J. K. Klingner. *Differentiating Instruction in Inclusive Classrooms: The Special Educator's Guide.* Boston: Allyn and Bacon, 2004.

Emphasizes the importance of decision making based on students' academic and social needs. Illustrates important concepts and constructs with realistic examples and practical ideas.

Howard, V. F., B. F. Williams, and C. Lepper. *Very Young Children with Special Needs: A Formative Approach for Today's Children,* 3rd ed. Upper Saddle River, NJ: Merrill/Prentice Hall, 2005.

Provides an introduction for early childhood professionals who plan to provide services and intervention to very young children with disabilities.

Turnbull, A. R., and M. Wehmeyer. *Exceptional Lives: Special Education in Today's Schools,* 5th ed. Upper Saddle River, NJ: Merrill/Prentice Hall, 2007.

Equips the reader with principles, values, and practices that support teaching the majority of students with disabilities within the scope of general education programs.

ENDNOTES

1. Public Law 105-17 (1997).

2. Ibid.

3. This section adapted from Many Beth Bruder, "The Individual Family Service Plan (IFSP)," *Eric EC Digest #E605* (December 2000), http://ericec.org/digests/e605.html.

4. National Early Childhood Technical Assistance System, *Helping Our Nation's Infants and Toddlers with Disabilities and Their Families: A Briefing Paper on Part H of the Individuals with Disabilities Education Act (IDEA)* (Author, 1996). Also available online at http://www.nectas.unc.edu.

5. Center for Special Education Finance, "Total per Pupil Expenditures for School-Aged Special Education Students, by SEEP State, 2001–2002," *Maryland Special Education Expenditure Project Final Report* (2003), http://www.csef-air.org/publications/seep/data_tables/seep_state_comparison.html.

6. Council for Exceptional Children (1996), http://www.cec.sped.org/.

7. Material in this section on itinerant special educators contributed by Faith Haertig Sadler, MEd, itinerant special education teacher in Seattle, Washington.

8. Teaching Children with Attention Deficit Hyperactivity Disorder: Instructional Strategies and Practices. U.S. Office of Special Education Programs, 2004. http://www.ed.gov/teachers/needs/speced/adhd/adhd-resource-pt2.pdf.

9. Ibid.

10. Information in this section from the U.S. Department of Education, *Teaching Children with Attention Deficit Hyperactivity Disorder: Instructional Strategies and Practices 2004,* http://www.ed.gov/teachers/needs/speced/adhd/adhd-resource-pt2.doc.

11. J. Burnette, "Including Students with Disabilities in General Education Classrooms: From Policy to Practice," *The Eric Review* 4 (1996): 2–11.

12. Ibid.

13. Ibid.

14. Jacob K. Javits Gifted and Talented Students Education Act of 1988, http://www.ed.gov/programs/javits/index.html.

15. Child Welfare League of America, "Child Protection: Facts and Figures." (2002), http://www.nocanch.acf.hhs/gov/pubs/factsheets/canstats.cfm.

16. U.S. Statutes at Large, vol. 88, pt. 1 (Washington, DC: U.S. Government Printing Office, 1976), 5.

17. How Many People Experience Homelessness? NCH Fact Sheet #2. National Coalition for the Homeless, June 2005. http://www.nationalhomeless.org/publications/facts/How_Many.pdf

18. Public Law 100-77, McKinney–Vento Homeless Education Act, Title VII-Subtitle B-Education for Homeless Children and Youths, 2001.

CHAPTER 17

Parent, Family, and Community Involvement

COOPERATION AND COLLABORATION

When parents are involved in their children's education at home,
the children do better in school.
And when parents are involved at school,
children go farther in school, and the schools they go to are better.

UNKNOWN

One thing we can say with certainty about the educational landscape today is that parents, families, and communities are as much a part of the educational process as are children, teachers, and staff. At no other time in U.S. educational history has support for family and community involvement in schools and programs been so high. All concerned view the involvement of families and communities as critical for individual student success, as well as for the success of the American dream of providing all children with an education that will meet their needs and enable them to be productive members of society. In this chapter we look at some of the reasons that parent, family, and community involvement in education is so important and some ways you can confidently and effectively contribute to the process. The Voice from the Field on page 497 echoes the importance of broad-based involvement in children's education.

CHANGES IN SCHOOLING

Schooling used to consist mostly of teaching children social and basic academic skills. But as society has changed, so has the content of schooling. Early childhood programs have assumed many parental functions and responsibilities and now help parents and families with educational and social issues that affect them and their children.

Political and social forces have led to a strengthened relationship between families and schools. The accountability and reform movements of the past and present have convinced families that they should no longer be kept out of their children's schools. They have become more militant in their demand for quality education, and schools and other agencies have responded by seeking ways to involve families in the quest for quality. Education professionals and families now realize that mutual cooperation is in everyone's best interest. Early childhood professionals are working with parents and families to develop programs to help them and their children reach their full potential.

CHANGES IN FAMILIES

The family of today is not the family of yesterday, nor will the family of today be the family of tomorrow. Table 17.1 shows some of the ways families have changed over the years. In addition, as more mothers are entering the workforce, more children are spending eight hours a day or more in the care of others, often beginning at an early age. As a result, opportunities have blossomed for child-serving agencies, such as child care centers and preschools, to assist and support parents in their child-rearing efforts. One of the major trends of the next decade will be that more early childhood programs will provide more parents with child development, child-rearing, and educational help and information.

Focus Questions

How do changes in society and families influence children and early childhood programs?

Why is parent, family, and community involvement important in early childhood programs?

What are the benefits of involving parents and families in early childhood programs?

How can you encourage and support programs for involving families and communities?

Companion Website

To check your understanding of this chapter, go to the Companion Website at **www.prenhall.com/ morrison**, select chapter 17, answer Multiple Choice and Essay Questions, and receive feedback.

TABLE 17.1   How Families Have Changed

Types of Families	Numbers in Thousands	
	1960	2004
Married-couple families with children	55,877	49,603
Single-mother families with children	5,105	17,072
Single-father families with children	724	3,402
Children living with relative	1,601	2,360
Children living with nonrelative	420	769

Source: U.S. Census Bureau, "Living Arrangements of Children Under 18 Years Old: 1960 to Present" (2005), http://www.census.gov/population/socdemo/hh-fam/ch1.csv.

Families continue to change, and as they do, early childhood professionals must adapt, adopting new ways of involving family members and providing for their needs. What can professionals do to ensure the involvement of grandparents in their programs?

GRANDPARENTS AS PARENTS

Grandparents acting as parents for their grandchildren are a growing reality in the United States today. In the new millennium, more grandparents are rearing their grandchildren than ever before in American history. In 2005, 5.5 million children, or 8 percent of all children under age eighteen, were living in homes maintained by 4.2 million grandparents.[1] Many of these children are *skipped-generation children,* meaning that neither of their parents is living with them. Reasons for the increase in children living with grandparents include drug use, divorce, mental and physical illness, abandonment, teenage pregnancy, child abuse and neglect, incarceration, and death of the parents.

Grandparents in these skipped-generation households have all of the parenting responsibilities of parents—providing for their grandchildren's basic needs and care, as well as making sure that they do well in school. As a result, these grandparents need your support and educational assistance. You can help them learn to parent all over again, keeping in mind that they are rearing their grandchildren in a whole different generation from the one in which they reared their children:

- Provide refresher parenting courses to help grandparents understand how children and schooling have changed since they reared their children.
- Link grandparents to support groups, such as Raising Our Children's Children (ROCC) and the AARP Grandparent Information Center.

IMPLICATIONS OF FAMILY PATTERNS

Given the changes in families today, here are some things you can do to help parents:

- *Provide support services.* Support can range from being a listening ear to organizing support groups and seminars on single parenting. You can help families link up with other agencies and groups, such as Big Brothers and Big Sisters and Families without Partners. Through newsletters and fliers, you can offer families specific advice on how to help children become independent and how to meet the demands of living in single-parent families, stepfamilies, and other family configurations.
- *Promote child care.* As more families need child care, you can be an advocate for establishing care where none exists, extending existing services, and helping to arrange cooperative babysitting services.

A Message to the Teaching Profession
It Takes More Than One

In 1983 I graduated from the State University of West Georgia with a teaching degree in my hand, and I took off to set the education world on fire. I truly believed I would be the saving grace of every student I encountered. I alone would be the salvation of education in general. Little did I know that it takes more than one person to educate a child. It didn't take me long to conclude, as the African proverb says, "It takes a village to raise a child."

Parental support, by far, is the most important component of a child's education; that involvement begins at birth. We know that parents who read to their children before they enter school give them a head start toward reading success. And research has proven that when parents are involved in their children's education, the children do better in school.

Involvement does not necessarily mean volunteering at the school; there are many times when volunteering is impossible. Involvement in a child's education can mean reading to the child, checking homework on a regular basis, and discussing the child's progress with teachers.

Business involvement in schools is also vital because the students of today are the employees of tomorrow.

How can businesses become involved? Monetary donations are nice, but that's not the only way to become involved. Businesses can provide personnel to serve as mentors not only for students at risk, but for all students. Mentoring is a way to help students in and out of school. The long-term relationship between students and mentors is a definite benefit. Another way business can help is by allowing employees time away from their jobs to attend functions at school without loss of wages. Many companies now allow employees a certain number of documented hours for involvement in their children's education. What a positive policy—for everyone involved.

Community involvement in schools is necessary because schools are the heart of society. With the help of everyone involved, success is inevitable. But it does take a village to raise a child.

Contributed by Theresa Stephens Stapler, Central Elementary School, Carrollton, Georgia, *USA Today* 2002 All-USA Teacher Award winner.

- *Avoid criticism.* Be careful not to criticize parents for the jobs they are doing. Parents may not have enough time to spend with their children or know how to discipline them. Regardless of their circumstances, families need help, not criticism.
- *Avoid being judgmental.* You should examine your attitudes toward family patterns and remember that there is no right family pattern from which all children should come.
- *Arrange educational experiences.* Offer experiences children might not otherwise have because of their family organization. For example, outdoor activities such as fishing trips and sports events can be interesting and enriching learning experiences for children who may not have such opportunities.
- *Adjust programs.* Adjust classroom and center activities to account for children's home situations; children's needs depend on their experiences at home. Opportunities abound for role-playing, which can bring into the open situations that children need to talk about. You can also use program opportunities to discuss families and the roles they play. Make it a point to model, encourage, and teach effective interpersonal skills.
- *Be sensitive.* Avoid having children make presents for both parents when it is inappropriate to do so or awarding prizes for bringing both parents to meetings. Replace such terms as *broken home* with *single-parent family.* Be sensitive to the realities of children's home lives. For instance, when a teacher sent a field trip permission form home with children and told them to have their mothers or fathers sign it, one child said, "I don't have a father. If my mother can't sign it, can the man she sleeps with sign it?"

Clarify with families how they would like specific situations handled; for example, ask whether you should send notices of school events to both parents.

- *Seek training.* Request professional development training to help you work with families. Professional development programs can provide information about referral agencies, guidance techniques, and child abuse identification and prevention. You need to be alert to all kinds of child abuse, including mental, physical, and sexual abuse (see chapter 16).

- *Increase parent contacts.* Encourage greater and different kinds of **family involvement** by visiting homes; talking to families about children's needs; providing information and opportunities to parents, grandparents, and other family members; gathering information from families (such as through interest inventories); and keeping in touch with parents. Make parent contacts positive.

Family involvement The participation of parents and other family members in all areas of their children's education and development, based on the premise that parents are the primary influence in children's lives.

Family involvement is a process of helping families use their abilities to benefit themselves, their children, and the early childhood program. Families, children, and the program are all part of the process, and you must work with and through families if you want to be successful. Refer to the accompanying Program in Action "Six Types of Parent/Family Involvement" on pages 499–500. Read about them and then keep them in mind as you read the rest of the chapter and learn how to involve parents and families.

EDUCATION AS A FAMILY AFFAIR

Education starts in the home, and what happens there profoundly affects the trajectory of development and learning. The greater the family's involvement in children's learning, the more likely it is that students will receive a high-quality education. Research confirms the benefits of parent involvement; you can see the specific findings in Figure 17.1.

The central role families play in children's education is a reality that teachers and schools must address as they make plans for reforming schools and increasing student achievement.

In the Head Start segment of the DVD, observe how parent involvement is required— parents act as volunteers and learn about proper nutrition. What are the pros and cons of mandatory parent involvement?

FIGURE 17.1 Research Support for Parent Involvement

- The earlier in a child's educational process parent involvement begins, the more powerful the effects.

- The most effective forms of parent involvement are those that engage parents in working directly with their children on learning activities at home.

- The most consistent predictors of children's academic achievement and social adjustment are parent expectations of the child's academic attainment and satisfaction with their child's education at school.

- Parents of high-achieving students set higher standards for their children's educational activities than parents of low-achieving students.

- The strongest and most consistent predictors of parent involvement at school and at home are the specific school programs and teacher practices that encourage parent involvement at school and guide parents in how to help their children at home.

- School-initiated activities to help parents change the home environment can have a strong influence on children's school performance.

- Parents need specific information on how to help and what to do.

Source: Michigan Department of Education, "What Research Says About Parent Involvement in Children's Education in Relation to Academic Achievement" (2001), http://www.michigan.gov/documents/Final_Parent_Involvement_Fact_Sheet_14732_7.pdf.

SIX TYPES OF PARENT/FAMILY INVOLVEMENT

As you think about your role in involving parents and families, it would be helpful to review the six types of involvement shown in the figure included here. A worthy professional goal would be to have some of your parents involved in all six of these types of parental involvement during the program year. Let's take a closer look at what you can do with each type, along with examples from actual practice.

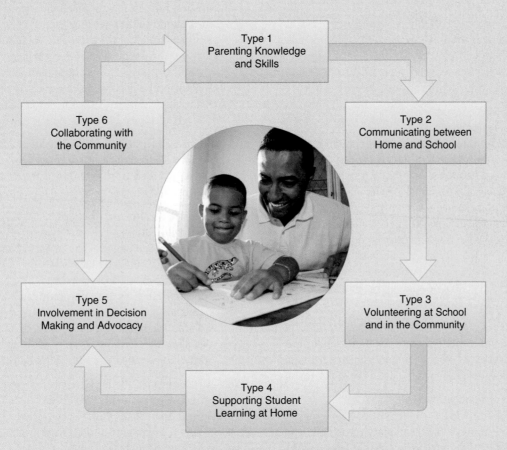

Type 1
Parenting Knowledge and Skills

Type 6
Collaborating with the Community

Type 2
Communicating between Home and School

Type 5
Involvement in Decision Making and Advocacy

Type 3
Volunteering at School and in the Community

Type 4
Supporting Student Learning at Home

Source: Figure content reprinted by permission from J. L. Epstein, *School, Family, and Community Partnerships: Your Handbook for Action,* 2nd ed. Thousand Oaks, CA: Corwin Press. Also see www.partnershipschools.org. Photo by Bill Lai/The Image Works.

1. *Parenting*—Assist families with parenting and child-rearing skills, understanding child and adolescent development, and setting home conditions that support children as students at each age and grade level. Assist schools in understanding families.

Windsor Hills Elementary School
Baltimore, Maryland

The Action Team planned activities to provide Windsor Hills' grandparents with the information and resources they need to foster a positive family structure and keep children focused on their education. The two Grandparent Gatherings also supported school improvement goals of increased attendance and achievement for students in preK through fifth grade and improved school climate.

2. *Communicating*—Communicate with families about school programs and student progress through effective school-to-home and home-to-school communications.

Freedom Elementary School
Freedom, Wisconsin
Everyone has heard the saying, "Serve food and they will come." Freedom Elementary proved that this strategy continues to work. In September the school hosted a family-school picnic supper immediately preceding open house. Nine hundred people attended, and they all visited classrooms for open house. This rural school has 730 students enrolled in preK to grade five.

3. *Volunteering*—Improve recruitment, training, tasks, and schedules to involve families as volunteers and audiences at school or in other locations to support students and school programs.

Clover Street School
Windsor, Connecticut
Every year it is difficult to recruit enough parents to volunteer for the library, classrooms, and other activities. The Action Team for Partnerships (ATP) worked to solve this challenge by reaching out to an untapped source—fathers and other male relatives. The goal was to involve men in the learning community and provide opportunities for them to be role models for students. Men participating in school activities also helps break the stereotype that only mothers volunteer and monitor student progress.

4. *Learning at home*—Involve families with their children in learning activities at home, including homework and other curriculum-related activities and decisions.

Monterey Elementary School
Grove City, Ohio
The ATP at Monterey Elementary throws a birthday party for Dr. Seuss to bring together families and the community during Read Across America Week. The birthday party encourages daily reading at home, models reading aloud for parents, and gives every child a new book. Monterey Elementary makes reading fun and interesting for a diverse group of people.

5. *Decision making*—Include families as participants in school decisions, governance, and advocacy through PTA/PTO, school councils, committees, and other parent organizations.

Highlands Elementary School
Naperville, Illinois
The School/Family/Community Partnership (SFCP) Team, the two parent cochairs, and the principal hosted a lunch for all parent SFCP team members the week after school began and two weeks prior to the first full SFCP team meeting. The objectives of the parent lunch were threefold:
- Introduce all of the parents to each other and make them feel comfortable talking to one another, the cochairs, and the principal
- Explain the goals and procedures of the team
- Provide an opportunity for everyone to make suggestions or present new ideas for the year

6. *Collaborating with the community*—Coordinate resources and services for families, students, and the school with businesses, agencies, and other groups, and provide services to the community.

Mill Street Elementary School
Naperville, Illinois
The Buddy Reading Program between North Central College and Mill Street Elementary School is a partnership of approximately sixty preservice education students and sixty fourth and fifth graders, discussing a specific novel on a one-to-one basis. Communication is via a college-based Web-board that allows students to exchange ideas and make connections using the latest computer technology.

You can learn more about partnership program development in J. L. Epstein et al., *School, Family, and Community Partnerships: Your Handbook for Action,* 2nd ed. (Thousand Oaks, CA: Corwin Press, 2002) or online at www. partnershipschools.org.

Reprinted by permission of National Network of Partnership Schools at Johns Hopkins University (2002), http://www.csos.jhu.edu/p2000/.

Partnering with parents is a process whose time has come, and the benefits far outweigh any inconveniences or barriers that may stand in the way of bringing schools and parents together.

FAMILY-CENTERED PROGRAMS

Family-centered programs focus on meeting the needs of children through the family unit, whatever that unit may be. And to most effectively meet the needs of children, early childhood teachers must also meet the needs of family members and the family unit. **Family-centered teaching** makes sense for a number of reasons. First, the family unit has the major responsibility for meeting children's needs; the family system is a powerful determiner of developmental processes, for both better and worse. Helping family members improve their roles benefits children and consequently promotes their success in school.

Second, family issues and problems must be addressed in order to really help children. For instance, helping parents gain access to adequate and affordable health care increases the chances that the whole family, including the children, will be healthy.

Third, teachers can do many things concurrently with children and their families that benefit both. Literacy is a good example. Adopting a family approach to literacy means helping parents learn the importance of literacy and of reading to their children to help ensure literacy development.

Even Start is an example of family-centered teaching. It combines adult literacy and parenting training with early childhood education to break the cycles of illiteracy that are often passed on from one generation to another. Even Start, as we discussed in chapter 8, helps parents become full partners in the education of their children, assists children in reaching their full potential, and provides literacy training for parents. Figure 17.2 diagrams family-centered teaching in action.

TWO-GENERATION AND INTERGENERATIONAL PROGRAMS

Two-generation programs involve parents and their children and are designed to help both generations, as well as strengthen the family unit. Delivery of two-generation services can and should begin before children's birth because many problems relating to children's health can be prevented by good prenatal care. **Intergenerational programs** involve grandparents and others as well.

A preventive approach to maternal and prenatal health is reflected in the growing numbers of schools that have on-site health clinics. Services often include both health and education, through which students and parents receive medical care and information that will support their efforts to lead healthy lives. This approach also includes programs in which young people provide services to older persons, those in which older persons provide services to youth, and those in which two generations work cooperatively on a project.

Avance. One example of a parenting program is Avance (from the Spanish word for "advance" or "progress"), which serves the needs of the hardest-to-reach, primarily Hispanic families. Founded in San Antonio, Texas, the organization focuses on teaching parents of children from birth through three years of age the skills parents need to nurture children to

In the Head Start segment of the DVD, observe how a father in an Even Start program is helping his child with literacy skills while a teacher looks on.

Family-centered teaching Instruction that focuses on meeting the needs of students through the family unit.

Companion Website To learn more about involving families in children's education, go to the Companion Website at **www.prenhall.com/morrison**, select chapter 17, then choose the Linking to Learning module.

Two-generation programs Programs that involve parents and their children and are designed to help both generations, as well as strengthen the family unit.

Intergenerational programs Programs that involve grandparents and others and are designed to help all generations.

FIGURE 17.2 Family-Centered Teaching
What else besides literacy can be taught to children and family members at the same time?

Early childhood education teachers

- Parent education
- Literacy programs
- Counseling programs
- Referrals to community agencies
- Assistance with problems of daily living

Outcomes/benefits

- Increased knowledge, skills, and understanding of education process
- Help for families and children in addressing and solving problems
- A greater range of resources and more experts than school alone can provide
- Less stress for families and children, making learning more possible

success in school and life. Avance provides a comprehensive parenting-education program, including a twenty-seven lesson/nine-month bilingual curriculum. While parents attend the once-a-week, three-hour parenting program—incorporating lessons in child growth and development, toy making, and family support—Avance provides transportation and quality developmental care for their children. Avance also includes a home visiting component, offers special programs for fathers, and provides literacy training. For more information about this organization, visit its website at *www.avance.org*.

GUIDELINES FOR INVOLVING PARENTS AND FAMILIES

As an early childhood professional, you can use the tips presented in Table 17.2 to develop programs for parent and family involvement.

ACTIVITIES TO ENCOURAGE INVOLVEMENT

There are unlimited possibilities for a meaningful program of family involvement. Families can make a significant difference in their children's education, and with your assistance they can join teachers and schools in a productive partnership. The accompanying Program in Action on pages 504–505 is a Competency Builder that shares effective strategies you can use to create parent-friendly schools, which will encourage that partnership. The following activities also allow for significant family involvement; they are organized according to the six types of parent/ family involvement outlined earlier.

Type 1: Parenting Knowledge and Skills

- *Workshops*—Introduce families to the school's policies, procedures, and programs. Most families want to know what is going on in the school and would do a better job of parenting and educating if they knew how.
- *Adult education classes*—Provide families with opportunities to learn about a range of subjects.
- *Training programs*—Give parents and other family members skills as classroom aides, club and activity sponsors, curriculum planners, and policy decision makers. When parents and other family members are viewed as experts, empowerment results.
- *Classroom and center activities*—Although not all families can be directly involved in classroom activities, encourage those who can. But remember that those who are involved must have guidance, direction, and training. Involving parents and others as paid aides can be an excellent way to provide both employment and training. Many programs, such as Head Start, actively support such a policy.
- *Libraries and materials centers*—Families benefit from books and other articles relating to parenting. Some programs furnish resource areas with comfortable chairs to encourage families to use these materials.

Type 2: Communicating between Home and School

- *Support services such as car pools and babysitting*—These can make attendance and involvement possible.
- *Performances and plays*—These, especially ones in which children have a part, tend to bring families to school; however, the purpose of children's performances should not be solely to get families involved.
- *Telephone hotlines*—When staffed by families, they can help allay fears and provide information relating to child abuse, communicable diseases, and special events. Telephone networks are also used to help children and parents with homework and to monitor latchkey children.

Companion
Website
To complete a
Program in Action activity
related to family involvement,
go to the Companion Website
at **www.prenhall.com/
morrison**, select chapter 17,
then choose the Program in
Action module.

In the Child
Care segment of the DVD, the
narrator says that parents are
looking for child care that they
can trust. What qualities in a
program or in a teacher
contribute to trust?

Companion
Website
To complete a
Program in Action activity
related to creating a parent-
friendly school, go to the
Companion Website at **www.
prenhall.com/morrison**,
select chapter 17, then
choose the Program in Action
module.

TABLE 17.2 Guidelines for Involving Parents and Families

Objective	Strategies
• Get to know your children's parents and families.	• Conduct home visits, especially in early childhood programs with a limited number of students. Teachers with a large number of students may find that visiting a few homes with special circumstances can be helpful and informative. • Call parents and introduce yourself. • Offer to e-mail parents and to answer their questions about their children and the school.
• Find out what goals parents have for their children. Encourage them to have realistically high expectations, and use these goals in your planning.	• Send home a parent questionnaire on the first day of school. • Talk about goals for children when you conference with parents. • Ask children to set goals for their learning, and then have them share the goals with their parents. • Send home to all parents the state standards for your grade.
• Make all parents and family members feel welcome.	• Talk face to face with parents. • Send out letters. • Have a notice board for parents.
• Build relationships with parents.	• Hold a parent–teacher conference several times throughout the school year to discuss children's success and strengths.
• Learn how to best communicate with parents according to their cultural preferences.	• Ask parents to share their interests, ideas, and goals for family involvement. Take into account cultural features that can inhibit collaboration. • Ask parents their involvement preferences.
• Support parents in their roles as the first teachers of their children.	• Share information, materials, help with parenting problems, and help with homework, and be available to answer questions. • Set up a School-Home Links Reading Kit program that involves all parents, even those who are unable to come into school. The reading kits are a collection of research-based activities designed to help families reinforce the reading and language arts skills that their children are learning at school.
• Provide frequent, open communication and feedback on student progress, including good news.	• Send home individual reports, report cards, progress reports. • Hold parent–teacher conferences to discuss children's progress. • Use the telephone and e-mail to let parents know about student progress.
• Train parents as mentors, classroom aides, tutors, and homework helpers.	• Communicate guidelines for helping students prepare for tests. • Let parents know what needs you have and invite them to help.
• Support fathers in their role as parents.	• Encourage fathers to read, play games, and help their children with homework and class projects. • Inform fathers that volunteering at school can enhance their children's learning.
• Work with and through families.	• Ask parents to help you work with and involve other parents.

HOW TO CREATE A PARENT-FRIENDLY SCHOOL

Parent and community involvement makes the difference between schools being a place to go and a place to learn. "Our PTA brings the school community together and encourages student involvement in affective and academic areas," says Dr. Jesse D. Baker, principal of Stadium Drive Elementary School of the Arts in Lake Orion, Michigan. He cites events such as mother–son dances, daddy–daughter outings, family swim night at the local high school, and a parent-directed spirit week and fun run as examples of parent involvement. In addition, it is usual to have one or two parent volunteers in each classroom on most days. "When parents are welcomed and their decisions are respected, their involvement increases," says Baker.

Parent-friendly schools and programs do not just happen. They require hard work and dedication by everyone involved. Here are some ideas from Stadium Drive Elementary School that you can use to make your classroom and school more parent friendly:

STRATEGY

1   Show that you care

Develop a compassionate culture toward students, families, and the community in general.

- Send flowers and letters and make telephone calls and visits to ill children or their families to show the extent of the staff's commitment to families.
- Welcome new families and encourage them to become involved.
- Encourage teachers to stand at their classroom doors each morning and greet youngsters as they enter.
- Organize a schoolwide effort to help a community member cope with a life-threatening condition. At Stadium Drive Elementary, students collected money. However, donations of food, offers of transportation, or care for children are other excellent ways to show you care.
- Collect canned goods for needy families at holiday times and throughout the year.
- Collect donations for victims of natural disasters. Stadium Drive's outpouring of donations for victims of the 2004 tsunami and hurricane Katrina in 2005 was overwhelming.

- Conduct a coats-for-kids drive before cold weather sets in.
- Reward students' caring behaviors. Stadium Drive Elementary has a Pause to Recognize program that acknowledges caring and respectful behavior.
- Create a scholarship fund. Staff members at Stadium Drive each pay a dollar on Fridays for the privilege of wearing blue jeans, thus creating a scholarship fund for a graduating senior alumnus.

STRATEGY

2   Communicate frequently with parents and the community

Through multiple media, highlight the school's philosophy and activities that support that philosophy. "Communication is key to maintaining a nurturing culture between staff and families," says Jan Seeds, PTA president. Parents at Stadium Drive, named a parent-friendly school by *Parent Magazine,* stay connected with the school through regular communication.

- Make a calendar of school events available on public access cable and the school's website.
- Publish a weekly newsletter in paper and electronic form.
- Ask the PTA to produce a student directory of addresses and phone numbers.
- Call or e-mail parents to update them on classroom activities.

STRATEGY

3   Solicit feedback from parents

Gather data from parents and the community regarding their needs and perceptions. Then use the data to set school goals. Gather written comments of parents regarding school climate. When requesting a teacher, one parent at Stadium Drive wrote, "My daughter was in her class last year. Through the different class volunteering I did, I was able to see how she managed her classroom and taught the children, and I was very impressed. Her attentiveness and compassion really helped bring out the best in children." Ask for opinions and suggestions.

STRATEGY 4 — Unite parents and staff in a common goal

Meeting the educational needs of all students should be everyone's top priority. Stadium Drive maintains a positive bond among all stakeholders and establishes school priorities as a result of formal and informal information gleaned from student, parent, and staff surveys.

- Provide funds for field trips and for visiting artists, musicians, dancers, and actors to come to your school to work with students. The PTA at Stadium Drive is responsible for this area.
- Extend the parent–teacher partnership whenever possible. At Stadium Drive's Curriculum Night, teachers explain grade-level curriculum and address specific issues. Fall and spring conferences update parents on their children's progress.

STRATEGY 5 — Create community partnerships

Cooperative relationships can showcase school efforts and involve businesses in school activities. Partnerships beyond the Stadium Drive school walls exist with both businesses and civic organizations.

- Establish mutually beneficial relationships with local businesses. For example, students can make deposits at school to their bank savings account. Or a local art shop can frame—at no cost—student art work going to state competition.
- Display student art and written work at local businesses and restaurants.
- Invite community artists, musicians, and journalists to judge student entries in competitions.
- Host senior citizens as special guests at school activities, recitals, concerts, and performances.
- Work with local charities. At Stadium Drive, staff and students work with the local Lions Club in an adopt-a-family program, with each classroom providing wrapped presents for a needy family during winter holidays.

STRATEGY 6 — Connect parents and students with the school

Programs and services that benefit and involve families can strengthen and unify the school community.

- Recruit parents at the beginning of the year, and then call them to volunteer for classroom help, special projects, and field trip chaperones, as well as in your school art room or media center. Stadium Drive uses this approach, and the growth in their volunteerism over the past six years has been significant—from 975 to nearly 5,000 volunteer hours.
- Tap into students from middle school and high school; they are often willing volunteers. At Stadium Drive these older students volunteered more than 600 hours last year.
- Thank all volunteers at the end of the year. For example, have a volunteer tea or picnic.
- Include nonacademic services for students and families, such as a school social worker, a county nurse, and special education ancillary staff.
- Offer counseling on child rearing, grief management, and conflict resolution.
- Recommend strategies for handling trauma, disruptive behavior, poor student choices, and psychological issues.
- Make referrals to outside agencies for child abuse, drug abuse, alcoholism, or domestic violence.
- Support students and parents with information and training on health issues.

STRATEGY 7 — Consider family needs

Make meeting times, child care arrangements, and other activities user friendly.

- Provide scholarships to aid students who would be otherwise unable to attend camp or field trips.
- Schedule PTA meetings, parent–teacher conferences, and personal contacts in the evening, before school, or immediately after school. Provide free child care.
- Encourage staff to meet at times convenient to parents.
- Provide before- and after-school child care and enrichment programs, such as cooking, dance, crafts, tumbling, magic, play-building, cartooning, art, and computer applications.
- Make school facilities available after hours to parents and the groups to which they belong for scouting, martial arts training, sports, home designing, or other community interests.
- Use the educational resources of the school and community to extend learning opportunities for families. For example, students at Stadium Drive design Web pages to exhibit classroom activities, and their concerts and musical productions are broadcast on local cable.
- Provide a parent section in the library for materials on child growth and parenting.

Contributed by Dr. Jesse D. Baker, principal, Stadium Drive Elementary School, Lake Orion, Michigan.

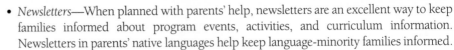

Companion Website To learn more about approaches to parent and family involvement, go to the Companion Website at **www.prenhall.com/morrison**, select chapter 17, then choose the Linking to Learning module.

- *Newsletters*—When planned with parents' help, newsletters are an excellent way to keep families informed about program events, activities, and curriculum information. Newsletters in parents' native languages help keep language-minority families informed.
- *Home learning materials and activities*—Putting out a monthly calendar of activities to be done at home is one good way to keep families involved in their children's learning.
- *IEPs for special needs children*—Involvement in writing an IEP is not only a legal requirement but also an excellent learning experience and an effective communication tool.

Type 3: Volunteering at School and in the Community

- *Child care*—Families may not be able to attend programs and become involved if they do not have child care for their children. Child care makes their participation possible and more enjoyable.
- *Service exchanges*—When operated by early childhood programs and other agencies, exchanges can help families with their need for services. For example, one parent might provide child care in her home in exchange for having her washing machine repaired. The possibilities for such exchanges are endless.
- *Welcoming committees*—A good way to involve families in any program is to have other families contact them when their children first join a program.

Type 4: Supporting Student Learning at Home

- *Books and other materials for home use*—Provide these for parents to read to their children.
- *Suggestions for parents*—Provide parents with tips on how to help their children with homework.
- *A website for parents*—This can inform them about the activities of your classroom. Give suggestions on how parents can extend and enrich classroom projects and activities at home.

Parents can be involved in early childhood programs in many ways—for example, accompanying children on field trips. How could you go about determining the best ways to involve parents in your programs?

- *A home learning kit*—This can consist of activities and materials (books, activity packets, etc.). Send such kits home with children.

Type 5: Involvement in Decision Making and Advocacy

- *Fairs and bazaars*—Involve families in fund-raising.
- *Hiring and policy making*—Parents and community members can and should serve on committees that hire staff and set policy.
- *Curriculum development and review*—Parents' involvement in curriculum planning helps them learn about and understand what constitutes a quality program and what is involved in a developmentally appropriate curriculum. When families know about the curriculum, they are more supportive of it.

Type 6: Collaborating with the Community

- *Family nights, cultural dinners, carnivals, and potluck dinners*—Such events bring families and the community to the school in nonthreatening, social ways.
- *Parent support groups*—Parents need support in their roles. Support groups can provide parenting information, community agency information, and speakers.

In the Head Start segment of the DVD, observe the role of the teacher with the parent and child during the home visit.

HOME VISITS

Home visits are becoming more commonplace for early childhood professionals. Plan now for how you will visit in the homes of your children's families. Teachers who do home visiting are trained prior to going on the visits.

A home visiting program can show that the school is willing to go more than halfway to involve parents in their children's education. Home visits also help teachers demonstrate their interest in students' families and understand their students better by seeing them in their home environment.

These visits should not replace parent–teacher conferences or be used to discuss children's progress. When completed early, before any school problems arise, visits avoid putting any parents on the defensive and signal that teachers are eager to work with parents. Teachers who have made home visits say that visits build stronger relationships with parents and children and improve attendance and achievement.

Planning and Scheduling. Administrators and teachers must be willing to participate in a home visiting program and be involved in planning it. These suggestions may be helpful:

- Teachers' schedules must be adjusted so that they have the necessary time.
- Home visits should be scheduled during just one month of the school year, preferably early.
- Visits should be logged so that teachers and administrators can measure their benefits.
- Some schools have scheduled home visits in the afternoon right after school. Others have found that early evening is more convenient for parents. Some schedule visits right before a new school year begins. A mix of times may be needed to reach all families.
- Teachers should be given flexibility to schedule their visits during a targeted time period.
- Wherever possible, teachers should visit the homes of children in their classes. If this is

not possible, the principal should ensure that every home that requests a visit receives one.
- Teachers of siblings may want to visit these children's homes together but should take care not to overwhelm parents.
- Some schools work with community groups (e.g., boys' and girls' clubs, housing complexes, 4-H, Y's, and community centers) to schedule visits in neutral but convenient places.

Making Parents Feel Comfortable. Here are some useful tips:

- Send a letter home to parents explaining the desire to have teachers make informal visits to all students' homes. Include a form that parents can mail back to accept or decline the visit and to request that a translator accompany the teacher.
- The letter should state clearly that the intent of this fifteen- to thirty-minute visit is only to introduce the teacher and family members to each other, not to discuss the child's progress.
- The letter might suggest that families think about special things their children would want to share with the teacher.
- The tone of the letter should try to lessen any parents' worries. One school included a note to parents that said, "No preparation is required. In fact, our own homes need to be vacuumed, and all of us are on diets!" This touch of humor and casualness helped to set a friendly and informal tone.

Many early childhood professionals conduct home visits to help parents learn how to support their children's learning at home. What useful information can parents provide to professionals about children's learning, experiences, and growth and development?

- A phone call to parents who have not responded can explain the plan for home visits and reassure parents that it is to get acquainted and not to evaluate students or parents.
- Enlist community groups, religious organizations, and businesses to help publicize the home visits.

PARENT CONFERENCES

Significant parent involvement occurs through well-planned and well-conducted conferences between parents and early childhood professionals, informally referred to as **parent–teacher conferences.** Such conferences are often the first contact many families have with a school and are critical both from a public relations point of view and as a vehicle for helping families and professionals accomplish their goals. The following guidelines will help you prepare for and conduct successful conferences:

Parent–teacher conferences Meetings between parents and early childhood professionals to inform the parents of the child's progress and allow them to actively participate in the educational process.

In the Primary Grade segment of the DVD, observe the parent–teacher conference and the ways the teacher encourages the father's involvement with his daughter's education.

- *Plan ahead.* Be sure of the reason for the conference. What do you want to accomplish? List the points you want to cover and think about what you are going to say.
- *Get to know the parents.* This is not wasted time; the more effectively you establish rapport with a parent, the more you will accomplish in the long run.
- *Avoid an authoritative atmosphere.* Do not sit behind your desk while the parent sits in a child's chair. Treat parents and others like the adults they are.
- *Communicate at the parent's level.* Do not condescend or patronize. Instead, use words, phrases, and explanations the parent understands and is familiar with. Do not use jargon or complicated explanations, and speak in your natural, conversational style.
- *Accentuate the positive.* Make every effort to show and tell the parent what the child is doing well. When you deal with problems, put them in the proper perspective: identify what the child is able to do, what the goals and purposes of the learning program are, what specific skill or concept you are trying to get the child to learn, and what problems the child is having in achieving. Most important, explain what you plan to do to help the child achieve and what specific role the parent can play in meeting the achievement goals.
- *Give families a chance to talk.* You will not learn much about them if you do all the talking, nor are you likely to achieve your goals. Professionals are often accustomed to dominating a conversation, but many parents will not be as verbal as you, so you will have to encourage families to talk.
- *Learn to listen.* An active listener holds eye contact, uses body language such as head nodding and hand gestures, does not interrupt, avoids arguing, paraphrases as a way of clarifying ideas, and keeps the conversation on track.
- *Follow up.* Ask the parent for a definite time for the next conference as you are concluding the current one. Another conference is the best method of solidifying gains and extending support, but other acceptable means of follow-up are telephone calls, written reports, notes sent with children, and brief visits to the home. Even though these types of contacts may appear casual, they should be planned for and conducted as seriously as any regular parent–professional conference. No matter which approach you choose, parent–professional conferences have many benefits:
  - Families see that you genuinely care about their children.
  - Participants can clarify problems, issues, advice, and directions.
  - Parents, family members, and children are encouraged to continue to do their best.
  - Conferences offer opportunities to extend classroom learning to the home.
  - You can extend programs initiated to help families or formulate new plans.
- *Develop an action plan.* Never leave the parent with a sense of frustration, unsure of what you will be doing or what they are to do. Every communication with families should end on a positive note, so that everyone knows what is to be done and how.

Children and Conferences. A frequently asked question is, Should children be present at parent–teacher conferences? The answer is, Yes, of course . . . if it is appropriate for them to be present. In most instances, it is appropriate and offers a number of benefits:

- Children have much to contribute. They can talk about their progress and behavior, offer suggestions for improvement and enrichment, and discuss their interests.
- The locus of control is centered in the child. Children learn that they have a voice and that others think their opinions are important.
- Children's self-esteem is enhanced because they are viewed as an important part of the conference and because a major purpose of the conference is to help them and their families.
- Children become more involved in their classroom and education. Students take pride not only in their own accomplishments and their ability to share them, but also in the opportunity to help each other prepare for their conferences. A team spirit—a sense of community—can emerge and benefit everyone involved.[2]
- Children learn that education is a cooperative process between home and school.

Telephone Contacts. When it is impossible to arrange a face-to-face conference as a follow-up, a telephone call is an efficient way to contact families (although, unfortunately, not all families have a telephone). The same guidelines apply to face-to-face and telephone conferences, in addition to these special tips:

- Because you cannot see someone on the phone, it takes a little longer to build rapport and trust. However, the time you spend overcoming families' initial fears and apprehensions will pay dividends later.
- Constantly clarify what you are talking about and what you and the families have agreed to do, using such phrases as, "What I heard you say then . . . ," and "So far, we have agreed that. . . . "
- Do not act hurried. Even though there is a limit to the amount of time you can spend on the phone, you may be one of the few people who cares about the parent and the child, and your telephone contact may be a major part of the family's support system.

SINGLE-PARENT FAMILIES

Many of the children you teach will be from single-parent families. Depending on where you teach, as many as 50 percent of your children could be from single-parent families. Here are some things you can do to ensure that single-parent families are involved.

First, many adults in one-parent families are employed during school hours and may not be available for conferences or other activities during that time. You must be willing to accommodate family schedules by arranging conferences at other times, perhaps early morning, noon, late afternoon, or early evening. Some employers, sensitive to these needs, give release time to participate in school functions, but others do not. In addition, professionals and principals need to think seriously about going to families, rather than having families always come to them.

Second, remember that single parents have a limited amount of time to spend on involvement with their children's school and with their children at home. Therefore, when you talk with single-parent families, make sure that (a) the meeting starts on time, (b) you have a list of items to discuss, (c) you have sample materials available to illustrate all points, (d) you make specific suggestions relative to one-parent environments, and (e) the meeting ends on time. Because one-parent families are more likely to need child care assistance to attend meetings, child care should be planned for every parent meeting or activity.

FIGURE 17.3 Involving Single and Working Parents

An increasing number of children live in single-parent and stepfamilies. Many also live in foster families and other nontraditional family forms. In addition, in many two-parent families, both parents work full days, so children come home to an empty house. Thus, involving single and working parents presents many challenges to schools.

Communication

- Avoid making the assumption that students live with both biological parents.
- Avoid the traditional "Dear Parents" greeting in letters and other messages; instead use "Dear Parent," "Dear Family," "Friends," or some other form of greeting.
- Develop a system of keeping noncustodial parents informed of their children's school progress.
- Demonstrate sensitivity to the rights of noncustodial parents. Inform parents that schools may not withhold information from noncustodial parents who have the legal right to see their children's records.
- Develop a simple unobtrusive system to keep track of family changes:
  - At the beginning of the year ask for the names and addresses of individuals to be informed about each child and involved in school activities.
  - At midyear send a form to each child's parent or guardian to verify that the information is still accurate. Invite the parent or guardian to indicate any changes.
- Place flyers about school events on bulletin boards of major companies in the community that are family friendly to learning.

Involvement

- Hold parent–teacher conferences and other school events in the evenings.
- Welcome other children at such events, and provide organized activities or child care services.
- Provide teachers and counselors with in-service training that sensitizes them to special problems faced by children of single and working parents and by the parents themselves.
- Gather information on whether joint or separate parent conferences need to be scheduled with parents.
- Sponsor evening and weekend learning activities at which parents can participate and learn with their children.
- Work with local businesses to arrange released time from work so that parents can attend conferences, volunteer, or otherwise spend time at their child's school when it is in session.

Source: U.S. Department of Education, Office of Educational Research and Improvement, *Reaching All Families: Creating Family-Friendly Schools* (1996).

In the Primary Grade segment of the DVD, listen to the teacher talk about the rewards of teaming with parents to help children achieve. Review the ideas in this chapter and identify several things you plan to do to team with parents.

Third, suggest some ways that single parents can make their time with their children meaningful. If a child has trouble following directions, show families how to use home situations to help in this area. For example, children can learn to follow directions while helping with errands, meal preparation, or housework.

Fourth, get to know families' lifestyles and living conditions. For instance, you can recommend that every child have a quiet place to study, but this may be an impossible demand for some households. You need to visit some of the homes in your community before you set meeting times, decide what family involvement activities to implement, and determine what you will ask of families during the year. All professionals, particularly early childhood professionals, need to keep in mind the condition of the home environment when they request that children bring certain items to school or carry out certain tasks at home. And when asking for parents' help, be sensitive to their talents and time constraints.

Fifth, help develop support groups for one-parent families within your school, such as discussion groups and classes on parenting for singles. And be sure to include the needs and abilities of one-parent families in your family involvement activities and programs. After all, single-parent families may represent the majority of families in your program. Figure 17.3 provides some additional suggestions that can guide your involvement of single and working parents.

LANGUAGE-MINORITY PARENTS AND FAMILIES

Language-minority parents are individuals whose English proficiency is minimal and who lack a comprehensive knowledge of the norms and social systems in the United States. Language-minority families often face language and cultural barriers that greatly hamper their ability to become actively involved in their children's education, although many have a great desire and willingness to participate.

Because the culture of language-minority families often differs from that of the majority in a community, those who seek a truly collaborative involvement must take into account the cultural features that can inhibit collaboration. Styles of child rearing and family organization, attitudes toward schooling, organizations around which families center their lives, life goals and values, political influences, and methods of communication within the cultural group all have implications for parent participation.

Language-minority families often lack information about the U.S. educational system—including basic school philosophy, practice, and structure—which can result in misconceptions, fear, and a general reluctance to become involved. Furthermore, this educational system may be quite different from the one these families are used to. They may even have been taught to avoid active involvement in the educational process, preferring to leave all decisions concerning their children's education to professionals and administrators.

The U.S. ideal of a community-controlled and community-supported educational system must be explained to families from cultures in which this concept is not so highly valued. The traditional roles of children, professionals, and administrators in the United States also have to be explained. Many families need to be taught to assume their roles and obligations in their children's schooling. The Diversity Tie-In on page 512 includes some useful suggestions for involving Hispanic parents in their children's schools.

The following culturally sensitive suggestions are provided by Janet Gonzalez-Mena[3]:

- *Know what each parent in your program wants for his or her child.* Find out families' goals. What are their caregiving practices? What concerns do they have about their child? Encourage them to talk about all of this. Encourage them to ask questions. Encourage the conflicts to surface—to come out in the open.
- *Become clear about your own values and goals.* Know what you believe in. Have a bottom line, but leave space above it to be flexible. When you are clear, you are less likely to present a defensive stance in the face of conflict. When we are ambiguous, we come on the strongest.
- *Become sensitive to your own discomfort.* Tune in on those times when something bothers you instead of just ignoring it and hoping it will go away. Work to identify what specific behaviors of others make you uncomfortable. Try to discover exactly what in yourself creates this discomfort. A conflict may be brewing.
- *Build relationships.* When you do this, you enhance your chances for conflict management or resolution. Be patient. Building relationships takes time, but it enhances communications and understandings. You'll communicate better if you have a relationship, and you'll have a relationship if you learn to communicate.
- *Become effective cross-cultural communicators.* It is possible to learn these communication skills. Learn about communication styles that are different from your own. Teach your own communication styles. What you think a person means may not be what he or she *really* means. Do not make assumptions. Listen carefully. Ask for clarification. Find ways to test for understanding.
- *Learn how to create dialogue*—how to open communication instead of shutting it down. Often, if you accept and acknowledge the other person's feelings, you encourage him or her to open up. Learn ways to let others know that you are aware of and sensitive to their feelings.
- *Use a problem-solving rather than a power approach to conflicts.* Be flexible—negotiate when possible. Look at your willingness to share power. Is it a control issue you are dealing with?

GETTING HISPANIC PARENTS INVOLVED IN SCHOOLS

Because parents play such a powerful role in their children's educational development, early childhood programs must make every effort to involve the parents and families of *all* children. Unfortunately, many minority parents are not included at all or not to the extent to which they should be. The urgency of involving minority parents becomes more evident when we look at the population growth of minorities. For example, the Bureau of the Census estimates that by 2025, 25 percent of all school-age children in the United States will be Hispanic.

"Historically, we know that Hispanics don't feel welcome in schools, and that's been a barrier to recruiting Hispanic parents," said Mark Townsend, Colorado PTA president and a board member of the National PTA.[*]

In order to welcome and involve Hispanic parents, the National PTA launched its Hispanic outreach initiative in 2002 in California, Florida, and Texas, using billboards and other advertisements in Spanish, such as "Los buenos padres no nacen. Se hacen." ("Good parents are not born. They are developed.")

Across the country more emphasis will be placed on how to make Hispanic and other minority parents feel welcome and involved in their children's schools. According to Delia Pompa, chair of the National PTA Hispanic Outreach Advisory Board, "Whether or not your PTA serves a community that is heavily Hispanic, this initiative is just a first step in helping all PTAs reach out to parents of many languages and cultures. Through this Hispanic outreach initiative, we hope to learn and model best practices for reaching out to and including all parents in PTA."[†]

Programs that have successfully involved Hispanic parents recommend the following strategies:

- *Personal touch*—Use face-to-face communication in the Hispanic parents' primary language when first making contact. It may take several personal meetings before parents gain sufficient trust to actively participate.
  - Make home visits if possible, taking Spanish-speaking parents with you to interpret for you. Remember, parents trust parents!
  - Have parents invite other parents to school, where you can talk personally to a small group.
    - Always greet parents whenever they come to school for any reason.
- *Nonjudgmental communication*—Avoid making Hispanic parents feel that they are to blame for or are doing something wrong. Support parents for their strengths rather than judging them for perceived failings.
  - Be an active listener—pay close attention to what parents are saying and how they are saying it.
  - Be willing to compromise.
- *Bilingual support*—Communicate with Hispanic parents in both Spanish and English.
  - Send all notes and flyers home in Spanish. Spanish-speaking parents can help you compose notes and announcements.
  - Designate a Hispanic parent as the contact for your classroom to keep other parents informed about upcoming meetings.
  - Establish a Spanish book corner where students and parents can check out bilingual or Spanish books to read together.
- *Staff development focused on Hispanic culture*—All staff must understand the key features of Hispanic culture—Latino history, traditions, values, and customs—and their impact on students' behavior and learning styles. For example, Hispanic children like peer-oriented learning, so mixed-age grouping and cooperative learning strategies work well. You should learn as much as possible about the children and their culture.
- *Community outreach*—Many Hispanic families can benefit from family literacy programs, vocational training, ESL programs, improved medical and dental services, and other community-based social services.[‡]

---

[*] Medina, "Push on to Recruit Latinos for Parent-Teacher Groups, *New York Times* (Sept. 16, 2002) A: 14.

[†] Ibid.

[‡] Linda Espinosa, "Hispanic Parent Involvement in Early Childhood Programs," *ERIC Digest* (1995), http://www.ericdigests.org/1996-1/hispanic.htm.

- *Commit yourself to education*—both your own and that of the families. Sometimes lack of information or understanding of each other's perspective is what keeps the conflict going.

TEENAGE PARENTS

At one time most teenage parents were married, but today the majority are not. Further, most teenage mothers elect to keep their children rather than put them up for adoption and are rearing them in single-parent families. Teenage families frequently live within extended families, and the child's grandmother often serves as the primary caregiver. Regardless of their living arrangements, teenage parents have the following needs:

- *Support in their role as parents.* Support can include information about child-rearing practices and child development and help in implementing the information in their interactions with their children.
- *Support in their continuing development as adolescents and young adults.* Remember that younger teenage parents are really children themselves. They need assistance in meeting their own developmental needs, as well as those of their children.
- *Help with completing their own education.* Some early childhood programs provide parenting courses as well as classes designed to help teenage parents complete requirements for a high school diploma. Remember that a critical influence on children's development is the mother's education level.

As early childhood programs enroll more children of teenage families, they must attend to creatively and sensitively involving these families in order to support the development of families and children.

FATHERS

More fathers are involved in parenting responsibilities today than ever before; more than one fifth of preschool children are cared for by their fathers while their mothers work outside the home.[4] The implication is clear: early childhood professionals must make special efforts to involve all fathers in their programs.

More professionals now recognize that fathering and mothering are complementary processes. Many fathers are competent caregivers, directly supervising children, helping set the tone for family life, providing stability in a relationship, supporting a mother's parenting role and career goals, and representing a masculine role model for the children. And more fathers are turning to professionals for support and advice.

There are many styles of fathering. Some fathers are at home while their wives work; some have custody of their children; some are single; some dominate home life and control everything; some are passive and exert little influence in the home; some are frequently absent because their work requires travel; some take little interest in their homes and families; some are surrogates. Regardless of the roles fathers play, as an early childhood professional you must make special efforts to involve them. Here are some father-friendly ideas you can use to encourage their involvement:

- Invite fathers to your class or program. Make sure they are included in all your parent/family initiatives.
- Make fathers feel welcome in your program.
- Send a simple survey home to fathers, asking them how they would like to be involved in their children's education. Keep in mind the six types of parent/family involvement.
- Provide special fatherhood and parenting classes for fathers.

• Have fathers invite other fathers to be involved. Fathers may think no other fathers are involved until they themselves get involved.

OTHER CAREGIVERS

Children of two-career and single-parent families often are cared for by nannies, au pairs, babysitters, or housekeepers. Whatever their title, these adults usually play significant roles in children's lives. Many early childhood programs and schools are reaching out to involve them in activities, such as professional conferences, help with field trips, and supervision of homework. Their involvement should begin with family approval in order to achieve a cooperative working relationship.

COMMUNITY INVOLVEMENT AND MORE

Early childhood professionals are realizing that neither they alone nor the limited resources of their programs are sufficient to meet the needs of many children and families. Consequently, professionals are seeking ways to link families to community services and resources. For example, if a child needs clothing, a professional who is aware of community resources might contact the local Salvation Army for assistance.

COMMUNITY RESOURCES

The community offers a vital and rich array of resources to help you meet the needs of parents and children. Following are suggested actions you can take to learn to use your community in your teaching:

• *Know your students and their needs.* Through observations, conferences with parents, and discussions with students, you can identify barriers to children's learning and discover what kind of help to seek.
• *Know your community.* Walk or drive around the community. Ask a parent to give you a tour to help familiarize you with agencies and individuals. Read the local newspaper, and attend community events and activities.
• *Ask for help and support from parents and the community.* Keep in mind that many parents will not be involved unless you personally ask them. The only encouragement many individuals and local businesses need is your invitation.
• *Develop a directory of community agencies.* Consult the business pages of local phone books, contact local chambers of commerce, and ask parents what agencies are helpful to them.
• *Compile a list of people who are willing to come to your classroom to speak to or work with your students.* You can start by asking parents to volunteer and to give suggestions and recommendations of others.

Only by helping families meet their needs and those of their children will you create opportunities for these children to reach their full potential. For this reason alone, family involvement programs and activities must be an essential part of every early childhood program.

SCHOOL-BUSINESS INVOLVEMENT

One good way to build social capital in the community is through school-business involvement. More early childhood programs are developing this link as a means of strengthening their programs and helping children and families. For their part, businesses are anxious to develop the connection in order to help schools better educate children.

NATIONAL ORGANIZATIONS

National programs dedicated to family involvement are another rich resource for information and support. Some of these are listed here:

- Institute for Responsive Education (IRE), http://www.responsiveeducation.org
- National Committee for Citizens in Education (NCCE), 800-638-9675
- Mega Skills Education Center, http://www.megaskillshsi.org
- National PTA, www.pta.org

Another organization, the Family Involvement Partnership for Learning, promotes children's learning through the development of family/school/community partnerships. This organization began as a cooperative effort between the U.S. Department of Education and the National Coalition for Parent Involvement in Education (NCPIE). A coalition of more than one hundred national education and advocacy organizations, NCPIE has been meeting for more than twenty years to advocate the involvement of families in their children's education and to promote relationships among home, school, and community that can enhance the education of all children and youth. NCPIE represents parents, schools, communities, religious groups, and businesses.[6]

WEBSITE CONNECTIONS

Many websites are available to help parents become more involved in their children's education. For example, the Family Education Network (http://www.familyeducation.com) offers resources and features on a wide array of educational topics. You can find other sites by entering the following keywords into one of the Internet's many available search engines:

- parent involvement
- community involvement
- school partnerships
- school/business relationships
- school/community collaboration

The challenge to early childhood professionals today is quite clear. Merely seeking ways to involve parents in school activities is no longer sufficient. Our challenge is to make families the focus of our involvement activities so that their lives and their children's lives are made better. We must help families and children access the opportunities of the twenty-first century.

Companion Website To learn more about the Institute for Responsive Education, the National Parent Teacher Association, and other national organizations, go to the Companion Website at **www.prenhall.com/morrison,** select chapter 17, then choose the Linking to Learning module.

Companion Website
For additional Internet resources or to complete an online activity for this chapter, go to the Companion Website at **www.prenhall.com/morrison,** select chapter 17, then choose the Linking to Learning or Making Connections module.

LINKING TO LEARNING

Edvantia
http://www.edvantia.org/

> *Offers ways to keep abreast of what's happening with school-community partnerships to address the pressing needs of children and their families.*

Early Childhood Educators' and Family Web Corner
http://users.sgi.net/~cokids/

> *Provides links to teacher pages, family pages, articles, and staff development resources.*

Family Education Network
http://www.familyeducation.com

> *Committed to strengthening and empowering families by providing communities with the counseling, education, resources, information, and training needed to promote a positive and nurturing environment in which to raise children.*

Institute for Responsive Education
http://www.responsiveeducation.org

> *A research-based assistance and advocacy agency promoting the partnership of schools, families, and communities with the ultimate goal of success for all children. Focused on urban educational reform in the United States; enriched and informed by also examining, communicating, and working with rural and urban schools throughout the world.*

National Coalition for Parent Involvement in Education
http://www.ncpie.org/

> *Dedicated to developing family-school partnerships throughout America, involving parents and families in their children's lives and fostering relationships among home, school, and community, all of which can enhance the education of our nation's young people.*

National Parent Teacher Association (PTA)
http://www.pta.org/

> *Calls for schools to promote partnerships that will increase parent involvement and participation in the social, emotional, and academic growth of children; has voluntary National Standards for Parent/Family Involvement Programs.*

Single & Custodial Fathers Network
http://www.scfn.org/index.html

> *A place for men who are primary caregivers to go to explore everything from cooking to balancing work and family. Also provides articles and links to more than twenty other sites.*

ACTIVITIES FOR FURTHER ENRICHMENT

ETHICAL DILEMMA: "I REALLY DON'T WANT TO GET INVOLVED."

Your school has enrolled a number of new families who were displaced by a recent hurricane. Six-year-old Tamika and her family arrived in town with only the clothes on their backs. You notice that Tamika has not had a change of clothing in several days. You mention to her teacher that there are several community agencies that could provide the family with clothing and other resources, but she responds, "I know, Wendy, but I don't have the time to mess around with this stuff. I've got all I can do to keep up with the things I have to do in the classroom. I don't want to make a lot of extra work for myself. Besides, I really don't want to get involved with these families; they just don't fit into our community."

What should you do to help Tamika and her family? Should you report her teacher to the principal or offer to buy Tamika and her family clothing or call your friend at the Salvation Army for help or develop another strategy?

APPLICATIONS

1. List the various ways early childhood professionals communicate pupils' progress to families. Which methods do you think are the most and least effective? What specific methods do you plan to use?
2. Describe the methods and techniques you would use to publicize a parent meeting about plans to involve families in their children's education.
3. You have just been appointed the program director for a family involvement program targeting first grade. Write objectives for the program. Develop specific activities for involving families and providing services to them.
4. Develop specific guidelines that a child care center could use to facilitate the involvement of fathers, language-minority families, and families of children with disabilities.

FIELD EXPERIENCES

1. Arrange with a local school district to be present during a parent–teacher conference. Discuss with the teacher, prior to the visit, his or her objectives and procedures. After the conference, assess its success with the teacher.
2. As discussed in this chapter, there are many ways to involve parents, family members, and the community.
   a. Identify your goals for family involvement and support.
   b. Develop a plan for implementing the goals that you identified.
   c. Develop a plan for specifically involving fathers in your program.
3. List six reasons that early childhood professionals might resist involving families. For each reason, give two strategies for overcoming the resistance.
4. Conduct a poll of parents to find out (a) how they think early childhood programs and schools can help them educate their children, (b) how they think they can be involved in early childhood programs, (c) what specific help they feel they need in child rearing/educating, and (d) what activities they would like in a home visitation program.

RESEARCH

1. Visit social services agencies in your area, and list the services they offer.
   a. Describe how early childhood professionals can work with these agencies to meet the needs of children and families.
   b. Invite agency directors to meet with your class to discuss how they and early childhood professionals can work cooperatively to help families and children.

2. As families change, so, too, do the services they need. Interview families in as many settings as possible (e.g., urban, suburban, rural), from as many socioeconomic backgrounds as possible, and from as many kinds of families as possible. Determine what services they believe could help them most, and then tell how you as a professional could help provide those services.
3. For the grade level that you plan to teach, develop a list of bilingual books and other materials that you could include in your classroom's Spanish book corner.
4. Develop plans for a one-hour workshop to help parents improve their children's grades and study skills. How would you tailor your workshop to Hispanic families?

READINGS FOR FURTHER ENRICHMENT

Barbour, Chandler, Nita Barbour, and Patricia Scully. *Families, Schools, and Communities: Building Partnerships for Educating Children,* 3rd ed. Upper Saddle River, NJ: Merrill/Prentice Hall, 2005.

Explores the interconnectedness of children's circles—home, school, and community. Advocates teaching strategies and curricula that are developmentally and culturally appropriate and that enfold each child's family and community into his or her education as equal partners with the school, its teachers, and its administration.

Gonzalez-Mena, Janet. *The Young Child in the Family and the Community,* 4th ed. Upper Saddle River, NJ: Merrill/Prentice Hall, 2006.

Recognizes that socialization is one of the most important aspects of child development and examines socialization issues of young children during child rearing, in child care facilities, and in the early education system.

Mierzwik, Diane. *Quick and Easy Ways to Connect with Students and Their Parents, Grades K–8: Improving Student Achievement Through Parent Involvement.* London: Sage, 2004.

Offers teachers clear, practical activities they can use to fine-tune the things they are already doing, in order to build effective relationships with students, parents, and the community.

Olsen, G., and M. L. Fuller. *Home-School Relations: Working Successfully with Parents and Families,* 2nd ed. Boston: Allyn and Bacon, 2003.

Examines the nature of the contemporary family and its relationship to the school and provides practical advice for developing strong home-school relationships. Discusses the need for educators to have positive working relationships with their students and describes the techniques they must use to understand the families from which their students come.

Wright, K., D. A. Stegelin, and L. Hartle. *Building Family, School, and Community Partnerships,* 3rd ed. Upper Saddle River, NJ: Merrill/Prentice Hall, 2007.

Profiles today's diverse American family structures and examines the special relationships among them, their children's schools, and their communities. Through an ecological systems approach, explores the family as a child's first teacher. Provides a wealth of strategies for involving parents and other family members in a child's education.

ENDNOTES

1. U.S. Census Bureau, "Facts for Features: Grandparents Day 2005: Sept. 11," www.census.gov/Press-Release/www/releases/archives/facts_for_features_special_editions/005353.html.

2. Richard J. Stiggins, *Student-Centered Classroom Assessment,* 2nd ed. (Upper Saddle River, NJ: Merrill/Prentice Hall, 1997), 499.

3. Reprinted by permission from J. González-Mena, "Taking a Culturally Sensitive Approach in Infant-Toddler Programs," *Young Children* 1 (1992): 8–9.

4. J. S. Coleman, *Parental Involvement in Education* (Washington, DC: U.S. Department of Education, 1991), 7.

5. Family Involvement Partnership for Learning, *Community Update #23* (Washington, DC: Author, April 1995).

Appendix A

NAEYC Code of Ethical Conduct and Statement of Commitment

PREAMBLE

NAEYC recognizes that those who work with young children face many daily decisions that have moral and ethical implications. The **NAEYC Code of Ethical Conduct** offers guidelines for responsible behavior and sets forth a common basis for resolving the principal ethical dilemmas encountered in early childhood care and education. The **Statement of Commitment** is not part of the Code but is a personal acknowledgement of an individual's willingness to embrace the distinctive values and moral obligations of the field of early childhood care and education. The primary focus of the Code is on daily practice with children and their families in programs for children from birth through 8 years of age, such as infant/toddler programs, preschool and prekindergarten programs, child care centers, hospital and child life settings, family child care homes, kindergartens, and primary classrooms. When the issues involve young children, then these provisions also apply to specialists who do not work directly with children, including program administrators, parent educators, early childhood adult educators, and officials with responsibility for program monitoring and licensing. (Note: See also the "Code of Ethical Conduct: Supplement for Early Childhood Adult Educators," online at http://www.naeyc.org/about/positions/asp/ethics04.)

CORE VALUES

Standards of ethical behavior in early childhood care and education are based on commitment to the following core values that are deeply rooted in the history of the field of early childhood care and education. We have made a commitment to

- Appreciate childhood as a unique and valuable stage of the human life cycle

- Base our work on knowledge of how children develop and learn
- Appreciate and support the bond between the child and family
- Recognize that children are best understood and supported in the context of family, culture,[1] community, and society
- Respect the dignity, worth, and uniqueness of each individual (child, family member, and colleague)
- Respect diversity in children, families, and colleagues
- Recognize that children and adults achieve their full potential in the context of relationships that are based on trust and respect

CONCEPTUAL FRAMEWORK

The Code sets forth a framework of professional responsibilities in four sections. Each section addresses an area of professional relationships: (1) with children, (2) with families, (3) among colleagues, and (4) with the community and society. Each section includes an introduction to the primary responsibilities of the early childhood practitioner in that context. The introduction is followed by a set of ideals (I) that reflect exemplary professional practice and by a set of principles (P) describing practices that are required, prohibited, or permitted.

The **ideals** reflect the aspirations of practitioners. The **principles** guide conduct and assist practitioners in resolving ethical dilemmas.[2] Both ideals and principles are intended to direct practitioners to those questions which, when responsibly answered, can provide the basis for conscientious decision making. While the Code provides specific direction for addressing

Source: From the National Association for the Education of Young Children, Washington, DC, 2005. Reprinted by permission. Revised April 2005. Endorsed by the Association for Childhood Education International.

[1]*Culture* includes ethnicity, racial identity, economic level, family structure, language, and religious and political beliefs, which profoundly influence each child's development and relationship to the world.

[2]There is not necessarily a corresponding principle for each ideal.

some ethical dilemmas, many others will require the practitioner to combine the guidance of the Code with professional judgment.

The ideals and principles in this Code present a shared framework of professional responsibility that affirms our commitment to the core values of our field. The Code publicly acknowledges the responsibilities that we in the field have assumed, and in so doing supports ethical behavior in our work. Practitioners who face situations with ethical dimensions are urged to seek guidance in the applicable parts of this Code and in the spirit that informs the whole.

Often "the right answer"—the best ethical course of action to take—is not obvious. There may be no readily apparent, positive way to handle a situation. When one important value contradicts another, we face an ethical dilemma. When we face a dilemma, it is our professional responsibility to consult the Code and all relevant parties to find the most ethical resolution.

SECTION I: ETHICAL RESPONSIBILITIES TO CHILDREN

Childhood is a unique and valuable stage in the human life cycle. Our paramount responsibility is to provide care and education in settings that are safe, healthy, nurturing, and responsive for each child. We are committed to supporting children's development and learning; respecting individual differences; and helping children learn to live, play, and work cooperatively. We are also committed to promoting children's self-awareness, competence, self-worth, resiliency, and physical well-being.

IDEALS

I-1.1—To be familiar with the knowledge base of early childhood care and education and to stay informed through continuing education and training.

I-1.2—To base program practices upon current knowledge and research in the field of early childhood education, child development, and related disciplines, as well as on particular knowledge of each child.

I-1.3—To recognize and respect the unique qualities, abilities, and potential of each child.

I-1.4—To appreciate the vulnerability of children and their dependence on adults.

I-1.5—To create and maintain safe and healthy settings that foster children's social, emotional, cognitive, and physical development and that respect their dignity and their contributions.

I-1.6—To use assessment instruments and strategies that are appropriate for the children to be assessed, that are used only for the purposes for which they were designed, and that have the potential to benefit children.

I-1.7—To use assessment information to understand and support children's development and learning, to support instruction, and to identify children who may need additional services.

I-1.8—To support the right of each child to play and learn in an inclusive environment that meets the needs of children with and without disabilities.

I-1.9—To advocate for and ensure that all children, including those with special needs, have access to the support services needed to be successful.

I-1.10—To ensure that each child's culture, language, ethnicity, and family structure are recognized and valued in the program.

I-1.11—To provide all children with experiences in a language that they know, as well as support children in maintaining the use of their home language and in learning English.

I-1.12—To work with families to provide a safe and smooth transition as children and families move from one program to the next.

PRINCIPLES

P-1.1—**Above all, we shall not harm children. We shall not participate in practices that are emotionally damaging, physically harmful, disrespectful, degrading, dangerous, exploitative, or intimidating to children.** *This principle has precedence over all others in this Code.*

P-1.2—We shall care for and educate children in positive emotional and social environments that are cognitively stimulating and that support each child's culture, language, ethnicity, and family structure.

P-1.3—We shall not participate in practices that discriminate against children by denying benefits, giving special advantages, or excluding them from programs or activities on the basis of their sex, race, national origin, religious beliefs, medical condition, disability, or the marital status/ family structure, sexual orientation, or religious beliefs or other affiliations of their families. (Aspects of this principle do not apply in programs that have a lawful mandate to provide services to a particular population of children.)

P-1.4—We shall involve all those with relevant knowledge (including families and staff) in decisions concerning a child, as appropriate, ensuring confidentiality of sensitive information.

P-1.5—We shall use appropriate assessment systems, which include multiple sources of information, to provide information on children's learning and development.

P-1.6—We shall strive to ensure that decisions such as those related to enrollment, retention, or assignment to special education services, will be based on multiple sources of information and will never be based on a single assessment, such as a test score or a single observation.

P-1.7—We shall strive to build individual relationships with each child; make individualized adaptations in teaching strategies, learning environments, and curricula; and consult with the family so that each child benefits from the program. If after such efforts have been exhausted, the current placement does not meet a child's needs, or the child is seriously jeopardizing the ability of other children to benefit from the program, we shall collaborate with the child's family and appropriate specialists to determine the additional services needed and/or the placement option(s) most likely to ensure the child's success. (Aspects of this principle may not apply in programs that have a lawful mandate to provide services to a particular population of children.)

P-1.8—We shall be familiar with the risk factors for and symptoms of child abuse and neglect, including physical, sexual, verbal, and emotional abuse and physical, emotional, educational, and medical neglect. We shall know and follow state laws and community procedures that protect children against abuse and neglect.

P-1.9—When we have reasonable cause to suspect child abuse or neglect, we shall report it to the appropriate community agency and follow up to ensure that appropriate action has been taken. When appropriate, parents or guardians will be informed that the referral will be or has been made.

P-1.10—When another person tells us of his or her suspicion that a child is being abused or neglected, we shall assist that person in taking appropriate action in order to protect the child.

P-1.11—When we become aware of a practice or situation that endangers the health, safety, or well-being of children, we have an ethical responsibility to protect children or inform parents and/or others who can.

SECTION II: ETHICAL RESPONSIBILITIES TO FAMILIES

Families[3] are of primary importance in children's development. Because the family and the early childhood practitioner have a common interest in the child's well-being, we acknowledge a primary responsibility to bring about communication, cooperation, and collaboration between the home and early childhood program in ways that enhance the child's development.

IDEALS

I-2.1—To be familiar with the knowledge base related to working effectively with families and to stay informed through continuing education and training.

I-2.2—To develop relationships of mutual trust and create partnerships with the families we serve.

I-2.3—To welcome all family members and encourage them to participate in the program.

I-2.4—To listen to families, acknowledge and build upon their strengths and competencies, and learn from families as we support them in their task of nurturing children.

I-2.5—To respect the dignity and preferences of each family and to make an effort to learn about its structure, culture, language, customs, and beliefs.

I-2.6—To acknowledge families' childrearing values and their right to make decisions for their children.

I-2.7—To share information about each child's education and development with families and to help them understand and appreciate the current knowledge base of the early childhood profession.

I-2.8—To help family members enhance their understanding of their children and support the continuing development of their skills as parents.

I-2.9—To participate in building support networks for families by providing them with opportunities to interact with program staff, other families, community resources, and professional services.

PRINCIPLES

P-2.1—We shall not deny family members access to their child's classroom or program setting unless access is denied by court order or other legal restriction.

P-2.2—We shall inform families of program philosophy, policies, curriculum, assessment system, and personnel qualifications, and explain why we teach as we do—which should be in accordance with our ethical responsibilities to children (see Section I).

P-2.3—We shall inform families of and, when appropriate, involve them in policy decisions.

P-2.4—We shall involve the family in significant decisions affecting their child.

P-2.5—We shall make every effort to communicate effectively with all families in a language that they understand. We shall use community resources for translation and interpretation when we do not have sufficient resources in our own programs.

P-2.6—As families share information with us about their children and families, we shall consider this information to plan and implement the program.

P-2.7—We shall inform families about the nature and purpose of the program's child assessments and how data about their child will be used.

P-2.8—We shall treat child assessment information confidentially and share this information only when there is a legitimate need for it.

P-2.9—We shall inform the family of injuries and incidents involving their child, of risks such as exposures to communicable diseases that might result in infection, and of occurrences that might result in emotional stress.

P-2.10—Families shall be fully informed of any proposed research projects involving their children and shall have the opportunity to give or withhold consent without penalty. We shall not permit or participate in research that could in any way hinder the education, development, or well-being of children.

P-2.11—We shall not engage in or support exploitation of families. We shall not use our relationship with a family for private advantage or personal gain, or enter into relationships with family members that might impair our effectiveness working with their children.

P-2.12—We shall develop written policies for the protection of confidentiality and the disclosure of children's records. These

---

[3]The term *family* may include those adults, besides parents, with the responsibility of being involved in educating, nurturing, and advocating for the child.

policy documents shall be made available to all program personnel and families. Disclosure of children's records beyond family members, program personnel, and consultants having an obligation of confidentiality shall require familial consent (except in cases of abuse or neglect).

P-2.13—We shall maintain confidentiality and shall respect the family's right to privacy, refraining from disclosure of confidential information and intrusion into family life. However, when we have reason to believe that a child's welfare is at risk, it is permissible to share confidential information with agencies, as well as with individuals who have legal responsibility for intervening in the child's interest.

P-2.14—In cases where family members are in conflict with one another, we shall work openly, sharing our observations of the child, to help all parties involved make informed decisions. We shall refrain from becoming an advocate for one party.

P-2.15—We shall be familiar with and appropriately refer families to community resources and professional support services. After a referral has been made, we shall follow up to ensure that services have been appropriately provided.

SECTION III: ETHICAL RESPONSIBILITIES TO COLLEAGUES

In a caring, cooperative workplace, human dignity is respected, professional satisfaction is promoted, and positive relationships are developed and sustained. Based upon our core values, our primary responsibility to colleagues is to establish and maintain settings and relationships that support productive work and meet professional needs. The same ideals that apply to children also apply as we interact with adults in the workplace.

A—Responsibilities to co-workers

IDEALS

I-3A.1—To establish and maintain relationships of respect, trust, confidentiality, collaboration, and cooperation with co-workers.

I-3A.2—To share resources with co-workers, collaborating to ensure that the best possible early childhood care and education program is provided.

I-3A.3—To support co-workers in meeting their professional needs and in their professional development.

I-3A.4—To accord co-workers due recognition of professional achievement.

PRINCIPLES

P-3A.1—We shall recognize the contributions of colleagues to our program and not participate in practices that diminish their reputations or impair their effectiveness in working with children and families.

P-3A.2—When we have concerns about the professional behavior of a co-worker, we shall first let that person know of our concern in a way that shows respect for personal dignity and for the diversity to be found among staff members, and then attempt to resolve the matter collegially and in a confidential manner.

P-3A.3—We shall exercise care in expressing views regarding the personal attributes or professional conduct of co-workers. Statements should be based on firsthand knowledge, not hearsay, and relevant to the interests of children and programs.

P-3A.4—We shall not participate in practices that discriminate against a co-worker because of sex, race, national origin, religious beliefs or other affiliations, age, marital status/family structure, disability, or sexual orientation.

B—Responsibilities to employers

IDEALS

I-3B.1—To assist the program in providing the highest quality of service.

I-3B.2—To do nothing that diminishes the reputation of the program in which we work unless it is violating laws and regulations designed to protect children or is violating the provisions of this Code.

PRINCIPLES

P-3B.1—We shall follow all program policies. When we do not agree with program policies, we shall attempt to effect change through constructive action within the organization.

P-3B.2—We shall speak or act on behalf of an organization only when authorized. We shall take care to acknowledge when we are speaking for the organization and when we are expressing a personal judgment.

P-3B.3—We shall not violate laws or regulations designed to protect children and shall take appropriate action consistent with this Code when aware of such violations.

P-3B.4—If we have concerns about a colleague's behavior, and children's well-being is not at risk, we may address the concern with that individual. If children are at risk or the situation does not improve after it has been brought to the colleague's attention, we shall report the colleague's unethical or incompetent behavior to an appropriate authority.

P-3B.5—When we have a concern about circumstances or conditions that impact the quality of care and education within the program, we shall inform the program's administration or, when necessary, other appropriate authorities.

C—Responsibilities to employees

IDEALS

I-3C.1—To promote safe and healthy working conditions and policies that foster mutual respect, cooperation, collaboration, competence, well-being, confidentiality, and self-esteem in staff members.

I-3C.2—To create and maintain a climate of trust and candor that will enable staff to speak and act in the best interests of children, families, and the field of early childhood care and education.

I-3C.3—To strive to secure adequate and equitable compensation (salary and benefits) for those who work with or on behalf of young children.

I-3C.4—To encourage and support continual development of employees in becoming more skilled and knowledgeable practitioners.

PRINCIPLES

P-3C.1—In decisions concerning children and programs, we shall draw upon the education, training, experience, and expertise of staff members.

P-3C.2—We shall provide staff members with safe and supportive working conditions that honor confidences and permit them to carry out their responsibilities through fair performance evaluation, written grievance procedures, constructive feedback, and opportunities for continuing professional development and advancement.

P-3C.3—We shall develop and maintain comprehensive written personnel policies that define program standards. These policies shall be given to new staff members and shall be available and easily accessible for review by all staff members.

P-3C.4—We shall inform employees whose performance does not meet program expectations of areas of concern and, when possible, assist in improving their performance.

P-3C.5—We shall conduct employee dismissals for just cause, in accordance with all applicable laws and regulations. We shall inform employees who are dismissed of the reasons for their termination. When a dismissal is for cause, justification must be based on evidence of inadequate or inappropriate behavior that is accurately documented, current, and available for the employee to review.

P-3C.6—In making evaluations and recommendations, we shall make judgments based on fact and relevant to the interests of children and programs.

P-3C.7—We shall make hiring, retention, termination, and promotion decisions based solely on a person's competence, record of accomplishment, ability to carry out the responsibilities of the position, and professional preparation specific to the developmental levels of children in his/her care.

P-3C.8—We shall not make hiring, retention, termination, and promotion decisions based on an individual's sex, race, national origin, religious beliefs or other affiliations, age, marital status/ family structure, disability, or sexual orientation. We shall be familiar with and observe laws and regulations that pertain to employment discrimination. (Aspects of this principle do not apply to programs that have a lawful mandate to determine eligibility based on one or more of the criteria identified above.)

P-3C.9—We shall maintain confidentiality in dealing with issues related to an employee's job performance and shall respect an employee's right to privacy regarding personal issues.

SECTION IV: ETHICAL RESPONSIBILITIES TO COMMUNITY AND SOCIETY

Early childhood programs operate within the context of their immediate community made up of families and other institutions concerned with children's welfare. Our responsibilities to the community are to provide programs that meet the diverse needs of families, to cooperate with agencies and professions that share the responsibility for children, to assist families in gaining access to those agencies and allied professionals, and to assist in the development of community programs that are needed but not currently available.

As individuals, we acknowledge our responsibility to provide the best possible programs of care and education for children and to conduct ourselves with honesty and integrity. Because of our specialized expertise in early childhood development and education and because the larger society shares responsibility for the welfare and protection of young children, we acknowledge a collective obligation to advocate for the best interests of children within early childhood programs and in the larger community and to serve as a voice for young children everywhere.

The ideals and principles in this section are presented to distinguish between those that pertain to the work of the individual early childhood educator and those that more typically are engaged in collectively on behalf of the best interests of children—with the understanding that individual early childhood educators have a shared responsibility for addressing the ideals and principles that are identified as "collective."

IDEAL (INDIVIDUAL)

I-4.—To provide the community with high-quality early childhood care and education programs and services.

IDEALS (COLLECTIVE)

I-4.2—To promote cooperation among professionals and agencies and interdisciplinary collaboration among professions concerned with addressing issues in the health, education, and well-being of young children, their families, and their early childhood educators.

I-4.3—To work through education, research, and advocacy toward an environmentally safe world in which all children receive health care, food, and shelter; are nurtured; and live free from violence in their home and their communities.

I-4.4—To work through education, research, and advocacy toward a society in which all young children have access to high-quality early care and education programs.

I-4.5—To work to ensure that appropriate assessment systems, which include multiple sources of information, are used for purposes that benefit children.

I-4.6—To promote knowledge and understanding of young children and their needs. To work toward greater societal acknowledgment of children's rights and greater social acceptance of responsibility for the well-being of all children.

I-4.7—To support policies and laws that promote the well-being of children and families, and to work to change those that impair their well-being. To participate in developing policies and laws that are needed, and to cooperate with other individuals and groups in these efforts.

I-4.8—To further the professional development of the field of early childhood care and education and to strengthen its commitment to realizing its core values as reflected in this Code.

PRINCIPLES (INDIVIDUAL)

P-4.1—We shall communicate openly and truthfully about the nature and extent of services that we provide.

P-4.2—We shall apply for, accept, and work in positions for which we are personally well-suited and professionally qualified. We shall not offer services that we do not have the competence, qualifications, or resources to provide.

P-4.3—We shall carefully check references and shall not hire or recommend for employment any person whose competence, qualifications, or character makes him or her unsuited for the position.

P-4.4—We shall be objective and accurate in reporting the knowledge upon which we base our program practices.

P-4.5—We shall be knowledgeable about the appropriate use of assessment strategies and instruments and interpret results accurately to families.

P-4.6—We shall be familiar with laws and regulations that serve to protect the children in our programs and be vigilant in ensuring that these laws and regulations are followed.

P-4.7—When we become aware of a practice or situation that endangers the health, safety, or well-being of children, we have an ethical responsibility to protect children or inform parents and/or others who can.

P-4.8—We shall not participate in practices that are in violation of laws and regulations that protect the children in our programs.

P-4.9—When we have evidence that an early childhood program is violating laws or regulations protecting children, we shall report the violation to appropriate authorities who can be expected to remedy the situation.

P-4.10—When a program violates or requires its employees to violate this Code, it is permissible, after fair assessment of the evidence, to disclose the identity of that program.

PRINCIPLES (COLLECTIVE)

P-4.11—When policies are enacted for purposes that do not benefit children, we have a collective responsibility to work to change these practices.

P-4.12—When we have evidence that an agency that provides services intended to ensure children's well-being is failing to meet its obligations, we acknowledge a collective ethical responsibility to report the problem to appropriate authorities or to the public. We shall be vigilant in our follow-up until the situation is resolved.

P-4.13—When a child protection agency fails to provide adequate protection for abused or neglected children, we acknowledge a collective ethical responsibility to work toward the improvement of these services.

Glossary of Terms Related to Ethics

Code of Ethics. Defines the core values of the field and provides guidance for what professionals should do when they encounter conflicting obligations or responsibilities in their work.

Values. Qualities or principles that individuals believe to be desirable or worthwhile and that they prize for themselves, for others, and for the world in which they live.

Core Values. Commitments held by a profession that are consciously and knowingly embraced by its practitioners because they make a contribution to society. There is a difference between personal values and the core values of a profession.

Morality. Peoples' views of what is good, right and proper; their beliefs about their obligations; and their ideas about how they should behave.

Ethics. The study of right and wrong, or duty and obligation, that involves critical reflection on morality and the ability to make choices between values and the examination of the moral dimensions of relationships.

Professional Ethics. The moral commitments of a profession that involve moral reflection that extends and enhances the personal morality practitioners bring to their work, that concern actions of right and wrong in the workplace, and that help individuals resolve moral dilemmas they encounter in their work.

Ethical Responsibilities. Behaviors that one must or must not engage in. Ethical responsibilities are clear-cut and are spelled out in the Code of Ethical Conduct (for example, early childhood educators should never share confidential information about a child or family with a person who has no legitimate need for knowing).

Ethical Dilemma. A moral conflict that involves determining appropriate conduct when an individual faces conflicting professional values and responsibilities.

Sources for Glossary Terms and Definitions

Feeney, S., & N. Freeman. 1999. *Ethics and the early childhood educator: Using the NAEYC code.* Washington, DC: NAEYC.

Kidder, R. M. 1995. *How good people make tough choices: Resolving the dilemmas of ethical living.* New York: Fireside.

Kipnis, K. 1987. How to discuss professional ethics. *Young Children* 42 (4): 26–30.

STATEMENT OF COMMITMENT[4]

As an individual who works with young children, I commit myself to furthering the values of early childhood education as they are reflected in the ideals and principles of the NAEYC Code of Ethical Conduct. To the best of my ability I will

- Never harm children.
- Ensure that programs for young children are based on current knowledge and research of child development and early childhood education.
- Respect and support families in their task of nurturing children.
- Respect colleagues in early childhood care and education and support them in maintaining the NAEYC Code of Ethical Conduct.
- Serve as an advocate for children, their families, and their teachers in community and society.
- Stay informed of and maintain high standards of professional conduct.
- Engage in an ongoing process of self-reflection, realizing that personal characteristics, biases, and beliefs have an impact on children and families.
- Be open to new ideas and be willing to learn from the suggestions of others.
- Continue to learn, grow, and contribute as a professional.
- Honor the ideals and principles of the NAEYC Code of Ethical Conduct.

---

[4]This Statement of Commitment is not part of the Code but is a personal acknowledgment of the individual's willingness to embrace the distinctive values and moral obligations of the field of early childhood care and education. It is recognition of the moral obligations that lead to an individual becoming part of the profession.

Appendix B

NAEYC Guidelines for Developmentally Appropriate Practice in Early Childhood Programs

This statement defines and describes principles of developmentally appropriate practice in early childhood programs for administrators, teachers, parents, policymakers, and others who make decisions about the care and education of young children. An early childhood program is any group program in a center, school, or other facility that serves children from birth through age 8. Early childhood programs include child care centers, family child care homes, private and public preschools, kindergartens, and primary-grade schools.

The early childhood profession is responsible for establishing and promoting standards of high-quality, professional practice in early childhood programs. These standards must reflect current knowledge and shared beliefs about what constitutes high-quality, developmentally appropriate early childhood education in the context within which services are delivered.

This position paper is organized into several components, which include the following:

1. a description of the current context in which early childhood programs operate;
2. a description of the rationale and need for NAEYC's position statement;

Source: From the National Association for the Education of Young Children, Washington, DC, 1997. Reprinted by permission.

3. a statement of NAEYC's commitment to children;
4. the statement of the position and definition of *developmentally appropriate practice;*
5. a summary of the principles of child development and learning and the theoretical perspectives that inform decisions about early childhood practice;
6. guidelines for making decisions about developmentally appropriate practices that address the following integrated components of early childhood practice:creating a caring community of learners, teaching to enhance children's learning and development, constructing appropriate curriculum, assessing children's learning and development, and establishing reciprocal relationships with families;
7. a challenge to the field to move from *either/or* to *both/and* thinking; and
8. recommendations for policies necessary to ensure developmentally appropriate practices for all children.

This statement is designed to be used in conjunction with NAEYC's "Criteria for High Quality Early Childhood Programs," the standards for accreditation by the National Academy of Early Childhood Programs (NAEYC 1991), and with "Guidelines for Appropriate Curriculum Content and Assessment in Programs Serving Children Ages 3 through 8" (NAEYC & NAECS/SDE 1992; Bredekamp & Rosegrant 1992, 1995).

THE CURRENT CONTEXT OF EARLY CHILDHOOD PROGRAMS

The early childhood knowledge base has expanded considerably in recent years, affirming some of the profession's cherished beliefs about good practice and challenging others. In addition to gaining new knowledge, early childhood programs have experienced several important changes in recent years. The number of programs continues to increase not only in response to the growing demand for out-of-home child care but also in recognition of the critical importance of educational experiences during early years (Willer et al. 1991; NCES 1993). For example, in the late 1980s Head Start embarked on the largest expansion in its history, continuing this expansion into the 1990s with significant new services for families with infants and toddlers. The National Education Goals Panel established as an objective of Goal 1 that by the year 2000 all children will have access to high-quality, developmentally appropriate preschool programs (NEGP 1991). Welfare reform portends a greatly increased demand for child care services for even the youngest children from very-low-income families.

Some characteristics of early childhood programs have also changed in recent years. Increasingly, programs serve children and families from diverse cultural and linguistic backgrounds, requiring that all programs demonstrate understanding of and responsiveness to cultural and linguistic diversity. Because culture and language are critical components of children's development, practices cannot be developmentally appropriate unless they are responsive to cultural and linguistic diversity.

The Americans with Disabilities Act and the Individuals with Disabilities Education Act now require that all early childhood programs make reasonable accommodations to provide access for children with disabilities or developmental delays (DEC/CEC & NAEYC 1993). This legal right reflects the growing consensus that young children with disabilities are best served in the same community settings where their typically developing peers are found (DEC/CEC 1994).

The trend toward full inclusion of children with disabilities must be reflected in descriptions of recommended practices, and considerable work has been done toward converging the perspectives of early childhood and early childhood special education (Carta et al. 1991; Mallory 1992, 1994; Wolery, Strain, & Bailey 1992; Bredekamp 1993b; DEC Task Force 1993; Mallory & New 1994b; Wolery & Wilbers 1994).

Other important program characteristics include age of children and length of program day. Children are now enrolled in programs at younger ages, many from infancy. The length of the program day for all ages of children has been extended in response to the need for extended hours of care for employed families. Similarly, program sponsorship has become more diverse. The public schools in the majority of states now provide prekindergarten programs, some for children as young as 3, and many offer before- and after-school child care (Mitchell, Seligson, & Marx 1989; Seppanen, Kaplan deVries, & Seligson 1993; Adams & Sandfort 1994).

Corporate America has become a more visible sponsor of child care programs, with several key corporations leading the way in promoting high-quality programs (for example, IBM, AT&T, and the American Business Collaboration). Family child care homes have become an increasingly visible sector of the child care community, with greater emphasis on professional development and the National Association for Family Child Care taking the lead in establishing an accreditation system for high-quality family child care (Hollestelle 1993; Cohen & Modigliani 1994; Galinsky et al. 1994). Many different settings in this country provide services to young children, and it is legitimate—even beneficial—for these settings to vary in certain ways. However, since it is vital to meet children's learning and developmental needs wherever they are served, high standards of quality should apply to all settings.

The context in which early childhood programs operate today is also characterized by ongoing debates about how best to teach young children and discussions about what sort of practice is most likely to contribute to their development and learning. Perhaps the most important contribution of NAEYC's 1987 position statement on developmentally appropriate practice (Bredekamp 1987) was that it created an opportunity for increased conversation within and outside the early childhood field about practices. In revising the position statement, NAEYC's goal is not only to improve the quality of current early childhood practice but also to continue to encourage the kind of questioning and debate among early childhood professionals that are necessary for the continued growth of professional knowledge in the field. A related goal is to express NAEYC's position more clearly so that energy is not wasted in unproductive debate about apparent rather that real differences of opinion.

RATIONALE FOR THE POSITION STATEMENT

The increased demand for early childhood education services is partly due to the increased recognition of the crucial importance of experiences during the earliest years of life. Children's experiences during early childhood not only influence their later functioning in school but can have effects throughout life. For example, current research demonstrates the early and lasting effects of children's environments and experiences on brain development and cognition (Chugani, Phelps, & Mazziotta 1987; Caine & Caine 1991; Kuhl 1994). Studies show that, "From infancy through about age 10, brain cells not only form most of the connections they will maintain throughout life but during this time they retain their greatest malleability" (Dana Alliance for Brain Initiatives 1996, 7).

Positive, supportive relationships, important during the earliest years of life, appear essential not only for cognitive development but also for healthy emotional development and social attachment (Bowlby 1969; Stern 1985). The preschool years are an optimum time for development of fundamental motor skills (Gallahue 1993), language development (Dyson & Genishi 1993), and other key foundational aspects of development that have lifelong implications.

Recognition of the importance of the early years has heightened interest and support for early childhood education programs. A number of studies demonstrating long-term, positive consequences of participation in high-quality early childhood programs for children from low-income families influenced the expansion of Head Start and public school prekindergarten (Lazar & Darlington 1982; Lee, Brooks-Gunn, & Schuur 1988; Schweinhart, Barnes, & Weikart 1993; Campbell & Ramey 1995). Several decades of research clearly demonstrate that high-quality, developmentally appropriate early childhood programs produce short- and long-term positive effects on children's cognitive and social development (Barnett 1995).

From a thorough review of the research on the long-term effects of early childhood education programs, Barnett concludes that "across all studies, the findings were relatively uniform and constitute overwhelming evidence that early childhood care and education can produce sizeable improvements in school success" (1995, 40). Children from low-income families who participated in high-quality preschool programs were significantly less likely to have been assigned to special education, retained in grade, engaged in crime, or to have dropped out of school. The longitudinal studies, in general, suggest positive consequences for programs that used an approach consistent with principles of developmentally appropriate practice (Lazar & Darlington 1982; Berreuta-Clement et al. 1984; Miller & Bizzell 1984; Schweinhart, Weikart, & Larner 1986; Schweinhart, Barnes, & Weikart 1993; Frede 1995; Schweinhart & Weikart 1996).

Research on the long-term effects of early childhood programs indicates that children who attend good-quality child care programs, even at very young ages, demonstrate positive outcomes, and children who attend poor-quality programs show negative effects (Vandell & Powers 1983; Phillips, McCartney, & Scarr 1987; Fields et al. 1988; Vandell, Henderson, & Wilson 1988; Arnett 1989; Vandell & Corasanti 1990; Burchinal et al. 1996). Specifically, children who experience high-quality, stable child care engage in more complex play, demonstrate more secure attachments to adults and other children, and score higher on measures of thinking ability and language development. High-quality child care can predict academic success, adjustment to school, and reduced behavioral problems for children in first grade (Howes 1988).

While the potential positive effects of high-quality child care are well documented, several large-scale evaluations of child care find that high-quality experiences are not the norm (Whitebook, Howes, & Phillips 1989; Howes, Phillips, & Whitebook 1992; Layzer, Goodson, & Moss 1993; Galinsky et al. 1994; Cost, Quality, & Child Outcomes Study Team 1995). Each of these studies, which included observations of child care and preschool quality in several states, found that good quality that supports children's health and social and cognitive development is being provided in only about 15% of programs.

Of even greater concern was the large percentage of classrooms and family child care homes that were rated "barely adequate" or "inadequate" for quality. From 12 to 20% of the children were in settings that were considered dangerous to their health and safety and harmful to their social and cognitive development. An alarming number of infants and toddlers (35 to 40%) were found to be in unsafe settings (Cost, Quality, & Child Outcomes Study Team 1995).

Experiences during the earliest years of formal schooling are also formative. Studies demonstrate that children's success or failure during the first years of school often predicts the course of later schooling (Alexander & Entwisle 1988; Slavin, Karweit, & Madden 1989). A growing body of research indicates that more developmentally appropriate teaching in preschool and kindergarten predicts greater success in the early grades (Frede & Barnett 1992; Marcon 1992; Charlesworth et al. 1993).

As with preschool and child care, the observed quality of children's early schooling is uneven (Durkin 1987, 1990; Hiebert & Papierz 1990; Bryant, Clifford, & Peisner 1991; Carnegie Task Force 1996). For instance, in a statewide observational study of kindergarten classrooms, Durkin (1987) found that despite assessment results indicating considerable individual variation in children's literacy skills, which would call for various teaching strategies as well as individual and small-group work, teachers relied on one instructional strategy—whole-group, phonics instruction—and judged children who did not learn well with this one method as unready for first grade. Currently, too many children—especially children from low-income families and some minority groups—experience school failure, are retained in grade, get assigned to special education, and eventually drop out of school (Natriello, McDill, & Pallas 1990; Legters & Slavin 1992).

Results such as these indicate that while early childhood programs have the potential for producing positive and lasting effects on children, this potential will not be achieved unless more attention is paid to ensuring that all programs meet the highest standards of quality. As the number and type of early childhood programs increase, the need increases for a shared vision and agreed-upon standards of professional practice.

NAEYC'S COMMITMENT TO CHILDREN

It is important to acknowledge at the outset the core values that undergird all of NAEYC's work. As stated in NAEYC's Code of Ethical Conduct, standards of professional practice in early childhood programs are based on commitment to certain fundamental values that are deeply rooted in the history of the early childhood field:

- appreciating childhood as a unique and valuable stage of the human life cycle [and valuing the quality of children's lives in the present, not just as preparation for the future];
- basing our work with children on knowledge of child development [and learning];
- appreciating and supporting the close ties between the child and family;
- recognizing that children are best understood in the context of family, culture, and society;
- respecting the dignity, worth, and uniqueness of each individual (child, family member, and colleague); and

- helping children and adults achieve their full potential in the context of relationships that are based on trust, respect, and positive regard (Feeney & Kipnis 1992, 3).

Taken together, these core values define NAEYC's basic commitment to children and underline its position on developmentally appropriate practice.

STATEMENT OF THE POSITION

Based on an enduring commitment to act on behalf of children, NAEYC's mission is to promote high-quality, developmentally appropriate programs for all children and their families. Because we define developmentally appropriate programs as programs that contribute to children's development, we must articulate our goals for children's development. The principles of practice advocated in this position statement are based on a set of goals for children: what we want for them, both in their present lives and as they develop to adulthood, and what personal characteristics should be fostered because these contribute to a peaceful, prosperous, and democratic society.

As we enter the twenty-first century, enormous changes are taking place in daily life and work. At the same time, certain human capacities will undoubtedly remain important elements in individual and societal well-being—no matter what economic or technological changes take place. With a recognition of both the continuities in human existence and the rapid changes in our world, broad agreement is emerging (e.g., Resnick 1996) that when today's children become adults they will need the ability to

- communicate well, respect others, and engage with them to work through differences of opinion, and function well as members of a team;
- analyze situations, make reasoned judgments, and solve new problems as they emerge;
- access information through various modes, including spoken and written language, and intelligently employ complex tools and technologies as they are developed; and
- continue to learn new approaches, skills, and knowledge as conditions and needs change.

Clearly, people in the decades ahead will need, more than ever, fully developed literacy and numeracy skills, and these abilities are key goals of the educational process. In science, social studies (which includes history and geography), music and the visual arts, physical education, and health, children need to acquire a body of knowledge and skills, as identified by those in the various disciplines (e.g., Bredekamp & Rosegrant 1995).

Besides acquiring a body of knowledge and skills, children must develop positive dispositions and attitudes. They need to understand that effort is necessary for achievement, for example, and they need to have curiosity and confidence in themselves as learners. Moreover, to live in a highly pluralistic society and world, young people need to develop a positive self-

identity and a tolerance for others whose perspective and experience may be different from their own.

Beyond the shared goals of the early childhood field, every program for young children should establish its own goals in collaboration with families. All early childhood programs will not have identical goals; priorities may vary in some respects because programs serve a diversity of children and families. Such differences notwithstanding, NAEYC believes that all high-quality, developmentally appropriate programs will have certain attributes in common. A high-quality early childhood program is one that provides a safe and nurturing environment that promotes the physical, social, emotional, aesthetic, intellectual, and language development of each child while being sensitive to the needs and preferences of families.

Many factors influence the quality of an early childhood program, including (but not limited to) the extent to which knowledge about how children develop and learn is applied in program practices. Developmentally appropriate programs are based on what is known about how children develop and learn; such programs promote the development and enhance the learning of each individual child served.

Developmentally appropriate practices result from the process of professionals making decisions about the well-being and education of children based on at least three important kinds of information or knowledge:

1. *what is known about child development and learning*—knowledge of age-related human characteristics that permits general predictions within an age range about what activities, materials, interactions, or experiences will be safe, healthy, interesting, achievable, and also challenging to children;
2. *what is known about the strengths, interests, and needs of each individual child in the group* to be able to adapt for and be responsive to inevitable individual variation; and
3. *knowledge of the social and cultural contexts in which children live* to ensure that learning experiences are meaningful, relevant, and respectful for the participating children and their families.

Furthermore, each of these dimensions of knowledge—human development and learning, individual characteristics and experiences, and social and cultural contexts—is dynamic and changing, requiring that early childhood teachers remain learners throughout their careers.

An example illustrates the interrelatedness of these three dimensions of the decision-making process. Children all over the world acquire language at approximately the same period of the life span and in similar ways (Fernald 1992). But tremendous individual variation exists in the rate and pattern of language acquisition (Fenson et al. 1994). Also, children acquire the language or languages of the culture in which they live (Kuhl 1994). Thus, to adequately support a developmental task such as language acquisition, the teacher must draw on at least all three interrelated dimensions of knowledge to determine a develop mentally appropriate strategy or intervention.

PRINCIPLES OF CHILD DEVELOPMENT AND LEARNING THAT INFORM DEVELOPMENTALLY APPROPRIATE PRACTICE

Developmentally appropriate practice is based on knowledge about how children develop and learn. As Katz states, "In a developmental approach to curriculum design, . . . [decisions] about what should be learned and how it would best be learned depend on what we know of the learner's developmental status and our understanding of the relationships between early experience and subsequent development" (1995, 109). To guide their decisions about practice, all early childhood teachers need to understand the developmental changes that typically occur in the years from birth through age 8 and beyond, variations in development that may occur, and how best to support children's learning and development during these years.

A complete discussion of the knowledge base that informs early childhood practice is beyond the scope of this document (see, for example, Seefeldt 1992; Sroufe, Cooper, & DeHart 1992; Kostelnik, Soderman, & Whiren 1993; Spodek 1993; Berk 1996). Because development and learning are so complex, no one theory is sufficient to explain these phenomena. However, a broad-based review of the literature on early childhood education generates a set of principles to inform early childhood practice. *Principles* are generalizations that are sufficiently reliable that they should be taken into account when making decisions (Katz & Chard 1989; Katz 1995). Following is a list of empirically based principles of child development and learning that inform and guide decisions about developmentally appropriate practice.

1. **Domains of children's development—physical, social, emotional, and cognitive—are closely related. Development in one domain influences and is influenced by development in other domains.**

   Development in one domain can limit or facilitate development in others (Sroufe, Cooper, & DeHart 1992; Kostelnik, Soderman, & Whiren 1993). For example, when babies begin to crawl or walk, their ability to explore the world expands, and their mobility, in turn, affects their cognitive development. Likewise, children's language skill affects their ability to establish social relationships with adults and other children, just as their skill in social interaction can support or impede their language development.

   Because developmental domains are interrelated, educators should be aware of and use these interrelationships to organize children's learning experiences in ways that help children develop optimally in all areas and that make meaningful connections across domains.

   Recognition of the connections across developmental domains is also useful for curriculum planning with the various age groups represented in the early childhood period. Curriculum

with infants and toddlers is almost solely driven by the need to support their healthy development in all domains. During the primary grades, curriculum planning attempts to help children develop conceptual understandings that apply across related subject-matter disciplines.

2. **Development occurs in a relatively orderly sequence, with later abilities, skills, and knowledge building on those already acquired.**

   Human development research indicates that relatively stable, predictable sequences of growth and change occur in children during the first nine years of life (Piaget 1952; Erikson 1963; Dyson & Genishi 1993; Gallahue 1993; Case & Okamoto 1996). Predictable changes occur in all domains of development—physical, emotional, social, language, and cognitive—although the ways that these changes are manifested and the meaning attached to them vary in different cultural contexts. Knowledge of typical development of children within the age span served by the program provides a general framework to guide how teachers prepare the learning environment and plan realistic curriculum goals and objectives and appropriate experiences.

3. **Development proceeds at varying rates from child to child as well as unevenly within different areas of each child's functioning.**

   Individual variation has at least two dimensions: the inevitable variability around the average or normative course of development and the uniqueness of each person as an individual (Sroufe, Cooper, & DeHart 1992). Each child is a unique person with an individual pattern and timing of growth, as well as individual personality, temperament, learning style, and experiential and family background. All children have their own strengths, needs, and interests; for some children, special learning and developmental needs or abilities are identified. Given the enormous variation among children of the same chronological age, a child's age must be recognized as only a crude index of developmental maturity.

   Recognition that individual variation is not only to be expected but also valued requires that decisions about curriculum and adults' interactions with children be as individualized as possible. Emphasis on individual appropriateness is not the same as "individualism." Rather, this recognition requires that children be considered not solely as members of an age group, expected to perform to a predetermined norm and without adaptation to individual variation of any kind. Having high expectations for all children is important, but rigid expectations of group norms do not reflect what is known about real differences in individual development and learning during the early years. Group-norm expectancy can be especially harmful for children with special learning and developmental needs (NEGP 1991; Mallory 1992; Wolery, Strain, & Bailey 1992).

4. **Early experiences have both cumulative and delayed effects on individual children's development; optimal**

periods exist for certain types of development and learning.

Children's early experiences, either positive or negative, are cumulative in the sense that if an experience occurs occasionally, it may have minimal effects. If positive or negative experiences occur frequently, however, they can have powerful, lasting, even "snowballing," effects (Katz & Chard 1989; Kostelnik, Soderman, & Whiren 1993; Wieder & Greenspan 1993). For example, a child's social experiences with other children in the preschool years help him develop social skills and confidence that enable him to make friends in the early school years, and these experiences further enhance the child's social competence. Conversely, children who fail to develop minimal social competence and are neglected or rejected by peers are at significant risk to drop out of school, become delinquent, and experience mental health problems in adulthood (Asher, Hymel, & Renshaw 1984; Parker & Asher 1987).

Similar patterns can be observed in babies whose cries and other attempts at communication are regularly responded to, thus enhancing their own sense of efficacy and increasing communicative competence. Likewise, when children have or do not have early literacy experiences, such as being read to regularly, their later success in learning to read is affected accordingly. Perhaps most convincing is the growing body of research demonstrating that social and sensorimotor experiences during the first three years directly affect neurological development of the brain, with important and lasting implications for children's capacity to learn (Dana Alliance for Brain Initiatives 1996).

Early experiences can also have delayed effects, either positive or negative, on subsequent development. For instance, some evidence suggests that reliance on extrinsic rewards (such as candy or money) to shape children's behavior, a strategy that can be very effective in the short term, under certain circumstances lessens children's intrinsic motivation to engage in the rewarded behavior in the long term (Dweck 1986; Kohn 1993). For example, paying children to read books may over time undermine their desire to read for their own enjoyment and edification.

At certain points in the life span, some kinds of learning and development occur most efficiently. For example, the first three years of life appear to be an optimal period for verbal language development (Kuhl 1994). Although delays in language development due to physical or environmental deficits can be ameliorated later on, such intervention usually requires considerable effort. Similarly, the preschool years appear to be optimum for fundamental motor development (that is, fundamental motor skills are more easily and efficiently acquired at this age) (Gallahue 1995). Children who have many opportunities and adult support to practice large-motor skills (running, jumping, hopping, skipping) during this period have the cumulative benefit of being better able to acquire more sophisticated, complex motor skills (balancing on a beam or riding a two-wheel bike) in subsequent years. On the other hand, children whose early motor experiences are severely limited may struggle to acquire physical competence and may also experience delayed effects when attempting to participate in sports or personal fitness activities later in life.

5. **Development proceeds in predictable directions toward greater complexity, organization, and internalization.**

Learning during early childhood proceeds from behavioral knowledge to symbolic or representational knowledge (Bruner 1983). For example, children learn to navigate their homes and other familiar settings long before they can understand the words *left* and *right* or read a map of the house. Developmentally appropriate programs provide opportunities for children to broaden and deepen their behavioral knowledge by providing a variety of firsthand experiences and by helping children acquire symbolic knowledge through representing their experiences in a variety of media, such as drawing, painting, construction of models, dramatic play, verbal and written descriptions (Katz 1995).

Even very young children are able to use various media to represent their understanding of concepts. Furthermore, through representation of their knowledge, the knowledge itself is enhanced (Edwards, Gandini, & Forman 1993; Malaguzzi 1993; Forman 1994). Representational modes and media also vary with the age of the child. For instance, most learning for infants and toddlers is sensory and motoric, but by age 2 children use one object to stand for another in play (a block for a phone or a spoon for a guitar).

6. **Development and learning occur in and are influenced by multiple social and cultural contexts.**

Bronfenbrenner (1979, 1989, 1993) provides an ecological model for understanding human development. He explains that children's development is best understood within the sociocultural context of the family, educational setting, community, and broader society. These various contexts are interrelated, and all have an impact on the developing child. For example, even a child in a loving, supportive family, within a strong, healthy community is affected by the biases of the larger society, such as racism or sexism, and may show the effects of negative stereotyping and discrimination.

We define *culture* as the customary beliefs and patterns of and for behavior, both explicit and implicit, that are passed on to future generations by the society they live in and/or by a social, religious, or ethnic group within it. Because culture is often discussed in the context of diversity or multiculturalism, people fail to recognize the powerful role that culture plays in influencing the development of *all* children. Every culture structures and interprets children's behavior and development (Edwards & Gandini 1989; Tobin, Wu, & Davidson 1989; Rogoff et al. 1993). As Bowman states, "Rules of development are the same for all children, but social contexts shape children's development into different configurations" (1994, 220). Early childhood teachers need to understand the influence of sociocultural contexts on learning, recognize children's developing competence, and accept a variety of ways for children to express their developmental achievements (Vygotsky 1978; Wertsch 1985; Forman, Minick, & Stone 1993; New 1993, 1994; Bowman & Stott 1994; Mallory & New 1994a; Phillips 1994; Bruner 1996; Wardle 1996).

Teachers should learn about the culture of the majority of the children they serve if that culture differs from their own. However, recognizing that development and learning are influenced by social and cultural contexts does not require teachers to understand all the nuances of every cultural group they may encounter in their practice; this would be an impossible task. Rather, this fundamental recognition sensitizes teachers to the need to acknowledge how their own cultural experiences shape their perspective and to realize that multiple perspectives, in addition to their own, must be considered in decisions about children's development and learning.

Children are capable of learning to function in more than one cultural context simultaneously. However, if teachers set low expectations for children based on their home culture and language, children cannot develop and learn optimally. Education should be an additive process. For example, children whose primary language is not English should be able to learn English without being forced to give up their home language (NAEYC 1996a). Likewise, children who speak only English benefit from learning another language. The goal is that all children learn to function well in the society as a whole and move comfortably among groups of people who come from both similar and dissimilar backgrounds.

7. **Children are active learners, drawing on direct physical and social experience as well as culturally transmitted knowledge to construct their own understandings of the world around them.**

Children contribute to their own development and learning as they strive to make meaning out of their daily experiences in the home, the early childhood program, and the community. Principles of developmentally appropriate practice are based on several prominent theories that view intellectual development from a constructivist, interactive perspective (Dewey 1916; Piaget 1952; Vygotsky 1978; DeVries & Kohlberg 1990; Rogoff 1990; Gardner 1991; Kamil & Ewing 1996).

From birth, children are actively engaged in constructing their own understandings from their experiences, and these understandings are mediated by and clearly linked to the sociocultural context. Young children actively learn from observing and participating with other children and adults, including parents and teachers. Children need to form their own hypotheses and keep trying them out through social interaction, physical manipulation, and their own thought processes—observing what happens, reflecting on their findings, asking questions, and formulating answers. When objects, events, and other people challenge the working model that the child has mentally constructed, the child is forced to adjust the model or alter the mental structures to account for the new information. Throughout early childhood, the child in processing new experiences continually reshapes, expands, and reorganizes mental structures (Piaget 1952; Vygotsky 1978; Case & Okamoto 1996). When teachers and other adults use various strategies to encourage children to reflect on their experiences by planning beforehand and "revisiting" afterward, the knowledge and understanding gained from the experience is deepened (Copple,

Sigel, & Saunders 1984; Edwards, Gandini, & Forman 1993; Stremmel & Fu 1993; Hohmann & Weikart 1995).

In the statement of this principle, the term "physical and social experience" is used in the broadest sense to include children's exposure to physical knowledge, learned through first-hand experience of using objects (observing that a ball thrown in the air falls down), and social knowledge, including the vast body of culturally acquired and transmitted knowledge that children need to function in the world. For example, children progressively construct their own understanding of various symbols, but the symbols they use (such as the alphabet or numerical system) are the ones used within their culture and transmitted to them by adults.

In recent years, discussions of cognitive development have at times become polarized (see Seifert 1993). Piaget's theory stressed that development of certain cognitive structures was a necessary prerequisite to learning (i.e., development precedes learning), while other research has demonstrated that instruction in specific concepts or strategies can facilitate development of more mature cognitive structures (learning precedes development) (Vygotsky 1978; Gelman & Baillargheon 1983). Current attempts to resolve this apparent dichotomy (Seifert 1993; Sameroff & McDonough 1994; Case & Okamoto 1996) acknowledge that essentially both theoretical perspectives are correct in explaining aspects of cognitive development during early childhood. Strategic teaching, of course, can enhance children's learning. Yet, direct instruction may be totally ineffective; it fails when it is not attuned to the cognitive capacities and knowledge of the child at that point in development.

8. **Development and learning result from interaction of biological maturation and the environment, which includes both the physical and social worlds that children live in.**

The simplest way to express this principle is that human beings are products of both heredity and environment and these forces are interrelated. Behaviorists focus on the environmental influences that determine learning, while maturationists emphasize the unfolding of predetermined, hereditary characteristics. Each perspective is true to some extent, and yet neither perspective is sufficient to explain learning or development. More often today, development is viewed as the result of an interactive, transactional process between the growing, changing individual and his or her experiences in the social and physical worlds (Scarr & McCartney 1983; Plomin 1994a, b). For example, a child's genetic makeup may predict healthy growth, but inadequate nutrition in the early years of life may keep this potential from being fulfilled. Or a severe disability, whether inherited or environmentally caused, may be ameliorated through systematic, appropriate intervention. Likewise, a child's inherited temperament—whether a predisposition to be wary or outgoing—shapes and is shaped by how other children and adults communicate with that child.

9. **Play is an important vehicle for children's social, emotional, and cognitive development, as well as a reflection of their development.**

Understanding that children are active constructors of knowledge and that development and learning are the result of interactive processes, early childhood teachers recognize that children's play is a highly supportive context for these developing processes (Piaget 1952; Fein 1981; Bergen 1988; Smilansky & Shefatya 1990; Fromberg 1992; Berk & Winsler 1995). Play gives children opportunities to understand the world, interact with others in social ways, express and control emotions, and develop their symbolic capabilities. Children's play gives adults insights into children's development and opportunities to support the development of new strategies. Vygotsky (1978) believed that play leads development, with written language growing out of oral language through the vehicle of symbolic play that promotes the development of symbolic representation abilities. Play provides a context for children to practice newly acquired skills and also to function on the edge of their developing capacities to take on new social roles, attempt novel or challenging tasks, and solve complex problems that they would not (or could not) otherwise do (Mallory & New 1994b).

Research demonstrates the importance of sociodramatic play as a tool for learning curriculum content with 3- through 6-year-old children. When teachers provide a thematic organization for play; offer appropriate props, space, and time; and become involved in the play by extending and elaborating on children's ideals, children's language and literacy skills can be enhanced (Levy, Schaefer, & Phelps 1986; Schrader 1989, 1990; Morrow 1990; Pramling 1991; Levy, Wolfgang, & Koorland 1992).

In addition to supporting cognitive development, play serves important functions in children's physical, emotional, and social development (Herron & Sutton-Smith 1971). Children express and represent their ideas, thoughts, and feelings when engaged in symbolic play. During play a child can learn to deal with emotions, to interact with others, to resolve conflicts, and to gain a sense of competence—all in the safety that only play affords. Through play, children also can develop their imaginations and creativity. Therefore, child-initiated, teacher-supported play is an essential component of developmentally appropriate practice (Fein & Rivkin 1986).

10. **Development advances when children have opportunities to practice newly acquired skills as well as when they experience a challenge just beyond the level of their present mastery.**

Research demonstrates that children need to be able to successfully negotiate learning tasks most of the time if they are to maintain motivation and persistence (Lary 1990; Brophy 1992). Confronted by repeated failure, most children will simply stop trying. So most of the time, teachers should give young children tasks that with effort they can accomplish and present them with content that is accessible at their level of understanding. At the same time, children continually gravitate to situations and stimuli that give them the chance to work at their "growing edge" (Berk & Winsler 1995; Bodrova & Leong 1996). Moreover, in a task just beyond the child's independent reach, the adult and more-competent peers contribute significantly to development by providing the supportive "scaffolding" that allows the child to take the next step.

Development and learning are dynamic processes requiring that adults understand the continuum, observe children closely to match curriculum and teaching to children's emerging competencies, needs, and interests, and then help children move forward by targeting educational experiences to the edge of children's changing capacities so as to challenge but not frustrate them. Human beings, especially children, are highly motivated to understand what they almost, but not quite, comprehend and to master what they can almost, but not quite, do (White 1965; Vygotsky 1978). The principle of learning is that children can do things first in a supportive context and then later independently and in a variety of contexts. Rogoff (1990) describes the process of adult-assisted learning as "guided participation" to emphasize that children actively collaborate with others to move to more complex levels of understanding and skill.

11. **Children demonstrate different modes of knowing and learning and different ways of representing what they know.**

For some time, learning theorists and developmental psychologists have recognized that human beings come to understand the world in many ways and that individuals tend to have preferred or stronger modes of learning. Studies of differences in learning modalities have contrasted visual, auditory, or tactile learners. Other work has identified learners as field-dependent or independent (Witkin 1962). Gardner (1983) expanded on this concept by theorizing that human beings possess at least seven "intelligences." In addition to having the ones traditionally emphasized in schools, linguistic and logical-mathematical, individuals are more or less proficient in at least these other areas: musical, spatial, bodily-kinesthetic, intrapersonal, and interpersonal.

Malaguzzi (1993) used the metaphor of "100 languages" to describe the diverse modalities through which children come to understand the world and represent their knowledge. The processes of representing their understanding can with the assistance of teachers help children deepen, improve, and expand their understanding (Copple, Sigel, & Saunders 1984; Forman 1994; Katz 1995). The principle of diverse modalities implies that teachers should provide not only opportunities for individual children to use their preferred modes of learning to capitalize on their strengths (Hale-Benson 1986) but also opportunities to help children develop in the modes or intelligences in which they may not be as strong.

12. **Children develop and learn best in the context of a community where they are safe and valued, their physical needs are met, and they feel psychologically secure.**

Maslow (1954) conceptualized a hierarchy of needs in which learning was not considered possible unless physical and psychological needs for safety and security were first met. Because children's physical health and safety too often are threatened today, programs for young children must not only provide adequate health, safety, and nutrition but may also need to ensure more comprehensive services, such as physical, dental, and mental health and social services (NASBE 1991; U.S. Department of Health & Human Services 1996). In addition, children's development in all areas is influenced by their ability to establish and maintain a limited number of positive, consistent primary relationships with adults and other children (Bowlby 1969; Stern 1985; Garbarino et al. 1992). These primary relationships begin in the family but extend over time to include children's teachers and members of the community; therefore, practices that are developmentally appropriate address children's physical, social, and emotional needs as well as their intellectual development.

A linear listing of principles of child development and learning, such as the above, cannot do justice to the complexity of the phenomena that it attempts to describe and explain. Just as all domains of development and learning are interrelated, so, too, there are relationships among the principles. Similarly, the following guidelines for practice do not match up one-to-one with the principles. Instead, early childhood professionals draw on all these fundamental ideas (as well as many others) when making decisions about their practice.

GUIDELINES FOR DECISIONS ABOUT DEVELOPMENTALLY APPROPRIATE PRACTICE

An understanding of the nature of development and learning during the early childhood years, from birth through age 8, generates guidelines that inform the practices of early childhood educators. Developmentally appropriate practice requires that teachers integrate the many dimensions of their knowledge base. They must know about child development and the implications of this knowledge for how to teach, the content of the curriculum—what to teach and when—how to assess what children have learned, and how to adapt curriculum and instruction to children's individual strengths, needs, and interest. Further, they must know the particular children they teach and their families and be knowledgeable as well about the social and cultural context.

The following guidelines address five interrelated dimensions of early childhood professional practice: creating a caring community of learners, teaching to enhance development and learning, constructing appropriate curriculum, assessing children's development and learning, and establishing reciprocal relationships with families. (The word *teacher* is used to refer to any adult responsible for a group of children in any early childhood program, including infant/toddler caregivers, family child care providers, and specialists in other disciplines who fulfill the role of teacher.)

Examples of appropriate and inappropriate practice in relation to each of these dimensions are given for infants and tod-

dlers (Part 3, pp. 72–90), children 3 through 5 (Part 4, pp. 123–35), and children 6 through 8 (Part 5, pp. 161–78). In the references at the end of each part, readers will be able to find fuller discussion of the points summarized here and strategies for implementation.

1. CREATING A CARING COMMUNITY OF LEARNERS
Developmentally appropriate practices occur within a context that supports the development of relationships between adults and children, among children, among teachers, and between teachers and families. Such a community reflects what is known about the social construction of knowledge and the importance of establishing a caring, inclusive community in which all children can develop and learn.

A. The early childhood setting functions as a community of learners in which all participants consider and contribute to each other's well-being and learning.

B. Consistent, positive relationships with a limited number of adults and other children are a fundamental determinant of healthy human development and provide the context for children to learn about themselves and their world and also how to develop positive, constructive relationships with other people. The early childhood classroom is a community in which each child is valued. Children learn to respect and acknowledge differences in abilities and talents and to value each person for his or her strengths.

C. Social relationships are an important context for learning. Each child has strengths or interests that contribute to the overall functioning of the group. When children have opportunities to play together, work on projects in small groups, and talk with other children and adults, their own development and learning are enhanced. Interacting with other children in small groups provides a context for children to operate on the edge of their developing capacities. The learning environment enables children to construct understanding through interactions with adults and other children.

D. The learning environment is designed to protect children's health and safety and is supportive of children's physiological needs for activity, sensory stimulation, fresh air, rest, and nourishment. The program provides a balance of rest and active movement for children throughout the program day. Outdoor experiences are provided for children of all ages. The program protects children's psychological safety; that is, children feel secure, relaxed, and comfortable rather than disengaged, frightened, worried, or stressed.

E. Children experience an organized environment and an orderly routine that provides an overall structure in which learning takes place; the environment is dynamic and changing but predictable and comprehensible from a child's point of view. The learning environment provides a variety of materials and opportunities for children to have firsthand, meaningful experiences.

2. TEACHING TO ENHANCE DEVELOPMENT AND LEARNING

Adults are responsible for ensuring children's healthy development and learning. From birth, relationships with adults are critical determinants of children's healthy social and emotional development and serve as well as mediators of language and intellectual development. At the same time, children are active constructors of their own understanding, who benefit from initiating and regulating their own learning activities and interacting with peers. Therefore, early childhood teachers strive to achieve an optimal balance between children's self-initiated learning and adult guidance or support.

Teachers accept responsibility for actively supporting children's development and provide occasions for children to acquire important knowledge and skills. Teachers use their knowledge of child development and learning to identify the range of activities, materials, and learning experiences that are appropriate for a group or individual child. This knowledge is used in conjunction with knowledge of the context and understanding about individual children's growth patterns, strengths, needs, interests, and experiences to design the curriculum and learning environment and guide teachers' interactions with children. The following guidelines describe aspects of the teachers' role in making decisions about practice:

A. Teachers respect, value, and accept children and treat them with dignity at all times.

B. Teachers make it a priority to know each child well.
  (1) Teachers establish positive, personal relationships with children to foster the child's development and keep informed about the child's needs and potentials. Teachers listen to children and adapt their responses to children's differing needs, interests, styles, and abilities.
  (2) Teachers continually observe children's spontaneous play and interaction with the physical environment and with other children to learn about their interests, abilities, and developmental progress. On the basis of this information, teachers plan experiences that enhance children's learning and development.
  (3) Understanding that children develop and learn in the context of their families and communities, teachers establish relationships with families that increase their knowledge of children's lives outside the classroom and their awareness of the perspectives and priorities of those individuals most significant in the child's life.
  (4) Teachers are alert to signs of undue stress and traumatic events in children's lives and aware of effective strategies to reduce stress and support the development of resilience.
  (5) Teachers are responsible at all times for all children under their supervision and plan for children's increasing development of self-regulation abilities.

C. Teachers create an intellectually engaging, responsive environment to promote each child's learning and development.
  (1) Teachers use their knowledge about children in general and the particular children in the group as well as their familiarity with what children need to learn and develop in each curriculum area to organize the environment and plan curriculum and teaching strategies.
  (2) Teachers provide children with a rich variety of experiences, projects, materials, problems, and ideas to explore and investigate, ensuring that these are worthy of children's attention.
  (3) Teachers provide children with opportunities to make meaningful choices and time to explore through active involvement. Teachers offer children the choice to participate in a small-group or a solitary activity, assist and guide children who are not yet able to use and enjoy child-choice activity periods, and provide opportunities for practice of skills as a self-chosen activity.
  (4) Teachers organize the daily and weekly schedule and allocate time so as to provide children with extended blocks of time in which to engage in play, projects, and/or study in integrated curriculum.

D. Teachers make plans to enable children to attain key curriculum goals across various disciplines, such as language arts, mathematics, social studies, science, art, music, physical education, and health (see "Constructing Appropriate Curriculum," p. 555).
  (1) Teachers incorporate a wide variety of experiences, materials and equipment, and teaching strategies in constructing curriculum to accommodate a broad range of children's individual differences in prior experiences, maturation rates, styles of learning, needs, and interests.
  (2) Teachers bring each child's home culture and language into the shared culture of the school so that the unique contributions of each group are recognized and valued by others.
  (3) Teachers are prepared to meet identified special needs of individual children, including children with disabilities and those who exhibit unusual interests and skills. Teachers use all the strategies identified here, consult with appropriate specialists, and see that the child gets the specialized services he or she requires.

E. Teachers foster children's collaboration with peers on interesting, important enterprises.
  (1) Teachers promote children's productive collaboration without taking over to the extent that children lose interest.
  (2) Teachers use a variety of ways of flexibly grouping children for the purposes of instruction, supporting collaboration among children, and building a sense of community. At various times, children have opportunities to work individually, in small groups, and with the whole group.

F. Teachers develop, refine, and use a wide repertoire of teaching strategies to enhance children's learning and development.
  (1) To help children develop their initiative, teachers encourage them to choose and plan their own learning activities.
  (2) Teachers pose problems, ask questions, and make comments and suggestions that stimulate children's thinking and extend their learning.

(3) Teachers extend the range of children's interests and the scope of their thought through presenting novel experiences and introducing stimulating ideas, problems, experiences, or hypotheses.

(4) To sustain an individual child's effort or engagement in purposeful activities, teachers select from a range of strategies, including but not limited to modeling, demonstrating specific skills, and providing information, focused attention, physical proximity, verbal encouragement, reinforcement and other behavioral procedures, as well as additional structure and modification of equipment or schedules as needed.

(5) Teachers coach and/or directly guide children in the acquisition of specific skills as needed.

(6) Teachers calibrate the complexity and challenge of activities to suit children's level of skill and knowledge, increasing the challenge as children gain competence and understanding.

(7) Teachers provide cues and other forms of "scaffolding" that enable the child to succeed in a task that is just beyond his or her ability to complete alone.

(8) To strengthen children's sense of competence and confidence as learners, motivation to persist, and willingness to take risks, teachers provide experiences for children to be genuinely successful and to be challenged.

(9) To enhance children's conceptual understanding, teachers use various strategies that encourage children to reflect on and "revisit" their learning experiences.

G. Teachers facilitate the development of responsibility and self-regulation in children.

(1) Teachers set clear, consistent, and fair limits for children's behavior and hold children accountable to standards of acceptable behavior. To the extent that children are able, teachers engage them in developing rules and procedures for behavior of class members.

(2) Teachers redirect children to more acceptable behavior or activity or use children's mistakes as learning opportunities, patiently reminding children of rules and their rationale as needed.

(3) Teachers listen and acknowledge children's feelings and frustrations, respond with respect, guide children to resolve conflicts, and model skills that help children to solve their own problems.

3. CONSTRUCTING APPROPRIATE CURRICULUM

The content of the early childhood curriculum is determined by many factors, including the subject matter of the disciplines, social or cultural values, and parental input. In developmentally appropriate programs, decisions about curriculum content also take into consideration the age and experience of the learners. Achieving success for all children depends, among other essentials, on providing a challenging, interesting, developmentally appropriate curriculum. NAEYC does not endorse specific curricula. However, one purpose of these guidelines is as a framework for making decisions about developing curriculum or selecting a curriculum model. Teachers who use a validated curriculum model benefit from the evidence of its effectiveness and the accumulated wisdom and experience of others.

In some respects, the curriculum strategies of many teachers today do not demand enough of children and in other ways demand too much of the wrong thing. On the one hand, narrowing the curriculum to those basic skills that can be easily measured on multiple-choice tests diminishes the intellectual challenge for many children. Such intellectually impoverished curriculum underestimates the true competence of children, which has been demonstrated to be much higher than is often assumed (Gelman & Baillargeon 1983; Gelman & Meck 1983; Edwards, Gandini, & Forman 1993; Resnick 1996). Watered-down, oversimplified curriculum leaves many children unchallenged, bored, uninterested, or unmotivated. In such situations, children's experiences are marked by a great many missed opportunities for learning.

On the other hand, curriculum expectations in the early years of schooling sometimes are not appropriate for the age groups served. When next-grade expectations of mastery of basic skills are routinely pushed down to the previous grade and whole group and teacher-led instruction is the dominant teaching strategy, children who cannot sit still and attend to teacher lectures or who are bored and unchallenged or frustrated by doing workbook pages for long periods of time are mislabeled as immature, disruptive, or unready for school (Shepard & Smith 1988). Constructing appropriate curriculum requires attention to at least the following guidelines for practice:

A. Developmentally appropriate curriculum provides for all areas of a child's development: physical, emotional, social, linguistic, aesthetic, and cognitive.

B. Curriculum includes a broad range of content across disciplines that is socially relevant, intellectually engaging, and personally meaningful to children.

C. Curriculum builds upon what children already know and are able to do (activating prior knowledge) to consolidate their learning and to foster their acquisition of new concepts and skills.

D. Effective curriculum plans frequently integrate across traditional subject-matter divisions to help children make meaningful connections and provide opportunities for rich conceptual development; focusing on one subject is also a valid strategy at times.

E. Curriculum promotes the development of knowledge and understanding, processes and skills, as well as the dispositions to use and apply skills and to go on learning.

F. Curriculum content has intellectual integrity, reflecting the key concepts and tools of inquiry of recognized disciplines in ways that are accessible and achievable for young children, ages 3 through 8 (e.g., Bredekamp & Rosegrant 1992, 1995). Children directly participate in study of the disciplines, for instance, by conducting scientific experiments, writing, performing, solving mathematical problems, collecting and analyzing data, collecting oral history, and performing other roles of experts in the disciplines.

G. Curriculum provides opportunities to support children's home culture and language while also developing all children's abilities to participate in the shared culture of the program and the community.

H. Curriculum goals are realistic and attainable for most children in the designated age range for which they are designed.

I. When used, technology is physically and philosophically integrated in the classroom curriculum and teaching. (See "NAEYC Position Statement: Technology and Young Children—Ages Three through Eight" [NAEYC 1996b].)

4. ASSESSING CHILDREN'S LEARNING AND DEVELOPMENT

Assessment of individual children's development and learning is essential for planning and implementing appropriate curriculum. In developmentally appropriate programs, assessment and curriculum are integrated, with teachers continually engaging in observational assessment for the purpose of improving teaching and learning.

Accurate assessment of young children is difficult because their development and learning are rapid, uneven, episodic, and embedded within specific cultural and linguistic contexts. Too often, inaccurate and inappropriate assessment measures have been used to label, track, or otherwise harm young children. Developmentally appropriate assessment practices are based on the following guidelines:

A. Assessment of young children's progress and achievements is ongoing, strategic, and purposeful. The results of assessment are used to benefit children—in adapting curriculum and teaching to meet the developmental and learning needs of children, communicating with the child's family, and evaluating the program's effectiveness for the purpose of improving the program.

B. The content of assessments reflects progress toward important learning and developmental goals. The program has a systematic plan for collecting and using assessment information that is integrated with curriculum planning.

C. The methods of assessment are appropriate to the age and experiences of young children. Therefore, assessment of young children relies heavily on the results of observations of children's development, descriptive data, collections of representative work by children, and demonstrated performance during authentic, not contrived, activities. Input from families as well as children's evaluations of their own work are part of the overall assessment strategy.

D. Assessments are tailored to a specific purpose and used only for the purpose for which they have been demonstrated to produce reliable, valid information.

E. Decisions that have a major impact on children, such as enrollment or placement, are never made on the basis of a single developmental assessment or screening device but are based on multiple sources of relevant information, particularly observations by teachers and parents.

F. To identify children who have special learning or developmental needs and to plan appropriate curriculum and teaching for them, developmental assessments and observations are used.

G. Assessment recognizes individual variation in learners and allows for differences in styles and rates of learning. Assessment takes into consideration such factors as the child's facility in English, stage of language acquisition, and whether the child has had the time and opportunity to develop proficiency in his or her home language as well as in English.

H. Assessment legitimately addresses not only what children can do independently but what they can do with assistance from other children or adults. Teachers study children as individuals as well as in relationship to groups by documenting group projects and other collaborative work.

(For a more complete discussion of principles of appropriate assessment, see the position statement *Guidelines for Appropriate Curriculum Content and Assessment for Children Ages 3 through 8* [NAEYC & NAECS/SDE 1992]; see also Shepard 1994.)

5. ESTABLISHING RECIPROCAL RELATIONSHIPS WITH FAMILIES

Developmentally appropriate practices derive from deep knowledge of individual children and the context within which they develop and learn. The younger the child, the more necessary it is for professionals to acquire this knowledge through relationships with children's families. The traditional approach to families has been a parent education orientation in which the professionals see themselves as knowing what is best for children and view parents as needing to be educated. There is also the limited view of parent involvement that sees PTA membership as the primary goal. These approaches do not adequately convey the complexity of the partnership between teachers and parents that is a fundamental element of good practice (Powell 1994).

When the parent education approach is criticized in favor of a more family-centered approach, this shift may be misunderstood to mean that parents dictate all program content and professionals abdicate responsibility, doing whatever parents want regardless of whether professionals agree that it is in children's best interest. Either of these extremes oversimplifies the importance of relationships with families and fails to provide the kind of environment in which parents and professionals work together to achieve shared goals for children; such programs with this focus are characterized by at least the following guidelines for practice:

A. Reciprocal relationships between teachers and families require mutual respect, cooperation, shared responsibility, and negotiation of conflicts toward achievement of shared goals.

B. Early childhood teachers work in collaborative partnerships with families, establishing and maintaining regular, frequent two-way communication with children's parents.

C. Parents are welcome in the program and participate in decisions about their children's care and education. Parents observe and participate and serve in decision-making roles in the program.

D. Teachers acknowledge parents' choices and goals for children and respond with sensitivity and respect to parents' preferences and concerns without abdicating professional responsibility to children.

E. Teachers and parents share their knowledge of the child and understanding of children's development and learning as part of day-to-day communication and planned conferences. Teachers support families in ways that maximally promote family decision-making capabilities and competence.

F. To ensure more accurate and complete information, the program involves families in assessing and planning for individual children.

G. The program links families with a range of services, based on identified resources, priorities, and concerns.

H. Teachers, parents, programs, social service and health agencies, and consultants who may have educational responsibility for the child at different times should, with family participation, share developmental information about children as they pass from one level or program to another.

MOVING FROM EITHER/OR TO BOTH/AND THINKING IN EARLY CHILDHOOD PRACTICE

Some critical reactions to NAEYC's (1987) position statement on developmentally appropriate practice reflect a recurring tendency in the American discourse on education: the polarizing into *either/or* choices of many questions that are more fruitfully seen as *both/ands*. For example, heated debates have broken out about whether children in the early grades should receive whole-language or phonics instruction, when, in fact, the two approaches are quite compatible and most effective in combination.

It is true that there are practices that are clearly inappropriate for early childhood professionals—use of physical punishment or disparaging verbal comments about children, discriminating against children or their families, and many other examples that could be cited (see Parts 3, 4, and 5 for examples relevant to different age groups). However, most questions about practice require more complex responses. It is not that children need food **or** water; they need both.

To illustrate the many ways that early childhood practice draws on *both/and* thinking and to convey some of the complexity and interrelationship among the principles that guide our practice, we offer the following statements as **examples:**

- Children construct their own understanding of concepts, **and** they benefit from instruction by more competent peers and adults.
- Children benefit from opportunities to see connections across disciplines through integration of curriculum **and** from opportunities to engage in in-depth study within a content area.
- Children benefit from predictable structure and orderly routine in the learning environment **and** from the teachers' flexibility and spontaneity in responding to their emerging ideas, needs, and interests.
- Children benefit from opportunities to make meaningful choices about what they will do and learn **and** from hav-

ing a clear understanding of the boundaries within which choices are permissible.

- Children benefit from situations that challenge them to work at the edge of their developing capacities **and** from ample opportunities to practice newly acquired skills and to acquire the disposition to persist.
- Children benefit from opportunities to collaborate with their peers and acquire a sense of being part of a community **and** from being treated as individuals with their own strengths, interests, and needs.
- Children need to develop a positive sense of their own self-identity **and** respect for other people whose perspectives and experiences may be different from their own.
- Children have enormous capacities to learn and almost boundless curiosity about the world, **and** they have recognized, age-related limits on their cognitive and linguistic capacities.
- Children benefit from engaging in self-initiated, spontaneous play, **and** from teacher-planned and-structured activities, projects, and experiences.

The above list is not exhaustive. Many more examples could be cited to convey the interrelationships among the principles of child development and learning or among the guidelines for early childhood practice.

POLICIES ESSENTIAL FOR ACHIEVING DEVELOPMENTALLY APPROPRIATE EARLY CHILDHOOD PROGRAMS

Early childhood professionals working in diverse situations with varying levels of funding and resources are responsible for implementing practices that are developmentally appropriate for the children they serve. Regardless of the resources available, professionals have an ethical responsibility to practice, to the best of their ability, according to the standards of their profession. Nevertheless, the kinds of practices advocated in this position statement are more likely to be implemented within an infrastructure of supportive policies and resources. NAEYC strongly recommends that policymaking groups at the state and local levels consider the following when implementing early childhood programs:

1. A comprehensive professional preparation and development system is in place to ensure that early childhood programs are staffed with qualified personnel (NAEYC 1994).
   - A system exists for early childhood professionals to acquire the knowledge and practical skills needed to practice through college-level specialized preparation in early childhood education/ child development.
   - Teachers in early childhood programs are encouraged and supported to obtain and maintain, through study and participation in inservice training, current knowledge of

child development and learning and its application to early childhood practice.

- Specialists in early childhood special education are available to provide assistance and consultation in meeting the individual needs of children in the program.
- In addition to management and supervision skills, administrators of early childhood programs have appropriate professional qualifications, including training specific to the education and development of young children, and they provide teachers time and opportunities to work collaboratively with colleagues and parents.

2. Funding is provided to ensure adequate staffing of early childhood programs and fair staff compensation that promotes continuity of relationships among adults and children (Willer 1990).

- Funding is adequate to limit the size of the groups and provide sufficient numbers of adults to ensure individualized and appropriate care and education. Even the most well-qualified teacher cannot individualize instruction and adequately supervise too large a group of young children. An acceptable adult–child ratio for 4- and 5-year-olds is two adults with no more than 20 children. (Ruopp et al. 1979; Francis & Self 1982; Howes 1983; Taylor & Taylor 1989; Howes, Philips, & Whitebook 1992; Cost, Quality, & Child Outcomes Study Team 1995; Howes, Smith & Galinsky 1995). Younger children require much smaller groups. Group size and ratio of children to adults should increase gradually through the primary grades, but one teacher with no more than 18 children or two adults with no more than 25 children is optimum (Nye et al. 1992; Nye, Boyd-Zaharias, & Fulton 1994). Inclusion of children with disabilities may necessitate additional adults or smaller group size to ensure that all children's needs are met.
- Programs offer staff salaries and benefits commensurate with the skills and qualifications required for specific roles to ensure the provision of quality services and the effective recruitment and retention of qualified, competent staff. (See *Compensation Guidelines for Early Childhood Professionals* [NAEYC 1993].)
- Decisions related to how programs are staffed and how children are grouped result in increased opportunities for children to experience continuity of relationships with teachers and other children. Such strategies include but are not limited to multiage grouping and multiyear teacher–child relationships (Katz, Evangelou, & Hartman 1990; Zero to Three 1995; Burke 1996).

3. Resources and expertise are available to provide safe, stimulating learning environments with a sufficient number and variety of appropriate materials and equipment for the age group served (Bronson 1995; Kendrick, Kaufmann, & Messenger 1995).

4. Adequate systems for regulating and monitoring the quality of early childhood programs are in place (see position on licensing [NAEYC 1987]; accreditation criteria and procedures [NAEYC 1991]).

5. Community resources are available and used to support the comprehensive needs of children and families (Kagan 1991; NASBE 1991; Kagan et al. 1995; NCSL 1995).

6. When individual children do not make expected learning progress, neither grade retention nor social promotion are used; instead, initiatives such as more focused time, individualized instruction, tutoring, or other individual strategies are used to accelerate children's learning (Shepard & Smith 1989; Ross et al. 1995).

7. Early childhood programs use multiple indicators of progress in all development domains to evaluate the effect of the program on children's development and learning and regularly report children's progress to parents. Group-administered, standardized, multiple- choice achievement tests are not used before third grade, preferably before fourth grade. When such tests are used to demonstrate public accountability, a sampling method is used (see Shepard 1994).

REFERENCES

Adams, G., & J. Sandfort. 1994. *Frist steps, promising futures: State prekindergarten initiatives in the early 1990s.* Washington. DC: Children's Defense Fund.

Alexander, K.L., & D.R. Entwisle. 1988. *Achievement in the first 2 years of school: Patterns and processes.* Monographs of the Society for Research in Child Development, vol. 53, no.2, serial no. 218. Ann Arbor: University of Michigan.

Arnett, J. 1989. Caregivers in day-care centers: Does training matter? *Journal of Applied Developmental Psychology* 10 (4): 541–52.

Asher, S., S. Hymel, & P. Renshaw. 1984. Loneliness in children. *Child Development* 55: 1456–64.

Barnett, W.S. 1995. Long-term effects of early childhood programs on cognitive and school outcomes. *The Future of Children* 5 (3): 25–50.

Bergen, D. 1988. *Play as a medium for learning and development.* Portsmouth, NH: Heinemann.

Berk, L.E. 1996. *Infants and children: Prenatal through middle childhood.* 2d ed. Needham Heights, MA: Allyn & Bacon.

Berk, L., & A. Winsler. 1995. *Scaffolding children's learning: Vygotsky and early childhood education.* Washington, DC: NAEYC.

Berrueta-Clement, J.R., L.J. Schweinhart, W.S. Barnett, A.S. Epstein, & D.P. Weikart. 1984. *Changed lives: The effects of the Perry Preschool Program on youths through age 19.* Monographs of the High/Scope Educational Research Foundation, no. 8. Ypsilanti, MI: High/Scope Press.

Bodrova, E., & D. Leong. 1996. *Tools of the mind: The Vygotskian approach to early childhood education.* Englewood Cliffs, NJ: Merrill/Prentice Hall.

Bowlby, J. 1969. *Attachment and loss: Vol.1. Attachment.* New York: Basic.

Bowman, B. 1994. The challenge of diversity. *Phi Delta Kappan* 76 (3): 218–25.

Bowman, B., & F. Stott. 1994. Understanding development in a cultural context: The challenge for teachers. In *Diversity and developmentally appropriate practices: Challenges for early childhood education,* eds. B. Mallory & R. New, 119–34. New York: Teachers College Press.

Bredekamp, S., ed. 1987. *Developmentally appropriate practice in early childhood programs serving children from birth through age 8.* Exp. ed. Washington, DC: NAEYC.

Bredekamp, S. 1993a. Reflections on Reggio Emilia. *Young Children* 49 (1): 13–17.

Bredekamp, S. 1993b. The relationship between early childhood education and early childhood special education: Healthy marriage or family feud? *Topics in Early Childhood Special Education* 13 (3): 258–73.

Bredekamp, S., & T. Rosegrant, eds. 1992. *Reaching potentials: Appropriate curriculum and assessment for young children, volume 1.* Washington, DC: NAEYC.

Bredekamp, S., & T. Rosegrant, eds. 1995. *Reaching potentials: Transforming early childhood curriculum and assessment, volume 2.* Washington, DC: NAEYC.

Bronfenbrenner, U. 1979. *The ecology of human development: Experiments by nature and design.* Cambridge, MA: Harvard University Press.

Bronfenbrenner, U. 1989. Ecological systems theory. In *Annals of child development,* Vol. 6, ed. R. Vasta, 187–251. Greenwich, CT: JAI Press.

Bronfenbrenner, U. 1993. The ecology of cognitive development: Research models and fugitive findings. In *Development in context,* eds. R.H. Wozniak & K.W. Fischer, 3–44. Hillsdale, NJ: Erlbaum.

Bronson, M.B. 1995. *The right stuff for children birth to 8: Selecting play materials to support development.* Washington. DC: NAEYC.

Brophy, J. 1992. Probing the subtleties of subject matter teaching. *Educational Leadership* 49 (7): 4–8.

Bruner, J.S. 1983. *Child's talk: Learning to use language.* New York: Norton.

Bruner, J.S. 1996. *The culture of education.* Cambridge, MA: Harvard University Press.

Bryant, D.M., R. Clifford, & E.S. Peisner. 1991. Best practices for beginners: Developmental appropriateness in kindegarten. *American Educational Research Journal* 28 (4): 783–803.

Burchinal, M., J. Robert, L. Nabo, & D. Bryant. 1996. Quality of center child care and infant cognitive and language development. *Child Development* 67 (2): 606–20.

Burke, D. 1966. Multi-year teacher/student relationships are a long-overdue arrangement. *Phi Delta Kappan* 77 (5): 360–61.

Caine, R., & G. Caine. 1991. *Making connections: Teaching and the human brain.* New York: Addison-Wesley.

Campbell, F., & C. Ramey. 1995. Cognitive and school outcomes for high-risk African-American students at middle adolescence: Positive effects of early intervention. *American Educational Research Journal* 32 (4): 743–72.

Carnegie Task Force on Learning in the Primary Grades. 1996. *Years of promise: A comprehensive learning strategy for America's children.* New York: Carnegie Corporation of New York.

Carta, J., I. Schwartz, J. Atwater, & S. McConnell. 1991. Developmentally appropriate practice: Appraising its usefulness for young children with disabilities. *Topics in Early Childhood Special Education* 11 (1): 1–20.

Case, R., & Y. Okamoto. 1996. *The role of central conceptual structures in the development of children's thought.* Monographs of the Society of Research in Child Development, vol. 61, no. 2, serial no. 246. Chicago: University of Chicago Press.

Charlesworth, R., C.H. Hart, D.C. Burts, & M. DeWolf. 1993. The LSU studies: Building a research base for developmentally appropriate practice. In *Perspectives on developmentally appropriate practice,* vol. 5 of *Advances in early education and day care,* ed. S. Reifel, 3–28. Greenwich, CT: JAI Press.

Chugani, H., M.E. Phelps, & J.C. Mazziotta. 1987. Positron emission tomography study of human brain functional development. *Annals of Neurology* 22 (4): 495.

Cohen, N., & K. Modigliani. 1994. The family-to-family project: Developing family child care providers. In *The early childhood career lattice: Perspectives on professional development,* eds. J. Johnson & J.B. McCracken, 106–10. Washington, DC: NAEYC.

Copple, C., I.E. Sigel, & R. Saunders. 1984. *Educating the young thinker: Classroom strategies for cognitive growth.* Hillsdale, NJ: Erlbaum.

Cost, Quality, & Child Outcomes Study Team. 1995. *Cost, quality, and child outcomes in child care centers, public report.* 2d ed. Denver: Economics Department, University of Colorado at Denver.

Dana Alliance for Brain Initiatives. 1996. *Delivering results: A progress report on brain research.* Washington, DC: Author.

DEC/CEC (Division for Early Childhood of the Council for Exceptional Children). 1994. Position on inclusion. *Young Children* 49 (5): 78.

DEC (Division for Early Childhood) Task Force on Recommended Practices. 1993. *DEC recommended practices: Indicators of quality in programs for infants and young children with special needs and their families.* Reston, VA: Council for Exceptional Children.

DEC/CEC & NAEYC (Division for Early Childhood of the Council for Exceptional Children & the National Association for the Education of Young Children). 1993. *Understanding the ADA—The Americans with Disability Act: Information for early childhood programs.* Pittsburgh, PA, & Washington, DC: Authors.

DeVries, R., & W. Kohlberg. 1990. *Constructivist early education: Overview and comparison with other programs.* Washington, DC: NAEYC.

Dewey, J. 1916. *Democracy and education: An introduction to the philosophy of education.* New York: Macmillan.

Durkin, D. 1987. A classroom-observation study of reading instruction in kindergarten. *Early Childhood Research Quarterly* 2 (3): 275–300.

Durkin, D. 1990. Reading instruction in kindergarten: A look at some issues through the lens of new basal reader materials. *Early Children Research Quarterly* 5 (3): 299–316.

Dweck, C. 1986. Motivational processes affecting learning. *American Psychologist* 41: 1030–48.

Dyson, A.H., & C. Genishi. 1993. Visions of children as language users: Language and language education in early childhood. In *Handbook of research on the education of young children,* ed. B. Spodek, 122–36. New York: Macmillan.

Edwards, C.P., & L. Gandini. 1989. Teachers' expectations about the timing of developmental skills: A cross-cultural study: *Young Children* 44 (4): 15–19.

Edwards, C., L. Gandini, & G. Forman, eds. 1993. *The hundred languages of children: The Reggio Emilia approach to early childhood education.* Norwood, NJ: Ablex.

Erikson, E. 1963. *Childhood and society.* New York: Norton.

Feeney, S., & K. Kipnis. 1992. *Code of ethical conduct & statement of commitment.* Washington, DC: NAEYC.

Fein, G. 1981. Pretend play: An integrative review. *Child Development* 52: 1095–118.

Fein, G., & M. Rivkin, eds. 1986. *The young child at play: Reviews of research.* Washington, DC: NAEYC.

Fenson, L., P. Dale, J.S. Reznick, E. Bates, D. Thal, & S. Pethick. 1994. *Variability in early communicative development.* Monographs of the Society for Research in Child Development, vol. 59, no. 2, serial no. 242. Chicago: University of Chicago Press.

Fernald, A. 1992. Human Maternal vocalizations in infants as biologically relevant signals: An evolutionary perspective. In *The adapted mind: Evolutionary psychology and the generation of culture,* eds. J.H. Barkow, L. Cosmides, & J. Tooby, 391–428. New York: Oxford University Press.

Fields, T., W. Masi, S. Goldstein, S. Perry, & S. Parl. 1988. Infant day care facilities preschool social behavior. *Early Childhood Research Quarterly* 3 (4): 341–59.

Forman, E.A., N. Minick, & C.A. Stone. 1993. *Contexts for learning: Sociocultural dynamics in children's development.* New York: Oxford University Press.

Forman, G. 1994. Different media, different languages. In *Reflections on the Reggio Emilia approach,* eds. L. Katz & B. Cesarone, 37–46. Urbana, IL: ERIC Clearinghouse on EECE.

Francis, P., & P. Self. 1982. Imitative responsiveness of young children in day care and home settings: The importance of the child to caregiver ratio. *Child Study Journal* 12: 119–26.

Frede, E. 1995. The role of program quality in producing early childhood program benefits. *The Future of Children,* 5 (3): 115–132.

Frede, E., & W.S. Barnett. 1992. Developmentally appropriate public school preschool: A study of implementation of the High/Scope curriculum and its effects on disadvantaged children's skills at first grade. *Early Childhood Research Quarterly* 7 (4): 483–99.

Fromberg, D. 1992. Play. In *The early childhood curriculum: A review of current research,* 2d ed., ed. C. Seefeldt, 35–74. New York: Teachers College Press.

Galinsky, E., C. Howes, S. Kontos, & M. Shinn. 1994. *The study of children in family child care and relative care: Highlights of findings.* New York: Families and Work Institute.

Gallahue, D. 1993. Motor development and movement skill acquisition in early childhood education. In *Handbook of research on the education of young children,* ed. B. Spodek, 24–41. New York: Macmillan.

Gallahue, D. 1995. Transforming physical education curriculum. In *Reaching potentials: Transforming early childhood curriculum and assessment, volume 2,* eds. S. Bredekamp & T. Rosegrant, 125–44. Washington, DC: NAEYC.

Garbarino, J., N. Dubrow, K. Kostelny, & C. Pardo. 1992. *Children in danger: Coping with the consequences of community violence.* San Francisco: Jossey-Bass.

Gardner, H. 1983. *Frames of mind: The theory of multiple intelligences.* New York: Basic.

Gardner, H. 1991. *The unschooled mind: How children think and how schools should teach.* New York: Basic.

Gelman, R., & R. Baillargeon. 1983. A review of some Piagetian concepts. In *Handbook of Child Psychology,* vol. 3, ed. P.H. Mussen, 167–230. New York: Wiley.

Gelman, R., & E. Meck. 1983. Preschoolers' counting: Principles before skill. *Cognition* 13: 343–59.

Hale-Benson, J. 1986. *Black children: Their roots, cultures, and learning styles.* Rev. ed. Baltimore: Johns Hopkins University Press.

Herron, R., & B. Sutton-Smith. 1971. *Child's play.* New York: Wiley.

Hiebert, E.H., & J.M. Papierz. 1990. The emergent literacy construct and kindergarten and readiness books of basal reading series. *Early Childhood Research Quarterly* 5 (3): 317–34.

Hohmann, M., & D. Weikart. 1995. *Educating young children: Active learning practices for preschool and child care programs.* Ypsilanti, MI: High/Scope Educational Research Foundation.

Hollestelle, K. 1993. At the core: Entrepreneurial skills for family child care providers. In *The early childhood career lattice: Perspectives on professional development,* eds. J. Johnson & J. B. McCracken, 63–65. Washington, DC: NAEYC.

Howes, C. 1983. Caregiver behavior in center and family day care. *Journal of Applied Developmental Psychology* 4: 96–107.

Howes, C. 1988. Relations between early child care and schooling. *Developmental Psychology* 24 (1): 53–57.

Howes, C., D.A. Phillips, M. Whitebook. 1992. Thresholds of quality: Implications for the social development of children in center-based child care. *Child Development* 63 (2): 449–60.

Howes, C., E. Smith, & E. Galinsky. 1995. *The Florida child care quality improvement study.* New York: Families and Work Institute.

Kagan, S., S. Goffin, S. Golub, & E. Pritchard. 1995. *Toward systematic reform: Service integration for young children and their families.* Falls Church, VA: National Center for Service Integration.

Kagan, S.L. 1991. *United we stand: Collaboration for child care and early education services.* New York: Teachers College Press.

Kamii, C., & J.K. Ewing. 1996. Basing teaching on Piaget's constructivism. *Childhood Education* 72 (5): 260–64.

Katz, L. 1995. *Talks with teachers of young children: A collection.* Norwood, NJ: Ablex.

Katz, L., & S. Chard. 1989. *Engaging children's minds: The project approach.* Norwood, NJ: Ablex.

Katz, L., D. Evangelou, & J. Hartman. 1990. *The case for mixed-age grouping in early education.* Washington, DC: NAEYC.

Kendrick, A., R. Kaufmann, & K. Messenger, eds. 1995. *Healthy young children: A manual for programs.* Washington, DC: NAEYC.

Kohn, A. 1993. *Punished by rewards.* Boston: Houghton Mifflin.

Kostelnik, M., A. Soderman, & A. Whiren. 1993. *Developmentally appropriate programs in early childhood education.* New York: Macmillan.

Kuhl, P. 1994. Learning and representation in speech and language. *Current Opinion in Neurobiology* 4: 812–22.

Lary, R.T. 1990. Successful students. *Education Issues* 3 (2): 11–17.

Layzer, J.I., B.D. Goodson, & M. Moss. 1993. *Life in preschool: Volume one of an observational study of early childhood programs for disadvantaged four-year-olds.* Cambridge, MA: Abt Association.

Lazar, I., & R. Darlington. 1982. *Lasting effects of early education: A report from the consortium for longitudinal studies.* Monographs of the Society for Research in Child Development, vol. 47, nos. 2–3, serial no. 195. Chicago: University of Chicago Press.

Lee, V.E., J. Brooks-Gunn, & E. Schuur. 1988. Does Head Start work? A 1-year follow-up comparison of disadvantaged children attending Head Start, no preschool, and other preschool programs. *Developmental Psychology* 24 (2): 210–22.

Legters, N., & R.E. Slavin. 1992. Elementary students at risk: A status report. Paper commissioned by the Carnegie Corporation of New York for meeting on elementary-school reform. 1–2 June.

Levy, A.K., L. Schaefer, & P.C. Phelps. 1986. Increasing preschool effectiveness: Enhancing the language abilities of 3- and 4-year-old children through planned sociodramatic play. *Early Childhood Research Quarterly* 1 (2): 133–40.

Levy, A.K., C.H. Wolfgang, & M.A. Koorland. 1992. Sociodramatic play as a method for enhancing the language performance of kindergarten age students. *Early Childhood Research Quarterly* 7 (2): 245–62.

Malaguzzi, L. 1993. History, ideas, and basic philosophy. In *The hundred languages of children: The Reggio Emilia approach to early childhood education,* eds. C. Edwards, L. Gandini, & G. Forman, 41–89. Norwood, NJ: Ablex.

Mallory, B. 1992. Is it always appropriate to be developmental? Convergent models for early intervention practice. *Topics in Early Childhood Special Education* 11 (4): 1–12.

Mallory, B. 1994. Inclusive policy, practice, and theory for young children with developmental differences. In *Diversity and developmentally appropriate practices: Challenges for early childhood education,* eds. B. Mallory & R. New, 44–61. New York: Teachers College Press.

Mallory, B.L., & R.S. New. 1994a. *Diversity and developmentally appropriate practices: Challenges for early childhood education.* New York: Teachers College Press.

Mallory, B.L., & R.S. New. 1994b. Social constructivist theory and principles of inclusion: Challenges for early childhood special education. *Journal of Special Education* 28 (3): 322–37.

Marcon, R.A. 1992. Differential effects of three preschool models on inner-city 4-year-olds. *Early Childhood Research Quarterly* 7 (4): 517–30.

Maslow, A. 1954. *Motivation and personality*. New York: Harper & Row.

Miller, L.B., & R.P. Bizzell. 1984. Long-term effects of four preschool programs: Ninth- and tenth-grade results. *Child Development* 55 (4): 1570–87.

Mitchell, A., M. Seligson, & F. Marx. 1989. *Early childhood programs and the public schools*. Dover, MA: Auburn House.

Morrow, L.M. 1990. Preparing the classroom environment to promote literacy during play. *Early Childhood Research Quarterly* 5 (4): 537–54.

NAEYC. 1987. *NAEYC position statement on licensing and other forms of regulation of early childhood programs in centers and family day care*. Washington, DC: Author.

NAEYC. 1991. *Accreditation criteria and procedures of the National Academy of Early Childhood Programs*. Rev. ed. Washington, DC: Author.

NAEYC. 1993. *Compensation guidelines for early childhood professionals*. Washington, DC: Author.

NAEYC. 1994. NAEYC position statement: A conceptual framework for early childhood professional development, adopted November 1993. *Young Children* 49 (3): 68–77.

NAEYC. 1996a. NAEYC position statement: Responding to linguistic and cultural diversity—Recommendations for effective early childhood education. *Young Children* 51 (2): 4–12.

NAEYC. 1996b. NAEYC position statement: Technology and young children—Ages three through eight. *Young Children* 51 (6): 11–16.

NAEYC & NAECS/SDE (National Association of Early Childhood Specialists in State Departments of Education). 1992. Guidelines for appropriate curriculum content and assessment in programs serving children ages 3 through 8. In *Reaching potentials: Appropriate curriculum and assessment for young children, volume 1*, eds. S. Bredekamp & T. Rosegrant, 9–27. Washington, DC: NAEYC.

NASBE (National Association of State Boards of Education). 1991. *Caring communities: Supporting young children and families*. Alexandria, VA: Author.

Natriello, G., E. McDill, & A. Pallas. 1990. *Schooling disadvantaged children: Racing against catastrophe*. New York: Teachers College Press.

NCES (National Center for Education Statistics). 1993. *The condition of education, 1993*. Washington, DC: U.S. Department of Education.

NCSL (National Conference of State Legislatures). 1995. *Early childhood care and education: An investment that works*. Denver: Author.

NEGP (National Education Goals Panel). 1991. *National education goals report: Building a nation of learners*. Washington, DC: Author.

New, R. 1993. Cultural variations on developmentally appropriate practice: Challenges to theory and practice. In *The hundred languages of children: The Reggio Emilia approach to early childhood education*, eds. C. Edwards, L. Gandini, & G. Forman, 215–32. Norwood, NJ: Ablex.

New, R. 1994. Culture, child development, and developmentally appropriate practices: Teachers as collaborative researchers. In *Diversity and developmentally appropriate practices: Challenges for early childhood education*, eds. B. Mallory & R. New, 65–83. New York: Teachers College Press.

Nye, B.A., J. Boyd-Zaharias, & B.D. Fulton. 1994. *The lasting benefits study: A continuing analysis of the effect of small class size in kindergarten through third grade on student achievement test scores in subsequent grade levels—seventh grade (1992–93)*, technical report. Nashville: Center of Excellence for Research in Basic Skills. Tennessee State University.

Nye, B.A., J. Boyd-Zaharias, B.D. Fulton, & M.P. Wallenhorst. 1992. Smaller classes really are better. *The American School Board Journal* 179 (5): 31–33.

Parker, J.G., & S.R. Asher. 1987. Peer relations and later personal adjustment: Are low-accepted children at risk? *Psychology Bulletin* 102 (3): 357–89.

Phillips, C.B. 1994. The movement of African-American children through sociocultural contexts: A case of conflict resolution. In *Diversity and developmentally appropriate practices: Challenges for early childhood education*, eds. B. Mallory & R. New, 137–54. New York: Teachers College Press.

Phillips, D.A., K. McCartney, & S. Scarr. 1987. Child care quality and children's social development. *Developmental Psychology* 23 (4): 537–43.

Piaget, J. 1952. *The origins of intelligence in children*. New York: International Universities Press.

Plomin, R. 1994a. *Genetics and experience: The interplay between nature and nurture*. Thousand Oaks, CA: Sage.

Plomin, R. 1994b. Nature, nurture, and social development. *Social Development* 3: 37–53.

Powell, D. 1994. Parents, pluralism, and the NAEYC statement on developmentally appropriate practice. In *Diversity and developmentally appropriate practices: Challenges for early childhood education*, eds. B. Mallory & R. New, 166–82. New York: Teachers College Press.

Pramling, I. 1991. Learning about "the shop": An approach to learning in preschool. *Early Children Research Quarterly* 6 (2): 151–66.

Resnick, L. 1996. Schooling and the workplace: What relationship? In *Preparing youth for the 21st century*, 21–27. Washington, DC: Aspen Institute.

Rogoff, B. 1990. *Apprenticeship in thinking: Cognitive development in social context*. New York: Oxford University Press.

Rogoff, B., J. Mistry, A. Goncu, & C. Mosier. 1993. *Guided participation in cultural activity by toddlers and caregivers*. Monographs of the Society for Research in Child Development, vol. 58, no. 8, serial no. 236. Chicago: University of Chicago Press.

Ross, S.M., L.J. Smith, J. Casey, & R.E. Slavin. 1995. Increasing the academic success of disadvantaged children: An examination of alternative early intervention programs. *American Educational Research Journal* 32 (4): 773–800.

Ruopp, R., J. Travers, F. Glantz, & C. Coelen. 1979. *Children at the center: Final report of the National Day Care Study*. Cambridge, MA: Abt Associates.

Sameroff, A., & S. McDonough. 1994. Educational implications of developmental transition: Revisiting the 5- to 7-year shift. *Phi Delta Kappan* 76 (3): 188–93.

Scarr, S., & K. McCartney. 1983. How people make their own environments: A theory of genotype–environment effects. *Child Development* 54: 425–35.

Schrader, C.T. 1989. Written language use within the context of young children's symbolic play. *Early Childhood Research Quarterly* 4 (2): 225–44.

Schrader, C.T. 1990. Symbolic play as a curricular tool for early literacy development. *Early Childhood Research Quarterly* 5 (1): 79–103.

Schweinhart, L.J., & D.P. Weikart. 1996. *Lasting differences: The High/Scope preschool curriculum comparison study through age 23*. Monographs of the High/Scope Educational Research Foundation, no. 12. Ypsilanti, MI: High/Scope Press.

Schweinhart, L.J., H.V. Barnes, & D.P. Weikart. 1993. *Significant benefits: The High/Scope Perry Preschool Study through age 27*. Monographs of the High/Scope Educational Research Foundation, no. 10. Ypsilanti, MI: High/Scope Press.

Schweinhart, L.J., D.P. Weikart, & M.B. Larner. 1986. Child-initiated activities in early childhood programs may help prevent delinquency. *Early Childhood Research Quarterly* 1 (3): 303–12.

Seefeldt, C., ed. 1992. *The early childhood curriculum: A review of current research.* 2d ed. New York: Teachers College Press.

Seifert, K. 1993. Cognitive development and early childhood education. In *Handbook of research on the education of young children,* ed. B. Spodek, 9–23. New York: Macmillan.

Seppanen, P.S., D. Kaplan deVries, & M. Seligson. 1993. *National study of before and after school programs.* Portsmouth, NH: RMC Research Corp.

Shepard, L. 1994. The challenges of assessing young children appropriately: *Phi Delta Kappan* 76 (3): 206–13.

Shepard, L.A., & M.L. Smith. 1988. Escalating academic demand in kindergarten: Some nonsolutions. *Elementary School Journal* 89 (2): 135–46.

Shepard, L.A., & M.L. Smith. 1989. *Flunking grades: Research and policies on retention.* Bristol, PA: Taylor & Francis.

Slavin, R., N. Karweit, & N. Madden, eds. 1989. *Effective programs for students at-risk.* Boston: Allyn & Bacon.

Smilansky, S., & L. Shefatya. 1990. *Facilitating play: A medium for promoting cognitive, socioemotional, and academic development in young children.* Gaithersburg, MD: Psychosocial & Educational Publications.

Spodek, B., ed. 1993. *Handbook of research on the education of young children.* New York: Macmillan.

Sroufe, L.A., R.G. Cooper, & G.B. DeHart. 1992. *Child development: Its nature and course.* 2d ed. New York: Knopf.

Stern, D. 1985. *The psychological world of the human infant.* New York: Basic.

Stremmel, A.J., & V.R. Fu. 1993. Teaching in the zone of proximal development: Implications for responsive teaching practice. *Child and Youth Care Forum* 22 (5): 337–50.

Taylor, J.M., & W.S. Taylor. 1989. *Communicable diseases and young children in group settings.* Boston: Little, Brown.

Tobin, J., D. Wu, & D. Davidson. 1989. *Preschool in three cultures.* New Haven, CT: Yale University Press.

U.S. Department of Health & Human Services. 1996. *Head Start performance standards.* Washington, DC: Author.

Vandell, D.L., & M.A. Corasanti. 1990. Variations in early child care: Do they predict subsequent social, emotional, and cognitive differences? *Early Childhood Research Quarterly* 5 (4): 555–72.

Vandell, D.L., & C.D. Powers. 1983. Day care quality and children's freeplay activites. *American Journal of Orthopsychiatry* 53 (4): 493–500.

Vandell, D.L., V.K. Henderson, & K.S. Wilson. 1988. A longitudinal study of children with day-care experiences of varying quality. *Child Development* 59 (5): 1286–92.

Vygotsky, L. 1978. *Mind in society: The development of higher psychological processes.* Cambridge. MA: Harvard University Press.

Wardle, F. 1996. Proposal: An anti-bias and ecological model for multicultural education. *Childhood Education* 72 (3): 152–56.

Wertsch, J. 1985. *Culture, communication, and cognition: Vygotskian perspectives.* New York: Cambridge University Press.

White, S.H. 1965. Evidence for a hierarchical arrangement of learning processes. In *Advances in child development and behavior,* eds. L.P. Lipsitt & C.C. Spiker, 187–220. New York: Academic Press.

Whitebook, M., C. Howes, & D. Philips. 1989. *The national child care staffing study: Who cares? Child care teachers and the quality of care in America.* Final report. Oakland, CA: Child Care Employee Project.

Wieder, S., & S.I. Greenspan. 1993. The emotional basic of learning. In *Handbook of research on the education of young children,* ed. B. Spodek, 77–104. New York: Macmillan.

Willer, B. 1990. *Reaching the full cost of quality in early childhood programs.* Washington, DC: NAEYC.

Willer, B., S.L. Hofferth, E.E. Kisker, P. Divine-Hawkins, E. Farquhar, & F.B. Glantz. 1991. *The demand and supply of child care in 1990.* Washington, DC: NAEYC.

Witkin, H. 1962. *Psychological differentiation: Studies of development.* New York: Wiley.

Wolery, M., & J. Wilbers, eds. 1994. *Including children with special needs in early childhood programs.* Washington, DC: NAEYC.

Wolery, M., & P. Strain, & D. Bailey. 1992. Reaching potentials of children with special needs. In *Reaching Potentials: Appropriate curriculum and assessment for young children,* volume 1, eds. S. Bredekamp & T. Rosegrant, 92–111. Washington, DC: NAEYC.

Zero to Three: The National Center. 1995. *Caring for infants and toddlers in groups: Developmentally appropriate practice.* Arlington, VA: Author.

Appendix C

Time Line: The History of Early Childhood Education

1524   Martin Luther argued for public support of education for all children in his *Letter to the Mayors and Aldermen of All the Cities of Germany in Behalf of Christian Schools.*

1628   John Amos Comenius's *The Great Didactic* proclaimed the value of education for all children according to the laws of nature.

1762   Jean-Jacques Rousseau wrote *Emile,* explaining that education should take into account the child's natural growth and interests.

1780   Robert Raikes initiated the Sunday School movement in England to teach Bible study and religion to children.

1801   Johann Pestalozzi wrote *How Gertrude Teaches Her Children,* emphasizing home education and learning by discovery.

1816   Robert Owen set up a nursery school in Great Britain at the New Lanark Cotton Mills, believing that early education could counteract bad influences of the home.

1817   In Hartford, Connecticut, Thomas Gallaudet founded the first residential school for the deaf.

1824   The American Sunday School Union was started with the purpose of initiating Sunday schools around the United States.

1836   William McGuffey began publishing the *Eclectic Reader* for elementary school children; his writing had a strong impact on moral and literary attitudes in the nineteenth century.

1837   In Blankenburgh, Germany, Friedrich Froebel established the first kindergarten; he later became known as the father of the kindergarten.

1837   Horace Mann began his job as secretary of the Massachusetts State Board of Education; he is often called the father of the common schools because of the role he played in helping set up the elementary school system in the United States.

1837   In France Edouard Seguin, influenced by Jean Itard, started the first school for the feebleminded.

1856   Mrs. Margaretha Schurz established the first kindergarten in the United States in Watertown, Wisconsin; the school was founded for children of German immigrants, and the program was conducted in German.

1860   Elizabeth Peabody opened a private kindergarten in Boston, Massachusetts, for English-speaking children.

1869   The first special education class for the deaf was founded in Boston.

1871   The first public kindergarten in North America was started in Ontario, Canada.

1873   Susan Blow opened the first public school kindergarten in the United States in St. Louis, Missouri, as a cooperative effort with superintendent of schools William Harris.

1876   A model kindergarten was shown at the Philadelphia Centennial Exposition.

1880   The first teacher-training program for teachers of kindergarten began in Oshkosh Normal School, Philadelphia.

1884   The American Association of Elementary, Kindergarten, and Nursery School Educators was founded to serve in a consulting capacity for other educators.

1892   The International Kindergarten Union (IKU) was founded.

1896   John Dewey started the Laboratory School at the University of Chicago, basing his program on child-centered learning with an emphasis on life experiences.

1905   Sigmund Freud wrote *Three Essays of the Theory of Sexuality,* emphasizing the value of a healthy emotional environment during childhood.

1907   In Rome, Maria Montessori started her first preschool, called Children's House; her now-famous teaching method was based on the theory that children learn best by themselves in a properly prepared environment.

1909 Theodore Roosevelt convened the first White House Conference on Children.

1911 Arnold Gesell, well known for his research on the importance of the preschool years, began child development study at Yale University.

1911 Margaret and Rachel McMillan founded an open-air nursery school in Great Britain in which the class met outdoors; emphasis was on healthy living.

1912 Arnold and Beatrice Gesell wrote *The Normal Child and Primary Education.*

1915 In New York City Eva McLin started the first U.S. Montessori nursery school.

1915 The Child Education Foundation of New York City founded a nursery school using Montessori's principles.

1918 The first public nursery schools were started in Great Britain.

1919 Harriet Johnson started the Nursery School of the Bureau of Educational Experiments, later to become the Bank Street College of Education.

1921 Patty Smith Hill started a progressive laboratory nursery school at Columbia Teachers College.

1921 A. S. Neill founded Summerhill, an experimental school based on the ideas of Rousseau and Dewey.

1922 With Edna Noble White as its first director, the Merrill-Palmer Institute Nursery School opened in Detroit, with the purpose of preparing women in proper child care; the Institute was known as the Merrill-Palmer School of Motherhood and Home Training.

1922 Abigail Eliot, influenced by the open-air school in Great Britain and basing her program on personal hygiene and proper behavior, started the Ruggles Street Nursery School in Boston.

1924 *Childhood Education,* the first professional journal in early childhood education, was published by the IKU.

1926 The National Committee on Nursery Schools was initiated by Patty Smith Hill at Columbia Teachers College; now called the National Association for the Education of Young Children, it provides guidance and consultant services for educators.

1926 The National Association of Nursery Education (NANE) was founded.

1930 The IKU changed its name to the Association for Childhood Education.

1933 The Works Projects Administration (WPA) provided money to start nursery schools so that unemployed teachers would have jobs.

1935 The first toy-lending library, Toy Loan, was founded in Los Angeles.

1940 The Lanham Act provided funds for child care during World War II, mainly for day care centers for children whose mothers worked in the war effort.

1943 Kaiser Child Care Centers opened in Portland, Oregon, to provide twenty-four-hour child care for children of mothers working in war-related industries.

1944 The journal *Young Children* was first published by NANE.

1946 Dr. Benjamin Spock wrote the *Common Sense Book of Baby and Child Care.*

1950 Erik Erickson published his writings on the eight ages or stages of personality growth and development and identified tasks for each stage of development; the information, known as Personality in the Making, formed the basis for the 1950 White House Conference on Children and Youth.

1952 Jean Piaget's *The Origins of Intelligence in Children* was published in English.

1955 Rudolf Flesch's *Why Johnny Can't Read* criticized the schools for their methodology in teaching reading and other basic skills.

1957 The Soviet Union launched *Sputnik,* sparking renewed interest in other educational systems and marking the beginning of the rediscovery of early childhood education.

1958 The National Defense Education Act was passed to provide federal funds for improving education in the sciences, mathematics, and foreign languages.

1960 Katharine Whiteside Taylor founded the American Council of Parent Cooperatives for those interested in exchanging ideas about preschool education; it later became the Parent Cooperative Preschools International.

1960 The Day Care and Child Development Council of America was formed to publicize the need for quality services for children.

1964 At its Miami Beach conference, NANE became the National Association for the Education of Young Children (NAEYC).

1964 The Economic Opportunity Act of 1964 was passed, marking the beginning of the War on Poverty and the foundation for Head Start.

1965 The Elementary and Secondary Education Act was passed to provide federal money for programs for educationally deprived children.

1965 The Head Start program began with federal money allocated for preschool education; the early programs were known as child development centers.

1966 The Bureau of Education for the Handicapped was established.

1967 The Follow Through program was initiated to extend Head Start into the primary grades.

1968 B. F. Skinner wrote *The Technology of Teaching,* which outlined a programmed approach to learning.

1968 The federal government established the Handicapped Children's Early Education Program to fund model preschool programs for children with disabilities.

1970 The White House Conference on Children and Youth was held.

1971 The Stride Rite Corporation in Boston was the first to start a corporate-supported child care program.

1972 The National Home Start Program began for the purpose of involving parents in their children's education.

1975 Public Law 94-142, the Education for All Handicapped Children Act, was passed, mandating a free and appropriate education for all children with disabilities and extending many rights to the parents of such children.

1979 The International Year of the Child was sponsored by the United Nations and designated by executive order.

1980 The first American *lekotek* (toy-lending library) opened its doors in Evanston, Illinois.

1980 The White House Conference on Families was held.

1981 The Head Start Act of 1981 (Omnibus Budget Reconciliation Act of 1981, Public Law 97-35) was passed to extend Head Start and provide for effective delivery of comprehensive services to economically disadvantaged children and their families.

1981 The Education Consolidation and Improvement Act (ECIA) was passed, consolidating many federal support programs for education.

1981 Secretary of Education Terrell Bell announced the establishment of the National Commission on Excellence in Education.

1982 The Mississippi legislature established mandatory statewide public kindergartens.

1983 An Arkansas commission chaired by Hillary Clinton called for mandatory kindergarten and lower pupil–teacher ratios in the early grades.

1984 The High/Scope Educational Foundation released a study that documented the value of high-quality preschool programs for poor children, a study cited repeatedly in later years by those favoring expansion of Head Start and other early-years programs.

1985 Head Start celebrated its twentieth anniversary with a joint resolution of the Senate and House "reaffirming congressional support."

1986 The U.S. Secretary of Education proclaimed this the Year of the Elementary School, saying, "Let's do all we can this year to remind this nation that the time our children spend in elementary school is crucial to everything they will do for the rest of their lives."

1986 Public Law 99-457 (the Education of the Handicapped Act Amendments) established a national policy on early intervention that recognizes its benefits, provides assistance to states to build systems of service delivery, and recognizes the unique roles of families in the development of their children with disabilities.

1987 Congress created the National Commission to Prevent Infant Mortality.

1988 Vermont announced plans to assess student performance on the basis of work portfolios as well as test scores.

1989 The United Nations Convention on the Rights of the Child was adopted by the UN General Assembly.

1990 The United Nations Convention on the Rights of the Child went into effect, following its signing by twenty nations.

1990 Head Start celebrated its twenty-fifth anniversary.

1991 Education Alternatives, Inc., a for-profit firm, opened South Pointe Elementary School in Miami, Florida, the first public school in the nation to be run by a private company.

1991 The Carnegie Foundation issued "Ready to Learn," a plan to ensure children's readiness for school.

1994 The United Nations declared 1994 the Year of the Indigenous Child.

1995 Head Start reauthorization established a new program, Early Head Start, for low-income pregnant women and families with infants and toddlers.

1999 As part of the effort to strengthen educational opportunities for America's six million students with disabilities, the Department of Education issued final regulations for implementing the Individuals with Disabilities Education Act (IDEA) of 1997.

1999 Florida became the first state in the nation to pass a statewide school voucher plan; the law gives children in academically failing public schools a chance to attend private, secular, or religious schools with public money.

2000 Head Start celebrated its thirty-fifth anniversary.

2002 President George W. Bush signed Public Law 107-110, the No Child Left Behind Act of 2001. NCLB contains four basic provisions: stronger accountability for results, increased flexibility and local control, expanded options for parents, and an emphasis on teaching methods that have been proven to work.

2003 The United Nations launched the Literacy Decade (2003–2012) in order to reduce world illiteracy rates; the theme is Literacy as Freedom.

2005 Head Start celebrated forty years of success.

Glossary

Absorbent mind The idea that the minds of young children are receptive to and capable of learning. The child learns unconsciously by taking in information from the environment.

Accommodation Changing or altering existing schemes or creating new ones in response to new information.

Active learning (instructional) Involvement of the child with materials, activities, and projects in order to learn concepts, knowledge, and skills.

Active learning (theory) The view that children develop knowledge and learn by being physically and mentally engaged in learning activities.

Active listening The practice of giving full attention to the person speaking.

Adaptation The process of building schemes through interaction with the environment. Consists of two complementary processes—assimilation and accommodation.

Adaptive education Modifications in any classroom, program, environment, or curriculum that help students achieve desired educational goals.

Adult–child discourse The talk between an adult and a child, which includes adult suggestions about behavior and problem solving.

Advocacy The act of engaging in strategies designed to improve the circumstances of children and families. Advocates move beyond their day-to-day professional responsibilities and work collaboratively to help others.

Alignment The arrangement of standards, curriculum, and tests so they are in agreement.

Anthroposophy A philosophy developed by Rudolf Steiner that focuses on the spiritual nature of humanity and the universe.

Approaches to learning How children react to and engage in learning and activities associated with school.

Assessment The process of collecting information about children's development, learning, health, behavior, academic process, need for special services, and attainment in order to make decisions.

Assimilation The process of fitting new information into existing schemes.

Assistive technology Any device used to promote the learning of children with disabilities.

Atelier A special area or studio for creating projects.

Atelierista A teacher trained in the visual arts who works with teachers and children.

Attachment A strong affectional tie between a parent/caregiver and a child that endures over time.

Attention deficit hyperactivity disorder (ADHD) Difficulty with attention and self-control, which leads to problems with learning, social functioning, and behavior that occur in more than one situation and have been present for a significant length of time.

Authentic assessment Assessment conducted through activities that require children to demonstrate what they know and are able to do; also referred to as *performance-based assessment*.

Autoeducation The idea that children teach themselves through appropriate materials and activities.

Autonomy The stage of moral thinking in which children govern their own actions and thoughts about what is right and wrong.

Baby signing Teaching babies to use signs or gestures to communicate needs and emotions.

Behavior guidance The processes by which children are helped to identify appropriate behaviors and use them.

Blank tablet The belief that at birth the mind is blank and that experience creates the mind.

Block grants Sums of money given by the federal government to states to provide services according to broad, general guidelines.

Bonding A parent's initial emotional tie to an infant.

Center-based child care Child care and education provided in a facility other than a home.

Cephalocaudal development The principle that development proceeds from the head to the toes.

Child as sinful View that children are basically sinful, need supervision and control, and should be taught to be obedient.

Child care Comprehensive care and education of young children outside their homes.

Child development The sum total of the physical, intellectual, social, emotional, and behavioral changes that occur in children from conception through adolescence.

Children as investments View that investing in the care and education of children reaps future benefits for parents and society.

Children as property Belief that children are literally the property of their parents.

Children's House Montessori's first school especially designed to implement her ideas.

Chronosystem The environmental contexts and events that influence children over their lifetimes, such as living in a technological age.

549

Collaboration Working jointly and co-operatively with other professionals, parents, and administrators.

Concrete operations The stage of cognitive development during which children's thought is logical and can organize concrete experiences.

Constructive play Play involving the use of modules to build things.

Constructivism Theory that emphasizes the active role of children in developing their understanding and learning.

Consultation Seeking advice and information from colleagues.

Cooperative learning A teaching strategy in which small groups of children work together on a variety of learning activities to improve their understanding of a topic, with each member responsible for learning what is taught and helping teammates learn.

Cross-categorical classroom A classroom or other setting of students with a variety of disabilities or delays.

Culture A group's way of life, including basic values, beliefs, religion, language, clothing, food, and practices.

Curriculum alignment The process of making sure that what is taught matches the standards.

Curriculum framework A blueprint for implementing content standards.

Developmental kindergarten Designed to provide children with additional time for maturation and physical, social, emotional, intellectual development, and their individuality and culture.

Developmentally appropriate Based on how children grow, deveop, and on individual and cultural differences.

Documentation Records of children's work including recordings, photographs, art, work samples, projects, and drawings.

Early childhood professional An educator who successfully teaches all children, promotes high personal standards, and continually expands his or her skills and knowledge.

Early Head Start A federal program serving pregnant women, infants, toddlers, and their families.

Embedded instruction Instruction that is included as an integral part of normal classroom routines.

Emergent literacy Children's literacy development before receiving formal reading and writing instruction in school.

Émile Jean-Jacques Rousseau's famous book that outlines his ideas about how children should be reared.

Encouraging environment A classroom environment that rewards student accomplishment and independence.

Entitlement programs Programs and services children and families are entitled to because they meet the eligibility criteria for the services.

Environmentalism The theory that the environment, rather than heredity, exerts the primary influence on intellectual growth and cultural development.

Equilibrium A balance between existing and new schemes, developed through assimilation and accommodation of new information.

Ethical conduct Responsible behavior toward students and parents that allows you to be considered a professional.

Eurythmy Steiner's art of movement, which makes speech and music visible through action and gesture.

Even Start A federal program that provides literacy services for low-income families and children.

Exosystems Environments or settings in which children do not play an active role but which nonetheless influence their development.

Family child care Home-based care and education provided by a nonrelative outside the child's home; also known as family care.

Family-centered teaching Instruction that focuses on meeting the needs of students through the family unit.

Family involvement The participation of parents and other family members in all areas of their children's education and development, based on the premise that parents are the primary influence in children's lives.

Fantasy play Play involving unrealistic notions and superheroes.

Fatherhood initiatives Various efforts by federal, state, and local agencies to increase and sustain fathers' involvement with their children and families.

Free and appropriate education (FAPE) Education suited to children's age, maturity, condition of disability, past achievements, and parental expectations.

Full inclusion An approach whereby students with disabilities receive all instruction and support services in a general classroom.

Functional play Play involving muscular activities, the only play of the sensorimotor period.

Gifts Ten sets of learning materials designed to help children learn through play and manipulation.

Good Start, Grow Smart The federal government's early childhood initiative designed to help states and local communities strengthen early learning for young children.

Growing plants View of children popularized by Froebel, which equates children to plants and teachers and parents to gardeners.

Head Start A federal early childhood program serving poor children aged three to five and their families.

Heteronomy The stage of moral thinking in which children are governed by others regarding matters of right and wrong.

Hierarchy of needs Maslow's theory that basic needs must be satisfied before higher-level needs can be satisfied.

High/Scope An educational program for young children based on Piaget's and Vygotsky's ideas.

High-stakes assessment testing Tests used to make decisions about whether to admit or not to admit children into programs or to promote or not to promote them from one grade to the next.

Holophrase The single words children use to refer to what they see, hear, and feel (e.g., *up, doll*).

I message A method of communication in which speakers reflect on their true feelings about a situation or event.

Implementation Committing to a certain action based on interpretations of the observational data.

Individualization of instruction Providing for students' specific needs, disabilities, and preferences.

Individualized education program (IEP) A plan for meeting an exceptional learner's educational needs, specifying goals, objectives, services, and procedures for evaluating progress.

Individualized family service plan (IFSP) A plan designed to help families reach their goals for themselves and their children, with varied support services.

Individuals with Disabilities Education Act (IDEA) A federal act providing a free and appropriate education to youth between ages three and twenty-one with disabilities.

Infant/toddler mental health The overall health and well-being of young children in the context of family, school, and community relationships.

Informal, or free, play Play in which children play in activities of interest to them.

Instrumental-relativist orientation The second stage of preconventional moral development, when children's actions are motivated by satisfaction of their needs.

Intentional teaching Developing plans, selecting instructional strategies, and teaching to promote learning.

Intergenerational programs Programs that involve grandparents and others and are designed to help all generations.

Interpretation Forming a conclusion based on observational and assessment data with the intent of planning and improving teaching and learning.

Itinerant teachers Professionals who travel from school to school, providing assistance and teaching students.

Key experiences Activities that foster developmentally important skills and abilities.

Kindergarten The name Friedrich Froebel gave to his system of education for children aged three through six; means "garden of children."

Language-minority parents Individuals whose English proficiency is minimal and who lack a comprehensive knowledge of the norms and social systems in the United States.

Learning Cognitive and behavioral changes that result from experiences.

Learning centers Places in a classroom where children are free to explore, manipulate, create, and work where their interests take them (e.g., a writing center, a dramatic play center, an art center, a math center).

Least restrictive environment (LRE) Placement that meets disabled students' needs in as regular a setting as possible.

Literacy education Teaching that focuses on reading, writing, speaking, and listening.

Locus of control The source of control over personal behavior, either internal or external.

Looping A single-graded class of children staying with the same teacher for two or more years.

Macrosystem The broader culture in which children live (e.g., democracy, individual freedom, and religious freedom).

Mainstreaming The concept that a student with a disability should be integrated with nondisabled peers to the maximum extent possible and appropriate to the needs of the child.

Mesosystem Links or interactions between microsystems.

Microsystem The environmental settings in which children spend a lot of their time (e.g., children in child care spend about thirty-three hours a week there).

Migrant family A family with school-aged children that moves from one geographic location to another to engage in agricultural work.

Migrant Head Start A federal program designed to provide educational and other services to migrant children and their families.

Miniature adults Belief that children are similar to adults and should be treated as such.

Mixed-age grouping Students in two or three grade levels mixed in one classroom with one teacher.

Model early childhood program An exemplary approach to early childhood education that serves as a guide to best practices.

Montessori method A system of early childhood education founded on the ideas and practices of Maria Montessori.

Motherese or parentese The way parents and others speak to young children in a slow, exaggerated way that includes short sentences and repetition of words and phrases.

Multicultural infusion Making multiculturalism an explicit part of curriculum and programs.

Multiculturalism An approach to education based on the premise that all peoples in the United States should receive proportional attention in the curriculum.

National Association for the Education of Young Children (NAEYC) An organization of early childhood educators and others dedicated to improving the quality of programs for children from birth through the third grade.

Naturalism Education that follows the natural development of children and does not force the educational process on them.

Naturalistic methods Incorporating instruction into opportunities that occur naturally or routinely in the classroom.

Neural shearing (pruning) The selective elimination of synapses.

No Child Left Behind Act Federal law passed in 2001 that has significantly influenced early childhood education.

Object permanence The concept that people and objects have an independent existence beyond the child's perception of them.

Observation The intentional, systematic act of looking at the behavior of a child in a particular setting, program, or situation.

Occupations Materials designed by Friedrich Froebel to engage children in learning activities.

Operations Mental actions that enable children to reason logically.

Orbis Pictus The first picture book for children; written by John Amos Comenius.

Parent–teacher conferences Meetings between parents and early childhood professionals to inform the parents of the child's progress and allow them to actively participate in the educational process.

Partial inclusion An approach whereby students with disabilities receive some instruction in a general classroom and some in a specialized setting.

Performance standards Federal guidelines for Head Start and Early Head Start, designed to ensure that all children and families receive high-quality services.

Persons with rights View that children have certain basic rights of their own.

Philosophy of education Beliefs about children's development and learning and the best ways to teach them.

Planning Thinking about what to teach, how to teach, how to assess what is taught; includes selecting activities, deciding on a time allotment, creating the learning environment, considering the needs of individual children, and preparing assessment.

Planning time A time when children plan and articulate their ideas, choices, and decisions about what they will do.

Playing games with rules Playing within limits and rules.

Portfolio A compilation of children's work samples, products, and teacher observations collected over time.

Poverty The condition of having insufficient income to support a minimum standard of living.

Practical life Montessori activities that teach skills related to everyday living.

Preconventional level The first level in Kohlberg's theory of moral development, when morality is based on punishment and rewards.

Preoperational stage The stage of cognitive development in which young children are capable of mental representations.

Prepared environment A classroom or other space that is arranged and organized to support learning in general and/or special knowledge and skills.

Preschool years The period from three to five years of age, before children enter kindergarten and when many children attend preschool programs.

Primary circular reactions Repetitive actions that are centered on the infant's own body.

Progressivism Dewey's theory of education that emphasizes the importance of focusing on the needs and interests of children rather than teachers.

Project Approach An in-depth investigation of a topic worth learning more about.

Proximodistal development The principle that development proceeds from the center of the body outward.

Public policy All the plans that local, state, and national governmental and nongovernmental organizations have for implementing their goals.

Punishment and obedience orientation The first stage of preconventional moral development, when children make moral decisions based on physical consequences.

Recall time The time in which children form mental pictures of their work-time experiences and discuss them with their teachers.

Reggio Emilia An approach to education based on the philosophy and practice that children are active constructors of their own knowledge.

Relations of constraint Children's reliance on others to determine right and wrong.

Relations of cooperation Children's engagement with others in making decisions about good, bad, right, or wrong.

Reporting The process of providing to parents information gathered by means of observation, assessment, and children's work products.

Resource teachers Professionals who provide assistance with materials and planning for teachers of exceptional students.

Rubrics Scoring guides that differentiate among levels of performance.

Scaffolding The process of providing various types of support, guidance, or direction during the course of an activity.

Schemes Organized units of knowledge.

Screening measures Any assessment that gives a broad picture of what children know and are able to do, as well as their physical health and emotional status.

Secondary circular reactions Children's repetitive actions focused on the qualities of objects, such as their shapes, sizes, colors, and noises.

Self-actualization An inherent tendency to reach one's true potential.

Self-regulation The ability to keep track of and control one's behavior.

Self-talk Speech directed to oneself that helps to guide one's behavior.

Sensitive period (development) A period of developmental time during which certain things are learned more easily than at earlier or later times.

Sensitive period (Montessori) A relatively brief time during which learning is most likely to occur. Also called a critical period.

Sensorimotor stage The stage during which children learn through the senses and motor activities.

Sensory education Learning experiences involving the five senses: seeing, touching, hearing, tasting, and smelling.

Sensory materials Montessori learning materials designed to promote learning through the senses and to train the senses for learning.

Sexism Prejudice or discrimination based on sex.

Sexual harassment Unwelcome sexual behavior and talk.

Social constructivist approach Approaches to teaching that emphasize the social context of learning and behavior.

Social play Play of children with others and in groups.

Sociodramatic play Play involving realistic activities and events.

Standards Statements of what children should know and be able to do.

Students with disabilities Children with physical or mental/emotional impairments or specific learning disabilities who need special education and related services.

Supportive classroom Physical arrangement of the classroom so that it is conducive to the behaviors to be taught.

Symbolic play The ability of a young child to have an object stand for something else.

Symbolic play (stage) The let's-pretend stage of play.

Symbolic representation The ability to use mental images to stand for something else.

Synaptogenesis The rapid development of neural connections.

Technological literacy The ability to understand and apply technological devices to personal goals.

Technology The application of tools and information to make products and solve problems.

Telegraphic speech Two word sentences that express actions and relationships (e.g., "milk gone").

Temperament A child's general style of behavior.

Tertiary circular reactions Modifications that infants make in their behavior in order to explore the effects of those modifications.

Theory A set of explanations of how children develop and learn.

The plan-do-review A sequence in which children, with the help of the teacher, initiate plans for projects or activities; work in learning centers to implement their plans; and then review what they have done with the teacher and their fellow classmates.

Thinking Reasoning about or reflecting on something.

Transdisciplinary team model Professionals from various disciplines working together to integrate instructional strategies and therapy and to evaluate the effectiveness of their individual roles.

Transition A passage from one learning setting, grade, or program to another.

Transition kindergarten Designed to serve children who may be old enough to go to first grade but are not quite ready to handle all of its expectations.

Twice exceptional Students with dual exceptionalities, who may be gifted and have a disability, for example.

Two-generation programs Programs that involve parents and their children and are designed to help both generations, as well as strengthen the family unit.

Universal kindergarten The availability of kindergarten to all children.

Whole language approach Philosophy of literacy development that advocates the use of all dimensions of language—reading, writing, listening, and speaking—to help children become motivated to read and write.

Work time The period of time when children carry out their plans and are engaged in a project or activity.

Zone of proximal development The range of tasks that are too difficult to master alone but that can be learned with guidance and assistance.

Index

Photo Credits